Learning VMware App Volumes

Deliver applications to virtual desktop environments in seconds and at scale with the click of a button

Peter von Oven

BIRMINGHAM - MUMBAI

Learning VMware App Volumes

First published: March 2016

Production reference: 1220316

Published by Packt Publishing Ltd.
Livery Place
35 Livery Street
Birmingham B3 2PB, UK.

ISBN 978-1-78588-438-2

www.packtpub.com

Credits

Author
Peter von Oven

Reviewer
Barry Coombs

Commissioning Editor
Kunal Parikh

Acquisition Editor
Divya Poojari

Content Development Editor
Onkar Wani

Technical Editor
Gaurav Suri

Copy Editor
Madhusudan Uchil

Project Coordinator
Bijal Patel

Proofreader
Safis Editing

Indexer
Hemangini Bari

Graphics
Kirk D'Penha

Production Coordinator
Shantanu N. Zagade

Cover Work
Shantanu N. Zagade

About the Author

Peter von Oven is an experienced technical consultant and has spent the past 20 years of his IT career working with customers and partners in designing technology solutions aimed at delivering true business value. During his career, Peter has been involved in numerous large-scale enterprise projects and deployments and has presented at key IT events, such as VMWorld, IP EXPO, and various VMUGs across the UK. He has also worked in senior presales roles and presales management roles for some of the giants of IT, such as Fujitsu, HP, Citrix, and VMware, and has been awarded VMware vExpert for 2015 and 2016.

Over the past 10 years and more, Peter has focused his skills and experience by specializing in the desktop and application virtualization market and today works for the market-leading desktop transformation specialists, Liquidware Labs.

Peter got his first taste for writing when assisting with some of the chapters in the book *Building End-User Computing Solutions with VMware View*, which then lead to four other Packt titles, *VMware Horizon Mirage Essentials* and *VMware Horizon Workspace Essentials*, co-written with Peter Bjork and Joel Lindberg, and *VMware Horizon View Essentials* and *Mastering Horizon View*, co-written with Barry Coombs.

Acknowledgments

There are a few people I want to thank for the continued and ongoing support they have given me during the writing of this book. Firstly, and most importantly, I would like to thank my wife and daughters for their continued support while I spent many evenings and weekends writing—I couldn't do it without their support.

This book wouldn't have happened if I hadn't had support from some of the vendors. Firstly, I would like to thank my friend and colleague Arash Ghazanfari at Tintri for his support and knowledge of the storage market, and secondly, a thank you to Mark Maclean at Dell for lending me the server hardware used in the Lab examples.

I would also like to say, a big thank you to my reviewer, Barry Coombs, who I have collaborated with on a number of projects over the years. The other person I would like to than is friend and ex-colleague Steve Horne for his expertise and knowledge in defining how to approach any desktop or VDI transformation project.

Finally, a thank you to the Packt Publishing team for again giving me the opportunity to write this book and for their support, which has yet again been outstanding.

About the Reviewer

Barry Coombs is the operations director for Computerworld Systems Ltd., a UK-based, virtualization-focused, value-added reseller. He has been focusing on virtualization, storage, and end-user computing technologies as a customer, consultant, and architect for the past 9 years.

In his current role, Barry manages a team of technical architects and is actively involved in engaging with customers and designing solutions to meet their needs. He also works with the business to set implementation standards and act as a point of technical escalation. Barry is responsible for identifying new technologies as well as speaking and hosting customer-focused events surrounding virtualization, storage, and end-user computing.

Barry has been awarded VMware's vExpert award for contributions to the VMware community every year since 2010. He is also part of the VMUG leadership team for South West UK and blogs at `http://www.definetomorrow.co.uk`. He is active on Twitter (`@virtualisedreal`), particularly reporting live from many industry-related events.

Barry has been a co-author on two VMware Horizon books; more information can be found at `http://virtualisedreality.com/eucbook/`.

Table of Contents

Preface

When we talk about end-user computing, we are typically referring to the virtual desktop infrastructure (VDI), where desktop operating systems are virtualized and hosted centrally in a data center, and users connect remotely to them using some form of client endpoint device over an optimized network delivery protocol. But what about the applications?

Deploying VDI decouples the OS from the local hardware, making the OS portable. However, the applications still remain wedded to the OS, meaning you have to continually manage multiple OS images just to manage applications. After all, the only reason you have the OS in the first place is to run applications.

With the introduction of VMware App Volumes, you now have a solution that allows you to abstract applications from the OS of the virtual desktop and deliver them back individually and on demand to the end users' virtual desktop machine. This approach is now more commonly referred to as application layering. Application layering allows you to separate applications from the underlying OS and then deliver them back into the OS, merging the application files and the OS files together or layering the application in.

By doing this, you can not only manage applications independently of the OS, but also get one step closer to deploying the nirvanic solution of a truly stateless virtual desktop infrastructure.

What this book covers

Chapter 1, Introduction to App Volumes, gives you a high-level introduction to App Volumes. We talk about how it works and what benefits it can bring to your desktop environment. We also look at where it fits within the overall VMware EUC portfolio, where you would use App Volumes compared to some of the other application delivery/packaging technologies, before finally discussing some of the key use cases.

Chapter 2, Architectural and Feature Overview, takes you a little deeper into the different component parts that make up an App Volumes solution. Then, once you are familiar with these different components, we discuss how they fit and work together.

Chapter 3, Designing and Building an App Volumes Deployment, covers the recommendations for sizing, scalability, and making the solution ready for a production environment. The chapter starts by taking a step back and looking at what we have in our current environment, how we are going to approach the overall project, and how to move it forward. We look at both the business and technical elements of a project and break those down into three distinct project phases.

Chapter 4, Installing and Configuring the App Volumes Software, takes you through installing App Volumes and completing the initial configuration steps. Before we do that, we take a few minutes to walk through the prerequisites and what you need to have in place before you start the installation. We also cover the App Volumes infrastructure requirements.

Chapter 5, A Guided Tour of the Management Console, spends a short while walking you through an overview of the management console so that you can familiarize yourself with where the different options are located and how the console pages are laid out.

Chapter 6, Working with AppStacks, takes a deeper look into AppStacks, how they work, and how to start building them, before finally showing you how to assign them to end users. We also look at some of the best practices of how to build an AppStack. At the end of this chapter, you will be able to create, assign, and deliver an AppStack to an end user and then perform ongoing management tasks.

Chapter 7, Working with Writable Volumes, takes a much deeper look at the Writable Volumes feature of App Volumes, how they work, and how to create them, before finally demonstrating Writable Volumes in action. We also look at some of the best practices of how to build a Writable Volume, with particular attention to the dos and don'ts. At the end of this chapter, you will be able to create, assign, and deliver a Writable Volume to an end user as well as perform ongoing management tasks.

Chapter 8, Delivering ThinApp Packages with App Volumes, starts by discussing the background for the ThinApp solution and what it delivers, for those that have not used this solution before. We then go on to look at how and why you would deliver ThinApp packaged applications with App Volumes. Once we have an understanding of what ThinApp is and why you would use it, we use the Example Lab to create a ThinApp package and then build an AppStack that contains the ThinApp package. Once this is created, we go ahead and assign it to a user. In the final part of the chapter, we look at how you can use existing ThinApp packages in order to create AppStacks.

Chapter 9, Horizon View Integration, looks at how App Volumes integrates into the VMware Horizon View virtual desktop solution. We configure and build a VMware Horizon View deployment to deliver virtual desktop machines, with applications being delivered using App Volumes.

Chapter 10, Deploying App Volumes in a Citrix XenDesktop Environment, takes a closer look at how to deploy App Volumes to deliver just-in-time applications to a virtual desktop machine delivered by Citrix XenDesktop.

Chapter 11, Deploying App Volumes in a RemoteApp Environment, takes a closer look at how to deploy App Volumes to deliver just-in-time applications to a Microsoft RemoteApp environment. We build an environment and demonstrate how to deliver the AppStacks for hosted applications.

Chapter 12, Deploying App Volumes in a Citrix XenApp Environment, takes a closer look at the other key Citrix solution and how to deploy App Volumes to deliver applications that are published using Citrix XenApp.

Chapter 13, Deploying App Volumes in a Horizon View Hosted Apps Environment, looks at how to build and configure a Horizon View environment designed to deliver hosted applications to end users with the applications being configured as AppStacks and delivered using the Horizon View hosted app feature.

Chapter 14, Advanced Configuration and Other Options, is the final chapter and looks at some of the advanced configuration options, such as batch script files and App Volumes Agent configuration, as well as some other additional administrations tasks, such as how to customize the App Volumes templates used for creating AppStacks and Writable Volumes and how you can create your own template sizes.

What you need for this book

To get the most out of this book, you should have some experience of working as a desktop administrator with skills and knowledge around building and designing Windows-based environments—both operating system and application skills. Active Directory skills will also be a major benefit.

You should also be familiar with the VMware vSphere platform (ESXi and vCenter Server) and be comfortable with building and configuring virtual machines as well as storage and networking.

Who this book is for

This book is for administrators and IT teams who would like to take full advantage of App Volumes to deliver applications in real time while providing a solution that allows easier management. It will be useful for virtualization professionals and teams that work on VDI deployments with VMware, Citrix, and Microsoft end-user computing solutions.

Conventions

In this book, you will find a number of text styles that distinguish between different kinds of information. Here are some examples of these styles and an explanation of their meaning.

Code words in text, database table names, folder names, filenames, file extensions, pathnames, dummy URLs, user input, and Twitter handles are shown as follows: "If you look at the **Disk File** box you will see the `Win-Desktop-1.vmdk` file."

Any command-line input or output is written as follows:

```
change user /install
```

```
change user /execute
```

New terms and **important words** are shown in bold. Words that you see on the screen, for example, in menus or dialog boxes, appear in the text like this: "Click on the radio button for **I accept the terms in the license agreement**, and click on **Next >** to continue."

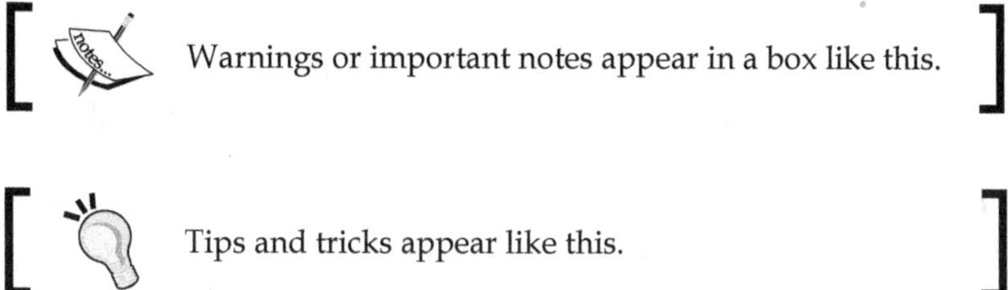

Warnings or important notes appear in a box like this.

Tips and tricks appear like this.

Reader feedback

Feedback from our readers is always welcome. Let us know what you think about this book—what you liked or disliked. Reader feedback is important for us as it helps us develop titles that you will really get the most out of.

To send us general feedback, simply e-mail `feedback@packtpub.com`, and mention the book's title in the subject of your message.

If there is a topic that you have expertise in and you are interested in either writing or contributing to a book, see our author guide at `www.packtpub.com/authors`.

Customer support

Now that you are the proud owner of a Packt book, we have a number of things to help you to get the most from your purchase.

Downloading the color images of this book

We also provide you with a PDF file that has color images of the screenshots/diagrams used in this book. The color images will help you better understand the changes in the output. You can download this file from `http://www.packtpub.com/sites/default/files/downloads/LearningVMwareAppVolumes_ColorImages.pdf`.

Errata

Although we have taken every care to ensure the accuracy of our content, mistakes do happen. If you find a mistake in one of our books—maybe a mistake in the text or the code—we would be grateful if you could report this to us. By doing so, you can save other readers from frustration and help us improve subsequent versions of this book. If you find any errata, please report them by visiting `http://www.packtpub.com/submit-errata`, selecting your book, clicking on the **Errata Submission Form** link, and entering the details of your errata. Once your errata are verified, your submission will be accepted and the errata will be uploaded to our website or added to any list of existing errata under the Errata section of that title.

To view the previously submitted errata, go to `https://www.packtpub.com/books/content/support` and enter the name of the book in the search field. The required information will appear under the **Errata** section.

Piracy

Piracy of copyrighted material on the Internet is an ongoing problem across all media. At Packt, we take the protection of our copyright and licenses very seriously. If you come across any illegal copies of our works in any form on the Internet, please provide us with the location address or website name immediately so that we can pursue a remedy.

Please contact us at `copyright@packtpub.com` with a link to the suspected pirated material.

We appreciate your help in protecting our authors and our ability to bring you valuable content.

Questions

If you have a problem with any aspect of this book, you can contact us at `questions@packtpub.com`, and we will do our best to address the problem.

1

Introduction to App Volumes

In this chapter, you will get a high-level introduction to **App Volumes**. We will talk about how it works and what benefits it can bring to your desktop environment.

We will also look at where it fits within the overall VMware **End User Computing (EUC)** portfolio, where you would use App Volumes compared to some of the other application delivery/packaging technology, before finally discussing some of its key use cases.

This book provides you with both the theory and the practical elements of App Volumes. Each chapter will explain specific areas of the solution and then give you the opportunity to try them out using an **Example Lab**. You will be introduced to the Example Lab at the end of this chapter.

What is App Volumes?

In August 2014, VMware acquired a start-up called **CloudVolumes**. The CloudVolumes technology provided a virtualized, real-time application-delivery engine for virtual desktop infrastructures as well as physical desktops.

In December 2014, CloudVolumes was rebranded and named App Volumes, and offered as a part of **Horizon Enterprise Edition**.

So, what does App Volumes give you? At a high-level, App Volumes provides a real-time application-delivery and life cycle management solution that is used as a delivery system for your virtual and physical desktops.

How does it work?

Let's start with our typical virtual desktop environment. Although the desktop operating system has been abstracted from the underlying hardware, the applications are still tightly integrated into that operating system. The ideal virtual desktop solution is to deliver fully stateless desktops and have the user elements added on the fly, depending on the user's profile. The fully stateless desktop model provides the most cost-effective solution by being easier to manage and requiring less infrastructure.

Today, there are a number of tools that can take care of delivering the user personalization, user data, and user profile elements to the desktop; however, applications are still delivered either as part of the base operating system image or using some form of application remoting or publishing.

App Volumes provides a layer of abstraction between the operating system and applications by delivering the applications in separate containers. These containers are called **AppStacks** and they integrate seamlessly into the operating system of the virtual desktop machine.

The following diagram shows the traditional, static model on the left and the App Volumes on-demand delivery method on the right:

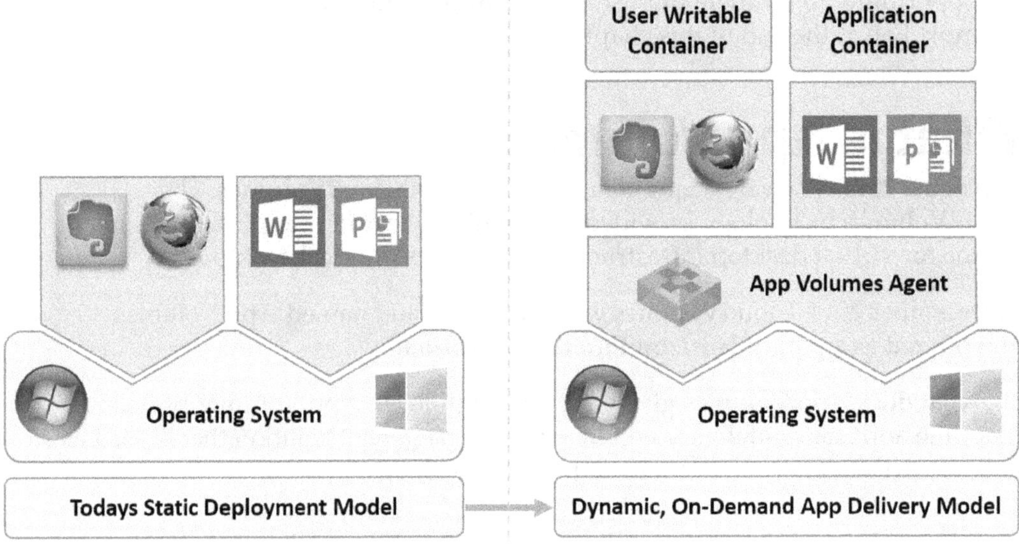

As well as application containers, App Volumes provides the end users with their own container or virtual hard disk, into which they can install their own applications. This container, called a **Writable Volume**, "follows" them when they log in to different virtual desktop machines, bringing all their applications with them.

The following diagram illustrates the App Volumes model of having application containers (AppStacks) and user-writable containers (Writable Volumes):

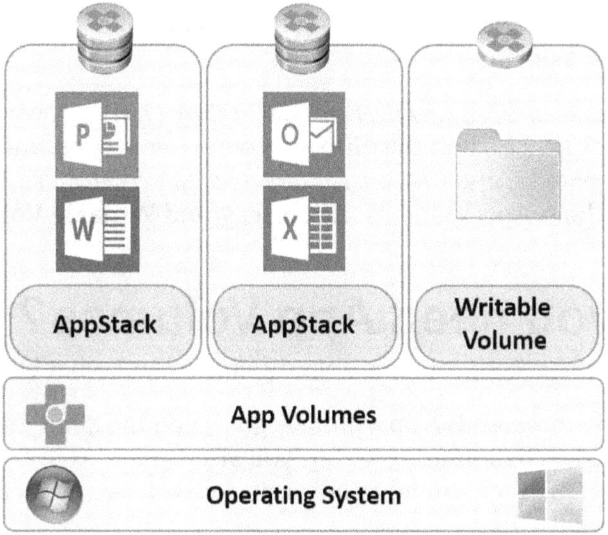

So how do you get started? The first thing you do is create or capture an application that can be delivered by App Volumes. You start the process by installing the application on a virtual desktop machine, which is referred to as the provisioning machine. This provisioning machine is basically a vanilla installation of the operating system, with no applications installed.

When you start the capture process, an empty **Virtual Machine Disk** (**VMDK**) file, called an AppStack, is mounted on to the provisioning machine. Next, you start the application installation as you would normally do. All the files associated with this application are then redirected to the AppStack or VMDK file.

Once you have completed the capture process, the AppStack is set to read-only mode and is ready to be assigned to end users based on their **Active Directory** group membership. AppStacks can also be assigned to individual users or other groups.

For the users to be able to access the applications in their assigned AppStack, an **App Volumes Agent** runs on their desktop, mounting the VMDK file and making the application appear as if it were fully integrated and installed locally rather than running from an additional drive. This is how applications are able to be delivered to a user in real time, as AppStacks can be assigned on the fly.

As well as the applications that get delivered as part of the AppStack, a user is able to have their own disk or VMDK file on which they can install their own applications. This is called a Writable Volume and will also follow the user when they roam among virtual desktops, making it perfect for developers to have non-persistent virtual desktops.

In the next chapter, *Chapter 2, Architectural and Feature Overview*, we will dive a little deeper into what exactly each of the different components does, and then in *Chapter 6, Working with AppStacks*, and *Chapter 7, Working with Writable Volumes*, we will take a deeper dive into how App Volumes, AppStacks, and Writable Volumes work.

Why do you need App Volumes?

So the question is what App Volumes does differently and what benefits it will bring.

As we have already discussed, App Volumes gives you the ability to deliver applications to users in real time; however, you also benefit from being able to manage application life cycles much more easily, as well as a reduction in costs.

Once you have created your AppStack, it's simply a case of a few clicks to assign it to a user or group of users. Conversely, it's that simple to remove it as well. This means that, when a user requests a new application, for example, it's very easy to assign it to them without having to go and install it.

If you are running a virtual desktop environment, then App Volumes helps you drive towards achieving a truly stateless desktop since applications are immediately and dynamically made available upon login, or even while the user is already logged in.

A comparison between App Volumes, Mirage, ThinApp, and RDSH

A question that comes up most of the time when talking about App Volumes and application delivery in general, in a VMware context, is this: which technology should you use and when?

People often ask whether or not App Volumes is going to replace ThinApp and Mirage, and whether these technologies are still required. The key thing to point out here is that each solution addresses a specific use case, and they actually do not all do the same thing. In fact, combining all three delivers a more complete solution.

To the question of whether or not App Volumes is going to replace ThinApp and Mirage, the answer is no. All three technologies are key to the VMware vision and strategy, and won't be going anywhere for the foreseeable future.

In this section, we will discuss which solution you will need, why you will need it, and then see how they are complementary to each other.

Let's start with Mirage. **Mirage** is a centralized, Windows image-management solution, primarily designed to manage physical desktop PCs and laptops. It is also used to deliver the containerized desktop solution, **Horizon FLEX**, for delivering virtual desktops in a **BYOD** (short for **Bring Your Own Device**) environment on both Mac and Windows laptops.

Next up is ThinApp. **ThinApp** is an application virtualization/packaging technology that is primarily used when you need isolation between applications. For example, you might need to deploy an older version of an application that doesn't run on your current operating system version. You may also need to run multiple versions of applications; for example, you may need to run different versions of Internet Explorer. This is one of the key differences in what the solutions deliver. ThinApp is an application-packaging technology. Mirage and App Volumes do not provide any packaging capabilities.

We have outlined what these technologies deliver and we have talked about them being complementary. Depending on your use case, you can use them in combination.

When it comes to managing a physical desktop environment or delivering containerized desktops with Horizon FLEX, Mirage is the technology you should use. If you have applications that need to be isolated, you will combine them with ThinApp to create Mirage application layers, with the application layers containing those ThinApp packages.

If we now take virtual desktop environments and, in particular, those that are built using linked clones and have a floating user assignment, then App Volumes will be the ideal solution for this use case. When they log in, end users will be assigned a vanilla desktop from a pool of floating desktops. Their applications will then be deployed by simply mounting the relevant VMDK file, thus containing the applications in real time.

That was the model for non-persistent, linked, clone desktops, but what about virtual desktops that are built using full clones and have a persistent assignment? For this use case, all three solutions can be combined: Mirage to manage the operating system element, App Volumes to deliver the applications, and the applications potentially being packaged using ThinApp, if you require the isolation between applications.

The VMware documentation for the latest version of App Volumes talks about being able to deliver AppStacks to physical desktops. Although this is possible, Mirage would be a better option for managing physical desktops.

As you can see, there are several use cases that lend themselves to the different technologies, and this is the key to deciding which ones to use and when.

The following diagram shows a high-level overview of how the technologies complement each other and work together:

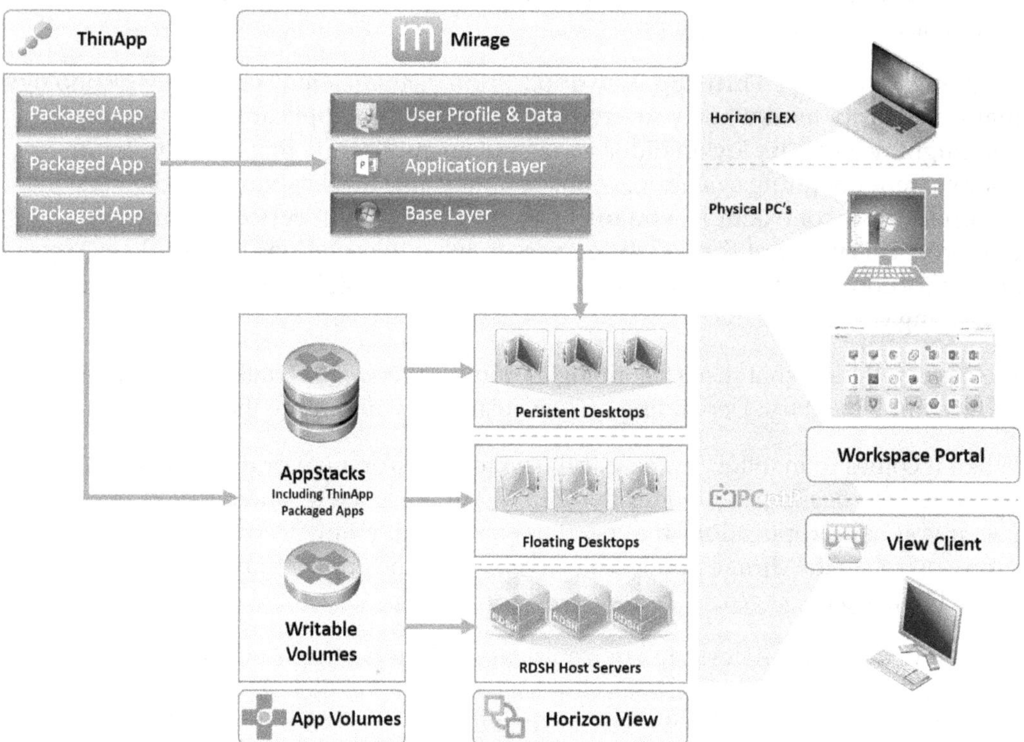

In the next section, we will discuss the key use cases for App Volumes in more detail.

App Volumes use cases

There are several key use cases for deploying App Volumes within your environment.

The first of these use cases is deploying App Volumes within a virtual desktop infrastructure environment.

VDI desktops

A **virtual desktop infrastructure** (**VDI**) is the primary use case for App Volumes. It allows IT administrators to deploy applications in real time and independent of the core operating system. The decision on who gets which applications is based on the user and group policies, depending on the user's membership in Active Directory.

So why is this important and a key use case?

In order to deploy the most optimized VDI, you would want to opt for a floating, non-persistent model. This means that virtual desktop machines are delivered on demand from a pool of available machines and that nobody owns their own desktop. Everything is delivered on demand, and when the user logs off the virtual desktop machine gets destroyed, ready for the next user to log on.

This model would suit the majority of users; however, there are some users, such as developers, who would still require a persistent virtual desktop machine so that they have the ability to install their own applications that will remain when they log off rather than being destroyed when the virtual desktop machine they have been using gets destroyed. Deploying these types of virtual desktop machines is more costly and puts a greater load on infrastructure resources as you need more computing power and more storage than you would in a non-persistent deployment.

By deploying App Volumes, and the Writable Volumes feature in particular, users essentially get their own hard drive with their own user-installed applications on that drive. As they log on to a non-persistent, floating virtual desktop, their writable volume or hard drive gets attached and mounted to that virtual desktop machine. To the user, it looks as if their applications are natively installed on their desktop and that it is their own desktop.

The end users also benefit from having their core applications delivered immediately, and for the IT department, this means they can easily manage application delivery in real time, allowing them to assign new applications on the fly as well as deploy any updates to existing applications.

Allowing users to work with this model of virtual desktop machine deployment also means that the overall infrastructure requirements, particularly storage, are significantly lowered.

It's also important to note that we are not just talking about VMware virtual desktop solutions. App Volumes also supports **Citrix** environments, and can be purchased specifically for this, which we will cover in the *How to license App Volumes* section of this chapter.

RDSH-delivered applications

This particular use case is one that often gets overlooked since **Remote Desktop Services Host** (**RDSH**) is in itself an application-delivery mechanism. So how can App Volumes help with this use case?

If you look at the basic infrastructure around RDSH, applications have to be installed onto the RDSH server before they can be published to the end users. This in itself makes the infrastructure pretty static in nature. By static we mean that if you need to scale up your RDSH deployment, you not only have to build a new server but also install the applications all over again afterwards. It's a similar story when you have to update applications.

App Volumes, in this use case, works in the same way it would with a VDI, but instead of mounting AppStacks on the virtual desktop machine's operating system this time you are mounting them on the RDSH server. It's just a case of installing the App Volumes Agent and capturing an AppStack for use in this environment. Obviously, your RDSH servers need to be running as virtual machines.

Essentially, you are creating a stateless RDSH server that allows you to add additional server resources and just mount the AppStacks on them rather than having to install the applications each time.

Citrix XenDesktop and XenApp environments

We already mentioned that App Volumes can be deployed in a Citrix environment and can deliver exactly the same benefits. **XenDesktop**-based virtual desktop machines work in exactly the same way as a VMware **Horizon View** virtual desktop machine when it comes to delivering applications; however, you can now support the **Virtual Hard Disk** (**VHD**) format.

XenApp works using the functionality of an RDSH server. This means that you can now deploy stateless XenApp Servers by mounting AppStacks to RDSH servers, as we discussed previously. Like XenDesktop deployments, this can also be done using VHD deployments if you use a virtualization platform based on XenServer or Hyper-V.

Project A^2

Announced at **VMworld** in 2015 as a tech preview, Project A^2 brings together AirWatch **enterprise mobile management** (**EMM**) and VMware App Volumes to deliver mobile-like management for their Microsoft Windows 10 devices and applications.

How to license App Volumes

There are several ways in which you can purchase and license App Volumes.

Firstly, App Volumes is a standard component of the Horizon Enterprise Edition license.

The second option is to purchase App Volumes as a part of the **VMware Horizon Application Management Bundle**. This bundle includes all the components except the core VDI solution, Horizon View, and is designed to complement existing Citrix environments.

Lastly, you can purchase App Volumes as a standalone product as part of an *à la carte* list of solutions. Whichever option you choose to purchase App Volumes, the product itself is licensed on a per-concurrent-user basis.

How does this book work?

Now that we have covered the introduction to App Volumes, let's just take five minutes to introduce you to how this book works and what you will need to get the most out of it.

This book will guide you through the key use cases for App Volumes, from the theory of how it works and how to design a solution, to the more practical elements, such as installation.

Each section of this book has been written based on everyday, real-world experiences of working with the product in both production and proof-of-concept/pilot environments.

In parallel with the chapters, you can set up your own lab environment, which will cover practical examples of how the technology works, giving you the option to follow the steps and try them for yourself. This can either be as an exercise while reading the chapters or to assist you in setting up a proof-of-concept, pilot, or live deployment.

Introducing the Example Lab

Accompanying this book, as previously mentioned, is an Example Lab that you can build along the way. In this introductory section, we are going to cover the requirements for this lab and what it will look like. The lab is optional, and you can choose to build your own environment.

What you will need for the lab

The lab environment used in this book was built on a Dell PowerEdge R720xd LE configured with two E5-2680V2 2.8-GHz 10-core processors and 64 GB RAM, running VMware vSphere 6 as the hypervisor.

Although the server had internal storage, the lab was built using a Tintri all-flash array. By using Tintri and its VM-aware capabilities, you can monitor right down to the virtual-machine level.

The reason I chose Tintri storage is the fact that it has been developed from the ground up for virtualized environments removing contention points and collision domains such as the LUN construct. Tintri was very easy to deploy. It was done in just under 15 minutes. The folks at Tintri have created a new storage category. They call it **VAS** (short for **VM Aware Storage**). This "awareness" is backed by Tintri's analytics engine learning the behavior of individual VMs underpinned by an intelligent filesystem. The architecture is designed to adapt to the fluidity that comes with virtualized workloads enabling it to deliver the right quality of service where and when it is needed. This makes Tintri ideal for VDI-type deployments as it has the ability to respond to performance bursts that can result from use cases such as App Volumes.

All of this was used to host the following virtual machines. The computer names of the virtual machines are shown in brackets and will be referred to in the lab examples throughout the book:

- Windows Server 2012 R2: configured with AD, DNS, and a file server (DC)
- VMware vCenter Server Appliance (VCSA)
- VMware ESXi v5.5 host server (ESX-1)
- Windows Server 2012 R2: App Volumes Manager (APP-VOL-MGR)
- Windows Server 2012 R2: Microsoft SQL 2008 Express*
- Windows Server 2012 R2: configured with the RDSH role**
- Windows Server 2012 R2: Horizon View Connection Server (VIEW-CS)***
- Windows 7: AppStack-provisioning desktop (AV-PROVISION)
- Windows 7: used as a virtual desktop machine (WIN7-DESKTOP-1)
- Windows 7: used as a virtual desktop machine (WIN7-DESKTOP-2)
- Windows 7: virtual desktop machine delivered by Horizon View (VIEW-1)
- Windows XP: used for ThinApp Setup Capture (WINXP-DESKTOP-1)

* In the Example Lab, the Microsoft SQL Express server is also installed on the same server as the App Volumes Manager. As this lab is just for testing, it is fine to configure it in this way. This is not recommended for production environments.

** Only required in *Chapter 11, Deploying App Volumes in a RemoteApp Environment*. If you don't plan to install and test this feature, there is no need to deploy an RDSH server.

*** Only required in *Chapter 9, Horizon View Integration*. If you don't plan to install and test Horizon View, there is no need to deploy a Horizon View connection server.

If you plan to build a lab as you follow the chapters, it's worth building the infrastructure detailed here beforehand. Build and install all the virtual machines, but with the exception of installing any of the App Volumes software components.

In writing this book, VMware vSphere 6 has been used as the hypervisor to host all of the VMs used in the Example Lab, but you could also run this in VMware Workstation.

If you choose not to follow the steps described, they will still help by providing you with a reference and foundation for building and managing your own environment.

A schematic diagram of the core lab environment used for the examples is detailed in the following diagram:

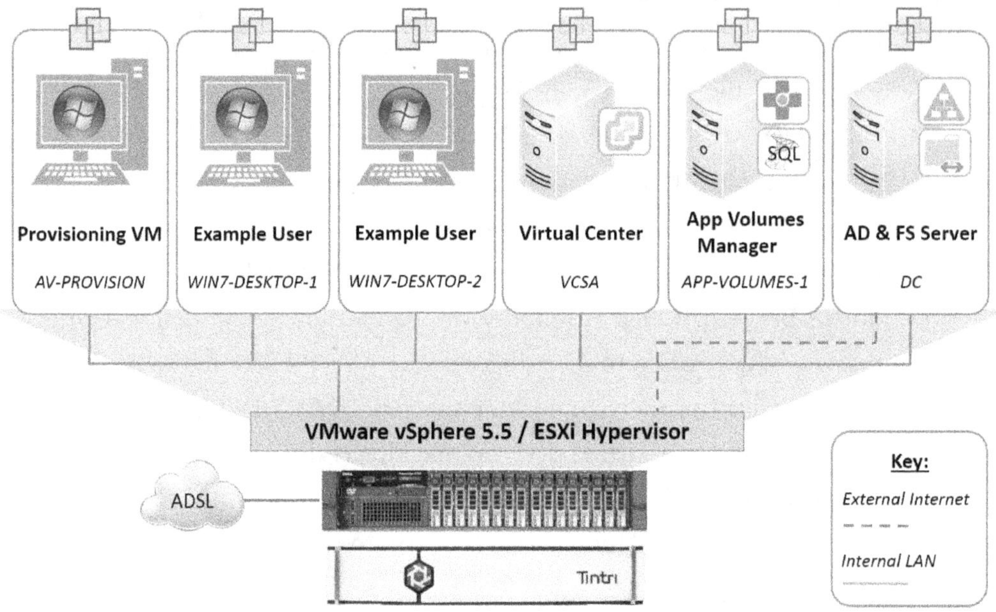

The next schematic diagram shows the optional lab components for integrating App Volumes with VMware Horizon View and RDSH servers:

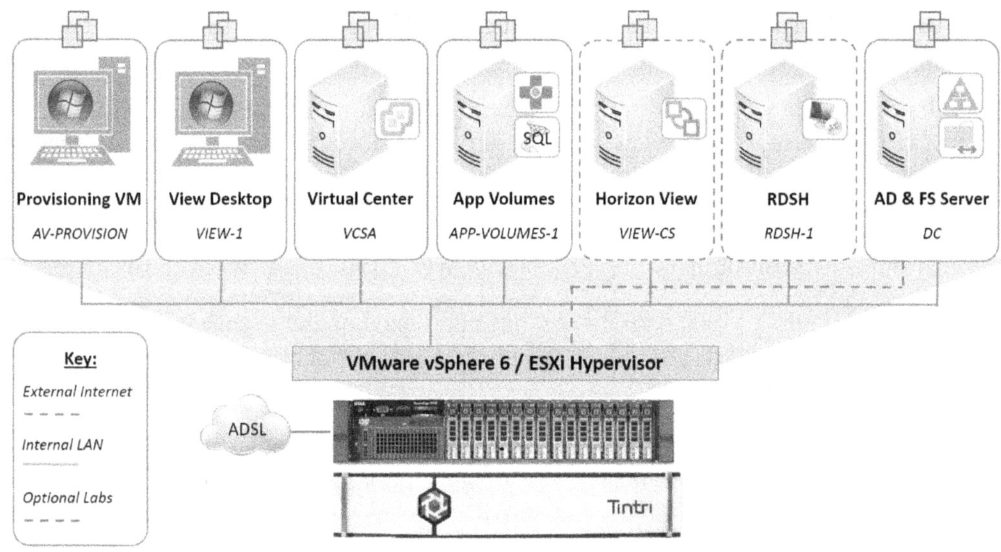

The file server in the lab environment was used to host a shared folder containing all the installation files so that they are accessible by all the other virtual machines.

This final schematic diagram shows the optional lab for *Chapter 8, Delivering ThinApp Packages with App Volumes*:

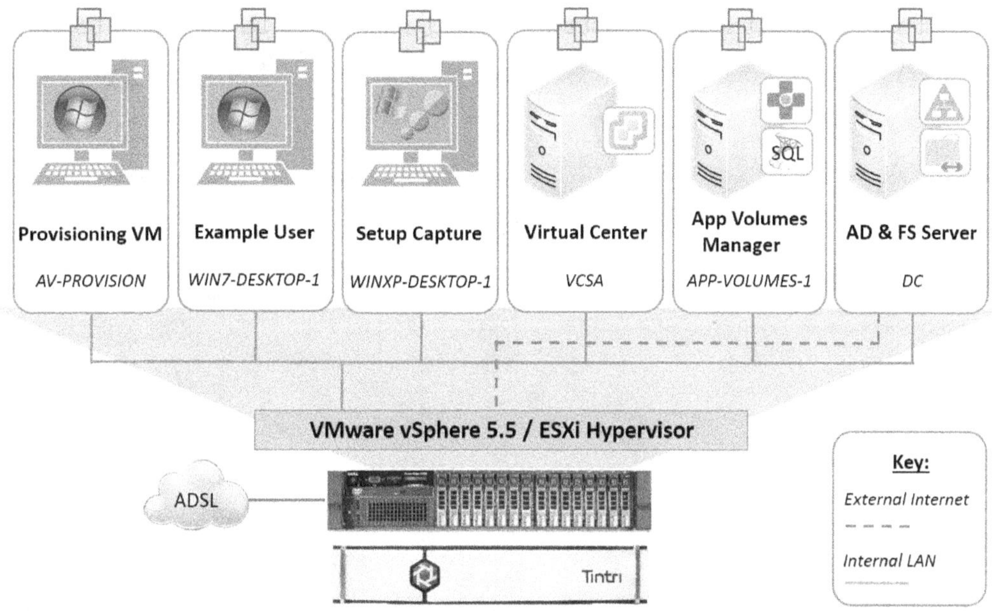

We also require an administrator account and a number of **Organizational Unit (OU)** groups and user accounts.

For administering App Volumes, a group called `AppVol Admin` was created. The administrator account was then added to this group. You can, of course, create other App Volumes administrator accounts.

In addition to the administrator account, we have created a number of Active Directory groups to reflect different departments. In each group, there are a few user accounts. These have been set up as shown in the following table:

Active Directory Group 1	Active Directory Group 2	User	Login Name
Domain Users	Sales	John Smith	jsmith@pvolab.com
		Sue Jones	sjones@pvolab.com
		Bob Cooper	bcooper@pvolab.com
	Engineering	Peter Owens	powens@pvolab.com
		James Thomas	jthomas@pvolab.com
		Ellie Richards	erichards@pvolab.com
	Finance	Tom Jackson	tjackson@pvolab.com
		Charlotte Edwards	cedwards@pvolab.com
		Nick Mason	nmason@pvolab.com

These users and groups will be used throughout the Example Lab to demonstrate user assignments.

Summary

In this chapter, we have covered a high-level introduction to App Volumes, looking at what it is, how it works, and what it can deliver.

We then went on to cover exactly where App Volumes fits into the overall VMware EUC portfolio, bearing in mind that products such as ThinApp and Mirage seem to deliver almost the same functionality.

Finally, we saw how to get the most out of this book, and you were introduced to the Example Lab that you can build along the way in each chapter.

In the next chapter, *Chapter 2, Architectural and Feature Overview*, we will start to look a little deeper into each of the App Volumes components.

2

Architectural and Feature Overview

In this chapter, we will start to look a little deeper into the different components that make up an App Volumes solution. Then, once you are familiar with these different components, we will discuss how they fit and work together.

App Volumes components

We will start by covering an overview of the different core components that make up the complete App Volumes solution—a glossary, if you like. These are either components of the actual App Volumes solution or additional components that are required to build your complete environment.

App Volumes Manager

App Volumes Manager is the heart of the solution. Installed on the Windows Server operating system, App Volumes Manager controls the application-delivery engine and provides you with access to a web-based dashboard and console from which you can manage your entire App Volumes environment.

You will get your first glimpse of App Volumes Manager in *Chapter 4, Installing and Configuring the App Volumes Software*, when you complete the installation and start the post-installation tasks, where you will configure details for your virtual host servers, storage, Active Directory, and other environment variables.

Once you have completed the installation tasks, you will use App Volumes Manager to perform tasks such as creating new and updating existing AppStacks, creating Writable Volumes, and then assigning both AppStacks and Writable Volumes to end users or virtual desktop machines.

App Volumes Manager also manages the virtual desktop machines that have an App Volumes Agent installed. Once a virtual desktop machine has the agent installed, it will appear within the App Volumes Manager inventory so that you are able to configure assignments.

In summary, App Volumes Manager performs the following functions:

- Orchestrating the key infrastructure components, such as Active Directory, AppStack/Writable Volumes attachments, and the virtual hosting infrastructure (ESXi hosts and vCenter Servers)
- Managing the assignment of AppStacks/Writable Volumes to users, groups, and virtual desktop machines
- Collating AppStacks and Writable Volumes usage
- Providing a history of administrative actions
- Acting as a broker for App Volumes Agents for the automated assignment of AppStacks and Writable Volumes when virtual desktop machines boot up and the end users log in
- Providing a web-based graphical interface from which to manage the entire environment

Throughout this book, you will see the following graphic used in drawings or schematics to denote App Volumes Manager:

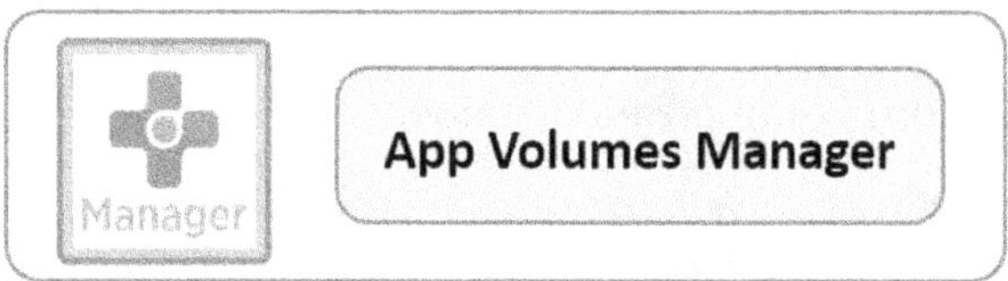

App Volumes Agents

An App Volumes Agent is installed onto a virtual desktop machine to which you want to be able to attach AppStacks or Writable Volumes and it runs as a service on that machine. As such, it is invisible to the end user.

When you attach an AppStack or Writable Volume to a virtual machine, then the agent acts as a filter driver and takes care of any application calls and file system redirects between the operating system and the AppStack or Writable Volume.

Rather than you seeing your AppStack, it appears as an additional hard drive within the operating system. The agent makes the applications appear as if they were natively installed. So, for example, the icons for your applications will automatically appear on your desktop/taskbar.

The App Volumes Agent is also responsible for registering the virtual machine with App Volumes Manager, as we discussed in the previous section.

Throughout this book, you will see the following graphic used in drawings or schematics to denote an App Volumes Agent:

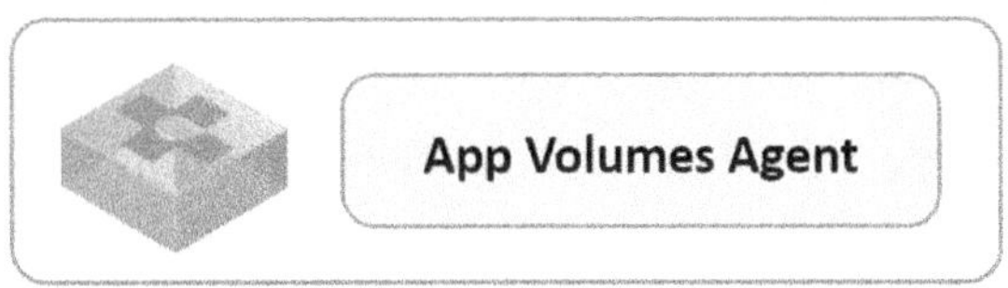

App Volumes Agents can also be installed onto an RDSH host server to allow the attachment of AppStacks within a hosted-applications environment. We will cover this in detail in *Chapter 11, Deploying App Volumes in a RemoteApp Environment.*

AppStacks

An AppStack is a read-only volume that contains your applications and is mounted as a VMDK file (VMware environments) or a VHD file (Citrix and Microsoft environments) on your virtual desktop machine or RDSH host server.

An AppStack is created using a provisioning machine that has an App Volumes Agent installed on it. Then, as part of the provisioning process, you mount an empty container (VMDK or VHD file) and then install the application(s) as you would normally do. The App Volumes Agent redirects the installation files, file system, and registry settings to the AppStack. Once this is completed, the AppStack is set to read-only mode, which allows one AppStack to be used for multiple users. This helps reduce the storage requirements (an App Stack is also thin-provisioned), but also allows any application that is delivered via an AppStack to be centrally managed and updated.

AppStacks are then delivered to the end users either as individual user assignments or via group membership using Active Directory.

Throughout this book, you will see the following graphic used in drawings or schematics to denote an AppStack:

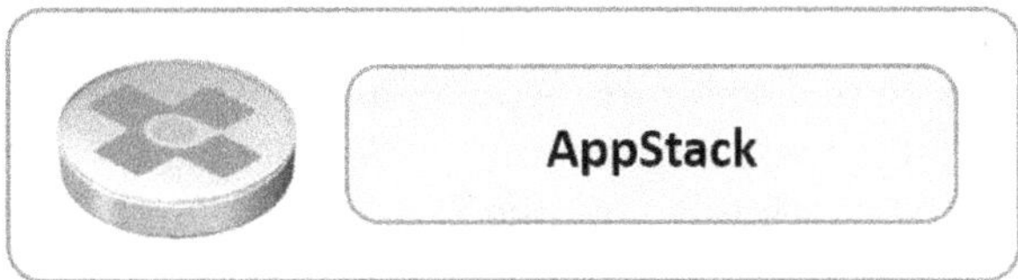

We will cover AppStacks in more detail in *Chapter 6, Working with AppStacks.*

Writable Volumes

One of the many use cases not best suited to a VDI has been that of developers, as they need to install various applications and her software. To cater to this use case, you need to deploy a dedicated, persistent desktop to meet their requirements. This method of deployment is not necessarily the most cost-effective one, potentially requiring additional infrastructure resources and management.

With App Volumes, all this changes with the Writable Volumes feature. In the same way that you assign an AppStack containing preinstalled and configured applications to an end user, with Writable Volumes you attach an empty container as a VMDK file to their virtual desktop machine, into which they can install their own applications.

This virtual desktop machine will be running an App Volumes Agent, which provides a filter between any application that the end user installs into the Writable Volume and the native operating system of the virtual desktop machine. The user then has their own drive onto which they can install applications.

Now, you can deploy non-persistent, floating desktops for these users and attach not only their corporate applications via AppStacks but also their own user-installed applications via a Writable Volume.

Throughout this book, you will see the following graphic used in drawings or schematics to denote a Writable Volume:

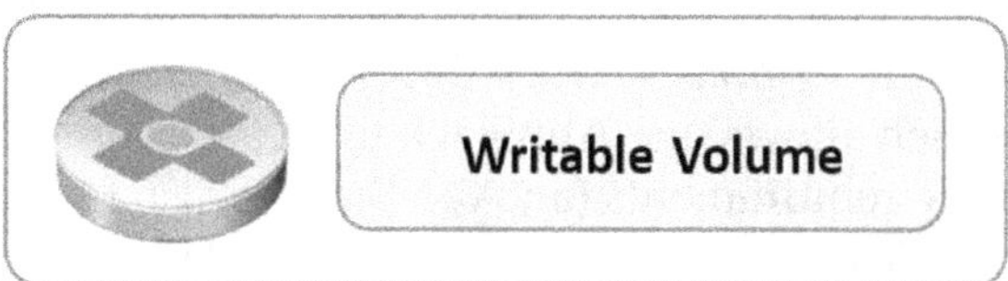

The provisioning virtual machine

Although not an actual part of the App Volumes software, a key component is a clean virtual desktop machine to use as a reference point to create your AppStacks from. This is known as a provisioning machine.

Once you have your provisioning virtual desktop machine, you firstly install an App Volumes Agent onto it. Then, from App Volumes Manager, you initiate the provisioning process, which attaches an empty VMDK file to the provisioning virtual desktop machine and then prompts you, the IT admin, to install the application.

Before you start the installation of the application(s) that you are going to create as an AppStack, it's good practice to take a snapshot. This way, you can roll back to the clean state of your virtual desktop machine prior to installation, ready to create the next AppStack.

Throughout this book, you will see the following graphic used in drawings or schematics to denote a provisioning machine:

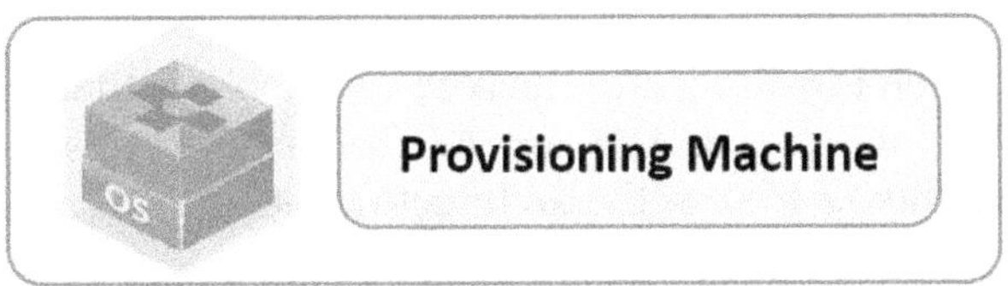

We will cover the use of the provisioning machine in more detail in *Chapter 6, Working with AppStacks*, when we create our first AppStack.

Storage groups

Again, although not a specific component of App Volumes, you have the ability to define storage groups for storing your AppStacks and Writable Volumes.

Storage groups are primarily used to provide replications of AppStacks and to distribute Writable Volumes across multiple datastores. With AppStack storage groups, you can define a group of datastores that will be used to store the same AppStacks, enabling replication to be automatically deployed on those datastores.

With Writable Volumes, only some of the storage group settings will apply attributes to the storage group, for example, the template location and distribution strategy.

The distribution strategy allows you to define how Writable Volumes are distributed across the storage group. There are two settings for this, as follows:

- **Spread**: This will distribute files evenly across all the storage locations. When a file is created, the storage location with the most available space is used.
- **Round-robin**: This works by distributing the Writable Volume files sequentially, using the storage location that hasn't been used for the longest time.

Throughout this book, you will see the following graphic used in drawings or schematics to denote storage groups:

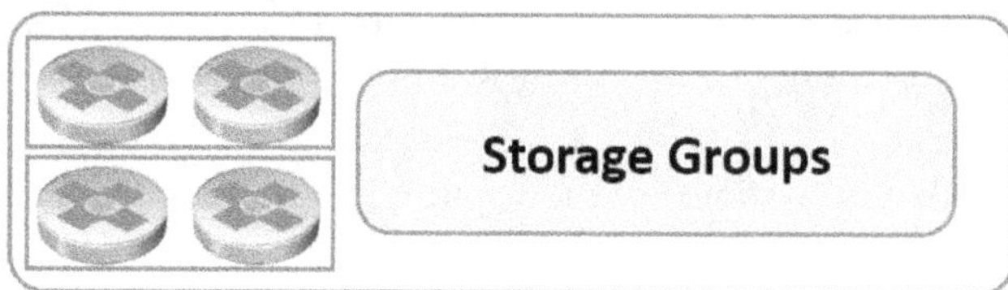

Now that you have been introduced to the core components that make up an App Volumes deployment, in the next section, we will start looking at how all these fit together, and we will take a look at the architecture.

The App Volumes architecture

Now that you understand what each of the individual components is used for, the next step is to look at how they all fit together to form the complete solution.

We are going to break the architecture down into three parts. The first part will be focused on the application-delivery and virtual desktop machines from an end user's perspective.

In the second part, we will look more closely at the supporting and underlying infrastructure, that is, from an IT administrator's point of view.

Finally, in the infrastructure section, we will look at the infrastructure with a networking hat on and illustrate the various network ports we will require to be available to us.

So let's go back and look at our first part: what the end user will see.

In this example, we have a virtual desktop machine running Windows as the starting point of our solution. Onto that virtual desktop machine, we have installed an App Volumes Agent.

We also have some core applications already installed onto this virtual desktop machine that part of the core/parent image. These will be applications that are delivered to every user, such as Adobe Reader. This is exactly the same best-practice method as we would normally follow in any other VDI. The updates here would be taken care of by updating the parent image and then using the recompose feature of linked clones in Horizon View.

With the agent installed, the virtual desktop machine will appear in the App Volumes Manager console, from where we can start assigning AppStacks to our Active Directory users and groups.

When a user who has been assigned an AppStack or Writable Volume logs in to a virtual desktop machine, the AppStack that has been assigned to them will be attached to that virtual desktop machine, and the applications within that AppStack will seamlessly appear on the desktop.

They will also have access to their Writable Volume, should one be assigned to them.

The following diagram illustrates an example deployment from the virtual desktop machine's perspective, as we have just described:

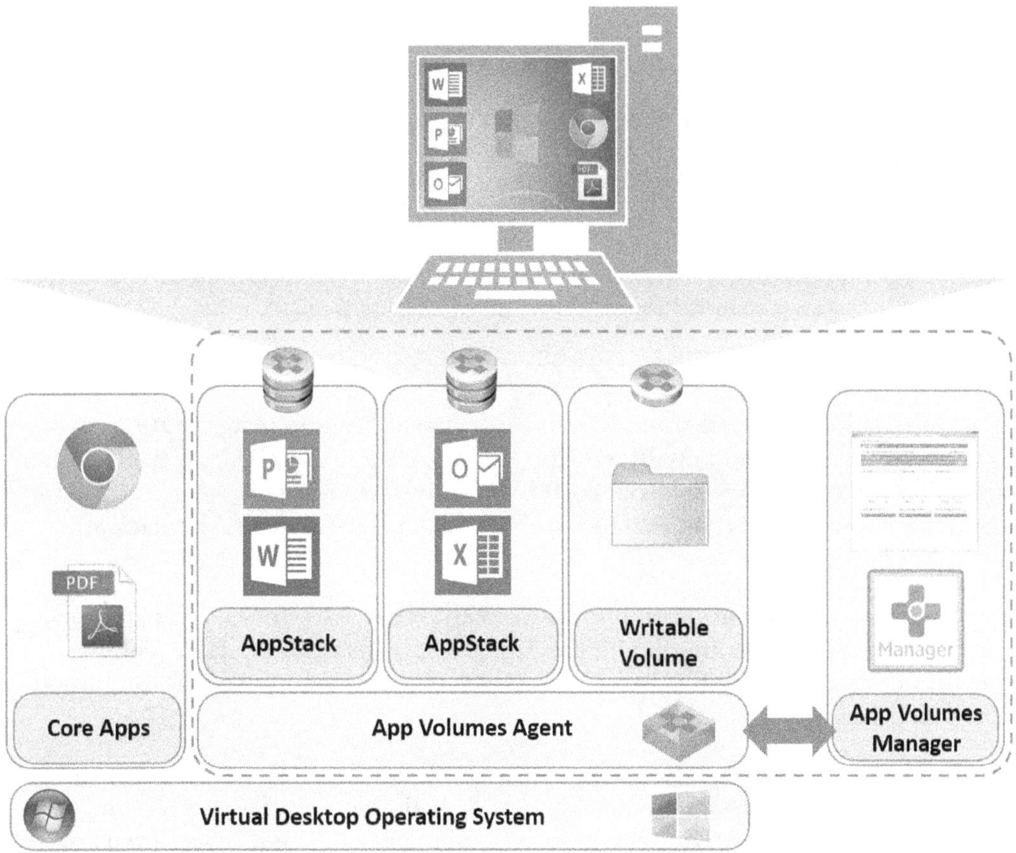

Moving on to the second part of our focus on the architecture, we are now going to look at the underlying/supporting infrastructure.

As a starting point, all of our infrastructure components have been deployed as virtual machines and are hosted on the VMware vSphere platform.

The following diagram illustrates the infrastructure components and how they fit together to deliver the applications to the virtual desktop machines:

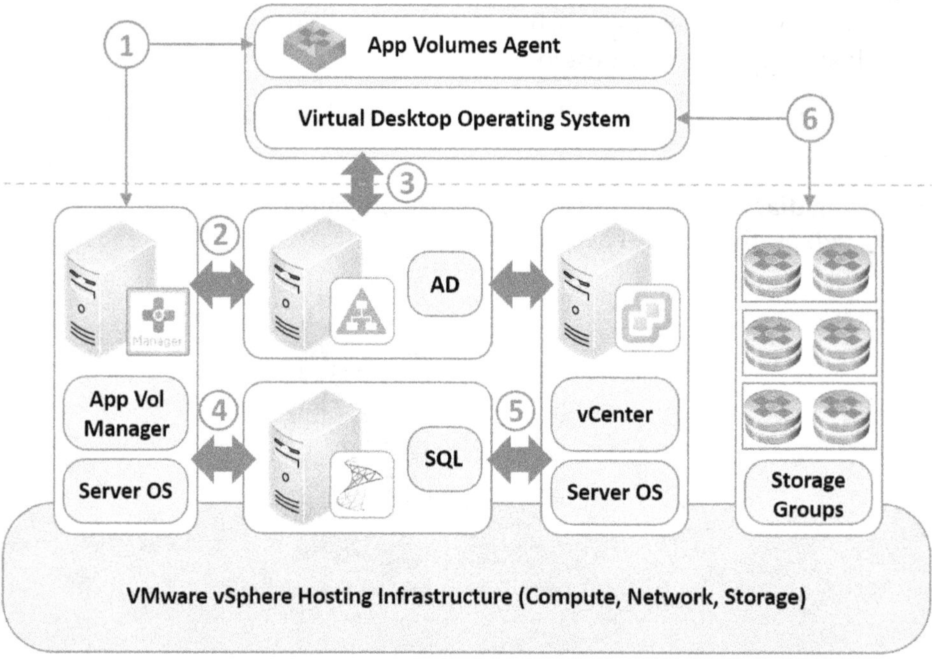

In the top section of the diagram, we have the virtual desktop machine running our Windows operating system with the App Volumes Agent installed. As well as acting as the filter driver, the agent also talks to App Volumes Manager **(1)** to read the user assignment information that describes who can access which AppStack and Writable Volume.

App Volumes Manager also communicates with Active Directory **(2)** to read user, group, and machine information for assigning AppStacks and Writable Volumes. The virtual desktop machine also talks to Active Directory for authenticating user logins **(3)**.

App Volumes Manager also needs access to a SQL database **(4)**, which stores the information about the assignments, AppStacks, Writable Volumes, and so on. A SQL database is also a requirement for vCenter Server **(5)**, and if you are using the linked clone function of Horizon View, then a database is required for the view composer.

We will discuss integration with Horizon View and the associated architecture in *Chapter 9, Horizon View Integration.*

The final part of the diagram shows the App Volumes storage groups that are used to store the AppStacks and Writable Volumes. These get mounted to the virtual desktop machines as virtual disks or VMDK files **(6)**.

Following on from the architecture and the way the different components fit together and communicate, in the next section we will cover which ports need to be open to allow communication between the various services and components.

Network ports

In this section, we are going to cover the firewall ports that are required to be open in order for the App Volumes components to communicate with the other infrastructure components.

The following diagram shows the port numbers (highlighted in boxes) that are required to be open for each component to communicate:

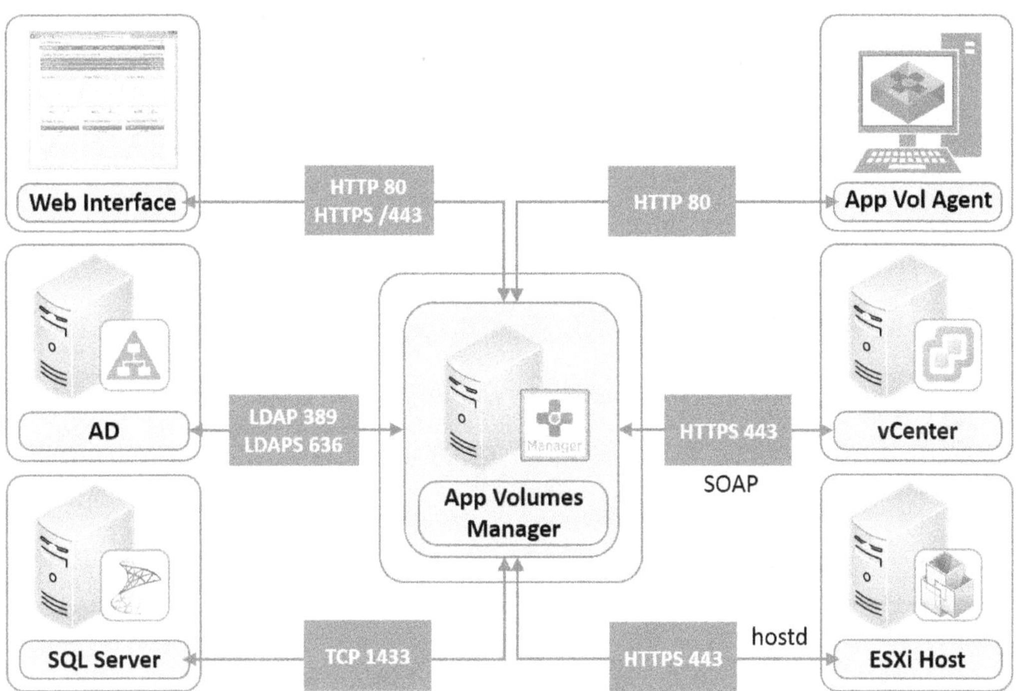

It's worth ensuring that these ports are configured before you start the deployment of App Volumes.

Summary

In this chapter, you were introduced to the individual components that make up an App Volumes solution and what task each of them performs. We then went on to look at how those components fit into the overall solution architecture as well as how the architecture works.

In the next chapter, we will start discussing how to design an App Volumes solution, what to look out for when dealing with applications, and how to generally approach a project such as this.

3

Designing and Building an App Volumes Deployment

In the previous chapter, we introduced you to the components and architecture that make up the App Volumes solution, but before we start to deploy anything in our environment, in this chapter, we are going to discuss the key points that you need to take into consideration when planning an App Volumes deployment.

In this chapter, we are going to cover the recommendations about sizing, scalability, and making the solution ready for a production environment, but before we get into the detail of all of that, we are going to take a step back and look at what we currently have in place today, and how we are going to approach the overall project and how to move it forward.

We are going to look at both the business and technical elements of a project, and break these down into three distinct project phases, as shown in the following diagram:

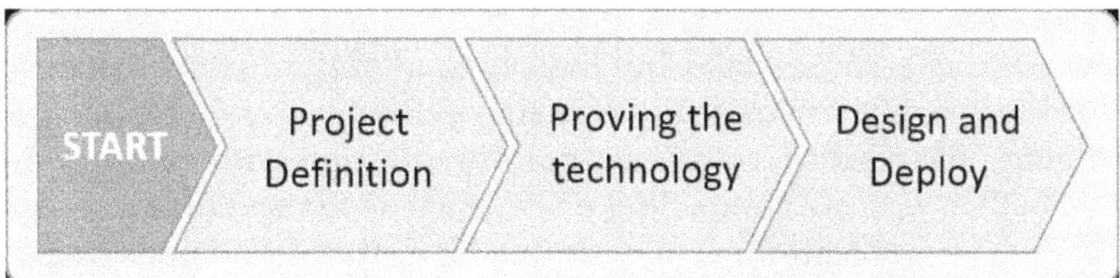

The three distinct phases can be explained as follows:

- **Phase I - Project Definition** is where we look at the business elements of the project, identifying both business and use cases
- **Phase II - Proving the technology** is the opportunity to test the solution in your environment
- **Phase III - Design and Deploy** takes the output and findings from the previous two phases, allowing you to design and deploy the solution in production

In the next sections, we are going to discuss the three phases in more detail.

Phase I – Project definition

In this first section, we are going to look at how we approach the project. This is broken down into four steps, as shown in the following diagram:

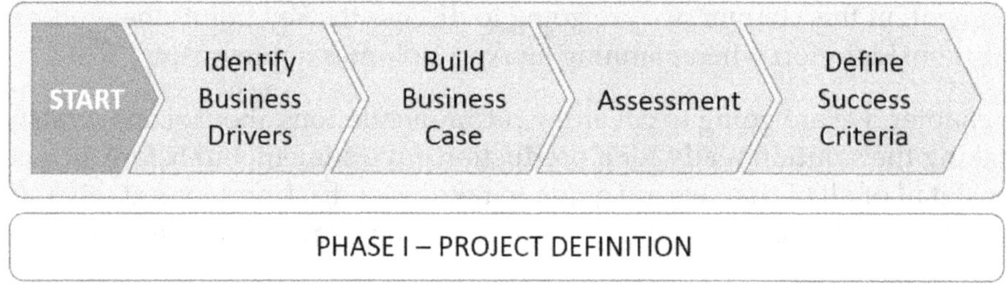

Let's start by looking at the business drivers.

Identifying business drivers

It may be an obvious point to make, but the key to identifying the business drivers is to really understand what you want to evaluate. By this, we mean is it a strategic decision based on the need to transform your organization with new working initiatives, or is there a more compelling event, such as the end of life of an operating system or application? It may simply be the need to reduce cost.

Whatever the case, you need to get that nailed down and written up on day one so the project has meaning and direction, and more importantly a baseline to refer back to when it comes to review time to gauge whether or not the project has been successful.

Primary drivers include things such as:

- Cost reduction - operating expenditure
- Centralized management of applications
- Scalability - faster, easier deployment of applications
- Reduced user downtime
- Reducing application refresh, deployment cycles, and updates
- Operating system migration

Now we have an understanding of why the business is considering this project, we can investigate further and start to build the specific business case.

Building the business case

Once we have defined the drivers behind an initiative or the compelling event that's kicked off the process, and understood the high-level objectives, the next stage is to start building the business case around these. By this, we mean to go to the next level of details and start to drill into the specific areas the solution needs to address.

To do this, you need to first understand the business strategy and then identify the key stakeholder for the project. We can then start to define the high-level requirements of each of the areas identified as drivers and also start to define user segmentation, for example, look at what different user types we have, how they work today, and what they need going forward. At the end of the day, it will be the end users who decide whether or not the project is a success. This leads us into the next section, the assessment phase.

Assessment

Once you have built your business case, validated it against your strategy, and identified that there is a requirement for a new way of delivering applications, the next stage is to run an assessment. It's quite fitting that this book is entitled "Learning", as this stage of the project is exactly that: learning about your current environment which is essential for a successful outcome.

So what do we mean by assessment? It comes down to several things that we are looking for. This includes examining your current application landscape by means of some form of application assessment so you can understand what applications are being delivered, to whom they are being delivered, and, more importantly, how they are being delivered.

The assessment is designed to build up a picture of what the current environment actually looks like. Some of the key metrics we are looking for include:

- Which users are using which applications?
- Application usage
- Are any applications being installed with a Windows Installer MSI?
- Identify any application virtualization/packaging technologies in use
- Unsuitable applications
- Which client operating systems are being used?
- Delivery methods (RDSH, XenApp, VDI, physical PCs, and so on)

If you have deployed a VDI solution already then you should have most of this data, but even so, if this was a while ago then it's worth re-running the assessment so you have up-to-date data, especially about the applications in your environment.

By gathering this assessment data, we are creating a baseline view of the environment. Then, as we move into defining the success criteria and proving the technology, we can refer back to the baseline as a reference point and use it to demonstrate how we have improved the current working environment and delivered on the business case and strategy.

There are a number of tools that can be used in the assessment phase to gather the information required and provide you with physical data, but don't forget to actually talk to the end users as well, so you are armed with the hard and fast facts from an assessment as well as from the user's perspective.

As part of the assessment, there are also some key things you need to understand about the existing application landscape and packaging strategy:

- Determine the existing application packaging strategy
- Is there a virtual first strategy, such as ThinApp or App Volume, or is it an MSI deployment with **System Center Configuration Manager** (**SCCM**)?
- Is the source media available?
- How does licensing work?
- Capture application usage per individual user

This information will help you to plan the number of applications per AppStack, bearing in mind that too many applications could increase the risk of conflicts between the different applications and also result in more complex management.

Defining the success criteria

The key objective in defining the success criteria is to document what a "good" solution should look like for the project to succeed and become production-ready.

We need to clearly define the elements that need to function correctly in order to move from proof of concept to proof of technology, and then into a pilot phase before deploying into production. You need to fully document what these elements are and get the end users or other project stakeholders to sign up to them. It's almost like creating a statement of work with a clearly defined list of tasks.

Another important factor is to ensure that during this phase of the project, the criteria don't start to grow beyond the original scope. By that, we mean other additional elements should not get added to the success criteria or at least not without discussing it first. It may well transpire that something key was missed; however, if you have conducted your assessment thoroughly, this shouldn't happen.

Another thing that works well at this stage is to involve the end users. Set up a steering committee or advisory panel by selecting people from different departments to act as sponsors within their area of business. Actively involve them in the application testing phases, but get them on board early as well to get their input in shaping the solution.

Too many projects fail when an end user tries something and it doesn't work. However, the thing those they tried is not actually a relevant use case or something that is used by the business as a critical line-of-business application and therefore shouldn't derail the project.

If we have a set of success criteria defined up front that the end users have signed up to, anything outside that criteria is not in scope. If it's not defined in the document then it should be disregarded as not being part of what success should look like.

Now that we have our assessment data and a scope of what we are setting out to achieve, in the next steps we are going to look at the options for proving the solution is fit for purpose and delivers the benefits required.

Phase II – Proving the technology

In this section, we are going to discuss the approach to proving the technology is fit for purpose. This is a key piece of work that needs to be successfully completed once we have completed phase I, and is somewhat different from how you would typically approach an IT project. This is the same approach you should take for any end user computing type of project. The transition from phase I to phase II can be seen in the following diagram:

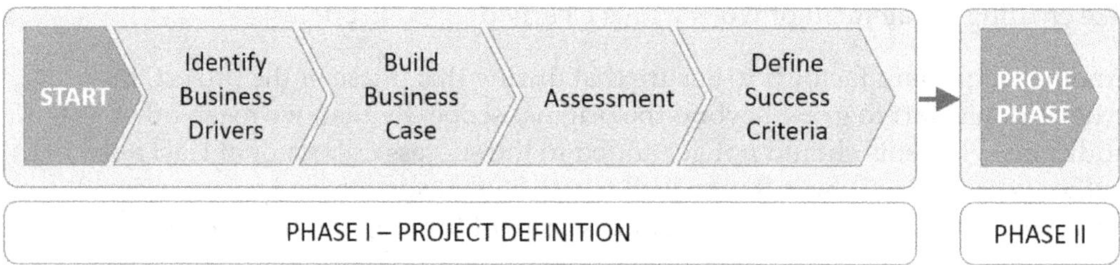

Our starting point is to focus on the end users rather than the IT department. After all, these are the people who will be using the applications on a daily basis and know what they need to get their jobs done. Rather than giving them what you think they need, let's ask them what they actually need and then, within reason, deliver their requirements. It's that old saying of don't try to fit a square peg into a round hole, as no matter how hard you try, it's just never going to fit.

First and foremost, we need to design the solution around the requirements of the end user rather than spending time and money on building an infrastructure, only to find that at the end of the project it doesn't deliver what the users require.

The App Volumes component could well be part of an overall EUC/VDI project or could be an additional component to an existing Citrix solution. Either way, it's worth following this methodology.

Once the previous steps have been discussed and documented, we should be able to build a picture about what's driving the project. You will understand what you are trying to achieve/deliver and, based on hard and fast facts from the assessment phase, be able to work on what success should look like. From there, we can then move into testing some form of the technology, should that be a requirement.

There are three distinct roads we can take within the testing cycle, and it might be the case that you don't need all of them. In actual fact, it is usually best to jump straight to the last one, and look at deploying a pilot. We will discuss why later in this chapter.

The three stages we are talking about are as follows:

- **Proof of concept** (**PoC**)
- **Proof of technology** (**PoT**)
- **Pilot**

In the next sections, we are briefly going to cover what each of these stages mean and why you might or might not need them.

Proof of concept

A proof of concept typically refers to a partial solution, typically built on any old hardware kicking about, that involves a relatively small number of users, usually within the confines of the IT department acting in business roles, to establish whether the system satisfies some aspect of the purpose it was designed for.

Once proven, one or two things happen. Firstly, nothing happens as it's just the IT department playing with technology and there wasn't a real business driver in the first place. This is usually down to the previous steps not having been defined. In a similar way, by not having any success criteria, it will also fail, as you don't know exactly what you are setting out to prove.

The second outcome is that the project moves into a pilot phase, which we will discuss in a later section. You could consider moving directly into this phase and bypass the PoC altogether. Maybe a demonstration of the technology would suffice, and using a demo environment over a longer period would show you how the technology works.

Proof of technology

In contrast to the PoC, the objective of a proof of technology is to determine whether or not the proposed solution or technology will integrate into your existing environment and therefore demonstrate compatibility. In this case, it is to ensure that your applications will work as an AppStack. The objective is to highlight any technical problems specific to your environment, such as how your bespoke systems might integrate.

As with the PoC, a PoT is typically run by the IT department and no business users would be involved. A PoT is purely a technical validation exercise.

Pilot

A pilot refers to what is almost a small-scale rollout of the solution in a production-style environment that would target a limited scope of the intended final solution. The scope may be limited by the number of users who can access the pilot system, the business processes affected, or the business partners involved.

The purpose of a pilot is to test, often in a production-like environment, whether the system is working as it was designed, while limiting business exposure and risk. It will also touch real users so as to gauge the feedback from what would ultimately become a live, production solution. This is a critical step in achieving success, as the users are the people who have to interact with the system on a daily basis, and the reason why you should set up some form of working group to gather their feedback.

That would also mitigate the project from failing, as the solution may deliver everything the IT department could ever wish for, but when it goes live and the first user logs on and reports a bad experience or performance, you may as well have not bothered.

The pilot should be carefully scoped, sized, and implemented, which breaks down nicely into the following four steps to a successful pilot.

The following diagram shows the workflow we will follow in defining the four steps in the pilot:

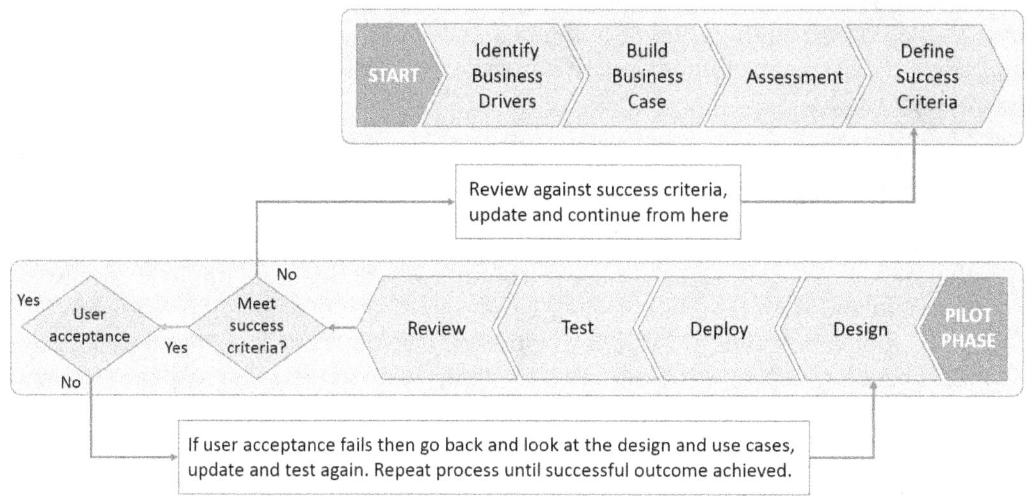

Design

The pilot infrastructure should be designed on the same hardware platforms on which the production solution is going to be deployed; for example, the same servers and storage. This takes into account any anomalies between platforms and configuration differences that could affect things such as scalability or, more importantly, performance.

Even at pilot stage, the design is absolutely key, and you should make sure you take into account the production design even at this stage. Why? Basically, because many pilot solutions end up going straight into production and more and more users and applications get added above and beyond those scoped for the pilot.

That's great, going live with the solution and not having to go back and rebuild it, but when you start to scale by adding more users and applications, you might have some issues due to the pilot sizing. It may sound obvious, but often with a successful pilot, the users just remain using it and additional applications get added, resulting in the recommended maximums being exceeded. If it's only ever going to be a pilot, that's fine, but keep this in mind and ask whether if you are planning on taking the pilot straight into production: design it for production from the outset.

It is always useful to work from a prerequisite document to understand the different elements that need consideration in the design. Key design elements include:

- Hardware sizing
- Application packaging requirements
- Storage design
- Active Directory (users and groups design)
- Number of applications
- How applications are going to be grouped in AppStacks

Once you have all this information, you can start to deploy the pilot.

Deploy

In the deployment phase of the pilot, we are going to start building out the infrastructure, create some AppStacks by capturing applications, assign users to the AppStacks, and then start testing.

Test

During the testing phase, the key thing is to work closely with the end users and your sponsors, showing them the solution and how it works, closely monitoring the users, and assessing the solution as it's being used. This allows you to keep in contact with the users and give them the opportunity to continually provide real-time feedback.

This in turn allows you to answer questions and make adjustments and enhancements on the fly rather than waiting until the end of the project and then being told it didn't work or they just simply didn't understand something.

This then leads us to the last section, the review.

Review

This final stage sometimes tends to get forgotten. We have deployed the solution, the users have been testing it, and then it ends there for whatever reason. However, there is one very important last thing to do to enable the customer to move to production.

We need to measure the user experience or the IT department's experience against the success criteria we set out at the start of this process. We need to get customer sign-off and agreement that we have successfully met all the objectives and requirements. If this is not the case, we need to understand the reasons why. Have we missed something in the use case, have the user requirements changed, or is it simply a perception issue?

Whatever the case, we need to cycle round the process again. Go back to the use case, understand and re-evaluate the user requirements (what it is that is seemingly failing or not behaving as expected), and then tweak the design or make the required changes and get them to test the solution again. We need to continue this process until we get acceptance and sign-off, otherwise we will not get to the final solution deployment phase.

When the project has been signed off after a successful pilot test, there is no reason why you cannot deploy the technology in production.

Now that we have talked about how to prove the technology and successfully demonstrate that it delivers against both your business case and your user requirements, in the next sections we are going to start looking at the design for our production environment, as shown in the following diagram:

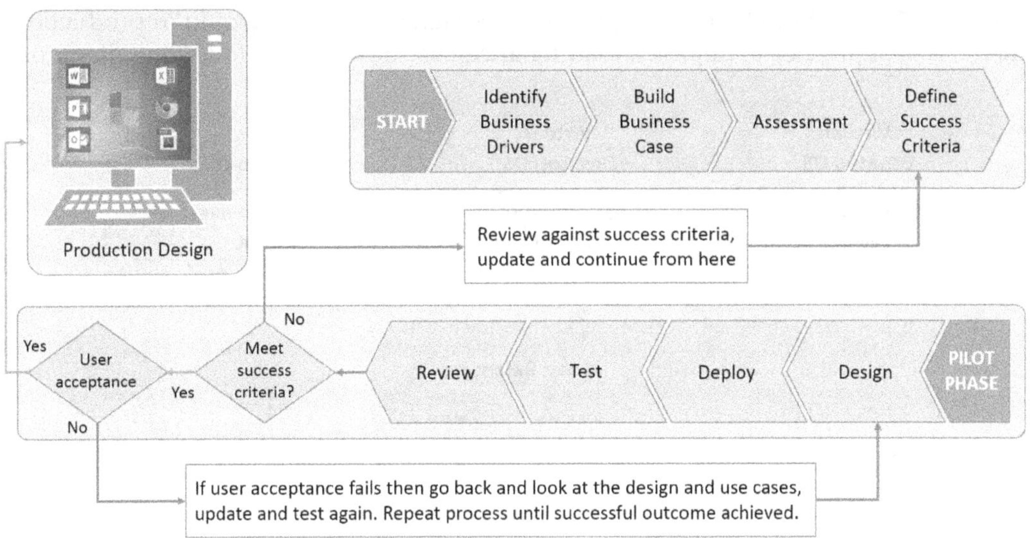

Phase III - Design and Deploy

Now that you have proved that the solution works within your environment, you can take all the findings from both the assessment and the pilot phases, and start to build out a design for production.

In this section, we are going to cover the main considerations for a successful design, and discuss the general rules of thumb and best practices and then move on to the specifics of sizing the storage requirement, scalability, availability, and also how to architect the solution when deployed as part of a VMware Horizon View virtual desktop solution.

Before we get into the specific areas we are going to touch on, let's look at a couple of best practices when it comes to the App Volumes server and the AppStacks themselves.

App Volumes Manager deployment best practice

In this book, we are using a single **App Volumes Manager** that is ideal for a test environment during the proof of concept and pilot stages of a project. However, when it comes to a production deployment then you should deploy a minimum of two App Volumes Managers. The minimum number of two servers allows you to effectively remove having a single point of failure in the event that one of the servers fails.

When deploying more than one App Volumes Manager, as you would in production, then it is best practice to deploy a **load balancer**, as shown in the following diagram:

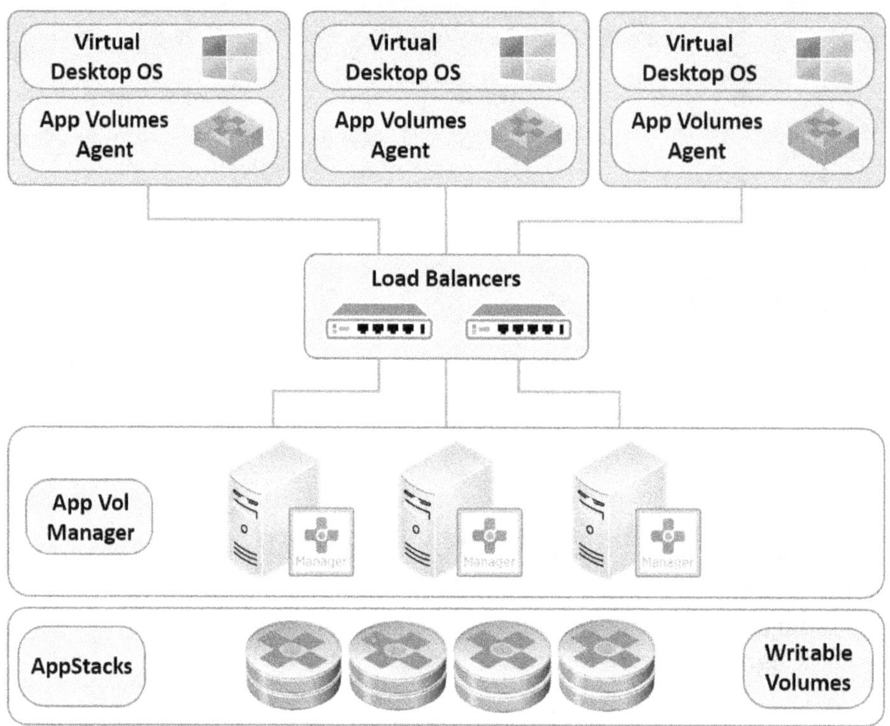

When using a load balancer, App Volumes will work with any load balancer that supports resolving to a single namespace. Configure your load balancer to use virtual IP addresses.

Configure each of the App Volumes Agents installed on your virtual desktop machines, RDSH servers, and physical desktops, and so on, to point at that virtual IP address of the load balancer.

You could also use a **Domain Name System** (**DNS**) server configured as round-robin that resolves to each of your App Volumes Managers in turn. It is also recommended to use DNS aliases when using Windows.

The actual number of servers you deploy is largely dependent on the size of your environment, although a minimum of two is the recommendation for any production environment. A single App Volumes Manager can support up to 10,000 users.

AppStack design considerations

In this next section, we are going to discuss how to design your AppStacks within your environment.

AppStack logical grouping

The first thing we are going to look at in more detail is how to group your AppStacks. This is going to determine who gets which applications, based on **Active Directory** (**AD**) membership, and where applications should ideally be grouped, based on AD groups.

Based on your assessment information, you should have built up a picture of your AD groups, your users, and the applications that they use. This should give you an understanding of which end users run which applications, and you can draw up an overview of how your AppStacks will be built and delivered. It may well mean that you need to perform some housekeeping when it comes to your users and their group membership.

If we look at your active directory then the highest level to which we can assign AppStacks is at the **Domain Users** level. This will basically assign AppStacks to everybody in your environment. As an example, this may be useful if you want to assign particular applications to all users, such as Adobe Reader. This will allow you to perform updates at the AppStack level and not per user.

The next level down might be to have groups at a departmental level; for example, sales, finance, marketing, and so on. This would allow AppStacks to be assigned to users who were just members of that particular active directory group. An example of this is where you have an application that is specific to a particular department. For example, the finance team may use a particular accounting package that is not relevant for other users, or indeed you don't want them to have access to it. This approach also helps with keeping tabs on the licensing of those particular applications, as only those who are members of that AD group will be able to run the application.

A final level may be a group within that group. If we use our previous example of the finance team, within that finance team there may be an application that only finance management can have access to. In this example, there will be another active directory group specifically for finance management to which these users can be assigned the AppStack containing that application.

The following diagram illustrates the scenario we have just described:

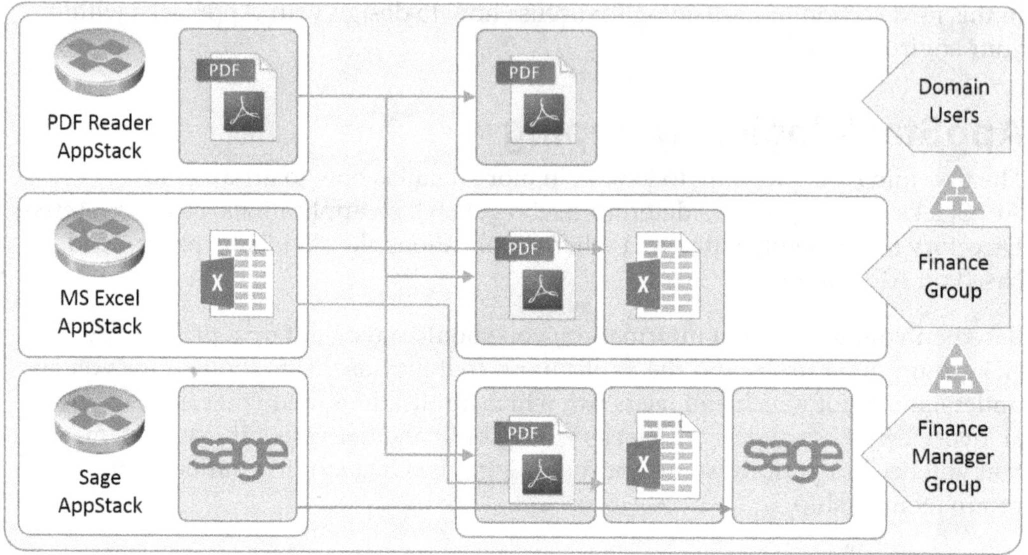

As you can see, the Domain Users group covers all users and in the example they all get assigned the **PDF Reader** AppStack.

The **Finance Group** has been assigned an AppStack that contains Microsoft Excel, but also, as that group falls under the Domain Users group, they also have access to the PDF Reader.

Finally, the **Finance Manager Group**, being a subgroup of the Finance Group, and part of Domain Users, will have all three AppStacks assigned to them: PDF Reader, MS Excel, and Sage.

One thing to be aware of when designing AppStack assignments in this way is to ensure that users are not assigned to more than three to five AppStacks. Having a large number of AppStacks could impact the performance for the users.

There are also some other important considerations when creating AppStacks for users with Microsoft Office applications. We will cover this in more detail in *Chapter 6, Working with AppStacks*, using our Example Lab, where we have created a number of Active Directory groups to represent various different departments, along with some example users.

AppStack deployment best practice

In this section, we are going to cover some of the best practices when it comes to deploying AppStacks in your environment.

How many AppStacks per VM can I have?

The current best practice is to limit each virtual desktop machine to having no more than 12 to 15 AppStacks attached at any one time. In theory, you could have up to 60 AppStacks attached at any one time, based on a virtual desktop machine being able to be configured with 4 virtual SCSI adapters, and each one being able to support 15 virtual SCSI disks; the rules of SCSI. After all, an AppStack is basically an attached disk or VMDK file. In reality, doing this will severely impact performance.

To limit the number of AppStacks in a production environment, it is a good practice to try to combine as many applications as possible into a single AppStack, and then use storage groups for AppStacks that are assigned to a large number of end users or desktops. This will help to distribute the aggregated **Input/Output Operations Per Second** (**IOPS**) across multiple datastores, while at the same time keep the assignments consistent and simpler to manage.

If you turn that around and now look at the number of connections to an AppStack, it is best practice to connect an AppStack to no more than 2,000 virtual desktop machines at any one time.

Application provisioning best practice

When it comes to the actual applications in an AppStack, there are a couple of points to note before we get to some of the best practices.

Firstly, any kernel mode drivers should be installed in the base image of the virtual desktop machine. You cannot have kernel mode drivers in an AppStack, as the applications in an AppStack run in user mode.

The second point to note is that any applications that need to run when an end user is logged out of their virtual desktop machine should also be installed in the base image.

When it comes to building your AppStacks on the provisioning virtual machine, then any AppStacks you create should be built on a clean and up-to-date base image that closely matches or is identical to the virtual desktop machines in your production environment.

By this, we mean that the provisioning virtual desktop machine and the virtual desktop machine in your production environment should all be running the same patches and service packs. This also applies to any applications. If you have any applications that are part of the base image, then they also need to be installed on the provisioning virtual desktop machine before creating any AppStacks.

The easiest way to manage the provisioning process is to create your provisioning virtual desktop machine as a dedicated VM using one of your production virtual desktop machines as the source. Once built exactly how you want it, including updates and applications, then take a snapshot to use as a reference point. It's now ready for you to create your AppStacks.

> Don't forget you will need to include the App Volumes Agent as part of the build of the virtual desktop machines used for provisioning AppStacks.

Once the provisioning process has been completed, the virtual desktop machine can then be rolled back to the initial snapshot ready to create the next AppStack. Before you start the "revert to previous snapshot" process, ensure that the virtual desktop machine has been powered off.

On the subject of the provisioning process itself, there are a few things to highlight as listed in the following:

- Do not use special characters when naming AppStacks and writable volumes. The following characters cannot be used:

  *~ ! @ $ ^ % ( ) { } [ ] | , ` ; # \ / : * ? < > ' " &*

- Perform provisioning on a virtual desktop machine that has not had any AppStacks attached to it before; that is, always start from a clean machine.
- Ensure the provisioning virtual desktop machine is joined to the same domain as your production virtual desktop machines.

> Some applications and licensing models require that the virtual desktop machine should share a common SID with the production virtual machines.

- Ensure you install applications for all users so that applications install in program files and not in a user's profile.

- The provisioning system should not have the following installed or enabled:
    - Anti-virus agents
    - VMware Horizon View Agent
    - Any other filter driver applications, such as VMware Mirage

VMware Horizon View integration with pod and block design

A feature of App Volumes is the ability to integrate with VMware Horizon View by installing the **Broker Integration Service** onto your **Horizon View Connection Servers**. We will cover the Broker Integration Service in *Chapter 9, Horizon View Integration*.

As well as installing the App Volumes Broker Integration Service onto the Horizon View Connection Servers, the App Volumes Managers can be included in the Horizon View pod and block reference architecture. To find out more about the VMware Horizon View specifics and the pod and block architecture, refer to, *Mastering VMware Horizon 6, Packt Publishing*.

The following diagram illustrates the reference architecture for a Horizon View block to support 2,000 users. It comprises a block containing the infrastructure to support the virtual desktop machines, and a separate block to support the management components:

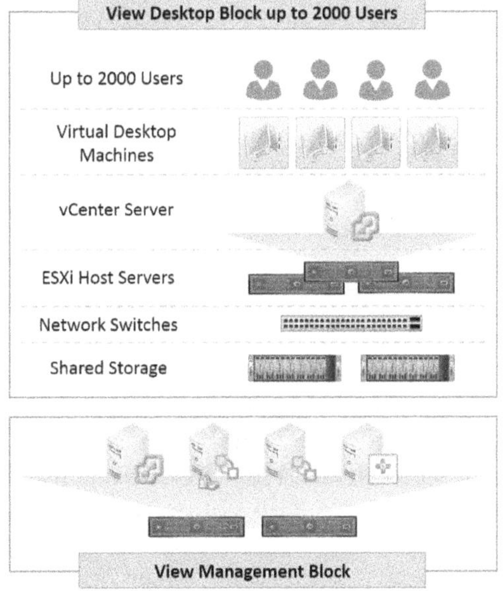

The App Volumes Managers would be part of the management block and therefore hosted on that part of the infrastructure.

However, the App Volumes Managers will be configured to point at the **vCenter Servers** in the desktop block, as these are managing the virtual desktop machines. AppStacks would be stored on the storage within the same block and mounted on the ESXi host servers in that block too.

In the previous example, we discussed an individual Horizon View desktop block. If we now scale this to a full pod configuration, consisting of 5 blocks of 2,000 users each to support 10,000 virtual desktop users, the architecture would look something like the following diagram:

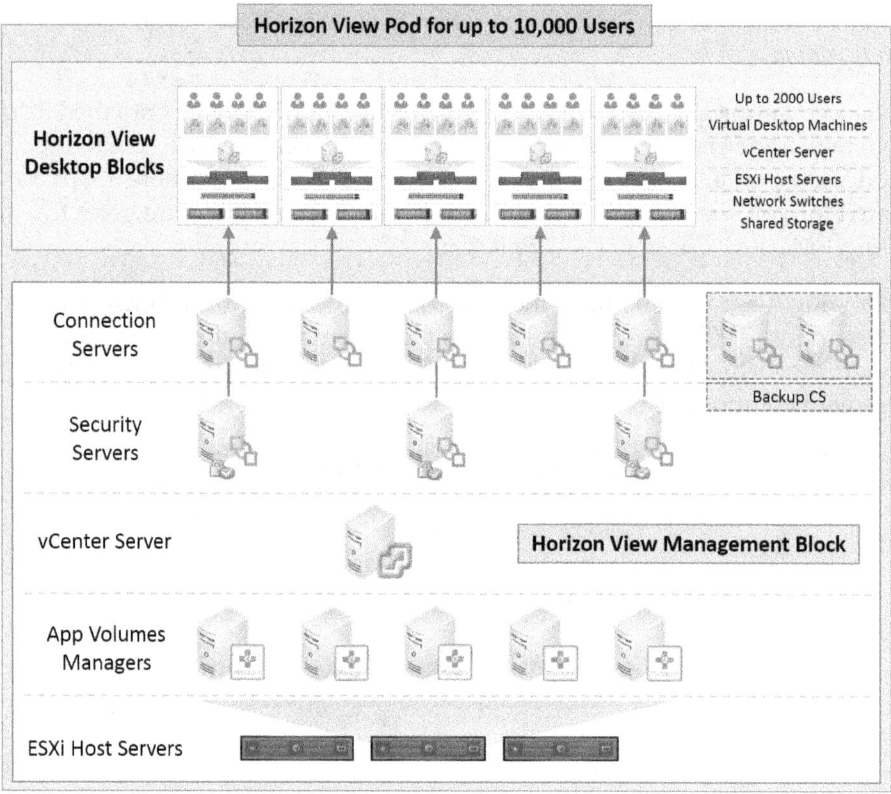

In this example, we have deployed 5 App Volumes Managers just for illustrative purposes, but you could deploy a single App Volumes Manager: given that each instance can support up to 10,000 users. However, as we discussed previously, best practice states that a minimum of two App Volumes Managers should be deployed in a production environment.

Each App Volumes Manager will be configured with the details of each of the vCenter Servers in the desktop blocks, a feature of App Volumes that allows support for multi-vCenter Servers. In App Volumes terms, the vCenter Servers are referred to as **Machine Managers**.

When configuring App Volumes with the multi-vCenter Server feature, the following list details a few points to be aware of:

- vCenter Servers must use the same credentials
- The hostnames must be unique
- Datastore names must be unique
- Once deployed, it's not recommended to revert back to a single vCenter Server

In the next section, we are going to look at some of the considerations when planning your storage for an App Volumes deployment

Storage considerations

The most important element when it comes to sizing is about the storage components. As AppStacks are essentially VMDK files containing the applications, you need to ensure your storage platform has both the capacity and performance to deliver these applications to the end users.

When you create and deploy new AppStacks or Writable Volumes, templates are used as the copy source, and by default are created as 20 GB in size. These templates, which get created as part of the installation process, should be hosted on a centralized, shared storage platform that is highly available, backed up, and even more importantly, has the ability to recover the data in the event of a failure.

Best practice would be to use a third-party data replication solution to ensure that App Volumes folders containing AppStacks and Writable Volumes are replicated across various locations.

The other key consideration is ensuring you have enough free storage space.

AppStack storage capacity considerations

It goes without saying that correctly sizing AppStacks and Writable Volumes is critical for a successful production deployment.

AppStacks should be configured so that they are of a big enough size to allow all the applications you want in that particular AppStack to be installed. You should also bear in mind that if the application is going to need to be updated during its lifecycle, you allow enough free space to accommodate these updates. Rule of thumb would say to leave about 20 percent of free space for future upgrades and updates.

Although AppStacks are created using standard templates, these templates can be resized if required.

[ The default size of an AppStack template is 20 GB.]

We will cover this in *Chapter 14, Advanced Configuration and Other Options*, and the *Customizing AppStack templates* section in that chapter.

Writable Volumes storage capacity considerations

In the same way as we discussed with AppStacks, Writable Volumes should also be sized correctly to ensure they can accommodate all the applications that a user could install into it. This should be a key piece of information you need to find from the assessment phase of any project that involves working with applications.

At first, this may seem like you require a large amount of storage capacity; however, all AppStacks and Writable Volumes use vSphere VMFS thin provisioning so that not all the storage space is utilized from day one, it's just allocated. This is where you will need to consider deploying tools that can monitor the free space in your environment.

When it comes to managing the free space for Writable Volumes, there are a couple of policy options to make you aware of that could complicate the management of that free space. These are about the Writable Volumes Delay Creation Option.

With this policy, you have the option to:

- **Create Writable Volumes on next login**: This means that any storage processes and capacity impacts occur based on user login behavior.

- **Restrict Writable Volume Access**: this allows you to restrict access to a certain virtual desktop machine or group of virtual desktop machines. This again means that login behavior dictates when a Writable Volume template is copied or initially created.

In a large-scale App Volumes deployment, it is not good practice to allow user behavior to dictate storage operations and capacity allocation. Writable Volumes should therefore be assigned to the end users at the same time as they are created, rather than waiting for the user to log in first and then create the Writable Volume. This allows you to manage and control the storage more effectively.

Scalability

An individual instance of an App Volumes Manager server has been tested with up to 10,000 active users connected to AppStacks. We have already talked about best practices where we limit each virtual desktop machine to having no more than 12 to 15 AppStacks attached to an individual virtual desktop machine and also to connect no more than 2,000 virtual desktop machines to an AppStack at any one time.

When it comes to scaling your deployment, in theory there isn't an upper limit to the number of App Volumes Managers you can deploy, or at least not one that has been tested today. In reality, even a deployment of 100,000 users would need only 10 App Volumes Managers.

Scaling your deployment is very straightforward. It's just a case of installing the App Volumes Manager software component onto a Windows server, and then connecting it to your existing App Volumes SQL database. When deploying additional App Volumes Manager servers, it is important not to overwrite the existing database.

Don't forget that when deploying multiple App Volumes Manager servers, that you will need to deploy a load balancer in front of the App Volumes Manager servers.

Availability

When it comes to making your App Volumes deployment highly available, it's more about the infrastructure that supports App Volumes that needs to be configured to be highly available.

The first and most obvious one is to configure some of the vSphere components to ensure that the App Volumes Manager servers are available. For example, you could enable VMware vSphere **HA** (short for **High Availability**) or even VMware **FT** (short for **Fault Tolerance**), although FT is probably a little overkill for App Volumes. As we have discussed previously, in a production environment you would have deployed multiple App Volumes Manager servers.

As part of the supporting infrastructure, you will have also deployed a SQL database or be using an existing SQL database. SQL is a critical component of App Volumes, as it keeps track of user assignments of AppStacks and Writable Volumes. If you lose the database, you will lose all of this information and effectively have to recreate all the assignments from scratch. With this in mind, and for production environments, you should deploy an enterprise-class level of SQL, using SQL clustering, for example.

You can of course use SQL Server Express as we are for the Example Lab in this book, and which is included with the App Volumes installation software; however, that should not be used in a production environment. When looking at your SQL deployment for App Volumes, ensure that the SQL Server is running on its own dedicated virtual machine, and that you place the datastore on storage that can satisfy the read/write IOPS that will be required.

Performance

There are a couple of components within App Volumes that you can configure to enhance the performance. The first of these is to enable the mounting of AppStacks and Writable Volumes to the vSphere host servers.

By enabling this feature, the App Volumes Manager will connect directly to the ESXi host server to issue a volume mount command. This could help increase the performance of mounting the AppStacks and Writable Volumes, as commands are not queued in the vCenter Server. It also provides a level of resiliency should the vCenter Server be down.

By default, if you do not enable this feature then the volume mount command will be issued indirectly to the vCenter Server via the vCenter SDK.

We have also talked previously about the number of App Volumes Manager servers that you should deploy based on 10,000 users per server, with a minimum of 2 servers for a production environment.

As a guideline for sizing your environment and to give you an idea of how many additional App Volumes Manager servers you may need in your environment, the rule of thumb is that each App Volumes Manager server supports a user login every second. So having 10 App Volume Manager servers would support 10 users every second.

When it comes to storage performance for your AppStacks, there are a couple of points to note. Firstly, you should ensure that your AppStacks, Writable Volumes, and virtual desktop machines are not stored on the same datastore. Keep them separate unless you are hosting your datastores on VMware Virtual SAN storage nodes.

You can find a reference architecture for Virtual SAN, Horizon View, and App Volumes by following this link: `http://tinyurl.com/qa4vnsf`.

The second point is more about the performance of the applications in the AppStack. It's best practice to install any application dependencies, such as Java or .NET, into the same AppStack in which the application is located.

Summary

In this chapter, we have covered everything concerned with designing your App Volumes environment. We started off by walking you through a typical approach to an App Volumes project, and how to get started and gather the information you need to take into the design phase of a project.

We then went on to discuss the key things you need to consider when creating your design, along with best practice.

In the next chapter, we are going to start to build out our Example Lab and install the App Volumes software.

4

Installing and Configuring the App Volumes Software

In this chapter, we will install the App Volumes software and complete the initial configuration steps. Before we do this, we are going to take a few minutes to walk through the prerequisites. We will also cover the App Volumes infrastructure requirements.

Prerequisites

Before you start the App Volumes installation, you need to have the following in place:

- An Active Directory account that has read access to the base DN so that App Volumes Manager can query Active Directory users and groups.
- An Active Directory user accounts with the following permissions:
    - Standard permissions for setup/connection
    - Administrator-level access to allow the installation of applications into Writable Volumes
- A vCenter administrator account that has administration permissions at the data center level.
- Local or remote access to a SQL database. In a production environment, the recommendation would be for a remote database with enterprise-class availability, but for a pilot or POC environment, you can use **SQL Express**. It is included as a part of the App Volumes software download package. App Volumes supports the following versions:
    - SQL Express 2008 R2
    - SQL 2008 R2 or 2012 (Standard or Enterprise Edition)

- In case a firewall is used between system components, ports `80/443` should be opened.
- If you deploy multiple App Volumes Manager instances, then a load balancer should be used to distribute the traffic between the managers.

App Volumes requirements

Now that we have covered the general environment prerequisites for an App Volume installation, the next step is to look at the specific requirements. We will break these into two categories: system requirements and software requirements.

System/hardware requirements

For App Volumes Manager, you will need a virtual machine with the following configuration:

- Hypervisor: ESXi and vCenter Server 5.x or higher
- 2 x vCPUs minimum (4 x vCPUs recommended)
- 4 GB of RAM
- 1 GB of disk space

For the App Volumes client (end user and provisioning/capture machine), you will need the following minimum configuration:

- Microsoft Windows 7 or 8.1
- 1 GB of RAM
- 5 MB of disk space

Software requirements

In addition to the system requirements detailed in the previous subsection, you will also need the following software components for App Volumes Manager:

- Microsoft Windows Server 2008 R2 or Windows 2012 R2
- Microsoft Active Directory Domain (2003 functional level or above)
- Supported browsers for the management console:
    - IE 9 and 10
    - Firefox 10 and 11
    - Safari 5.1.x

- For the App Volumes Agent instance used on end users' virtual desktops and the capture and provisioning machine, you will need Microsoft Windows 7 or higher

Downloading the App Volumes software

Now that you have met all the prerequisites and requirements, you can download the App Volumes software.

You can download the software from this link:

`http://tinyurl.com/hxml28f`

It will lead you to this page:

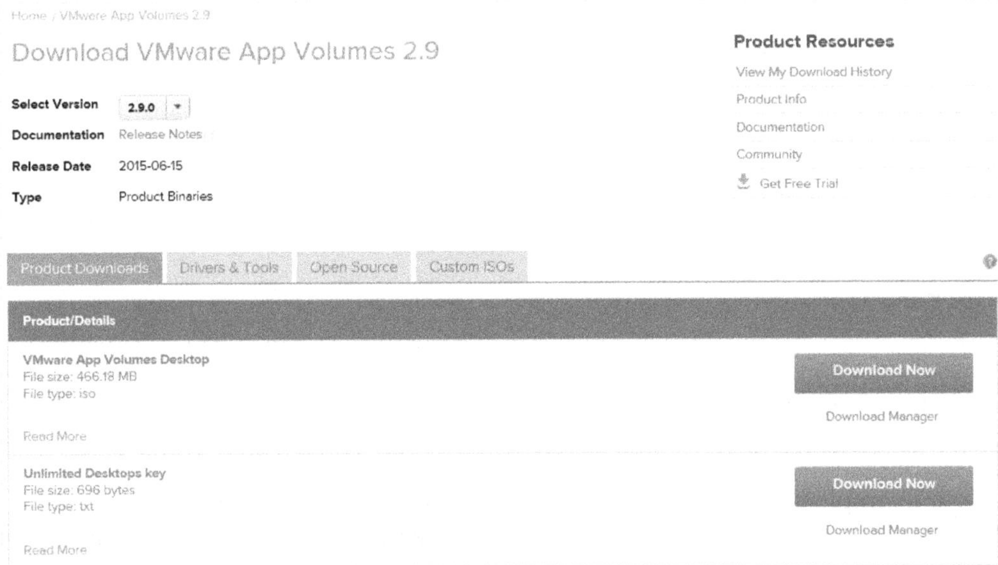

To download it, click on the **Download Now** button, which is next to both **VMware_App_Volumes_v210.iso** and **Unlimited Desktop key**, but note that you will need to log in to your **My VMware** account.

You can also download a trial version from the *VMware App Volumes Product Evaluation Center* by following this link:

`https://my.vmware.com/web/vmware/evalcenter?p=app-volumes`

Once it is downloaded, you will have a disc image file (ISO) containing the App Volumes software, as shown in the following screenshot:

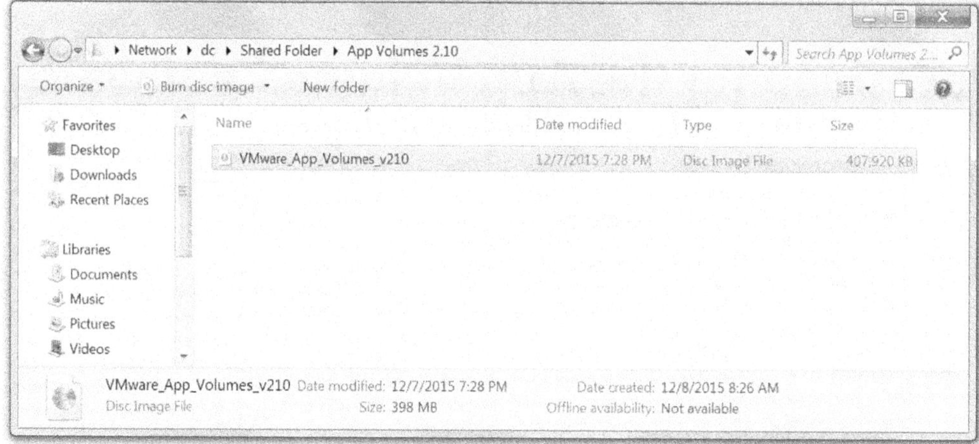

If you now double-click on this file to mount the ISO image, you will see the following:

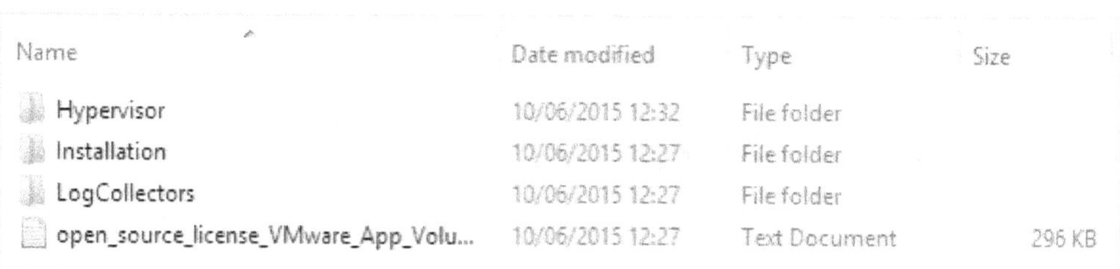

For our Example Lab, we are going to extract these software components and store them on a shared folder on the **domain controller**, which is also acting as our file server.

Installing the software

Now that we have downloaded the software, met our prerequisites and requirements, and have our infrastructure in place, it's time to start the installation. We will start with App Volumes Manager.

Installing App Volumes Manager

Locate the folder or shared folder where you have stored the App Volumes software.

Double-click on the **Installation** folder, then on the **Manager** folder, and then launch the **App Volumes Manager** Windows Installer file, as shown in the following screenshot:

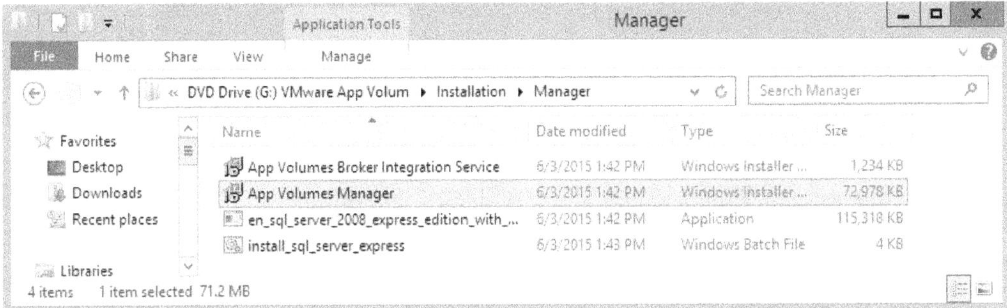

The **App Volumes Manager Installation Wizard** launches, as shown in the following screenshot:

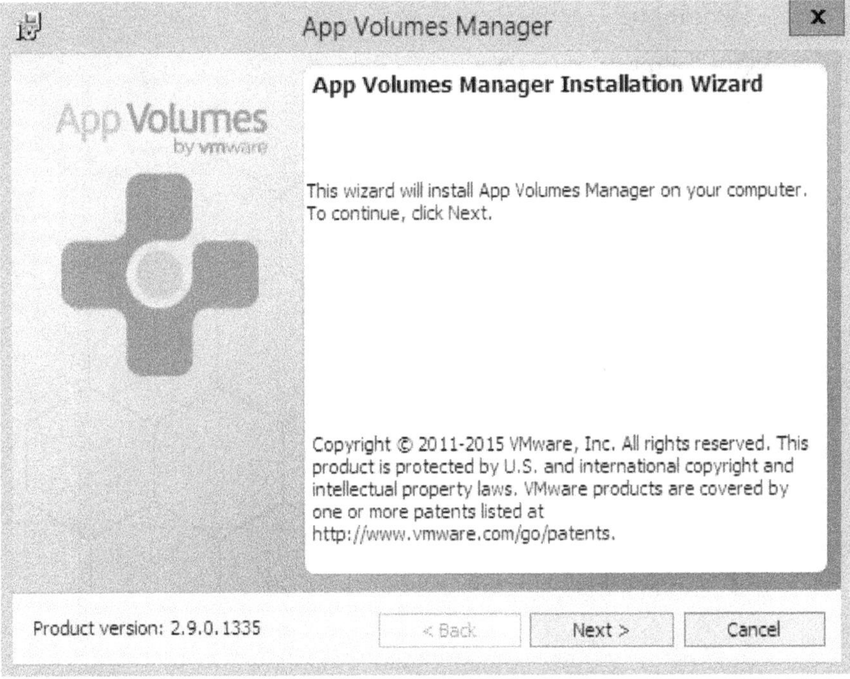

Click on **Next >** to start the installation. You will now see the **VMWARE END USER LICENSE AGREEMENT** window, as shown in the following screenshot:

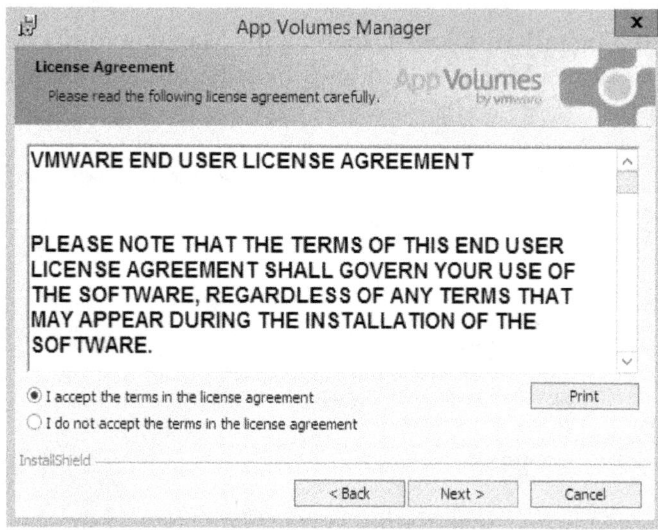

Click on the radio button for **I accept the terms in the license agreement**, and then click on **Next >** to continue.

You will now see the **Choose a Database** window, as shown in the following screenshot:

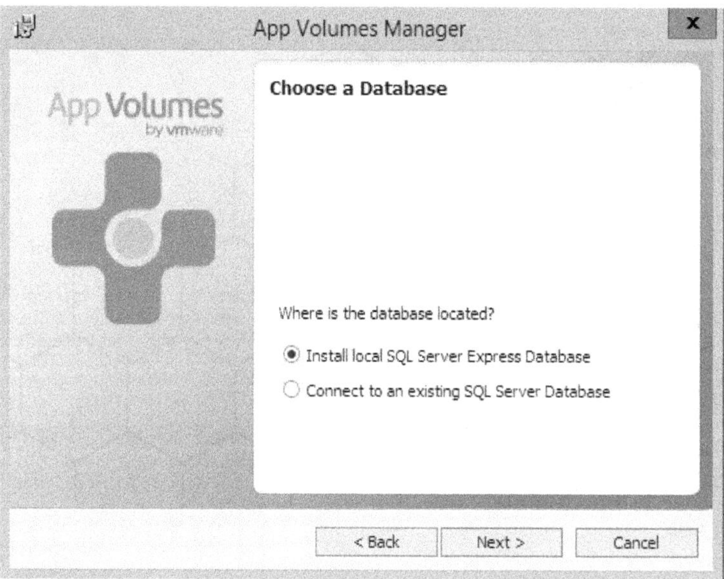

Here you have two options: you can install a local instance of SQL on this server, or you can connect to an existing SQL database. You would choose the second option for a production deployment, where the SQL database would be enterprise-class and therefore highly available.

In our Example Lab, we are going to install a local copy of SQL, so click on the radio button for **Install local SQL Server Express Database**, and then click on **Next >**.

You will now see, as shown in the following screenshot, that the App Volumes installer will automatically install a SQL Express database on your machine:

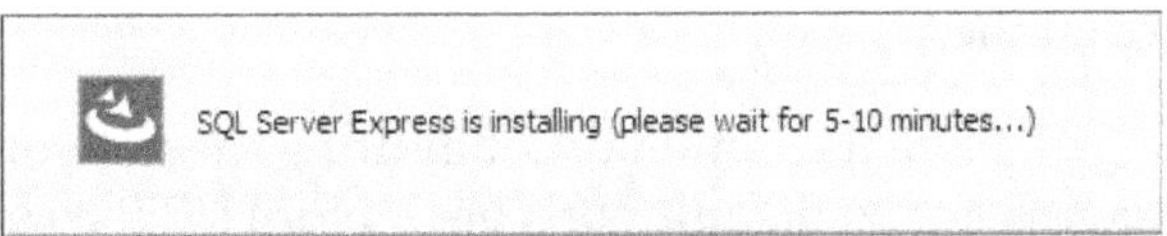

Once the installation is complete, you will see the following window. You will also see this window if you choose the option of connecting to an existing SQL database, as this is where you would enter the details of that existing database.

As we have chosen to install a local copy on the App Volumes Manager server, the default configuration is used.

You also have the option of changing the authentication method. In the Example Lab, we will use this server's account.

> You will also see that there is a checkbox to overwrite any existing database. If you are adding an additional App Volumes Manager instance, then make sure that you *DO NOT* check this box as it will overwrite the existing database. You would use this option for a new clean install, where you don't want to use an existing database.

Click on **Next >** to continue.

In the next window, you have the option of configuring the network, as shown in the following screenshot. The default ports are `80` for HTTP traffic and `443` for HTTPS traffic. Ensure that both of these ports are open and are configured in Windows Firewall.

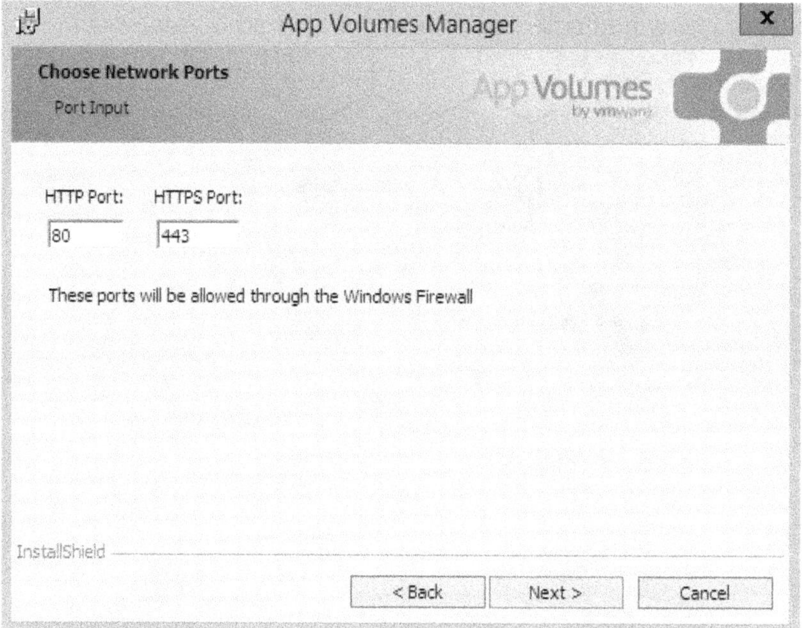

Click on **Next >** to continue.

In the next window, you can choose the features to install, as well as the location App Volumes Manager will be installed to. This is shown in the following screenshot:

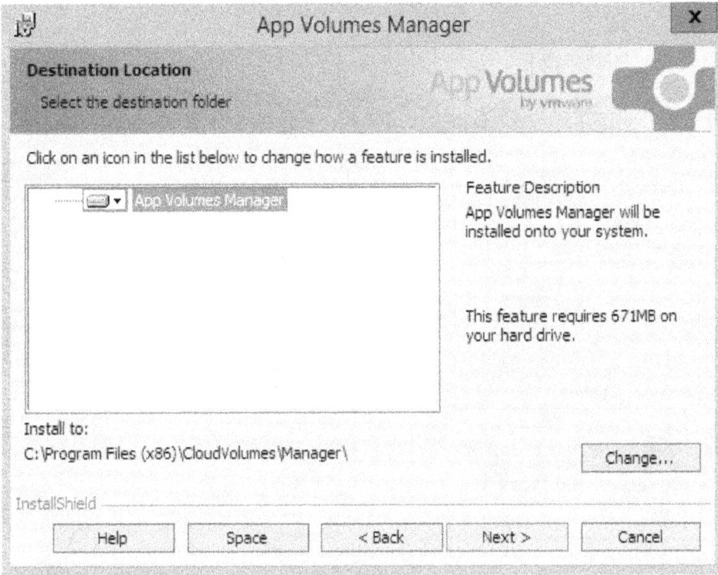

Click on **Next >** to continue. You will now see the **Ready to Install the Program** window:

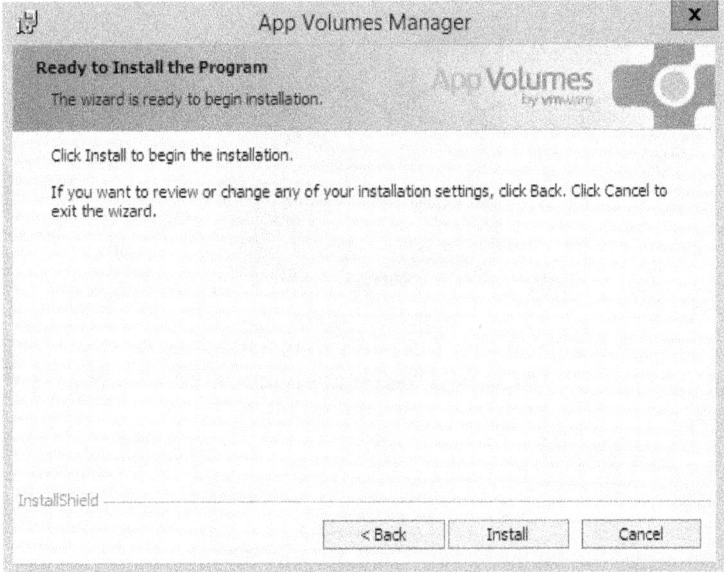

Click on **Install** to continue. You will see the following window:

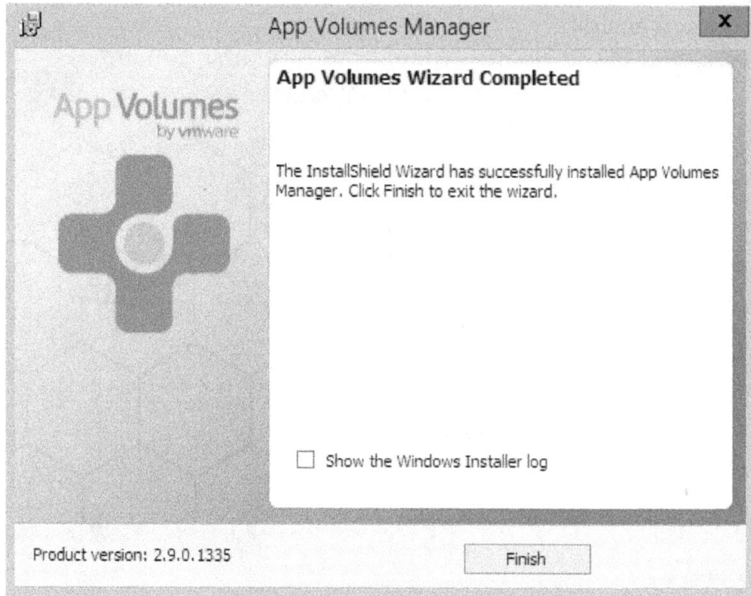

Finally, click on **Finish** to complete the installation.

Once it is completed, you will see the **App Volumes Manager** icon on the desktop, which looks like this:

You have now completed the initial installation tasks. In the next subsection, we are going to perform the next part of the installation: configuring App Volumes Manager.

Initial configuration tasks

To start the configuration, launch App Volumes Manager by double-clicking on the icon on the desktop. A browser will launch and show the **Welcome to App Volumes Manager** page, as shown in the following screenshot:

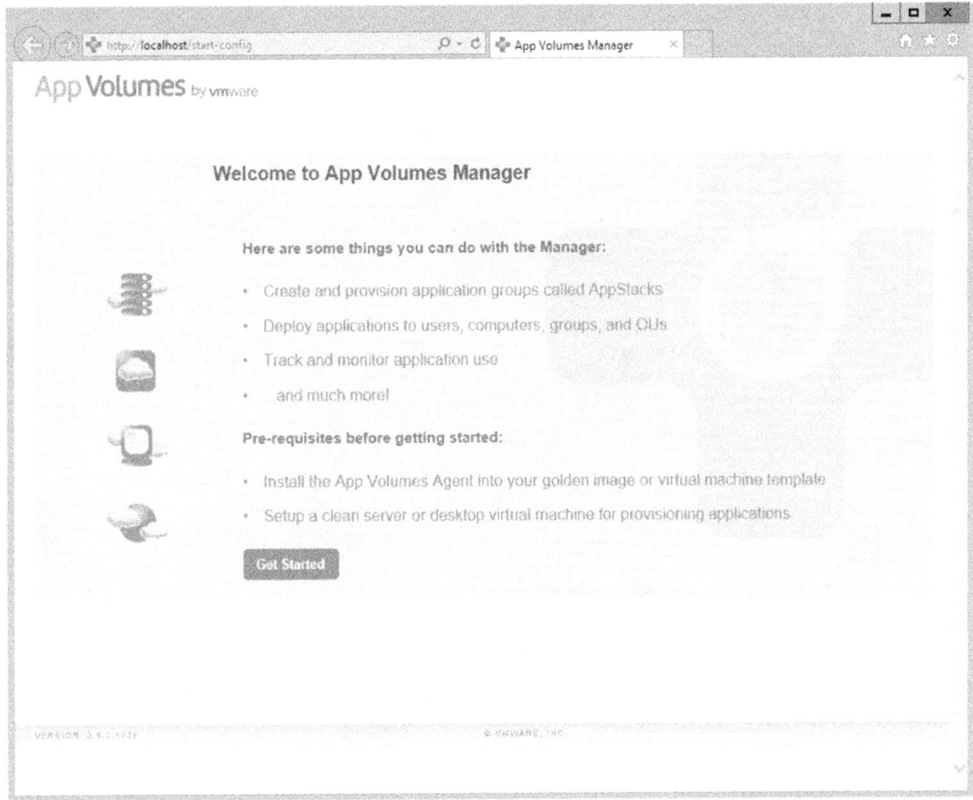

Click on the **Get Started** button to start configuring App Volumes Manager.

The first thing we need to configure is the licensing, which is shown in the following figure. This is the first configuration page that is displayed:

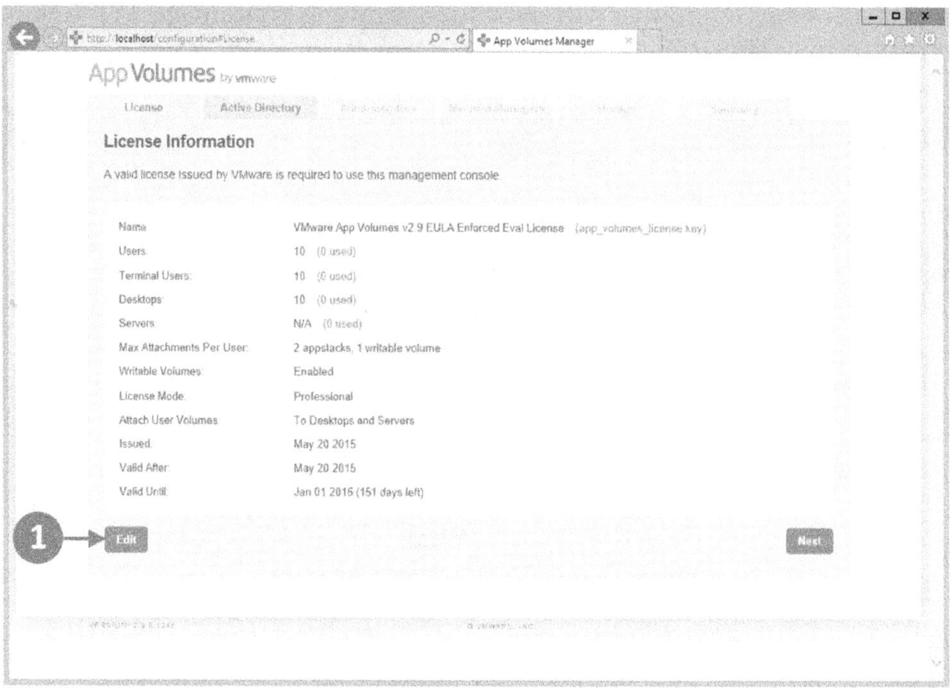

By default, you will be licensed for **10** users, each with 2 AppStacks and 1 Writable Volume. To add a license, click on the **Edit** button **(1)**. You will now see the following window:

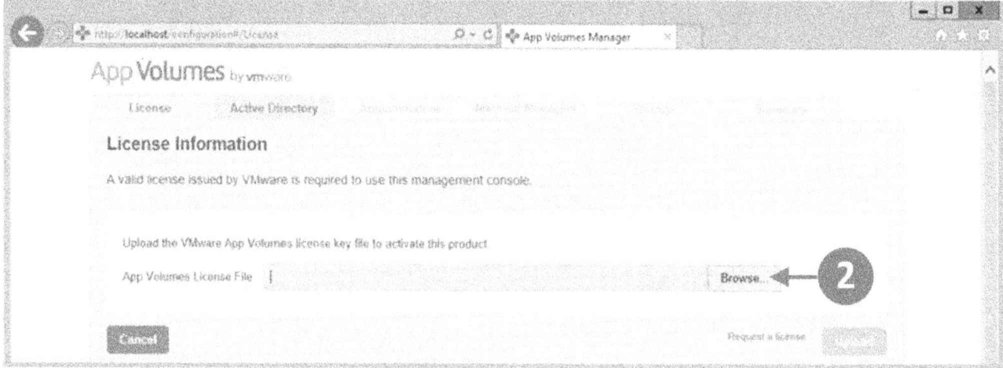

To add a license, click on the **Browse** button **(2)**, and then navigate to your license file.

Once you have located the license file, click on the **Upload** button.

When you have finished configuring the **License** page, click on the **Next** button. The next configuration page is for **Active Directory**, as shown in the following diagram:

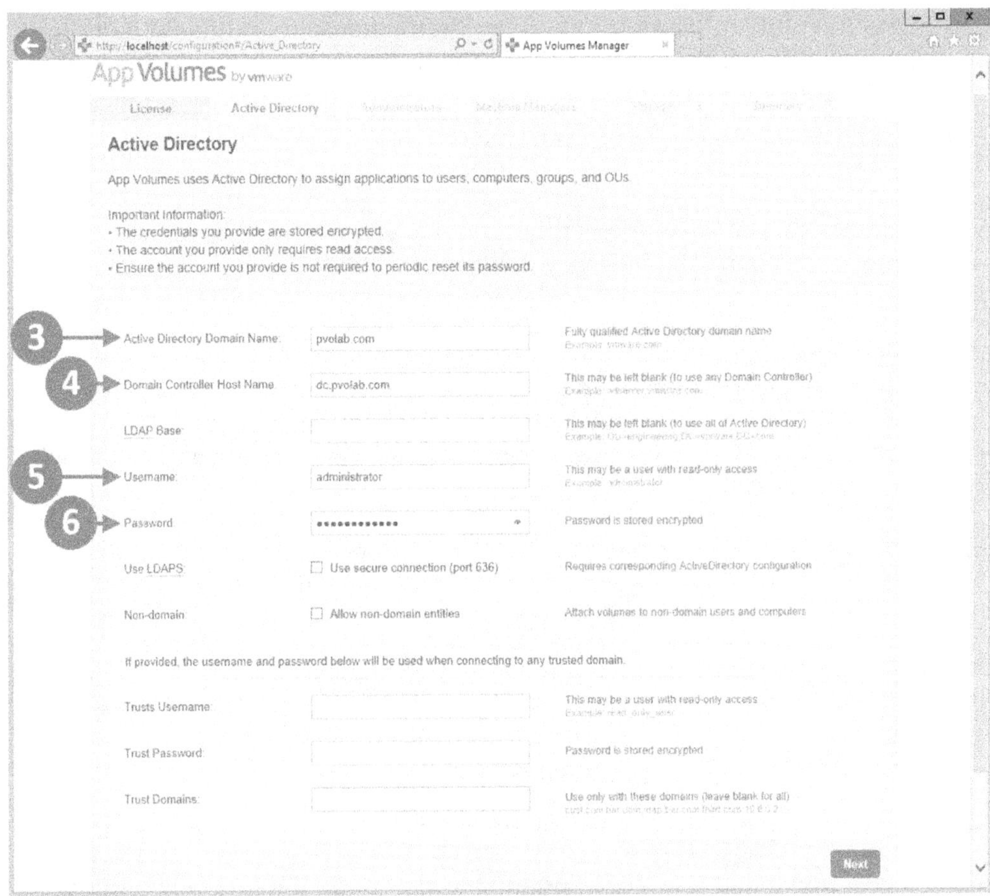

Complete the following steps:

1. In the **Active Directory Domain Name** box **(3)**, enter the fully qualified name of your domain. In our Example Lab, the entry will be `pvolab.com`.
2. In the **Domain Controller Host Name** box **(4)**, enter the fully qualified name of your domain controller. In our Example Lab, the domain controller's hostname is `dc`, so we will enter `dc.pvolab.com`.

3. You then have the option of filling in the **LDAP Base** box. This will be used to specify specific the organizational units (OUs) within Active Directory from which to search for users and groups. For example, if you had an OU called Sales, then every user or group that fell under this OU would be searchable. In our example, we want to search all of Active Directory, so we will leave it blank.
4. In the **Username** box **(5)**, enter a username that has read access to Active Directory. In our Example Lab, we are going to use the administrator account, but you can use any account so long as it has the ability to read the directory information.
5. Finally, in the **Password** box **(6)**, enter the password for the account you entered previously.

There are some other configuration options on this page, but in our environment, we are not going to configure them as they don't apply; however, we will explain what they are used for.

Firstly, if you check the **Use LDAPS** box, you can enable **secure connections when reading directory information**. If you select this option, then ensure that your Active Directory supports this and is configured correctly, because when you move on to the next configuration page, the directory connection will be tested and you won't be able to continue if it fails.

The next checkbox, **Non-domain**, is pretty self-explanatory. By checking this box, you are able to attach AppStacks to users, groups, and computers that are not part of the domain.

The final section at the bottom of this configuration page allows you to connect to other trusted domains. You will need to enter a trust username, trust password, and then you have a box into which you can enter a list of the domains that you want to use. If you want to use all trusted domains, then leave this box blank.

Once you have completed the configuration of this page, click on the **Next** button.

As mentioned previously, before moving to the next page, the connection to Active Directory will be tested to ensure that communication is working. You will see the following message displayed:

When the connection has successfully been tested, you will see the following message:

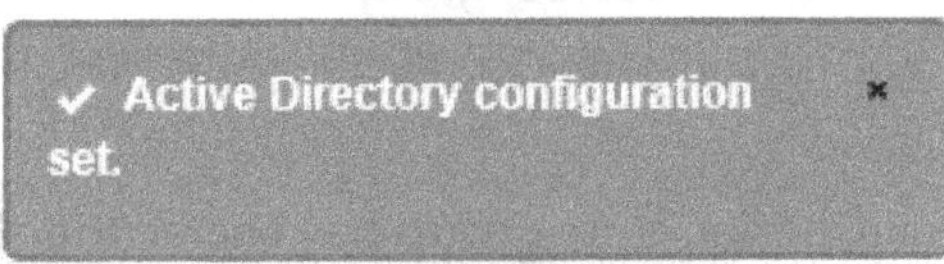

The next configuration page is for configuring **App Volumes Administrators Group**. This page is shown in the following diagram:

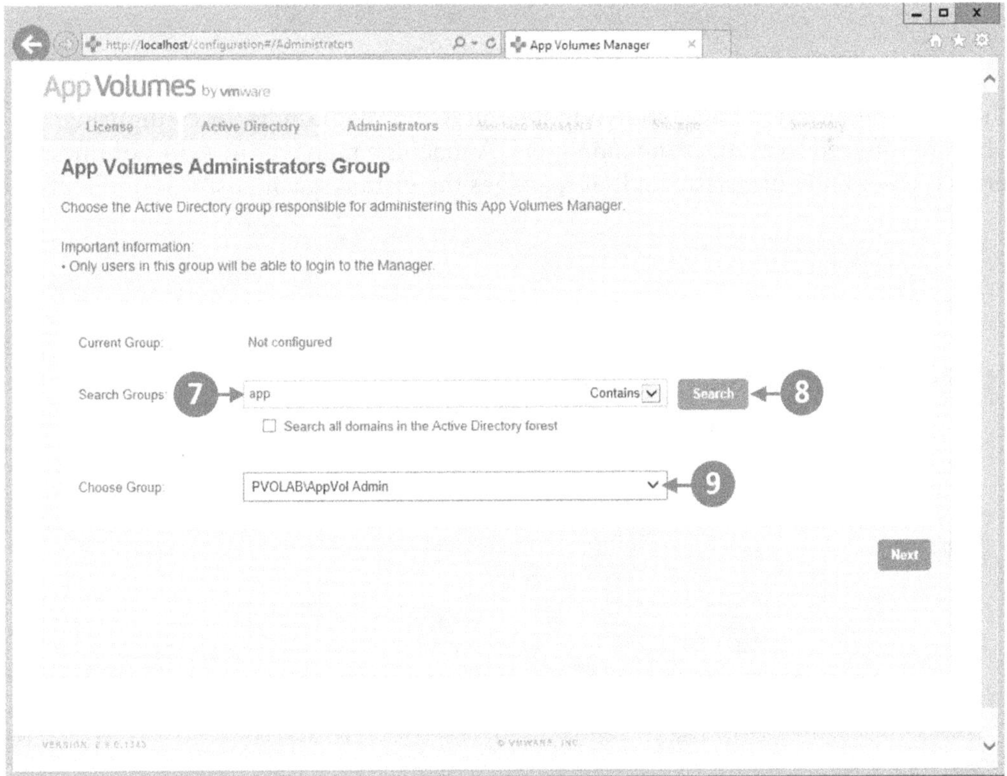

In the **Search Groups** box **(7)**, start typing in the name of the administrators group. This is the group that contains the App Volumes administrators that we set up as part of the prerequisites in *Chapter 1, Introduction to App Volumes*. The group we created is called `AppVol Admin`, so just type in the word `app` and click on the **Search** button **(8)**. Next to the **Search** button, you will also notice that there is a drop-down option for changing the filter. In this example, we will set that to **Contains** so that we pick out any groups that contain `app`, the first three letters of our group name.

The results of the search are displayed in the **Choose Group** box. If there is more than one group that matches the search criteria, then you would click on the drop-down box **(9)** and choose the correct group from the list shown. In our Example Lab, we will see the `PVOLAB\AppVol Admin` option, so select it and then click on the **Next** button.

When the App Volumes administrators group has been configured successfully, you will see the following message:

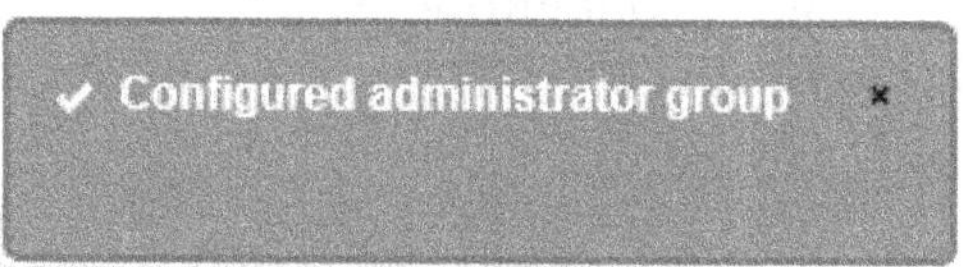

The next configuration page, shown in the following diagram, is for configuring what are referred to as **machine managers**. A machine manager in App Volumes terms is essentially the platform that manages the virtual machines.

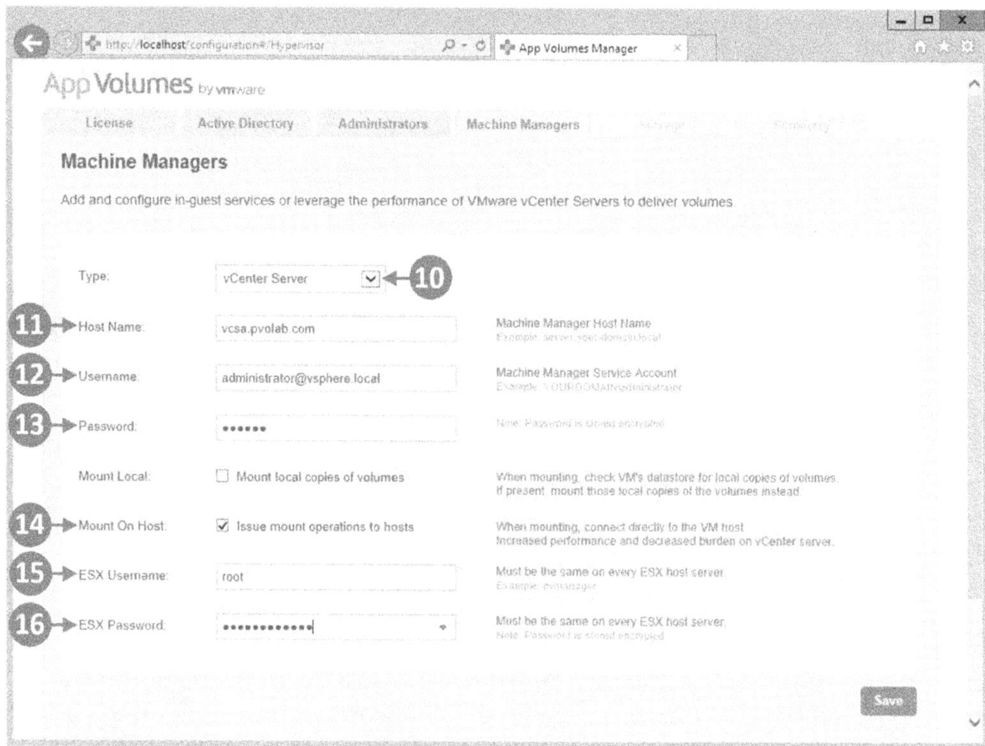

Complete the following steps:

1. In the **Type** box, click on the drop-down arrow **(10)** and select the type of machine manager. App Volumes supports the following machine managers:
    - vCenter Server
    - ESX host server
    - VHD In-Guest servers (App Volumes can support Citrix environments)

   In our Example Lab, we are going to use our vCenter Server instance as the machine manager, so select this from the drop-down menu.
2. In the **Host Name** box **(11)**, type in the fully qualified domain name of the vCenter Server instance. In our lab environment, this is `vcsa.pvolab.com`.
3. In the **Username** box **(12)**, type in the details of the administrator account for the chosen machine manager. In our Example Lab, we have chosen vCenter, so the username is `administrator@vshpere.local`.
4. Enter the password for this username in the **Password** box **(13)**.
5. The next two options configure where the AppStacks will be mounted, either mounting a local copy if it exists in the virtual machine's datastore, or mounting directly to the virtual machine's host. The latter of these options results in an increase in performance as the load is taken away from vCenter, and is therefore the option we are going to choose. Check the box for **Mount On Host (14)**.
6. As we have selected to mount the AppStacks on the ESX host servers, we now need to supply the credentials for the host servers. In the **ESX Username** box **(15)**, enter the username. In our Example Lab, we are using `root` as the username.
7. In the **ESX Password** box **(16)**, enter the password for the root user.

The username and password must be the same for all ESX servers.

Once you have completed all the details, click on the **Save** button. You will see the following message displayed:

Adding machine manager configuration...

When the machine manager information has been saved successfully, you will see the following message:

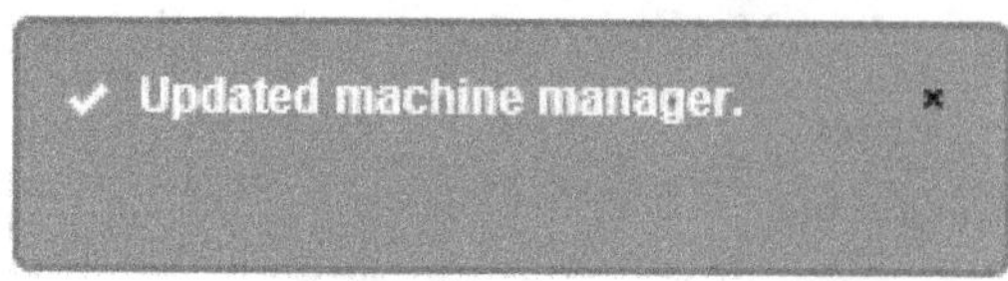
Updated machine manager.

There are also a number of vCenter permissions that you will need to configure.

First, you will need to check that datastore browsing is enabled. App Volumes Manager uses this in order to enumerate volumes on the datastore. It should be enabled by default, but it's worth checking.

The following figure is a table of the other permissions that need to be set:

Top Level Description	Next Level Description	Permission
Datastore		Allocate Space
		Browse Datastore
		Low Level File Operations
		Remove File
		Update Virtual Machine Files
Folder		Create Folder
		Delete Folder
Global		Cancel Task
Host	Local Operations	Reconfigure Virtual Machine
Sessions		View and Stop Sessions
Tasks		Create Task
Virtual Machine	Configuration	Add Existing Disk
		Add New Disk
		Add or Remove Device
		Change Resource
		Remove Disk
		Settings
	Inventory	Create New
		Move
		Register
		Remove Disk
		Unregister
	Provisioning	Promote Disks

Having clicked on the **Save** button, you will now see a summary screen detailing the machine manager that you have just configured.

This is shown in the following diagram:

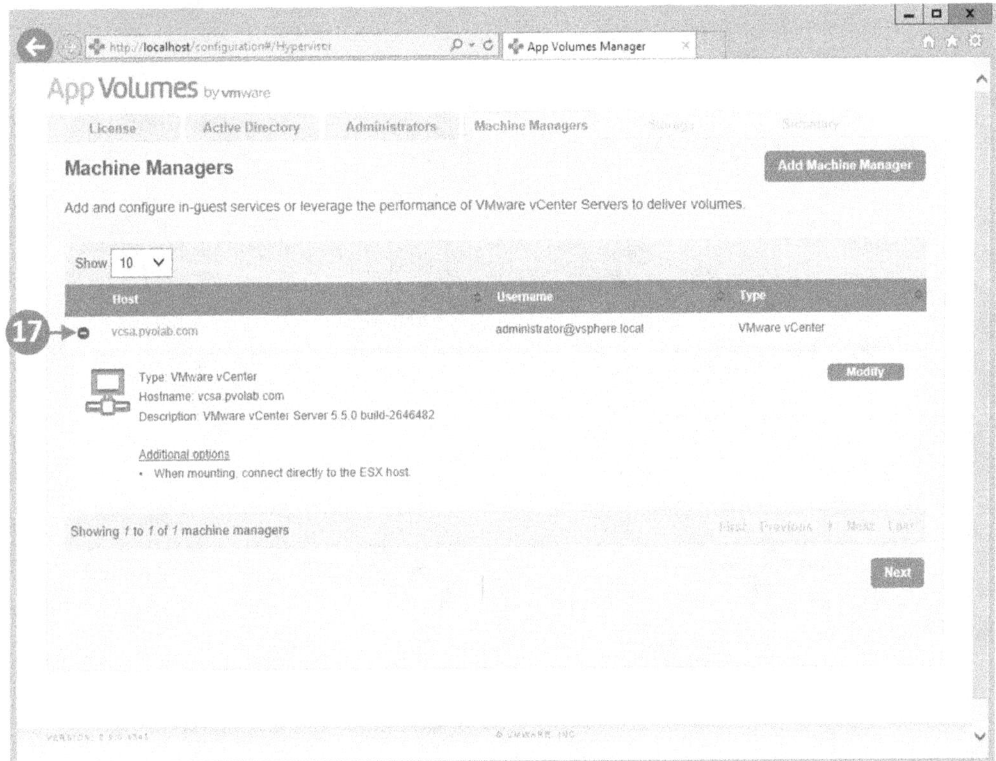

To expand the details, click on the **+/-** button **(17)**. You will see the details of the machine manager, including the hostname, a description of the version of vCenter, and the user details.

You also have the option of adding additional machine managers (App Volumes now has multi-vCenter support), or you can modify the current configuration.

Click on the **Next** button to continue the configuration.

The next configuration page is for configuring the storage options for AppStacks and Writable Volumes, as shown in the following diagram:

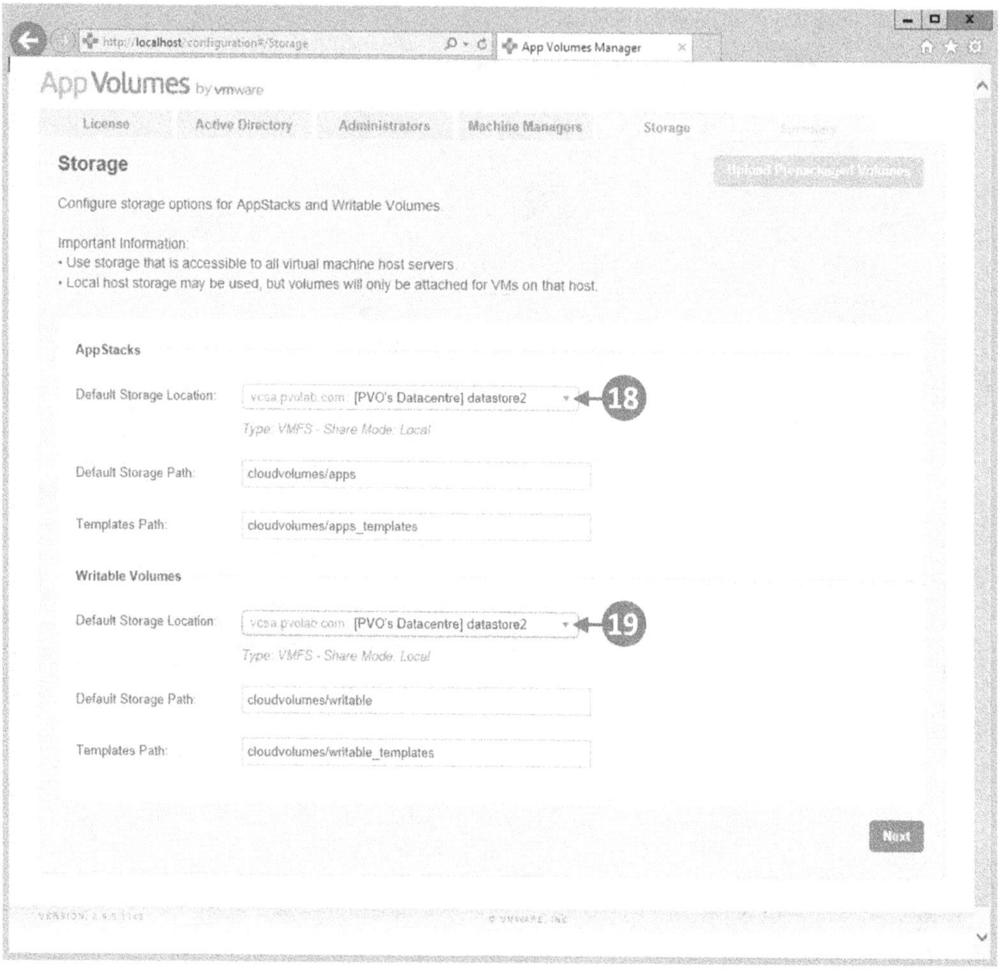

http://localhost/configuration#/Storage
App Volumes Manager
App Volumes by vmware
License | Active Directory | Administrators | Machine Managers | Storage | Summary
Storage
Upload Prepackaged Volumes
Configure storage options for AppStacks and Writable Volumes.
Important Information:
• Use storage that is accessible to all virtual machine host servers
• Local host storage may be used, but volumes will only be attached for VMs on that host.
AppStacks
Default Storage Location: vcsa.pvolab.com: [PVO's Datacentre] datastore2 — 18
Type: VMFS - Share Mode: Local
Default Storage Path: cloudvolumes/apps
Templates Path: cloudvolumes/apps_templates
Writable Volumes
Default Storage Location: vcsa.pvolab.com: [PVO's Datacentre] datastore2 — 19
Type: VMFS - Share Mode: Local
Default Storage Path: cloudvolumes/writable
Templates Path: cloudvolumes/writable_templates
Next

> Storage must be accessible to all host servers, so the best practice would be to use a shared storage platform. However, you can use local storage on the host servers, but remember that any volumes that are mounted can only be mounted by virtual machines that are on that particular host.

We need to configure the storage location for both the AppStacks and Writable Volumes.

In the **AppStacks** section of the configuration page, in the **Default Storage Location** box, click on the drop-down arrow **(18)** and select the location where you want to store your AppStacks. The options in this list are picked up from vCenter Server and reflect the already configured datastores. In our Example Lab, we have a data center in vCenter called `PVO's Datacenter`, and within that data center, we have two datastores. We are going to select the second datastore, `datastore2`, for our AppStacks.

Next, we need to do the same thing to configure the location for our Writable Volumes. Click on the drop-down arrow **(19)** and select the same datastore as we did in the previous configuration (`datastore2`).

Click on the **Next** button when you have completed the configuration. You will see the following message pop up:

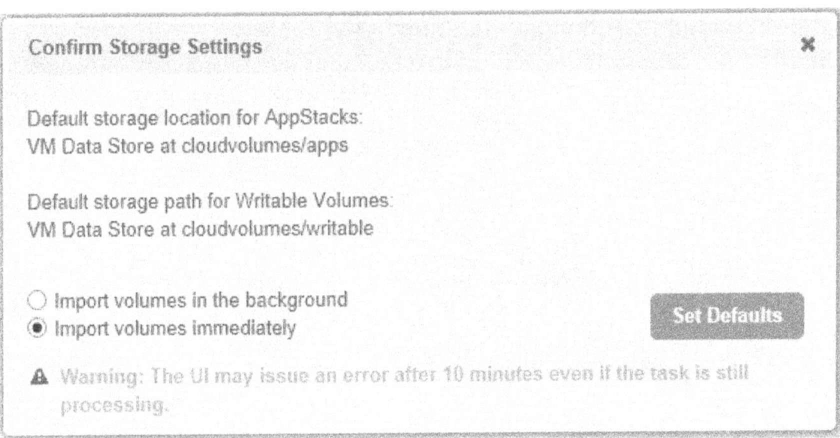

Here, you have the option of importing the volumes in the background or importing them immediately. Importing them immediately means exactly that, and you will have to wait until the volumes have been imported before you can continue. Choosing to import in the background means that you can continue while the operation executes in the background.

Click on the radio button for **Import volumes immediately**, and then click on **Set Defaults**.

You will see the following message displayed:

When the default storage location information has successfully been saved, you will see the following message:

The next configuration page is also storage related; on this page, we will configure the datastore to which we are going to upload the App Volumes templates. Templates are used to create either AppStacks or Writable Volumes.

This page is shown in the following diagram:

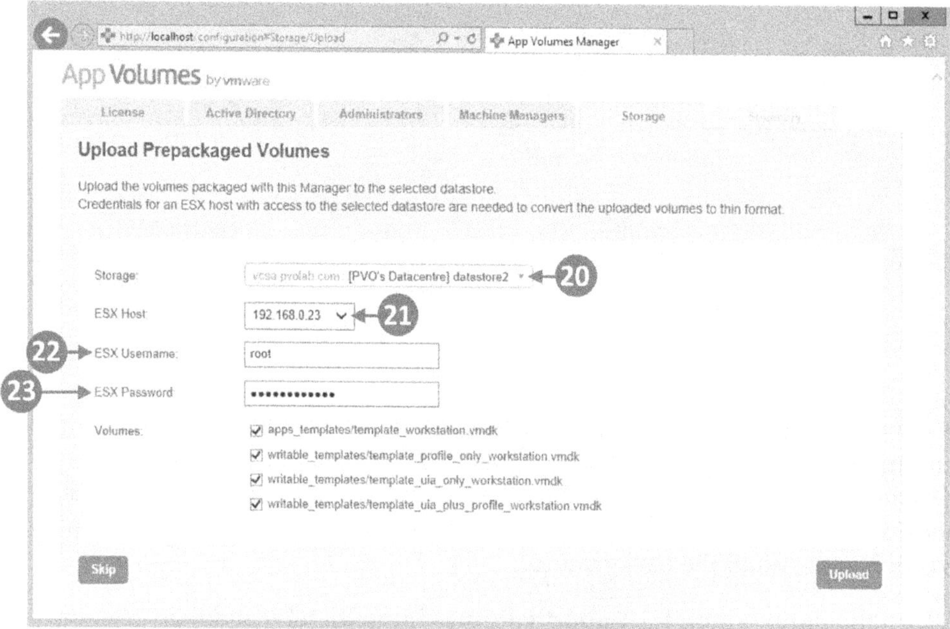

Let's complete the following configuration steps:

1. In the **Storage** drop-down box **(20)**, click on the drop-down arrow and select the datastore for storing the templates. In our Example Lab, we are going to select `datastore2`.
2. In the **ESX Host** box, click on the drop-down arrow **(21)** and select the ESX host with access to the chosen datastore. In our Example Lab, we have a single ESX server with the IP address `192.168.0.23`.
3. In the **ESX Username** box **(22)**, enter the username for the ESX host. We are going to use the root user.
4. In the **ESX Password** box **(23)**, enter the password for the username you entered in the previous box. So, in our example, this is the root password.

You need to enter the ESX server credentials so that the templates that get uploaded are converted to thin format and therefore take up less disk space.

5. Finally, check the box for the templates that you want to upload. In our example, we will upload all of them.
6. Once you have completed entering the configuration details, click on the **Upload** button.

   Before the upload is executed, you will see the **Confirm Upload Prepackaged Volumes** dialog box, as shown in the following screenshot:

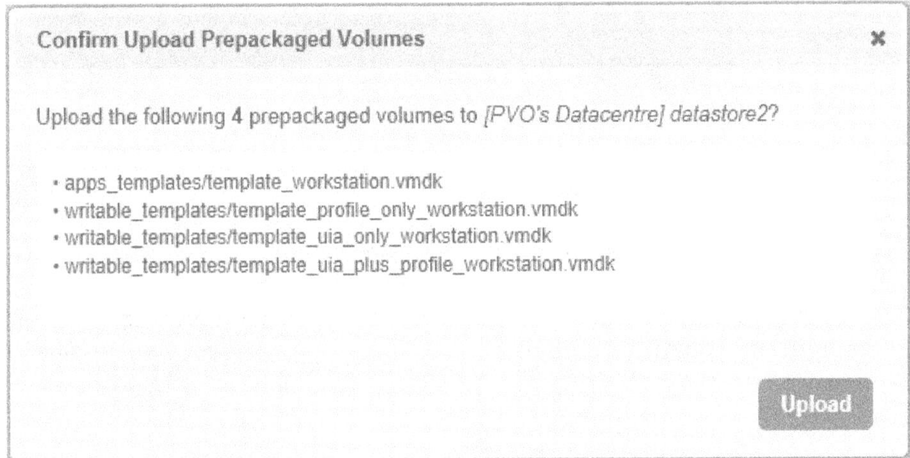
Confirm Upload Prepackaged Volumes
Upload the following 4 prepackaged volumes to [PVO's Datacentre] datastore2?
• apps_templates/template_workstation.vmdk
• writable_templates/template_profile_only_workstation.vmdk
• writable_templates/template_uia_only_workstation.vmdk
• writable_templates/template_uia_plus_profile_workstation.vmdk
Upload

7. Click on the **Upload** button to confirm and continue the upload process. You will see the following message:

The upload will now complete, after which you will see the **Summary** screen, as shown in the following screenshot:

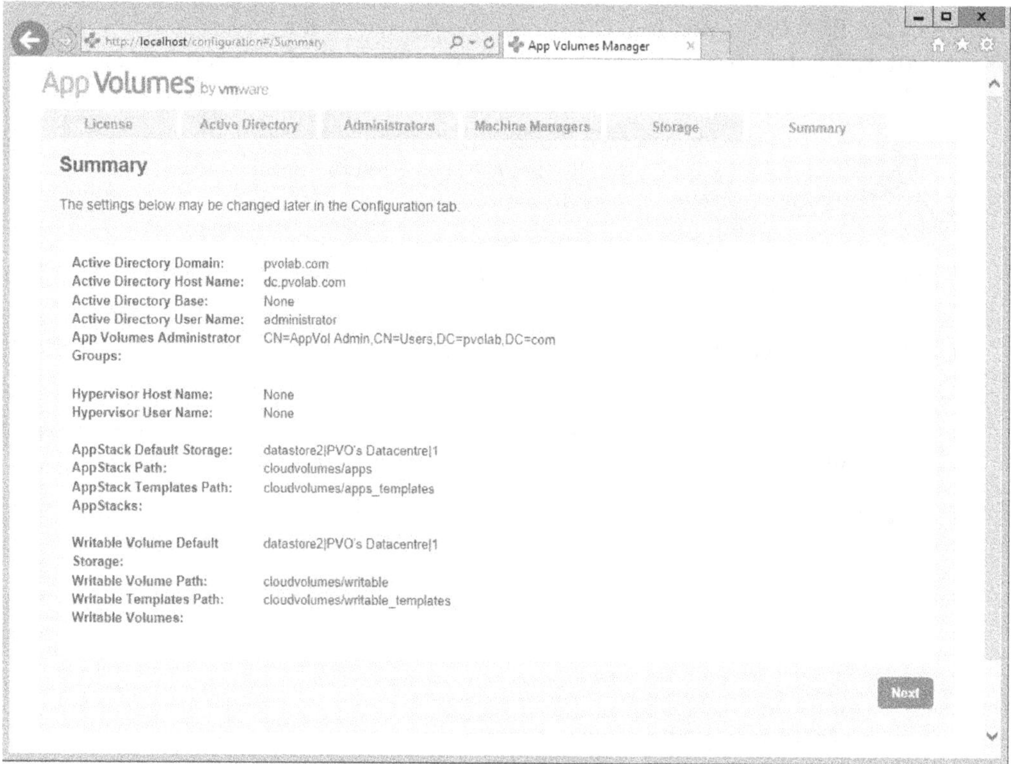

8. Once everything has been configured correctly, click on **Next** to complete the configuration of App Volumes.

At this stage, App Volumes has created the directories on the datastore in which your AppStacks and Writable Volumes are going to be stored, as well as having copied the default templates. You can check this by logging in to the vCenter Server, as shown in this diagram:

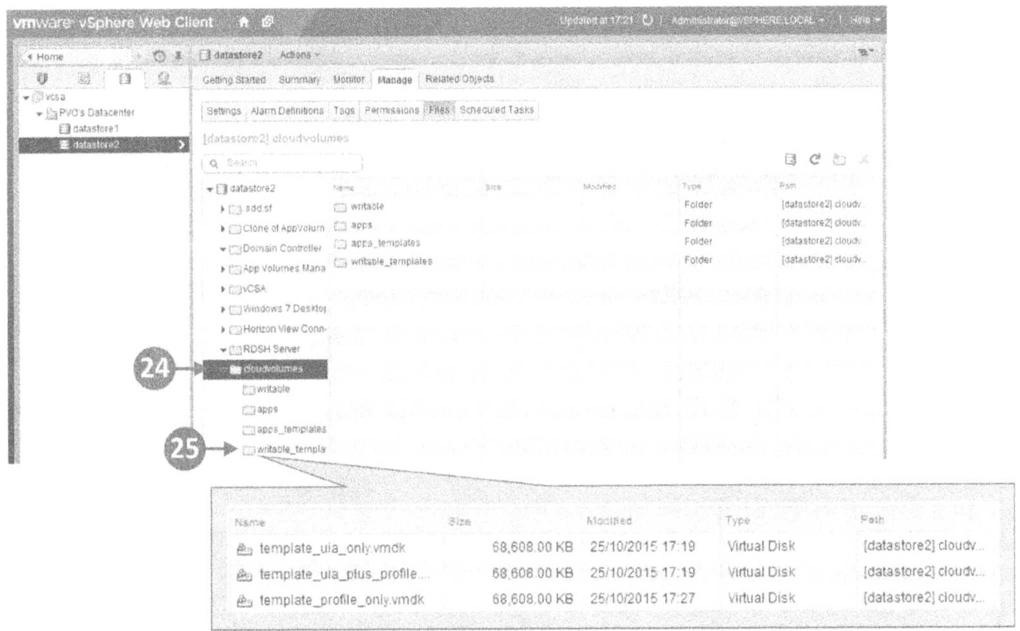

You can see that the `cloudvolumes` folder **(24)** has been created in the datastore. If you expand the folder by clicking on the arrow, you will see that the templates have also been created.

If you double-click on the `writable_template` folder **(25)**, you will see the VMDK files that make up the templates. In this case, there are a couple of templates for deployment.

Switch back to the App Volumes Manager summary screen, and if you need to go back and make any changes, simply click on the appropriate tab from the top of the page.

Click on the **Next** button to continue. When the App Volumes configuration has successfully completed, you will be taken to the **Volumes** menu, as shown in the following screenshot, in preparation for creating your first AppStack:

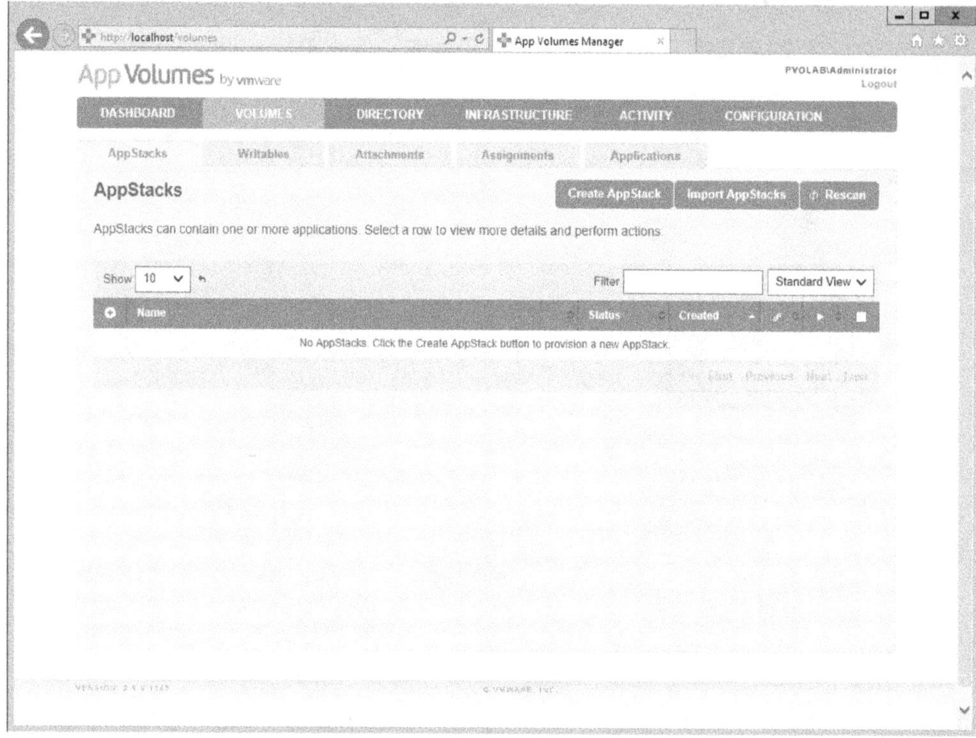

You have now completed the installation and configuration of App Volumes Manager. In the next subsection, we will install App Volumes Agent onto our virtual desktop that we will capture new AppStacks from.

Installing App Volumes Agent

Now that we have installed App Volumes Manager, the next step is to install App Volumes Agent instances onto each virtual desktop that we want to attach AppStacks to.

Ideally, we would install these onto the parent or master image, which we would then use to create our desktops. As we discussed previously, deploying App Volumes allows you to deploy a stateless, non-persistent virtual desktop model, taking advantage of features such as the linked clone feature in Horizon View.

Locate the folder or shared folder where you have stored the App Volumes software, and perform the following steps:

1. Double-click on the **Installation** folder, then on the **Agent** folder, and then launch the **App Volumes Agent** installer file, shown in the following screenshot:

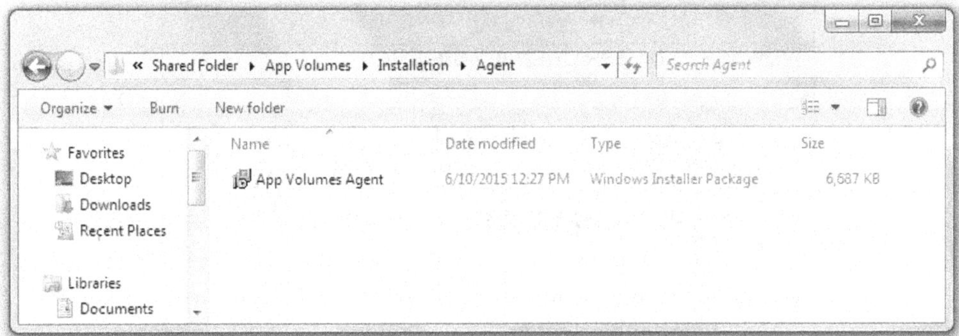

2. The **App Volumes Agent Installation Wizard** is launched, as shown in the following screenshot:

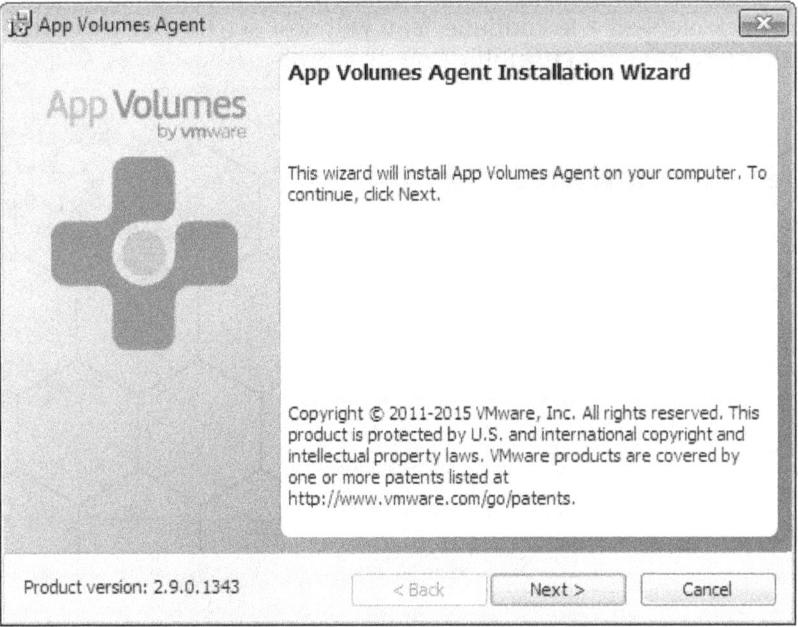

3. Click on the **Next >** button to start the installation. You will now see the **VMWARE END USER LICENSE AGREEMENT** window, as shown in the following screenshot:

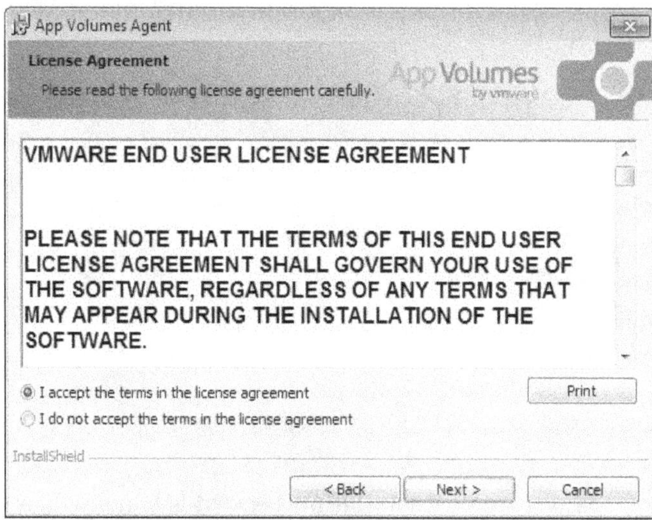

4. Click on the radio button for **I accept the terms in the license agreement**, and click on **Next >** to continue. You will now see the **Server Configuration** dialog box, shown in the following diagram:

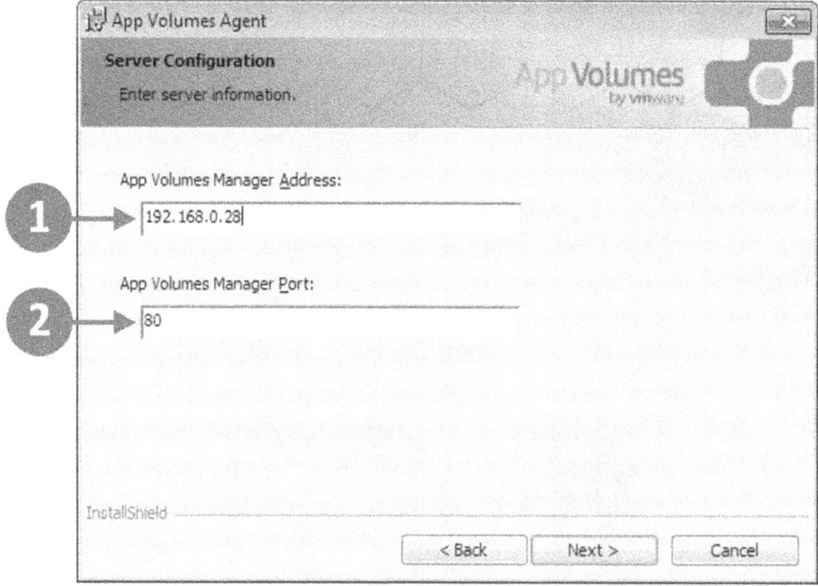

5. In the **App Volumes Manager Address** box **(1)**, type in the address of the App Volumes Manager instance. In our Example Lab, this is `192.168.0.28`.
6. Then, in the **App Volumes Manager Port** box **(2)**, enter the port number for the App Volumes Manager instance. In our Example Lab, we have left this as the default port, `80`.
7. Once you have entered the details, click on the **Next >** button. You will now see the **Ready to Install the Program** dialog box, shown in the following screenshot:

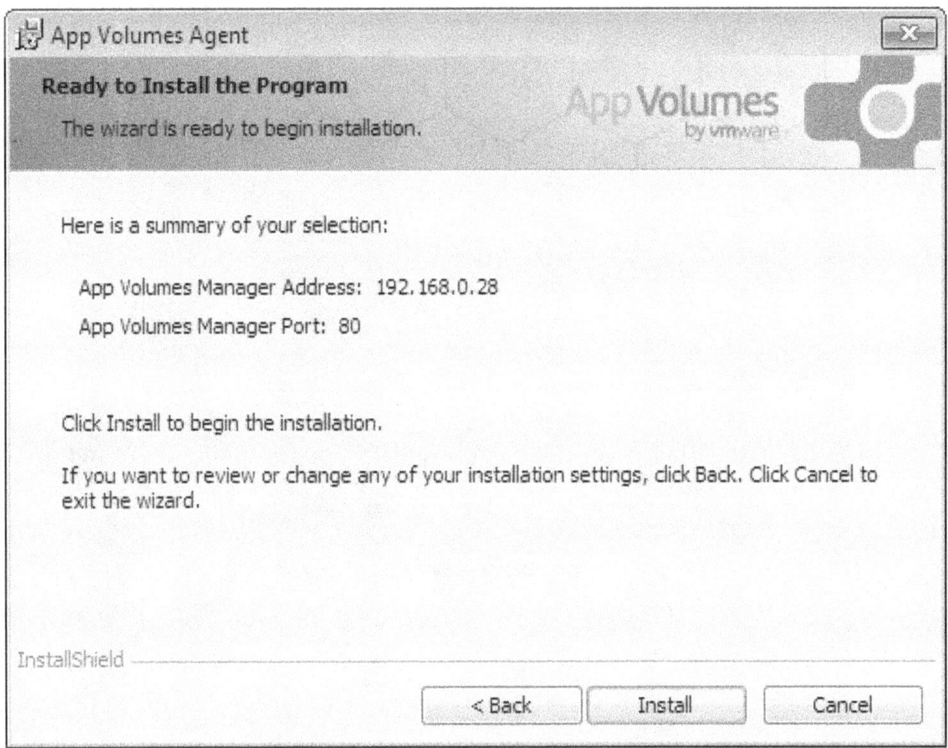

8. Check the summary details and whether you have entered the configuration details correctly, and then click on the **Install** button to continue the installation. You will now see the **Installing App Volumes Agent** progress bar, as shown in the following screenshot:

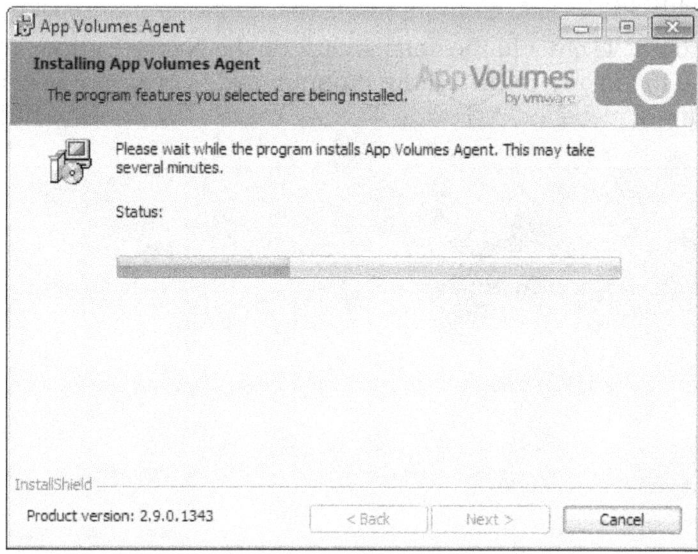

Once the installation is complete, you will see the following window:

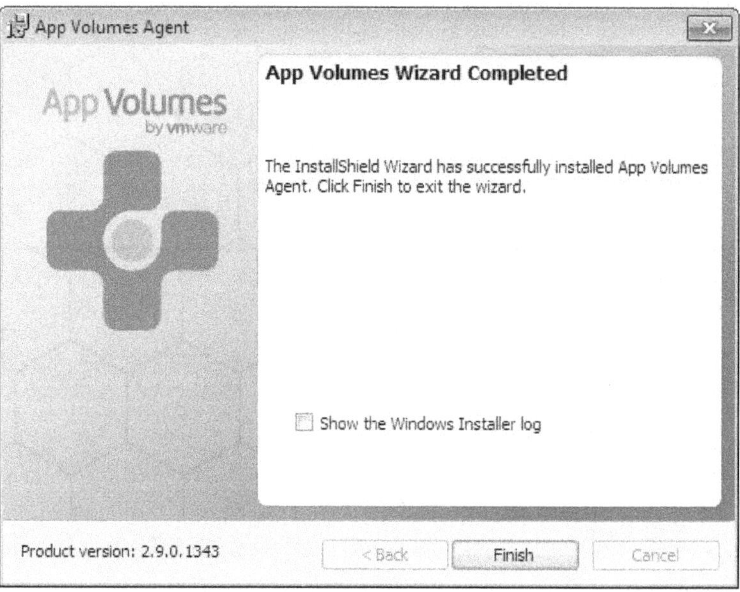

9. Click on the **Finish** button to complete the installation and close the App Volumes Agent installer. You will then be prompted to reboot the virtual desktop machine to complete the installation, as shown here:

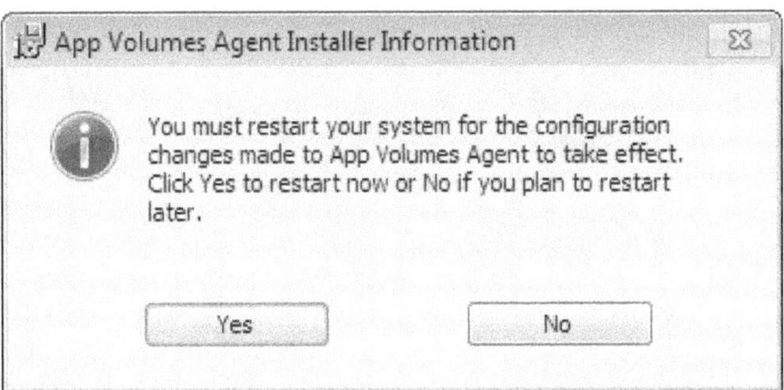

10. Click on the **Yes** button to reboot.

You have now successfully installed App Volumes Agent, and the virtual desktop machine will now appear in App Volumes Manager. We will use this machine later in this book in *Chapter 6, Working with AppStacks*, for capturing AppStacks.

Summary

In this chapter, we started by discussing the prerequisites for installing App Volumes Manager and then discussed the requirements from both a hardware and software perspective.

We then went on to download the software components and install the App Volumes Manager software onto our server (including a SQL Express database) before finishing off with the installation of App Volumes Agent onto one of our virtual desktop machines. In this case, it was the virtual desktop that we are going to use later in this book to capture AppStacks from.

In the next chapter, we will take a guided tour of App Volumes Manager so that you can familiarize yourself with how it works and where to perform the different tasks for managing your App Volumes environment.

5

A Guided Tour of the Management Console

Now that we have our App Volumes software installed and have completed the initial configuration tasks, we can start creating and managing our AppStacks and Writable Volumes.

Before we start doing this, we will spend five minutes walking through an overview of the management console so that you can familiarize yourself with where the different options are located and how the console pages are laid out.

Logging in to the management console

The App Volumes **management console** is a web-based console that allows you to configure App Stacks, Writable Volumes, and user assignments.

To launch App Volumes Manager, double-click on the icon on the desktop of the server where you installed it. This will launch a browser session displaying the login screen, as shown in the following screenshot:

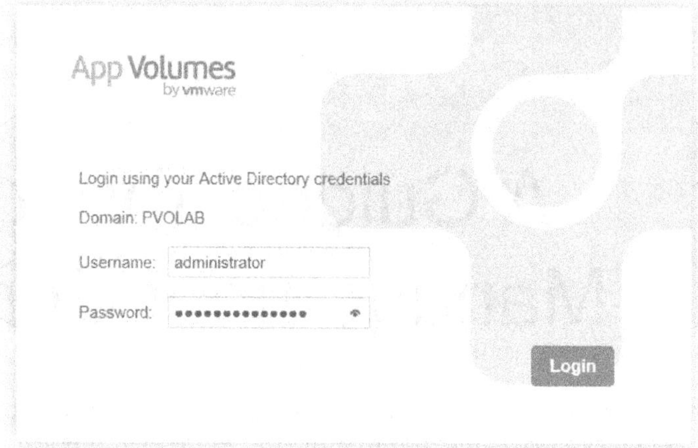

Enter the username and password. In our example, we are using the administrator account that was added to the App Volumes administrators group.

Once you have entered the credentials, click on the **Login** button.

The DASHBOARD page

The first page you will see is the **DASHBOARD** page, as shown in the following screenshot:

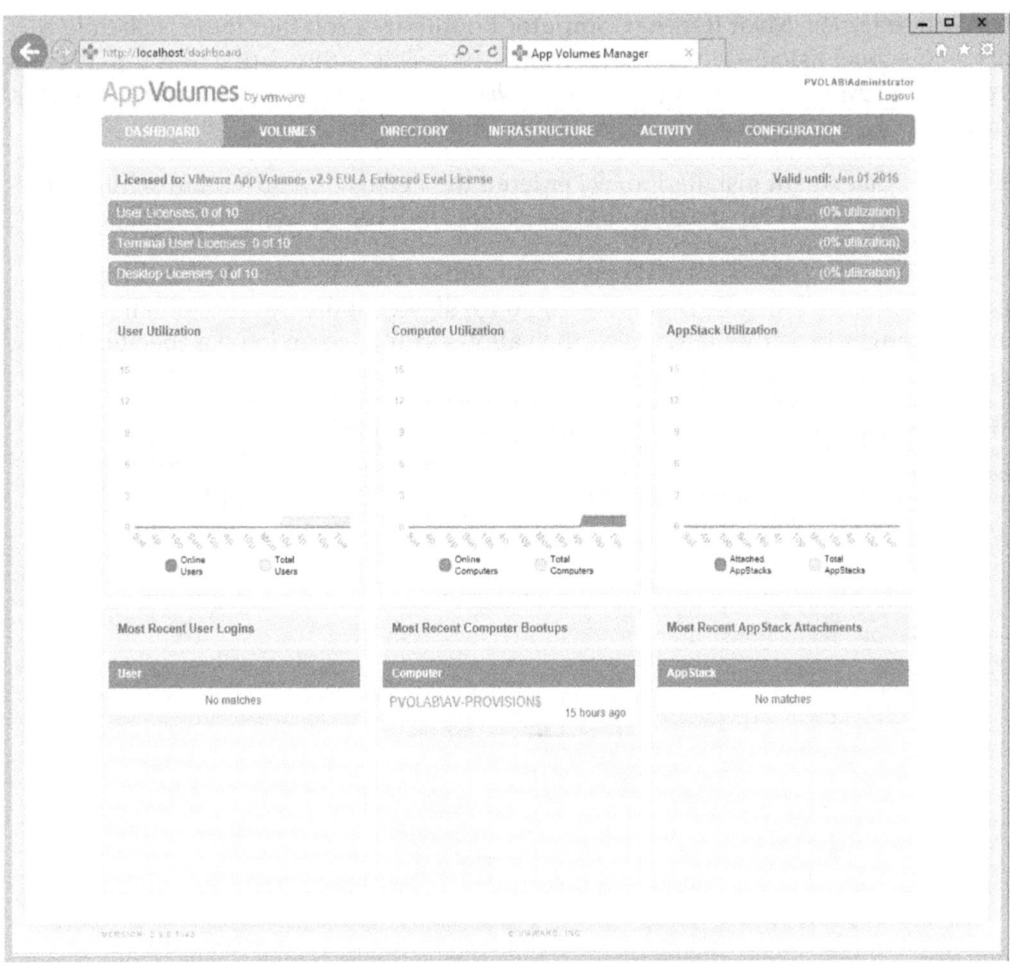

The **DASHBOARD** page gives you an instant view of your App Volumes deployment and what's going on. You can see at a glance useful utilization statistics on user, computer, and AppStacks utilization as well as recent user logins, computer bootups, and AppStack attachments.

You will see in the **Most Recent Computer Bootups** section that there is already a virtual machine listed – `PVOLAB\AV-PROVISION$`. This is the virtual desktop machine we installed App Volumes Agent onto in *Chapter 4, Installing and Configuring the App Volumes Software*, and it will be used to provision AppStacks.

As part of that Agent installation, we entered the details of App Volumes Manager and that virtual desktop machine has therefore "checked in" with the manager.

While still on the **DASHBOARD** page, you will also see that, if you hover your mouse over any of the utilization boxes, you will get another level of detail. The cursor changes to a crosshair, which then allows you to zoom in on a specific date and time.

An example of this is shown in the following screenshot:

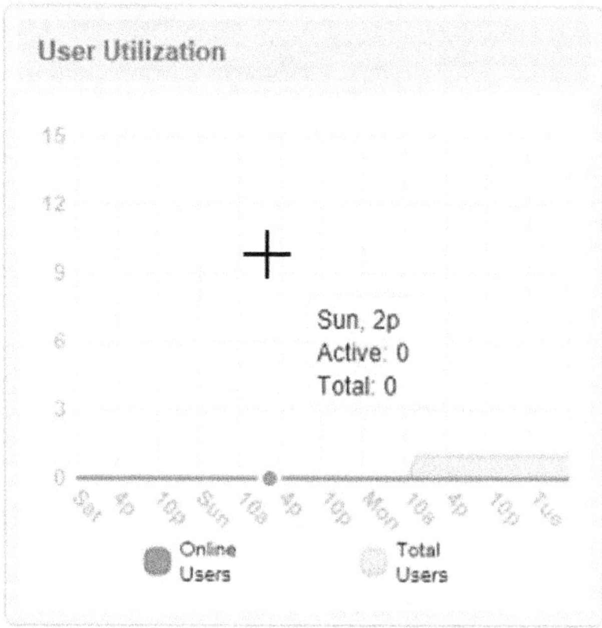

As you can see in the preceding example, we are looking at the number of active users from 2 pm on Sunday, during which time there were no active users.

Let's move back to the top of the **DASHBOARD** page and look at the menu options, as shown in the following diagram:

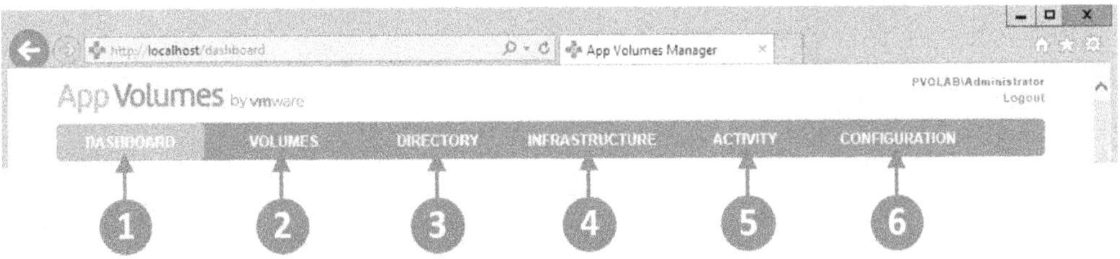

There are six different menu options for the various tasks. The following list describes each one at a high level:

1. **DASHBOARD**: This provides a high-level usage/utilization overview of your App Volumes environment.
2. **VOLUMES**: This is where you create AppStacks and Writable Volumes. It also shows you a breakdown of current attachments and assignments as well as a list of all the applications that are contained within the AppStacks.
3. **DIRECTORY**: This provides the details of your Active Directory environment, listing users, groups, computers, and OUs, as well as showing those that are currently online.
4. **INFRASTRUCTURE**: This details currently managed machines as well as storage locations and storage group configuration.
5. **ACTIVITY**: This shows details of logs, pending activities, and system-generated messages.
6. **CONFIGURATION**: This is the configuration section as per the initial configuration details that were completed as part of the installation. Here, you are able to change any of the configuration details, such as licensing, Active Directory, machine managers, and storage.

We will cover these menu options in a bit more depth in the following sections.

The final section on the **DASHBOARD** page displays the license information. It details the type of license and the date it is valid until, as well as how many licenses are currently being used. The following screenshot shows this information for our Example Lab:

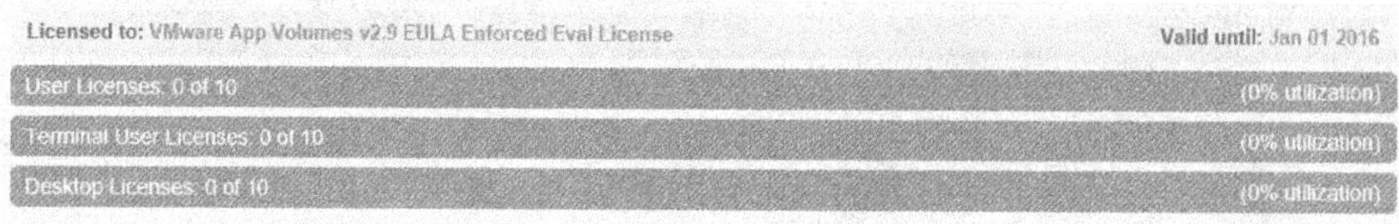

In the next sections, we will take a closer look at the other menu options, starting with the **VOLUMES** menu.

The VOLUMES menu

The **VOLUMES** menu presents you with all the tasks you need to create AppStacks and Writable Volumes and then assign them to users. Click on on the **VOLUMES** menu **(7)**. You will now see that you have five different options to choose from, displayed as tabs, as shown in the following diagram:

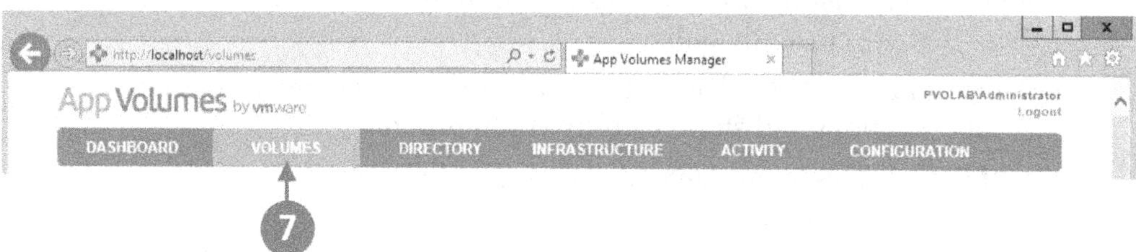

The first tab is for configuring AppStacks, so let's start there.

AppStacks

The **AppStacks** tab is shown in the following diagram:

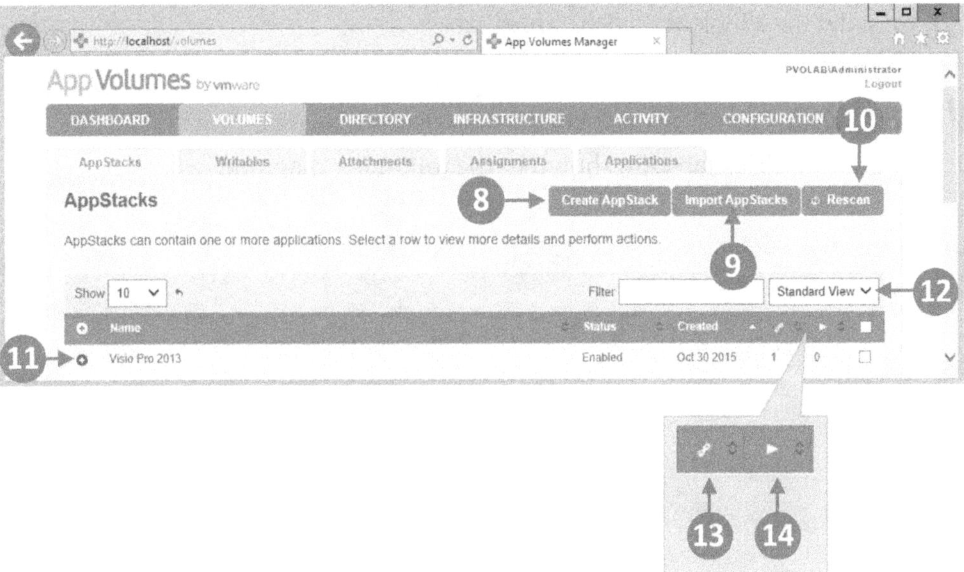

Within the **AppStacks** configuration tab, there are several configuration options. The first option you have is to create a new AppStack by clicking on the **Create AppStack** button **(8)**. This will launch the **Create an AppStack** page. We will cover the process for creating AppStacks in *Chapter 6, Working with AppStacks*.

Next, you have the option that imports existing AppStacks by clicking on the **Import AppStacks** button **(9)**. You can also rescan the storage by clicking on the **Rescan** button **(10)** to check the accessibility of any existing AppStacks.

At the bottom of the page **(11)**, the details of existing AppStacks are displayed. You can change how these are displayed by clicking on the drop-down arrow in the view options box **(12)**. You can show the **Standard View**, which details the name, status, and creation date; the **Usage View**, which shows when the AppStack was last mounted; and finally, the **File View**, which details the size of the AppStack and the policy applied to it.

Finally, there are also a couple of icons displayed along the title bar. The first one **(13)** shows the quantity that AppStack that is assigned. The second icon **(14)** shows how many of that particular AppStack are currently in use.

Next, we will take a look at the **Writables** tab.

Writables

Click on the **Writables** tab **(15)**, shown in the following diagram:

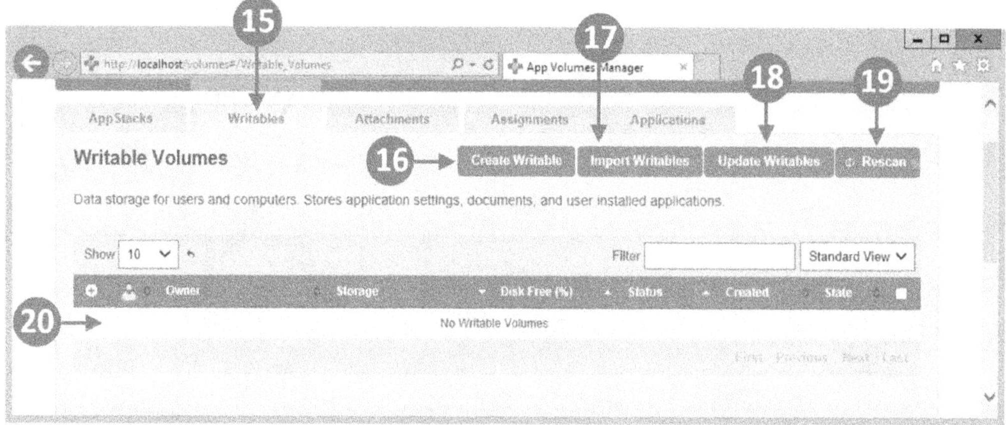

Within the **Writables** configuration tab, there are several configuration options.

The first option you have is to create a new Writable Volume by clicking on the **Create Writable** button **(16)**. This will launch the **Create Writable Volume** page. We will cover the process for creating and managing Writable Volumes in more detail in *Chapter 7, Working with Writable Volumes*.

Next, you have the option to import existing Writable Volumes by clicking on the **Import Writables** button **(17)**. From here, you will be able to point App Volumes Manager to a datastore and path where existing Writable Volumes that you want to import exist.

The next option is to **Update Writables (18)**. Clicking on this button allows you to upload a ZIP file that will then get written to all Writable Volumes the next time they are attached.

Finally, you can also rescan the storage by clicking on the **Rescan** button **(19)** to check that existing Writable Volumes are still accessible.

At the bottom of the page **(20)**, the details of existing Writable Volumes are displayed.

Next, we will take a look at the **Attachments** tab.

Attachments

Click on the **Attachments** tab **(21)**, as shown in the following diagram:

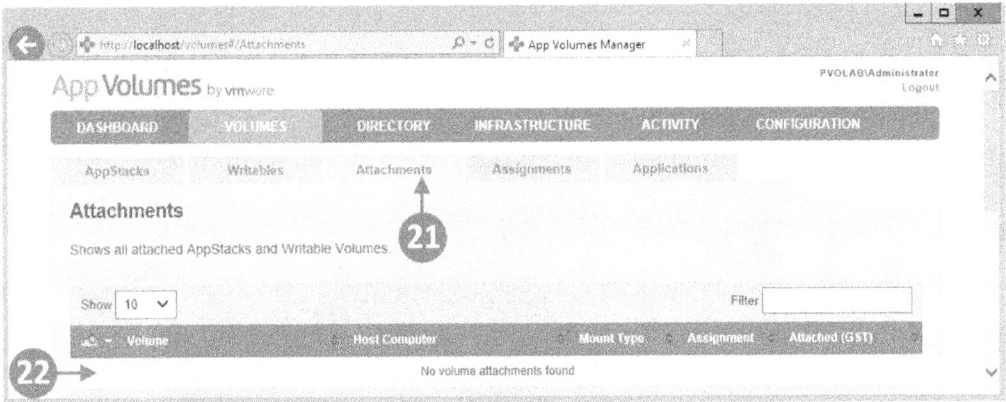

In the section. at the bottom of the page **(22)**, you can see the details of the currently attached AppStacks and Writable Volumes, along with information regarding the volume, host computer, mount type, and so on.

Next, we will take a look at the **Assignments** tab.

Assignments

Click on the **Assignments** tab **(23)**, shown in the following diagram:

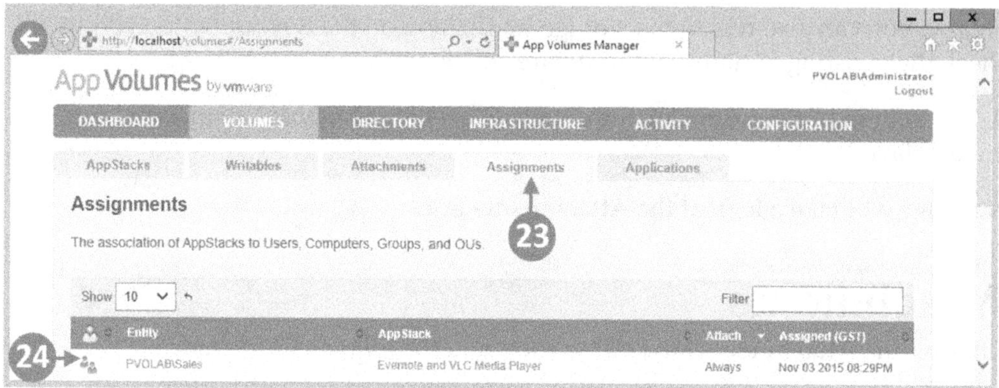

In the section at the bottom of the page **(24)**, App Volumes Manager displays details of which users, computer, or groups are assigned to which AppStacks.

The following icons are used to represent users, groups, and computers:

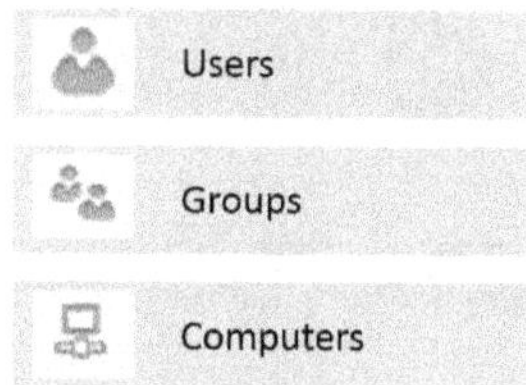

Next, we will take a look at the **Applications** tab.

Applications

Click on the **Applications** tab **(25)**, shown in the following diagram:

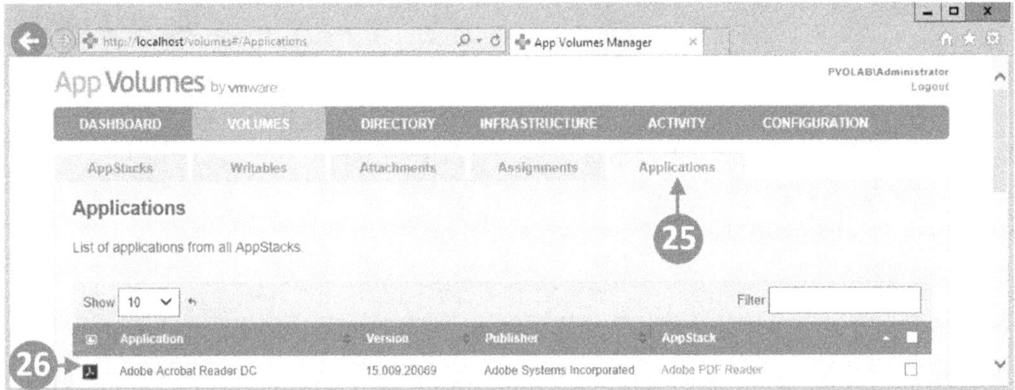

In the section at the bottom of the page **(26)**, App Volumes Manager displays details of all the applications that are contained within the AppStacks.

In the next section, we will explore the **DIRECTORY** menu and its options.

The DIRECTORY menu

The **DIRECTORY** menu is all about displaying details of App Volumes' interaction with Active Directory, showing details of your Active Directory environment, listing users, groups, computers, and OUs, as well as showing those that are currently online.

The first tab is for displaying users who are currently online, so let's start there.

Online

Click on the **DIRECTORY** menu **(1)**, shown in the following diagram:

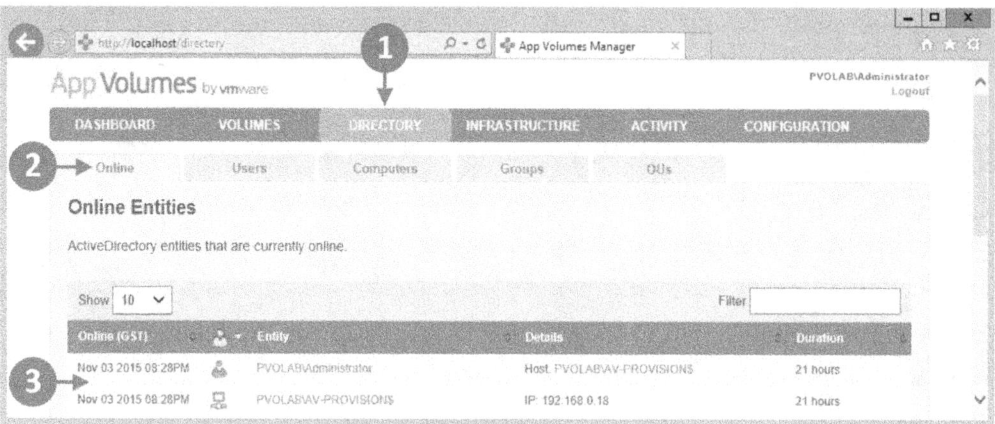

The first tab you will see is the **Online** tab **(2)**. This shows details of the current users or computers that are currently online **(3)**.

Next, we will take a look at the **Users** tab.

Users

Click on the **Users** tab **(4)**, shown in the following diagram:

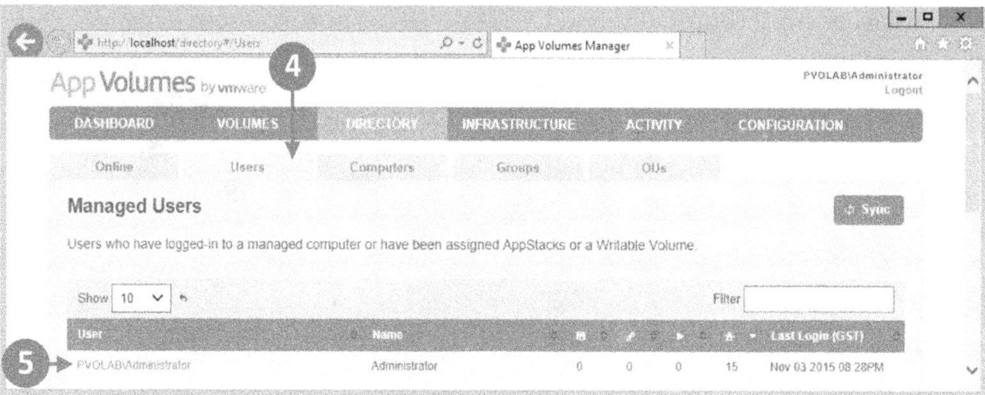

App Volumes Manager now shows you a list of users who are currently logged in to a virtual desktop machine that is running App Volumes Agent, have either an AppStack or Writable Volume attached, or have previously logged in to a virtual desktop machine running App Volumes Agent.

You can see in this example that the administrator is currently logged in **(5)** but has no AppStacks or Writable Volumes assigned to them. The icons represent the following:

Next, we will take a look at the **Computers** tab.

Computers

Click on the **Computers** tab **(6)**, shown in the following diagram:

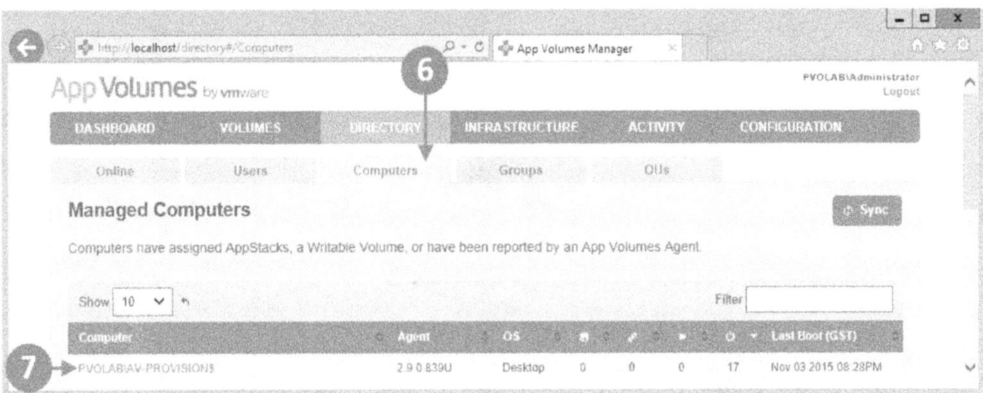

App Volumes Manager now shows you a list of computers that either currently have or have previously had AppStacks or Writable Volumes assigned to them.

In this example **(7)**, you can see that there is one computer listed, `PVOLAB\AV-PROVISION`. This is our AppStack provisioning virtual desktop. We can see that it is currently powered on, the time it booted, and that it currently has no AppStacks or Writable Volumes attached to it.

There is also a **Sync** button on this page. This allows you to perform a synchronization with Active Directory in order to update the list of computers.

Finally, the following icon denotes the number of times that particular machine has booted up:

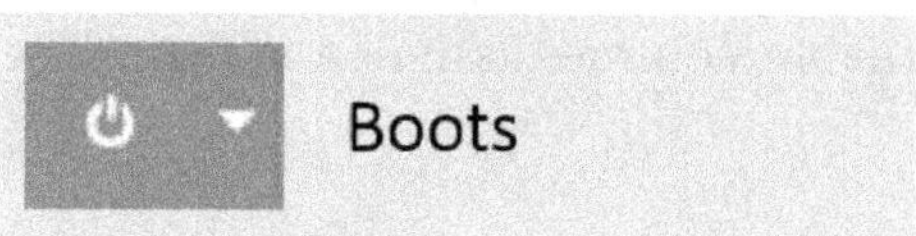

Next, we will take a look at the **Groups** tab.

Groups

Click on the **Groups** tab **(8)**, shown in the following diagram:

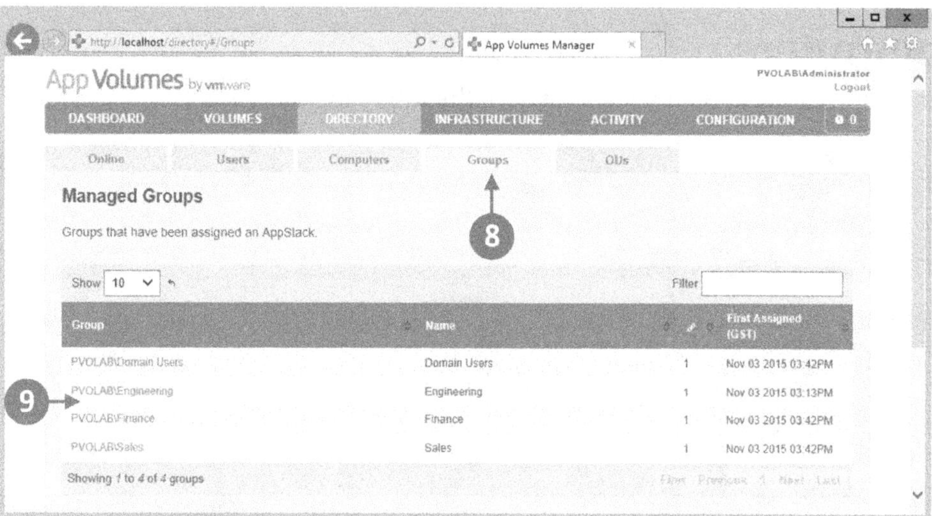

In this tab, App Volumes Manager shows you a list of Active Directory groups that have been assigned an AppStack **(9)**.

Next, we will take a look at the final tab in this section, the **OUs** tab.

OUs

Click on the **OUs** tab **(10)**, shown in the following diagram:

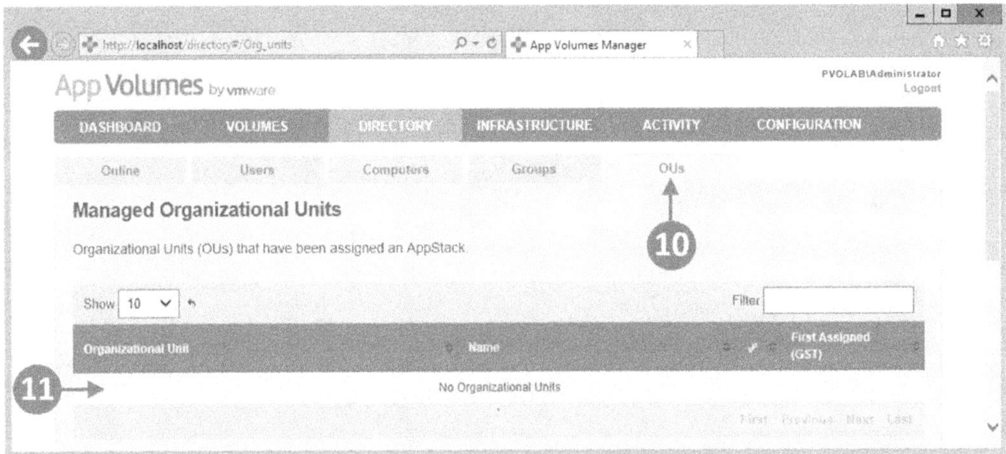

Similar to the **Groups** tab, on the **OUs** tab, App Volumes Manager shows you a list of the **Organizational Units** (**OUs**) that that have been assigned an AppStack **(11)**.

In the next section, we will explore the **INFRASTRUCTURE** menu and its options.

The INFRASTRUCTURE menu

The **INFRASTRUCTURE** menu is all about displaying details about the infrastructure components in your App Volumes environment, such as storage and storage groups.

The first tab is for displaying managed machines, so let's start there.

Machines

Click on the **INFRASTRUCTURE** menu **(1)**, shown in the following diagram:

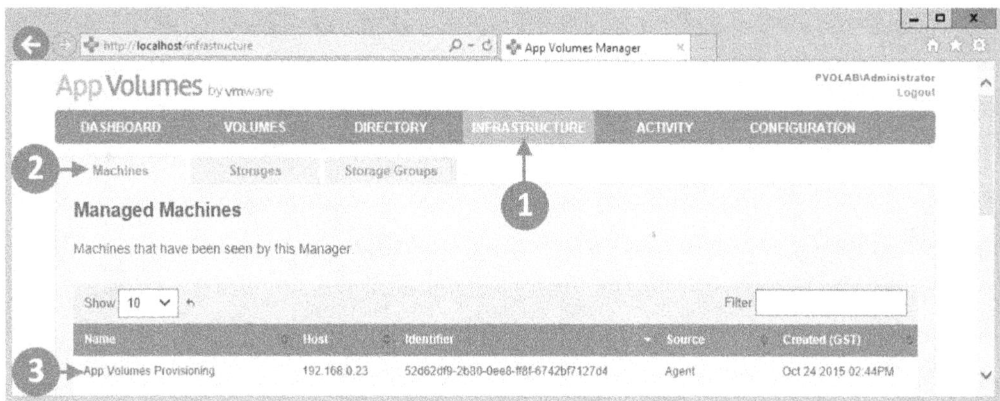

The first tab you will see is the **Machines** tab **(2)**. This shows details of the machines that have previously been or are being managed by App Volumes Manager **(3)**.

Next, we will take a look at the **Storage** tab.

Storage

Click on the **Storage** tab **(4)**, shown in the following diagram:

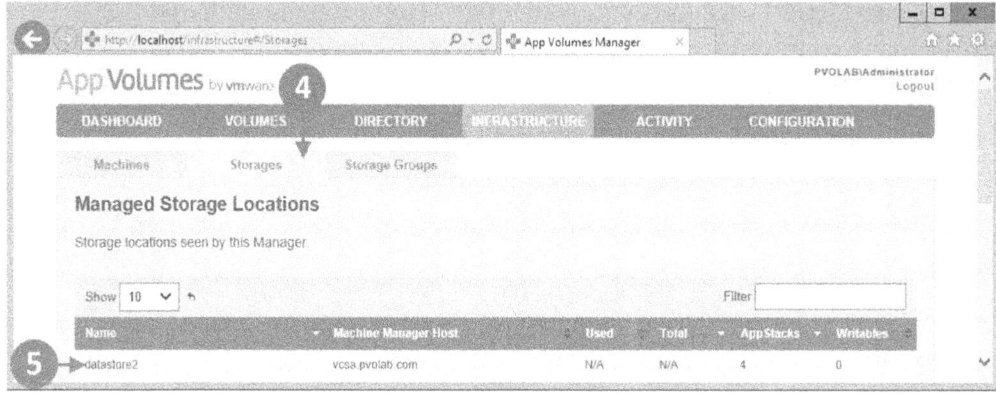

In this tab, App Volumes Manager shows you a list of the storage locations **(5)** that are being used. The information details the name of the datastore, which vCenter is managing it, and other details, such as the number of AppStacks and Writable Volumes that are stored in each datastore.

Next, we will take a look at the final tab in this section, the **Storage Groups** tab.

Storage Groups

Click on the **Storage Groups** tab **(6)**, shown in the following diagram:

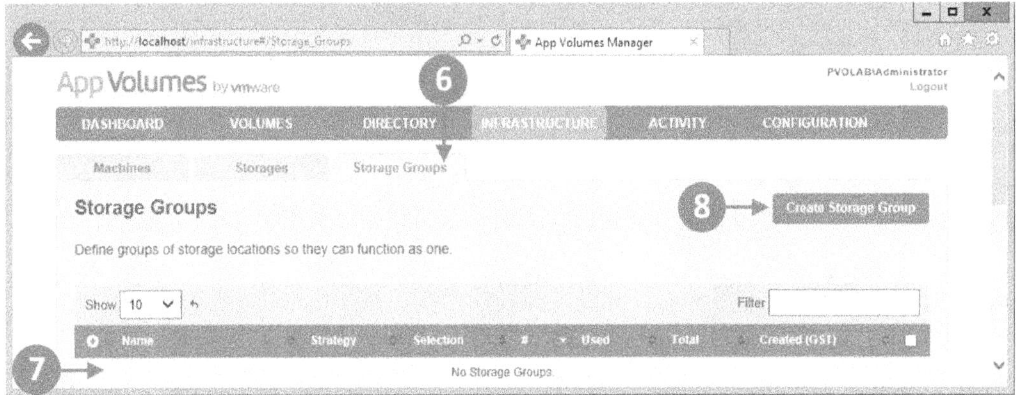

In this tab, App Volumes Manager shows you a list of storage groups **(7)**.

If you click on the **Create Storage Group** button **(8)**, you will see the following configuration page:

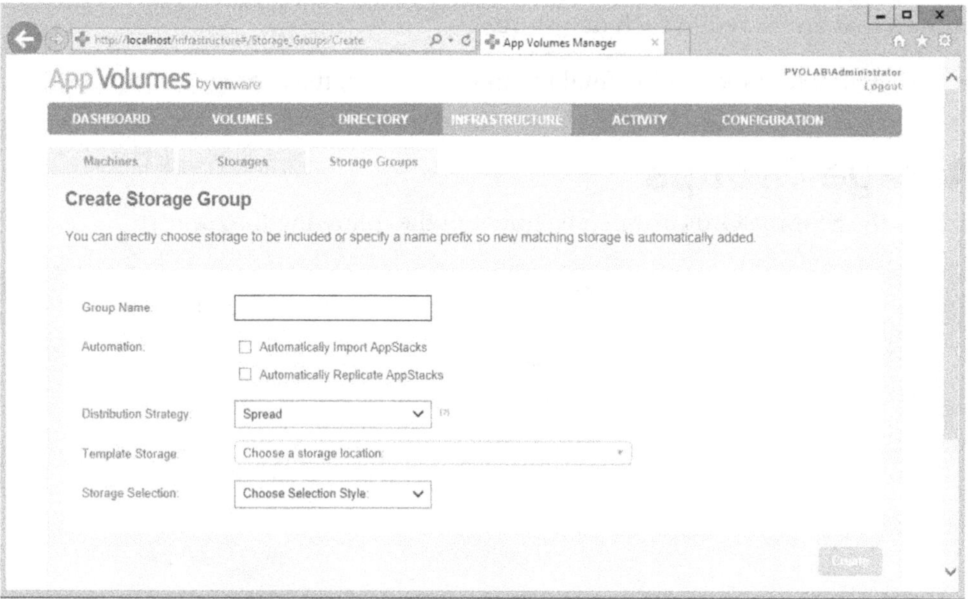

From here, you can create your storage groups. We will cover this in greater detail in *Chapter 12, Deploying App Volumes in a Citrix XenApp Environment*.

In the next section, we will explore the **ACTIVITY** menu options.

The ACTIVITY menu

The **ACTIVITY** menu is all about displaying log files, messages, and pending activities.

The first tab is for displaying pending actions, so let's start there.

Pending Actions

Click on the **ACTIVITY** menu **(1)**, shown in the following diagram:

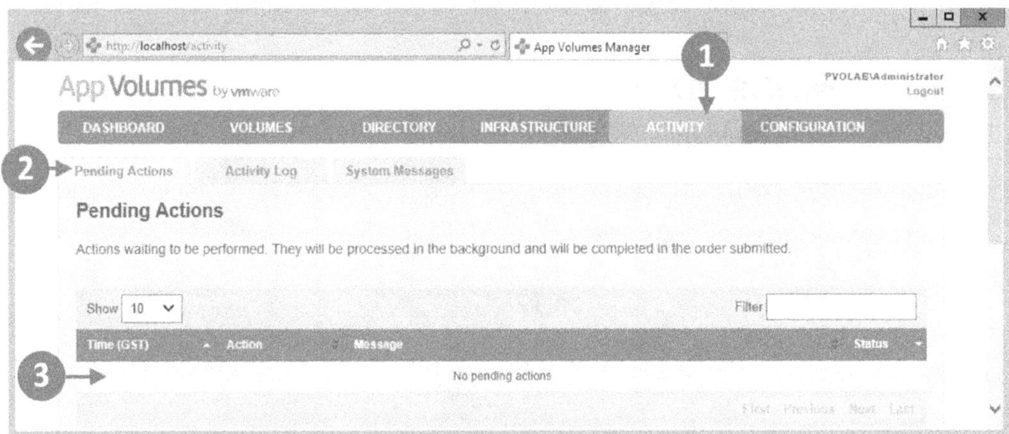

The first tab you will see is the **Pending Actions** tab **(2)**. This shows details of any actions that are queued and waiting to be actioned **(3)**.

Next, we will take a look at the **Activity Log** tab.

Activity Log

Click on the **Activity Log** tab **(4)**, shown in the following diagram:

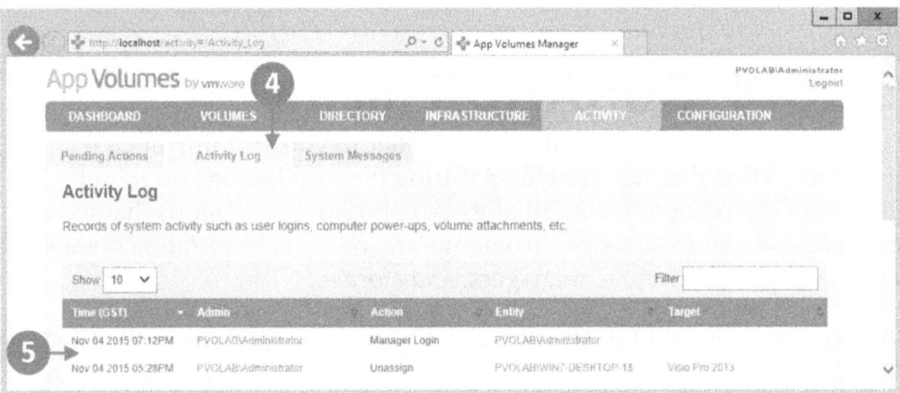

In this tab, App Volumes Manager shows you a list of all the events that have taken place **(5)**.

Next, we will take a look at the final tab in this menu, the **System Messages** tab.

System Messages

Click on the **System Messages** tab **(6)**, shown in the following diagram:

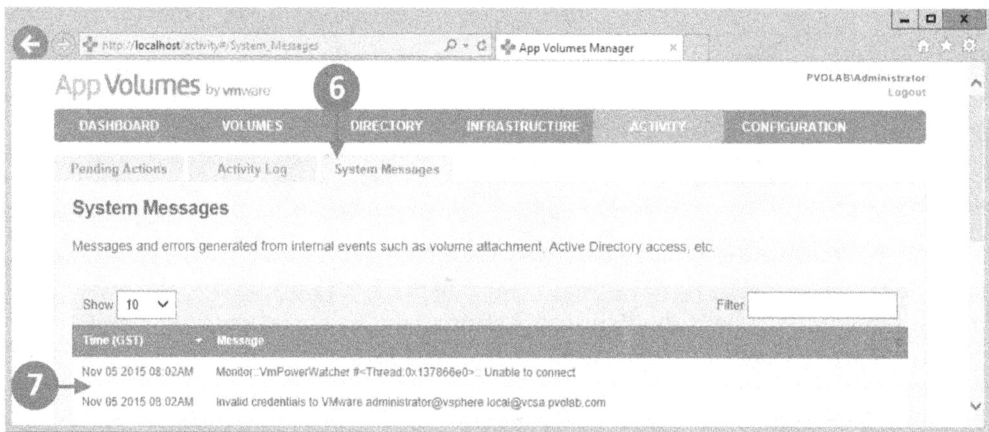

In this tab, App Volumes Manager shows you a list of all the system-generated messages and errors that have occurred **(7)**. This can help with troubleshooting.

Finally, in the next section, we will cover the last menu option: **CONFIGURATION**.

The CONFIGURATION menu

The **CONFIGURATION** menu will seem familiar to you as it mirrors the configuration section that we completed during the installation and initial configuration. This section details all of those configuration options that were entered previously and allows you to change any of the configuration details such as licensing, AD, machine managers, and storage.

Under this menu option, there are five tabs. The first tab is for licensing information, so let's start there.

License

First, click on the **CONFIGURATION** menu **(1)**, shown in the following diagram:

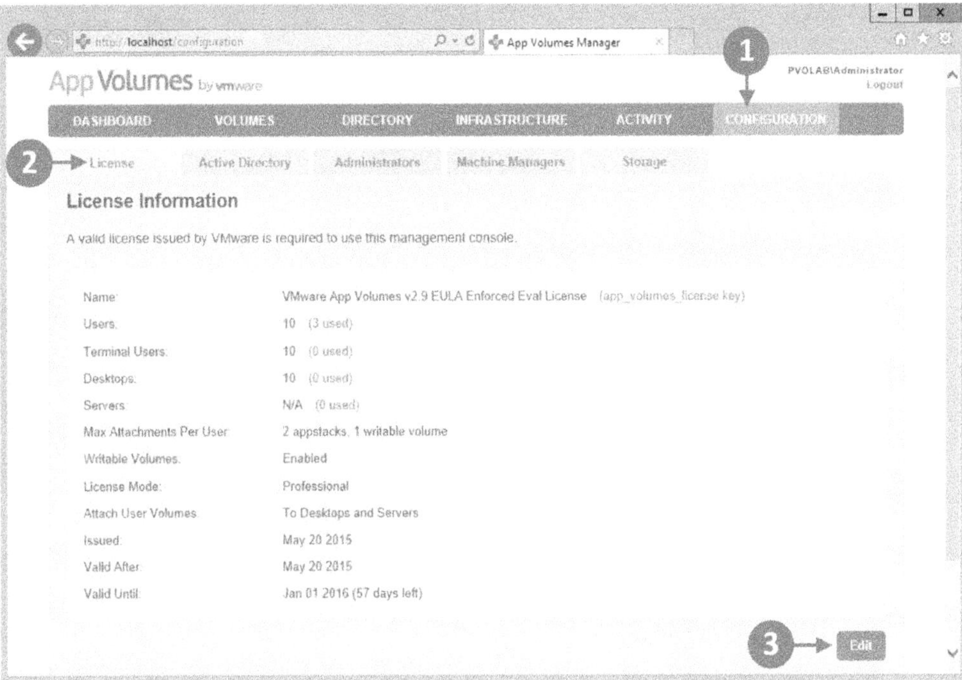

The first tab you will see is the **License** tab **(2)**. This shows details of how your App Volumes deployment is licensed, providing details on the number of users, type of license, maximum number of attachments, and the date when your license expires.

Licensing information can be updated by clicking on the **Edit** button **(3)**.

Next, we will take a look at the **Active Directory** tab.

Active Directory

Click on the **Active Directory** tab **(4)**, shown in the following diagram:

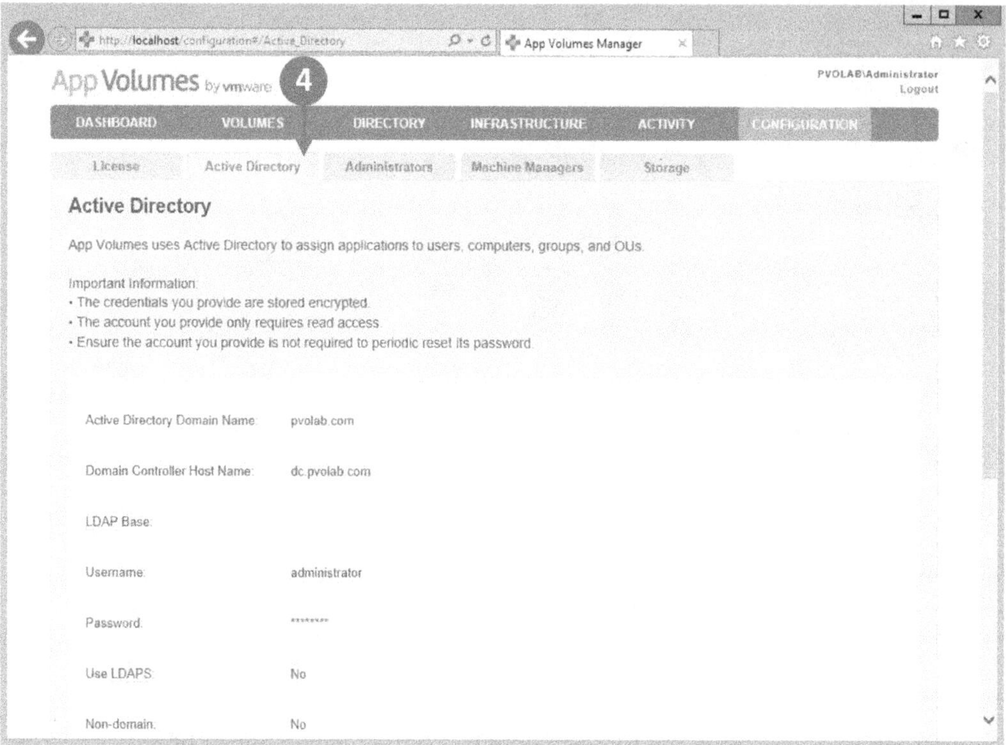

This will display all the information related to Active Directory.

Next, we will take a look at the **Administrators** tab.

Administrators

Click on the **Administrators** tab **(5)**, shown in the following diagram:

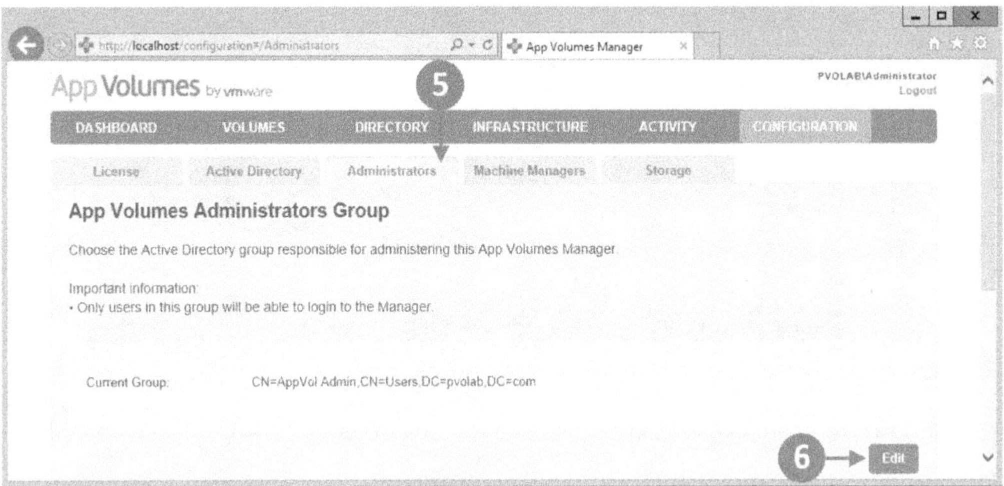

On this page, you will see the details of the administrators group that you entered during the installation process for the accounts that can administer App Volumes.

You can change or update this information by clicking on the **Edit** button **(6)**.

Next, we will take a look at the **Machine Managers** tab.

Machine Managers

Click on the **Machine Managers** tab **(7)**, shown in the following diagram:

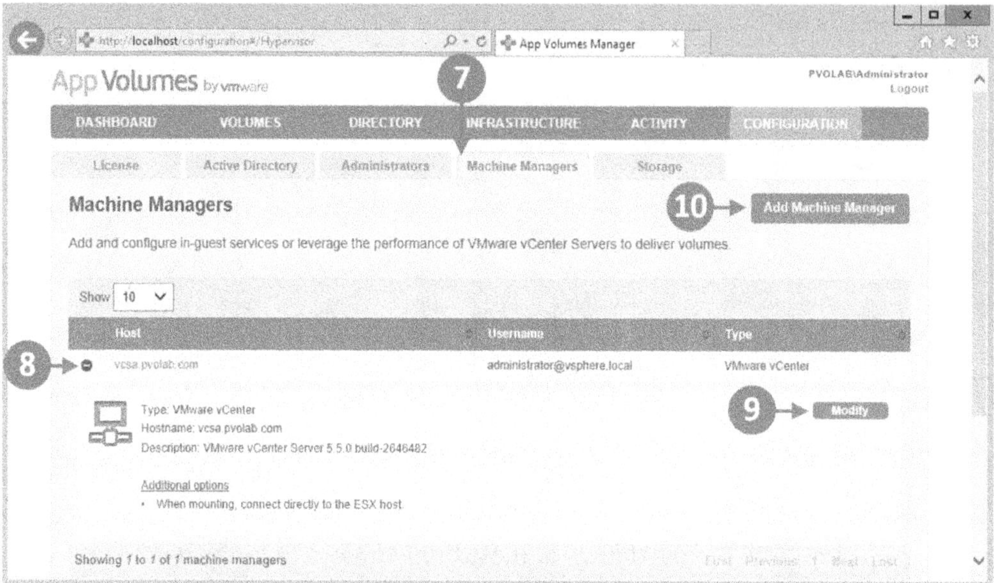

Click on the +/- button **(8)** to expand the information. You will now see the details of the machine managers or vCenter Servers linked to App Volumes Manager.

You can change the current information by clicking the **Modify** button **(9)**. If you want to add additional vCenter Servers, then click on the **Add Machine Manager** button **(10)**. As we discussed previously, App Volumes can support multiple -vCenter Servers.

The final tab we will explore is the **Storage** tab.

Storage

Click on the **Storage** tab **(10)**, shown in the following diagram:

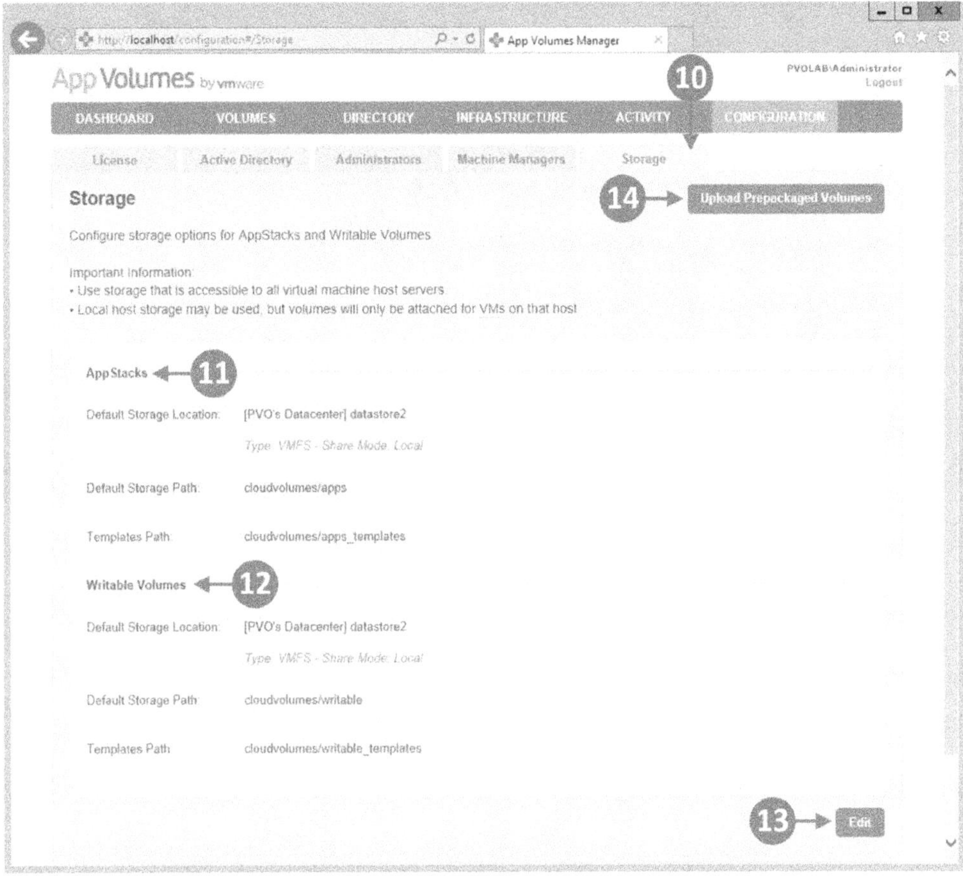

This page details the storage used for storing **AppStacks (11)** and **Writable Volumes (12)**. It shows the datastore location, path, and the templates being used.

You can change this information by clicking on the **Edit** button **(13)**.

The final option on this page is to upload any volumes to the datastores. The volumes in question are the templates used for creating AppStacks and Writable Volumes. This option would be used if you created new templates to use with this App Volumes Manager.

To perform this task, click on the **Upload Prepackaged Volumes** button **(14)**. You will then see this window:

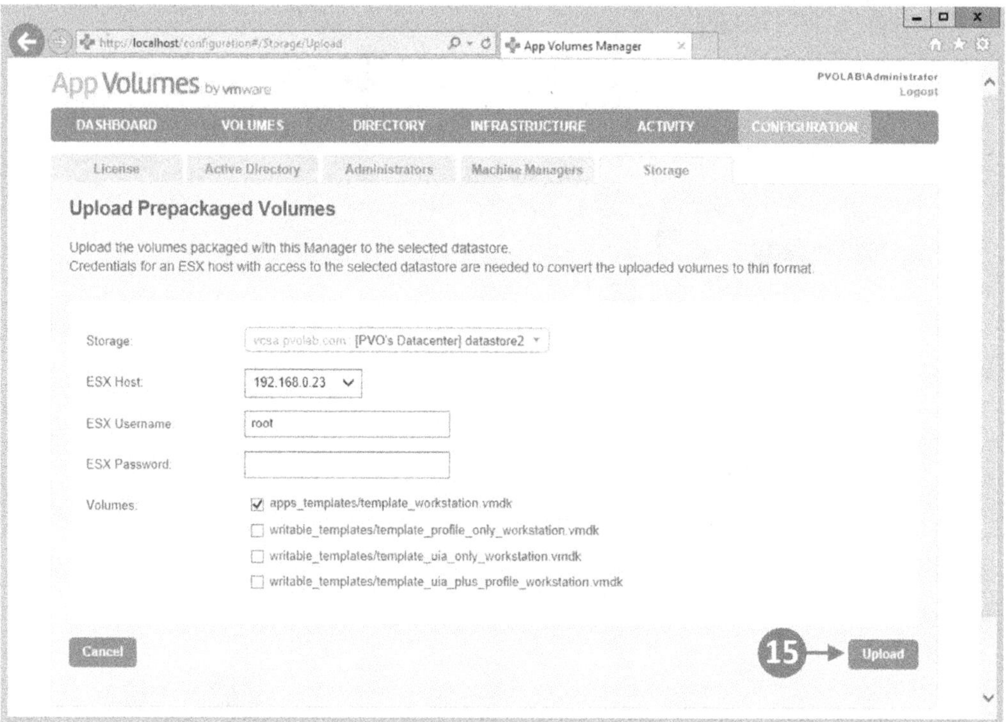

Once you have completed the configuration information, click on the **Upload** button **(15)**.

We will cover how to customize templates in *Chapter 12, Deploying App Volumes in a Citrix XenApp Environment*.

Summary

In this chapter, we explored the App Volumes Manager console. We looked at each of the configuration menu options and which tasks each one is responsible for in configuring and managing your environment.

You should now be able to confidently navigate your way around the management console and find the different tasks more easily. These tasks will be used in the coming chapters as we start to put the features of App Volumes to work in our Example Lab.

In the next chapter, we will discuss the first of these tasks and take a closer look at creating, building, and delivering AppStacks, so that we can deliver applications to our users in real time.

6 Working with AppStacks

In this chapter, we will take a deeper look into AppStacks, how they work, and how to start building them, before finally assigning them to end users. We will also look at some of the best practices for building AppStacks.

By the end of this chapter, you will be able to create, assign, and deliver an AppStack to an end user and then perform ongoing management tasks.

We are going to work through the following distinct steps: create, assign, and deliver.

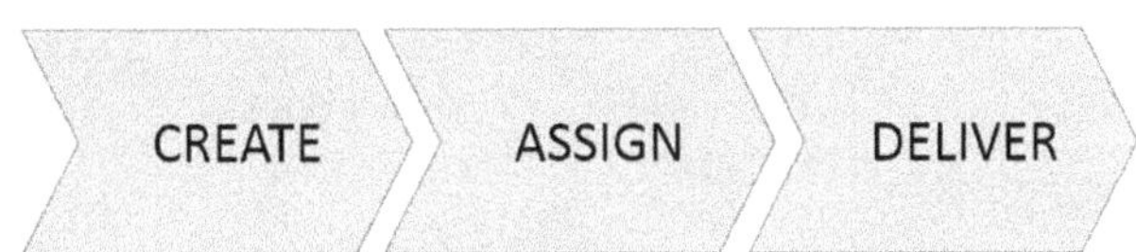

We will also cover some of the best-practice tips for deploying Microsoft Office applications as AppStacks.

So, just as a quick recap, an AppStack is a VMDK or VHD file that is attached to a virtual desktop machine when a user who has been assigned that particular AppStack logs in. The AppStack itself contains an application or set of applications that, once attached, are available to the end user to launch and consume as they would any other application. Don't forget; the applications are not installed or streamed onto the virtual desktop machine.

Creating your first AppStack

The first subject we are going to cover is how to create an AppStack.

Since we have covered the architecture and requirements for building our App Volumes environment in previous chapters, and you have the infrastructure deployed by either following the Example Lab or your own environment, you can now start to build and create your AppStacks, which is referred to as AppStack provisioning.

The following diagram illustrates the provisioning process we are going to follow to create an AppStack:

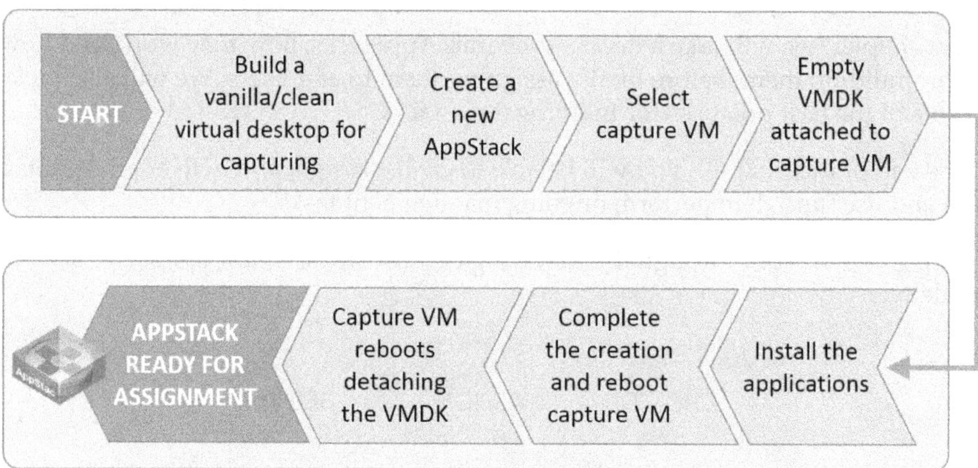

Before we start the actual capture process, we need to make sure that we have a cleanly built virtual desktop machine, complete with an up-to-date and patched operating system that we can use as our provisioning machine. The best practice is to use a virtual desktop machine in any case, as that way you can take a snapshot before you install the applications and then easily roll back to the original image for any subsequent provisioning you want to run.

We are also going to make sure we have Microsoft Office installed in the base image of our provisioning virtual desktop machine. We will discuss why in the next section.

In our Example Lab environment, we have a virtual desktop machine called `AV-PROVISION`, which is already set up for this task.

> The best practice is to create your AppStacks on the same operating system that is going to be used for deployment. So, if you are deploying AppStacks to a Windows 7 virtual desktop machine, then create those AppStacks on a Windows 7 capture virtual machine.
>
> Likewise, if you have Windows 8.1 or Windows 10 in your environment, use that operating system to capture your AppStacks.
>
> There is, however, the option of deploying a ThinApp packaged application as an AppStack, in which case you might not need to follow this guidance, but whichever method you use, make sure you test your applications thoroughly before assigning any applications to end users in a production environment.

Next, you log in to App Volumes Manager and select the option that creates an AppStack, followed by pointing App Volumes Manager to the virtual desktop machine you are going to use for provisioning. This machine will be visible in the App Volumes Manager console as we have installed App Volumes Agent onto it; it has registered itself with App Volumes Manager already.

You then install the application onto that virtual desktop machine in exactly the same way as you would install the application any other time, including any reboots that might need to take place during the installation process. The provisioning process only ends when you physically click the button to complete the process.

With the applications now installed, you can tell App Volumes Manager that the provisioning process is complete, which will trigger a reboot of the provisioning virtual desktop machine and therefore detach the newly created AppStack.

At the end of the process, you will have a newly created AppStack containing the applications that you installed, ready to be assigned to end users.

Before you start assigning the newly created AppStack, it's worth performing some tests to ensure that it attaches correctly and that the applications run as expected.

The following diagram illustrates the provisioning process:

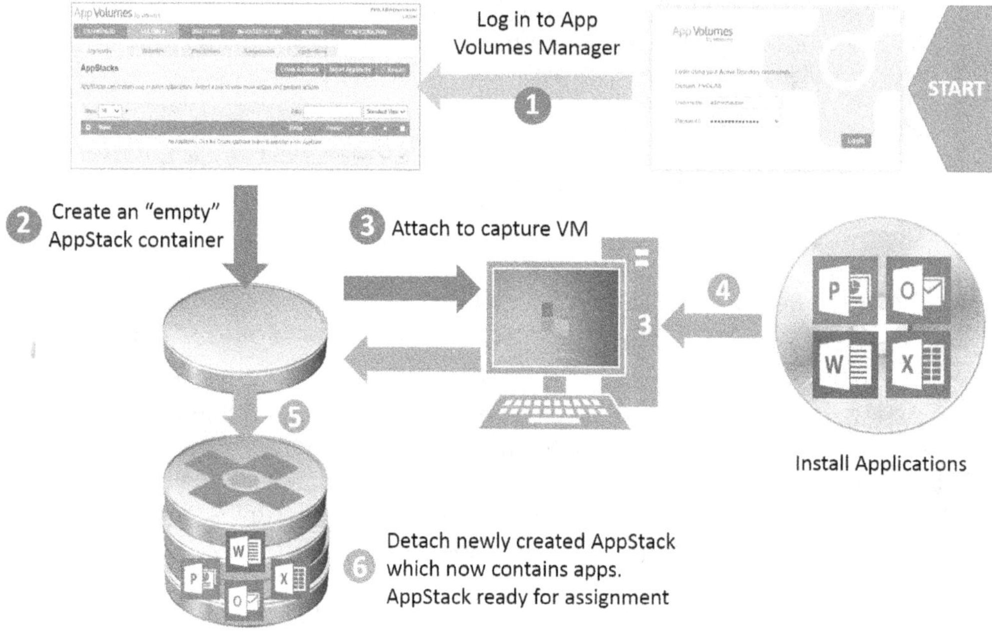

You can now roll the virtual desktop machine used for the provisioning process back to the snapshot of the previous state, ready for the next provisioning task.

Now that you are familiar with the theory behind the AppStack creation process, we are going to use the Example Lab to physically build a number of different AppStacks, each one for a different use case or type of user.

Before we create our AppStacks, and specifically because we are going to install Microsoft Office as one of our applications, there are some rules we need to discuss when delivering Microsoft Office applications as an AppStack. We will cover these in the next subsection.

Creating an AppStack for Microsoft Office

We are going to use some components of Microsoft Office as the applications in our Example Lab. The reason is that this is probably the most common application that will be installed, and also that there are a few things you need to be aware of.

You can only have *one* AppStack containing Microsoft Office products attached to a virtual desktop machine at any point in time.

So, for example, you could have Office installed as a part of your base image and deliver any additional Office components as an AppStack. Some example combinations could be:

Example 1: Office in the base + Visio as an AppStack

Example 2: Office in the base + Project as an AppStack

Example 3: Office in the base + Visio and Project together as one AppStack

Example 4: Office and Visio in the base + Project as an AppStack

Example 5: Office and Project in the base + Visio as an AppStack

Example 6: Office, Visio, and Project as *one* AppStack

Don't forget that even though you can have various Office components in multiple AppStacks, only one AppStack containing an Office product can be attached to a virtual desktop at any one point in time, regardless of whether or not Office is in the base image.

In our Example Lab, we are going to have the core Office components (Word, PowerPoint, and Excel) installed as a part of the core base image on the virtual desktop machine.

We are then going to create a total of four AppStacks, one containing Visio, one containing Evernote and VLC media player, one containing OpenOffice, and the final one containing Adobe Acrobat Reader.

You could argue that Adobe Reader would most likely be delivered as a part of a base image, but in our Example Lab, we are creating this as an AppStack to demonstrate that by keeping the applications separate from your base image, you can update and patch them independently on the virtual desktop machine's operating system.

The first AppStack we are going to create will contain Microsoft Visio.

Creating an AppStack for Microsoft Visio

In this subsection, we are going to work through the process of creating an AppStack that will contain Microsoft Visio Professional 2013, which will be assigned to the **Engineering** group:

1. Log in to App Volumes Manager by double-clicking on the App Volumes icon, entering your administrator credentials, and clicking on **Login**, as shown in the following screenshot:

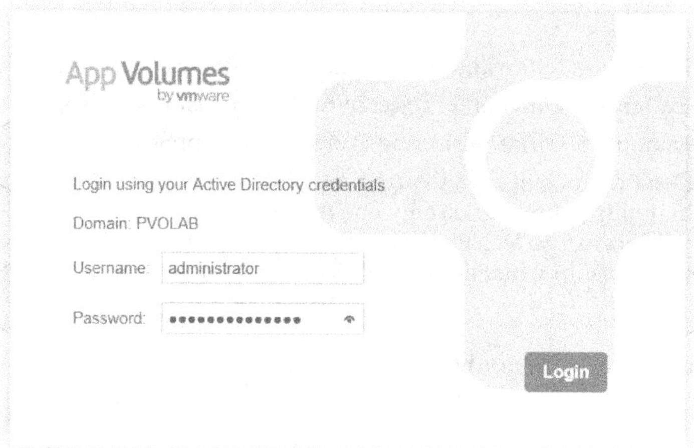

2. Once you have successfully logged in, click on the **VOLUMES** menu **(1)**, as shown in the next diagram, to display volumes configuration options.
3. Now, click on the **Create AppStack** button **(2)**, as shown here:

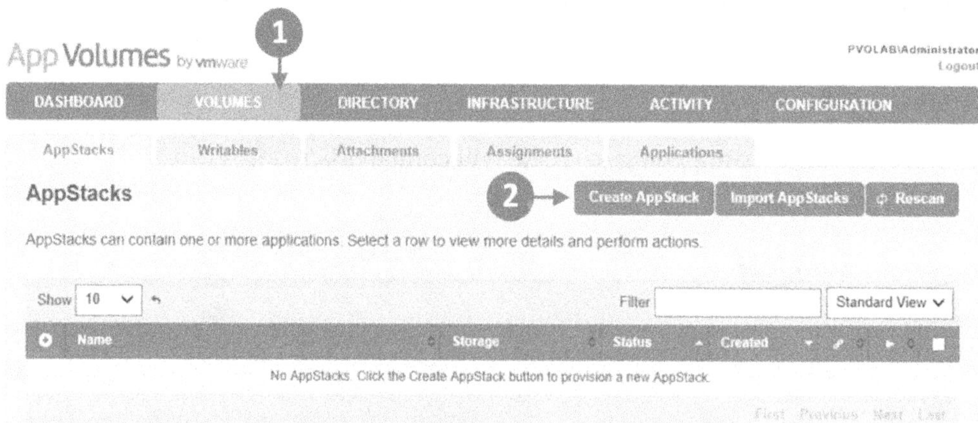

4. You will now see the **Create AppStack** page, as shown in the following diagram:

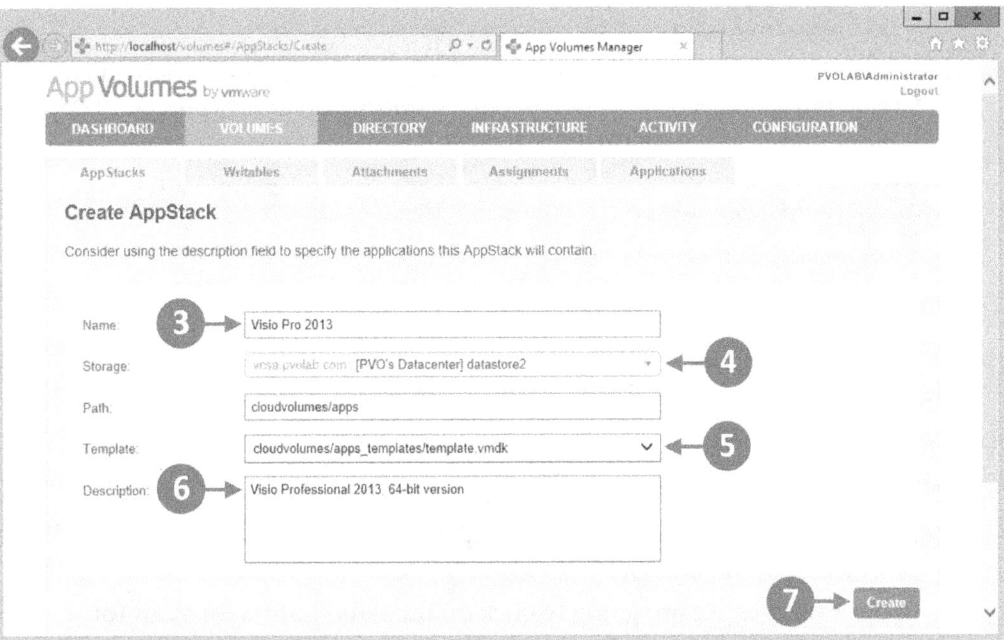

5. The first task is to enter a name for this AppStack in the **Name** box **(3)**. For our Example Lab, we are going to create an AppStack for Visio, so in this box, we are going to type in `Visio Pro 2013`.
6. In the next box, **Storage (4)**, click on the drop-down arrow and select the datastore where this AppStack is going to be stored. For our Example Lab, we are going to choose `datastore2`.

Don't forget that AppStacks should be kept on a separate datastore than the one in which your virtual desktop machines are stored.

7. Leave the **Path** box with the default value of `cloudvolumes/app`. This is the directory that was created during the setup configuration.
8. In the **Template** box **(5)**, click on the drop-down box and select the AppStack template you want to use. In our example, we will use the `apps_templates/template.vmdk` template. This is the default AppStack template.

9. Finally, in the **Description** box **(6)**, type in a description for this AppStack, ensuring that whatever you enter accurately describes the application(s) that is/are contained within this AppStack. In our example, we have entered `Visio Professional 2013, 64-bit version`.
10. Once you are happy with the information you have entered, click on the **Create** button **(7)**. You will now see the **Confirm Create AppStack** dialog box, as shown in the following screenshot:

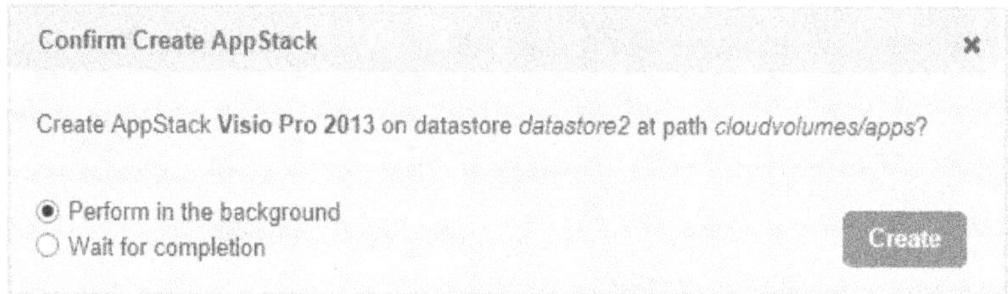

11. This dialog box displays the datastore and path details of where the AppStack in going to be created. You then have the option of either performing the task in the background and continuing with the configuration, or waiting for it to complete.

    In our example, we are going to click on the radio button for **Wait for completion,** as shown in the following screenshot:

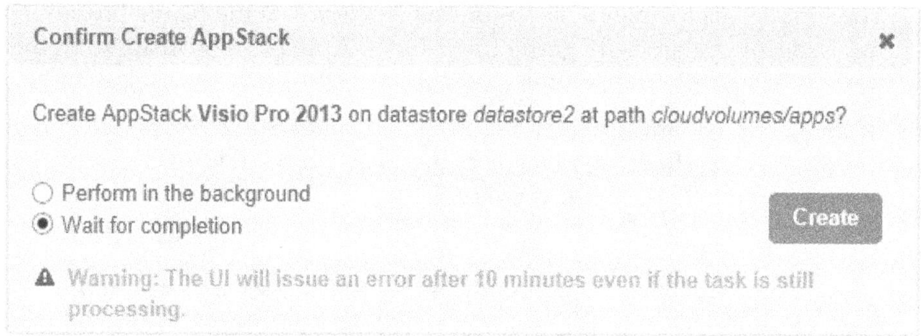

12. You will see that a warning is displayed telling you that after 10 minutes the user interface will issue an error, even if the task is still completing.

Click on **Create** to continue the process. You will see the following message displayed:

13. At this stage, App Volumes will create the AppStack by making a copy of the template. You can see this by logging in to vCenter Server and browsing the datastore.
14. Once logged in to our Example Lab, click on **Storage** under **Home**, select `datastore2`, and then select the **Files** tab. Expand the `cloudvolumes` folder and then click on `apps`, as shown in the following screenshot:

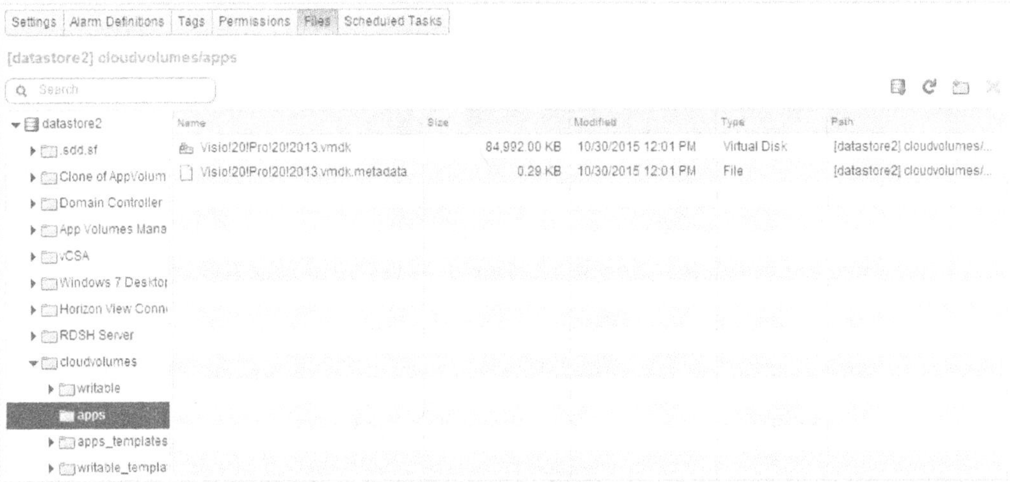

You will see that the virtual disk file that has been created for this AppStack is just under 85 MB in size. This is due to the App Volumes configuration files that get copied across as part of the template. We will cover this in more detail in *Chapter 12, Deploying App Volumes in a Citrix XenApp Environment*.

If you now return to App Volumes Manager, you will see the following window:

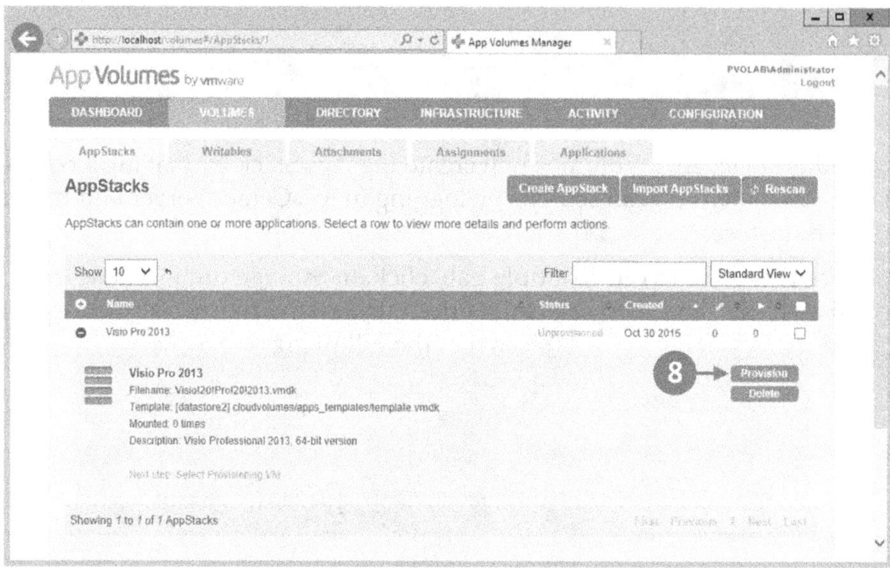

15. Click on the **Provision** button **(8)** to start the provisioning process. You will now see the **Provision AppStack** screen, as shown in the following diagram:

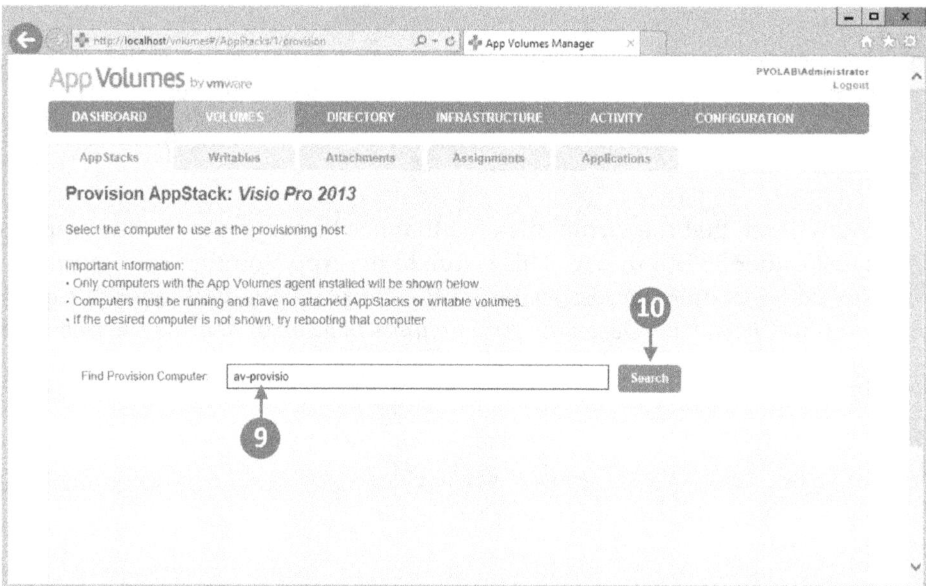

16. The first thing you need to do is select the virtual desktop machine that you are going to use to provision the AppStack. In our Example Lab, we have a virtual desktop machine named `AV-PROVISION`.

    In the **Find Provision Computer** box **(9)**, start typing in the name of this machine. You only need to type in enough unique text to display a list of matching machines.

    Once you have entered the text, click on the **Search** button **(10)**. App Volumes Manager will now display a list of matching machines, as shown in the following diagram:

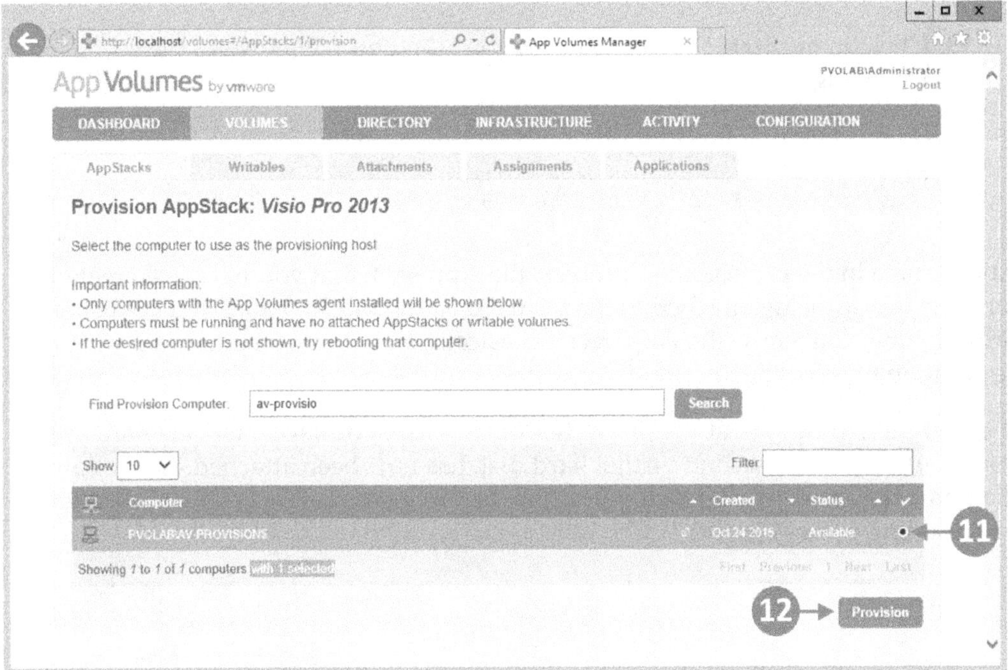

17. To select the provisioning machine, click on the radio button **(11)**. If you have more than one machine displayed, then select the appropriate virtual desktop machine for provisioning.

18. Once selected, click on the **Provision** button **(12)**. You will see the following dialog box:

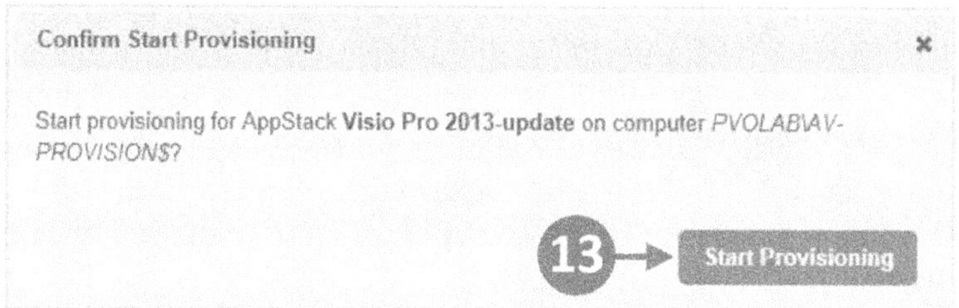

19. Click on the **Start Provisioning** button **(13)**. You will now see the following message:

At this stage in the provisioning process, the AppStack that you have just created for Visio is now being attached to the virtual desktop machine that you are using for provisioning. Currently, the AppStack is basically an empty container ready for the application to be installed.

If you were to now look at the properties of the virtual desktop machine hardware, you would see that a second virtual hard disk has now been attached. The following diagram show the virtual desktop machine before provisioning (left) and during the provisioning process (right):

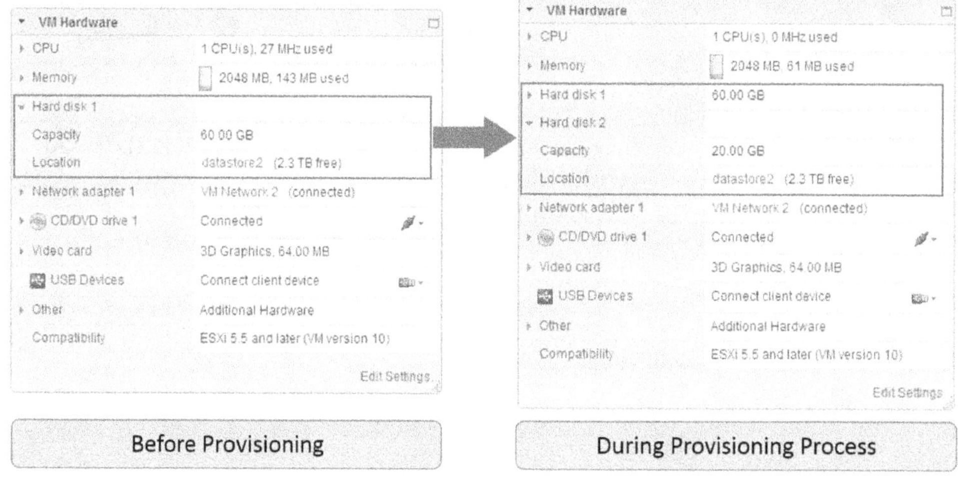

Once the AppStack has been attached to the provisioning virtual desktop machine, you will see the following window in App Volumes Manager:

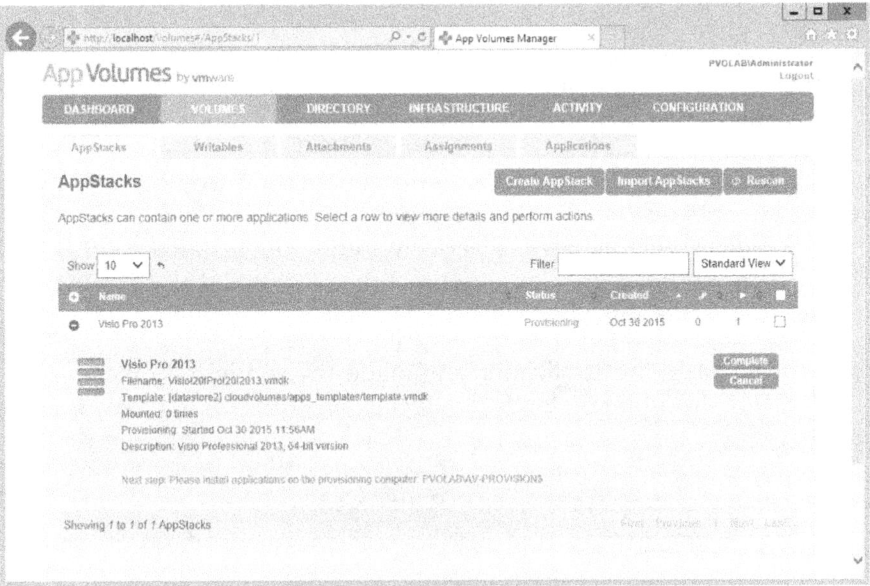

Leave this page as it is and *do not* click on anything yet. Clicking on the **Complete** button now will stop the provisioning process before you even start it! We will come back to this page a bit later to complete the provisioning process.

Now, switch over to the console of the virtual desktop machine that's being used for AppStack provisioning. In our Example Lab, this is the `AV-PROVISION` virtual desktop.

The first thing that you will see is the following message:

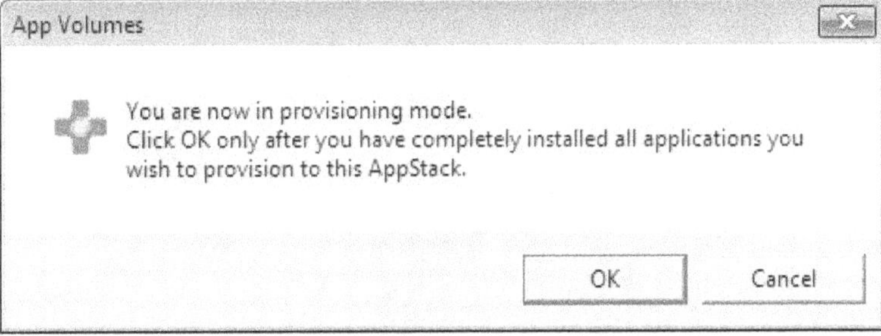

Only click on **OK** once you have finished installing applications.

The virtual desktop machine is now in provisioning mode, and you can start installing the application(s). In this example, we are going to install Visio Professional.

Launch the Visio installer and install the application as you would normally do. This includes any reboots that the application requires as part of the installation. There are no special tasks you need to perform during the installation of applications. App Volumes Agent will redirect the files copied and created during the installation to the newly created AppStack.

Once you have installed the application and made any configuration changes, you can go back to the initial dialog box and click on **OK**. You will now see the following dialog box:

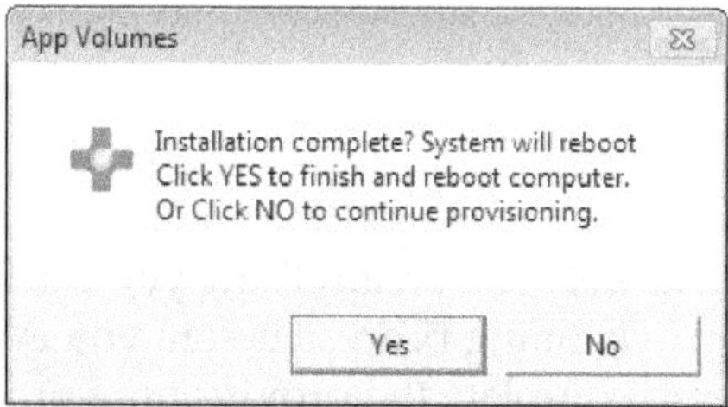
App Volumes
Installation complete? System will reboot
Click YES to finish and reboot computer.
Or Click NO to continue provisioning.
Yes
No

Click on the **Yes** button if you are happy that you have finished installing the applications that you want included as part of this AppStack. The application will now be analyzed, as shown in the following screenshot:

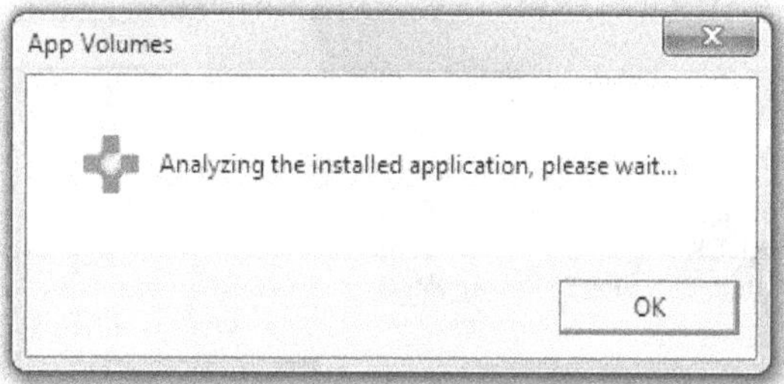
App Volumes
Analyzing the installed application, please wait...
OK

Click on **OK** and then reboot the virtual desktop machine.

Once the machine reboots, you will see the following dialog box stating that the provisioning completed successfully and the AppStack has been provisioned:

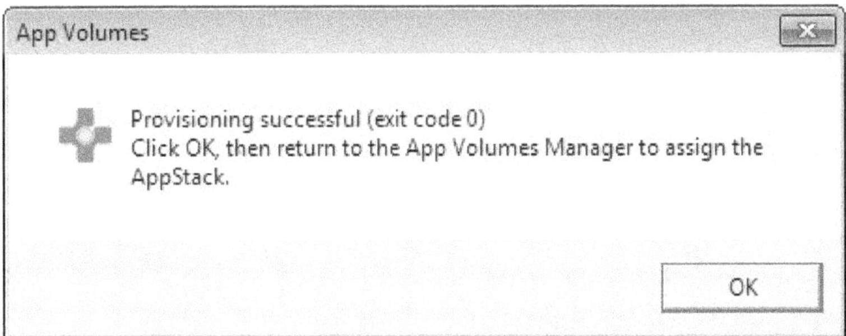

Click on **OK** to complete the provisioning process on the virtual desktop machine, and then switch back to the App Volumes Manager console, as shown in the following diagram:

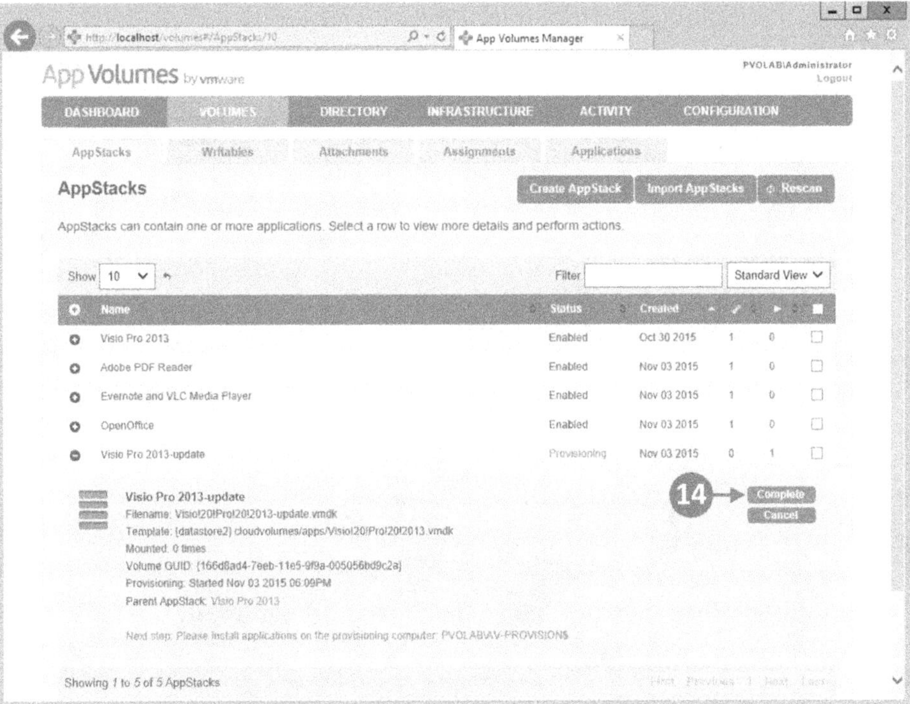

Now that the applications have been installed, you can click on the **Complete** button **(14)**. You will see the following dialog box:

Click on the **Complete Provisioning** button **(15)**.

The newly completed AppStack will now be detached from the virtual desktop machine used for provisioning, and is ready for assignment. You will see what is shown in the following diagram:

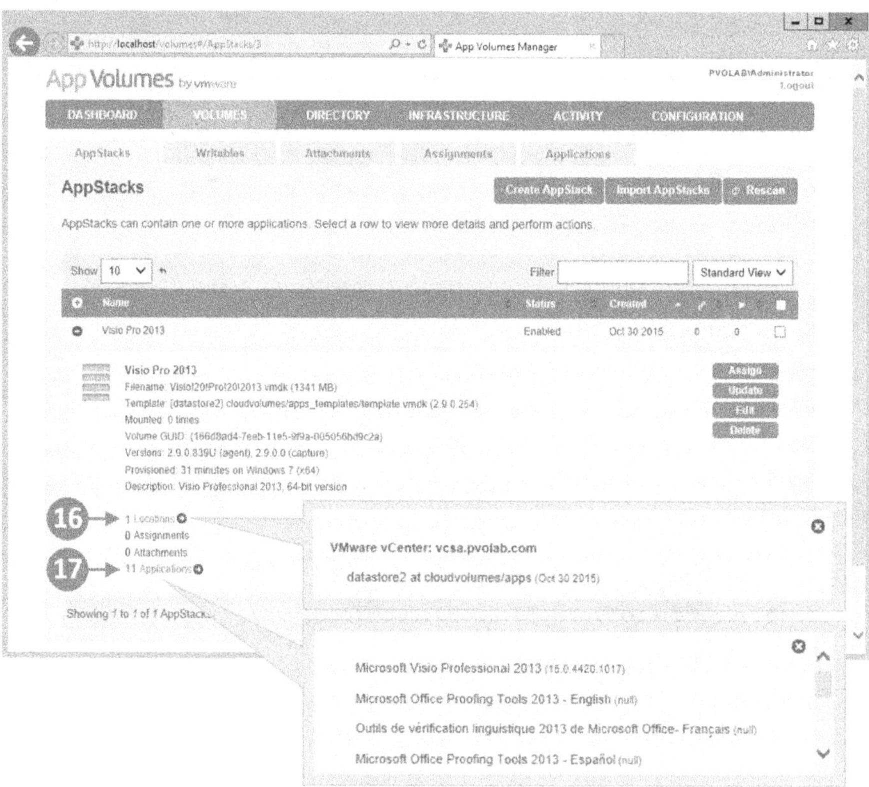

We will cover the assigning of an AppStack in a later section, but while we are on this page, it's worth pointing out a couple of other pieces of information.

If you click on the **Locations** link **(16)**, you can see that this AppStack is currently stored in `datastore2` in the `cloudvolumes/apps` folder.

You can also see all the individual applications that were installed by clicking on the **Applications** link **(17)**. As this is an Office product, you can see that other tools were installed as part of this AppStack.

If you log in to vCenter Server again and navigate to the datastore, you will see that the size of the virtual disk used for the AppStack has now grown to just under 1.4 GB, as shown in the following screenshot:

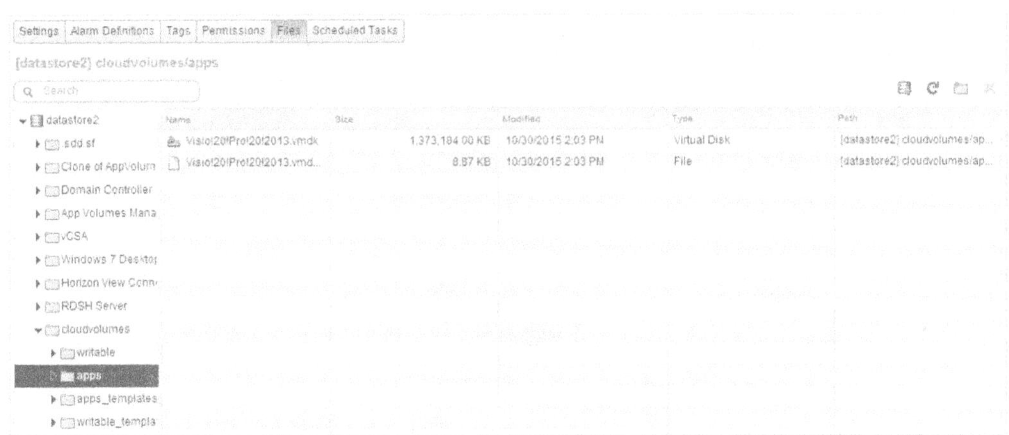

You have now successfully created your first AppStack. In the next couple of sections, we are going to repeat the process and create a number of additional AppStacks to demonstrate the assignment process.

A number of different applications have been chosen as examples to demonstrate this; however, you are free to choose your own.

Creating an AppStack for Evernote and VLC Media Player

Following the process we covered in the previous subsection, create an AppStack that contains both Evernote and VLC media player. We will use this AppStack for the **Sales** group.

To complete this task, install both applications as you normally would, one after the other.

Don't forget, before you start, to ensure that you have a clean virtual desktop machine. In the Example Lab, we would have rolled back to a snapshot taken before we started the first provisioning task.

Creating an AppStack for Adobe Reader

Next, follow the provisioning process to create an AppStack that contains Adobe Reader. We will use this AppStack for the **Domain Users** group.

Creating an AppStack for OpenOffice

Finally, follow the provisioning process to create an AppStack for OpenOffice. We will use this AppStack for the **Finance** group.

Now that you have created the four AppStacks, you should have a configuration that looks like this:

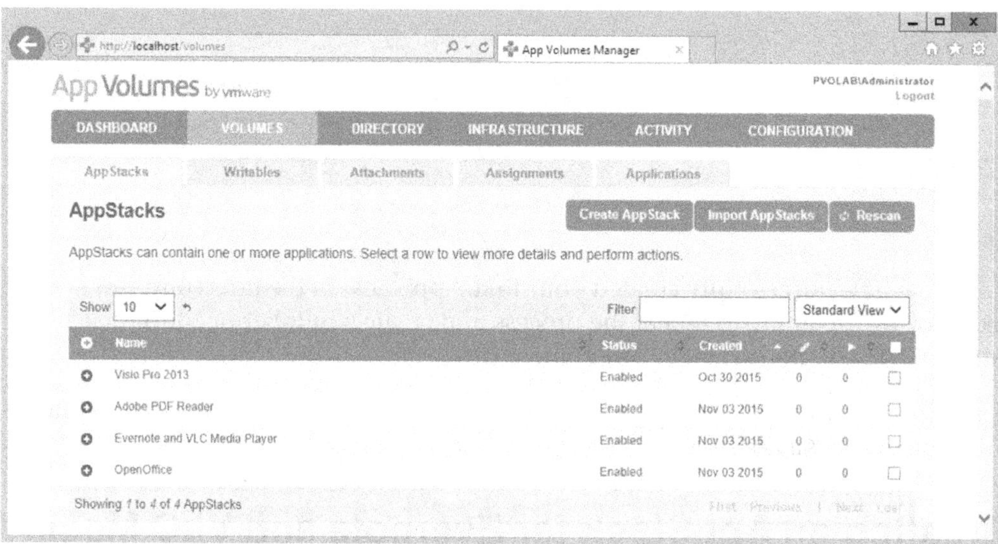

In the next section, we will start assigning the newly created AppStacks to our users and groups.

Assigning and delivering AppStacks to end users

In the previous section, we covered the process of creating AppStacks. If you followed the Lab examples, you will now have four AppStacks ready to be assigned to your end users.

In this section, we are going to cover the next phase and look at how we configure the assignment of those AppStacks to end users, as well as how the delivery process works.

Assigning the Visio and Adobe Reader AppStacks

We are going to demonstrate the assignment process using the Visio AppStack, by assigning it to the Engineering group. As part of this exercise, we are also going to assign the Adobe Reader AppStack to all end users. Follow these steps:

1. If you are not already logged in, log in to App Volumes Manager. Click on the **VOLUMES** menu option and then the **AppStacks** tab, as shown in the following diagram:

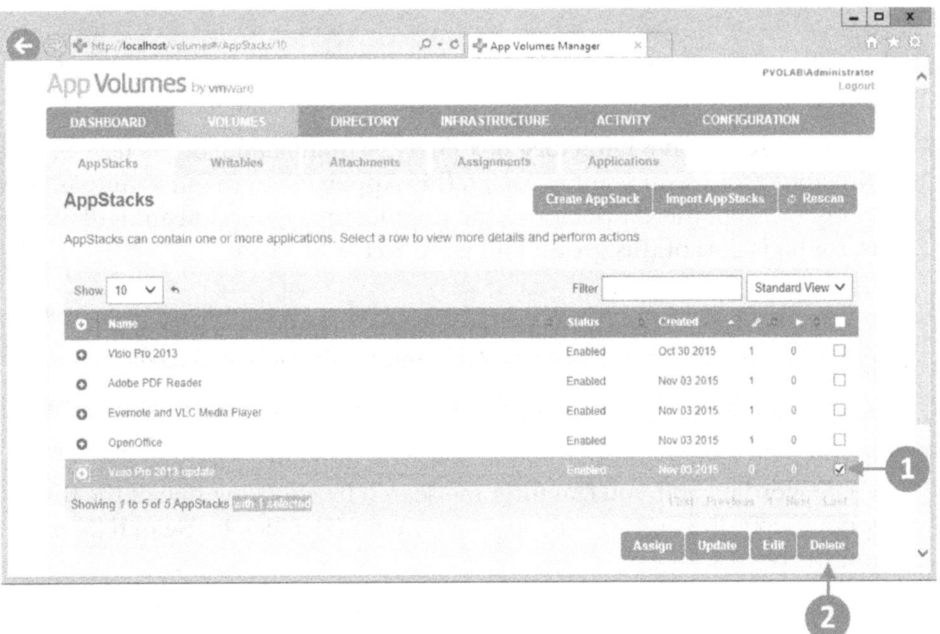

2. Check the box next to the AppStack you want to assign to a user. In our example, we will check the box for **Visio Pro 2013** **(1)**.
3. Click on the **Assign** button **(2)**. You will now see the **Assign AppStack: Visio Pro 2013** page, as shown in the following diagram:

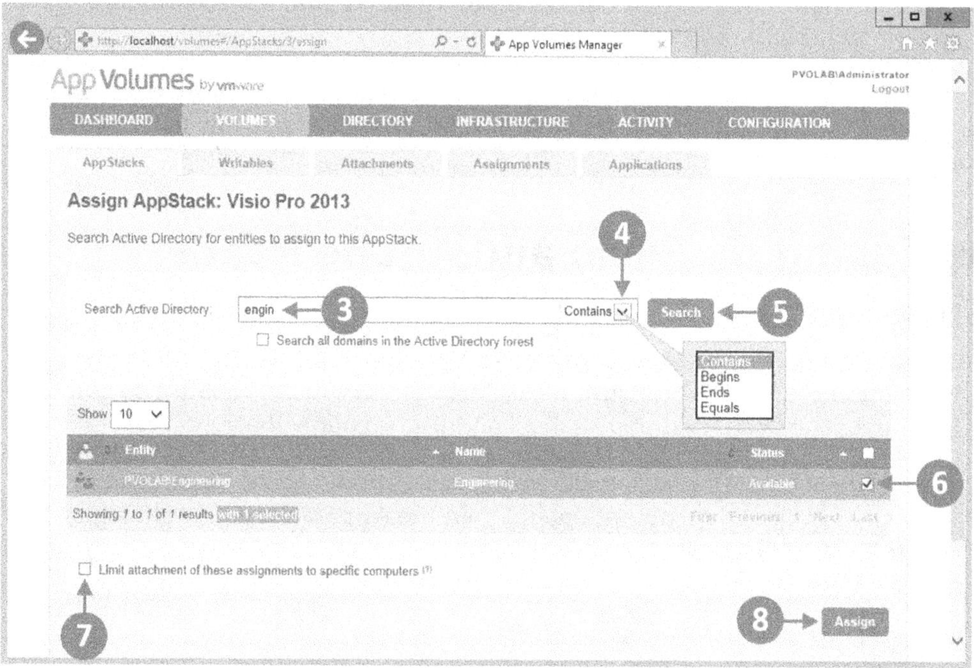

4. In the **Search Active Directory** box **(3)**, type in the name of the user or Active Directory group you want to assign this AppStack to. In our example, we are going to assign this AppStack to the Engineering group, meaning that every user who is part of this group will have access to Visio.

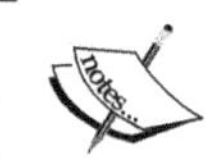

> You can assign an AppStack either to an individual user or a group of users. User and group information is read directly from Active Directory.

5. Start typing `engineering` into the box. You don't need to type the whole word in, and you can filter the search by choosing one of the filter options from the **Contains** drop-down menu **(4)**. Click on **Search** **(5)** to find the results.

   The Engineering group should now be listed in the results.

6. Check the box **(6)** to select the Engineering group. The line will now become highlighted. Before we go ahead and assign the AppStack, there is another option shown at the bottom of this page.
7. This option **(7)** is **Limit attachment of these assignments to specific computers**. In normal operation, all assigned AppStacks are attached to the virtual desktop machine during startup or when a user logs in. However, there may be some use cases that require a more selective approach to assignment, whereby an AppStack is only attached to a specific set of virtual desktop machines.

   This option allows you to specify the prefix of a computer name, resulting in an assigned AppStack only being attached to computers whose names begin with that prefix, and it is configured as per the following screenshot:

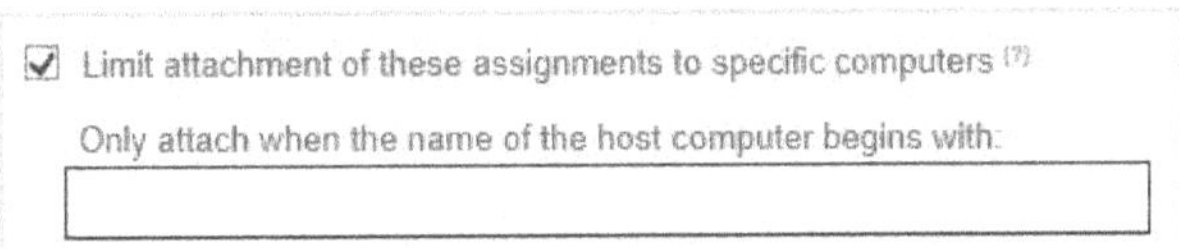

   For example, if our Lab user John Smith, who is in the Sales group, is assigned two AppStacks, one being his standard group assignment and the other one being the Visio AppStack from the Engineering group, which is limited to a specific virtual desktop machine named WIN7-TEST, what would be the result?

   When he logs in to the computer named WIN7-TEST, both AppStacks are attached, but if he logs in to any other machine, only his standard AppStack (Evernote and VLC) are attached. This could be due to the fact that the virtual desktop machine's configuration is different, in order to run this application.

   In our Example Lab, we are going to leave this option unchecked.

8. Click on the **Assign** button **(8)**. You will now see the dialog box shown in the following diagram:

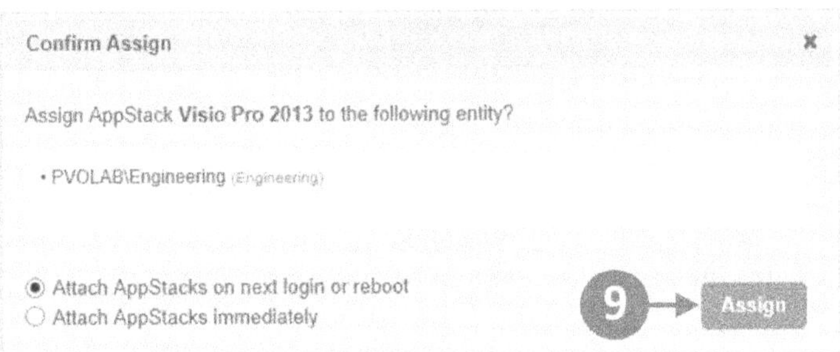

9. Click on the radio button for **Attach AppStacks on next login or reboot**. AppStacks will then be attached when the user next logs in or the virtual desktop machine powers on and boots.

   The other option is to attach the AppStack immediately. As per the description in our example, we are going to choose the option for attaching it on the next login as we currently have no users logged in.

10. Click on the **Assign** button **(9)**. You will see the following screen as the AppStack is assigned:

11. Once it is assigned, you will now return to the main AppStacks configuration page, as shown in the following diagram:

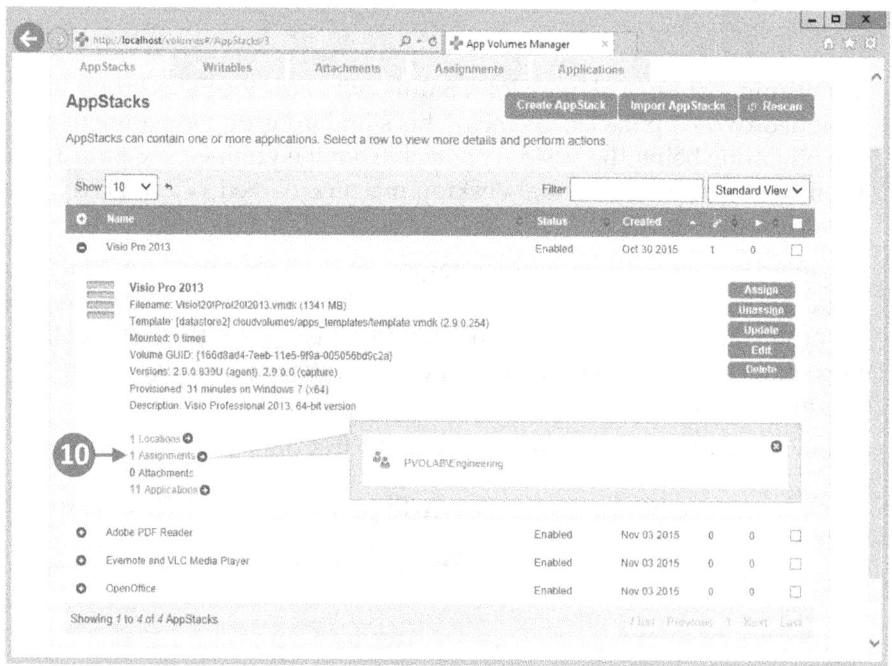

You will now see that this AppStack has one assignment **(10)**.

If you click on this link, you will see a list of who has been assigned this AppStack. In our example it's the Engineering group.

Now that you have created an assignment for this AppStack, repeat the process and assign each of the other AppStacks that were created in the previous section to the other Active Directory groups in the Example Lab, as follows:

- The Evernote and VLC media player AppStack to the Sales group
- The OpenOffice AppStack to the Finance group
- The Adobe Reader AppStack to all Domain Users group

Once you complete this, you should have something like the following screenshot:

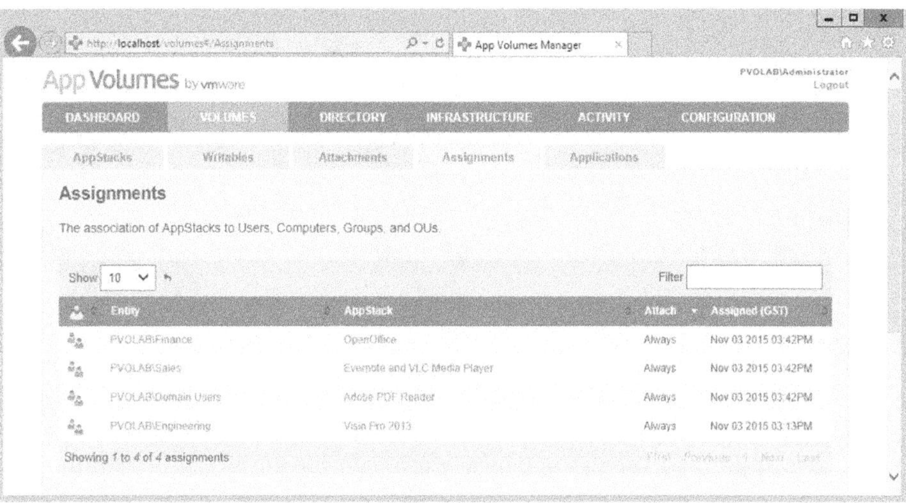

As you see, once you create your AppStacks, you can very quickly and easily assign them to end users.

We are now going to test whether these assignments work correctly by logging in as a user that is a member of each of our example groups and checking whether that user has access to the applications.

Testing AppStack assignments

To test our assignments, we are going to use two of the virtual desktop machines we created in the beginning of this book, `WIN7-DESKTOP-1` and `WIN7-DESKTOP-2`.

Before we can use them, ensure that they both have Office and App Volumes Agent installed. The quickest way of doing this is to make a copy of the provisioning virtual desktop machine.

Once this task has been completed, from the App Volumes Manager console, verify that the two virtual desktop machines are shown as online entities. To do this, click on the **DIRECTORY** menu option **(1)** and then the **Online** tab **(2)**.

The results should show that there are currently four entities online **(3)**. These are the App Volumes administrator, the provisioning virtual desktop machine, and finally, the two Win7 desktops. This is shown in the following diagram:

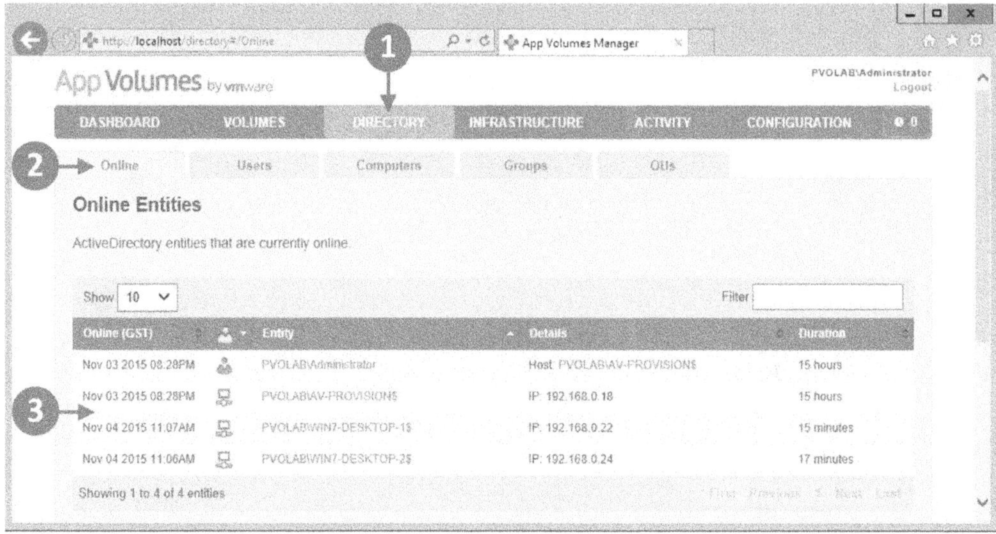

Now, switch to the console of `WIN7-DESKTOP-1` and log in as Peter Owens (the username is `powens@pvolab.com`). This is shown in the following diagram:

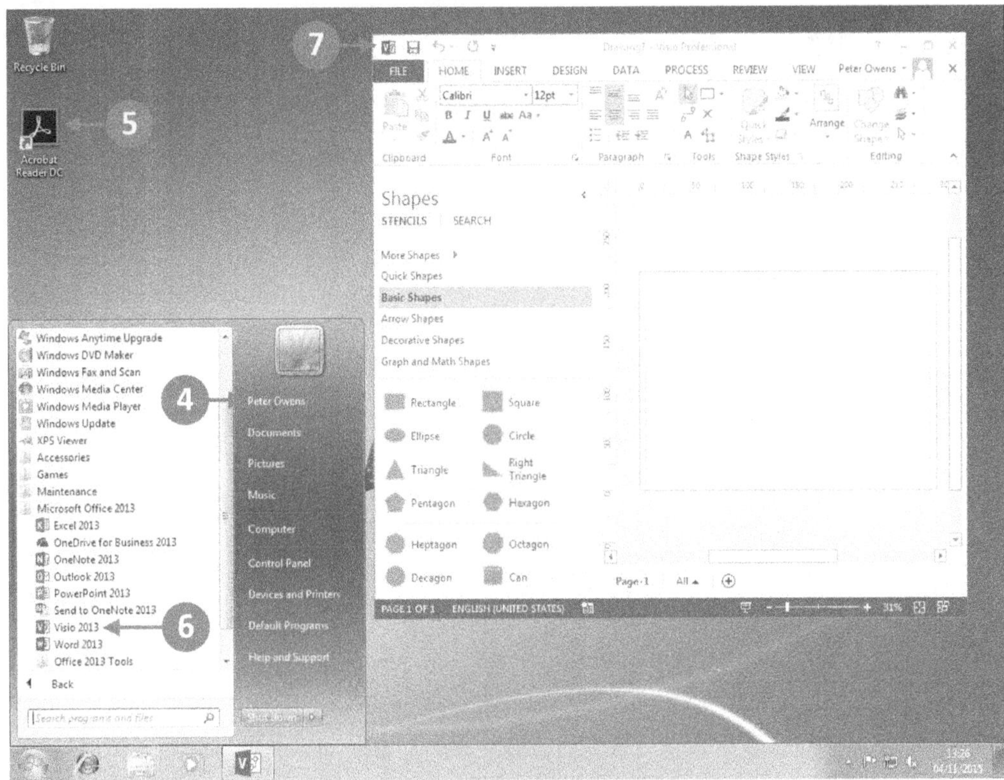

You can see that this user is now successfully logged in **(4)**.

This user is a part of the Domain Users group and the Engineering group and will therefore have been assigned two AppStacks: one will contain Adobe Acrobat Reader DC, and the other will contain Visio Pro 2013.

The first thing you will see is the shortcut icon for Adobe Acrobat Reader DC **(5)**.

If you click on the **Start** button and then on **Microsoft Office 2013**, you will see that **Visio 2013** is listed as an available application **(6)**. Launch Visio 2013 to test whether it runs correctly **(7)**.

Let's take a look at the virtual machine properties of this desktop, as shown in the following diagram:

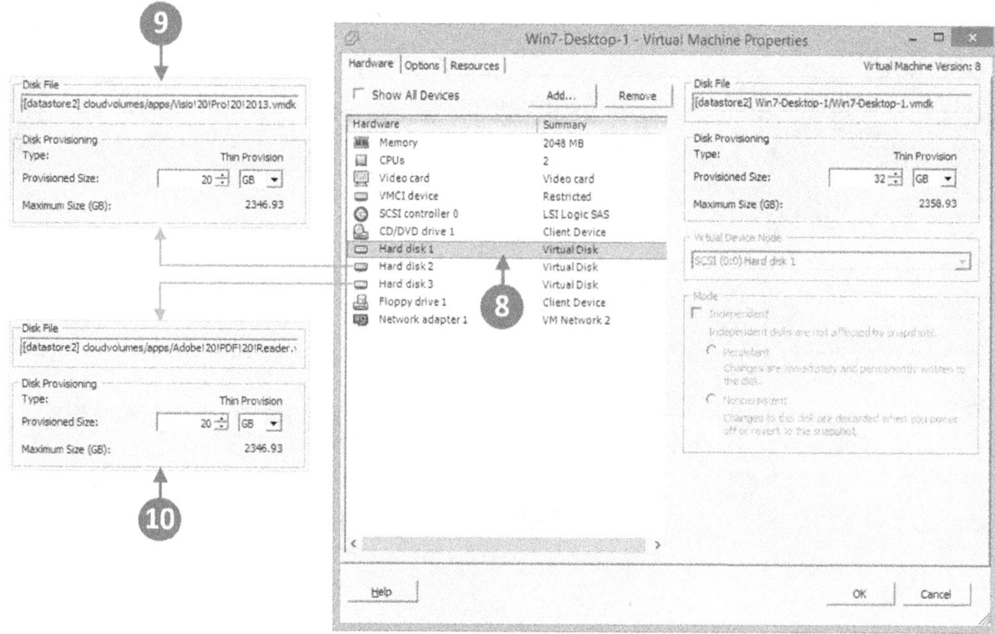

The first thing you will notice is that this virtual desktop machine has three hard disks attached to it.

Click on **Hard disk 1 (8)**. This is the hard disk containing the virtual desktop machine's operating system, or the C: drive. If you look at the **Disk File** box you will see the `Win-Desktop-1.vmdk` file.

If you click on **Hard disk 2** and look at the **Disk File** properties **(9)**, you will see that this second hard drive contains a file called `Visio!20!Pro!2014.vmdk`. This is the AppStack for Visio Pro 2013.

Finally, click on **Hard disk 3** and look at the **Disk File** properties **(10)**; you will see that this second hard drive contains a file called `Adobe!20!PDF!20!Reader.vmdk`. This is the AppStack for Adobe Acrobat Reader DC.

The !20! part shown in the filename represents the fact that we have included spaces within the name of the AppStack.

Log the current user, Peter Owens, out of the virtual desktop machine.

Finally, we are going to log in to the same desktop as another of our example users, John Smith, who is a member of the Sales Active Directory group. Once logged in, you will see this:

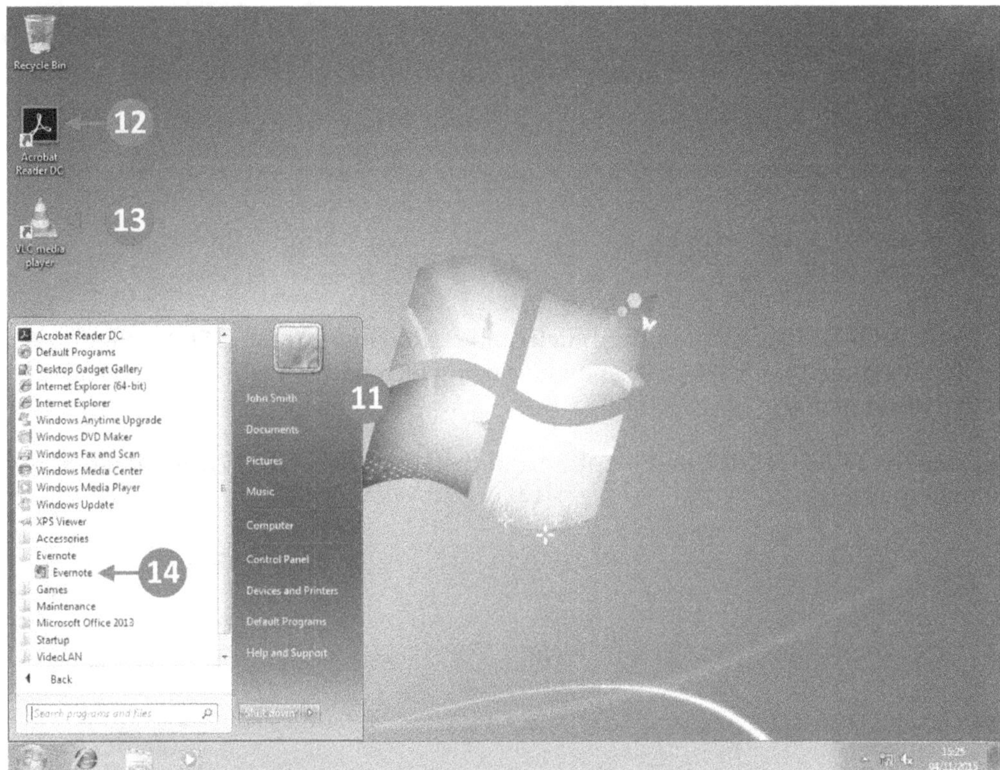

You can see that you are now logged in as **John Smith (11)**.

This user is a part of the Domain Users group and the Sales group and will therefore have been assigned two AppStacks: one will contain **Acrobat Reader DC (12)**, and the other will contain **VLC media player (13)** and **Evernote (14)**.

If we now switch back to the App Volumes Manager console, we will see this from the IT admin's perspective, as shown in the following diagram:

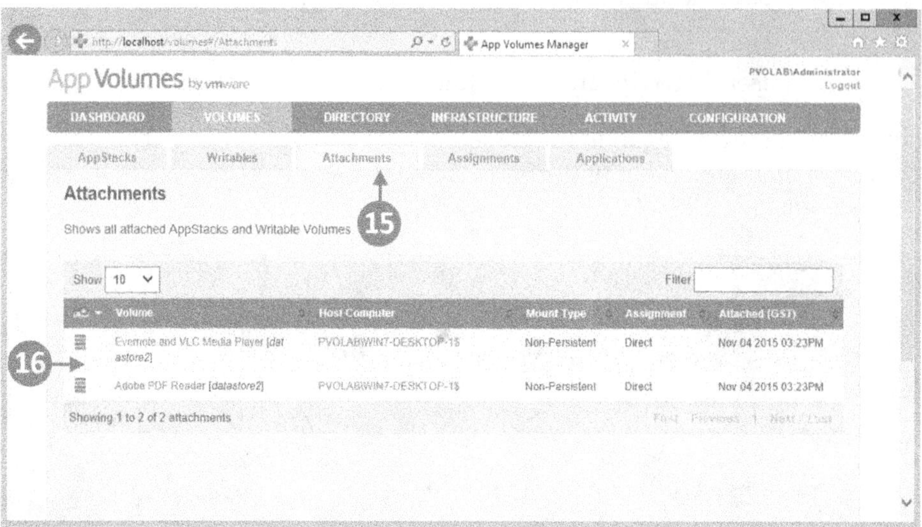

From the **VOLUMES** menu option, click on the **Attachments** tab **(15)**. You will see that there are two AppStacks shown as being attached to the `WIN7-DESKTOP-1` virtual desktop machine **(16)**.

Click on the **DIRECTORY** menu option and then the **Users** tab **(17)**, as shown in the following diagram:

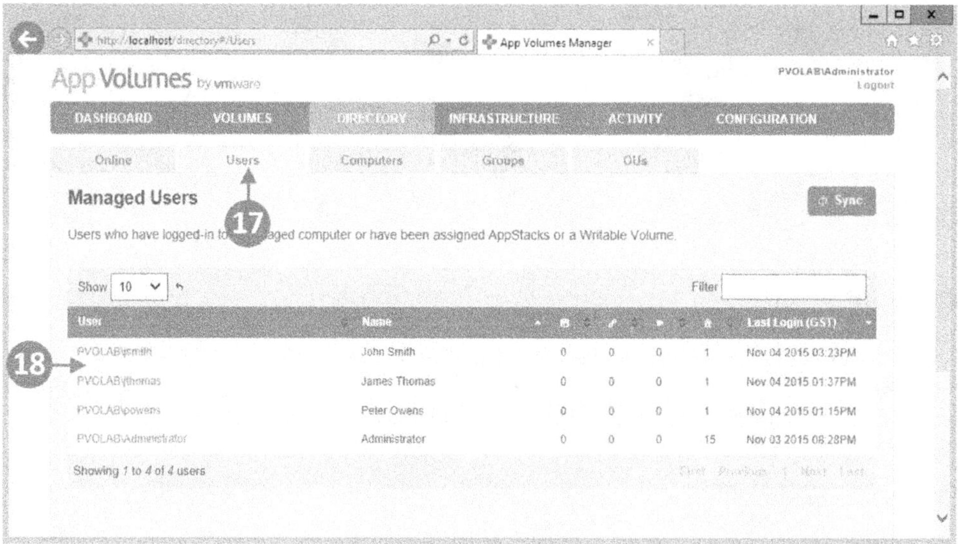

You will see the users that have logged in listed. You can see that each of our example users has logged in once but no longer has any AppStacks attached.

Now that we have demonstrated the AppStack delivery process in action, in the next section, we will look a little deeper into what's going on behind the scenes to make all this happen.

AppStack delivery process

Until now, we have created some AppStacks, assigned them to end users, and demonstrated that the applications work when the users log in. In this section, we will look at what's going on behind the scene to make this work.

As you have already experienced, the provisioning process and the assignment tasks are all performed in App Volumes Manager. Once all these elements have been put in place, it's down to App Volumes Agent to communicate with App Volumes Manager to ensure that AppStacks and Writable Volumes are delivered to the correct end users and virtual desktop machines.

In this section, we are going to take a deeper look into how App Volumes Agent works. We are going to break this down into two specific areas:

- App Volumes Agent startup and shutdown
- End user login and logout

Agent start up process

The following diagram illustrates the App Volumes Agent startup process:

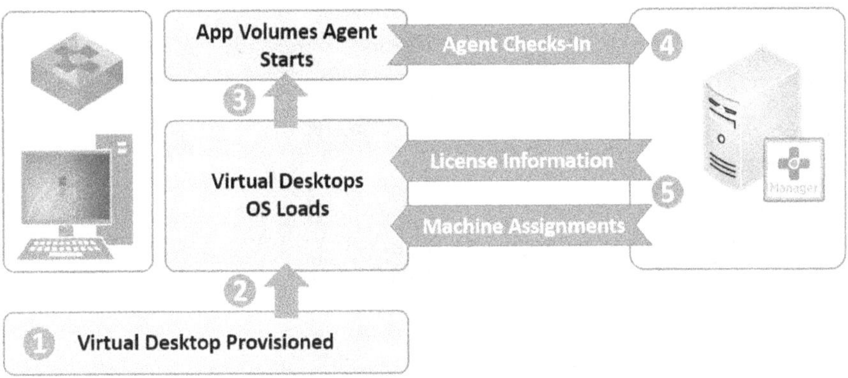

The startup process in this example is defined as the virtual desktop machine being powered on **(1)** and then booting up into the operating system **(2)**, ready for an end user to log in. As a part of this boot process, App Volumes Agent loads and the service starts running **(3)**.

Once it starts running, App Volumes Agent connects to the App Volumes Manager instance that you entered the details for during agent installation. This could also be the details of a load balancer, depending on your design.

When the check-in has completed and the agent has connected, App Volumes Manager will send license information to the virtual desktop machine to ensure that you have enough licenses to manage this virtual desktop machine.

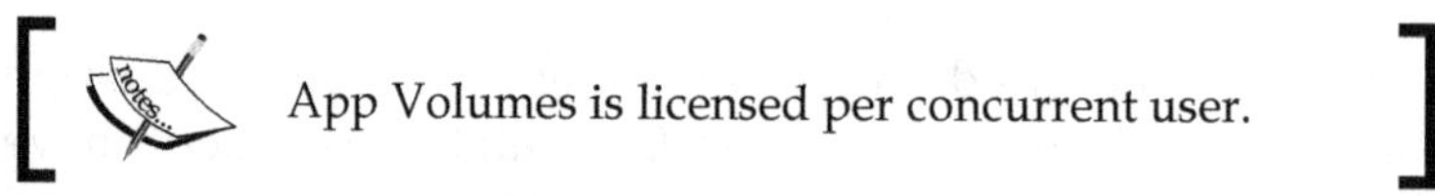

App Volumes is licensed per concurrent user.

Finally, App Volumes Manager sends the machine assignment information to the virtual desktop machine. A machine assignment is an AppStack that is assigned to a virtual desktop machine rather than to a specific user.

Agent shutdown process

The following diagram illustrates the App Volumes Agent shutdown process:

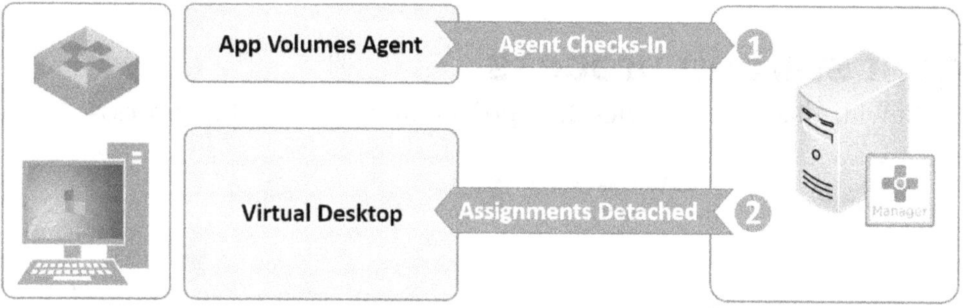

When a virtual desktop machine shuts down, as part of the process, App Volumes Agent connects with App Volumes Manager. App Volumes Manager then detaches any assigned AppStacks or Writable Volumes.

Agent login process

In the previous subsections, we described how App Volumes Agent works when a virtual desktop machine starts up and shuts down. In this subsection, we are going to look at what happens when a user logs in to a virtual desktop machine.

The following diagram illustrates the App Volumes Agent login process:

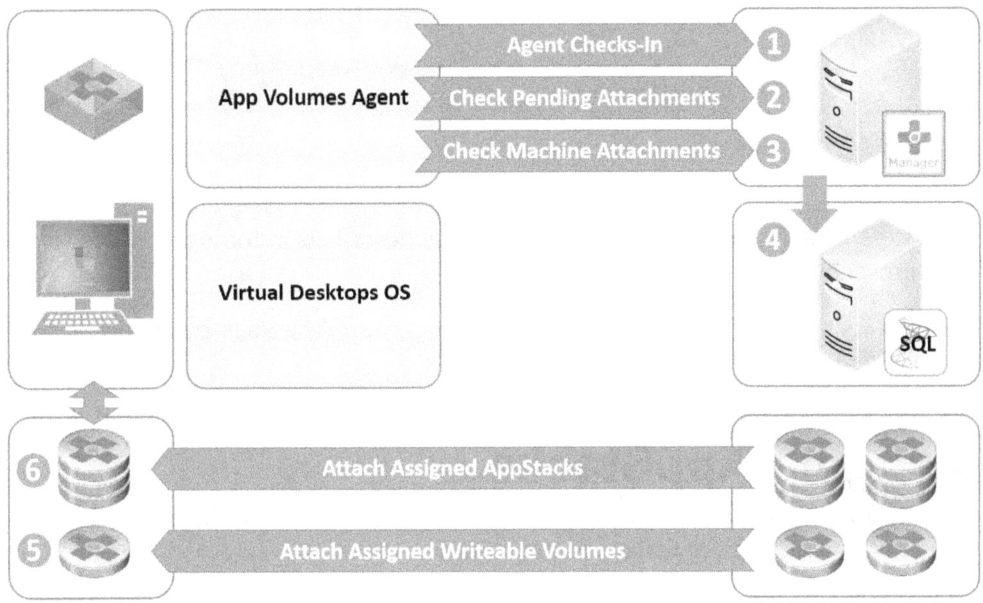

The following tasks describe this process:

1. App Volumes Agent connects to App Volumes Manager.
2. App Volumes Agent checks for any pending attachments or detachments.
3. App Volumes Agent checks for machine-based attachments; if it finds machine based attachments, no user-based attachments are honored.
4. App Volumes Manager checks the SQL database for logged-in user assignments.
5. Writable Volumes are attached to the virtual desktop machine.
6. AppStacks are attached to the virtual desktop machine.

Agent logout process

The following diagram illustrates the App Volumes Agent logout process:

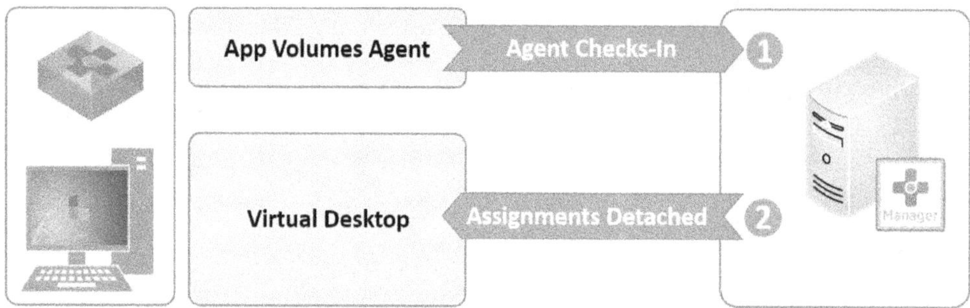

This process is identical to the shutdown process described in the *Agent shutdown process* subsection.

In the next section, we will look at how to customize an AppStack by changing the size of the disk used for the template.

Managing AppStacks

In this section, we will look at the tasks you can perform on your AppStacks, and other general management tasks and processes.

Editing AppStacks

Once you have created an AppStack, you have the ability to edit some of its settings. Here's how to edit an AppStack:

1. Click on the **VOLUMES** menu option and then, from the **AppStacks** tab, check the box next to the AppStack you want to edit.

   In this example, click on the **Visio Pro 2013** AppStack **(1)**. Click on the **Edit** button **(2)**, as shown in the following diagram:

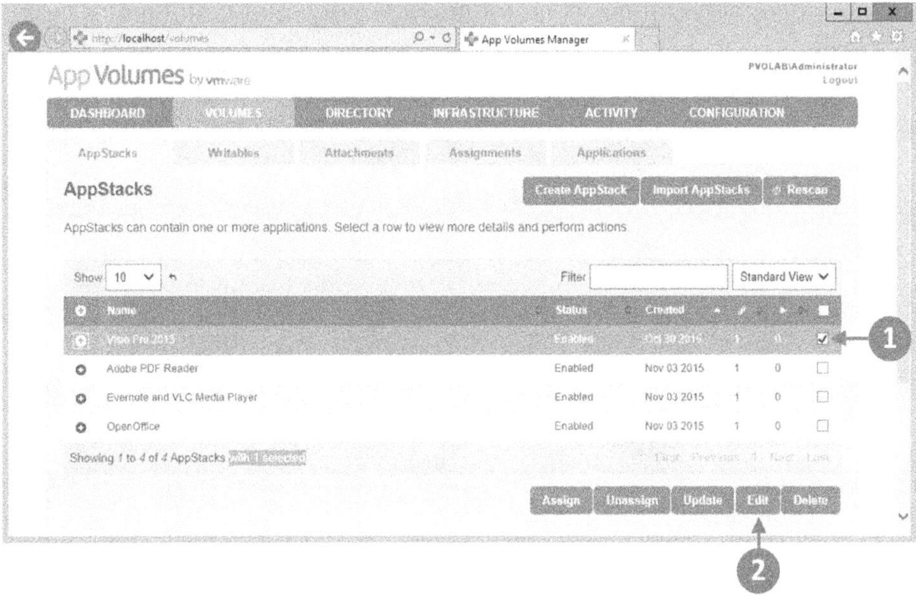

You will now see the **Edit AppStack** page, which looks like this:

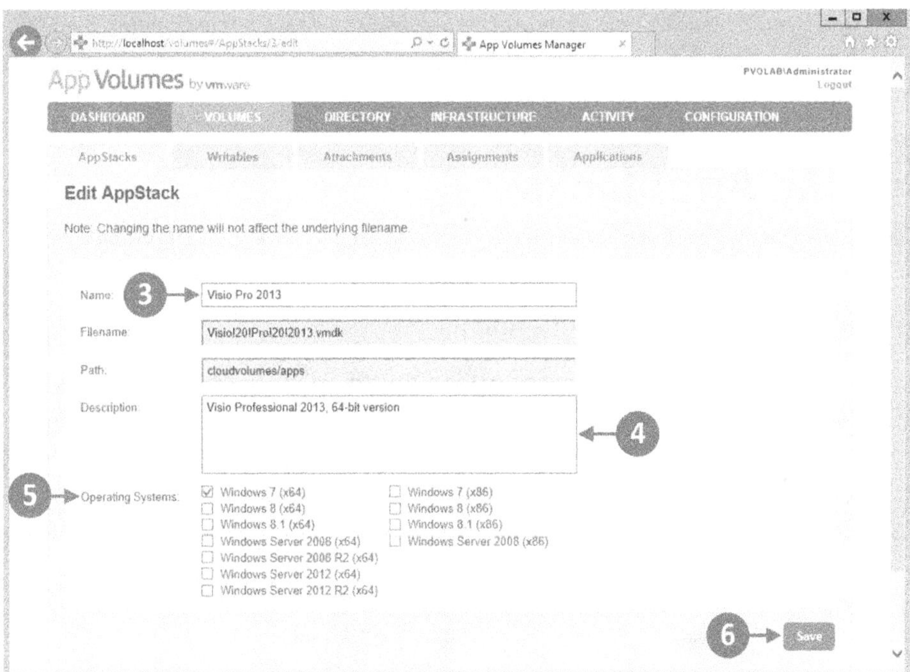

2. You can edit the AppStack name **(3)** and description **(4)**. Simply enter the new text.

   There is also the option of selecting operating system compatibility **(5)**. Here, you can select which operating systems the AppStack supports.

When selecting an operating system, ensure that the applications contained in the AppStack will run on the operating system you select. It's worth testing the application before making any changes.

   Once you have made your changes, click on the **Save** button **(6)**. You will be prompted to confirm the changes you have made, as shown in the following screenshot:

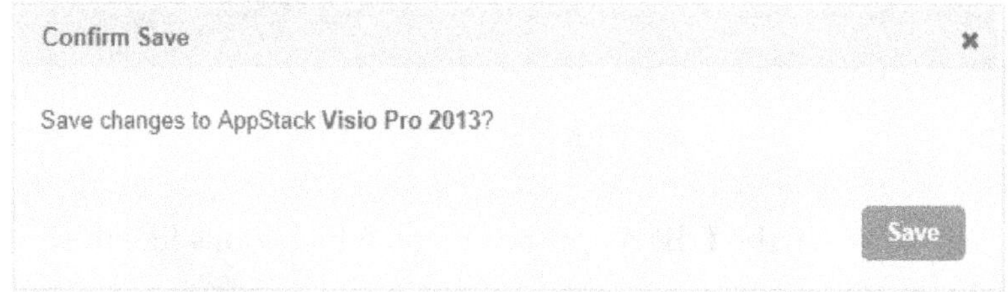
Confirm Save
Save changes to AppStack Visio Pro 2013?
Save

3. Click on the **Save** button if you are happy to confirm the changes you have made.

Updating AppStacks

In this subsection, we will look at how to update an existing AppStack to allow application updates and patches to the applications contained within the AppStack.

To update an AppStack, perform the following steps:

1. Click on the **VOLUMES** menu option and then, from the **AppStacks** tab, check the box next to the AppStack you want to edit.

   In this example, check the box for the **Visio Pro 2013** AppStack **(1)**, and click on the **Update** button **(2)**, as shown in the following diagram:

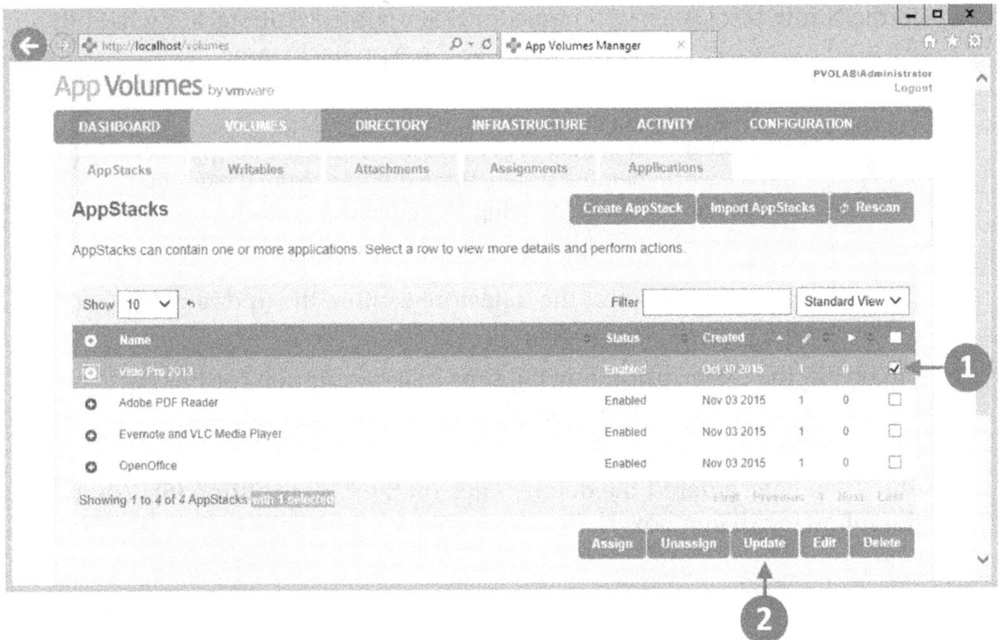

You will now see the **Update AppStack** page, which looks like this:

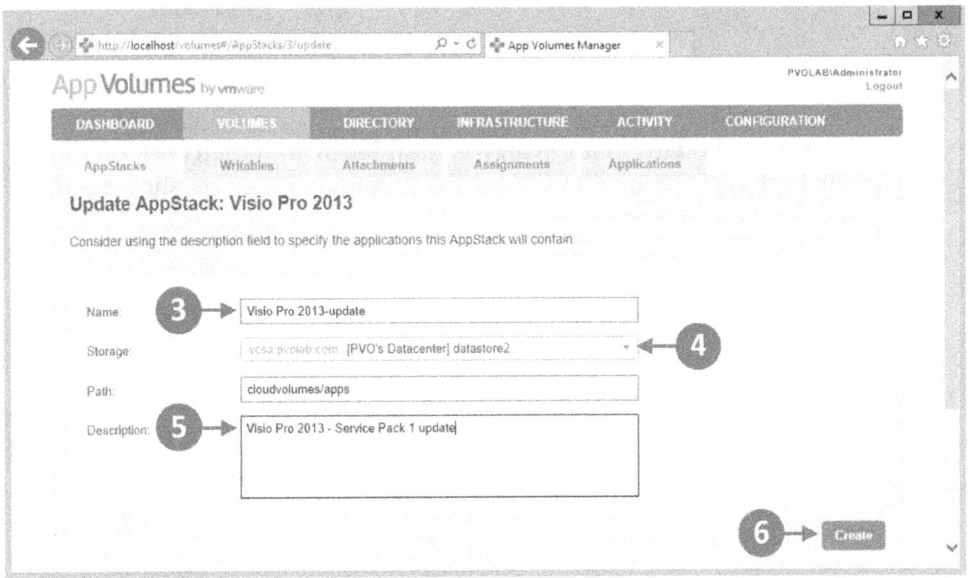

2. In the **Name** box **(3)**, enter a name for this updated AppStack. By default, App Volumes will append `-update` to the AppStack name.

> You can enter a name of your choice to identify the AppStack, but it's worth naming it something different from the original in order to identify it as being an updated AppStack.

3. In the **Storage** box **(4)**, select the datastore to store the updated AppStack on, and leave the path details as default.
4. Finally, in the **Description** box **(5)**, type in a description for this AppStack. In this example, we have entered details of what the update contains, just for reference.
5. Once you have entered the details, click on the **Create** button **(6)**. You will see the following dialog box:

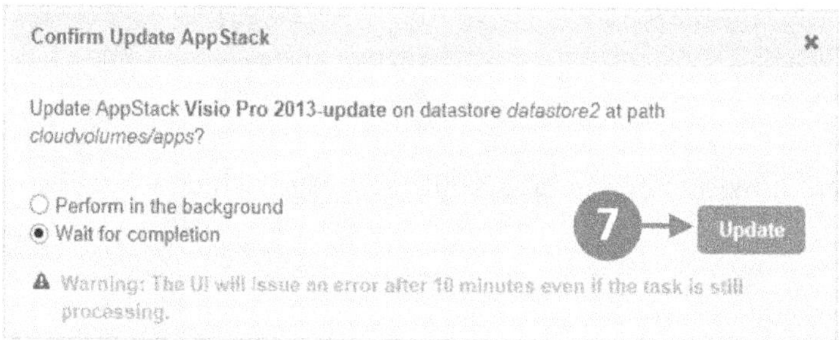
Confirm Update AppStack
Update AppStack Visio Pro 2013-update on datastore datastore2 at path cloudvolumes/apps?
Perform in the background
Wait for completion
7
Update
Warning: The UI will issue an error after 10 minutes even if the task is still processing.

6. Click on the radio button for **Wait for completion** and then click on the **Update** button **(7)**. You will now see the following message, showing the AppStack being created:

Creating AppStack

As this task is for updating an existing AppStack, rather than creating a brand new one from a template, App Volumes actually copies the original AppStack. So in this example, App Volumes will make a copy of the original Visio AppStack and name it as per the new name you entered in the previous step.

Depending on the size of your AppStack, this step might take a little longer than when you created the original AppStack.

Once the AppStack has been created, you will see the following page:

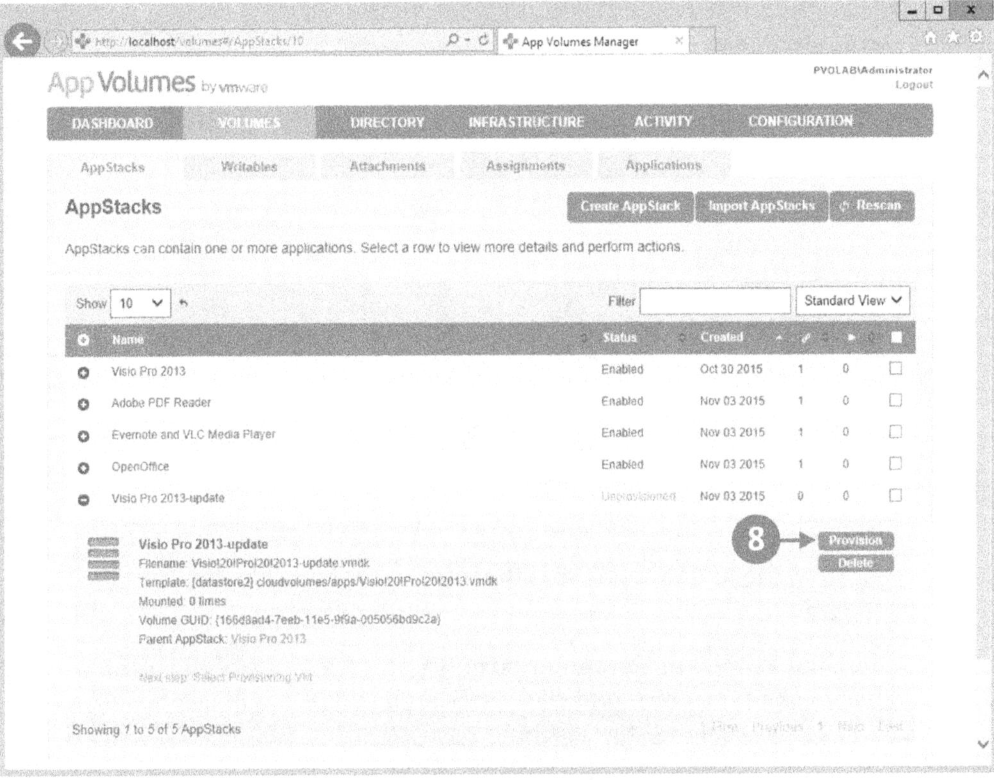

7. Now, click on the **Provision** button **(8)**. You will see the **Provision AppStack** page, which looks like this:

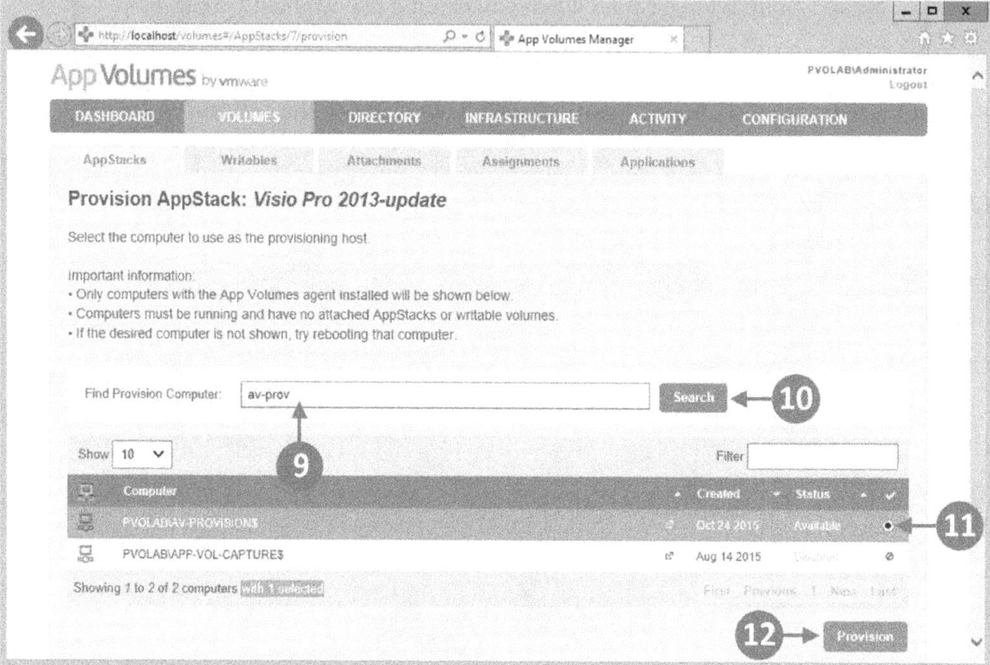

From here, the update process is the same as that used to create the AppStack.

8. In the **Find Provision Computer** box **(9)**, enter the name of the provisioning virtual desktop machine and click on **Search (10)**. We will use our `AV-PROVISION` virtual desktop machine.
9. The machine will now be listed in the results box. Click on the radio button next to the machine entry **(11)**, and then click on **Provision (12)**.

   You will now see the following dialog box:

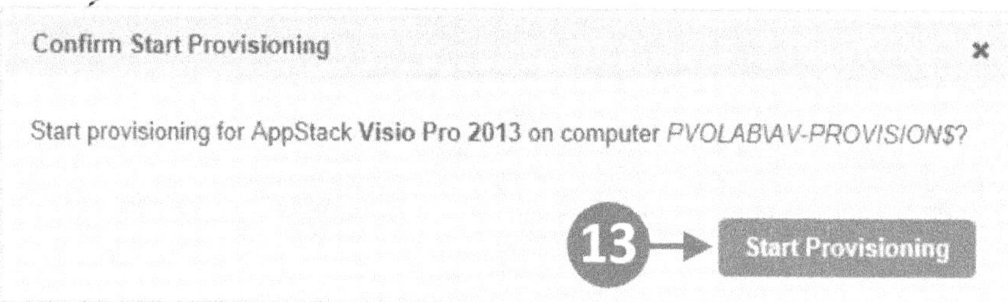

10. Click on the **Start Provisioning** button **(13)**. You will see the following message as the AppStack is attached to the provisioning virtual desktop machine:

Attaching AppStack To Computer

[Remember that this is the copy of the AppStack that already contains the original application installation.]

Once the AppStack has been attached, switch to the console of the virtual desktop machine. You will see the following dialog box displayed on the virtual desktop machine:

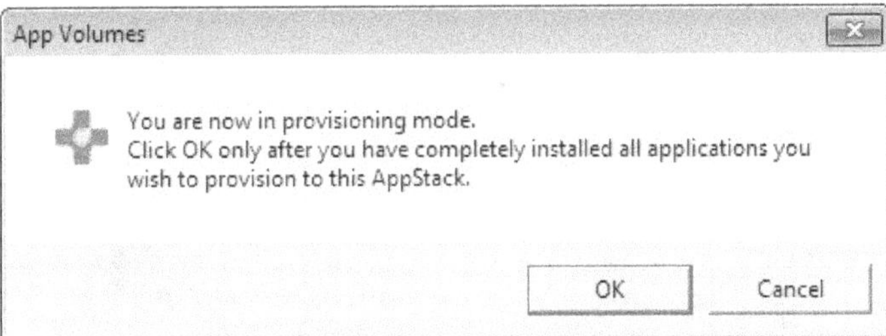
App Volumes
You are now in provisioning mode.
Click OK only after you have completely installed all applications you wish to provision to this AppStack.
OK
Cancel

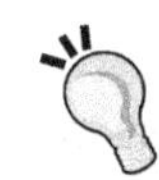

[Remember to only click on **OK** once you have finished installing the updates to the applications.]

The virtual desktop machine is now in provisioning mode, and you can start installing your updates. In our example, we are going to install some of the other Visio features.

Launch the Visio installer and update the application as you would normally do.

Once you have installed the updates, you can go back to the initial dialog box and click on **OK**. You will see the following dialog box:

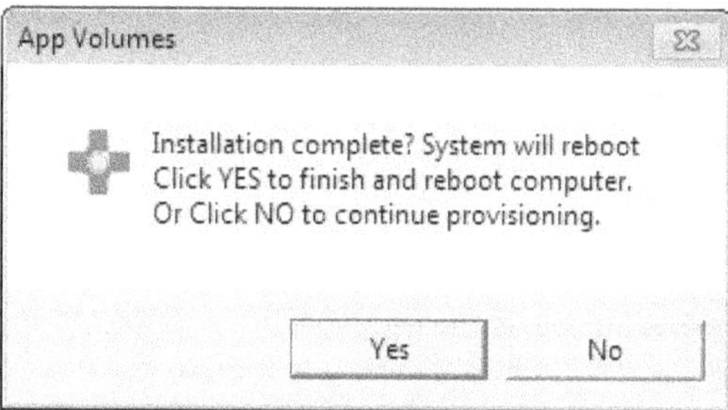
App Volumes
Installation complete? System will reboot
Click YES to finish and reboot computer.
Or Click NO to continue provisioning.
Yes
No

11. Click on the **Yes** button if you are sure that you have finished installing the updates you want included as part of this AppStack. The application will now be analyzed, as shown in the following screenshot:

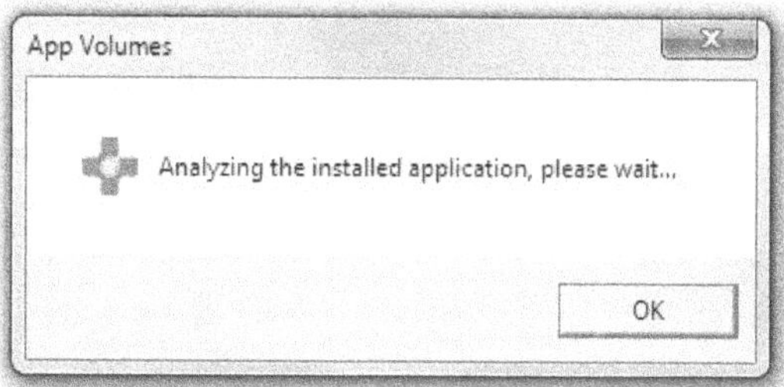
App Volumes
Analyzing the installed application, please wait...
OK

12. Click on **OK** and then reboot the virtual desktop machine.

    Once the machine reboots, you will see the following dialog box stating that the provisioning completed successfully and the AppStack has been provisioned or, in our example, updated:

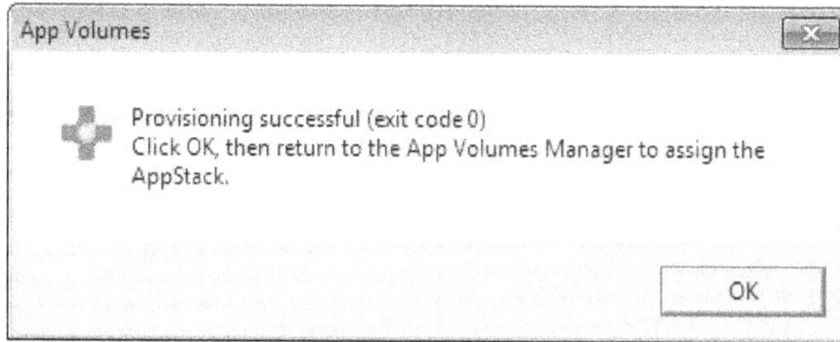
App Volumes
Provisioning successful (exit code 0)
Click OK, then return to the App Volumes Manager to assign the AppStack.
OK

13. Click on **OK** to complete the update process on the virtual desktop machine, and then switch back to the App Volumes Manager console, shown in the following diagram:

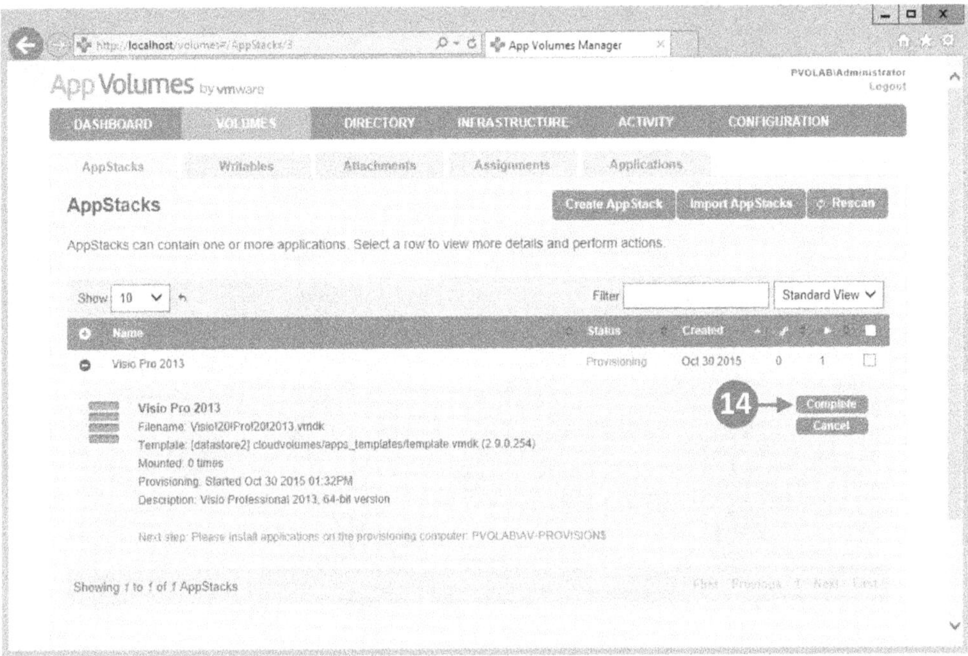

14. Click on the **Complete** button **(14)** to finish the update process. You will see the following dialog box:

15. Click on the **Complete Provisioning** button **(15)**.

You will now return to the **AppStacks** page, shown in the following screenshot:

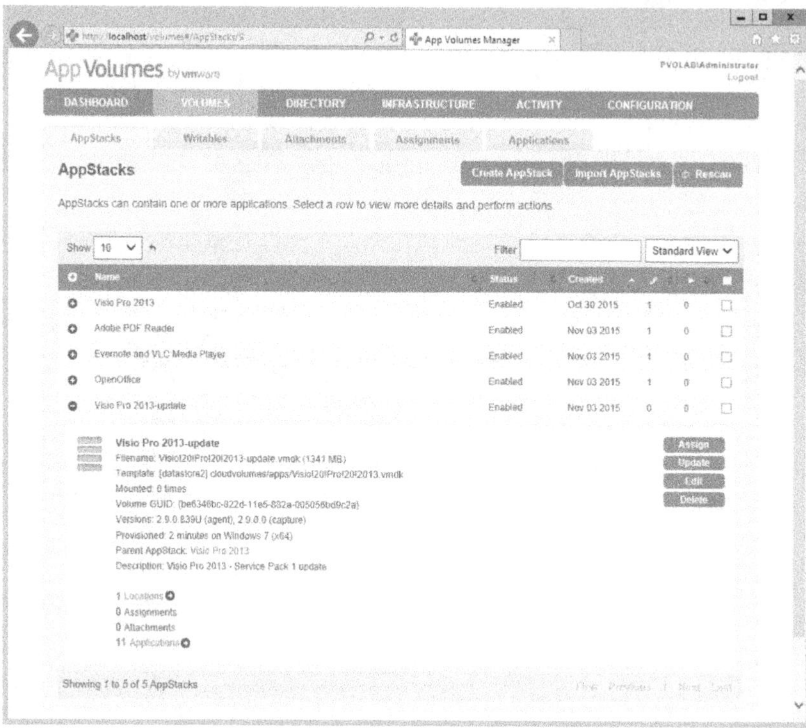

You should now have an updated AppStack for Visio Pro 2013. Actually, you have created a new AppStack that contains the original application plus the updates that you made, and the original AppStack is still in place and untouched. This is true for the AppStack assignments too.

> App Volumes does not copy over the assignments from the original AppStack. You will need to work through the assigning process in order to assign the new, updated AppStack to end users.

Not changing assignments immediately means less user disruption. Users can continue working with their applications while you update them in the background and then assign them when appropriate.

In the next subsection, we will look at how to delete an AppStack.

Deleting AppStacks

In the previous subsection, we created an updated AppStack, so it may be that since you now have a new version, you want to delete the old version in order to make management easier.

To delete an AppStack, perform the following steps:

1. Click on the **VOLUMES** menu option and then, from the **AppStacks** tab, check the box next to the AppStack you want to delete.

   In this example, check the box for the **Visio Pro 2013-update** AppStack **(1)**, and click on the **Delete** button **(2)**, as shown in the following diagram:

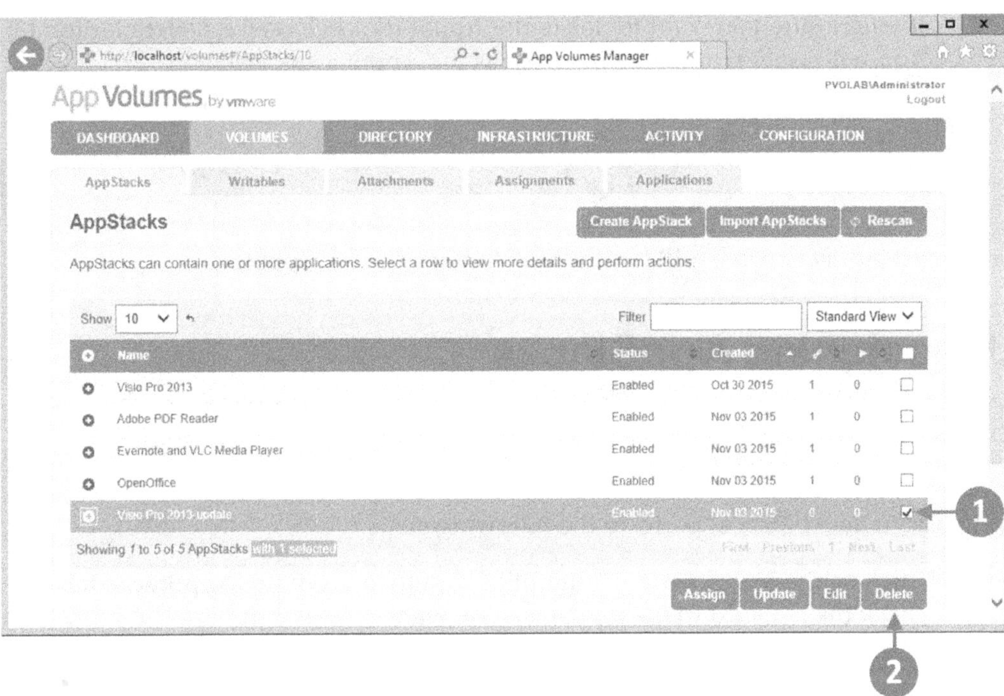

2. You will now see the **Confirm Delete** dialog box, which looks like this:

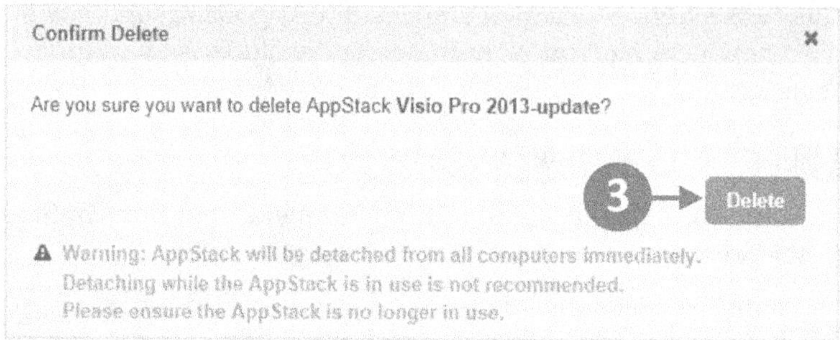
Confirm Delete
Are you sure you want to delete AppStack Visio Pro 2013-update?
3
Delete
Warning: AppStack will be detached from all computers immediately.
Detaching while the AppStack is in use is not recommended.
Please ensure the AppStack is no longer in use.

3. If you're sure you want to delete the AppStack, click on the **Delete** button **(3)**. You will see the following message as the AppStack is deleted:

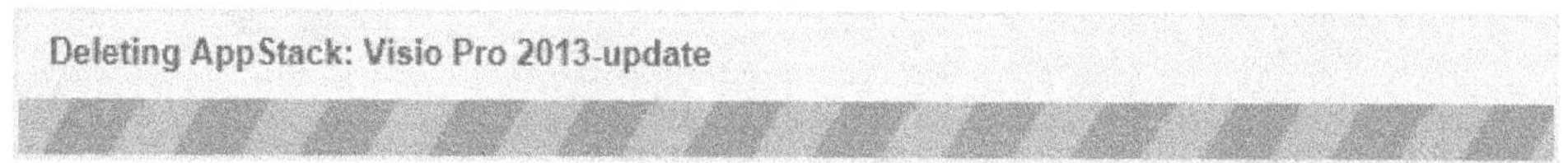
Deleting AppStack: Visio Pro 2013-update

In the next subsection, we will look at how to unassign an AppStack.

Unassigning AppStacks

As we saw in the *Assigning and delivering AppStacks to end users* section of this chapter, it is very easy to give users access to applications. It's just as simple to revoke access to applications.

To unassign an AppStack, perform the following steps:

1. Click on the **VOLUMES** menu option and then, from the **AppStacks** tab, check the box next to the AppStack you want to unassign.

In this example, check the box for the **Visio Pro 2013** AppStack **(1)** and click on the **Unassign** button **(2)**, as shown in the following diagram:

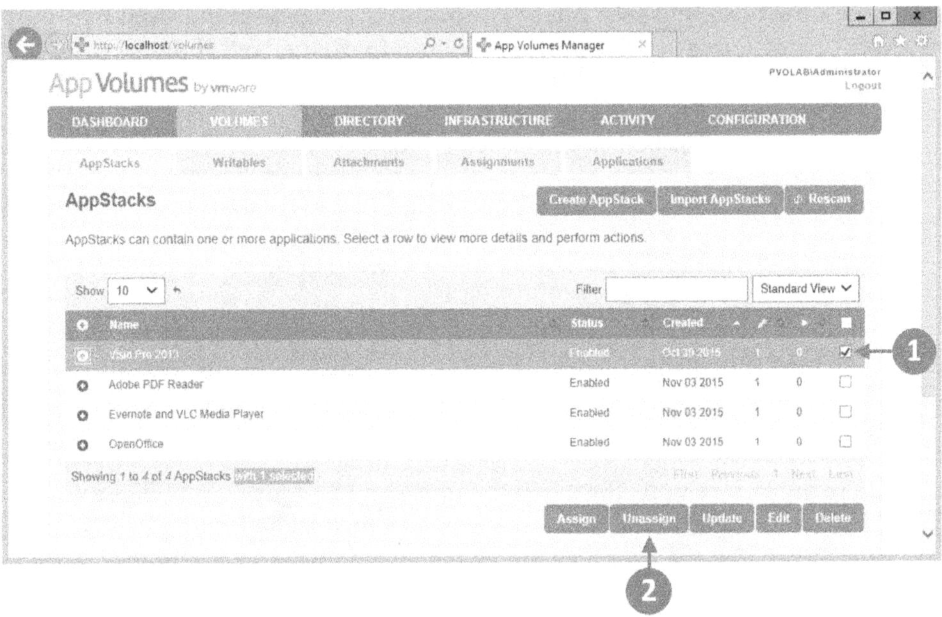

You will now see the **Unassign AppStack** page, which looks like this:

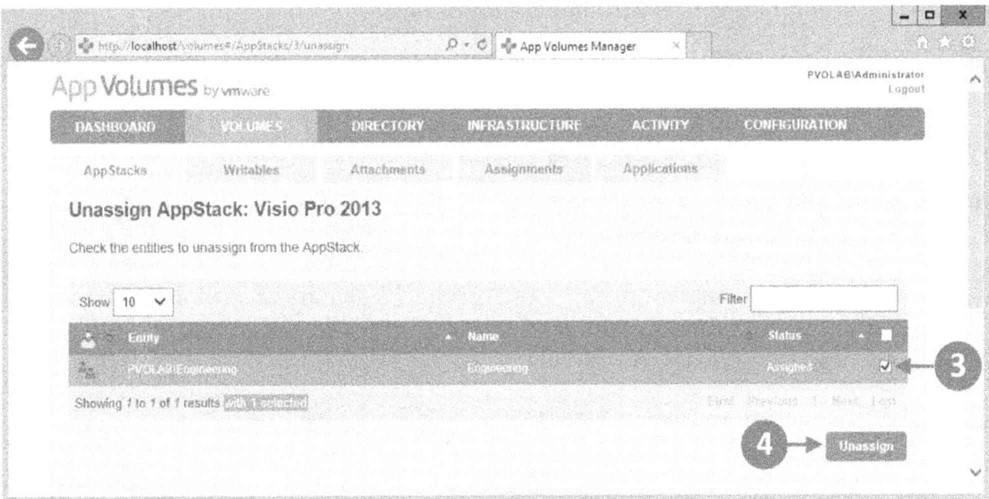

The current users and groups of this AppStack will be listed. In this example, it's the Engineering Active Directory group.

2. Check the box **(3)** to select this group, and then click on the **Unassign** button **(4)**. You will now see the **Confirm Unassign** dialog box, shown here:

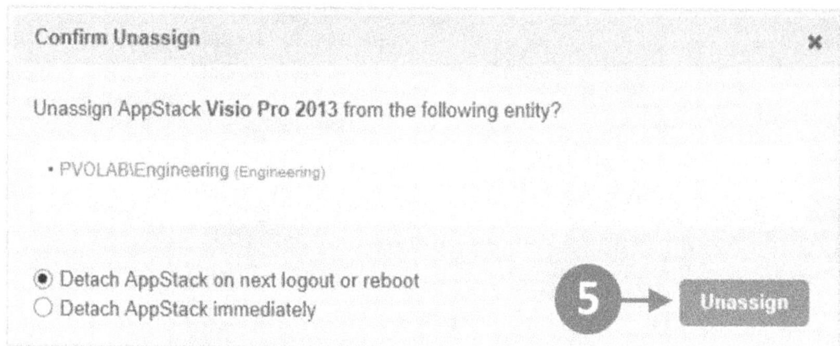

There are two options for when the unassignment task completes and the AppStack is detached: either the AppStack is detached immediately, or it is detached when the user logs out or the virtual desktop machine is rebooted.

3. For this example, click on the radio button for **Detach AppStack on next logout or reboot**, and click on the **Unassign** button **(5)**.

You have now successfully taken away that user's access to the AppStack, and the applications will no longer be available to them.

In the next subsection, we will look at how to import an AppStack.

Importing AppStacks

The **Import AppStacks** feature allows you to import existing AppStacks that are part of another App Volumes deployment.

For example, you may create a number of AppStacks as part of a pilot project, and when you deploy the technology in production, you could import the AppStacks rather than creating them again.

To import an AppStack, perform the following steps:

1. Click on the **VOLUMES** menu option and then, from the **AppStacks** tab, click on the **Import AppStacks** button **(1)**, as shown in the following diagram:

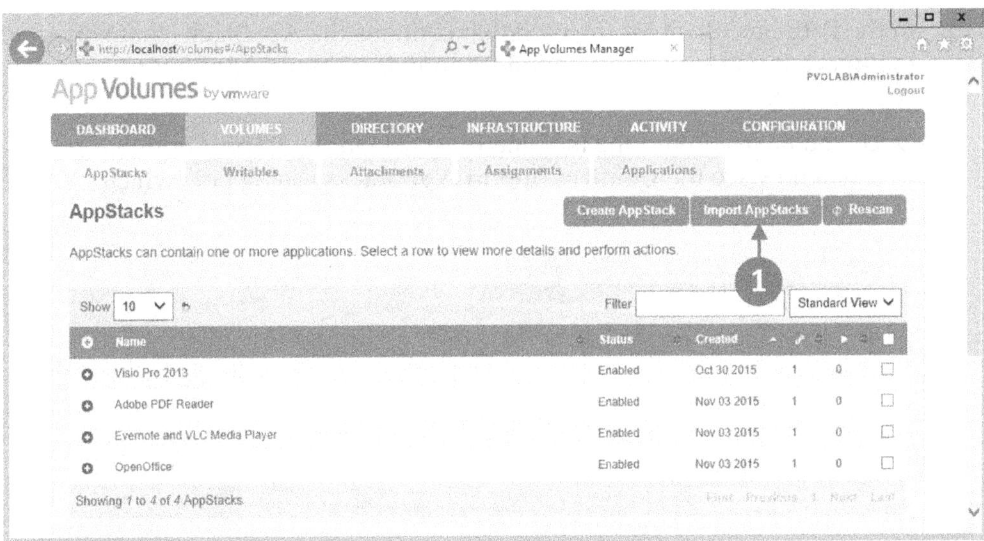

You will now see the **Import AppStacks** page, which looks like this:

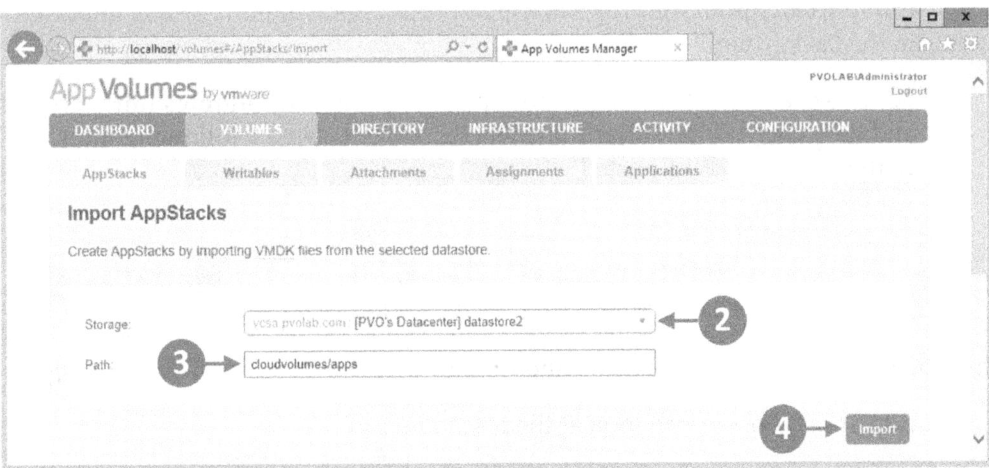

2. In the **Storage** box **(2)**, from the drop-down menu, select the datastore that contains the AppStacks that you want to import.

> You can either copy your existing AppStacks that you want to import into a different folder on the same datastore using the Datastore Browser feature in vCenter, or ensure that your vCenter Server instance has access to the other datastores.

3. In the **Path** box **(3)**, enter the path that contains the AppStacks that you want to import. If you created a new folder containing your AppStacks for import, enter it here.
4. Once you have entered the information, click on the **Import** button **(4)**. You will now see the **Confirm Import AppStacks** dialog box, which looks like this:

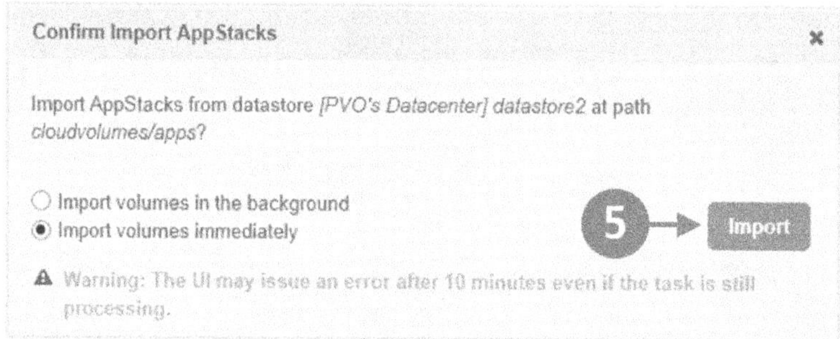
Confirm Import AppStacks
Import AppStacks from datastore [PVO's Datacenter] datastore2 at path cloudvolumes/apps?
Import volumes in the background
Import volumes immediately
5
Import
Warning: The UI may issue an error after 10 minutes even if the task is still processing.

There are two options for when the import task completes and the AppStack is imported. Either the AppStack is imported immediately, or it is imported in the background.

5. For this example, click on the radio button for **Import volumes immediately**, and then click on the **Import** button **(5)**. You will see the following message as the AppStack is imported:

Importing AppStacks

The AppStack will now be imported and then be displayed and available to assign.

In the next subsection, we will look at the rescan feature.

Rescanning AppStacks

The AppStack **rescan** feature updates the current AppStack inventory from the AppStack information held in the datastore to ensure that AppStacks still exist and are accessible.

To demonstrate the outcome of this, before performing the rescan, log in to vCenter, and, using the datastore browser, move one of the current AppStacks to a different datastore temporarily. In this example, the Evernote AppStack will be moved.

Now, perform the rescan exercise.

To perform a rescan, from the **AppStacks** tab under the **VOLUMES** menu option, click on the **Rescan** button **(1)**, as shown here:

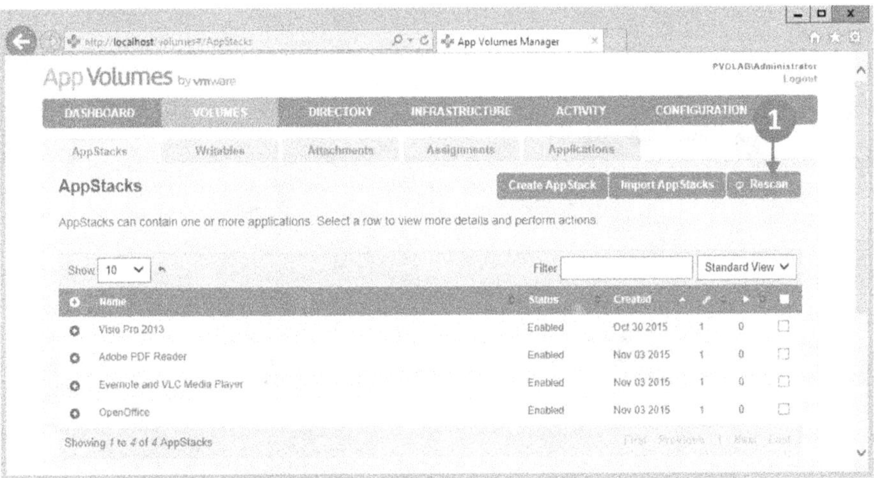

You will now see the **Confirm Rescan** dialog box, which looks like this:

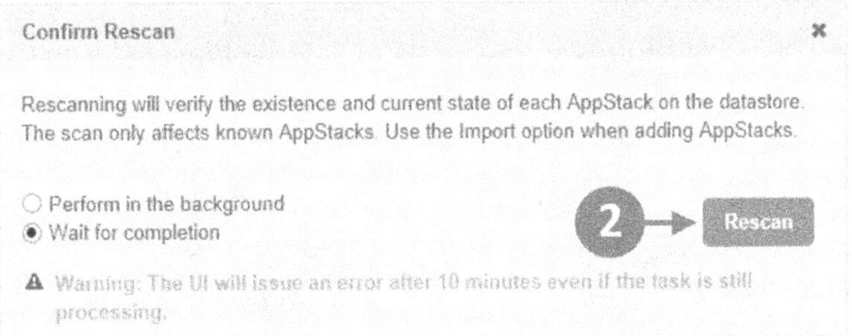

Confirm Rescan
Rescanning will verify the existence and current state of each AppStack on the datastore. The scan only affects known AppStacks. Use the Import option when adding AppStacks.
Perform in the background
Wait for completion
2
Rescan
Warning: The UI will issue an error after 10 minutes even if the task is still processing.

There are two options for when the rescan task is completed. You can either wait for the rescan to complete, or perform the rescan in the background.

For this example, click on the radio button for **Wait for completion** and then click on the **Rescan** button **(2)**.

You will see the following message as the datastore is scanned:

You will then see the results of the rescan displayed, as shown in the following diagram:

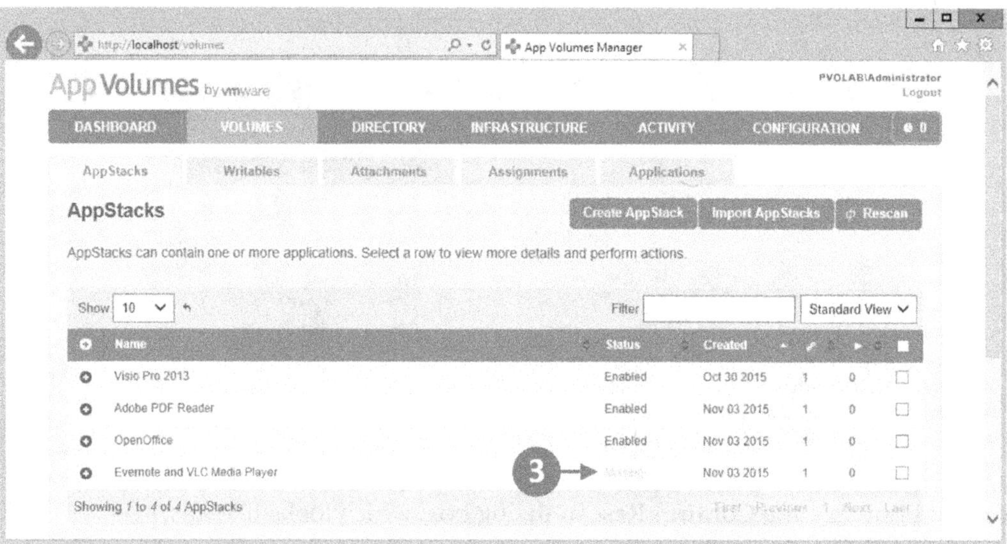

As you can see, the status for **Evernote and VLC Media Player** is listed as **Missing (3)**.

This is because App Volumes Manager has this listed as an AppStack but cannot verify its existence. Users will not be able to access this AppStack.

Now that the rescan feature has been demonstrated, copy the AppStack back to its original datastore and perform the rescan again so that it is listed in the inventory as **Enabled**.

This leads us to how to back up AppStacks, which we will see in the next subsection.

Backing up AppStacks

We are not really going to talk about specific backup tools, as App Volumes does not have anything built in for backing up AppStacks. However, it is important to back up your AppStacks; otherwise, you will end up having to recreate them.

App Volumes has a form of backup built in: the ability to create **storage groups**. You can then replicate AppStacks and Writable Volumes across these datastores.

We will cover this feature in more detail in *Chapter 14, Advanced Configuration and Other Options*.

Alternatively, you could use some form of SAN-based replication.

Don't forget that AppStacks and Writable Volumes are effectively unmounted VMDK files and may show up as being orphaned. They are only attached when a user who has been assigned these volumes is logged in. Any backup solution will need to work with unmounted VMDK files.

Summary

In this chapter, we covered the topic of AppStacks in more detail.

We started off by describing the provisioning process before moving on to creating an AppStack.

Once it was created, we went on to look at assignment and how to deliver AppStacks to some of our end users. We did this by assigning AppStacks to our example Active Directory groups, which reflected different departments within our organization.

Finally, we looked at how to perform some of the ongoing management of AppStacks, such as updates and other general admin tasks.

In the next chapter, we will take a deeper look into Writable Volumes.

7
Working with Writable Volumes

In this chapter, we will take a much deeper look into Writable Volumes, how they work, and how to create them, before finally demonstrating Writable Volumes in action.

We will also look at some of the best practices of how to build a Writable Volume with particular attention to the dos and don'ts.

At the end of this chapter, you will be able to create, assign, and deliver a Writable Volume to an end user as well as perform ongoing management tasks.

The steps we will work through follow three distinct topics: create, assign, and consume:

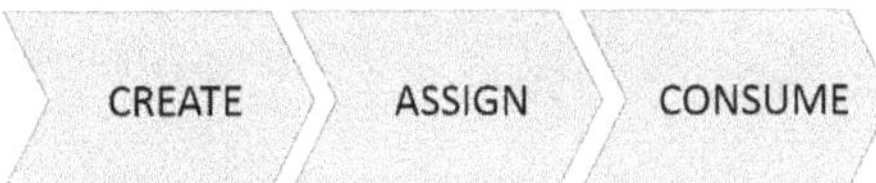

So, just as a quick recap, a Writable Volume is an empty virtual hard disk, or VMDK file, that is attached to a virtual desktop machine when a user who has been assigned a Writable Volume logs in. The Writable Volume itself contains any user-installed applications or user profile information.

The user effectively owns that Writable Volume and it will be attached to whichever virtual desktop machine they log in to.

A Writable Volume has a 1:1 relationship with a user and therefore becomes owned by that user and is attached to any virtual desktop machine that they log on to.

Writable Volumes allow persistent data and settings when you have deployed a non-persistent virtual desktop environment delivered using linked clone desktop pools. By adding this feature, you open up the ability to address more use cases for non-persistent desktops, such as developers and other users that need to install applications.

Usually, in a non-persistent desktop model, as the name suggests, any applications that a user installs onto the virtual desktop machine will be removed when they log out and the desktop is returned to its initial state. Now with the Writable Volume feature, anything that the end user installs is redirected to this drive, with this drive effectively becoming portable and being able to be attached to any virtual desktop machine that the user logs in to.

Creating Writable Volumes

The first thing we are going to do in this chapter is to create a Writable Volume, but before we do that, we will take a look at the process for doing this.

The process for creating a Writable Volume is far simpler than the one used for creating AppStacks, as you don't need to provision or install any applications up front, have provisioning machines, or have to then configure assignments as a separate task.

The following diagram illustrates the process we will follow to create a Writable Volume:

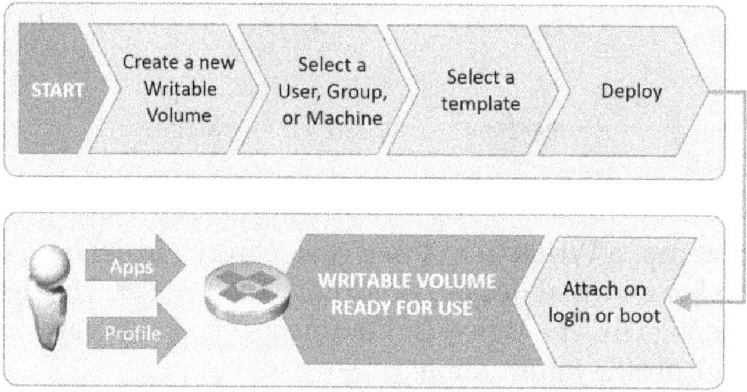

As you can see, it's simply a case of creating a Writable Volume from one of the three standard templates, which we will cover later in this chapter, assigning which user or group you want to assign the Writable Volume to, and then deploying it for use.

The end users can then install their own applications.

The following diagram illustrates the creation process and the subsequent user installation of applications in a little more detail. User-installed applications are exactly that: applications installed by the end users and not the IT admins.

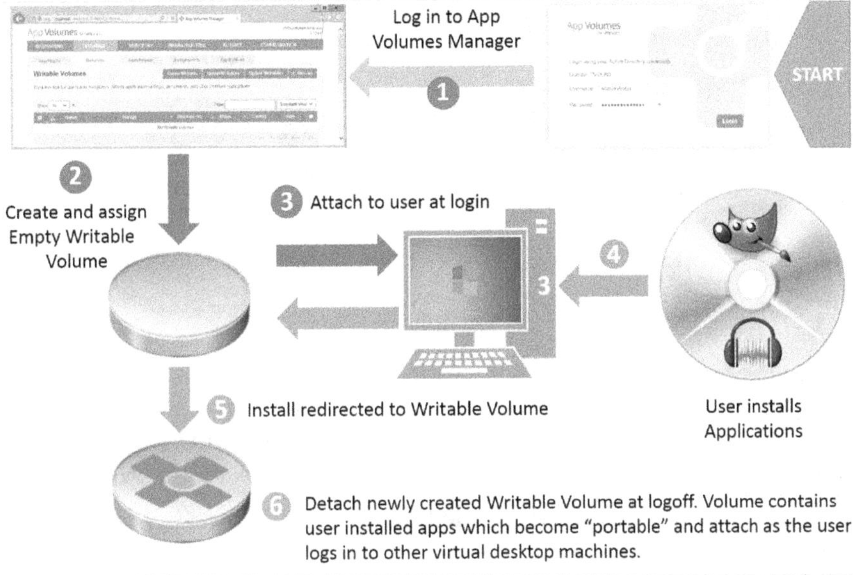

Having described the process, in the next section, we will create a new Writable Volume.

Creating your first Writable Volume

In this section, we will work through the process of creating a Writable Volume for one of our Example Lab end users. We will then go on to demonstrate installing an application onto the Writable Volume and show the outcome for when that user logs in to a virtual desktop machine.

We will also highlight what's going on with the backend infrastructure and what gets created. Perform the following steps:

1. Log in to App Volumes Manager by double-clicking on the App Volumes icon on the desktop of the App Volumes Manager machine, entering your administrator credentials, and clicking on **Login**, as shown in the following screenshot:

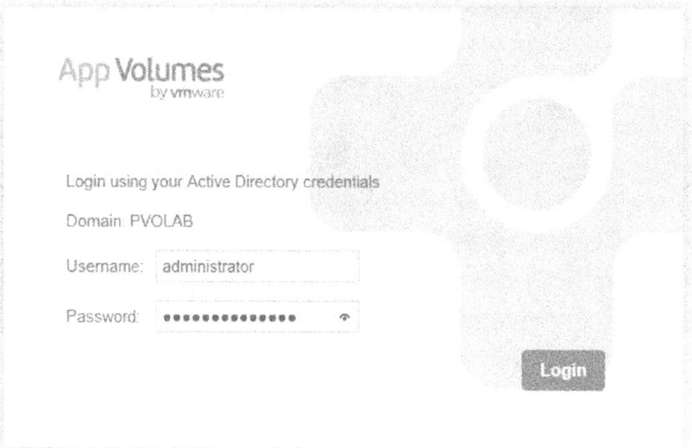

2. Once you have successfully logged in, click on the **VOLUMES** menu **(1)** to display volume configuration options, and then click on the **Writables** tab **(2)**.
3. Now, click on the **Create Writable** button **(3)**, as shown in the following diagram:

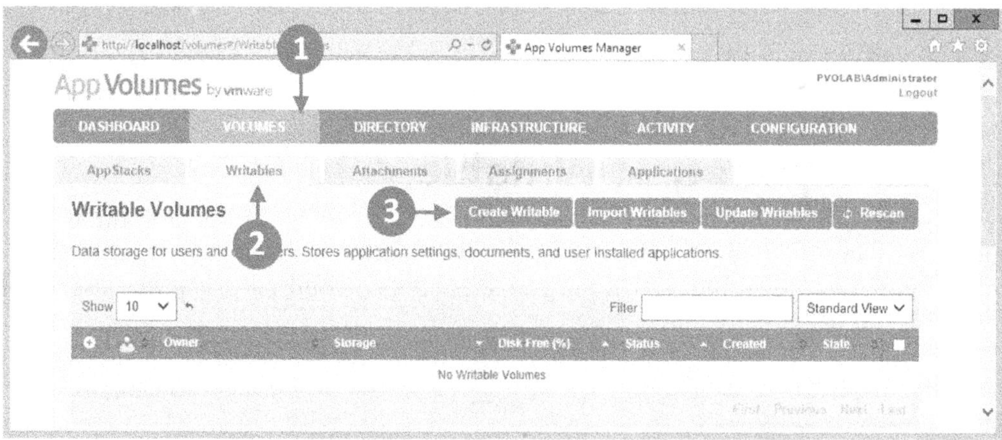

You will now see the **Create Writable Volume** page, shown in the following diagram:

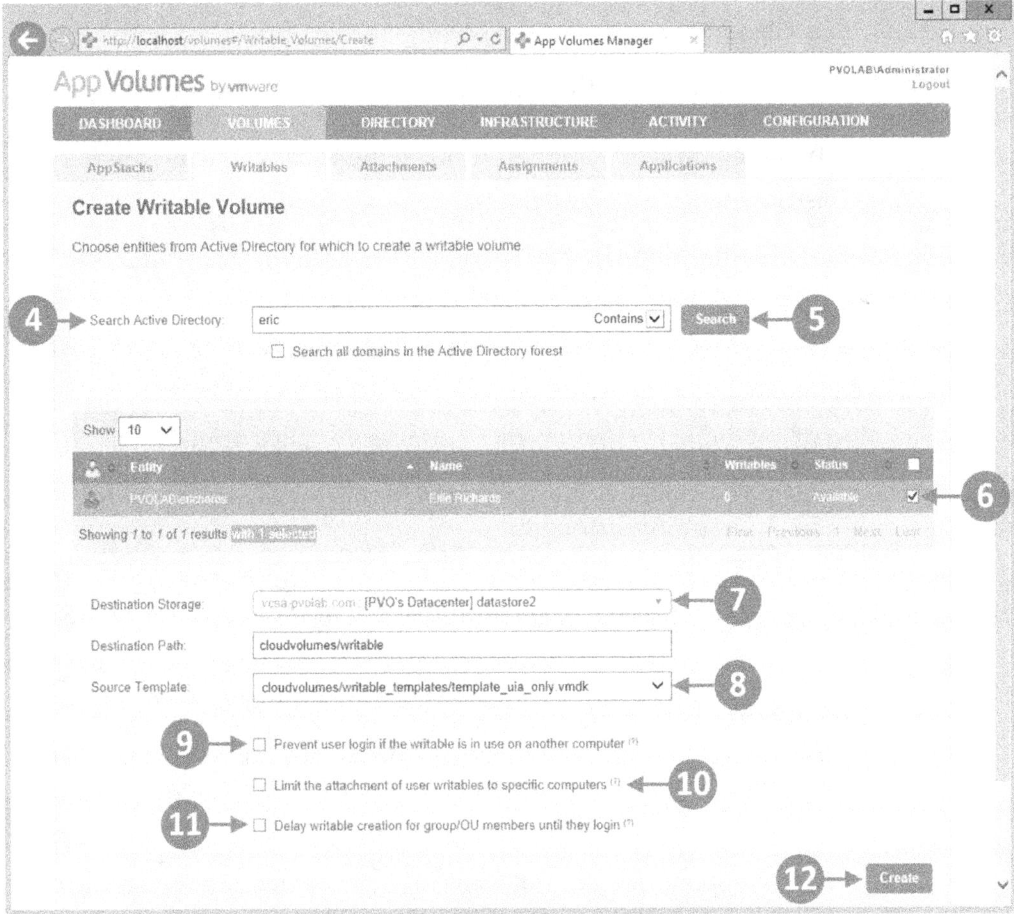

The first task is to search for and select the entity that you want to assign this Writable Volume to. This can be a user, group, or machine.

4. In this example, we are going to use one of the end users in the Example Lab, so start typing the user name into the **Search Active Directory** box **(4)**. The user we are using is `Ellie Richards`.
5. You don't need to type in the whole name, just the first part, and then click on the **Search** button **(5)**. You can also filter the search using the drop-down menu and selecting **Contains**, **Begins**, **Ends**, or **Equals** as the search criteria.

6. The result will now be displayed. From the results, select the entity you want to assign this Writable Volume to. In this example, we only have one option to select, so check the box **(6)** to highlight the user.

   Next, you will see that we have some configuration options to choose from.

7. The first of these is to select the **Destination Storage (7)**. From the drop-down menu, select the datastore where this Writable Volume is going to be stored. In this example, we are going to select `datastore2`.
8. Leave **Destination Path** as the default.

Next, you need to select the template that is going to be used for this Writable Volume. There are three to choose from:

- The Writable Volumes template for user-installed applications (10 GB)
- The Writable Volumes template for user profiles only (10 GB)
- The Writable Volume for user profiles and user-installed applications (10 GB)

Each template contains a number of preconfigured files to manage either user-installed application, user profiles, or both.

In this example, we are going to choose the option for user-installed applications or **UIA**, as it is called, so select this option from the drop-down menu.

There is also the option of using Writable Volumes to store user profiles; however, if you want a solution for managing user profiles, then it's worth looking at **Liquidware Labs' ProfileUnity**, or some other third-party **User Environment Management** (**UEM**) tool, instead of using App Volumes.

Finally, there are three options that control some of the behavior of how the Writable Volumes are deployed and attached.

The first of these, **Prevent user login if the writable is in use on another computer (9)**, is required for a Writable Volume to function correctly. An end user must have never logged in to a computer without their Writable Volume attached. This is required because their local profile can cause a conflict with their profile stored on the Writable Volume.

To prevent this conflict, check the box **(9)**, and App Volumes Manager will prevent a user from logging in to an additional computer when their Writable Volume is attached to another machine. You will need to do this on every Writable Volume a user has been assigned.

This feature is used to protect end users from logging in to persistent desktops without their Writable Volume. It is not required when using non-persistent pools as the virtual desktop machine will revert to a clean image when a user logs out.

The next option is **Limit the attachment of user writables to specific computers (10)**.

You can use this option when the end users may not need their Writable Volumes to be attached to all the virtual desktop machines they may use. There may also be a case where some users may need separate Writable Volumes that contain a specific application that will only run on a specific configuration of virtual desktop machine.

This option allows you to specify the prefix of a computer name so that the Writable Volume will only be attached to a computer with a name that begins with the prefix.

The following dialog box shows the result of enabling this option. Type the hostname in the box.

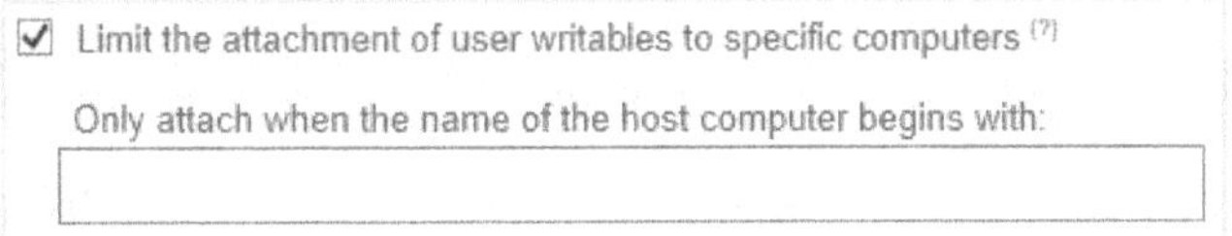

For example, our Lab user `Ellie Richards` is assigned two Writable Volumes, one being her standard assignment for standard applications and the other one containing a high-end engineering application. In this case, you may want to control which virtual desktop machine can have which Writable Volume attached.

The high-end engineering application may need a far higher specification of virtual desktop machine that potentially has access to accelerated GPU hardware, for example, and will only run on that type of platform. Therefore, you would only allow that machine to attach that particular Writable Volume.

In our Example Lab, we are going to leave this option unchecked.

The final option to choose is **Delay writable creation for group/OU members until they login (11)**.

If you want to create a Writable Volume and assign it to an entire group or **organizational unit** (**OU**), then an individual Writable Volume will then be created for each member of that group. Don't forget: a Writable Volume has a 1:1 relationship with an end user.

If the group or OU has hundreds or thousands of members, then this could create some performance issues as the Writable Volumes are created. It may also be the case that not every user in the group you assigned a Writable Volume to actually needs one; however, they will get one anyway, taking up unnecessary storage space and additional management overhead.

The **Delay writable creation for group/OU members until they login** option defers the creation of Writable Volumes for all the group and OU members until they next log in.

This option only applies to groups and OUs, and standard user and computer assignments will still have their Writable Volumes created immediately.

In our Example Lab, we are going to leave this option unchecked.

Now that we have completed the configuration options on this page, click on the **Create** button **(12)**.

You will now see the **Confirm Create Writable Volumes** dialog box as shown in the following figure:

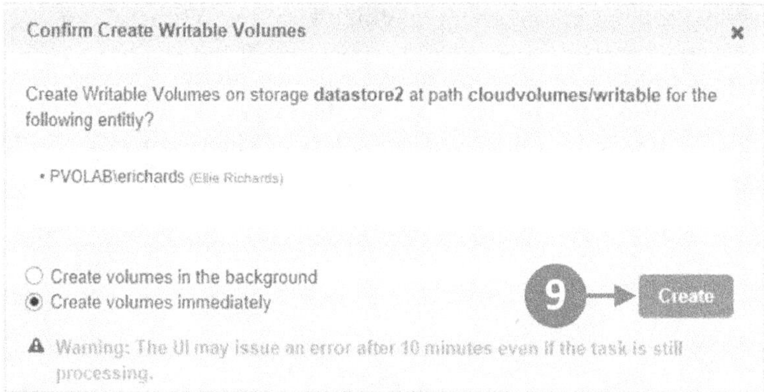

There are two options for creating a Writable Volume. It is either created immediately or in the background.

In this example, click on the radio button for **Create volumes immediately**, and click on the **Create** button **(9)**.

You will see the following message as the Writable Volume is created:

Once the task has completed, you will return to the Writable Volumes page, as shown in the following diagram:

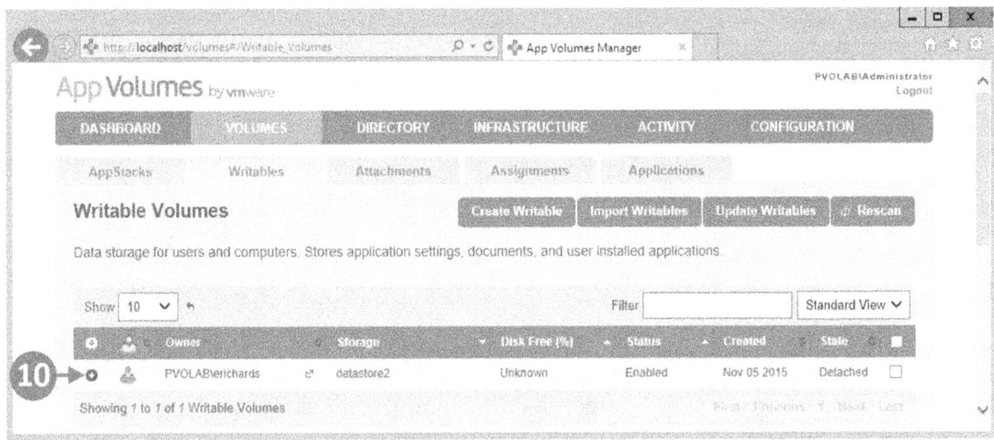

As you can see, we have successfully created a Writable Volume. As the user has not logged in, it currently shows up as being detached.

The next question is this: what has happened in the background?

So far, all we have done is create an empty Writable Volume. We can view this by logging in to the vSphere client or web client and using the datastore browser to view the contents of the datastore. This is shown in the following screenshot:

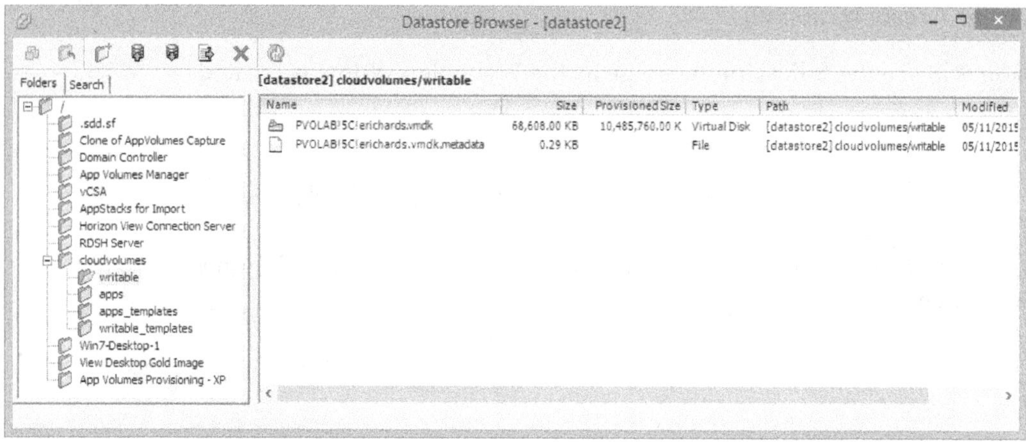

You can see that a file called `PVOLAB!5C!erichards.vmdk` has been created, along with a metadata file. The current size of the file is just under 69 MB. This is the size of the template, as the new Writable Volume is a copy of this template.

Now that the Writable Volume has been created, the next thing we are going to do is log in as that particular user.

For this example, we are going to use one of the Windows 7 desktops from the Example Lab: `Win7-Desktop-2`. Open a console to this desktop and log in as the user `Ellie Richards`.

Once logged in, you will see a dialog box with an App Volumes message asking you to reboot:

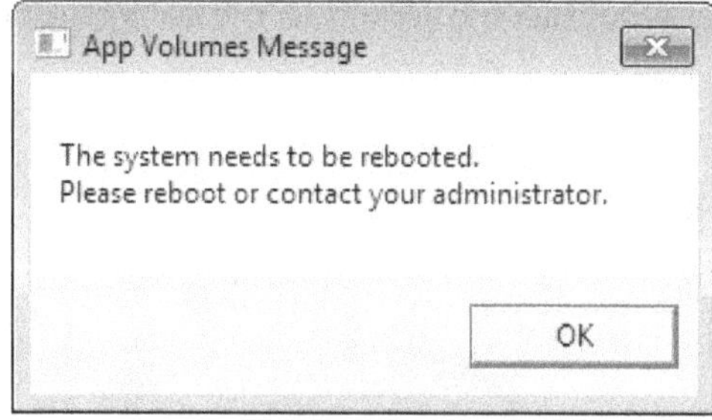

Click on **OK** to reboot. Once the virtual desktop machine has rebooted, log in again as the same user. You will now see the user's desktop, as shown in the following screenshot:

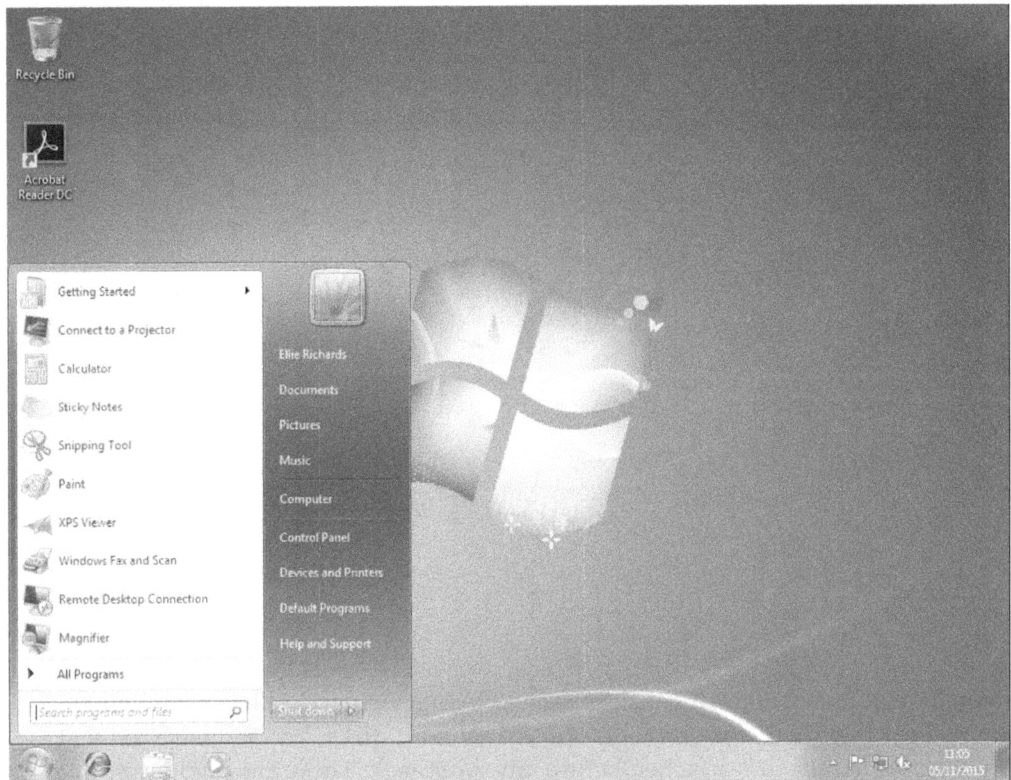

As well as now having a Writable Volume assigned, this user has also been assigned two AppStacks based on their Active Directory group membership: Adobe Acrobat Reader DC, which is part of the Domain Users group, and Visio Pro 2013, as this user is a part of the Engineering group.

Other than the obvious icons on the desktop, we can also see this from the admin perspective and the properties of the virtual desktop machine, as shown in the following figure:

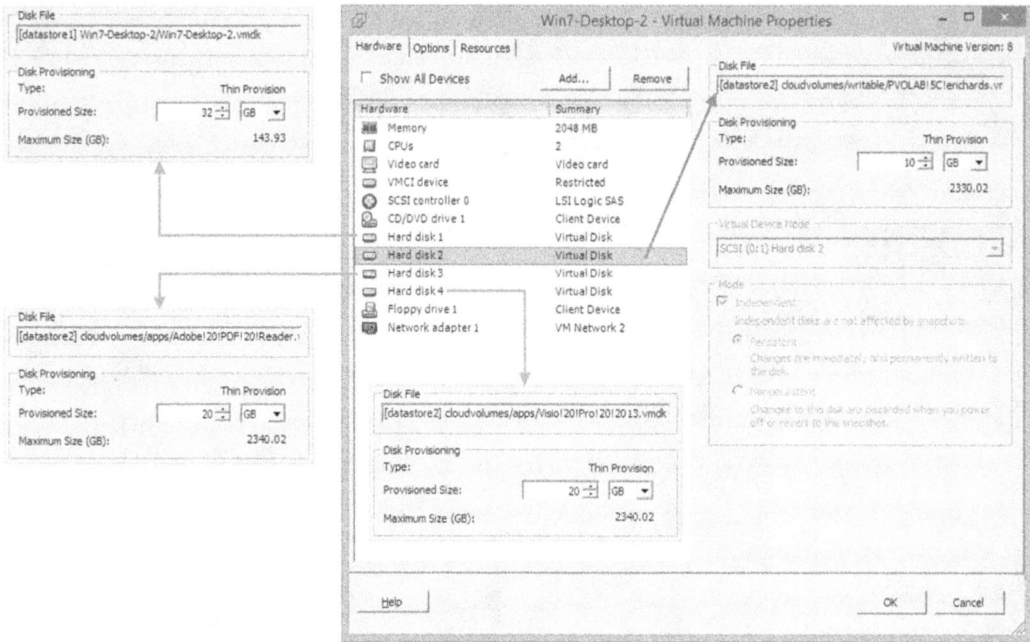

If you look at the virtual hard disks attached to this virtual desktop machine, you will see that there are a total of four virtual hard disks. You will also see that the Writable Volumes is attached before any AppStack. These are as follows:

- **Hard disk 1**: Virtual desktop operating system
- **Hard disk 2**: Writable Volume
- **Hard disk 3**: AppStack with Adobe Acrobat Reader
- **Hard disk 4**: AppStack with Visio Pro 2013

From the App Volumes Manager console, this looks like the following screenshot:

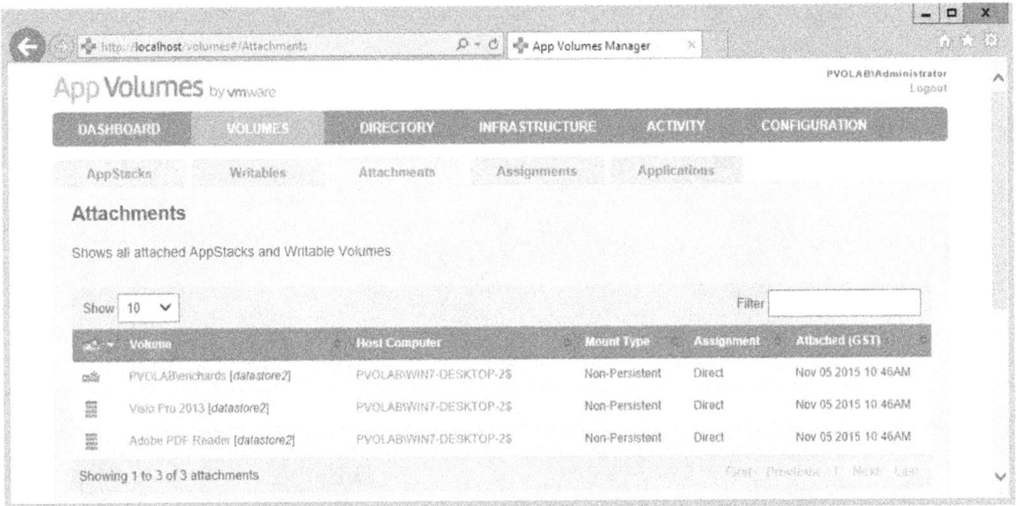

As a key to the icons shown in the screenshot, here are what the icons represent:

Now that we have seen what's going on behind the scenes, we are going to put the newly created Writable Volume to use and install an application as the user.

In this example, we are going to install **GIMP 2**.

While still logged in as the user `Ellie Richards`, install the application as you would normally install any other application. App Volumes Agent will redirect the installed files to the Writable Volume.

> It's worth remembering that any users that you are going to allow to install their own applications will need to have correct permission levels in order to allow them to do this. Ensure they have permission or are members of groups that have the correct permission levels.

Once the application has been installed, the desktop of the virtual desktop machine will look like the following screenshot:

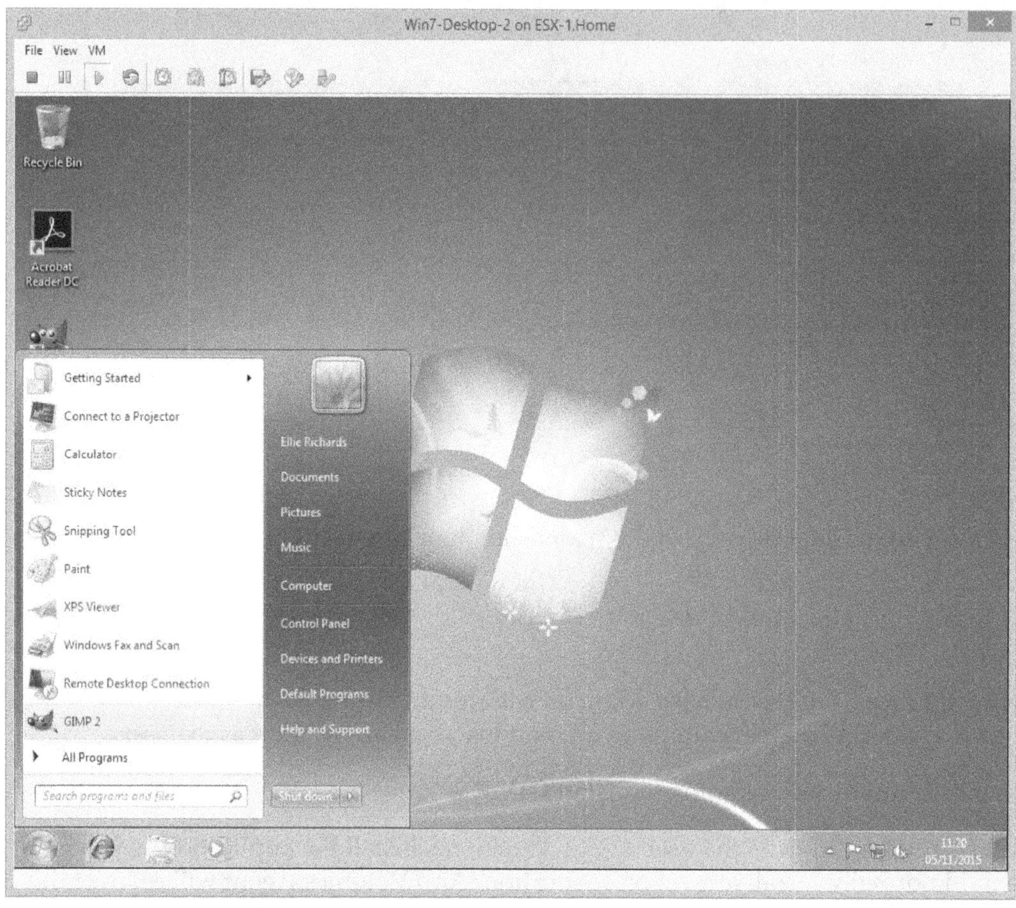

With the application now installed, we should see a change in the file size of the Writable Volume, as shown in the following screenshot:

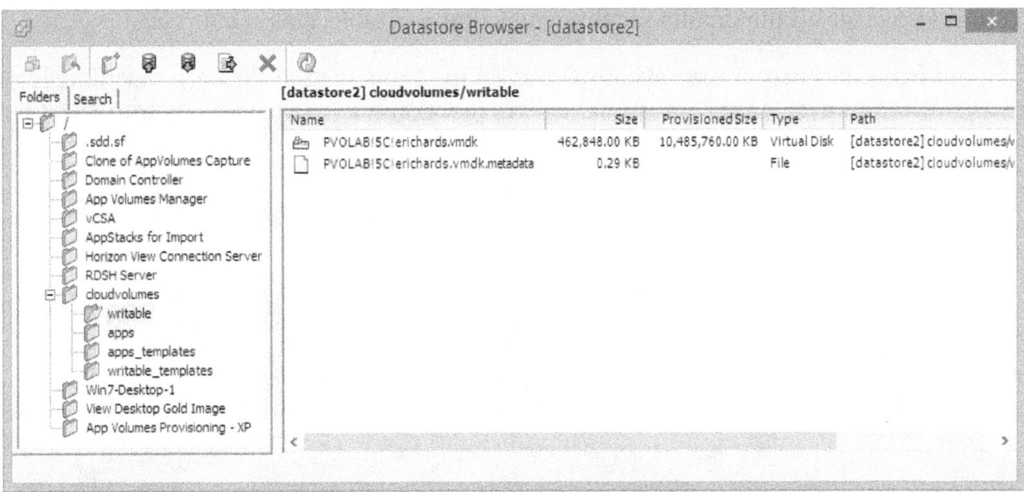

As you can see, the size of the Writable Volume is now nearly 463 MB as it now contains the files from the installation of the application.

You can switch back to App Volumes Manager console and look at the **Writables** tab. Click on the **+/- (11)** button to expand the details, as shown here:

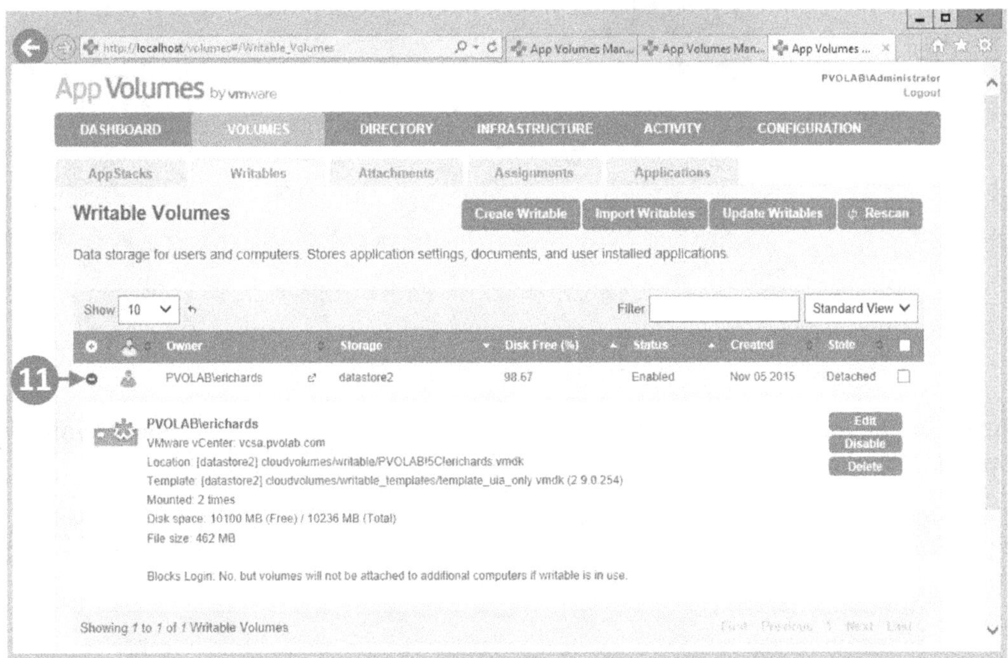

You can now see all the details for that particular Writable Volume.

Log out from the current user account, and on the same virtual desktop machine, log in as a different user. In this example, we are just going to log in as the administrator, as shown in the following screenshot:

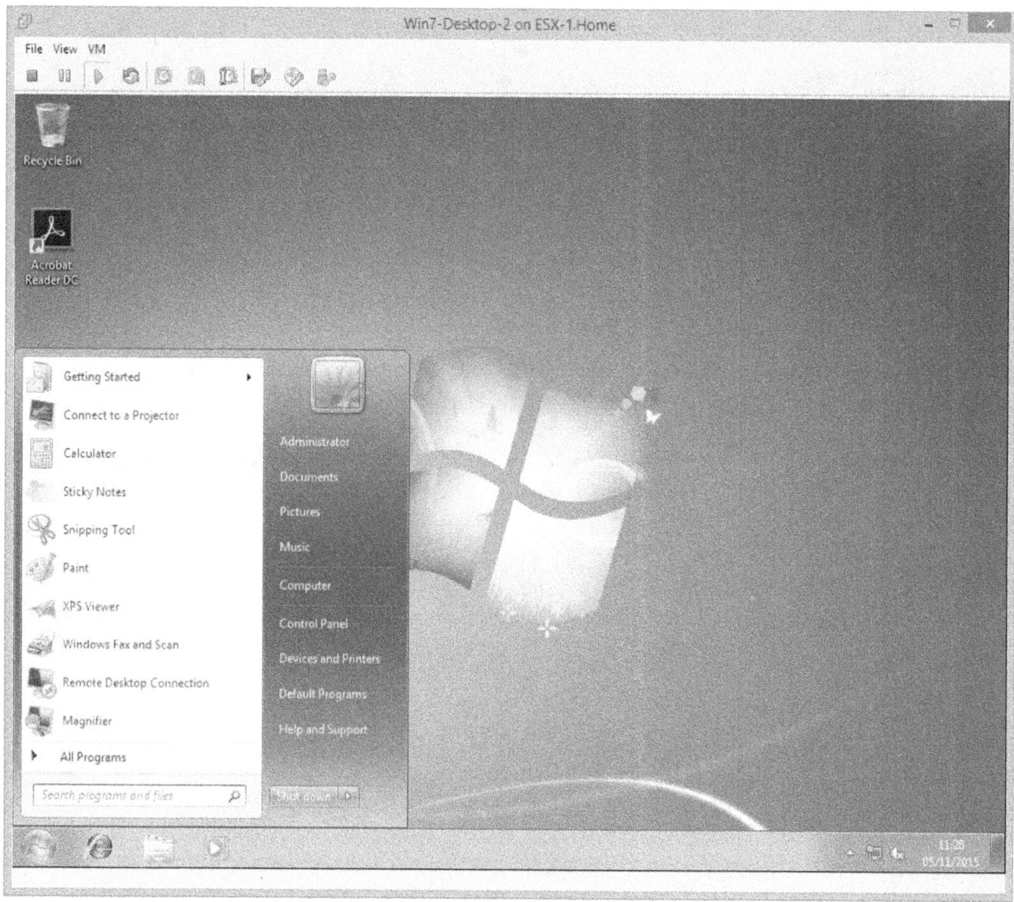

As we are now logged in as another user, the GIMP application is no longer available on this virtual desktop machine, even though it's the same machine.

The application is contained within the Writable Volume that belongs to the user `Ellie Richards` and as such, the Writable Volume will only be attached to a virtual desktop machine that she logs in to.

Managing Writable Volumes

In this section, we will look at the ongoing tasks you can perform on Writable Volumes, along with other general management tasks and processes.

All of these tasks are performed from the App Volumes Manager console.

Importing Writable Volumes

The import a Writable Volume feature allows you to import existing Writable Volumes that could be part of another App Volumes deployment.

For example, you may create a number of Writable Volumes as part of a pilot project, and when you deploy the technology in production, you could import those existing Writable Volumes rather than have the end users create them again.

To import a Writable Volume, perform the following steps:

1. Click on the **VOLUMES** menu option **(1)** and then, from the **Writables** tab **(2)**, click on the **Import Writables** button **(3)**, as shown in the following diagram:

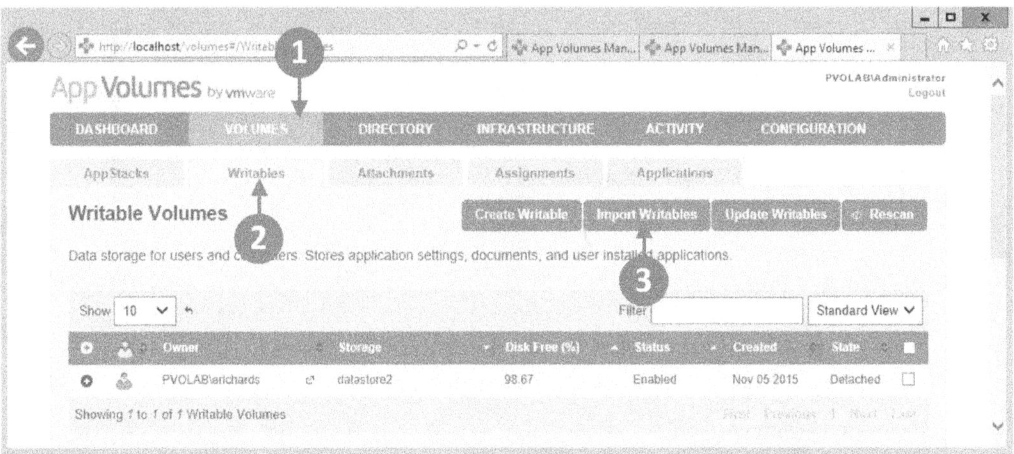

You will now see the **Import Writable Volumes** page, shown in the following diagram:

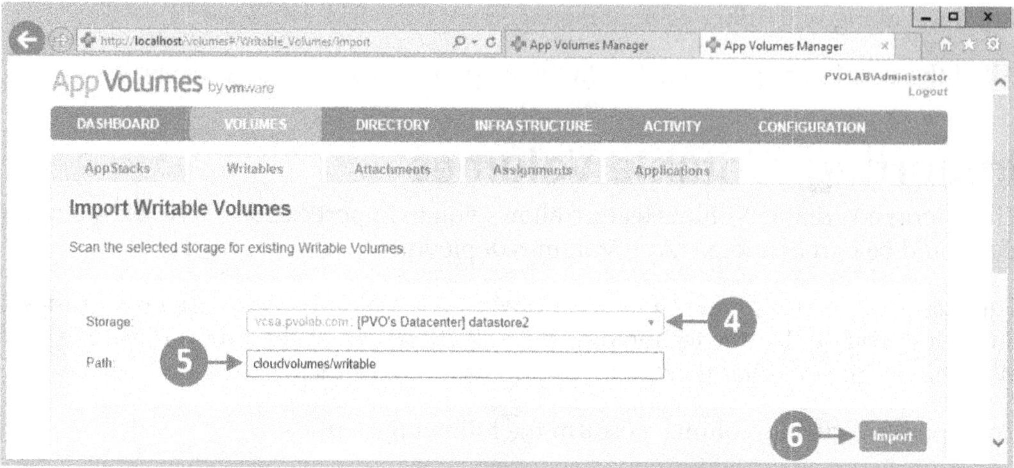

2. In the **Storage** box **(4)**, from the drop-down menu, select the datastore that contains the Writable Volume that you want to import.

> You can either copy your existing Writable Volumes that you want to import into a different folder on the same datastore using the datastore browser feature in vCenter, or ensure that your vCenter Server has access to the other datastore. From a management perspective, ensure that you know which is which.

3. In the **Path** box **(5)**, enter the path that contains the Writable Volumes that you want to import. If you have created a new folder, containing your AppStacks for import, which is the recommended option, then enter this information here.

4. Once you have entered the information, click on the **Import** button **(6)**. You will now see the **Confirm Import Writable Volumes** dialog box, shown in the following figure:

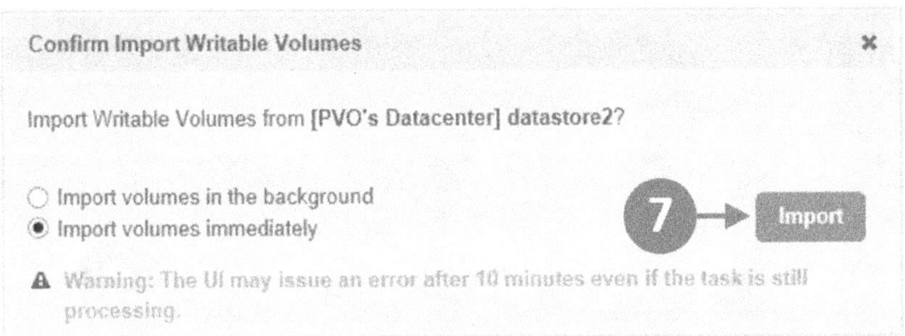
Confirm Import Writable Volumes
Import Writable Volumes from [PVO's Datacenter] datastore2?
Import volumes in the background
Import volumes immediately
7
Import
Warning: The UI may issue an error after 10 minutes even if the task is still processing.

There are two options for when the import task completes and the Writable Volumes are imported: the Writable Volume is either imported immediately or in the background.

5. In this example, click on the radio button for **Import volumes immediately**, and click on the **Import** button **(7)**. You will see the following message as the Writable Volumes are imported:

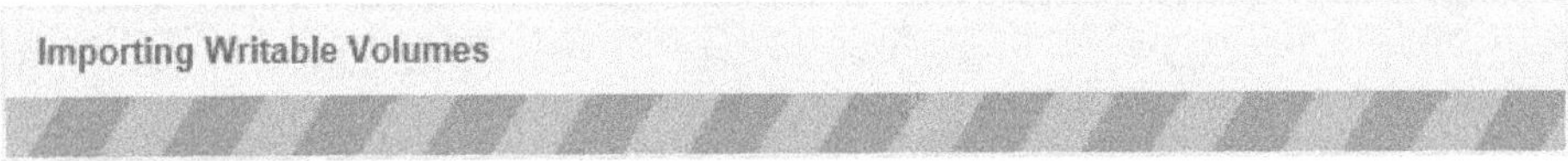
Importing Writable Volumes

The Writable Volumes will now be imported and displayed.

In the next section, we will look at updating Writable Volumes.

Updating Writable Volumes

In this section, we will look at how you can update an existing Writable Volume. A Writable Volume belongs to an end user and will likely contain applications that they have installed. As such, you as the IT admin cannot update these. The update feature for Writable Volumes will just allow you to add files to that hard disk.

To update a Writable Volume, perform the following steps:

1. Click on the **VOLUMES** menu option **(1)** and then, from the **Writables** tab **(2)**, click on the **Update Writables** button **(3)**, as shown in the following figure:

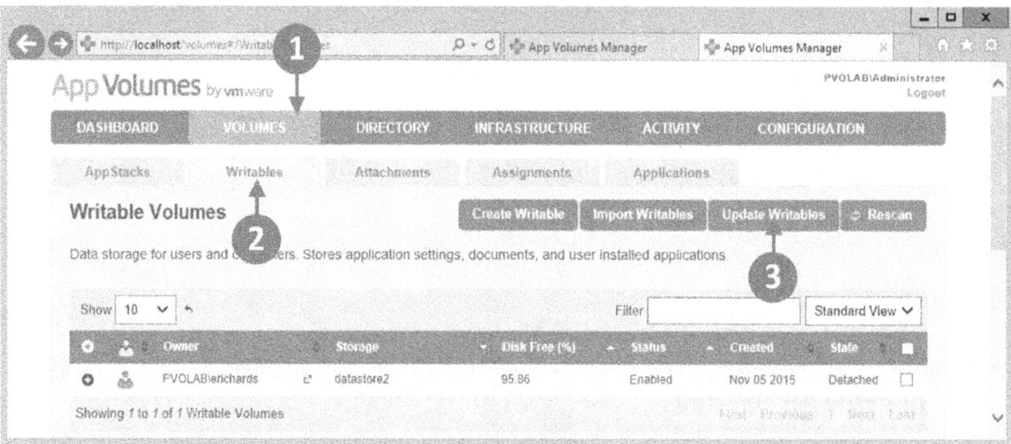

   You will now see the **Update Writable Volumes** page, shown in the following diagram:

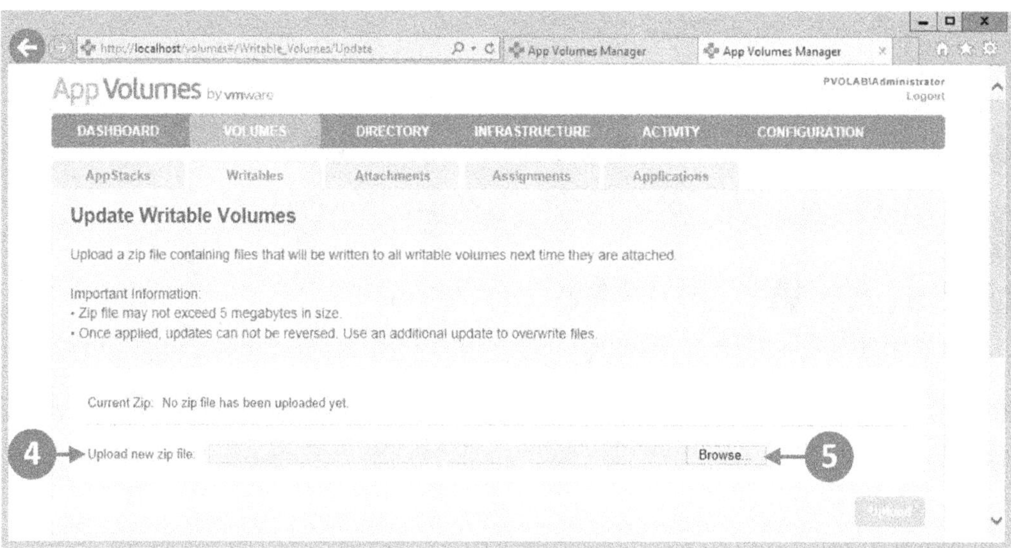

2. Here, in the **Upload new zip file** box **(4)**, you can enter the details of a ZIP file to upload to the Writable Volumes.
3. If you want to select a file, then click on **Browse (5)**. You will see the **Choose File to Upload** dialog box, shown in the following diagram:

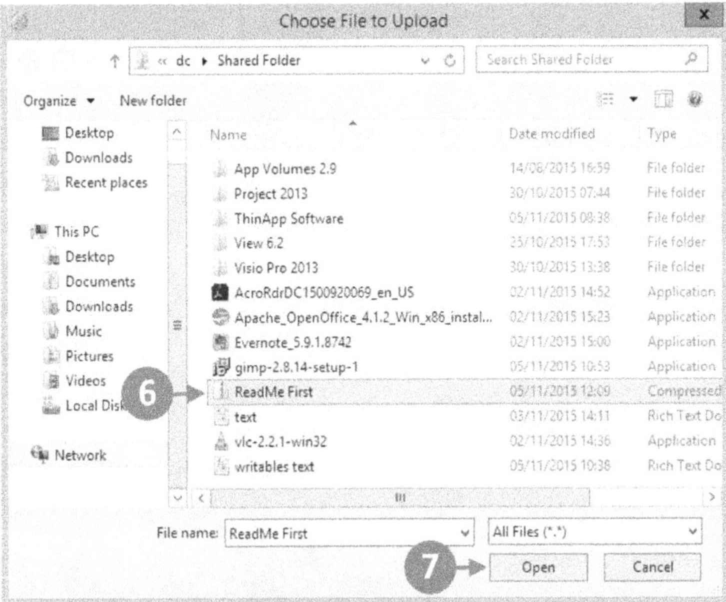

4. In this example, we have a ZIP file called **ReadMe First (6)**. Click to highlight this file and then click on the **Open** button **(7)**.

5. You will now return to the **Update Writable Volumes** screen, shown in the following diagram:

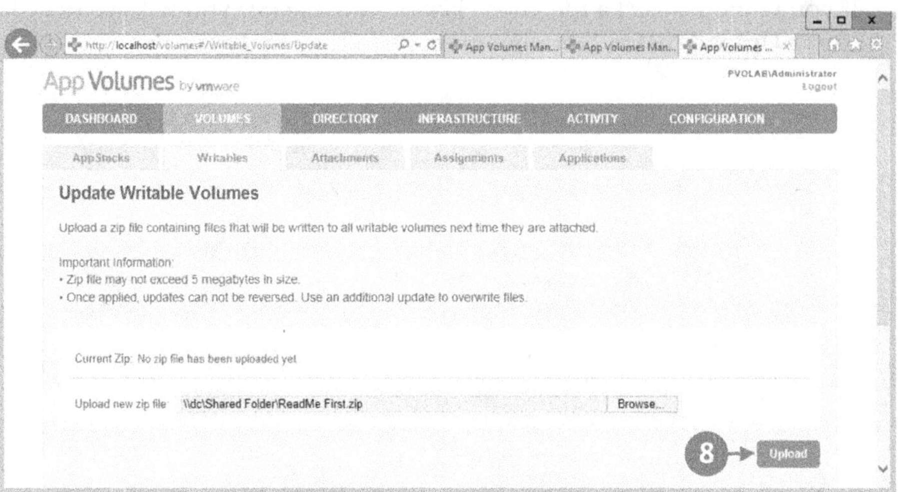

6. Click on the **Upload** button **(8)**. You will see the following progress bar as the file is uploaded to the Writable Volumes:

Once the upload has completed, you will return to the **Update Writable Volumes** page. You will now see the details of the upload, as shown in the following diagram:

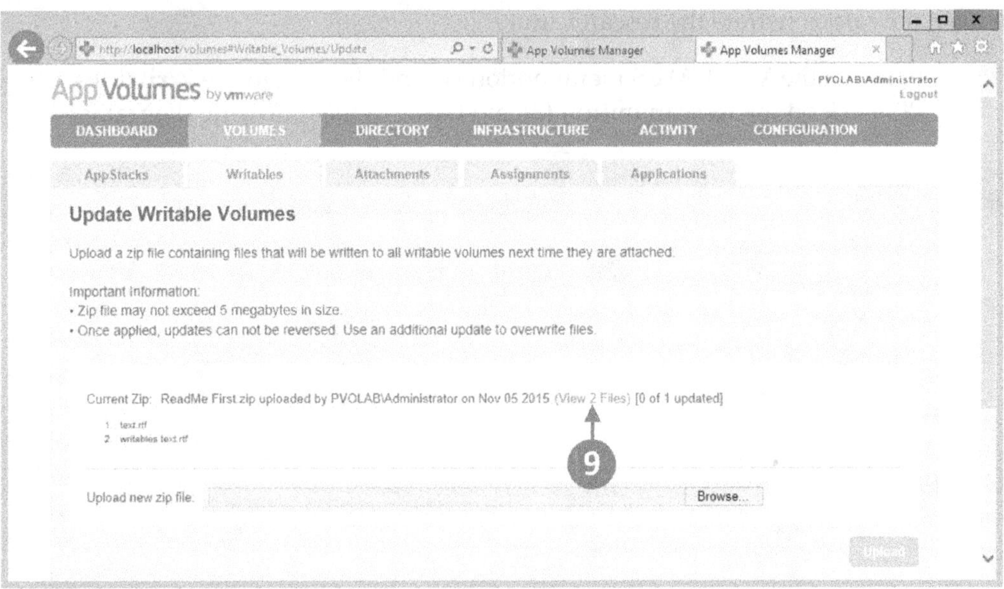

The details of the file that was uploaded are shown. If you click on the **View 2 Files** link **(9)**, the individual files will be listed.

You have now successfully updated a Writable Volume. In the next section, we will look at the rescan feature.

Rescanning Writable Volumes

The Writable Volumes rescan feature updates the current Writable Volumes inventory from the Writable Volumes information held on the datastore to ensure that the Writable Volumes still exist and are accessible.

To demonstrate the outcome of this, before performing the rescan, log in to vCenter, and using the datastore browser, temporarily move one of the current Writable Volumes to a different datastore.

In this example, browse to the `cloudvolumes/writable` directory. We only have a single Writable Volume called `PVOLAB!5C!erichards.vmdk`, so move this file from `datastore2` to `datastore1`.

We can now demonstrate the rescan feature:

1. Click on the **VOLUMES** menu option **(1)** and then, from the **Writables** tab **(2)**, click on the **Rescan** button **(3)**, as shown in the following diagram:

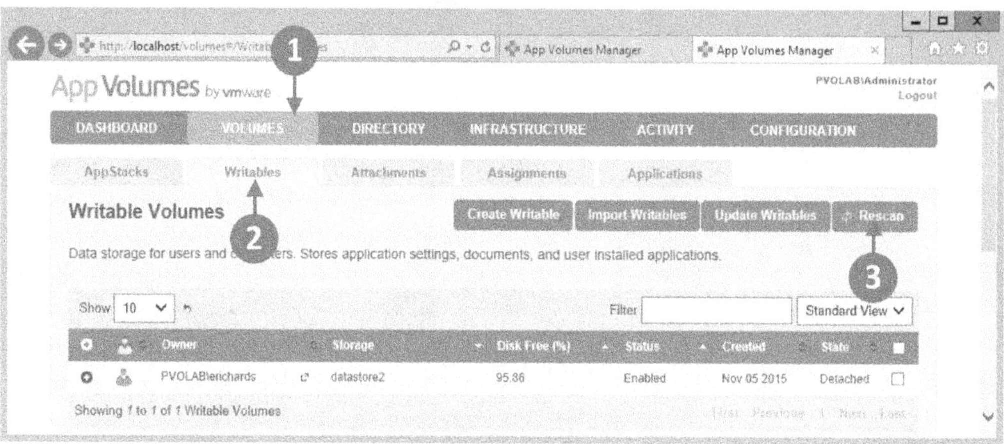

You will now see the following **Confirm Rescan** dialog box:

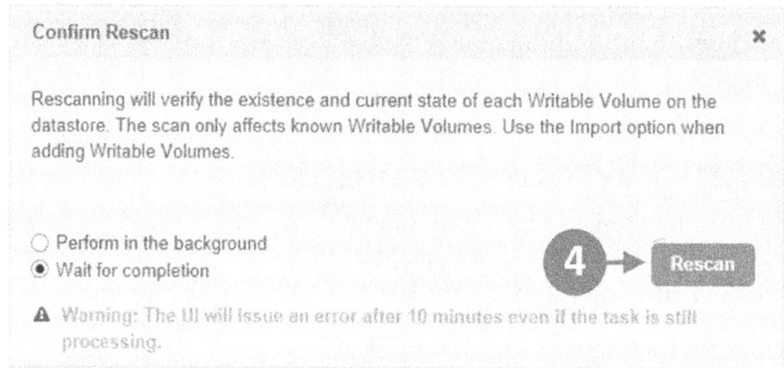

There are two options for when the rescan task completes. You can either wait for the rescan to complete or perform it in the background.

2. In this example, click on the radio button for **Wait for completion**, and click on the **Rescan** button **(4)**. You will see the following message as the datastore is scanned for Writable Volumes:

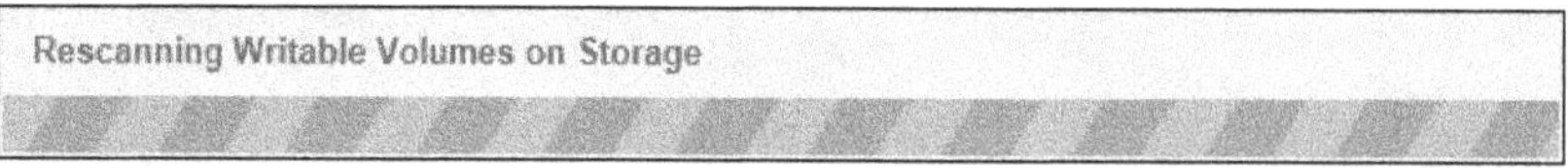

Once the rescan has completed, you will return to the Writable Volumes page, shown in the following diagram:

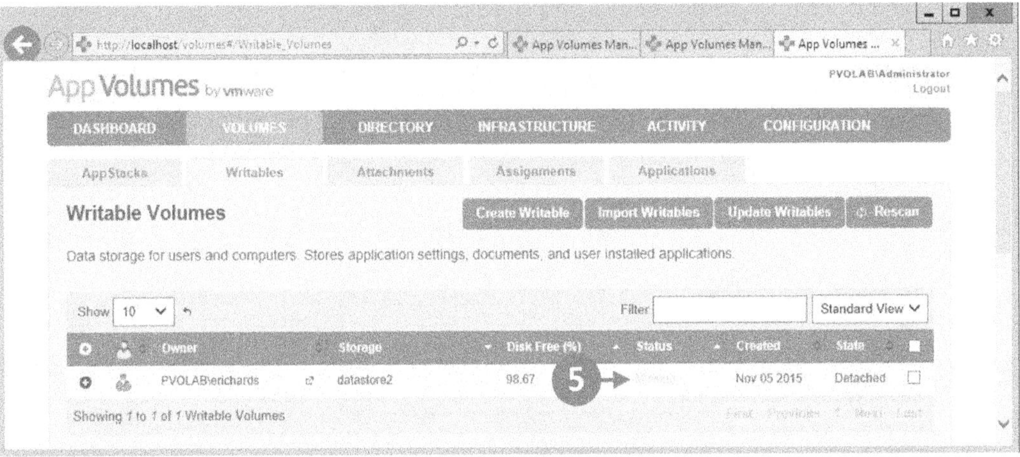

You will see that the **Status** column is now reporting the Writable Volume as **Missing (5)**.

Now, go back to vCenter, and using the datastore browser, move the Writable Volume back to its original storage location from `datastore1` back to `datastore2`, ensuring it goes back in the `cloudvolumes/writables` folder.

Once you have done that, perform the rescan again and make sure the Writable Volume now appears in the inventory with the status of **Enabled**.

You have now successfully performed a rescan of the Writable Volumes.

In the next section, we will look at how to edit a Writable Volume.

Editing a Writable Volume

Once you have created and assigned a Writable Volume, you have the ability to edit some of the settings.

To edit a Writable Volume, perform the following steps:

1. Click on the **VOLUMES** menu option **(1)** and then, from the **Writables** tab **(2)**, check the box next to the Writable Volume you want to edit. In this example we only have one Writable Volume, so check the box **(3)** to highlight it.

2. Now, click on the **Edit** button **(4)**, shown in the following diagram:

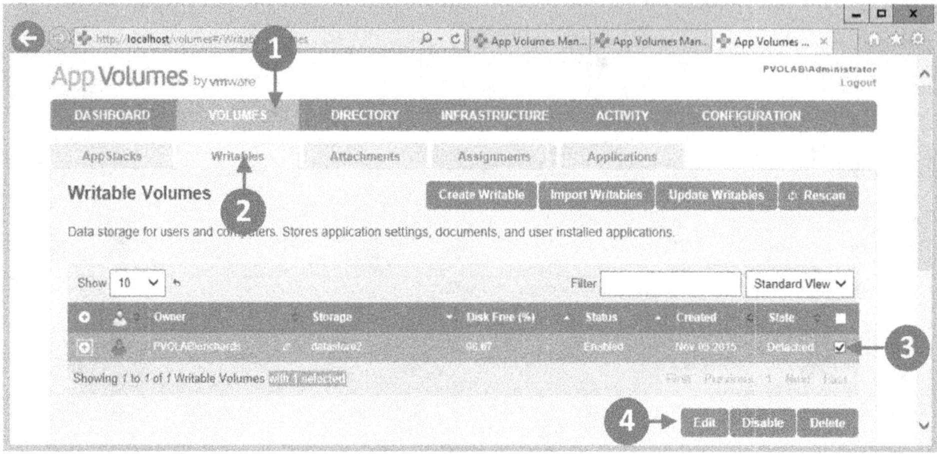

You will now see the **Edit Writable** page, shown in the following diagram:

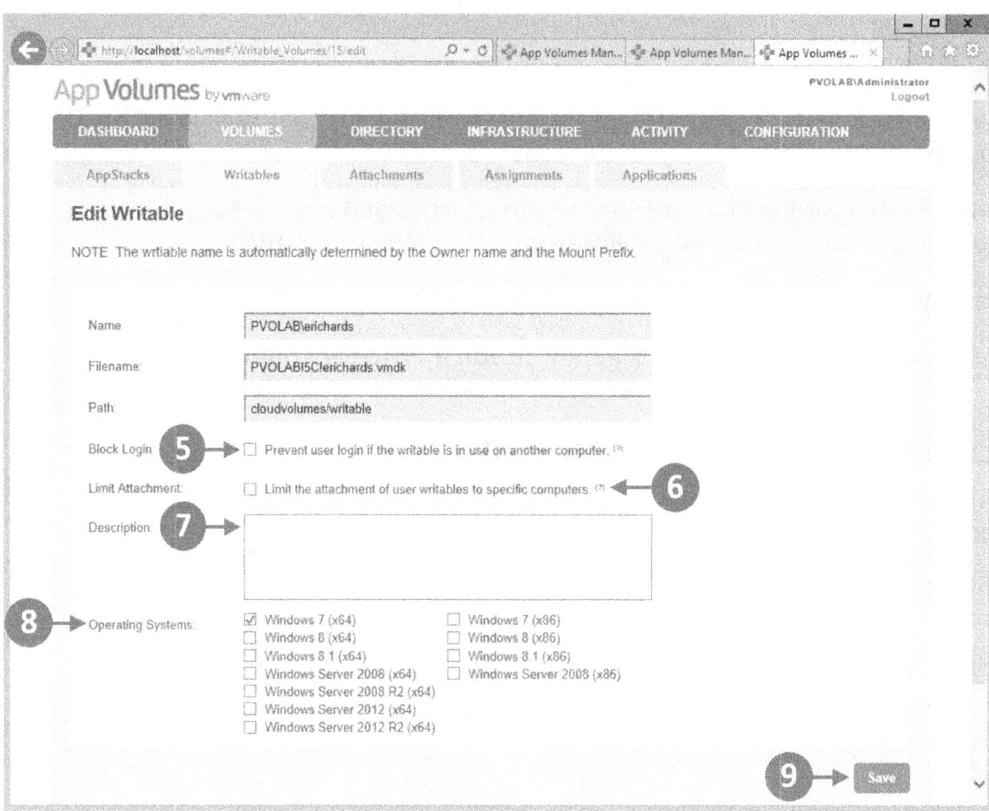

3. You cannot change the name, filename, or path details. The first options you can edit are the **Block Login** option **(5)** and the **Limit the attachment of user writables to specific computer** option **(6)**. Both of these options have been covered in the beginning of the *Creating your first Writable Volume* section of this chapter, so for more details on these settings, refer back to it.
4. The next option is **Description (7)**, which allows you to enter a description for this Writable Volume.
5. Finally, in the **Operating System** section **(8)**, there is also the option to select the operating system compatibility. Here, you can select which operating systems the Writable Volume supports.

> When selecting an operating system, ensure that the applications and data contained in the Writable Volume will run on the operating system you select. As these applications are end-user owned, it's worth checking with them before making any changes. This option would basically prevent them from using other operating systems, which, if part of a development role, would negatively impact the end users.

6. Once you have made your changes, click on the **Save** button **(9)**. You will be prompted to confirm the changes you have made, as shown in the following figure:

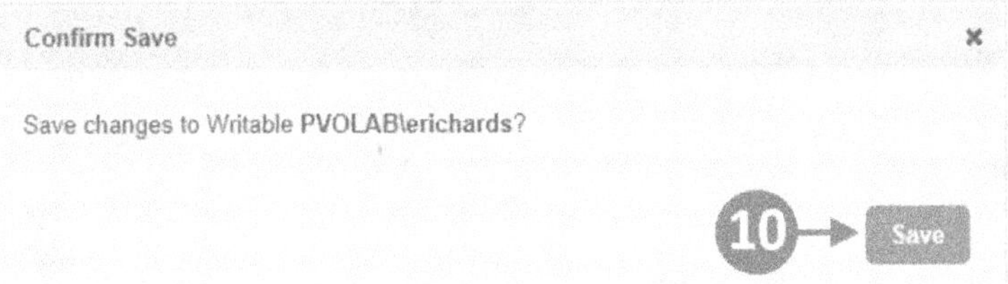

7. Click on the **Save** button **(10)**. You will see the following message as the Writable Volumes details are saved:

You have now successfully edited the Writable Volumes configuration.

In the next section, we will look at how to disable a Writable Volume.

Disabling a Writable Volume

In this section, we will look at how to disable a Writable Volume, effectively preventing the end user from having access to it. It does not delete the Writable Volume.

To disable a Writable Volume, perform the following steps:

1. Click on the **VOLUMES** menu option **(1)** and then, from the **Writables** tab **(2)**, check the box next to the Writable Volume you want to edit. In this example, we only have one Writable Volume, so check the box **(3)** to highlight it.

   Now, click on the **Disable** button **(4)**, as shown in the following diagram:

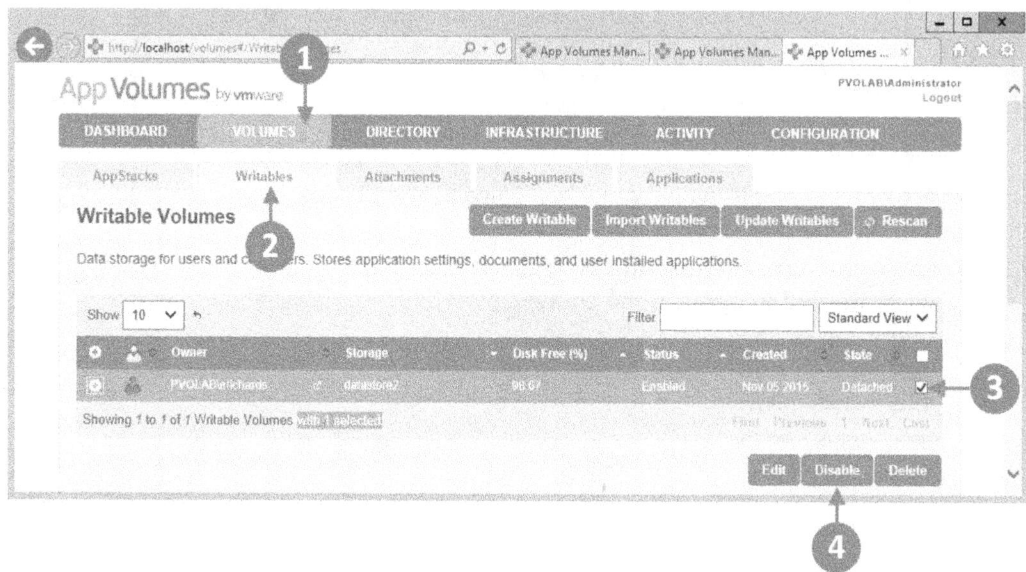

   You will now see the **Confirm Disable** dialog box, shown in the following figure:

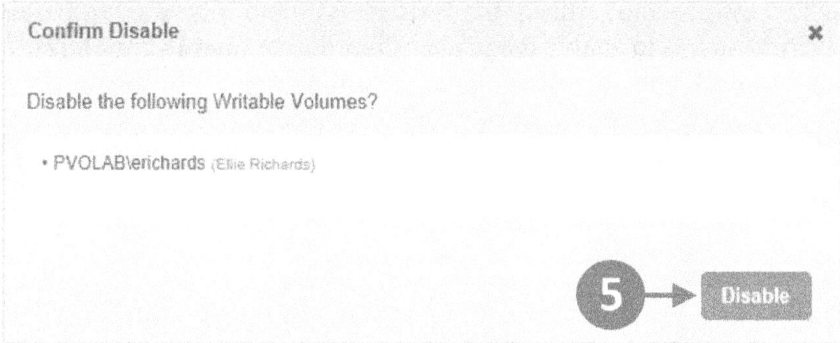

2. Click on **Disable (5)** to disable user access to the Writable Volume. You will see the following message as the Writable Volume is disabled:

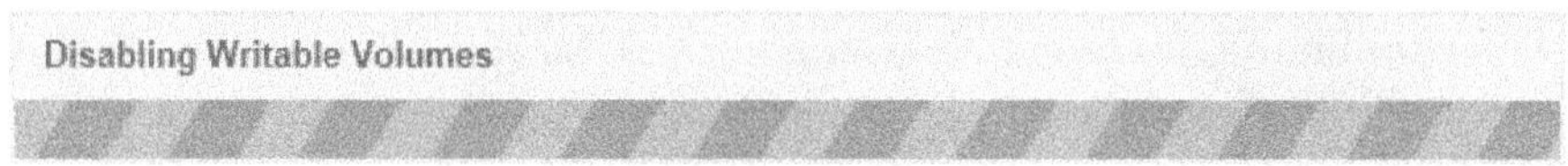

You will now return to the **Writable Volumes** page, shown in the following diagram:

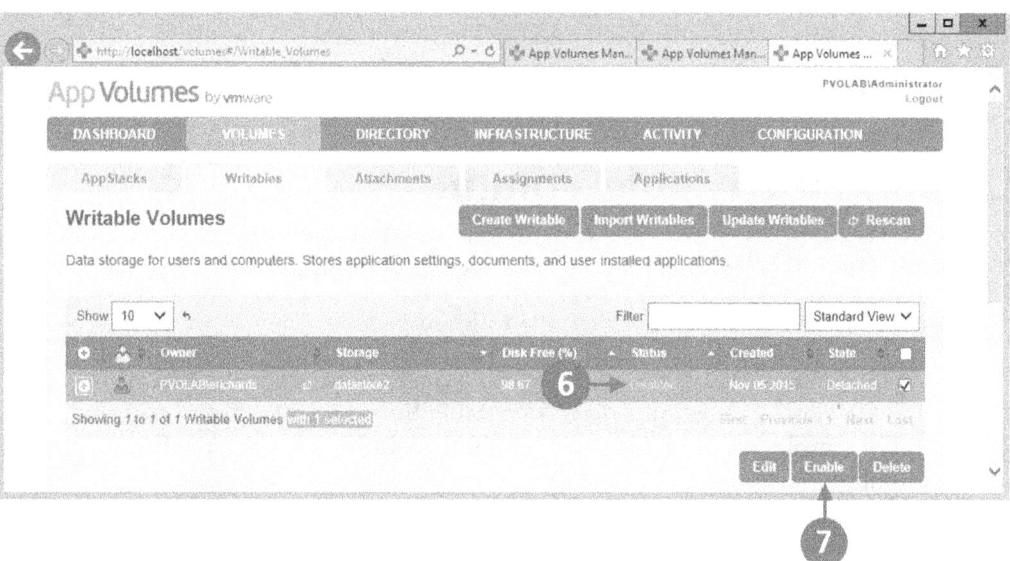

3. As you can see, the status of the Writable Volume is now set to **Disabled (6)**. The next step is to enable it again, so click on the **Enable** button **(7)**. You will now see the **Confirm Enable** dialog box, shown in the following diagram:

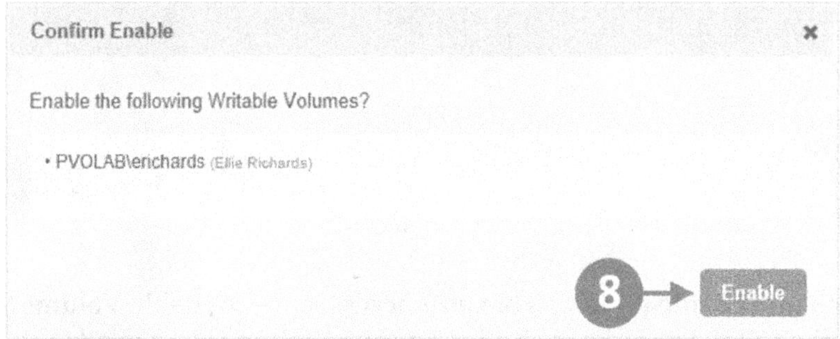

4. Click on **Enable (8)** to enable user access to the Writable Volume. You will see the following message as the Writable Volume is enabled:

You have now successfully disabled and enabled a Writable Volume.

In the next section, we will look at how to delete a Writable Volume.

Deleting a Writable Volume

In this final section, we will look at how to delete a Writable Volume, removing it completely from App Volumes Manager as well as deleting it from the datastore.

To delete a Writable Volume, perform the following steps:

1. Click on the **VOLUMES** menu option **(1)** and then, from the **Writables** tab **(2)**, check the box next to the Writable Volume you want to edit. In this example, we only have one Writable Volume, so check the box **(3)** to highlight it.
2. Now, click on the **Delete** button **(4)**, as shown in the following figure:

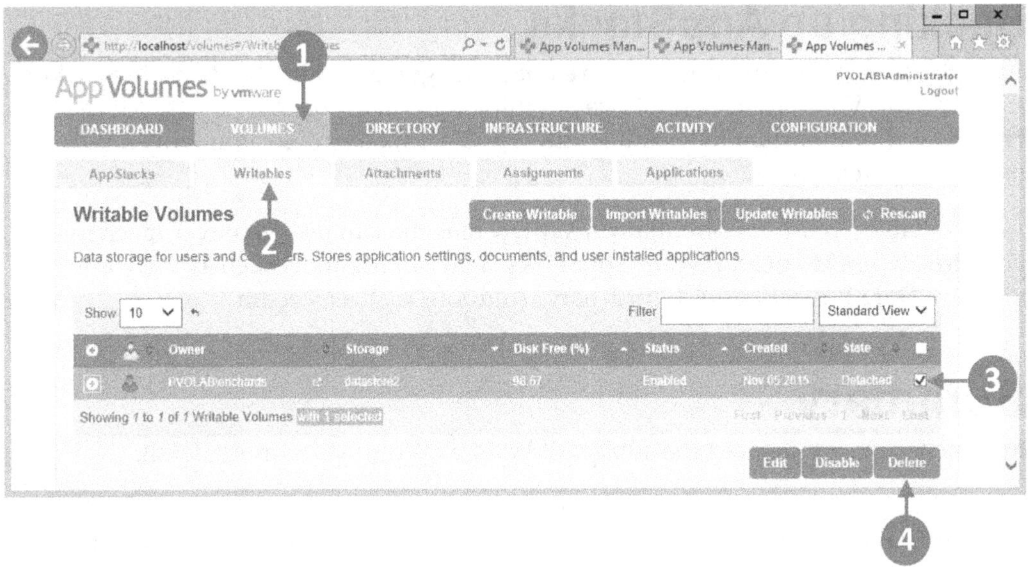

You will now see the **Confirm Delete** dialog box, shown in the following figure:

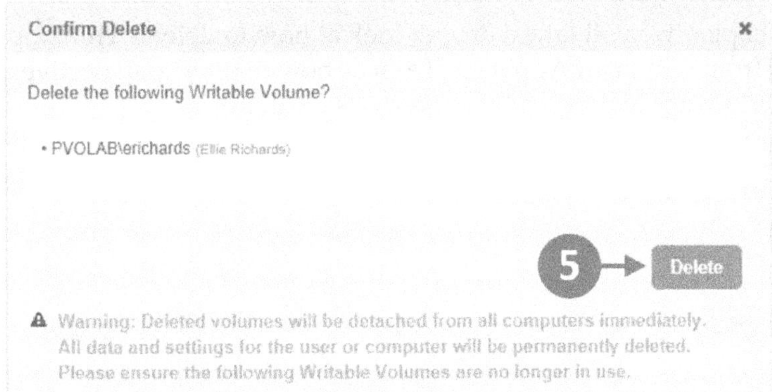

3. Click on the **Delete** button **(5)**.

You will see a message displayed as the Writable Volume is deleted, and once the task has completed, you will have successfully deleted the Writable Volume.

In the next section, we will touch on backing up your Writable Volumes.

Backing up AppStacks

As with the AppStacks chapter, we are not really going to talk about specific backup tools, as App Volumes does not have anything built in for backing up AppStacks. However, it is important to back up your AppStacks; otherwise, you will end up having to recreate them.

As a Writable Volume is essentially a VMDK file, you can use whatever mechanism you already use to back up your AppStacks. You can use tools such as VMware **vSphere Data Protection** or a third-party solution, such as **Veeam**.

Summary

In this chapter, we covered the subject of Writable Volumes in more detail.

We started off by describing the how Writable Volumes work from a process and architectural point of view, before moving on to create our first Writable Volume.

Once we created a Writable Volume, we went on to show how it worked, by logging is as an end user, installing applications, and then moving from one virtual desktop to another. Finally, we looked at how to perform some of the ongoing management of the Writable Volumes, such as updates and other general admin tasks.

In the next chapter, we will take a deeper look at how to deliver ThinApp packaged applications from within an AppStack, from a "how to do it" perspective as well as why you would want to do it and the use cases for doing so.

8
Delivering ThinApp Packages with App Volumes

In this chapter, for those that have not used this solution before, we will start by discussing what the ThinApp solution is and what it offers. We will then go on to look at the use cases and how and why you would deliver ThinApp packaged applications with App Volumes.

Once we have described the technology and the use cases, we will go on to look at a couple of scenarios: how to create and deliver a new ThinApp package, including how to create a simple package, and then how to deliver existing ThinApp packages with App Volumes.

What is ThinApp?

Let's quickly start off by describing what ThinApp is for those of you who are new to the technology or don't know that much about it.

ThinApp is an agentless application-virtualization or application-packaging solution that decouples applications from the underlying operating systems. It's designed to eliminate application conflict and streamline application delivery and management. ThinApp licenses come as part of the Horizon View license and can be used on both physical and virtual desktop machines, therefore providing a mechanism for delivering applications across your entire end-user estate.

What is application virtualization?

ThinApp encapsulates applications into a package consisting of a single `.exe` or `.msi` file and abstracts them from the following:

- The host operating system
- Any traditionally installed applications already running on the system
- All other virtual applications running on the system

It has the following features:

- Applications are run in a virtual environment with minimal or zero impact on the underlying operating system, **virtual file system**, and **virtual registry**
- They are easily deployed, upgraded, managed, and retired

Understanding ThinApp application virtualization

When you create a ThinApp package, you are basically capturing all the application files, registry settings, and file system that an application requires in order to run. As part of the capture process, it also captures its own agent, so the end client requires nothing to be installed.

Once packaged, the application can be deployed (either streamed or installed) onto the virtual desktop machine or even a physical desktop. The only requirement for a ThinApp package to run is the Windows operating system, irrespective of whether the desktop is virtual or physical. It's important to note that when it runs, the package makes no changes to the operating system of the machine it's running on.

There are no requirements for backend infrastructure either, and all your ThinApp packaged applications are stored on a file share on a file server. This means that you can centrally manage and update your packages so that all users receive the updates the next time they launch the application.

We can summarize ThinApp in the following points:

- It allows Windows applications to be packaged, distributed and executed as a single `.exe` or `.msi` file on either physical or virtual machines
- The build process "links" a **virtual operating system** (**VOS**) with a compressed embedded file system and registry into a single file
- It requires no preinstalled software on the end-user machine

- It has zero footprint on the underlying OS
- No traditional installation or changes to the local OS registry or file system are required
- No backend server infrastructure is required other than a file share to store your ThinApp packages.

For a detailed deep-dive of ThinApp, you can read *VMware ThinApp 4.7 Essentials, Peter Bjork, Packt Publishing*.

Why is this different from App Volumes?

As we have just discussed, ThinApp is an application-packaging technology that is used to create an isolated instance of an application that has no dependencies on the underlying Windows operating system, therefore allowing it to be portable and execute on other versions of the Windows operating system.

App Volumes provides a just-in-time delivery mechanism of applications.

Combining the two solutions now allows you to have real-time delivery of applications that are completely isolated from the operating system, meaning that you can deploy multiple versions of the same application knowing that there will be no conflicts.

Throughout this chapter, we will demonstrate this capability and look at how to deliver ThinApp packaged applications using App Volumes.

We will cover two specific scenarios: the first is how to create a brand-new ThinApp package and deliver it as an AppStack, and the second is how to update an existing ThinApp package that was originally created as an executable file (`.exe`) and create an AppStack for it. In this scenario, we will also look at an alternative option utilizing the tools available with ThinApp.

Let's look at the process for building a new ThinApp for an AppStack first.

Creating a new ThinApp

This section is going to start off by demonstrating how to build a new ThinApp package, before going on to create an AppStack to deliver it.

For this example, we are going to use the virtual desktop machine called `WinXP-Desktop-1`, which has ThinApp Enterprise 5.1.1 already installed on it.

The process we are going to follow is illustrated in the following diagram:

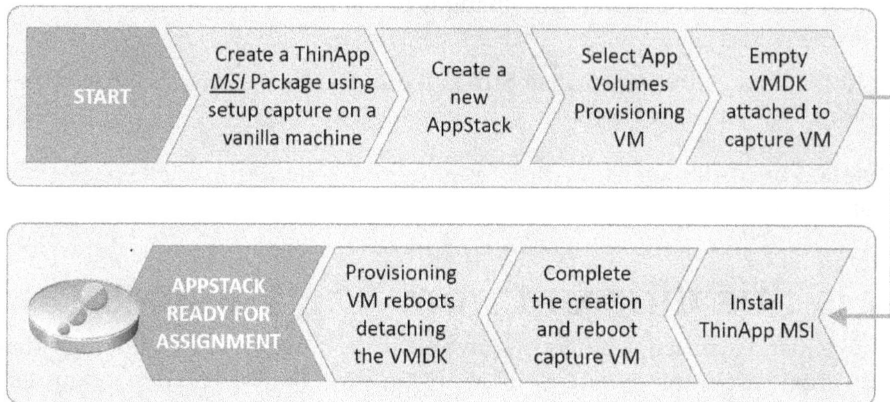

The first task we are going to cover is creating a new `.msi` packaged ThinApp using the Setup Capture utility.

Running Setup Capture

So, the first thing we need to do is capture the application we want to package. In this example, we are going to create a package for **GIMP 2**.

On the virtual desktop machine `WinXP-Desktop-1`, launch the ThinApp Setup Capture utility. You will see the **Setup Capture - Welcome** screen, shown in the following diagram:

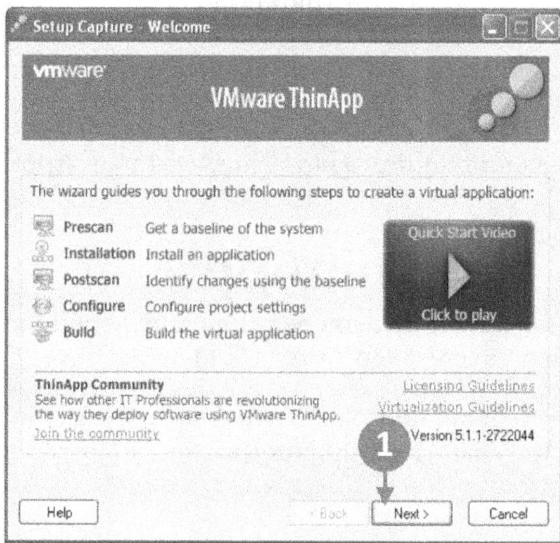

Perform the following steps:

1. Click on the **Next >** button **(1)** to continue. The next screen is the **Setup Capture - Ready to Prescan** screen. This step performs a scan of the machine state of your virtual desktop machine before you install any applications. This is shown in the following diagram:

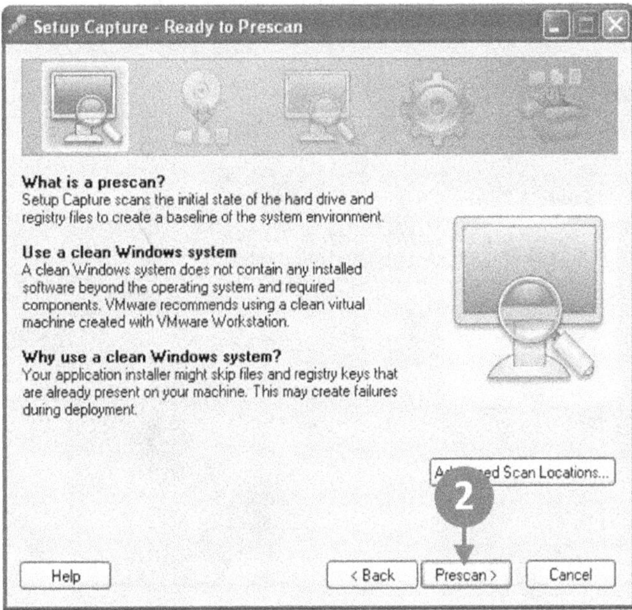

2. Click on the **Prescan >** button **(2)** to start the scan process.
3. The next screen displays the progress of the prescan process. Once it has completed, click on the **Next >** button to continue.

4. The next screen is the **Setup Capture -Install Application** screen, shown in the following diagram:

DO NOT click on anything on this screen until you have installed the application. Now go ahead and perform the installation. In our example, we are going to install GIMP 2, performing the installation as we would normally and making any configuration changes we need to make.

5. Once the application has been installed, click on the **Postscan >** button **(3)** to start the postscan process, as shown in the following screenshot:

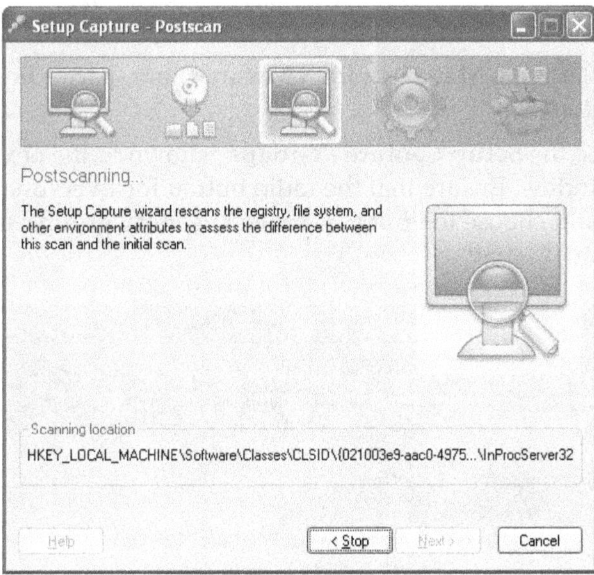

6. Once the postscan has completed, click on the **Next >** button. You will now see the **Setup Capture - Entry Points** screen, shown in the following diagram:

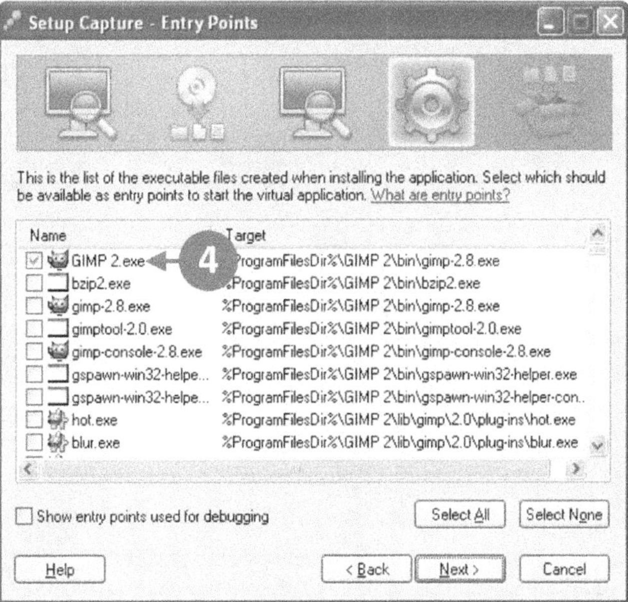

> Ensure that an entry point is selected. An entry point is where you would start the application from. In this case, ensure that `GIMP 2.exe` is selected, by checking the box **(4)**.

7. On the next screen, **Manage with VMware Workspace**, click on the **Next >** button.
8. You will see the **Setup Capture - Groups** , shown in the next diagramwindow. Ensure that the radio button for **Everyone** is selected **(5)**. You could choose to limit the Active Directory groups; however, App Volumes can do that:

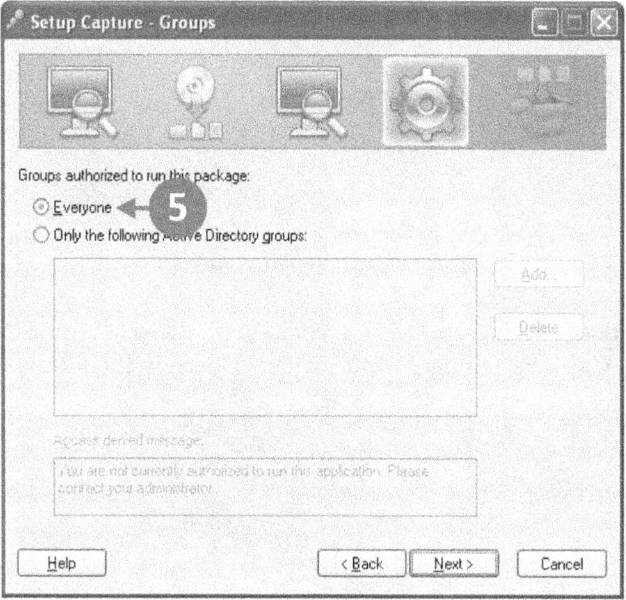

9. Click the **Next >** button to continue. Next you will see the **Setup Capture - Isolation** screen as shown in the following screenshot:

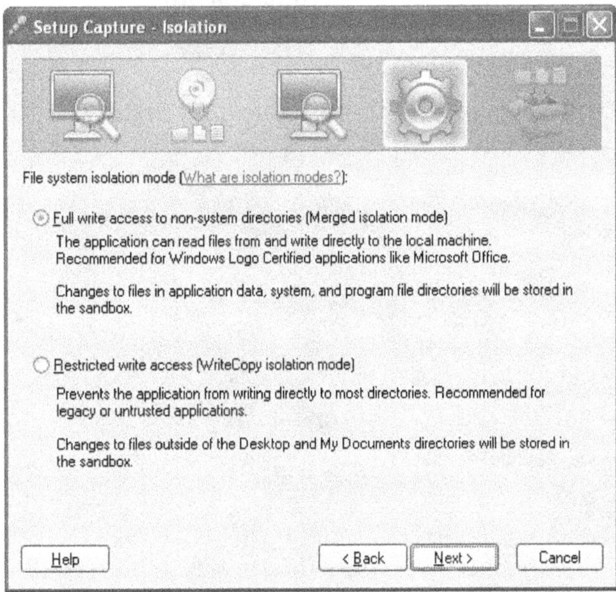

10. Check the radio button for full write access, and then click on the **Next >** button to continue. Next, you will see the **Setup Capture - Sandbox** screen, shown in the following screenshot:

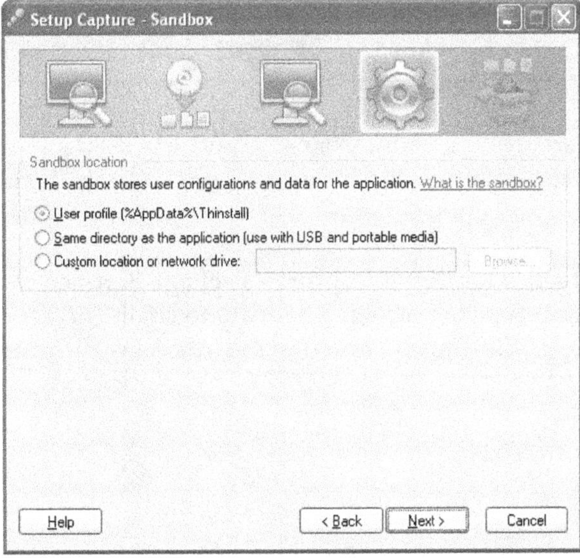

11. Check the radio button for **User profile (%AppData%Thinstall)**, and then click on the **Next >** button to continue.
12. Next, you will see the **Quality Assurance Statistics** screen. Check the radio button for **No – Do not send any information to VMware**, and then click on the **Next >** button to continue.

    Next, you will see the **Setup Capture - Project Settings** screen, shown in the following screenshot:

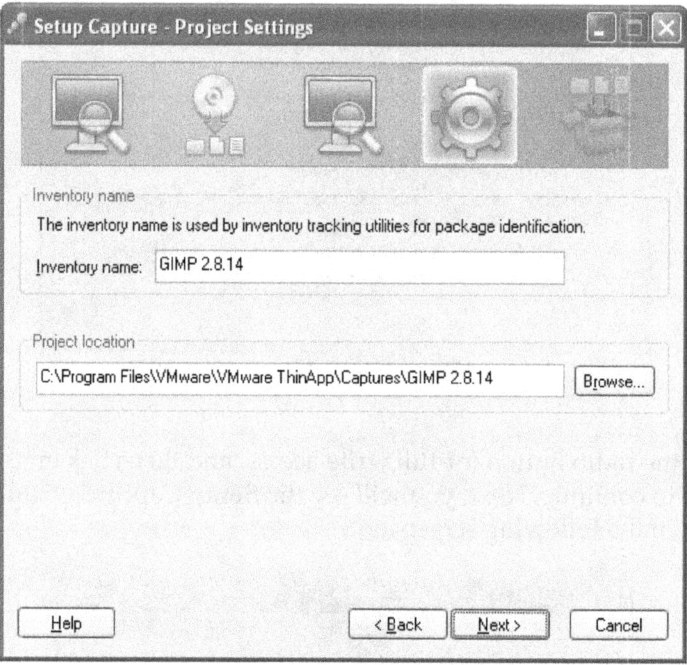

    Here, you can give the package a name and specify the location of the project and build files. In this example, we are going to leave them as the defaults.

13. Click on the **Next >** button to continue.
14. The next screen is for **Setup Capture - Package Settings**, which allows you to configure what type of package you want to create. In this example, we want to create a `.msi` file. This is shown in the following diagram:

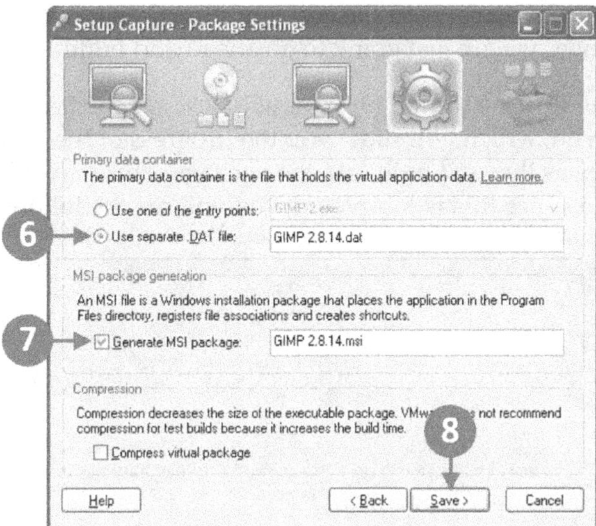

15. First, click on the radio button to select **Use separate .DAT file (6)**, and then check the box **(7)** for **Generate MSI package**. You can also change the filenames if you want to, but in this example, we will leave them as default.
16. Click on **Save > (8)** to continue.
17. The project files are then saved, and the progress is shown in the next screenshot. Once this is completed, click on the **Next >** button to continue. You will now see the **Setup Capture - Ready to Build** screen, shown in the following diagram:

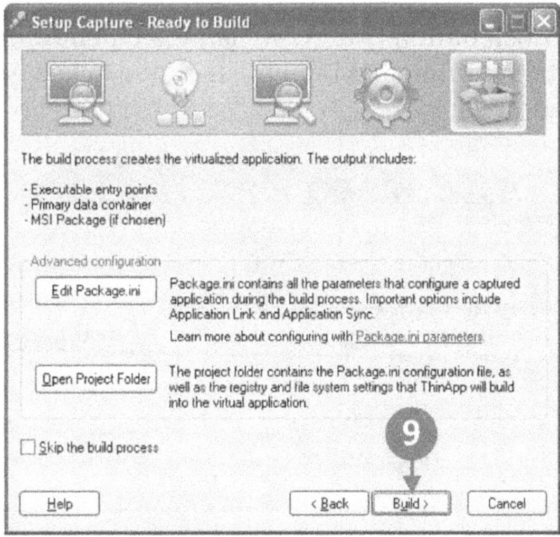

On this screen, you can edit the configuration details or look at the project files; however, we are just going to go ahead and build the package.

18. Click on the **Build >** button **(9)**. You will now see the **Setup Capture - Build Project** screen, which will show you the progress of the build and the files and settings as they get built into the package. This may take a few minutes to complete. Once this is completed, you will see the following window:

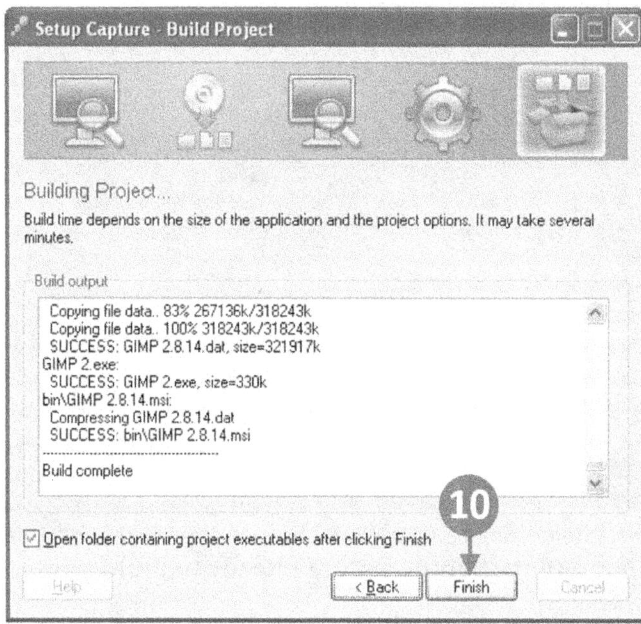

19. Click on the **Finish** button **(10)**. As we left the **Open folder containing project executables after clicking Finish** option ticked, you will see the following window:

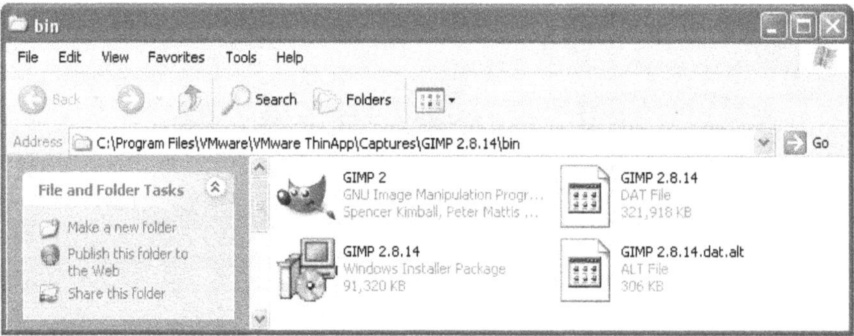

You can see the files that ThinApp has created, which we will use in the next section to provision our AppStack.

To make it easier, we are going to copy these files to a shared folder on our file server so that they are accessible to the provisioning virtual desktop machine.

Creating the ThinApp AppStack

Now that we have created our ThinApp package, the next step is to create the AppStack. We already covered this process in *Chapter 6, Working with AppStacks*, so we are going to pick up the provisioning process from the part where we install the application on the App Volumes provisioning virtual desktop machine.

So, to recap, make sure that at this point you have logged in to the App Volumes Manager console, created an AppStack, and attached it to the provisioning virtual desktop machine. In this example, we are using the machine named `AV-PROVISION`.

If we now open a console to the `AV-PROVISION` virtual desktop machine, we will see that the virtual desktop machine is in provisioning mode. This is shown in the following screenshot:

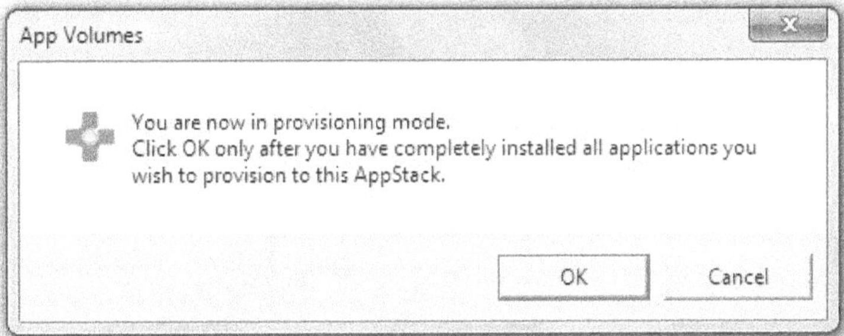
App Volumes
You are now in provisioning mode.
Click OK only after you have completely installed all applications you wish to provision to this AppStack.
OK
Cancel

Remember, *DO NOT* click on **OK** until you have completely finished the installation of the application.

Browse to the shared folder that contains the ThinApp package for the application we are going to install. In our Example Lab, the installation file is stored on our fileserver, as shown in the following screenshot:

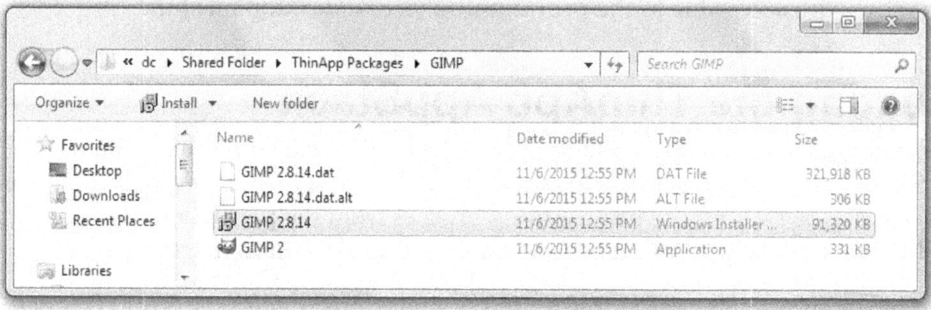

Double-click on the **GIMP 2.8.14** Windows installer.

The installation and configuration window will now launch and install the application. You will see the message shown in the following screenshot:

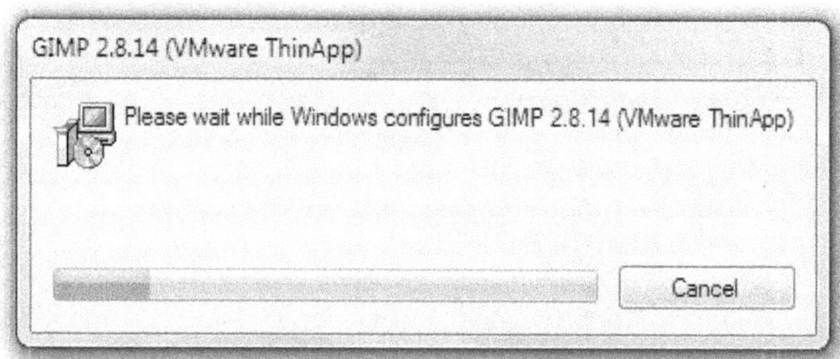

Once the task has completed, return to the App Volumes dialog box and click on **OK** to finish the provisioning process. Reboot the virtual desktop machine when prompted.

When it has rebooted, log back in and click on **OK** in the dialog box to acknowledge that the provisioning has been successful.

Now, switch back to the App Volumes Manager console and click on the **Complete** button and then, on the dialog box displayed, click on the **Complete Provisioning** button.

The AppStack that contains the ThinApp package containing GIMP 2 has now been successfully provisioned, as shown in the following screenshot:

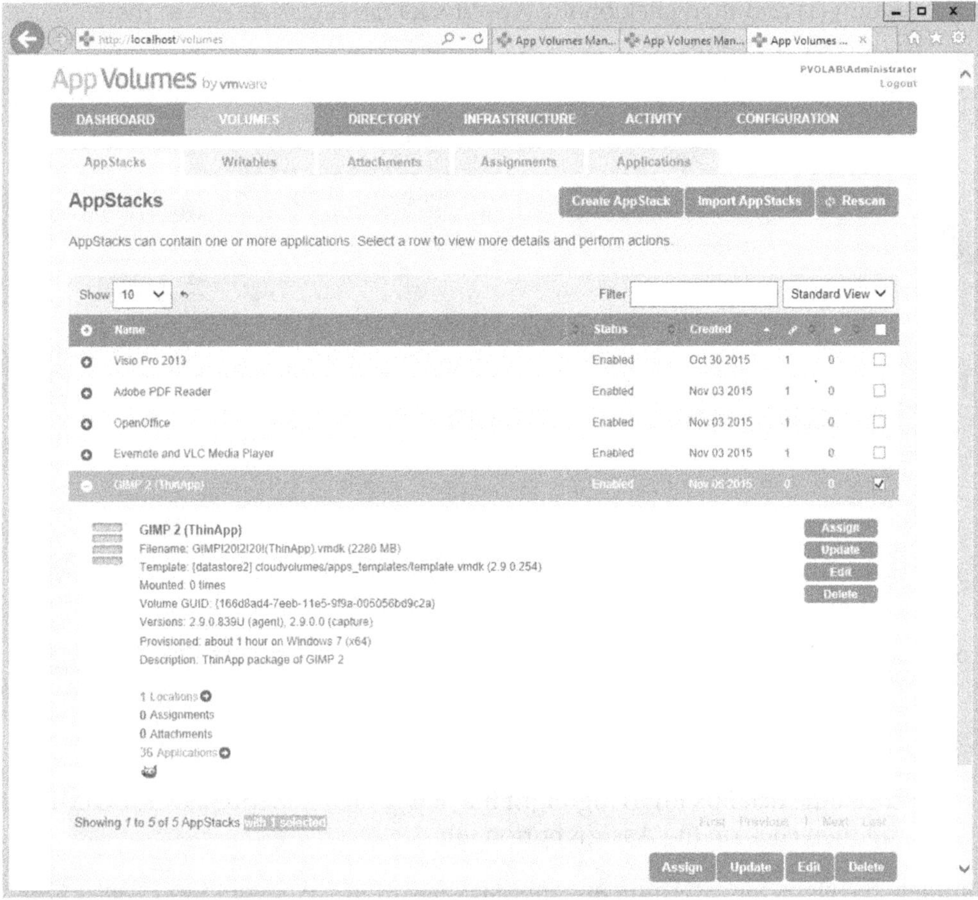

The next task is to assign this newly completed AppStack to an end user, which we will cover in the next section.

Assigning the new ThinApp AppStack

The next step now that we have created our new AppStack containing our ThinApp packaged application is to assign it to one of the end users. For this, perform the following steps:

1. From the App Volumes Manager console, click on the **VOLUMES** menu option **(1)** and then click on the **AppStacks** tab **(2)**, as shown in the following diagram:

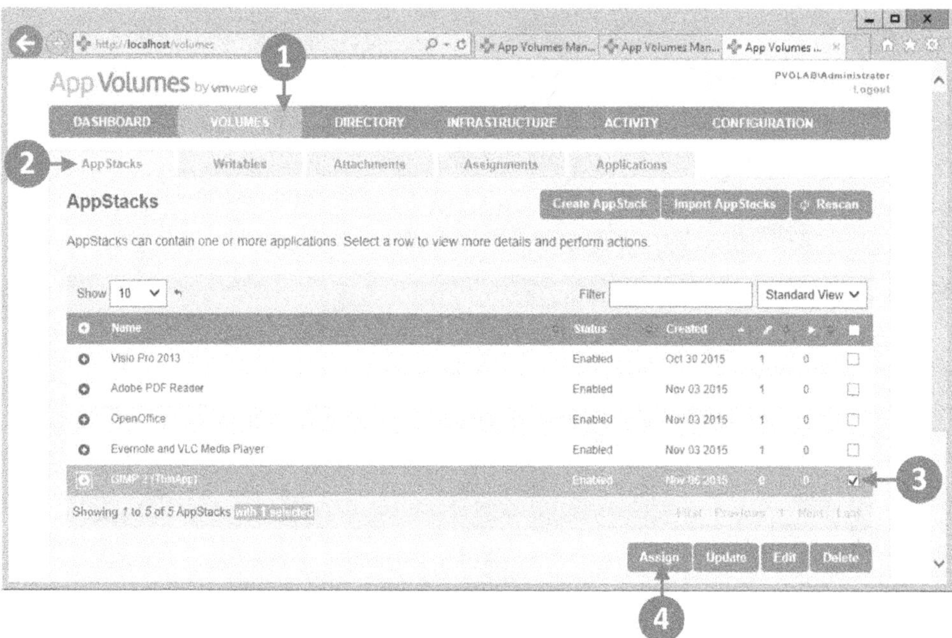

2. Check the tick box **(3)** to highlight the newly created AppStack for GIMP 2, and then click on the **Assign** button **(4)**.

Complete the steps for assigning an AppStack task that we covered in *Chapter 6, Working with AppStacks*, and in this example, assign the AppStack to a specific user. We are going to assign it to Bob Cooper (`bcooper@pvolab.com`).

As we have the licensed capability only of attaching two AppStacks to a user at any one time, you will need to unassign one of the existing attached AppStacks. In this example, we have unassigned the Adobe Acrobat Reader AppStack temporarily.

Next, we are going to test the AppStack by logging in as Bob Cooper, using the `Win7-Desktop-1` virtual desktop machine.

Once logged in, you will see the following view of the user's desktop:

You will see that the user's current AppStacks for VLC Media Player and Evernote have been attached, and now, you will also see a shortcut icon for GIMP 2.

If you double-click on the **GIMP 2** icon **(5)**, you will see the ThinApp message pop up at the bottom of the screen **(6)**, showing that a ThinApp package is launching. The GIMP application will now execute.

You have now successfully created a ThinApp package, created and assigned an AppStack for the package, and demonstrated it to be running on a virtual desktop machine.

In the next section, we will look at ways of updating existing ThinApp packages.

Updating existing ThinApp packages

In the previous section, we looked at how to create a brand-new ThinApp package to deliver as an AppStack; however, what if you already have a number of ThinApp packages in use today and they are not `.msi`-based packages? What now?

In this section, we are going to cover two ways of tackling this scenario.

The first involves taking an existing `.exe`-based ThinApp package containing `Audacity 2.1.1`; updating its configuration to allow it to be provisioned as an AppStack, basically turning it into a `.msi` file; creating the AppStack; and then assigning the AppStack to one of our Example Lab end users.

The second option is to take the original `.exe` and `.dat` ThinApp packaged files and then, using the `THINREG.EXE` command, create a new AppStack, attach it to the provisioning virtual desktop machine, and then register the package rather than install it, before assigning the AppStack to one of our Example Lab end users.

Before we start looking at either of these options, you need to make sure that you have access to the project folder that you used when you originally packaged the application. The path to this folder will look something like the following:

```
C:\Program Files\VMware\VMware ThinApp\Captures\Audacity 2.1.1
```

If you don't have the project folder, then, using the `WinXP-Desktop-1` machine, create a new ThinApp package, following the instructions described in the first part of this chapter. You can choose your own application if you wish to, but for this example, we will use `Audacity` as the example application.

Now that you have the project folder and the source files from the original Setup Capture process, in the next section, we will edit the `PACKAGE.ini` file that defines the behavior of the ThinApp package.

Updating the ThinApp Package to .msi

To update the ThinApp package, browse to the location of you project folder, as shown in the following diagram, and locate the `PACKAGE.ini` file **(1)**. This file contains the settings for the ThinApp package:

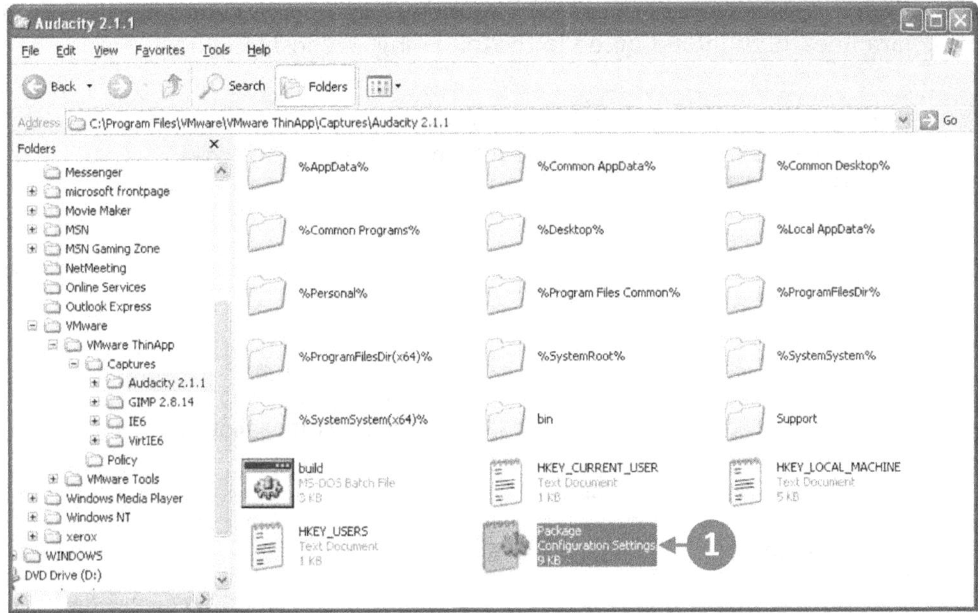

This ThinApp package was originally created as a `.exe` file, and what we are going to do in the following steps is to reconfigure it and rebuild it as a `.msi` file so that we can then install it as part of the AppStack provisioning process.

Open the `PACKAGE.ini` file in a text editor such as Notepad, as shown in the following diagram, and scroll down to the `[BuildOptions]` section **(2)**:

```
; This file can be used to configure build and runtime options for packages
; Lines that begin with a semicolon contain only comments and do not have any effect
; For documentation and to obtain a complete list of options available visit:
;
;   http://www.vmware.com/info?id=906
;
[Compression]
CompressionType=None

[Isolation]
DirectoryIsolationMode=Merged

[BuildOptions]
;-------- MSI Parameters ----------
;Enable MSIFilename if you want to generate a Windows Installer package.
;MSIFilename=Audacity 2.1.1.msi
;MSIManufacturer=PVO
;MSIProductVersion=1.0
;MSIDefaultInstallAllUsers=1
;MSIRequireElevatedPrivileges=1
;MSIInstallDirectory=Audacity 2.1.1 (VMware ThinApp)
;MSIProductCode={D3C6313B-E8C6-07C0-3AE2-08AFE28B038A}
;MSIUpgradeCode={E6F2C54D-0B35-09FA-BC81-72AF0694DBAC}
;MSIStreaming=0
;MSICompressionType=Fast
;MSIArpProductIcon=%ProgramFilesDir%\Audacity\audacity.exe
;MSIIs64Bit=0

;-------- AppSync Parameters ----------
;AppSyncURL=https://example.com/some/path/PackageName.exe
;AppSyncUpdateFrequency=1d
;AppSyncExpirePeriod=30d
;AppSyncWarningPeriod=5d
;AppSyncWarningFrequency=1d
```

We are going to enable some of the **MSI Parameters** settings by removing the `;` from the relevant lines, highlighted in red in the following screenshot:

```
;------- MSI Parameters ----------
;Enable MSIFilename if you want to generate a Windows
Installer package.
MSIFilename=Audacity 2.1.1.msi
MSIManufacturer=PVO
MSIProductVersion=1.0
MSIDefaultInstallAllUsers=1
MSIRequireElevatedPrivileges=1
MSIInstallDirectory=Audacity 2.1.1 (VMware ThinApp)
;MSIProductCode={D3C6313B-E8C6-07C0-3AE2-08AFE28B038A}
;MSIUpgradeCode={E6F2C54D-0B35-09FA-BC81-72AF0694DBAC}
MSIStreaming=0
;MSICompressionType=Fast
MSIArpProductIcon=%ProgramFilesDir%\Audacity\audacity.exe
;MSIIs64Bit=0
```

Once you have made the changes, save the file, ensuring you keep the same filename and folder location.

In your `Projects` folder, locate the `build.bat` file, shown here:

Double-click on the `build.bat` icon to launch the batch file. This will rebuild the ThinApp package to include the configuration changes that you made to the `PACKAGE.ini` file for the MSI parameters.

The build process is shown in the following screenshot:

```
C:\WINDOWS\system32\cmd.exe
Adding \%ProgramFilesDir%\Audacity\unins000.exe  1484489 bytes (100%)
Adding %ProgramFilesDir%\Audacity\FirstTime.ini  27 bytes (100%)
Adding amFilesDir%\Audacity\EQDefaultCurves.xml  4425 bytes (100%)
Adding lesDir%\Audacity\wxbase28u_vc_custom.dll  1198592 bytes (100%)
Adding sDir%\Audacity\wxmsw28u_qa_vc_custom.dll  104960 bytes (100%)
Adding Dir%\Audacity\wxmsw28u_adv_vc_custom.dll  705536 bytes (100%)
Adding ir%\Audacity\wxbase28u_net_vc_custom.dll  125440 bytes (100%)
Adding ir%\Audacity\wxbase28u_xml_vc_custom.dll  124928 bytes (100%)
Adding ir%\Audacity\wxmsw28u_core_vc_custom.dll  2918912 bytes (100%)
Adding ir%\Audacity\wxmsw28u_html_vc_custom.dll  485888 bytes (100%)
Adding es\VMware\VMware ThinApp\TASurrogate.exe  136192 bytes (100%)
Adding \VMware\VMware ThinApp\TASurrogate64.exe  167424 bytes (100%)
VMware ThinApp Runtime Linker Version 5.1.1-2722044, Built May  7 2015
Copyright 1998-2015, VMware, Inc. All rights reserved.
Enterprise Edition, licensed to Learning App Volumes
Audacity 2.1.1.dat:
  Copying file data.. 25% 13952k/54627
  Copying file data.. 79% 46016k/54627k
  SUCCESS: Audacity 2.1.1.dat, size=57792k
Audacity.exe:
  SUCCESS: Audacity.exe, size=549k
C:\Program Files\VMware\VMware ThinApp\Captures\Audacity 2.1.1\\bin\Audacity 2.1
.1.msi:
  Populating MSI tables
  Compressing Audacity 2.1.1.dat...
```

If you now browse to the `Captures` folder, you will see that you now have two `Audacity` packages: the original `.exe` file and now a new `.msi` package. This is shown in the following screenshot:

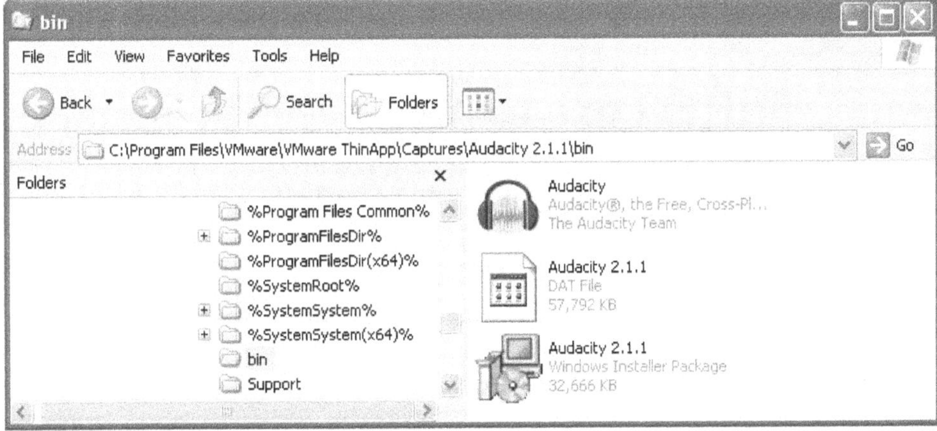

Now, we have our updated package—in this case, a new `.msi` file. In the next section, we will create an AppStack for it.

Creating an AppStack for the updated .msi package

We have created our updated ThinApp package for `Audacity`.

Having reconfigured the package as an `.msi`, file we could now simply follow the process we discussed in the first section of this chapter, where we created a new AppStack; attach it to the provisioning virtual desktop machine; and then just run the `.msi` installer to install the application into the AppStack.

This would install the application as a ThinApp package (packaging as a `.msi` allows us to install it as a ThinApp package).

You would then complete the AppStack provisioning process and assign the AppStack to an end user as you did previously. It's no different at this point.

This is all well and good, but what if you have multiple ThinApp packages that you need to install into the AppStack? If you use this manual update process, you will have to reconfigure and rebuild each and every ThinApp package you have that is currently not a `.msi` file, which could be rather time consuming depending on the number of ThinApp packages that you have in your environment.

This is where the ThinApp `THINREG.exe` command will come in useful, and we will cover it in more detail in the next section.

Using THINREG.exe to mass-deploy packages

Before we start working through registering the application for our new AppStack, we need to complete a few prerequisite tasks or ensure that they have been done in preparation of deploying our ThinApp package using the `THINREG.EXE` command. These are listed as follows:

1. Ensure that App Volumes Agent is installed on the `AV-PROVISION` virtual desktop machine and that you logged in as a user that currently has no assigned/attached AppStacks or Writable Volumes.

> If you have volumes attached, then the virtual desktop machine will not appear on the list of machines available for provisioning.

2. Copy the `THINREG.EXE` file into the `C:\Windows` folder on the `AV-PROVISION` virtual desktop machine.

You will find this file in `C:\Program Files\VMware\VMware ThinApp`.

3. Ensure that the ThinApp package files for `Audacity` are in a location accessible by the provisioning machine.

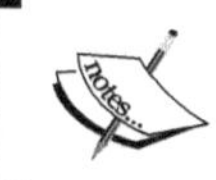

We just need the original ThinApp packaged files for this task. We do not require a `.msi` file.

With these pieces in place, we can now go ahead and start the AppStack creation process and then register the application using `THINREG.EXE`.

Creating the ThinApp AppStack

The first step in creating the ThinApp AppStack is to follow the normal AppStack creation process that we covered in *Chapter 6, Working with AppStacks*, which we will cover again briefly to get us started:

1. Log in to the App Volumes Manager console, click on the **VOLUMES** menu option, and then click on the **AppStacks** tab.
2. Click on the **Create AppStack** button, and you will see the **Create AppStack** page, which looks like this:

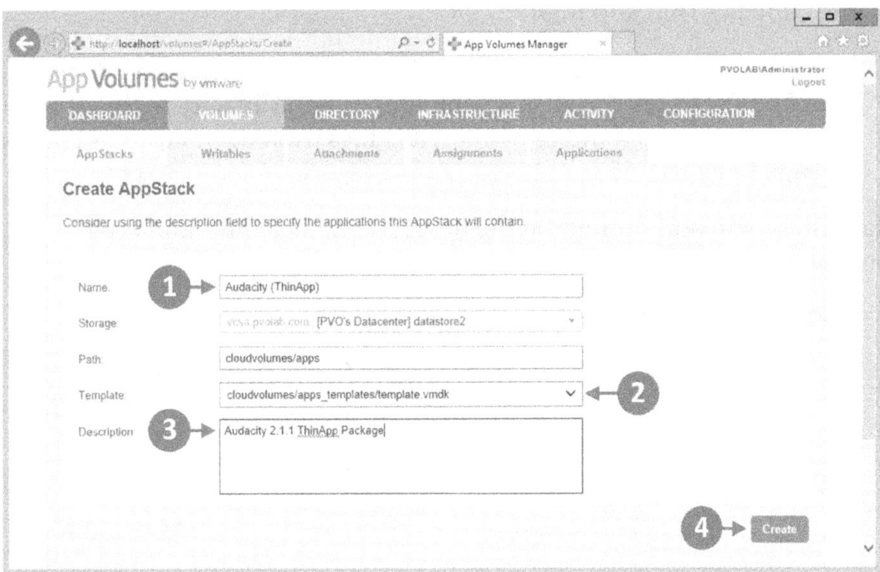

3. In the **Name** box **(1)**, type in a name for this AppStack. Leave the **Storage** and **Path** details as default, and then, in the **Description** box **(3)**, enter a description for this AppStack.
4. Click on the **Create** button **(4)** to continue.
5. Next, on the AppStacks page, check the box to highlight the AppStack you just created for `Audacity`, and then click on the **Provision** button.
6. Enter the name of the provisioning machine or type the first part of the name and then click on the **Search** button.
7. In the results that are displayed, click on the radio button next to the virtual desktop machine you are going to use for provisioning on order to highlight it, and click on the **Provision** button. In this example, we are using the virtual desktop machine called `AV-PROVISION`.
8. Click on the **Start Provisioning** button in the **Confirm Start Provisioning** dialog box, and you will now a message saying the new AppStack is being attached to the provisioning machine.
9. Now, switch to the console of the provisioning machine. You will see a dialog box stating that the machine is now in provisioning mode.

Remember: *DO NOT* click on **OK** until after you have completed the provisioning process.

The next step is to create a folder on the provisioning machine into which we will copy the ThinApp files.

10. In this example, in the root of the **C:** drive, we have created a folder called **ThinApp Packages** and then a subfolder called **Audacity** within this folder. We have then copied the `.exe` and `.dat` files from the `Audacity` ThinApp package into this folder.

Next, launch a command prompt on the provisioning machine, and type this command:

```
Thingreg.exe "c:\ThinApp Packages\*" /A
```

This is shown in the following screenshot:

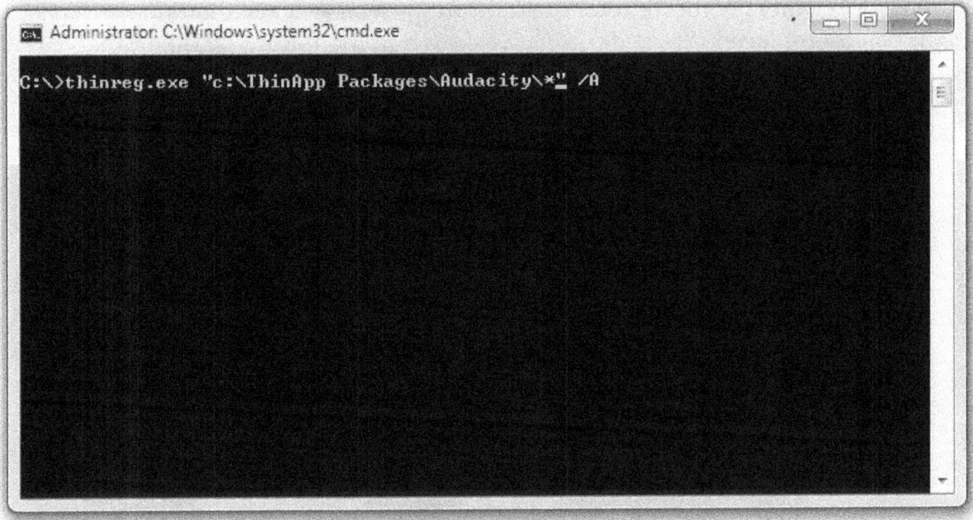
Administrator: C:\Windows\system32\cmd.exe
C:\>thinreg.exe "c:\ThinApp Packages\Audacity*" /A

This command will register the `Audacity` ThinApp package on the provisioning machine, and as it's in provisioning mode, App Volumes Agent redirects this to the attached AppStack, therefore creating a new AppStack containing the `Audacity` ThinApp package.

> If you wanted to register more than one ThinApp package, then you would use a `*` symbol as a wildcard. For example, if our ThinApp packages directory had multiple folders, each containing package files, we could use this command:
>
> **`thingreg.exe "c:\ThinApp Packages\*\*" /A`**
>
> This would mean that `THINGREG` would look in all the subfolders. The `/A` option just means that the package can be used by all users.

Command Prompt will not show the result of registering the application and will return you back to the cursor; however, as part of the ThinApp configuration was to add a desktop icon and shortcut to the application, you will see that the **Audacity** icon **(5)** has been placed on the desktop, as shown in the following diagram:

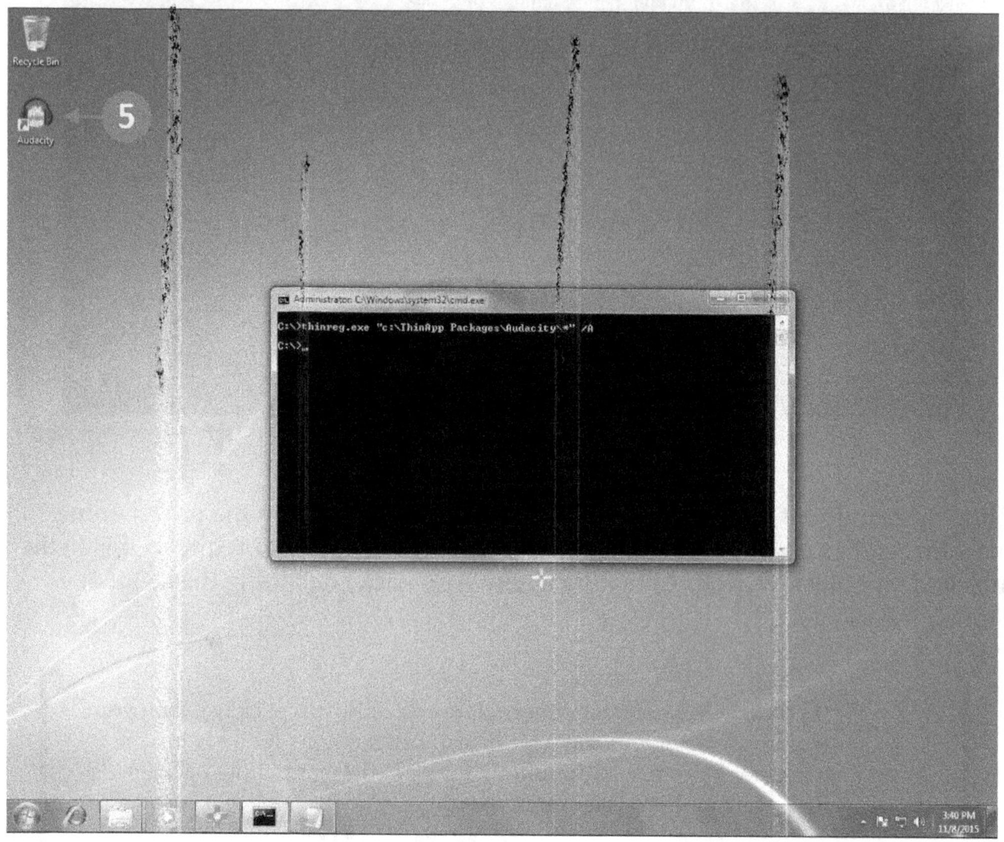

Launch the application to test whether it works properly.

Once you are happy it works, you can click on **OK** in the App Volumes provisioning dialog box. Click on **Yes** to finish, and finally, click on **OK** to reboot the provisioning machine.

When the provisioning machine reboots, log in and then click on **OK** to end the provisioning process on the provisioning machine.

Switch back to the App Volumes Manager console.

Click on the **Complete** button, and then in the **Confirm Provisioning Complete** dialog box, click on **Complete Provisioning**.

At this stage, we have completed the creation of our AppStack, which now contains a ThinApp packaged version of Audacity.

In the next section, we are going to assign this AppStack to one of the Example Lab end users and then test it.

Assigning the Audacity ThinApp packages AppStack

The final thing to do is to assign this AppStack to an end user. In this example, we are going to assign it to the user Nick Mason (`nmason@pvolab.com`).
Here are the steps:

1. From the AppStacks page, click on the **Assign** button. You will now see the **Assign AppStack** page, shown in the following diagram:

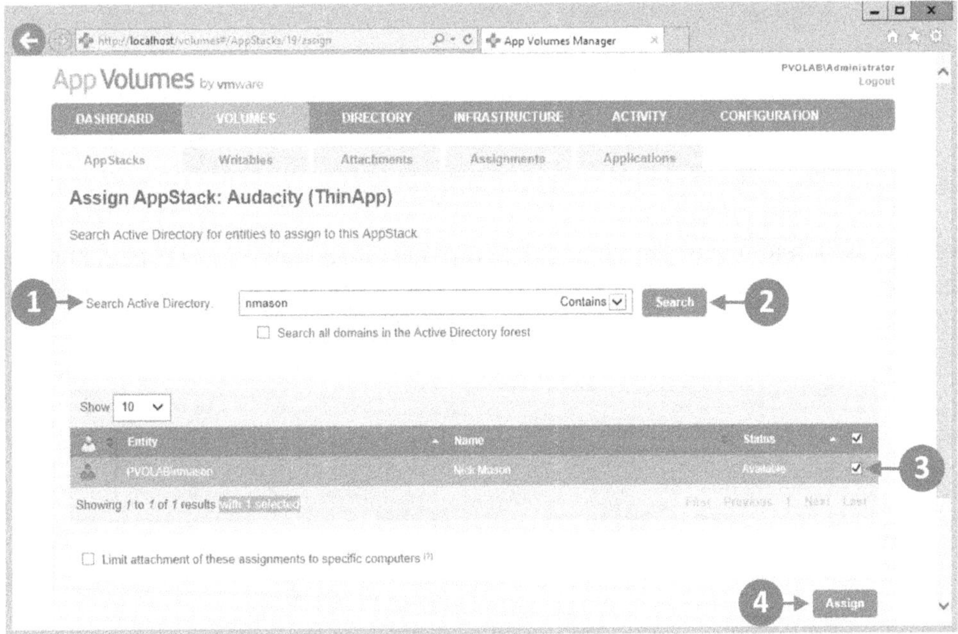

2. In the **Search Active Directory** box **(1)**, type the username or part of the username and then click on the **Search** button **(2)**.

3. In the displayed results, check the box for the user **(3)**, and then click on **Assign (4)**. The AppStack has now been assigned to the end user, as shown in the following screenshot:

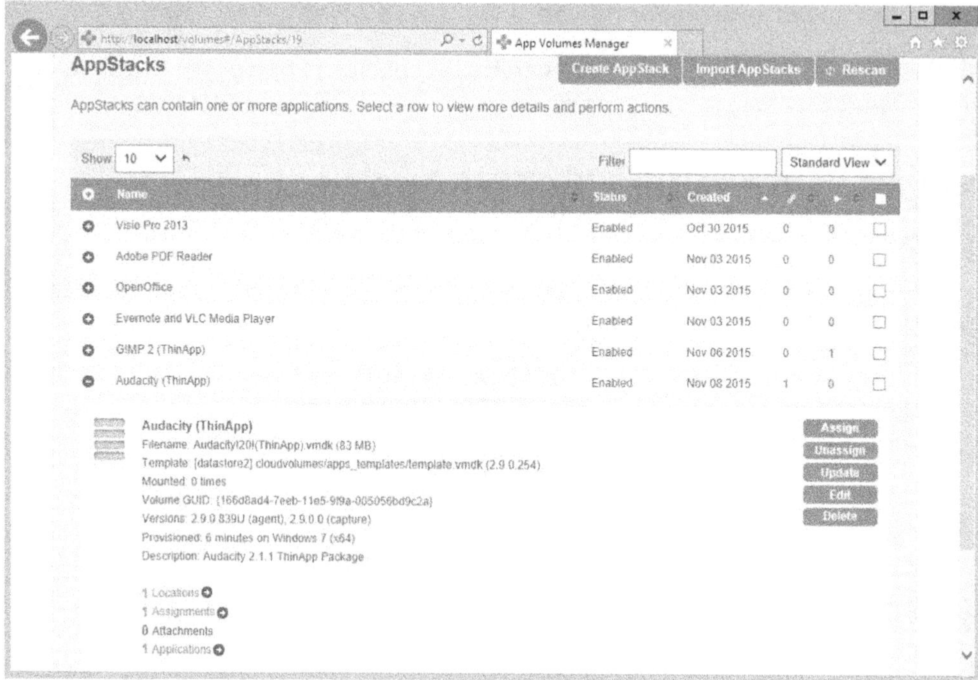

If we now switch to one of the virtual desktop machines, `Win7-Desktop-2`, and log in as the user `nmason`, you will see that the **Audacity** shortcut icon is on the desktop.

If you double-click on the icon, you will see the application launch, as shown in the following screenshot:

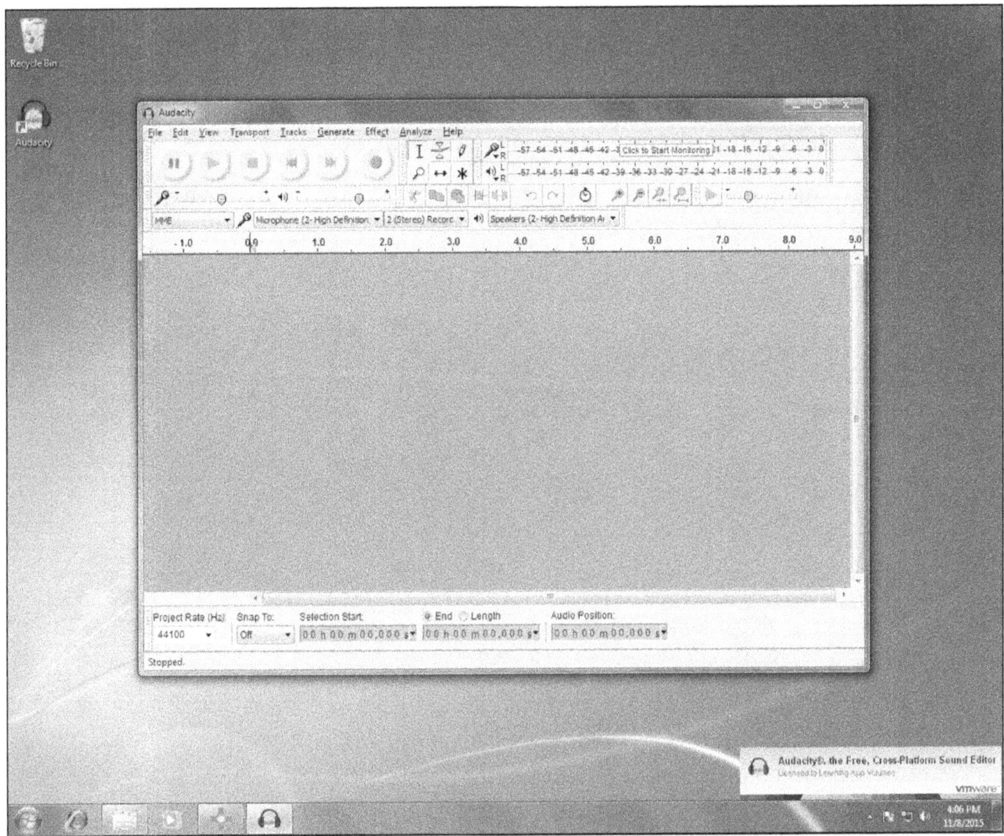

You have successfully deployed a ThinApp packaged application onto an AppStack using the `THINGREG` command.

Summary

In this chapter, we took a deeper look at how ThinApp works in conjunction with App Volumes to deliver AppStacks containing isolated applications.

We covered a few scenarios; firstly, how to create a new `.msi` ThinApp package and create an AppStack with it, and then we looked at a couple of ways of taking existing ThinApp packages and deploying them onto AppStacks.

In the next chapter, we will look at how App Volumes integrates with VMware Horizon View.

9
Horizon View Integration

In this chapter, we will look at how App Volumes integrates into the VMware Horizon View virtual desktop solution.

Back in *Chapter 3, Designing and Building an App Volumes Deployment*, we looked at the architecture of how App Volumes fits into the Horizon View pod and block reference architecture. Now we are going to complete the installation and configuration tasks to demonstrate how to build virtual desktop machines delivered by VMware Horizon View, with applications being delivered using App Volumes.

The following diagram illustrates how App Volumes is integrated with Horizon View:

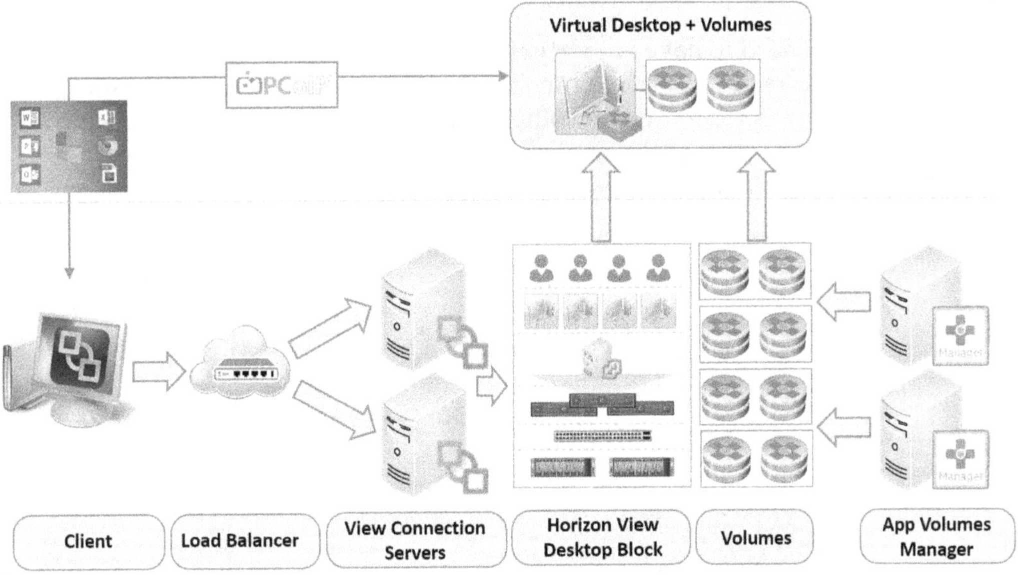

Basically, you build and deploy your Horizon View environment as you normally would, with the addition of the App Volumes Agent that needs to be installed onto each of the virtual desktop machines you want to deliver applications to.

In a virtual desktop environment, AppStacks and Writable Volumes should be assigned to users rather than individual virtual desktop machines when using floating assignments, as you don't know which virtual desktop machine the user is going to be allocated.

We are not going to cover building a Horizon View deployment in this book, so for details on how to build this environment if you don't have one and want to test this feature, refer to *Mastering VMware Horizon 6, Packt Publishing*.

For the Example Lab, we have deployed a simple environment with just a single **Horizon View Connection Server** and built a Windows 7 desktop image to use as a template from which to deploy virtual desktop machines.

Building and configuring a virtual desktop

So, now that we have described how App Volumes integrates with Horizon View, we can start building this scenario using the Example Lab.

The next thing we need to have is a virtual desktop machine image built, containing all the components required for it to run. This build process is exactly the same as you would follow for building any other Horizon View-based virtual desktop machine; however, as previously mentioned, you now need to include App Volumes Agent as part of the image.

The process is illustrated in the following diagram:

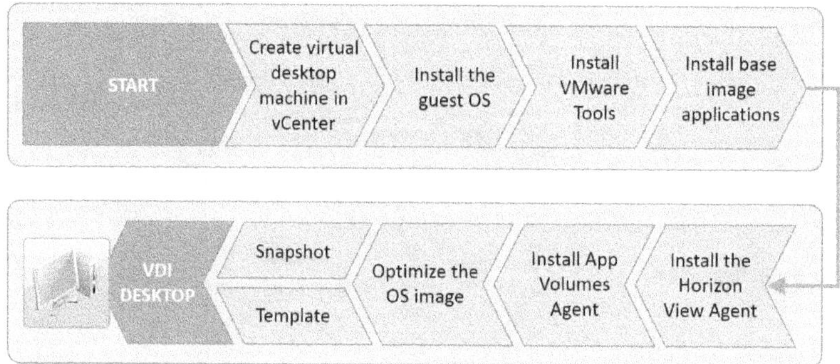

In the Example Lab, we have followed the process as described in the diagram and created a template called the Horizon View desktop template, which will be used to create some example virtual desktop machines.

We are not going to cover this process in any more detail, but if you want to find out more about VMware Horizon View desktop solutions, please refer to *Mastering VMware Horizon 6* by Peter von Oven and Barry Coombs.

Now that we have a virtual desktop machine built and ready to use, we can create and configure a **desktop pool** and entitle an end user to that pool so that they can use the virtual desktop machine.

Creating and configuring a desktop pool

In this example, we will create a very quick desktop pool to demonstrate how App Volumes works within a Horizon View environment.

When it comes to designing a production App Volumes and Horizon View deployment, you will need to look at how you create and configure the desktop pools so that the pool configuration and the desktops within it match the application requirement of the AppStacks that are going to be speed.

In previous chapters, we used virtual desktop machines that have not been managed by Horizon View, but now we are going to use Horizon View. The only difference is that Horizon View will now be allocated the virtual desktop machine rather than us connecting and logging in directly. App Volumes' behavior is no different.

For this example, we will create an automated desktop pool, with a floating user assignment. We will also create full clone virtual desktop machines.

In a production environment, you would use View Composer linked clone virtual desktop machines rather than full clones to save on infrastructure and management costs. We will use full clones just for quickness.

Continuing the configuration, we will set the ID for the pool as `AV-Sales` and the display name, which is what the user sees, is going to be App Volumes Sales pool.

We have also configured Horizon View to provision four virtual desktop machines from the Horizon View desktop template that we created, provision them up-front, and power them on. The virtual desktop machines will be stored in a folder called **View Desktops**.

Once the desktop pool has been created, you can entitle users to the virtual desktop machines.

Entitling desktops

The final step of the Horizon View configuration process is to entitle end users to the desktop pool that you just created, allowing them access to the virtual desktop machines within it.

In our example, we will entitle the user John Smith (`jsmith@pvolab.com`) to the desktop pool.

You should now have completed the desktop pool configuration, entitled an end user, and should see something like the following screenshot in the **VMware Horizon 6 View Administrator** console:

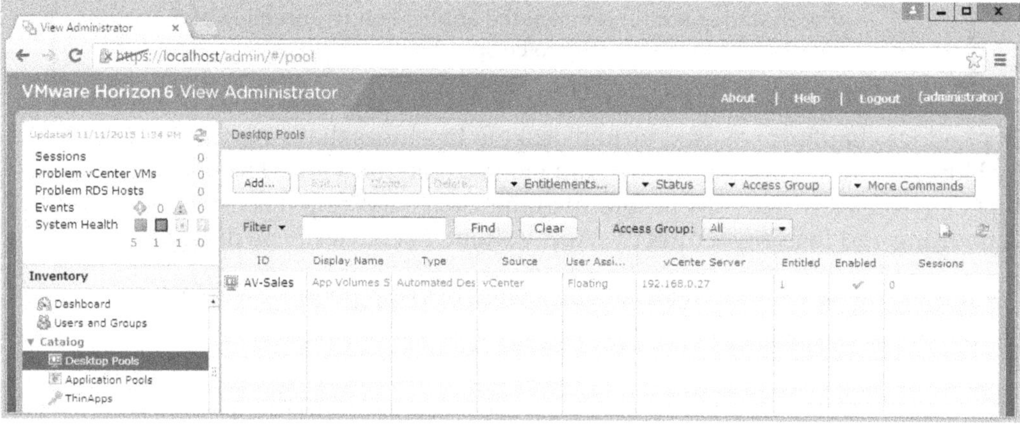

The next step is to test that the user can first of all log in to a virtual desktop machine, and secondly that they have all their applications available to them.

In the next section, we will log in and put that to the test, but before we do, you need to ensure that the user chosen in this example has been assigned an AppStack.

In the Example Lab, the user John Smith is part of the Sales group and therefore should be assigned two AppStacks, one containing Evernote and VLC Media Player and another containing Adobe Reader.

Logging on to a View desktop

Before logging on to a virtual desktop machine, you need to ensure you have VMware Horizon View Client installed. We have this already installed on one of the example desktop machines.

Launch VMware Horizon View Client and add the Horizon View Connection Server details. These are shown in the following screenshot:

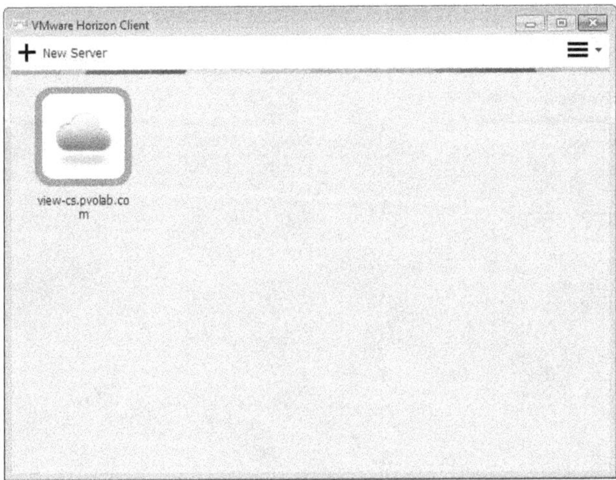

The client will now connect to Horizon View Connection Server and then prompt you to enter your username and password, as shown in the following screenshot:

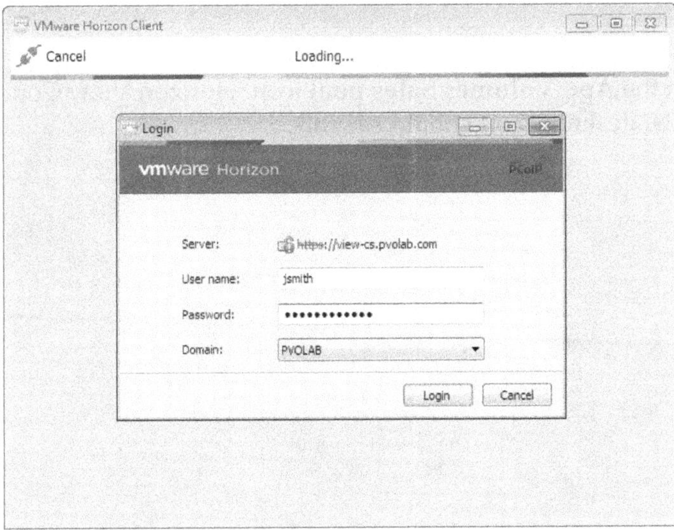

Enter the details of the example user, and click on the **Login** button.

Horizon View Connection Server will now authenticate the user against Active Directory and then, via **App Volumes Broker Integration Service**, look to see which AppStack and Writable Volumes that user has assigned to them.

You will now see which desktop pools are available to the end user. In this example, the user has been entitled to the App Volumes Sales pool we created previously, as shown in the following screenshot:

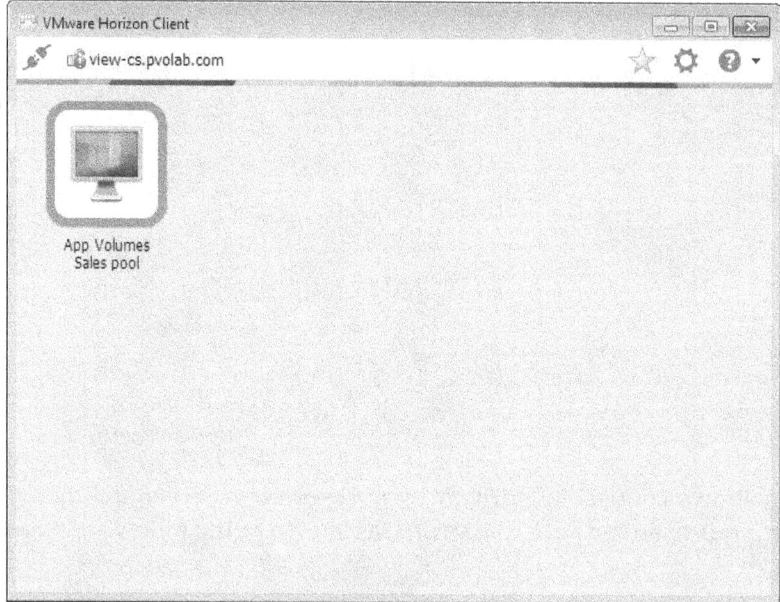

Double click on the **App Volumes Sales pool** icon. Horizon View Connection Server then prepares the desktop. You should see this:

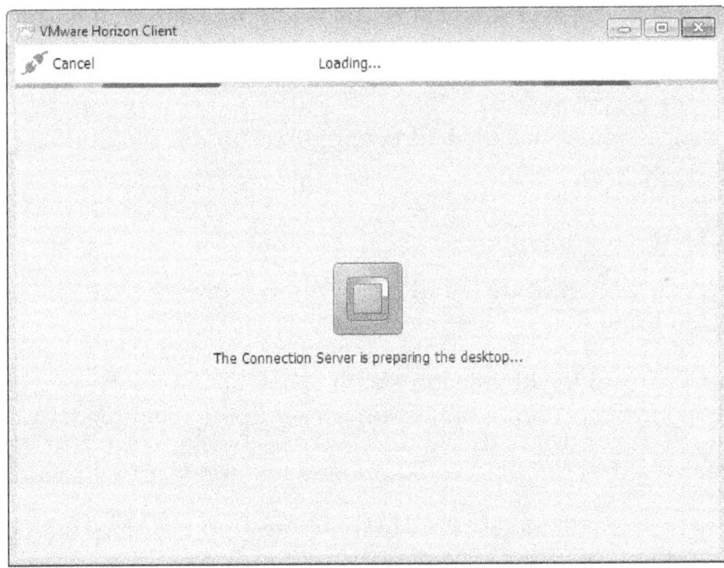

After configuring it, Horizon View Connection Server delivers the virtual desktop machine to the end user, complete with the assigned AppStacks attached, as shown in the following screenshot:

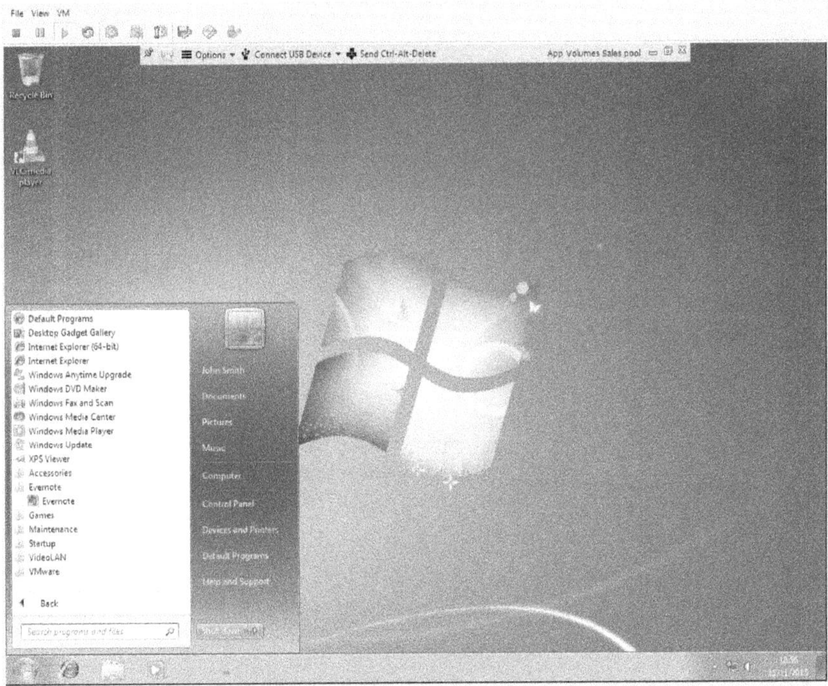

You will now see that the user John Smith is logged in to a virtual desktop machine and has his AppStack applications, Evernote and VLC Media Player, available to launch.

You have now successfully installed and configured Broker Integration Service.

Summary

In this chapter, you were introduced to App Volumes Broker Integration Service for VMware Horizon View.

We started by looking at the architecture with respect to how it works, before going on to install it on Horizon View Connection Server in the Example Lab.

Finally, we created a desktop pool and demonstrated the feature in action.

In the next chapter, we will look at how to integrate App Volumes with Citrix XenDesktop.

10

Deploying App Volumes in a Citrix XenDesktop Environment

One of the key features of App Volumes is that it is not restricted to working with just VMware technology and products. As we have already seen, as well as its ability to integrate with VMware Horizon View (both virtual desktop machine delivery and hosted applications), App Volumes complements Citrix XenDesktop, Citrix XenApp, and Microsoft RDSH solutions.

In this chapter, we will take a closer look at how to deploy App Volumes to deliver just-in-time applications to a virtual desktop machine delivered by Citrix XenDesktop.

Unlike the VMware Horizon View solution, there is no broker integration to install.

The following diagram illustrates how App Volumes would look within the Citrix XenDesktop architecture:

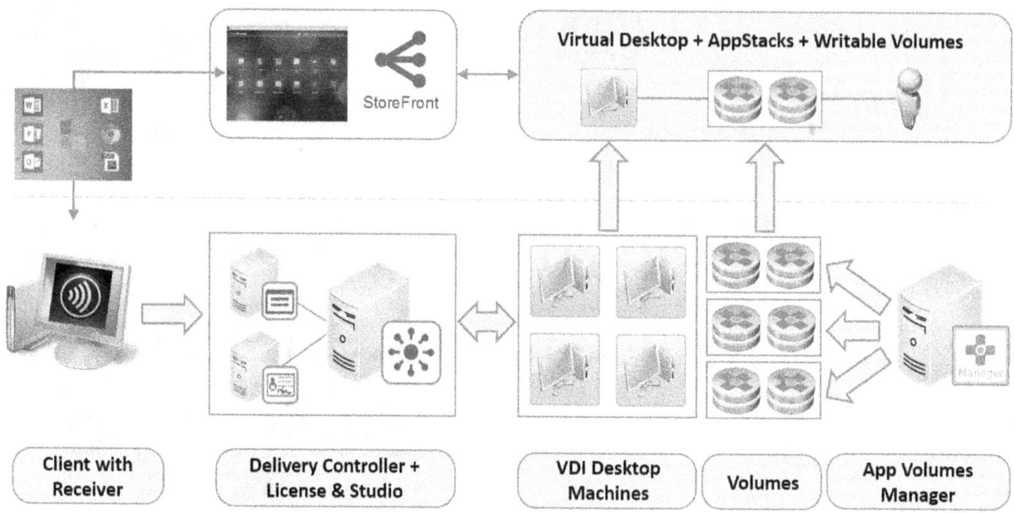

The Citrix XenDesktop process for logging on to desktops remains exactly as it would in any other Citrix deployment. However, by having App Volumes Agent installed onto the base images of the virtual desktop machines delivered by XenDesktop, when a user that has been assigned an AppStack or Writable Volumes logs in to that virtual desktop machine, those volumes will be automatically attached to the virtual desktop.

In this example, we are using VMware vSphere (ESXi and vCenter Server) as the underlying infrastructure to host the Citrix XenDesktop virtual desktop machines and infrastructure components (**Delivery Controller**, **Studio**, **StoreFront**, and **License Server**), and therefore using VMware-based virtual machines with VMDK files for the virtual disk files. However, you can use VHD-format virtual disk files, which we will cover in *Chapter 14, Advanced Configuration and Other Options*.

We will not cover how to build a Citrix XenDesktop environment in this chapter, so having an environment in place is a prerequisite for this chapter as we are going to configure a new **machine catalog** and **delivery group** for the App Volumes-enabled virtual desktop machines.

To build a Citrix environment, have a look at this link: `http://tinyurl.com/nla9k8u`. This takes you to the Citrix website and the Citrix XenDesktop reviewer's guide, which will walk you through *building a demo* environment as we have built in this guide.

If you have followed this guide to create the basic infrastructure, then in the later sections, we will briefly cover the final steps for delivering the virtual desktop machines.

In the next section, we will build and configure a virtual desktop machine.

Building and configuring a virtual desktop

Now that we have described the architecture of how App Volumes fits into a Citrix XenDesktop environment, the next thing we need to have is a virtual desktop machine image built, containing all the components required for it to run.

This build process is exactly the same as you would follow for building any other XenDesktop-based virtual desktop machine; however, you now need to include App Volumes Agent as part of the image build.

As previously mentioned, we are going to use a VMware vSphere environment to host the Citrix components of the lab environment.

The process is illustrated in the following diagram:

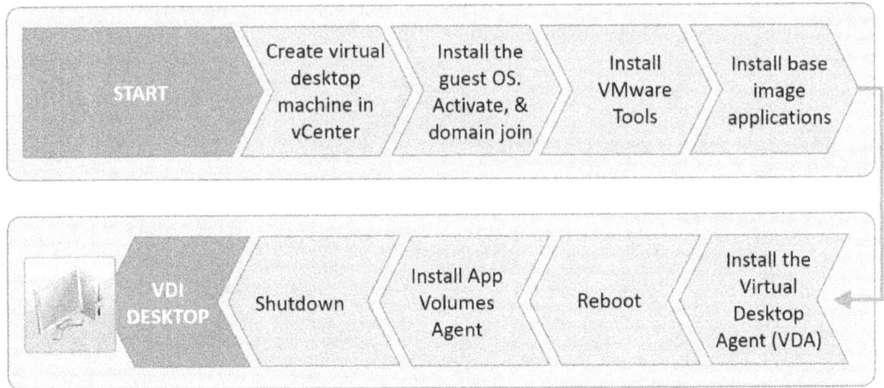

In the Example Lab, we have followed this process and created a template called **XenDesktop Gold Image**, which will be used to create example virtual desktop machines.

Now that we have a virtual desktop machine built and ready to use, we can create and configure a machine catalog and then a delivery group to entitle an end user to use the virtual desktop machine.

Creating a machine catalog

Now that you have a virtual desktop machine image built, the next step is to create a machine catalog, which will utilize this image to deploy virtual desktop machines.

We will walk through this process.

On the server onto which you installed XenDesktop Delivery Controller, launch Citrix Studio. This is a **Microsoft Management Console** (**MMC**)-based console used to manage the Citrix environment. You would have used this to complete the configuration stage when you built and configured the infrastructure components.

You will see the following window:

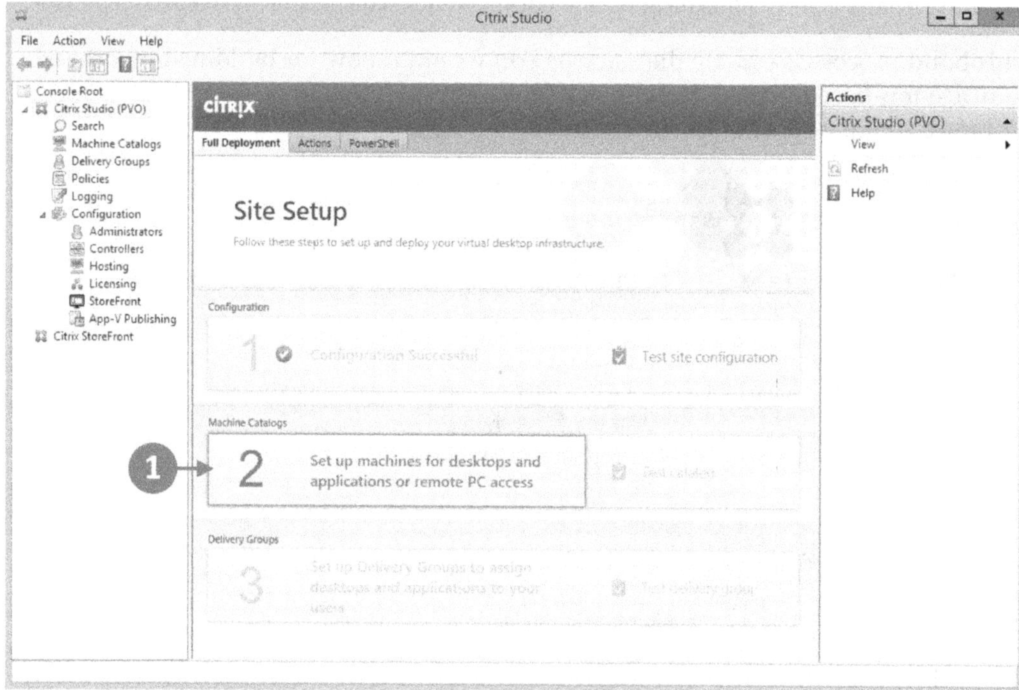

Follow these steps to create and configure the virtual desktop machines:

1. In the **Machine Catalogs** section, click on **Set up machines for desktops and applications or remote PC access (1)**.

[The first screen you see is the **Introduction** screen. In this example, the screenshot for this has not been shown.]

2. Click on the **Next** button in the **Introduction** screen to continue.
3. The next screen you will see is the **Operating System** screen, where you select the type of operating system deployment. As we are creating an environment for virtual desktop machines, click on the radio button for **Windows Desktop OS (2)**. This is shown in the following figure:

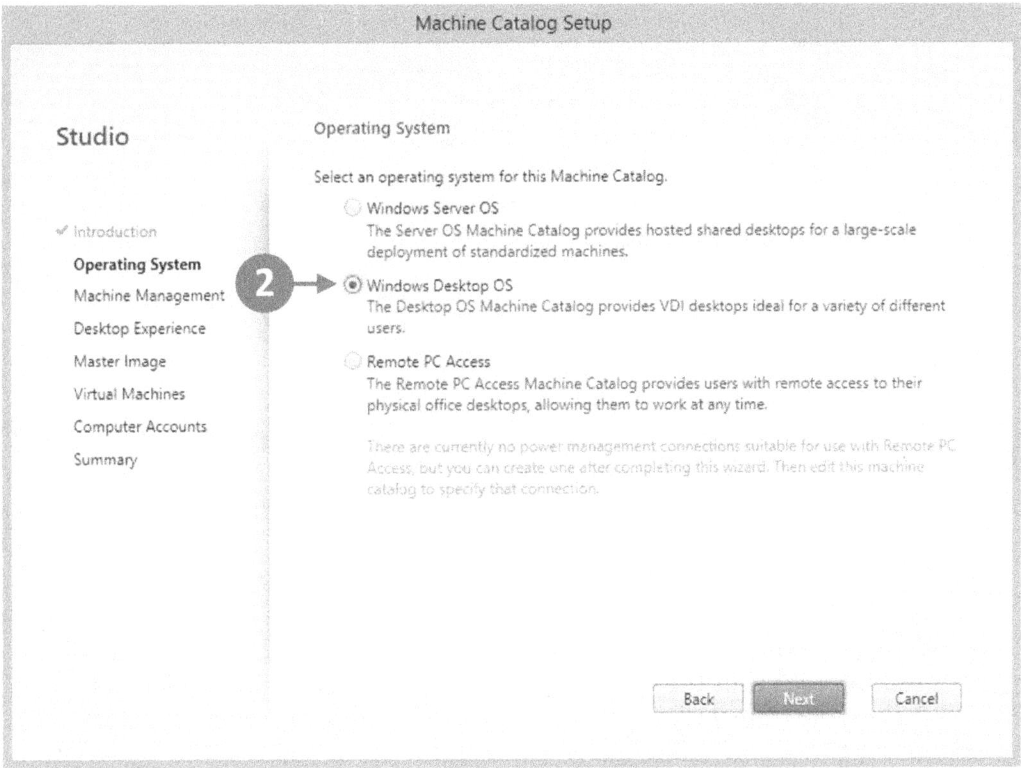

4. Click on the **Next** button to continue. The next screen is the **Machine Management** screen.
5. Click on the radio button for **Machines that are power managed (3)**, since we are configuring a virtual desktop environment, and then, in the **Deploy machine using:** section, click on the radio button for **Citrix Machine Creation Services (MCS) (4)**. This is shown in the following diagram:

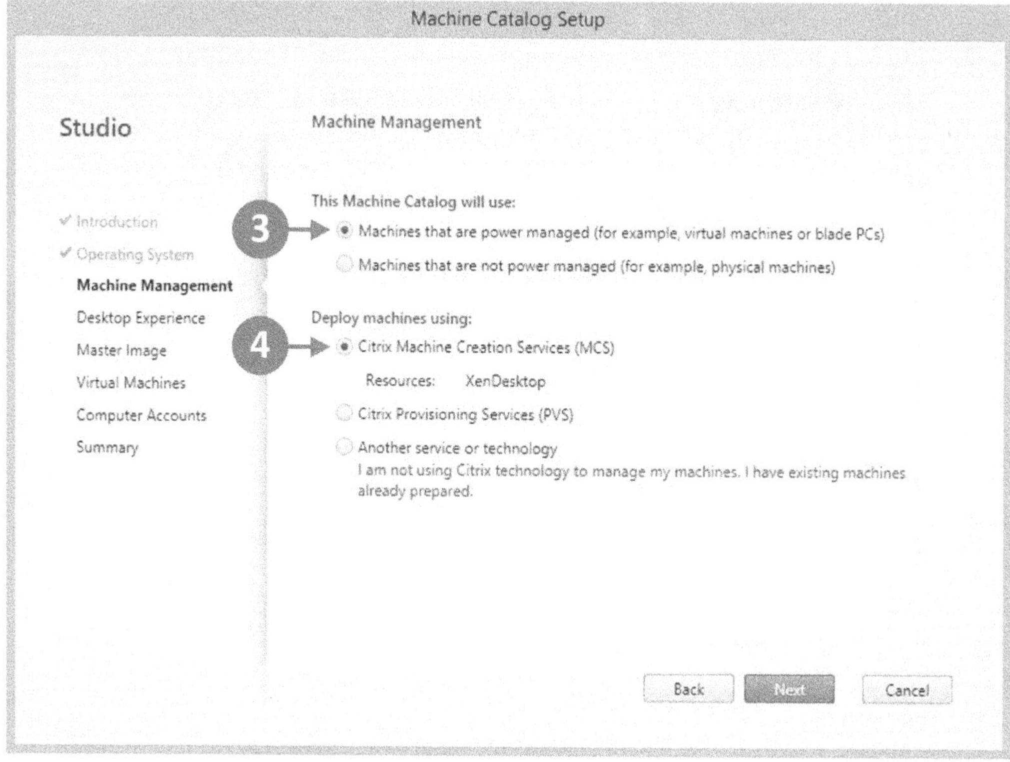

6. Click on the **Next** button to continue. The next screen is for selecting the desktop experience.
7. Click on the radio button for **I want users to connect to a new (random) desktop each time they log on. (5)**. This basically configures a floating desktop assignment.

8. Also ensure that you select the radio button for **No, discard all changes and clear virtual desktops when the user logs off. (6)**. This means that the virtual desktop machine is non-persistent and nothing will be saved to it. When the user logs off from the virtual desktop machine, it will revert to the original image.

   By choosing this option, we have configured a stateless virtual desktop machine environment. This is shown in the following diagram:

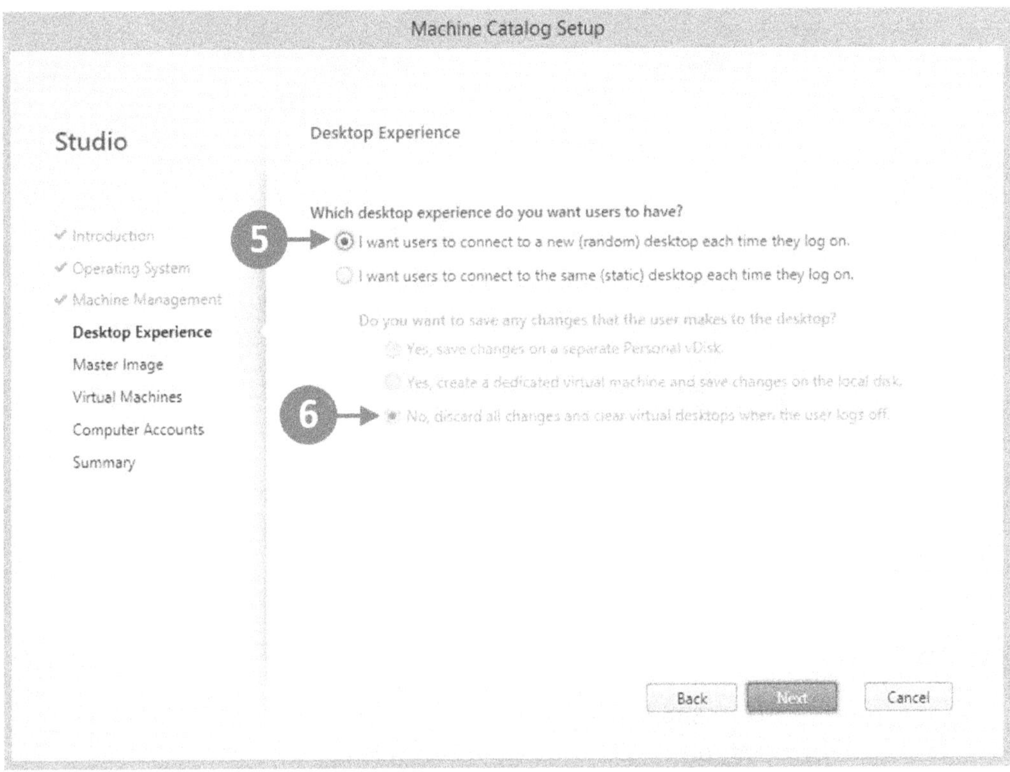

9. Click on the **Next** button to continue. You will now see the **Master Image** screen.
10. Scroll down the list in the **Master Image** screen, and select the image that you built in the previous section. In this example, the image is called **XenDesktop Gold Image (7)**.

11. From **Select the VDA version installed on this snapshot (or virtual machine):** drop-down menu **(8)**, select the correct version. In this example, we have installed version 7.6 onto the virtual desktop machine image. This is shown in the following figure:

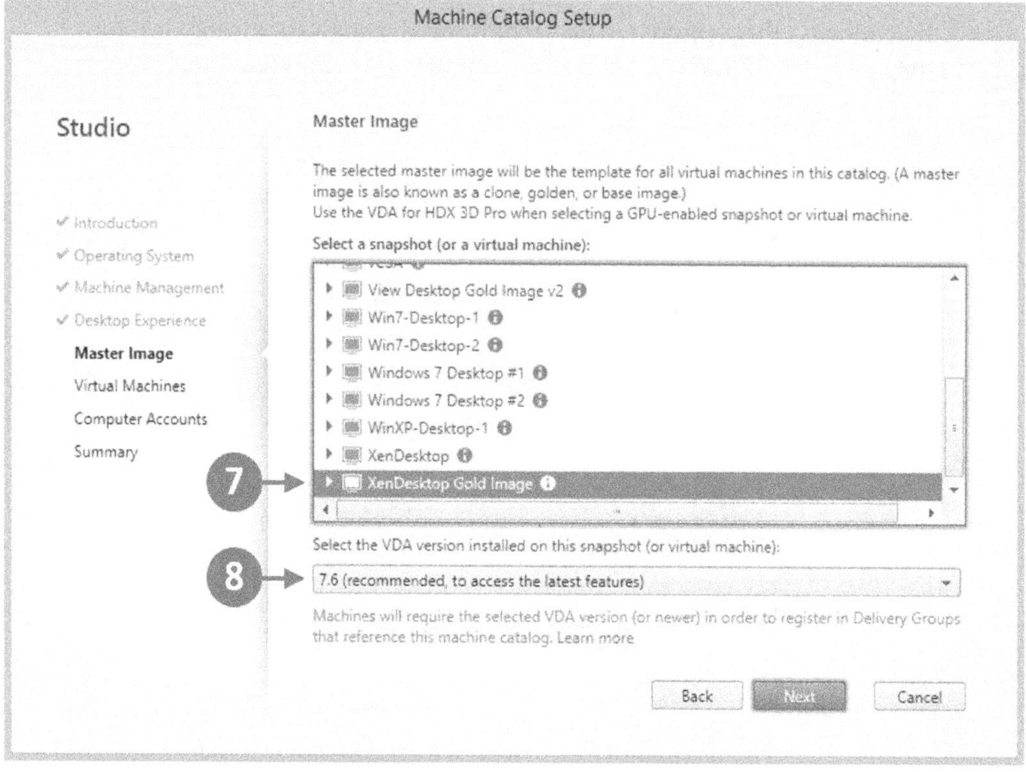

12. Click on the **Next** button to continue.
13. In the **Virtual Machines** screen, first of all select the number of virtual machines you want to create from the master image **(9)**. Then, configure the virtual hardware by selecting the number of virtual CPUs **(10)** and the amount of memory **(11)** you want each of the virtual desktop machines to have. The disk size will already be set at the same size as the original virtual desktop machine. This is shown in the following diagram:

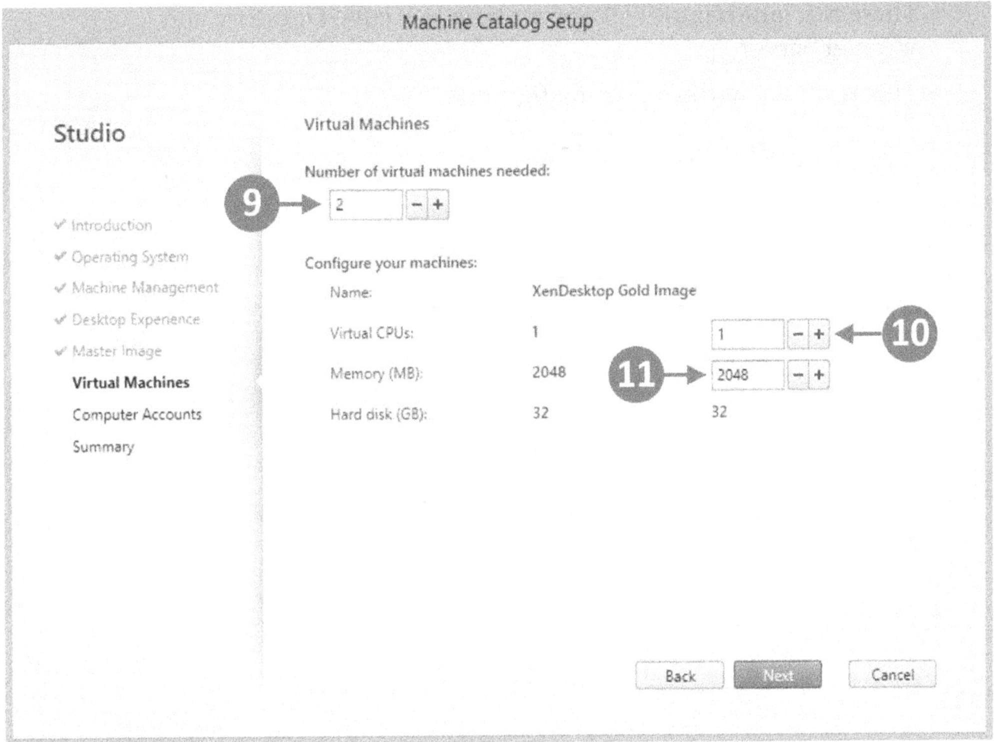

14. Click on the **Next** button to continue.

    You now have the option of configuring **Active Directory Computer Accounts**.

    Click on the radio button for **Create new Active Directory accounts (12)**, and ensure that the correct domain has been selected from the drop-down menu **(13)**. In this example, we are using the **pvolab.com** domain.

    You can then choose the location where these virtual desktop machines will be created. In this example, we have selected the **Computers** group **(14)** in Active Directory.

    The final option in this screen is to create an **Account naming scheme (15)**. This will be the names given to the virtual desktop machines that get created. In this example, we have used **XenDesktop-#**, which means that since we created two virtual desktop machines, you will see them created as **XenDesktop-1** and **XenDesktop-2**.

These machine names will appear both in Active Directory and vCenter Server.

This is shown in the following figure:

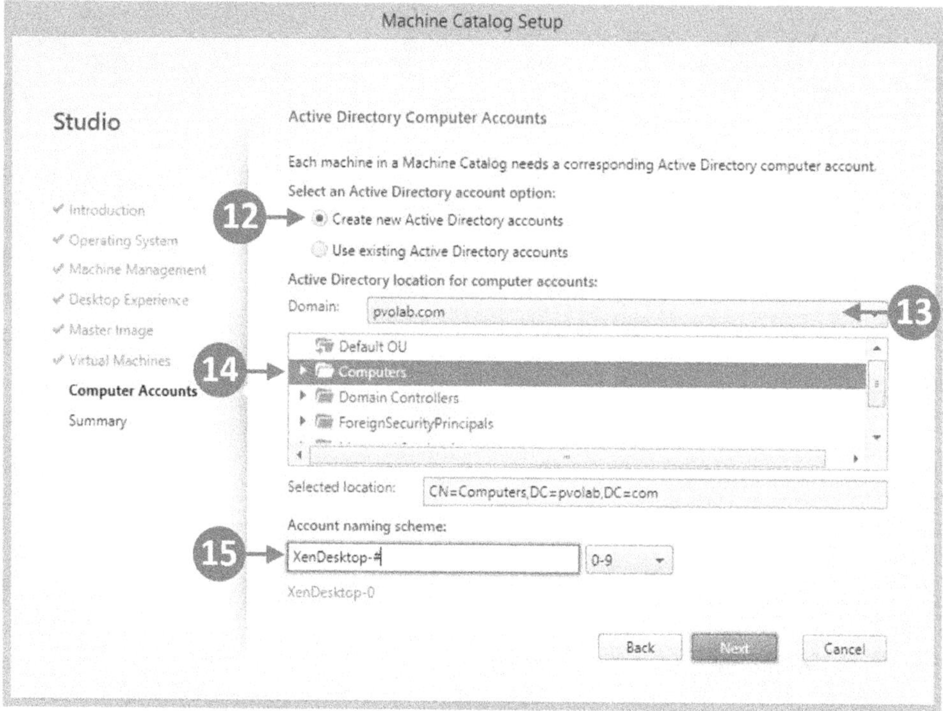

15. Click on the **Next** button to continue.

    Finally, you will see the **Summary** screen.

    Check whether the configuration is correct, but before finalizing, you need to enter a name for the machine catalog as well as an optional description. In this example, the machine catalog name is **App Volumes - Sales (16)**. For **Machine catalog description for administrators (17)**, in this example, we entered `Win 7 Desktops`. This is shown in the following diagram:

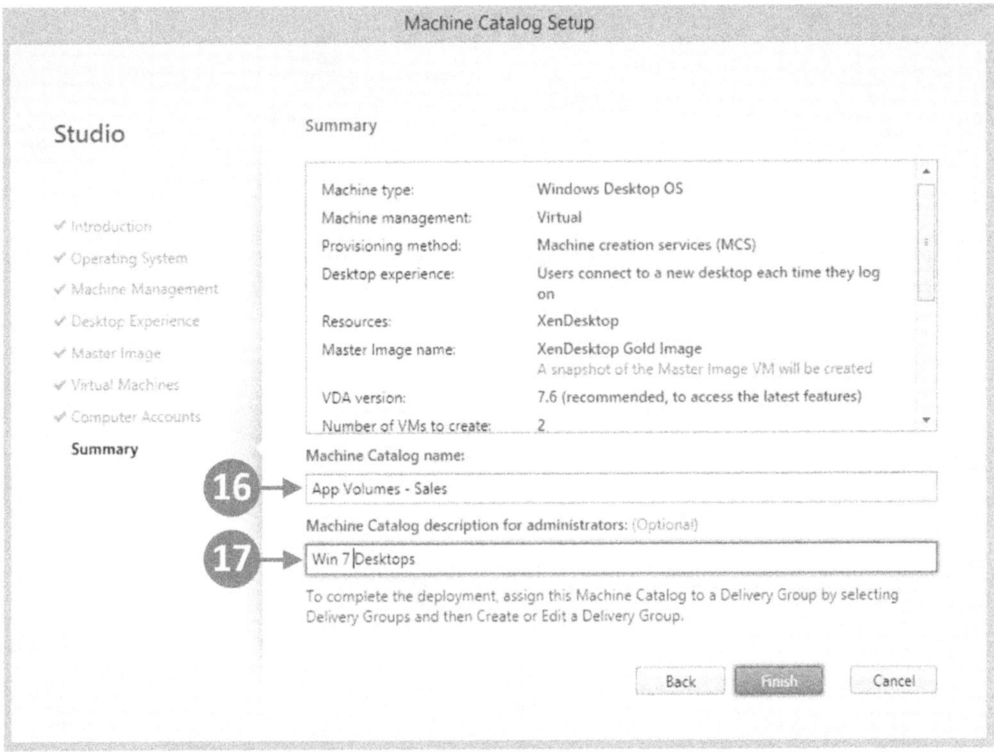

16. Click on the **Finish** button to complete the machine catalog configuration. You will see the following message displayed:

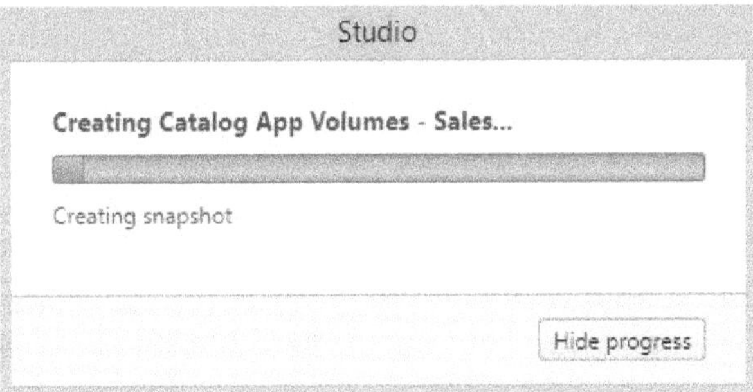

The virtual desktop machines will be created, configured, and will now appear in vCenter Server, along with having Active Directory machine accounts created.

The next step is to create a delivery group, which we will cover in the next section.

Creating a delivery group

At this stage, we have our infrastructure built, and we also have our virtual desktop machines built and configured, ready for delivery to the end users.

In this section, we will configure the assignment and delivery components. Here's how to do it:

1. From the Citrix Studio screen, in the **Delivery Groups** section, click on **Set up Delivery Groups to assign desktops and applications to your users (1)**, as shown in the following diagram:

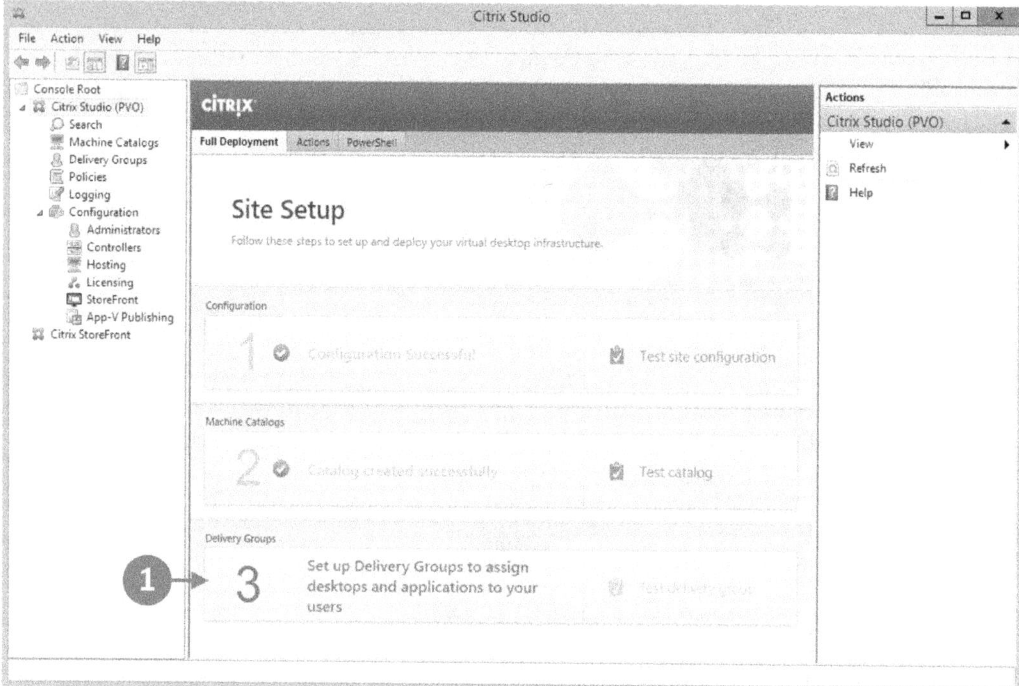

2. In the **Getting started with Delivery Groups** screen, click on the **Next** button to start the configuration. This screenshot is not shown. The first screen you will see is the **Machines** screen.

3. In the **Machines** screen, click on the radio button to select the machine catalog that contains the virtual desktop machines you want to assign. In this example, you will see the **App Volumes – Sales** machine catalog **(2)** that you created in the previous section.
4. Next, select the number of virtual desktop machines you want to use in this delivery group **(3)**. This is shown in the following figure:

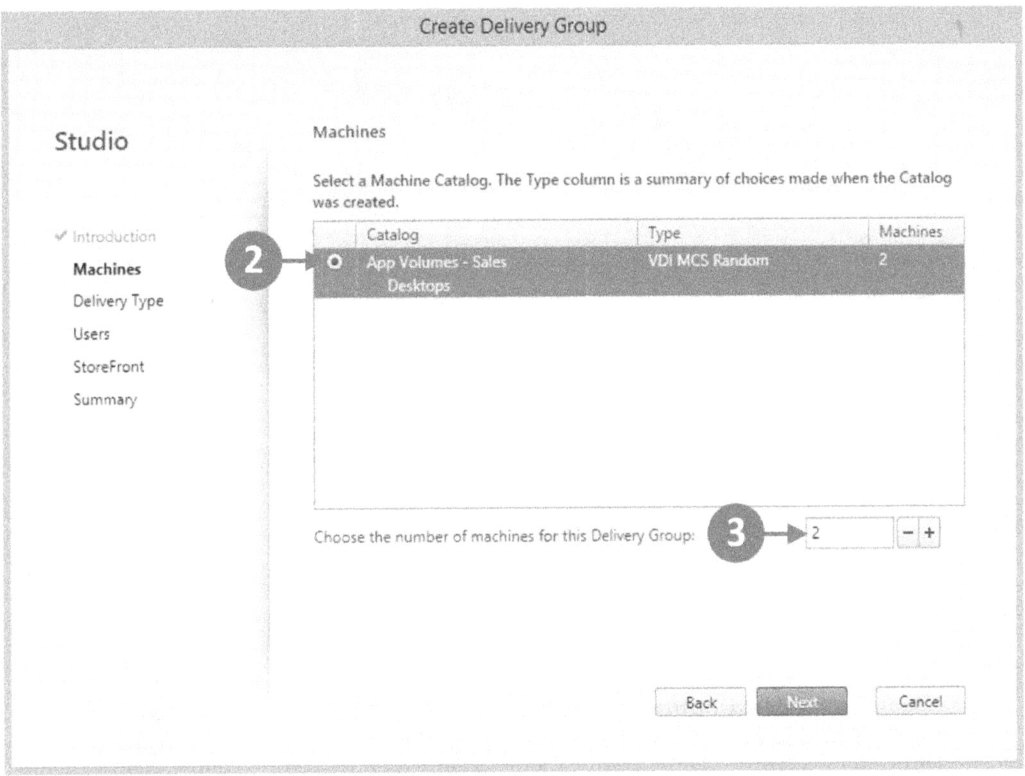

5. Click on the **Next** button to continue. The next screen allows you to select the **Delivery Type**. In this example, we are delivering virtual desktop machines, so click on the radio button for **Desktops (4)**. This is shown in the following diagram:

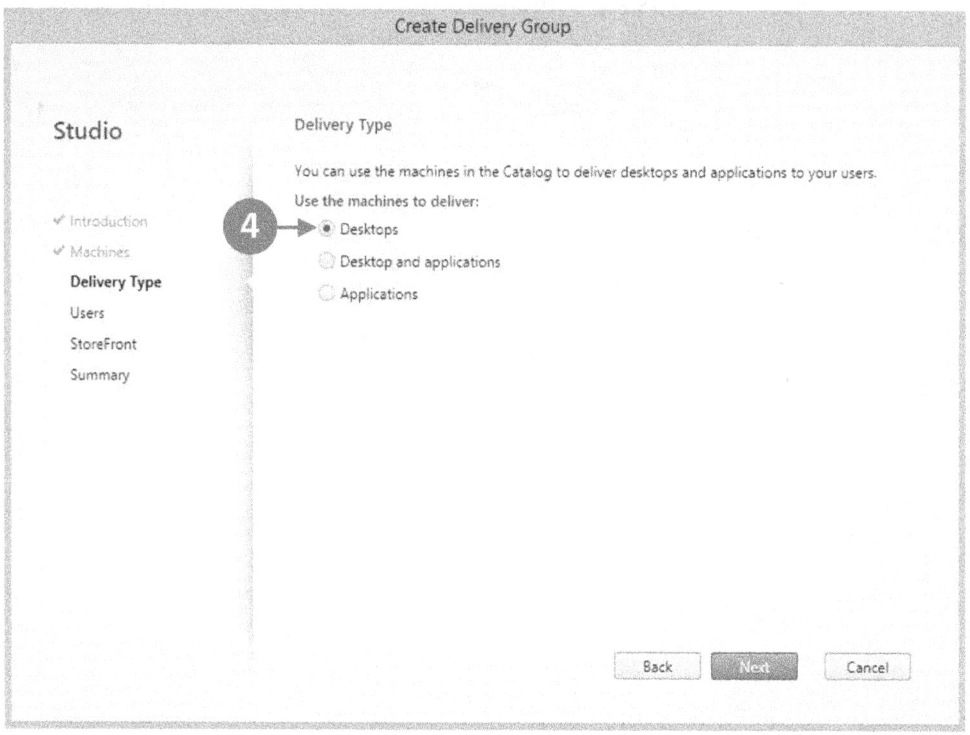

6. Click on the **Next** button to continue. Next, you need to select the users that will have access to this delivery group. In this example, we are going to assign an Active Directory group.

7. Click on the **Add...** button **(5)**, as shown in the following figure:

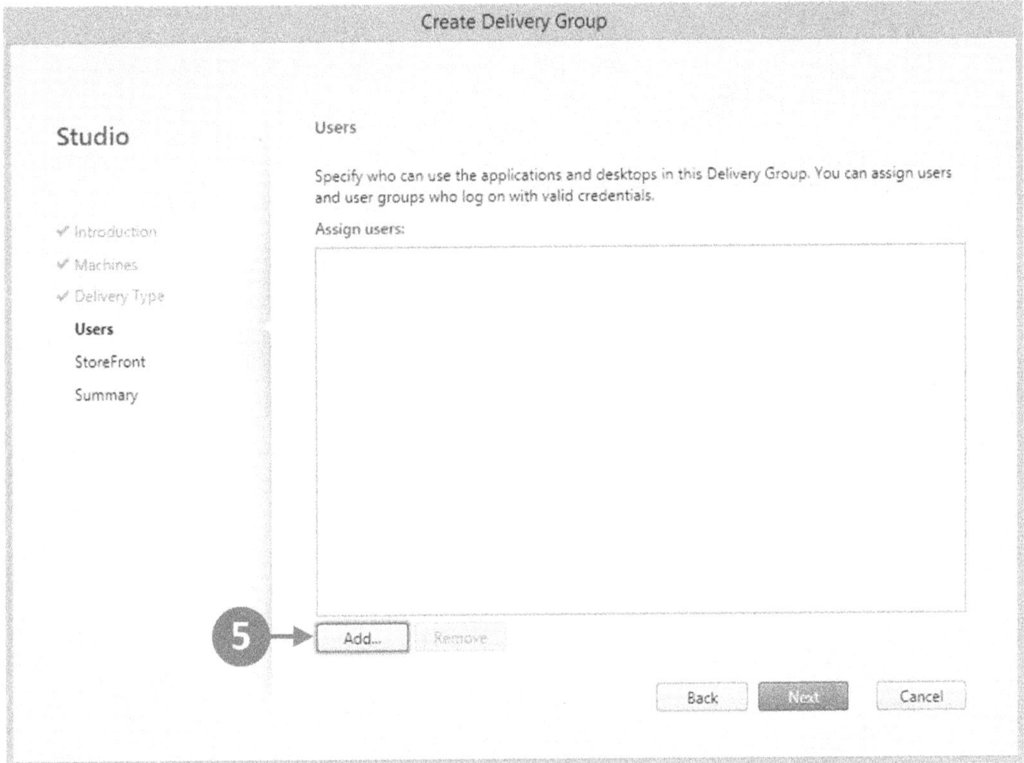

You will now see the **Select Users or Groups** dialog box, shown in the following screenshot:

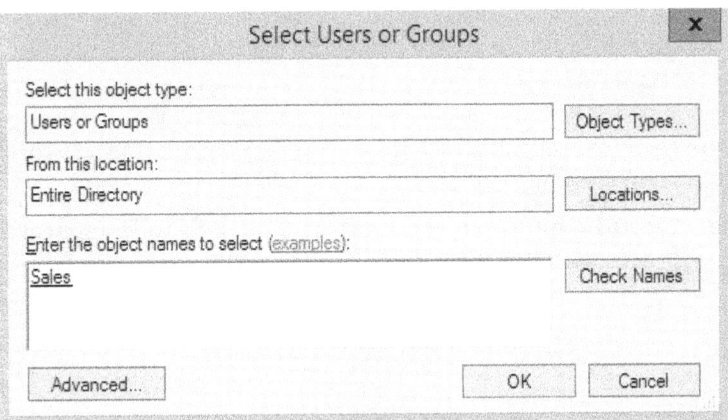

In the dialog box, type in the name of the user or group that you want to allow access to the virtual desktop machines. In this example, we are going to use the **Sales** group.

Type `Sales` into the box and then click on **Check Names**. The Sales group should now be listed.

8. Click on **OK** to close the box and return to the **Users** configuration screen. It should now look like the following screenshot:

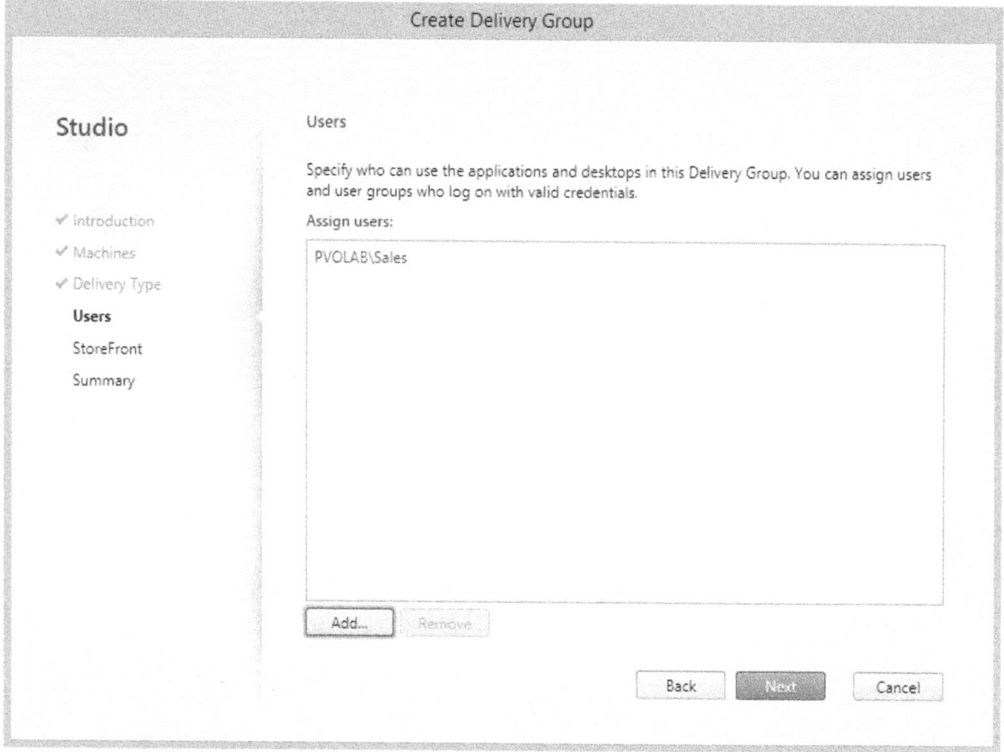

9. Click on the **Next** button to continue. The next screen is the **StoreFront** configuration screen.
10. Click on the radio button for **Manually, using a StoreFront server address that I will provide later (6)**. This is shown in the following figure:

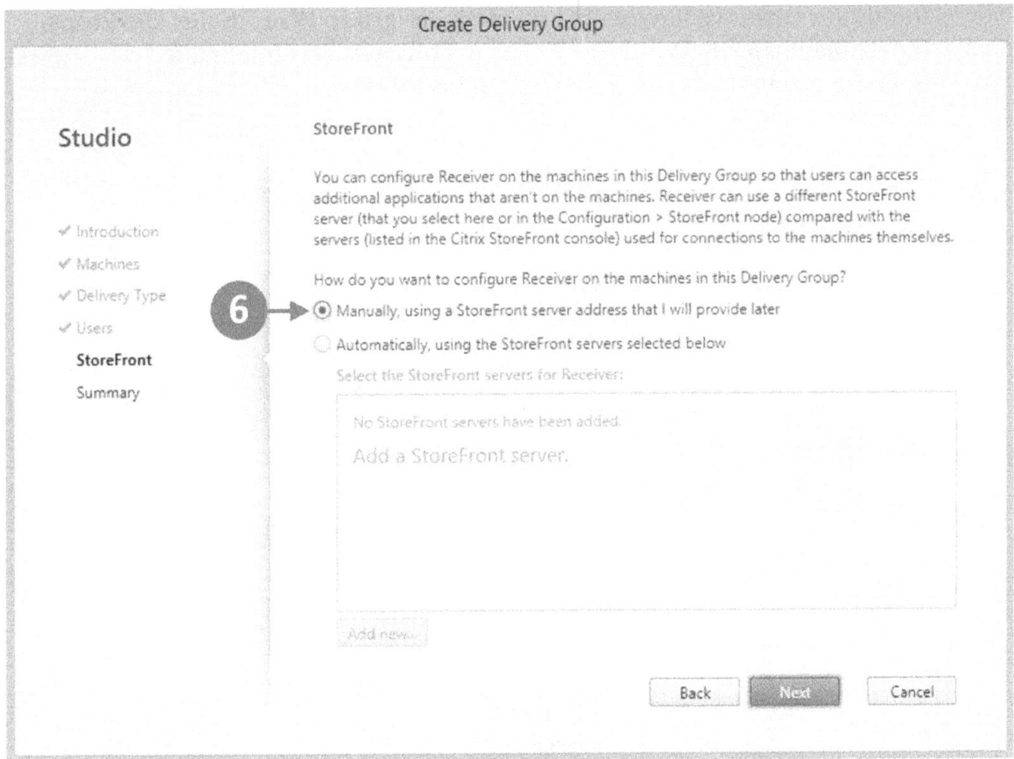

11. Click on the **Next** button to continue. The final screen you will see is the **Summary** screen. Check whether the configuration details have all been entered correctly. You can click on the **Back** button if you need to go back and correct any of the details.
12. Before you complete the details, there are a couple of things to configure in the summary screen. The last thing to configure is a **Delivery Group name (7)**, **Display name (8)**, and a **Delivery Group description (9)**.

In this example, we have called the delivery group **Win 7 Sales Desktops**, the display name is **Windows 7 + App Volumes**, and finally the delivery group description is **Win 7 Sales Desktops**. This is shown in the following diagram:

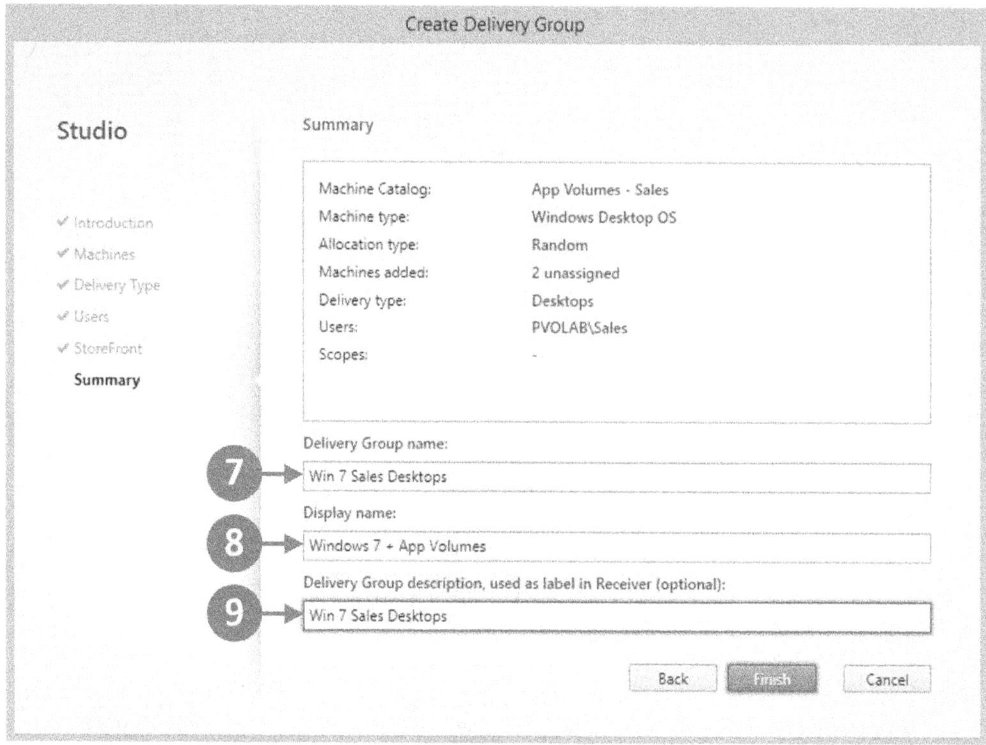

13. Click on the **Finish** button to complete the configuration of the delivery group. You will see the following progress bar:

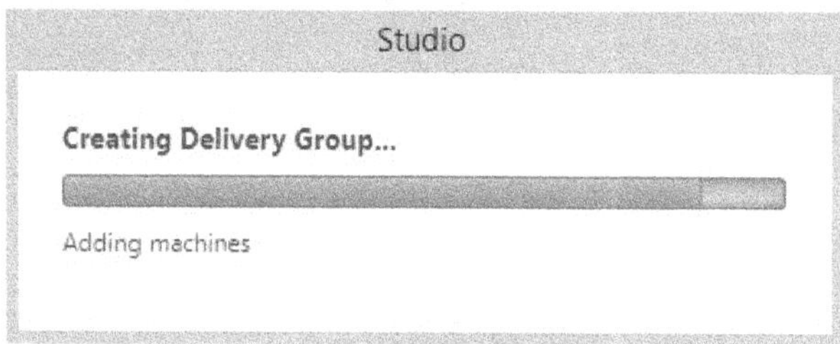

Once this is completed, you are ready to test whether everything works, which we will cover in the next chapter.

Logging on to a XenDesktop virtual desktop

We have completed the required configuration steps, built a desktop image ready for delivery, created a machine catalog, and finally created a delivery group.

The next step is to log in to XenDesktop and verify that the user can not only access a virtual desktop machine, but also that they have their App Volumes-delivered applications available.

We are going to use one of the example user desktop machines to log in from. You will need to ensure that **Citrix Receiver** is installed on this desktop machine.

The first step is to launch a browser and enter the address of the StoreFront server. In the Example Lab, a separate StoreFront server wasn't built, so we will use the default address. Enter `http://xendesktop.pvolab.com/Citrix/StoreWeb/` as the address:

You will now see the Citrix Receiver login screen, shown in the following screenshot:

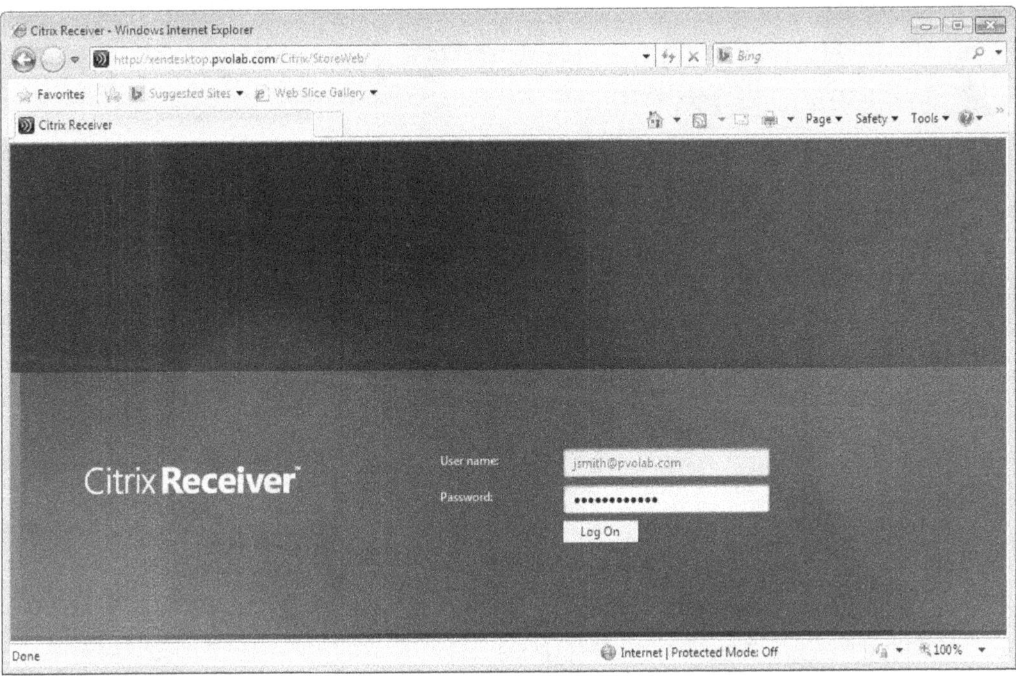

Enter the username `jsmith@pvolab.com` and the password for it, and then click on the **Log On** button. You will now see this window:

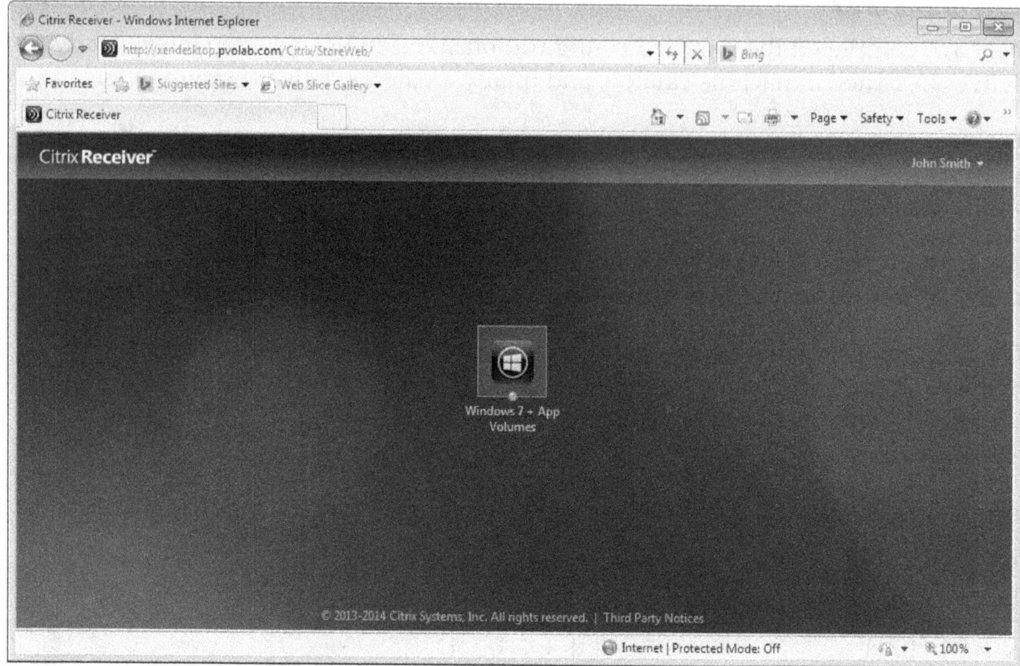

You will see an icon that represents the delivery group that was configured and a virtual desktop machine from within that group. Double-click on the icon to connect to the virtual desktop machine. You will see the following screen while the connection is established:

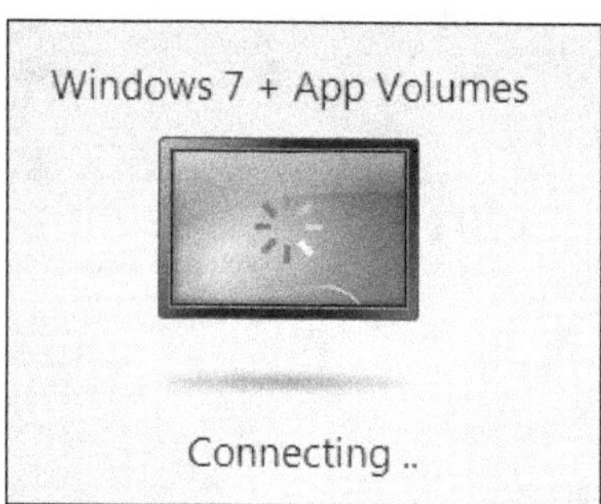

Once the connection has been established, you will see the following desktop:

As you can see, you now have a virtual desktop machine delivered by Citrix XenDesktop.

We configured the XenDesktop delivery group for the Sales group in Active Directory and then logged in as John Smith, who is a member of that group. The Sales group has also been assigned an AppStack containing VLC media player and Evernote, and therefore, these are attached to the virtual desktop machine as part of the AppStack assignment to that group.

You have now successfully set up a XenDesktop environment and delivered applications via an AppStack to an end user.

Summary

In this chapter, we started by taking a look at the architecture and describing how you can deliver applications using AppStacks as the delivery mechanism, but this time the virtual desktop machines were delivered using Citrix XenDesktop.

We then went on to configure an example Citrix XenDesktop deployment and build a virtual desktop image, complete with App Volumes Agent.

Finally, we demonstrated an end-user experience by logging in to the virtual desktop machine and showing that the application AppStack attached and the applications within it are available to the end user.

In the next chapter, we will look at another Citrix technology, Citrix XenApp, and how you can create stateless XenApp Servers using App Volumes.

11

Deploying App Volumes in a RemoteApp Environment

As we discussed in the previous chapter, a key feature of App Volumes is that it is not restricted to working with just VMware technology and products. In that chapter, we focused on how App Volumes can help deliver just-in-time applications when running a virtual desktop environment using Citrix XenDesktop, helping us create a truly stateless desktop environment for end users.

App Volumes is not just limited to working in a virtual desktop environment; it can also be used to deliver applications to servers that deliver application sessions or published applications to end users rather than a full desktop experience.

In *Chapter 1, Introduction to App Volumes*, we covered the published applications use case and that it is a perfect fit for App Volumes. Basically, you create a stateless application server farm with no actual applications physically installed on the servers. Instead, you attach AppStacks containing the applications, allowing you to scale the farm quickly without having to install applications on each individual server; you simply attach the relevant AppStack.

There are a few different solutions available on the market today for delivering published applications. We will cover the key technologies in the coming chapters, but in this chapter, we will take a closer look at how to deploy App Volumes to deliver just-in-time applications to a **Microsoft RemoteApp** environment.

We are going to start with Microsoft RemoteApp and **Remote Desktop Session Host** (**RDSH**), as it is used by other vendors as the foundation that underpins their application hosting/publishing solutions.

The following diagram illustrates how App Volumes works within a Microsoft RemoteApp architecture:

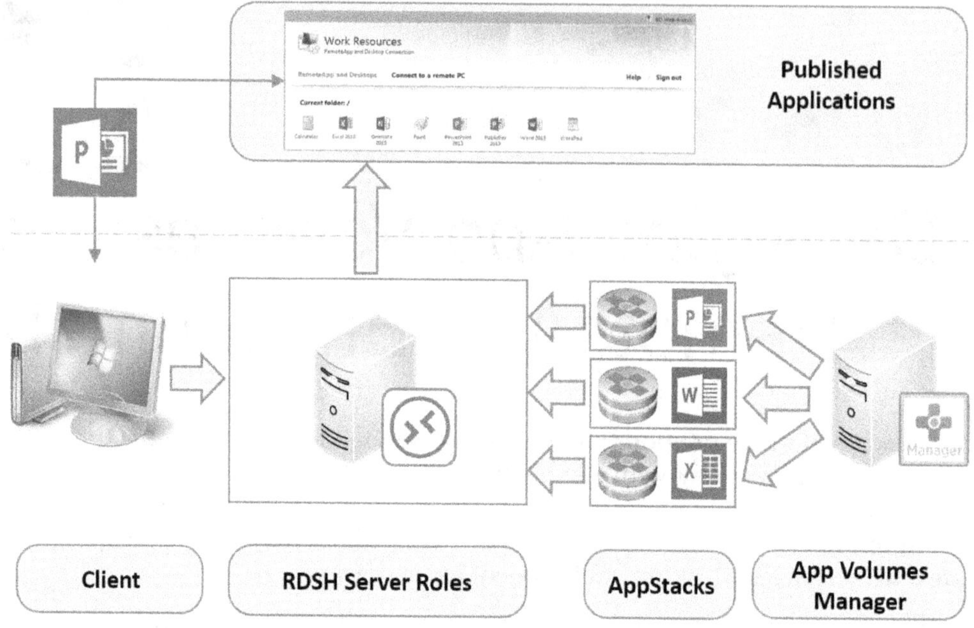

The Microsoft RemoteApp process for logging in and connecting to applications remains exactly as it would in any other RemoteApp deployment, so for users, the fact that the applications are delivered as AppStacks is completely transparent.

For IT administrators, the process is slightly different, as rather than having to install the applications onto each RDSH server, once you have provisioned an AppStack for use with RDSH and RemoteApp, you simply assign that provisioned AppStack containing the applications to each server.

In this example, we are using VMware vSphere (ESXi and vCenter Server) as the underlying infrastructure to host the RDSH servers as virtual machines, and therefore using VMware-based virtual machines with VMDK files for the virtual disk files.

In the next section, we will describe the process for building an AppStack for use with RDSH servers and then show how to deliver that back and publish the applications to the end users.

Building and configuring an AppStack for RemoteApp delivery

Now that we have described the architecture of how App Volumes fits into a Microsoft RDSH environment, we can start to build and configure the environment.

There are a number of steps involved in creating the environment, which are illustrated in the following diagram:

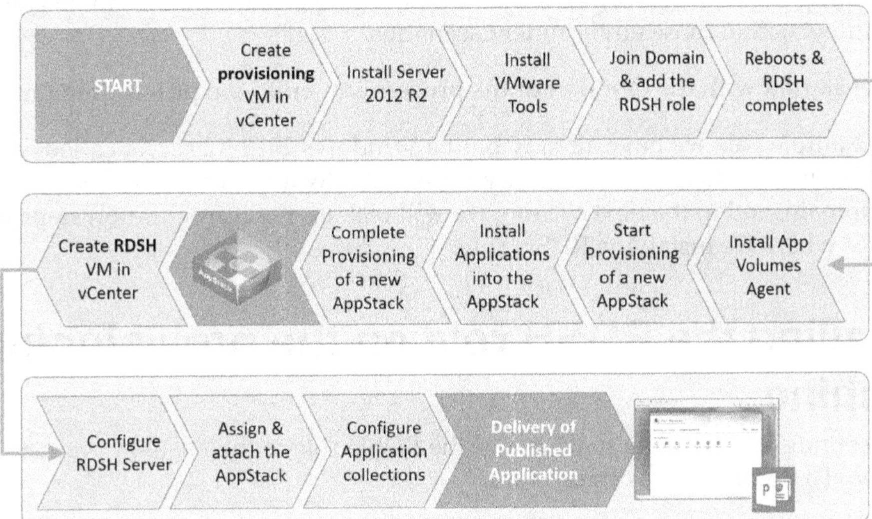

In this chapter, we will cover the complete scenario of building a Microsoft RemoteApp solution from the ground up, with the applications delivered using App Volumes.

> The steps described in the previous diagram are in the order in which they should be completed. It is important to note when to install App Volumes Agent in particular and will become more important in other chapters when we come to installing VMware Horizon View.

As with the process described for building AppStacks for use with virtual desktop machines, the first part of this process is to build a provisioning machine from which we can create AppStacks.

> AppStacks need to be provisioned using the same operating system that they are going to be delivered to.

In this example, the provisioning machine will be a Windows Server 2012 R2 virtual machine configured with the RDSH role.

This provisioning machine will be used to create an AppStack containing Microsoft Office 2013 Professional, and once created, the AppStack can then be used on other RDSH-enabled servers.

So, the AppStack that you will create in this chapter will also be used in *Chapter 12, Deploying App Volumes in a Citrix XenApp Environment*, and in *Chapter 13, Deploying App Volumes in a Horizon View Hosted Apps Environment*, to deliver the applications within those environment scenarios.

Let's get started with the first part of the process and build the provisioning machine.

In the Example Lab, we have already built a Windows 2012 R2 server called RDSH-Provision. This server is already running VMware tools and is also joined to the domain, and in the next section, we will pick up the configuration steps from the point where we install the RDSH role.

Installing the RDSH role on the provisioning machine

The first thing we are going to do is add the RDSH role to the `RDSH-Provision` machine. To do that, follow these steps:

1. Open a console to the server and launch Server Manager.
2. From the main screen, under **Configure this local server**, select the option for **Add roles and features (1)**, as shown in the following diagram:

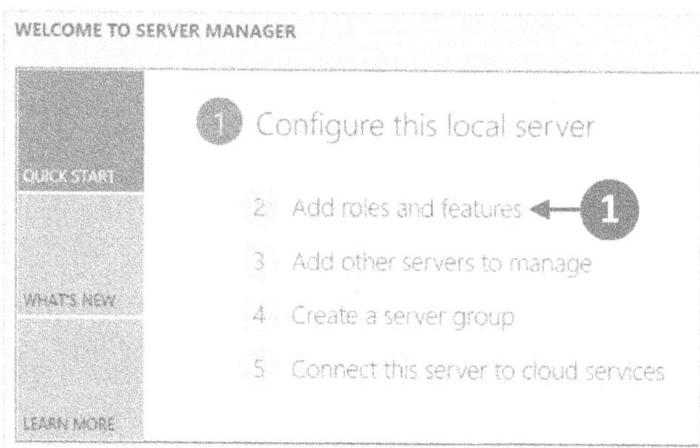

3. You will now see the **Before You Begin** screen. Click on the **Next >** button to continue.

4. On the **Installation Type** screen, click on the radio button for **Remote Desktop Services Installation (2)**, as shown in the following diagram:

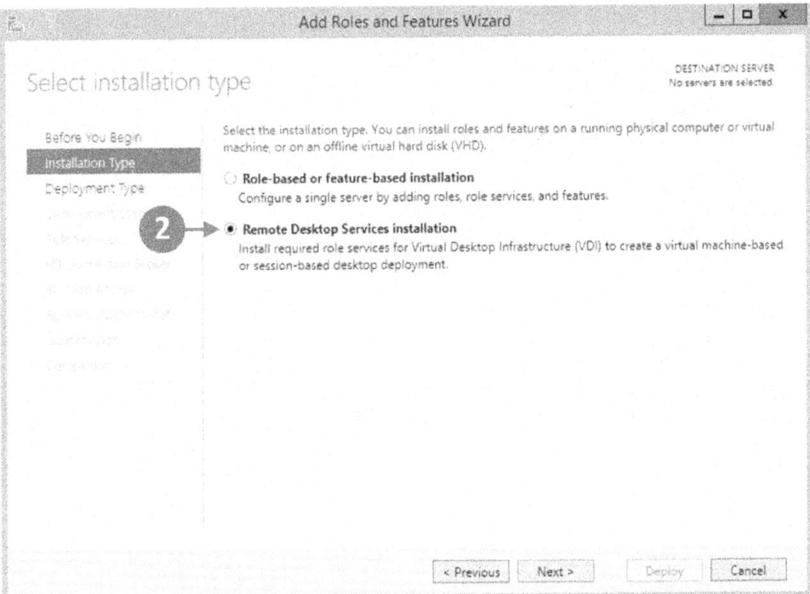

5. Click on the **Next >** button to continue. You will now see the **Deployment Type** screen.

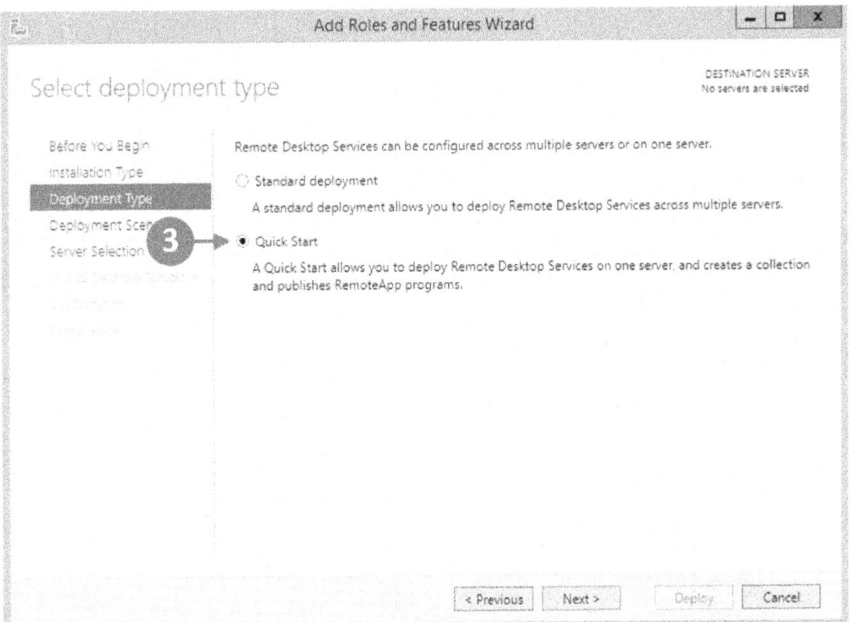

6. On the **Deployment Type** screen, click on the radio button for **Quick Start (3)**, and then click on the **Next >** button to continue. You will now see the **Deployment Scenario** screen, shown in the following diagram:

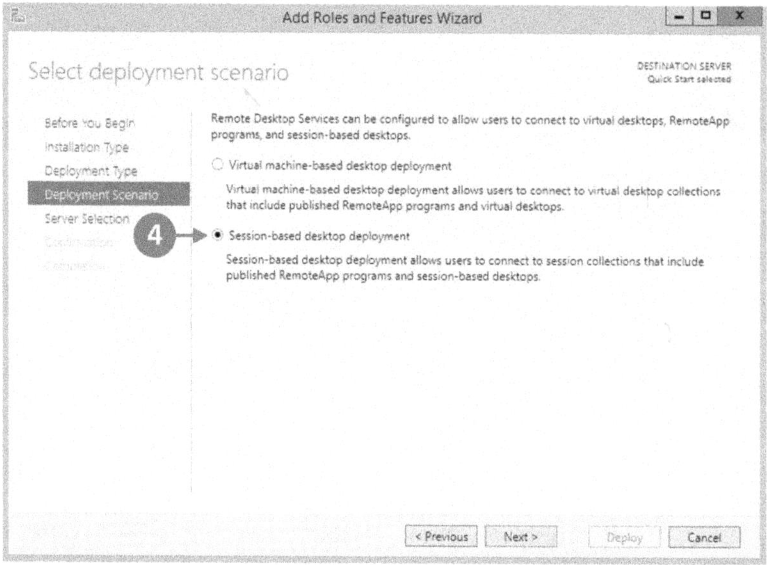

7. Click on the radio button for **Session-based desktop deployment (4)**, and then click on the **Next >** button to continue. You will now see the **Server Selection** screen, shown in the following diagram:

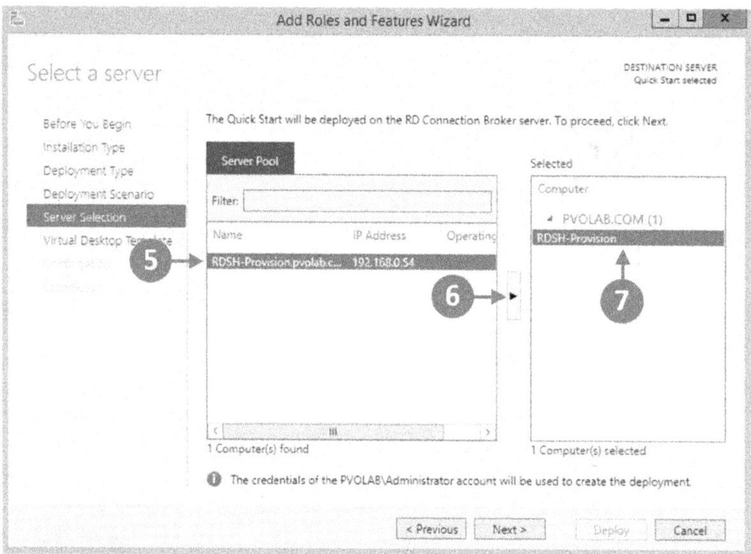

8. Select the server that you want to add the RDSH role to and use as the provisioning virtual machine. In this example, the machine's name is `RDSH-Provision.pvolab.com`.
9. Highlight the server name in the **Server Pool** box **(5)**, and then click on the arrow **(6)** to add it to the **Selected** box **(7)**.
10. Once this is complete, click on the **Next >** button to continue. You will now see the **Confirmation** screen, shown in the following diagram:

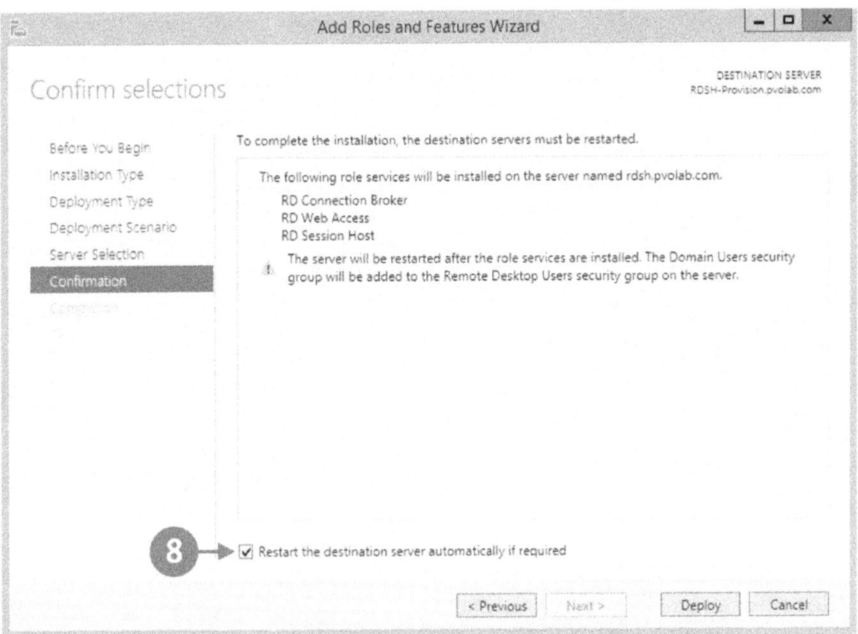

11. Check the **Restart the destination server automatically if required** box **(8)**, and finally, click on the **Deploy** button. You will now see the **Completion** screen:

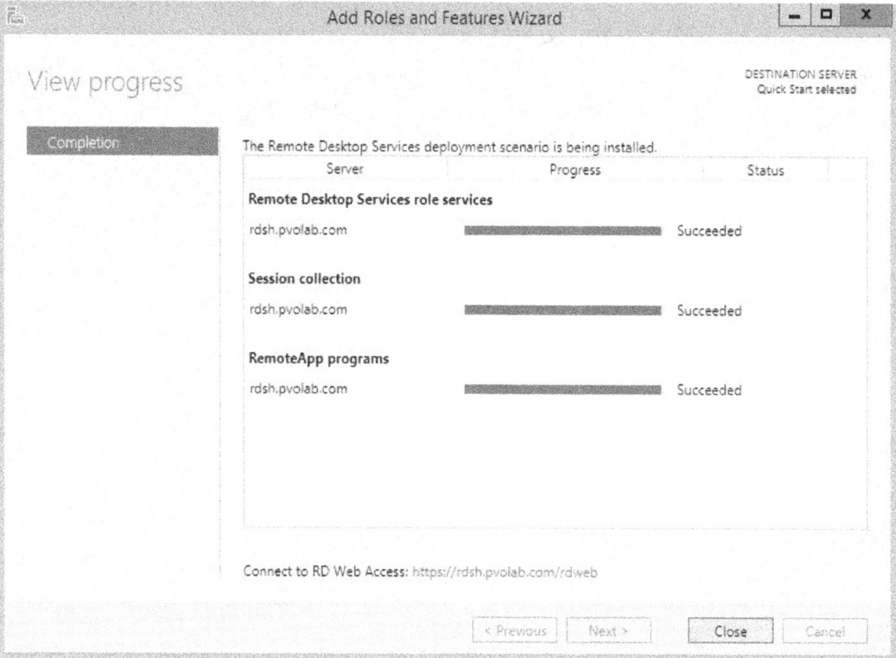

12. Check that the installation has completed successfully, and then click on the **Close** button.

13. You will now return to the Server Manager screen, which will show that the roles for **Remote Desktop Services** and **IIS** have been added, as shown in the following screenshot:

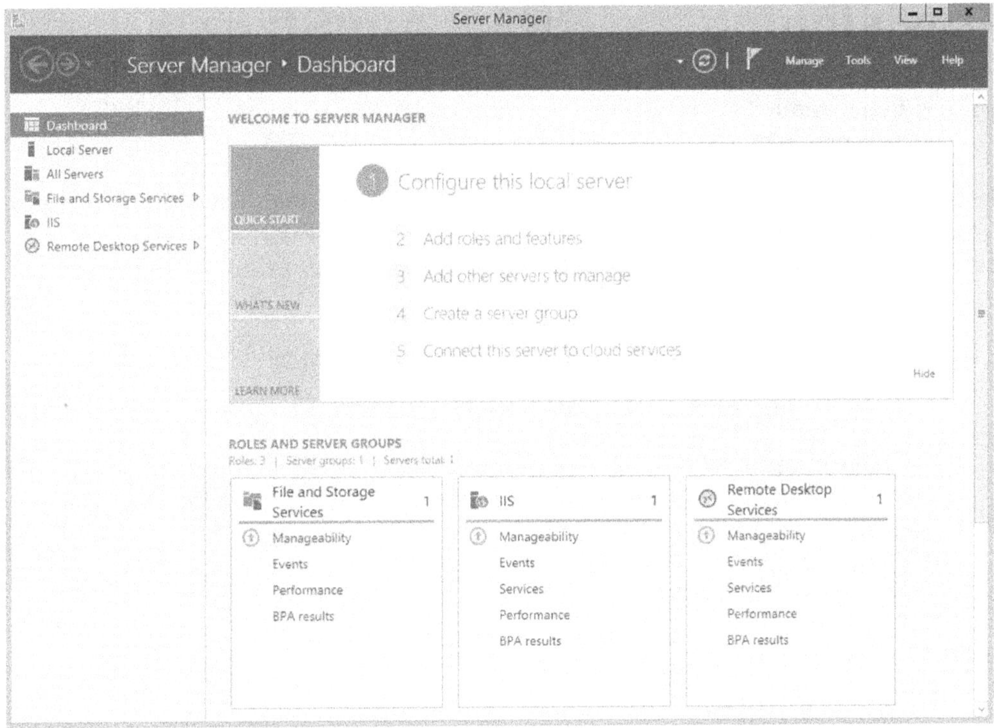

You should now have a server that has been configured as an RDSH host server.

The next step is to install App Volumes Agent.

Installing App Volumes Agent

The next part of the process is to install App Volumes Agent onto the RDSH host server so that it registers itself with App Volumes Manager, allowing us to start using it for application provisioning.

We have already covered the installation process in the *Installing App Volumes Agent* section of *Chapter 4, Installing and Configuring the App Volumes Software*, so refer back to that chapter on how to do this. The process is exactly the same for servers as it is for desktops.

Provisioning the RDSH AppStack

At this stage of the process, you have built a server and configured it with the RDSH role and then installed App Volumes Agent onto it. We are going to break the provisioning process into two stages.

First, we will walk through a reminder on how to perform the provisioning process and then, as we install applications on an RDSH server, we will detail the application installation process since it is different from installing on to a desktop machine.

Starting the provisioning process

Perform the following steps to start the provisioning process:

1. Open a console to the App Volumes Manager server and launch the App Volumes Manager management console. You will now see the login screen, shown in the following screenshot:

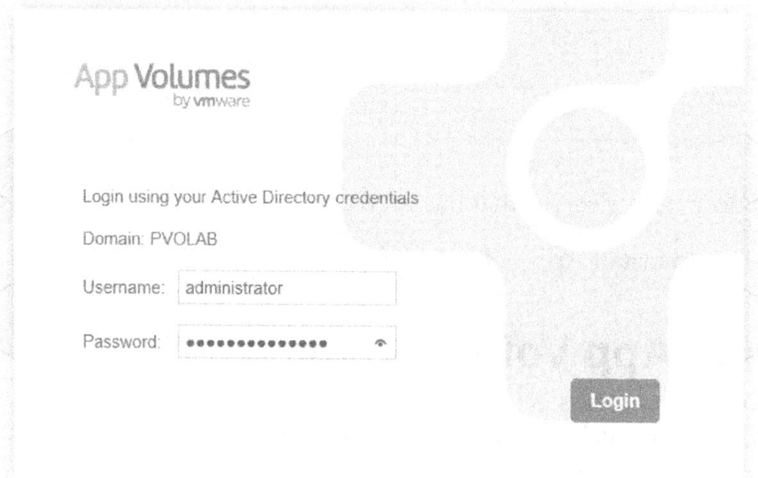

2. Enter the username and password of the administrator account and then click on the **Login** button.
3. From the App Volumes Manager console, click on the **Volumes** menu option **(1)**, and then click on the **AppStacks** tab **(2)**.

4. Now, click on the **Create AppStack** button **(3)**, as shown in the following diagram:

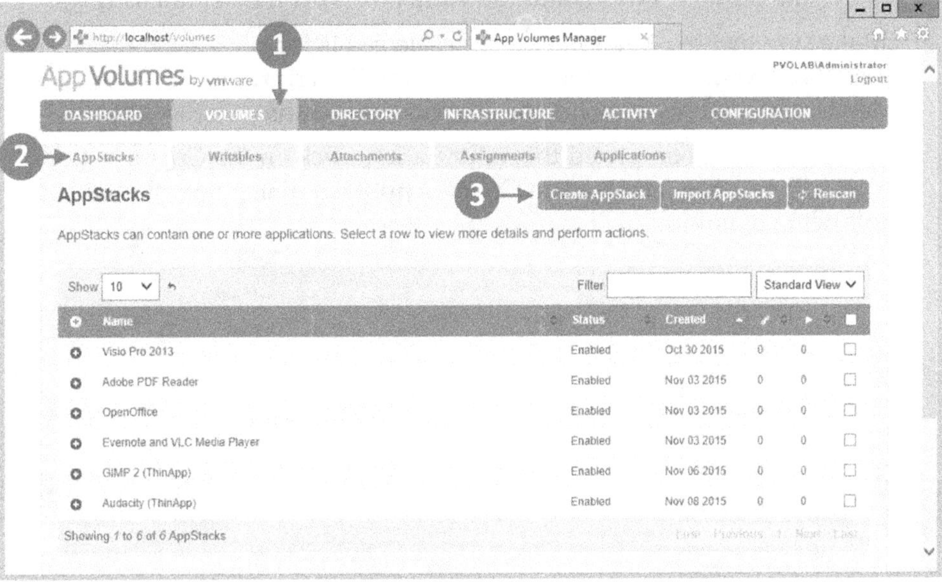

You will now see the **Create AppStack** screen, shown in the following diagram:

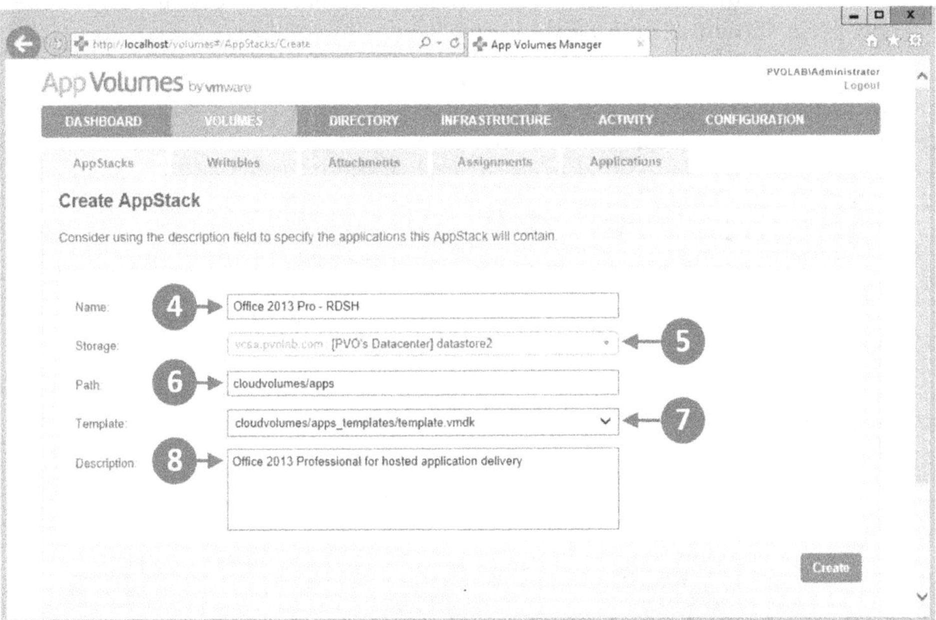

5. In the **Name:** box **(4)**, enter a name for the AppStack. In this example, we have called it `Office 2013 Pro - RDSH`.
6. Leave the **Storage:** box **(5)** and the **Path:** box **(6)** at the default settings.
7. Make sure that the **Template:** option selected is for `apps_templates/template.vmdk` **(7)**, and then finally, in the **Description:** box **(8)**, enter a description to describe what this AppStack contains.
8. When you have completed this information, click on the **Create** button. You will now see the **Confirm Create AppStack** dialog box, shown in the following diagram:

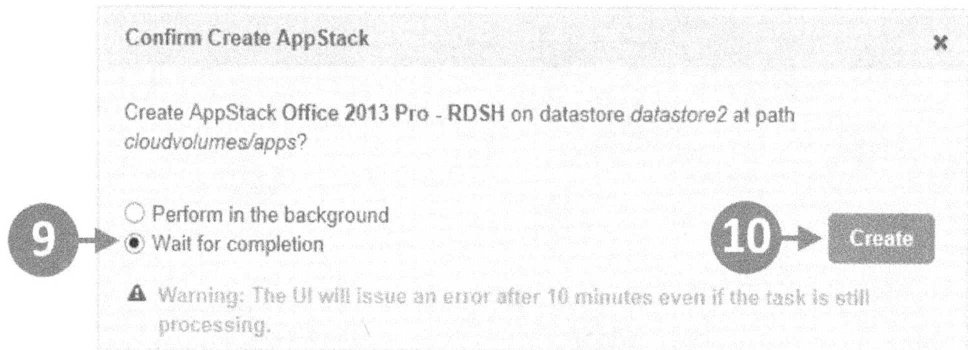
Confirm Create AppStack
Create AppStack Office 2013 Pro - RDSH on datastore datastore2 at path cloudvolumes/apps?
Perform in the background
Wait for completion
9
10
Create
Warning: The UI will issue an error after 10 minutes even if the task is still processing.

9. Click on the radio button for **Wait for completion (9)**, and then click on the **Create** button **(10)**. The AppStack is now created and you will see the progress shown with the following:

Creating AppStack

With the AppStack now created, you can start the provisioning of the applications. You will now see the **AppStacks** configuration screen, shown in the following diagram:

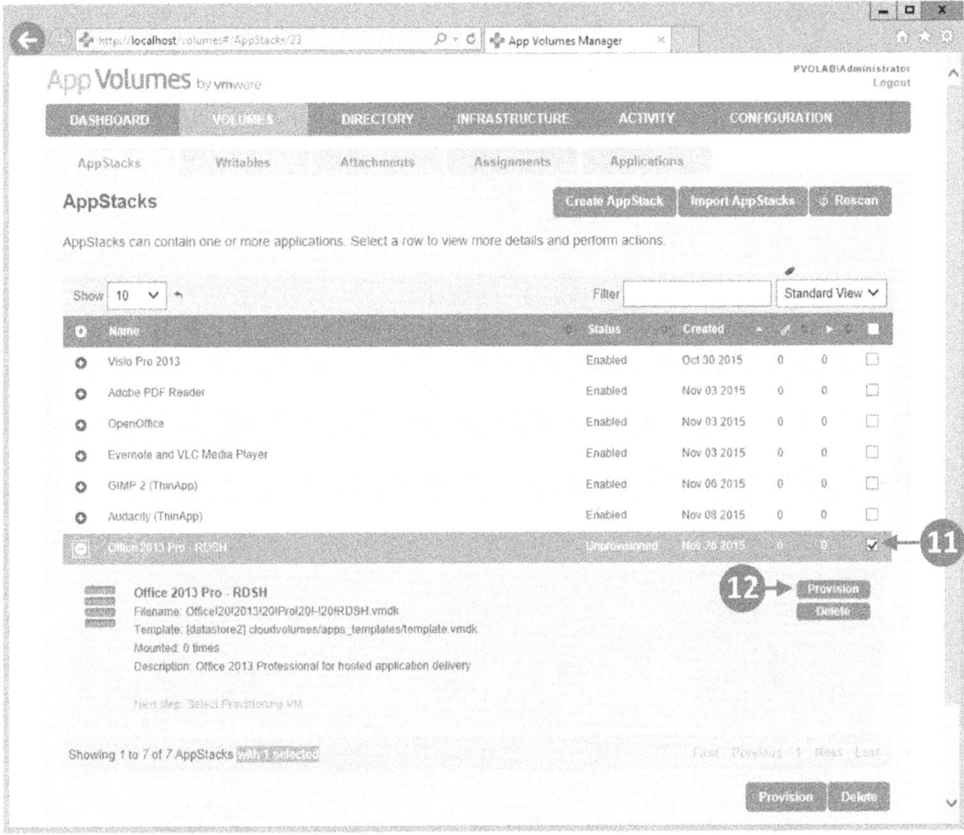

10. Select the AppStack that you just created by checking the tick box next to its entry on the inventory **(11)**. When selected, the entry will be highlighted in orange.
11. Now, click on the **Provision** button **(12)**.

12. Next, you will see the **Provision AppStack: Office 2013 Pro – RDSH** screen, where you need to choose which virtual machine you are going to use to provision this particular AppStack. This is shown in the following diagram:

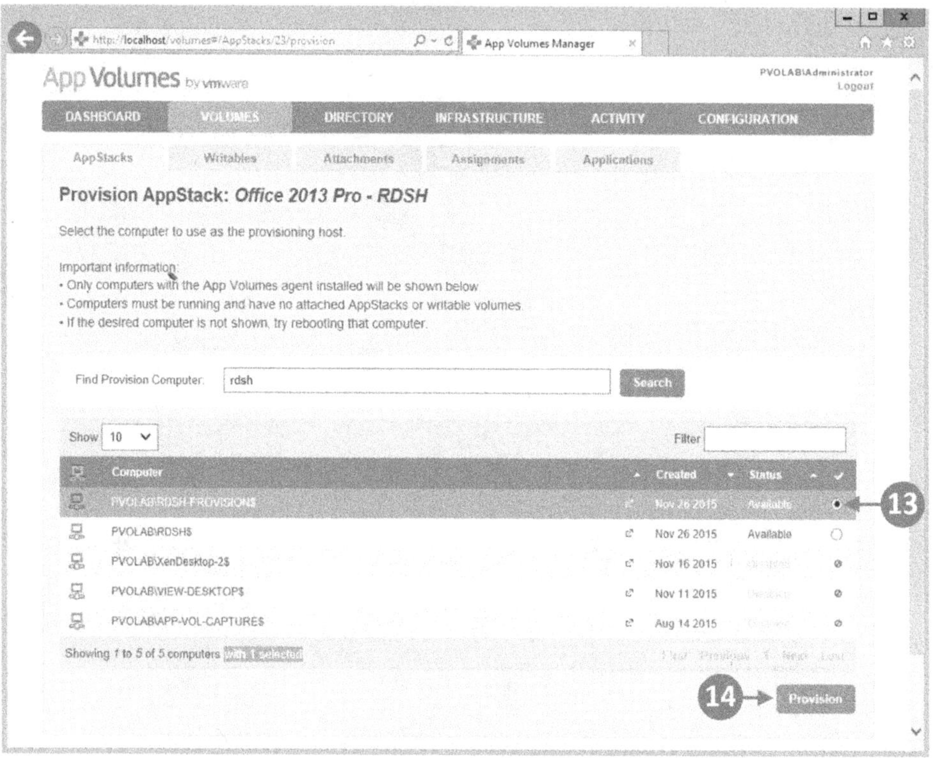

In this example, we are going to use the RDSH server that we built and configured at the beginning of this chapter. The machine name for the provisioning machine is `RDSH-Provision`.

13. Click on the radio button next to the entry for `PVOLAB\RDSH-PROVISION$` **(13)**, and then click on the **Provision** button **(14)**. You will now see the following dialog box:

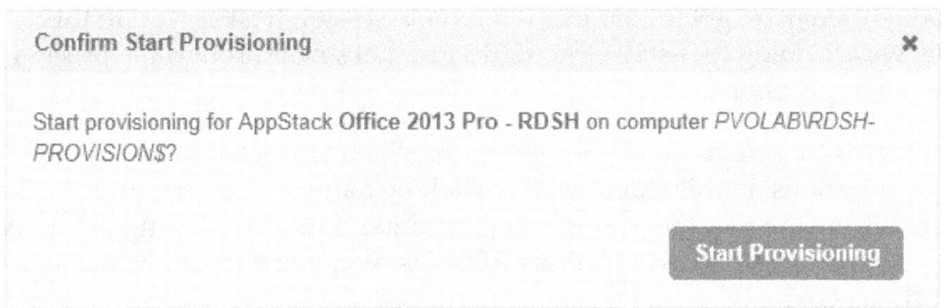

14. Click on the **Start Provisioning** button to continue the process. You will see the following message as the AppStack is attached:

The AppStack is now attached to the provisioning machine, as shown in the following screenshot:

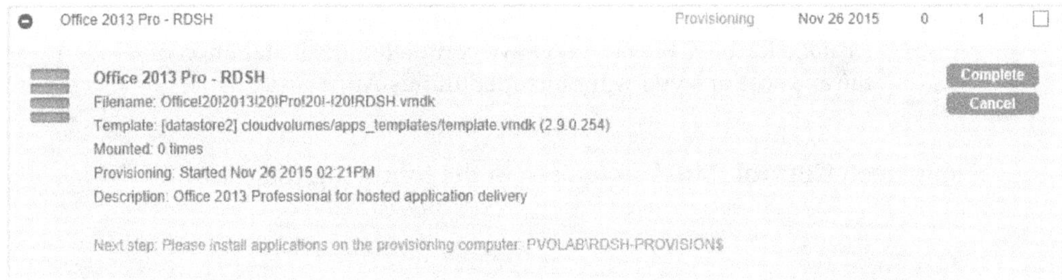

You can now start to install applications on the provisioning machine.

Remember, *do not* click on the **Complete** button until you have completely finished installing the applications.

In the next section, we will look at how to install applications on the provisioning machine, given the fact that it is an RDSH host.

Installing applications

Installing applications on an RDSH server is almost identical to installing applications on any other Windows-based machine. However, there are a few subtle differences, given that this is a remote session host server. In this example, we are going to install Office 2013 Pro. Let's run through the process of installing applications:

1. Open a console to the RDSH server on which you want to install the applications; in this example, the machine name is `RDSH-Provision`. First of all, ensure that the provisioning machine is in provisioning mode. When you switch to the console of the RDSH server, you should see the following dialog box:

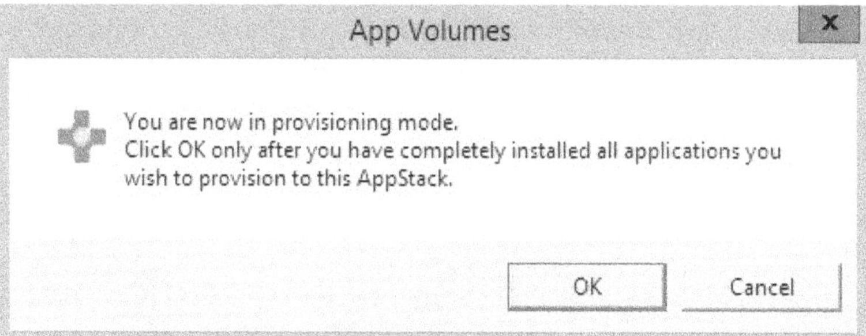
App Volumes
You are now in provisioning mode.
Click OK only after you have completely installed all applications you wish to provision to this AppStack.
OK
Cancel

Do not click on **OK** until you have completed the installation of all the applications you want included in this AppStack.

2. Next, open **Control Panel**, as shown in the following diagram:

Control Panel
Programs
1
Uninstall a program
Get programs
Turn Windows features on or off

3. From **Control Panel**, click on **Programs (1)**. The **Programs** dialog box opens, as shown in the following diagram:

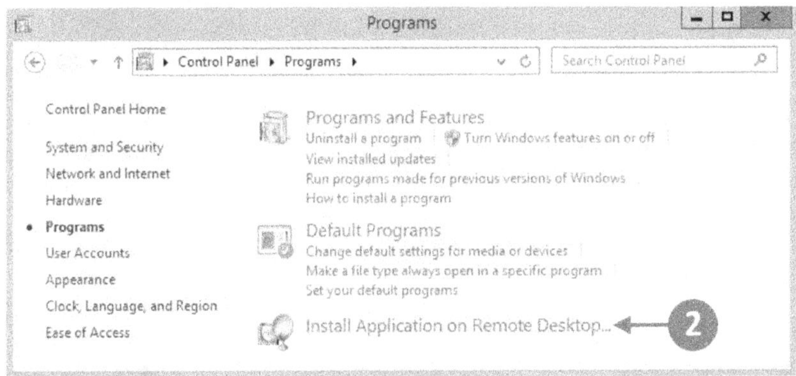

4. Click on **Install Application on Remote Desktop... (2)**. You will now see the **Install Program From Floppy Disk or CD-ROM** dialog box, shown in the following screenshot:

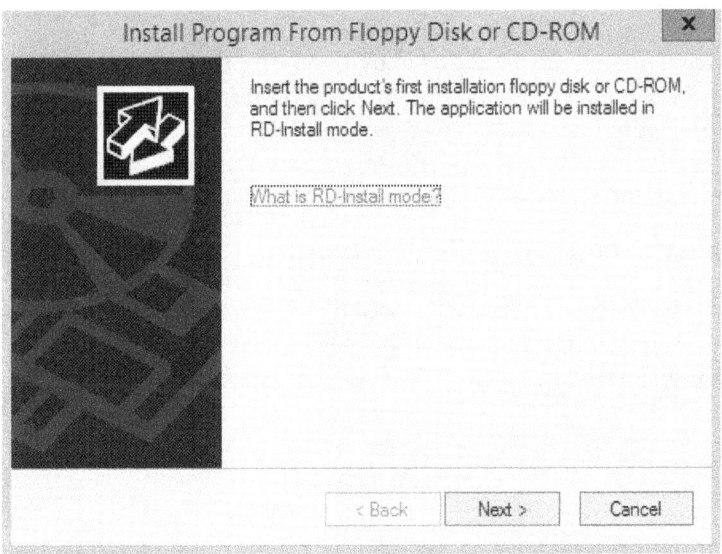

In this dialog box, you will see that it talks about something called RD-Install mode, with a link to **What is RD-Install mode?**

This is where the differences between a desktop installation and a server installation come into play. To install an application on an RDSH host server, the server needs to be switched into a special install mode known as RD-Install. This ensures that the applications are able to run in a multiuser environment, such as published applications, where multiple users run applications at the same time.

Once you have installed the applications on the RDSH server, the server needs to be switched back into normal mode, or what is called execution mode or RD-Execute, so that users can remotely connect to the server and the applications running on it.

This installation mode change can also be initiated from the command line, using the following commands:

```
change user /install
```

```
change user /execute
```

You can check the current installation mode of your RDSH server from the command line, using the following command:

```
change user /query
```

The easiest way to install applications is by installing them from the **Programs** option in **Control Panel**, which is how we are going to do it in this example. This option takes you through the installation process by automatically switching the server to RD-Install mode, installing the program, and switching the server back to RD-Execute mode once the installation is complete.

Click on the **Next >** button to continue the installation.

The server automatically checks for the installation media and installation files, first on the **A:** drive and then the **E:** drive. If it doesn't locate any media, then the **Run Installation Program** dialog box is displayed, as shown in the following screenshot:

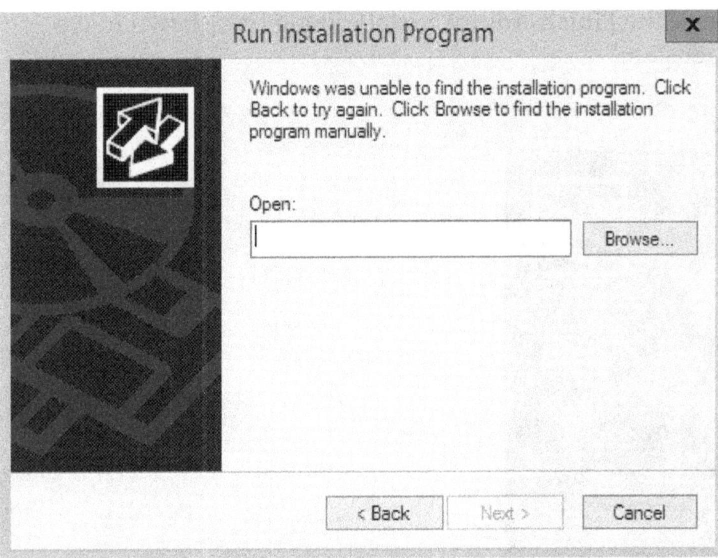

In the **Open:** box, type in the path to the application installer files if you know it. In this example, we are going to click on the **Browse...** button and in the window that opens, we are going to navigate to the location of where we have saved the Office 2013 ISO file, which happens to be located in the shared folder.

Once it is located, as shown in the following screenshot, click on the **Next >** button:

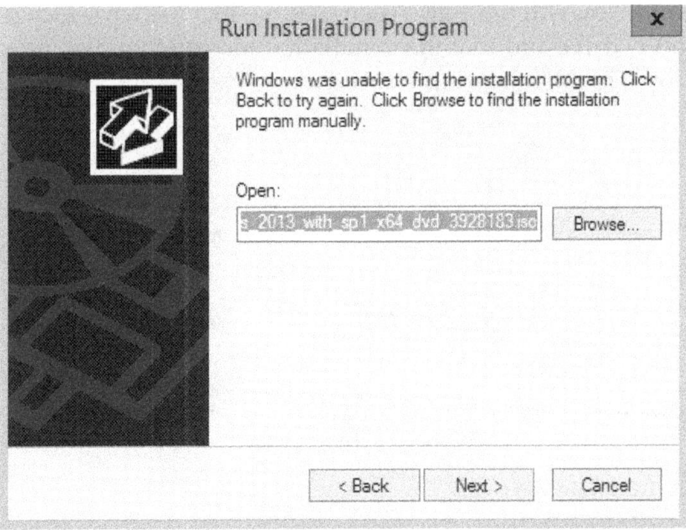

You will now see the **Finish Admin Install** dialog box, shown in the following screenshot:

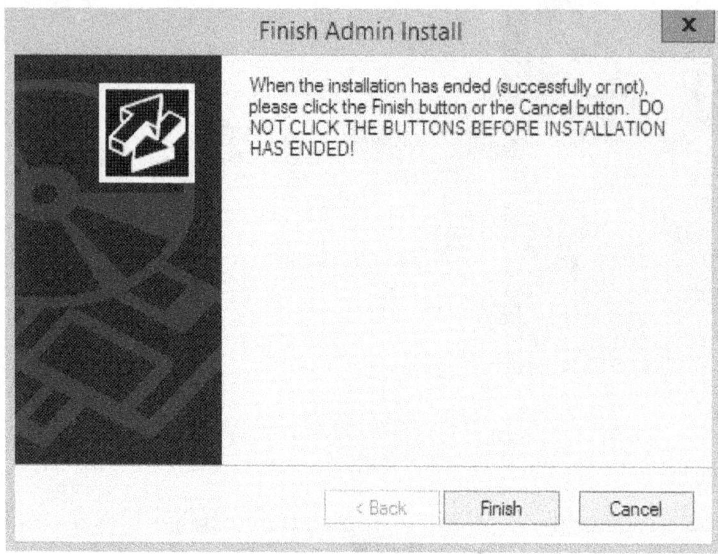

Do not click on **Finish** until you have completed the application installation.

In the background, you will have also seen that the ISO file we selected has been mounted as a DVD drive and that the installation files on that disk image are now available, as shown in the following screenshot:

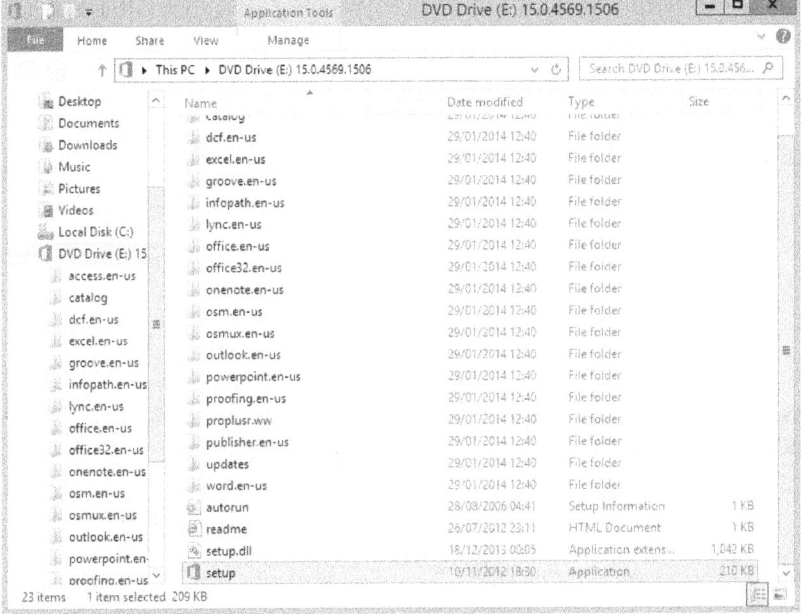

Locate and launch the setup program and start the installation of Office 2013. We are not to go through that process, so continue and install Office as you normally would.

> Make sure you have the appropriate license key, such as a Volume License key, in order to be able to run Office on an RDSH server.

Once the installation has successfully completed and you have completed any additional configuration tasks, return to the **Finish Admin Install** dialog box, and click on **Finish**.

Next, return to the App Volumes dialog box and click on **OK** to finish the provisioning process. You will see the following dialog box:

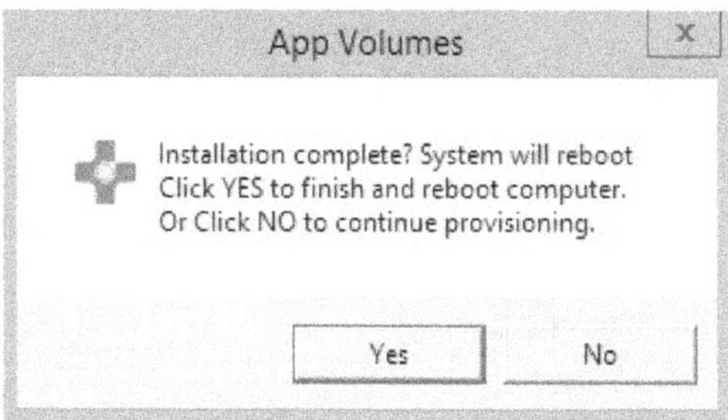
App Volumes
Installation complete? System will reboot
Click YES to finish and reboot computer.
Or Click NO to continue provisioning.
Yes
No

Click on **Yes** to confirm that you have completed the application installation. You will now see the following dialog box:

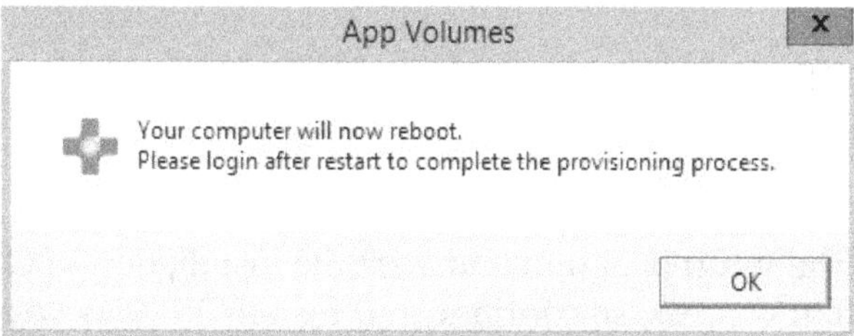
App Volumes
Your computer will now reboot.
Please login after restart to complete the provisioning process.
OK

Click on **OK** to confirm the reboot. The provisioning machine will now reboot and in the process detach the newly created and provisioned AppStack.

Once it has rebooted, you will see the following dialog box:

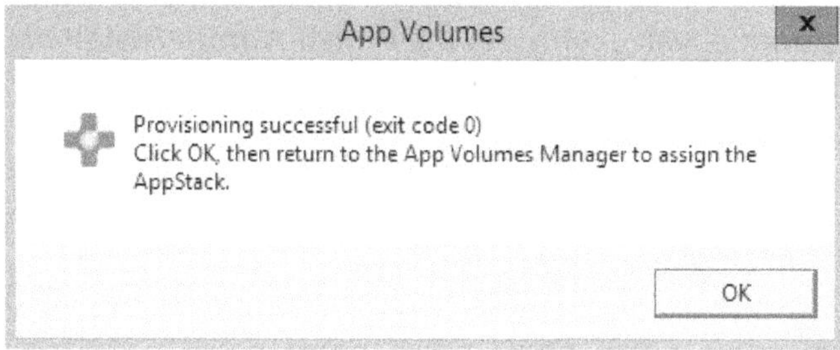
App Volumes
Provisioning successful (exit code 0)
Click OK, then return to the App Volumes Manager to assign the AppStack.
OK

Click on **OK** to close the box and finish the provisioning.

You now have an AppStack containing Office 2013 that can be attached to RDSH servers. In the next section, we will do exactly that and attach the newly created AppStack to an RDSH server.

Assigning the AppStack to the RDSH server

Now that we have our Office 2013 AppStack, we can assign and attach it to an RDSH server. In this example, we have a second RDSH server with the machine name `RDSH`.

This machine has already been built and configured with the RDSH role, but is currently missing applications.

If you go back to the App Volumes Manager console, you will see the AppStack listed, as shown in the following diagram:

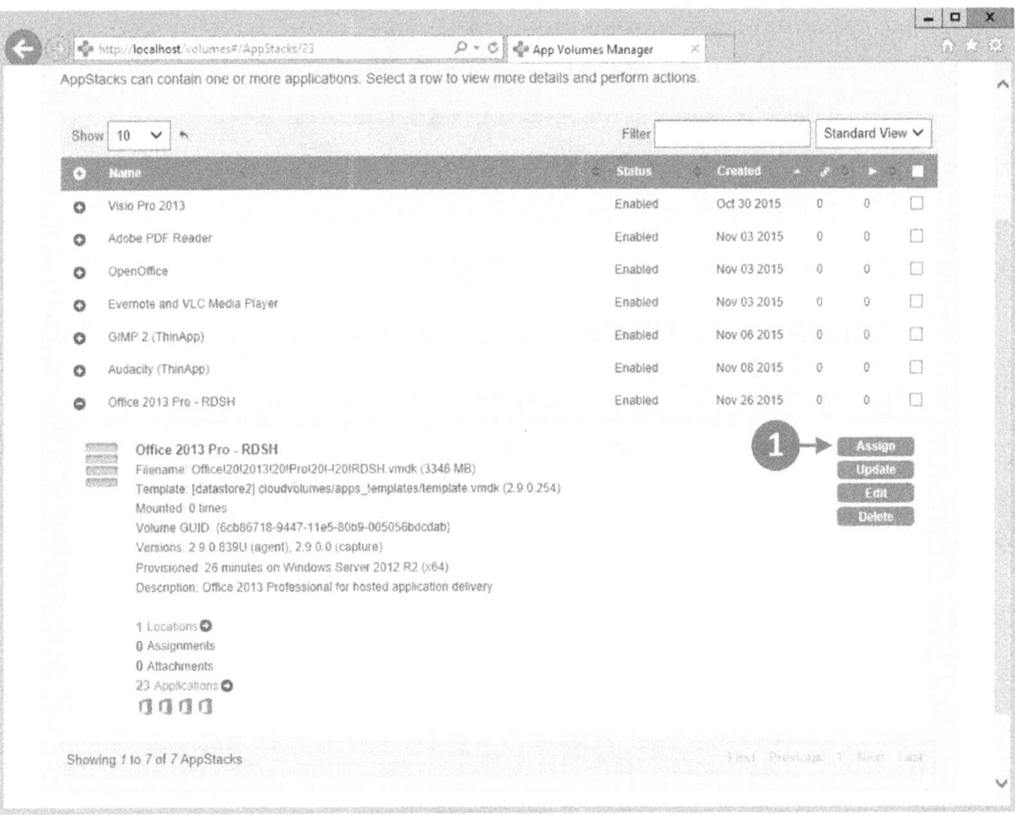

Perform the following steps:

1. Click on the **Assign** button **(1)**. You will now see the **Assign AppStack** screen, shown in the following diagram:

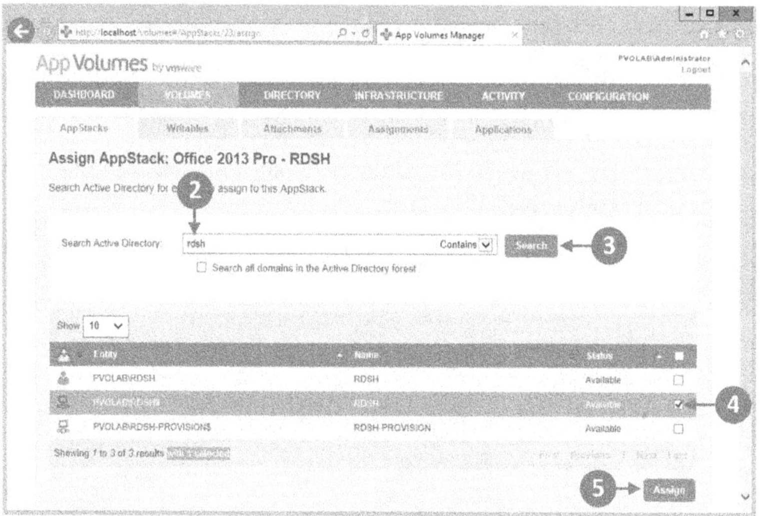

2. In the **Search Active Directory** box **(2)**, enter the name of the server to assign the AppStack to. In this example, the server we are searching for is **RDSH**, so type this into the box and then click on the **Search** button **(3)**.
3. From the results displayed, check the box next to the server you want to assign the AppStack to **(4)**, and then click on the **Assign** button **(5)**. You will now see the **Confirm Assign** dialog box, shown in the following diagram:

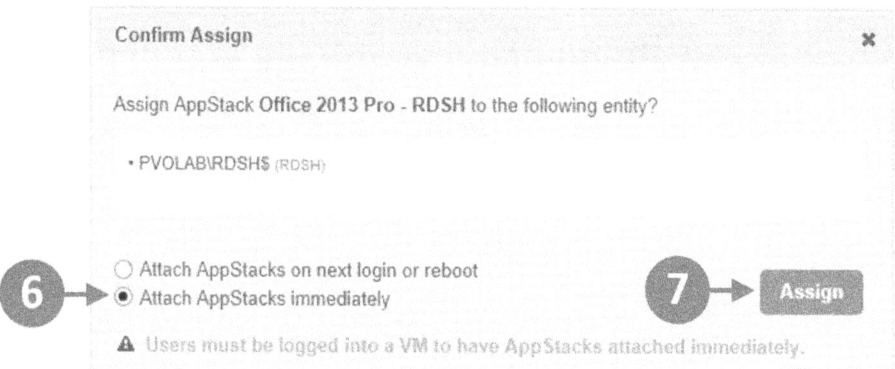

4. Click on the radio button for **Attach AppStacks immediately (6)**, and then click on the **Assign** button **(7)**. You will see the following message as the AppStack is assigned and attached:

Once the assignment has completed and the AppStack has been attached, you will see the following window:

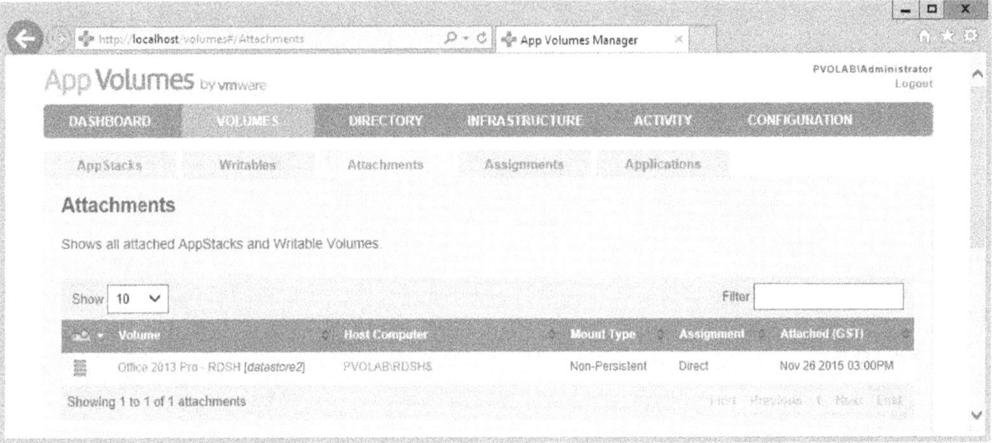

You can also double-check to make sure that the AppStack has been attached, by checking the virtual machine properties in vCenter, as shown in the following diagram:

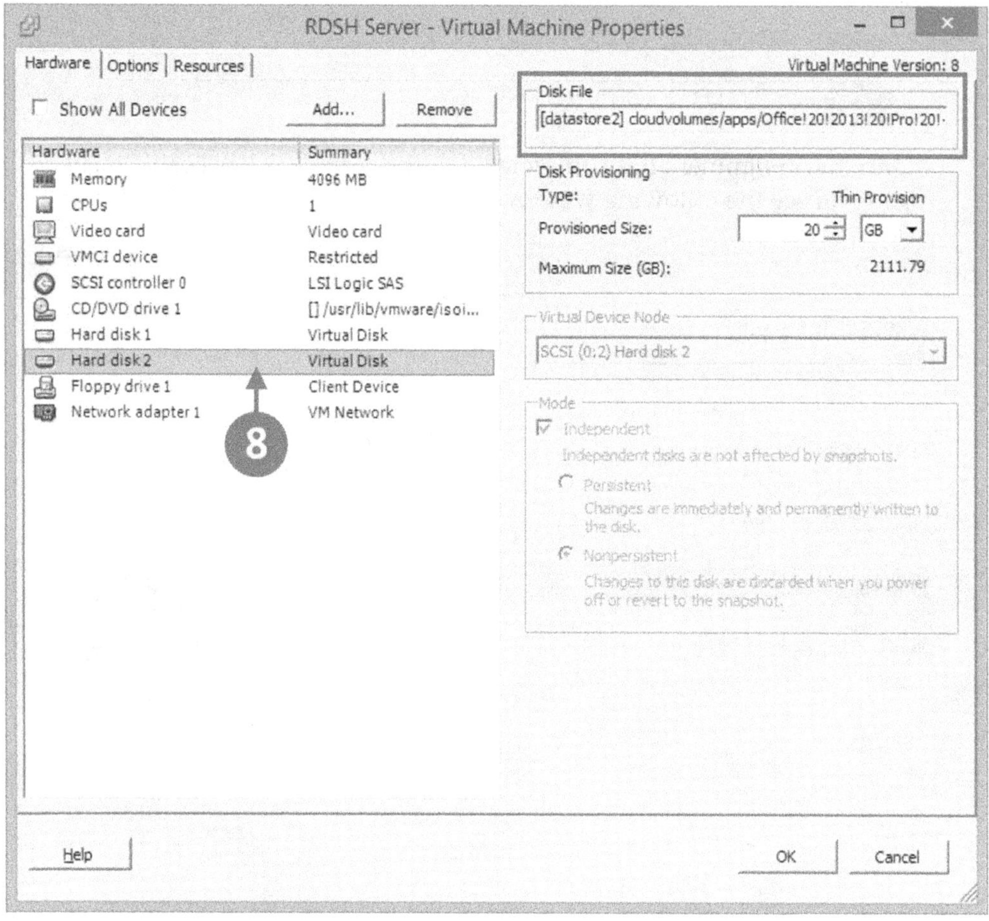

Here, you can clearly see the second virtual hard disk attached **(8)**, and in the **Disk File** box, you can see that it is the Office 2013 AppStack.

In the next section, we will configure the applications that you are going to publish.

Configuring applications for publishing

Before we continue, let's just quickly take stock of where in the process we are.

So far, we have built and configured an RDSH provisioning machine, including App Volumes Agent, and provisioned an AppStack that contains Office 2013. In the previous step, we assigned that AppStack to our second RDSH server and then made sure that it was attached.

The next step is to go back to the Remote Desktop Services configuration and publish the applications. Follow these steps:

1. Open a console to the RDSH server, and then launch **Server Manager**, as shown in the following diagram:

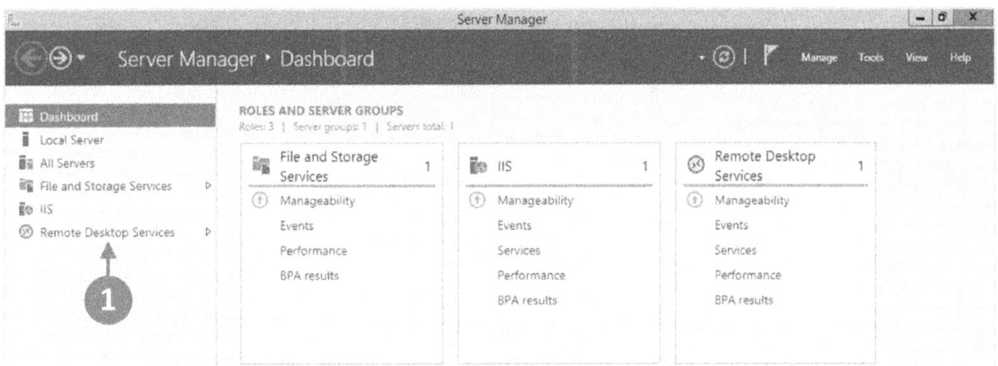

2. Click on **Remote Desktop Services (1)**. You will see the following window:

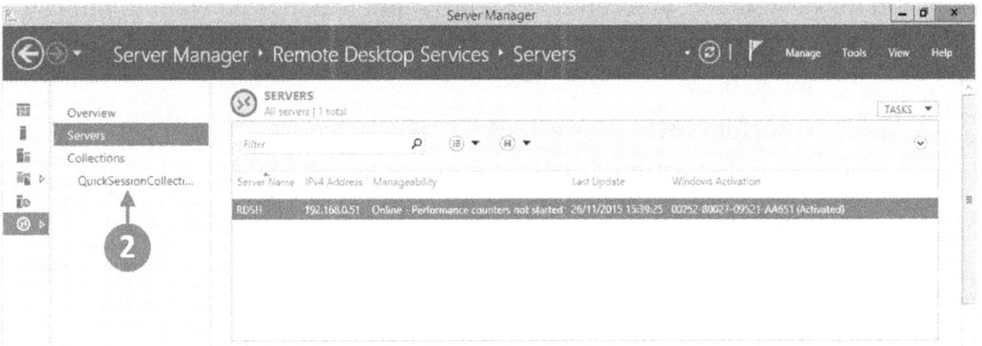

3. Ensure that the correct server is highlighted – in this example, the RDSH server – and then click on **QuickSessionCollection (2)**. You will now see the **QuickSessionCollection** configuration screen, shown in the following diagram:

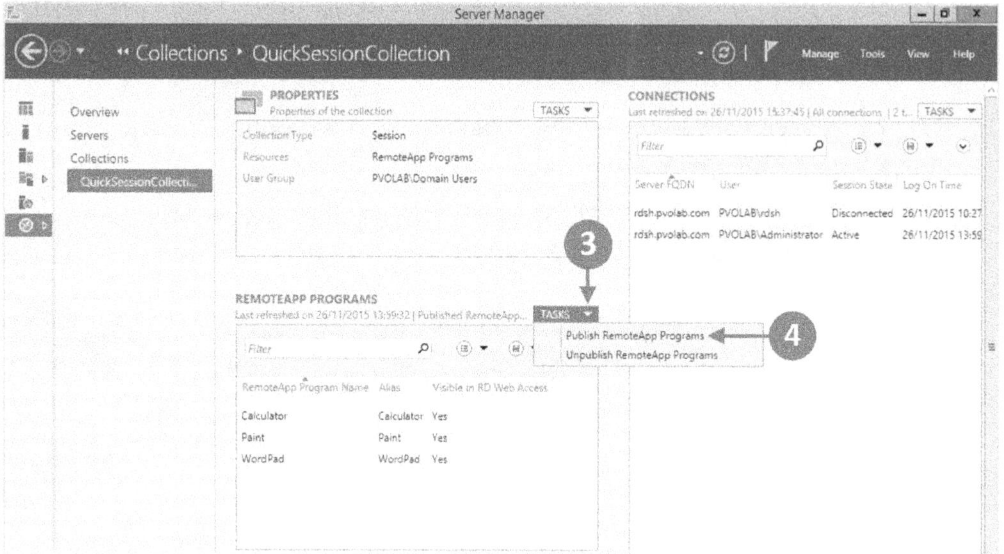

4. In the **REMOTEAPP PROGRAMS** box, click on the **TASKS** drop-down menu box **(3)**, and then select **Publish RemoteApp Programs (4)**.

   You can see that the default programs such as Calculator and Paint have already been published. In this example, we will leave that as it is.

   On the next screen, you can select which applications you want to publish. In this example, scroll down and select the following applications:

   - **Excel 2013**
   - **OneNote 2013**
   - **PowerPoint 2013**
   - **Publisher 2013**
   - **Word 2013**

This is shown in the following screenshot:

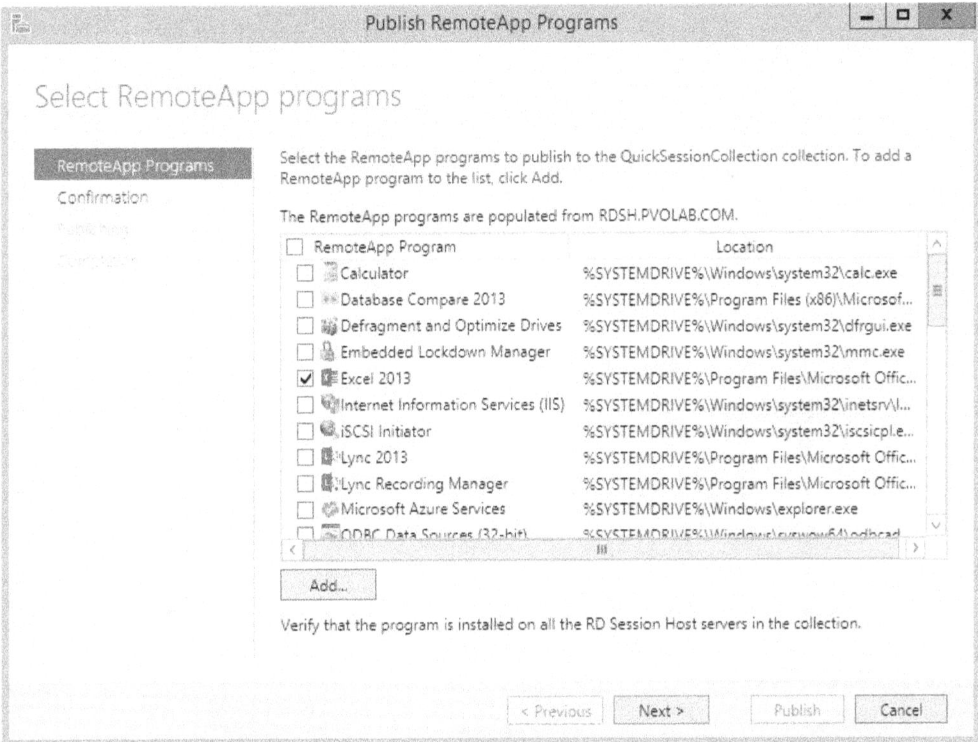

You will see that the list of applications also includes the Office 2013 components that are part of the AppStack we created at the beginning of this chapter. Those applications are not physically installed on this server; however, App Volumes Agent and the filter driver make them appear as if they were installed.

5. Once you have selected the applications that you want to publish, click on the **Next >** button. You will now see the **Confirmation** screen, listing the applications that are going to be published, as shown in the following screenshot:

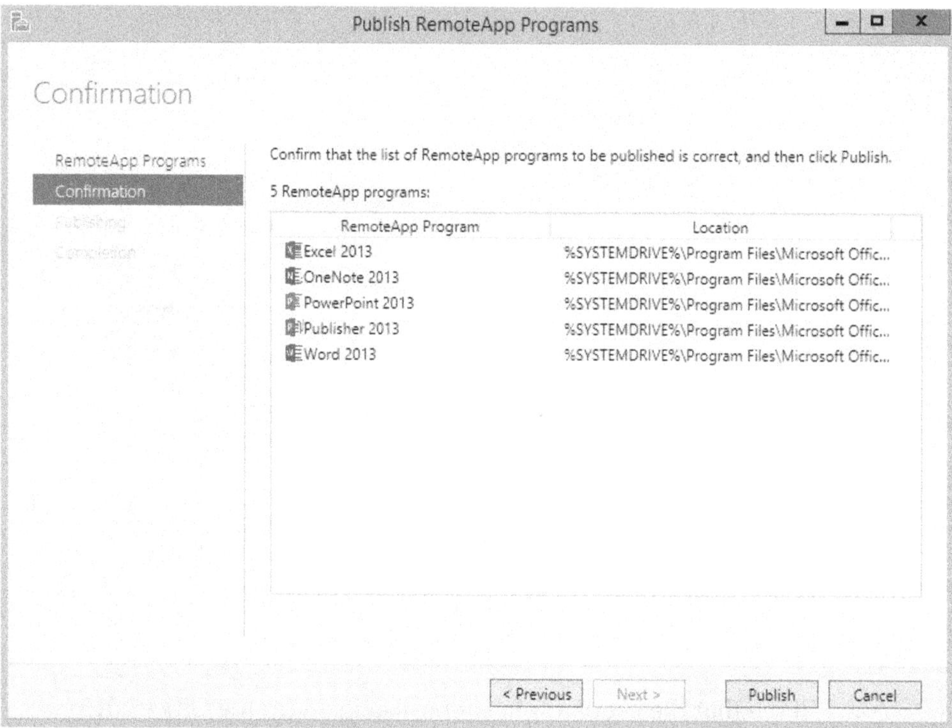

6. Click on the **Publish** button. You will now see the **Publishing** screen with a progress bar showing the process executing.
7. Once this is completed, you will see the final screen, the **Completion** screen. Click on the **Close** button to close the dialog box and return to the Server Manager screen.

If you look again at the **REMOTEAPP PROGRAMS** box, you will see the new applications that have been added, as shown in the following screenshot:

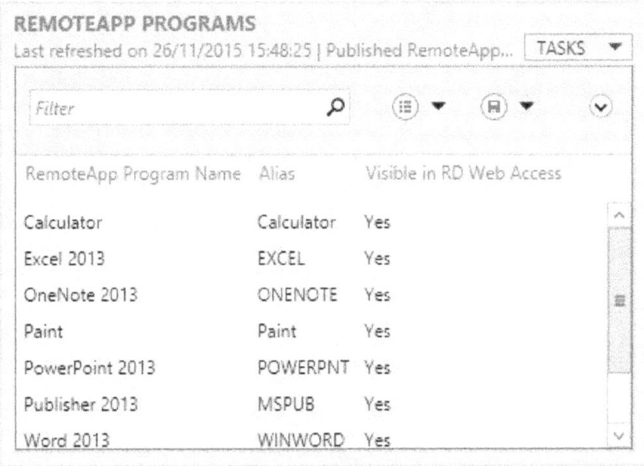

You have now successfully completed all the configuration steps and have a working RemoteApp solution that can deliver Office 2013 from an AppStack to the end users.

In the next section, we will test that this works as expected.

Launching AppStack-based published applications

In this final section, we are going to log in as an end user from one of the example desktop machines in order to make sure that the applications launch and run as we expect them to.

From the desktop, open a browser and enter `https://rdsh.pvolab.com/rdweb` in the address bar. If you see a warning about running an add-on for Microsoft Remote Desktop Web Access, then click on the message, and from the drop-down box, select **Run Add-on**.

You will now see the web page shown in the following screenshot:

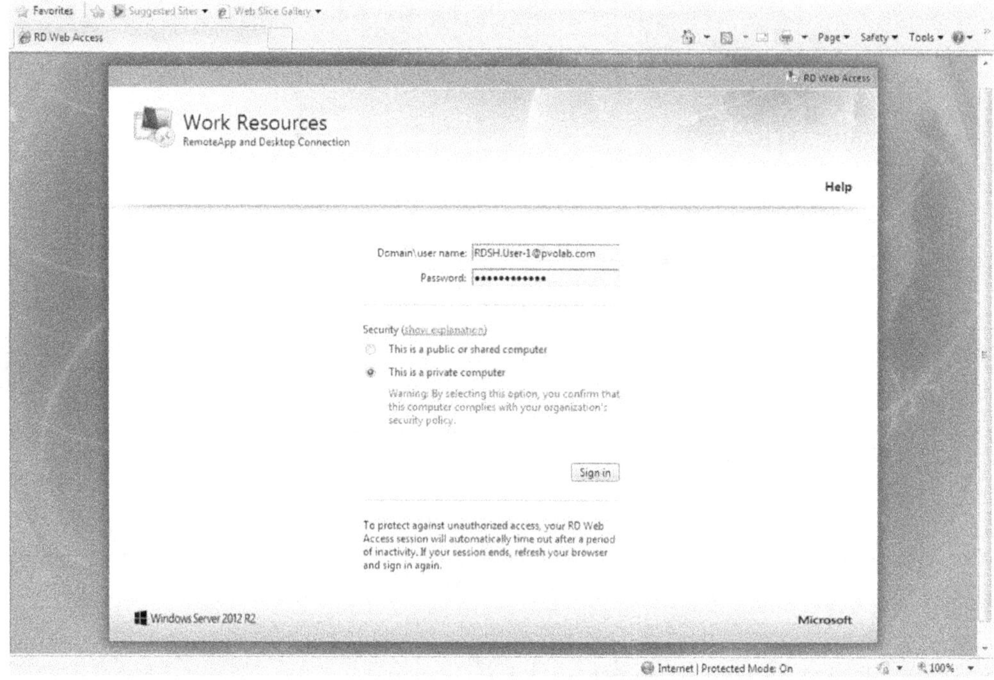

Log in as the user `rdsh.user-1@pvolab.com`, click on the button for **This is a private computer**, and then click on the **Sign in** button.

You will now see the **Work Resources** web page and the available RemoteApps. These should be the applications that were configured in the previous section, and are shown in the following screenshot:

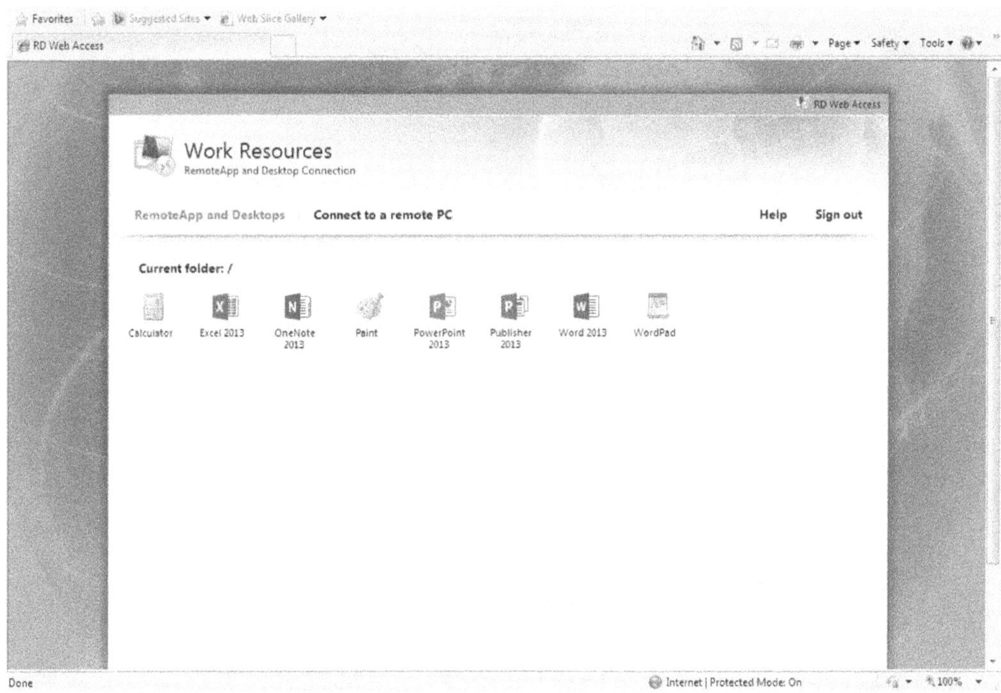

Now that you have the applications available and published from the RDSH server, let's launch one and make sure it runs correctly.

Double-click on the **Word 2013** icon. As the application launches, you will see the following pop-up message appear from the notification area of the taskbar, as shown in the following screenshot:

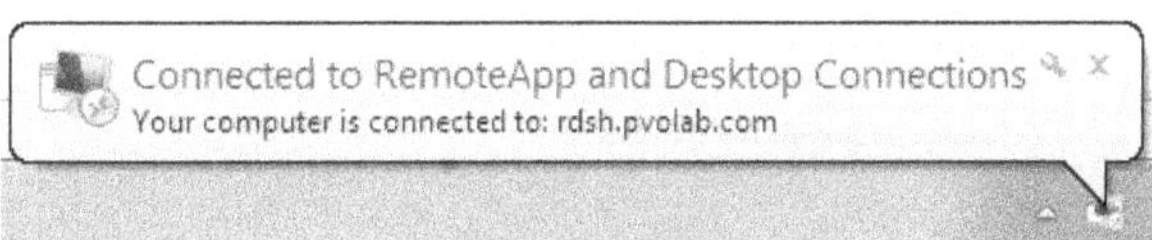

The connection to the RDSH server has been made and the application will now launch, as shown in the following screenshot:

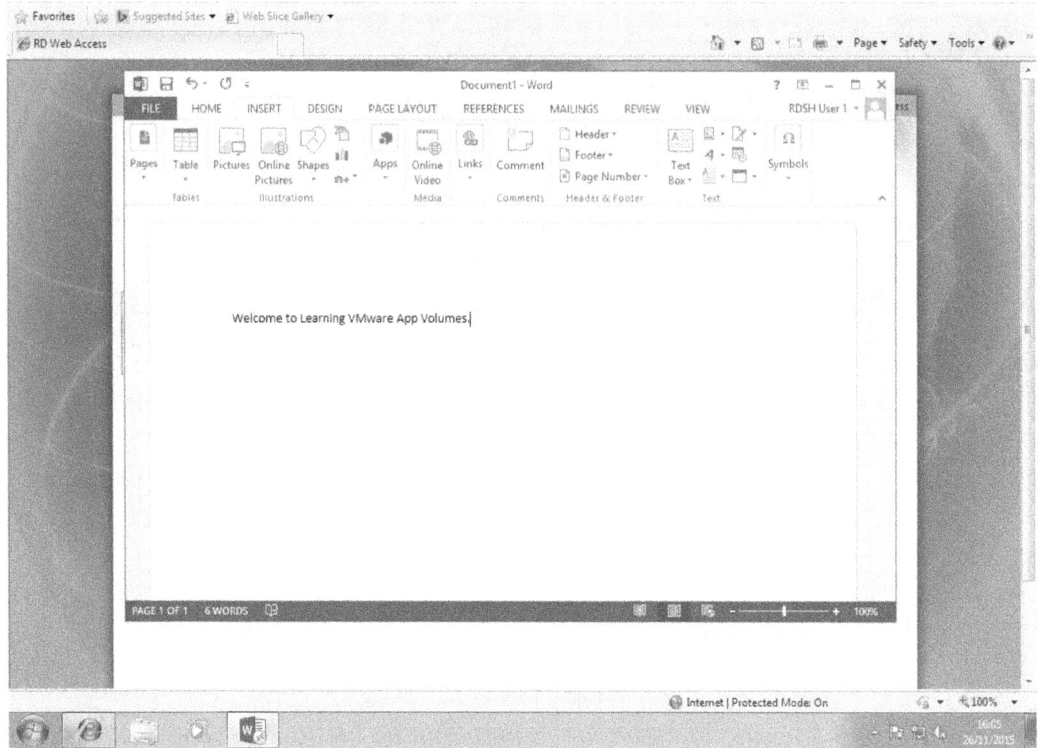

Just to make sure it's running, type in some text.

Once you are happy everything is working as expected, close Word and then, from the **Work Resources** page, click on **Sign out**.

You have now successfully configured and deployed an RDSH server running applications that are attached as AppStacks.

Summary

In this chapter, we started by talking about the use case for deploying App Volumes in an RDSH/published-application environment. We then went on the look at the architecture of how it all fits together.

Once familiar with the solution, we went on to build a provisioning machine to provision our RDSH AppStack for Office 2013, before going on to build an RDSH server, which was assigned the Office AppStack and then configured to publish some of the core Office applications.

Finally, we tested the solution to make sure it behaved as expected and that end users could log in and launch their applications.

In the next chapter, we will build on what we learned in this chapter, by adding a Citrix XenApp environment to the mix and configuring XenApp to deliver our Office 2013 AppStack.

12

Deploying App Volumes in a Citrix XenApp Environment

In the previous chapter, we looked at one of the key features of App Volumes: the ability to work with other vendor's solutions, and not just VMware technology and products. In that chapter, we specifically focused on building virtual desktop machines using Citrix XenDesktop and having the applications delivered by App Volumes, followed by how to deliver AppStack-based applications by publishing them using Microsoft RemoteApp.

In this chapter, we are going to take a closer look at the other key Citrix solutions and how to deploy App Volumes to deliver applications that are published using Citrix XenApp.

The following diagram illustrates how App Volumes would look within a Citrix XenApp architecture:

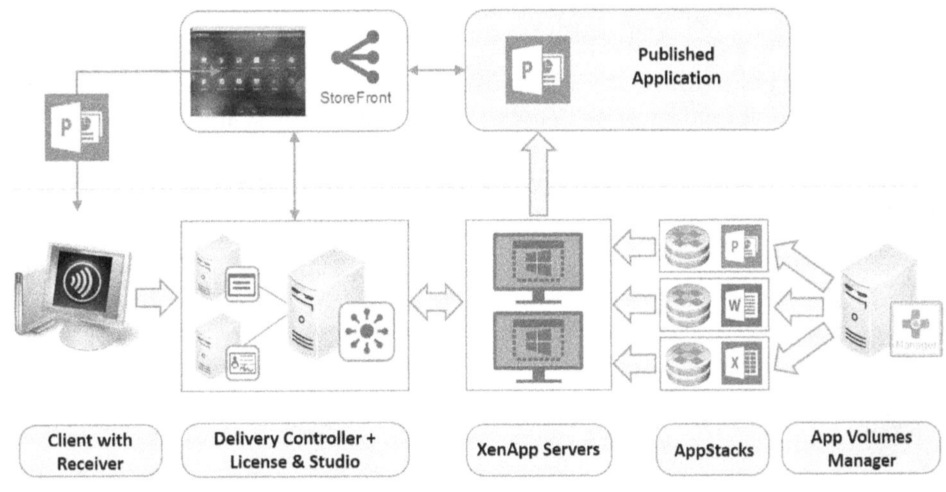

The Citrix XenApp process for publishing applications remains exactly as it is for any other Citrix XenApp deployment, but now, rather than having the applications physically installed onto each server that is hosting the applications, you instead just install the App Volumes Agent onto those servers. Applications are delivered via AppStacks and are assigned to the hosting servers rather than a user. When that server boots or starts up, the assigned AppStack is attached and delivers the applications to that server, ready to be published by XenApp to end users.

As we have already discussed in the use cases, adopting this approach allows you to create stateless hosting servers, as there are no applications installed directly onto these servers. You can quickly scale up the number of servers and simply attach the pre-built AppStacks ready for publication. It also means you can easily manage updates to any of the applications.

Again, we are using VMware vSphere (ESXi and vCenter Server) as the underlying infrastructure to host the Citrix infrastructure components (Delivery Controller, Studio, StoreFront, and License Server), and therefore using VMware-based virtual machines with VMDK files for the virtual disk files. However, you can use the VHD format virtual disk files, which we will cover in *Chapter 14, Advanced Configuration and Other Options*.

We are not going to cover how to build a Citrix XenDesktop environment in this chapter, so having an environment in place is a prerequisite for this chapter as we are going to configure a new machine catalogue and delivery group to deliver the published applications. If you have built the infrastructure in the previous chapter, then we are going to use that for publishing the applications.

To build a Citrix environment, have a look at this link: `http://tinyurl.com/nla9k8u`. This takes you to the Citrix website and the Citrix XenDesktop reviewers' guide which will walk you through the *building a demo* environment that we have built in this guide.

If you follow this guide to create the basic infrastructure, then in the next sections we will briefly cover the final steps to deliver the published applications.

In the next section, we are going to build and configure the application delivery master image.

Building and configuring an AppStack for XenApp

Now that we have described the architecture of how App Volumes fits into a Citrix XenApp environment, the next thing we need to have is to start building and configuring the environment.

There are a number of steps involved in creating the environment, which are illustrated in the following diagram:

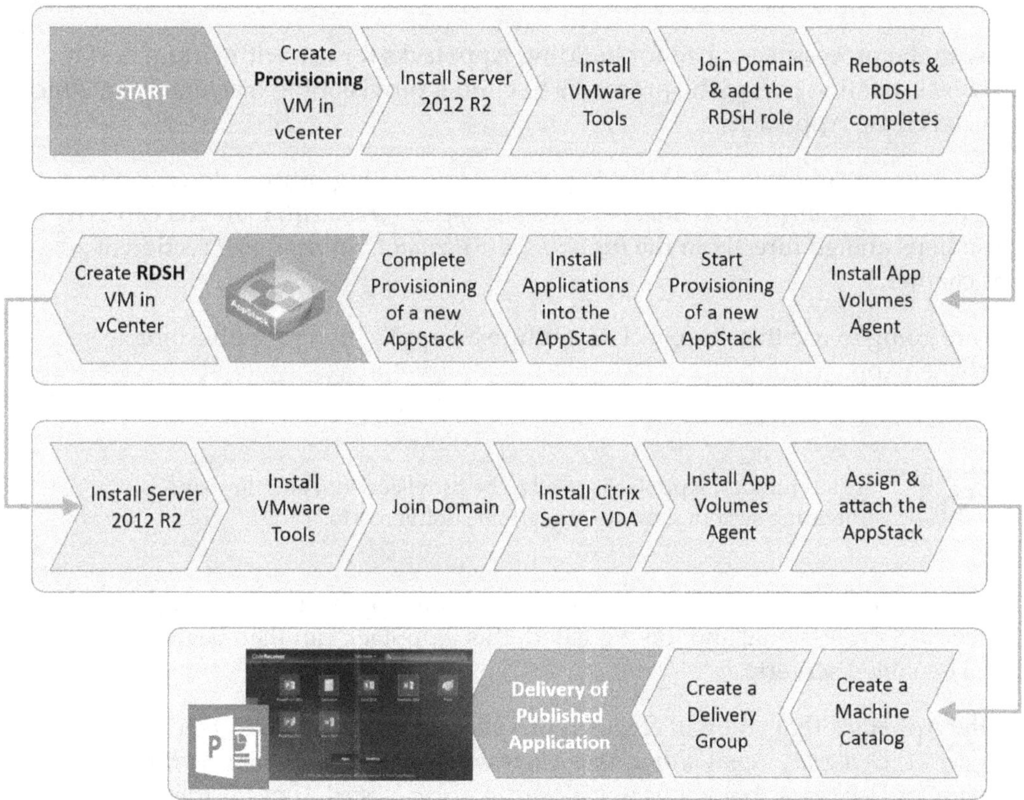

In this chapter, we are going to cover the complete scenario of building an AppStack for Office 2013 Professional, and then deliver this as a published application using Citrix XenApp.

To follow the Example Lab for this chapter, you will need to use two RDSH host servers (`RDSH-Provision` and XenApp). You will also use the Citrix XenDesktop virtual machine and the associated infrastructure components (Delivery Controller, Studio, StoreFront, and License Server). These were built in *Chapter 10, Deploying App Volumes in a Citrix XenDesktop Environment*. Please refer to that chapter to build out that environment.

The steps described in the previous diagram are in the order in which they should be completed. It is important to note when to install the App Volumes Agent in particular.

As with the process described for building AppStacks for use with virtual desktop machines, the first part of the process is to build a provisioning machine from which you can create AppStacks.

If you have already completed the AppStack provisioning process described in *Chapter 11, Deploying App Volumes in a RemoteApp Environment*, then you can skip these steps and go directly to the *Installing the Virtual Delivery Agent* section of this chapter.

We are going to use this AppStack to capture an application for publishing in Citrix XenApp.

As a reminder, AppStacks need to be provisioned using the same operating system they are going to be delivered to.

The provisioning machine will be used to create an AppStack containing Microsoft Office 2013 Professional and, once created, this AppStack can then be used on other RDSH-enabled servers.

So the AppStack that you will create in this chapter will also have been used in *Chapter 11, Deploying App Volumes in a Microsoft RemoteApp Environment*, and in *Chapter 13, Deploying App Volumes in a Horizon View Hosted Apps Environment*, to deliver the applications within those environment scenarios. If you have already created this AppStack, then you can skip these steps. If not, then continue with the process outlined in the following section.

Let's get started with the first part of the process and build the provisioning machine.

In the Example Lab, we have already built a Windows 2012 R2 server called `RDSH-Provision`. This server is already running VMware tools and is also joined to the domain, and in the next section we will pick up the configuration steps from the point where we install the RDSH role.

Installing the RDSH role on the provisioning machine

The first thing we are going to do is add the RDSH role to the `RDSH-Provision` machine.

Open a console to the server and launch the **Server Manager**. From the main screen, under **Configure this local server**, select the option for **Add roles and features (1)**, as shown in the following diagram:

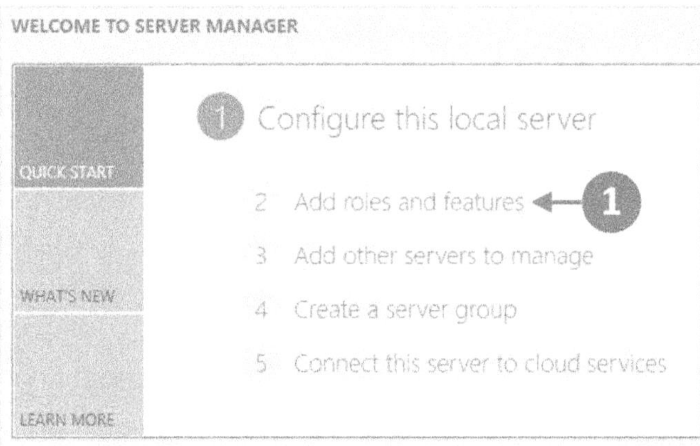

You will now see the **Before You Begin** screen. Click the **Next >** button to continue.

On the **Installation Type** screen, click the radio button for **Remote Desktop Services Installation (2)**, as shown in the following diagram:

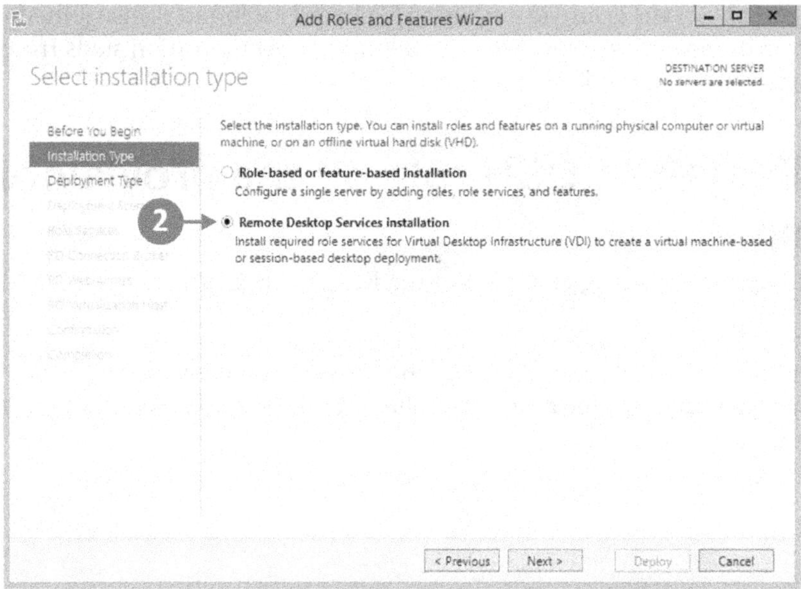

Click the **Next >** button to continue. You will now see the **Deployment Type** screen:

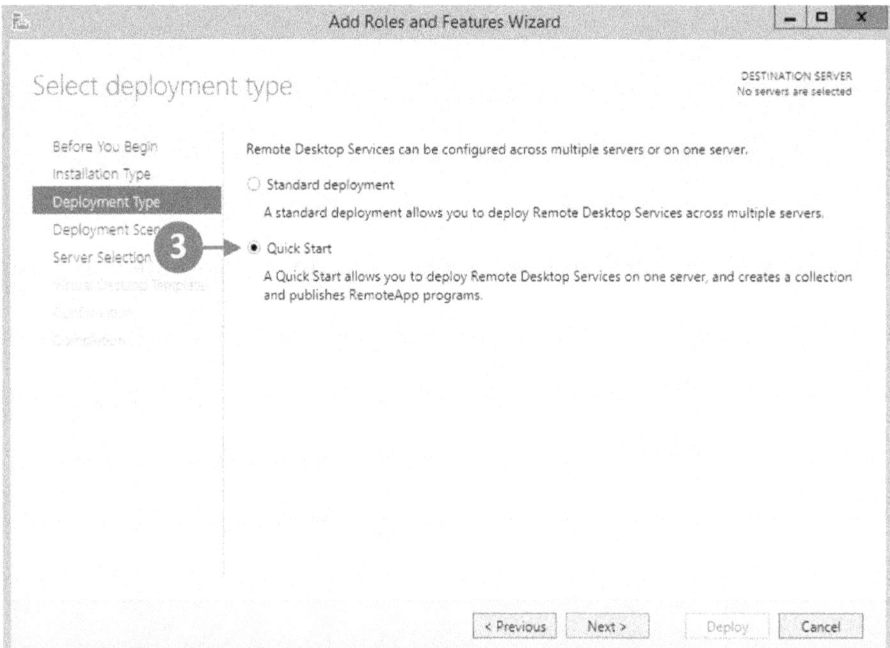

On the **Deployment Type** screen, click the radio button for **Quick Start (3)**, and then click the **Next >** button to continue.

You will now see the **Deployment Scenario** screen, as shown in the following diagram:

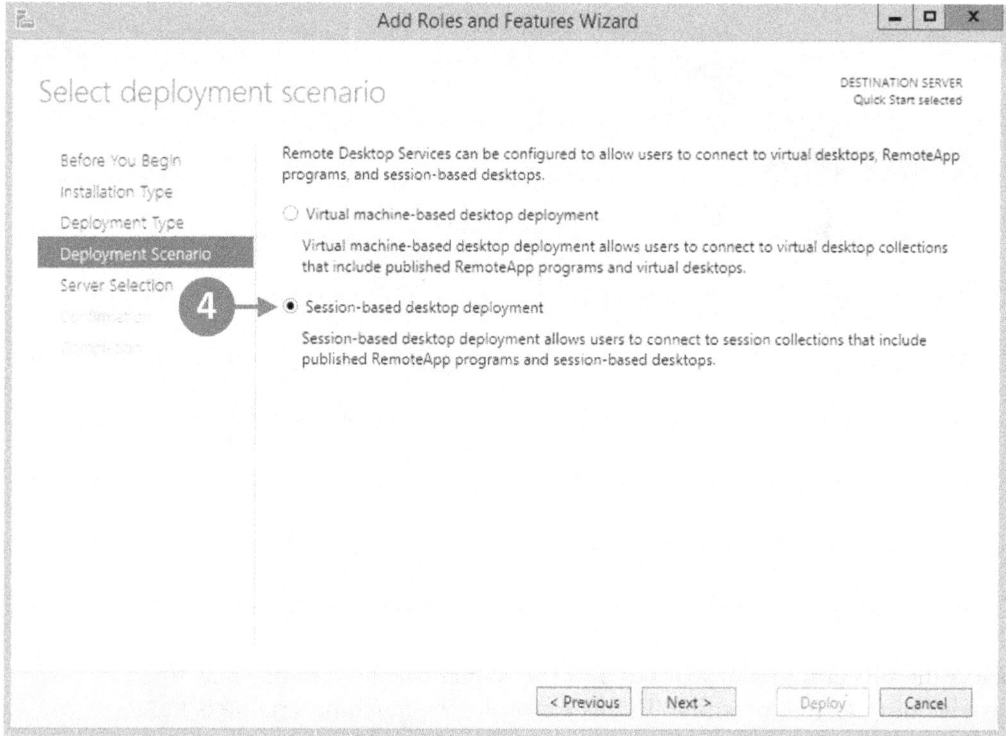

Click the radio button for **Session-based desktop deployment (4)**, and then click the **Next >** button to continue.

You will now see the **Server Selection** screen, as shown in the following diagram:

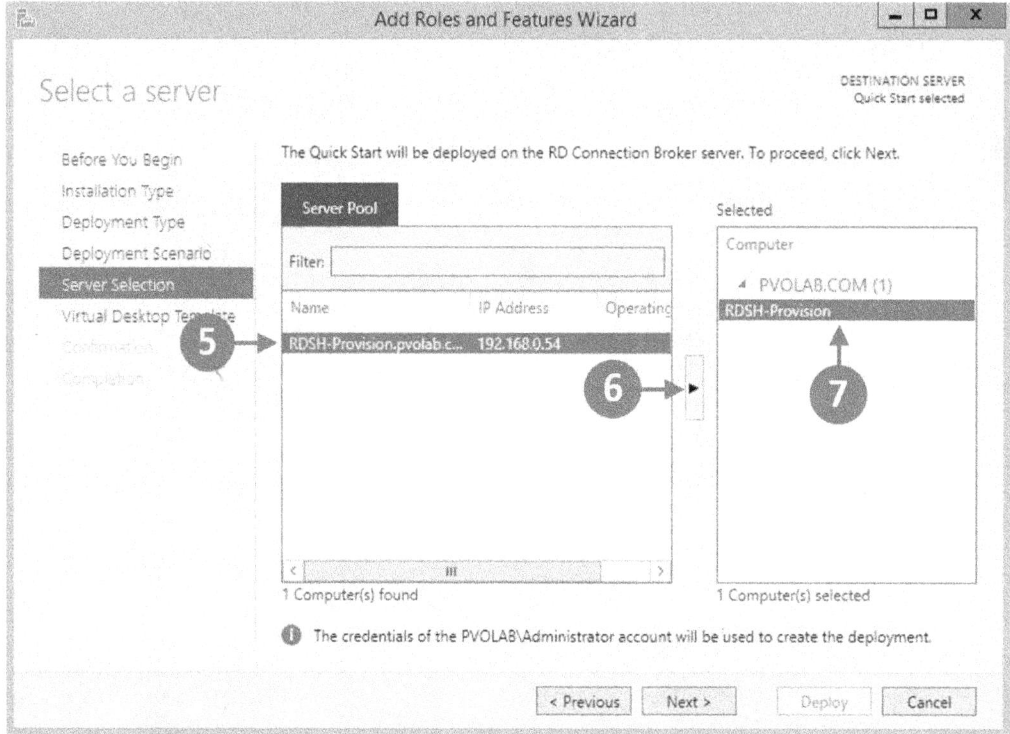

Select the server that you want to add the RDSH role to, and use it as the provisioning virtual machine. In this example, the machine's name is `RDSH-Provision.pvolab.com`.

Highlight the server name in the **Server Pool** box **(5)**, and then click the arrow **(6)** to add it to the **Selected** box **(7)**.

Once complete, click the **Next >** button to continue.

You will now see the **Confirmation** screen, as shown in the following diagram:

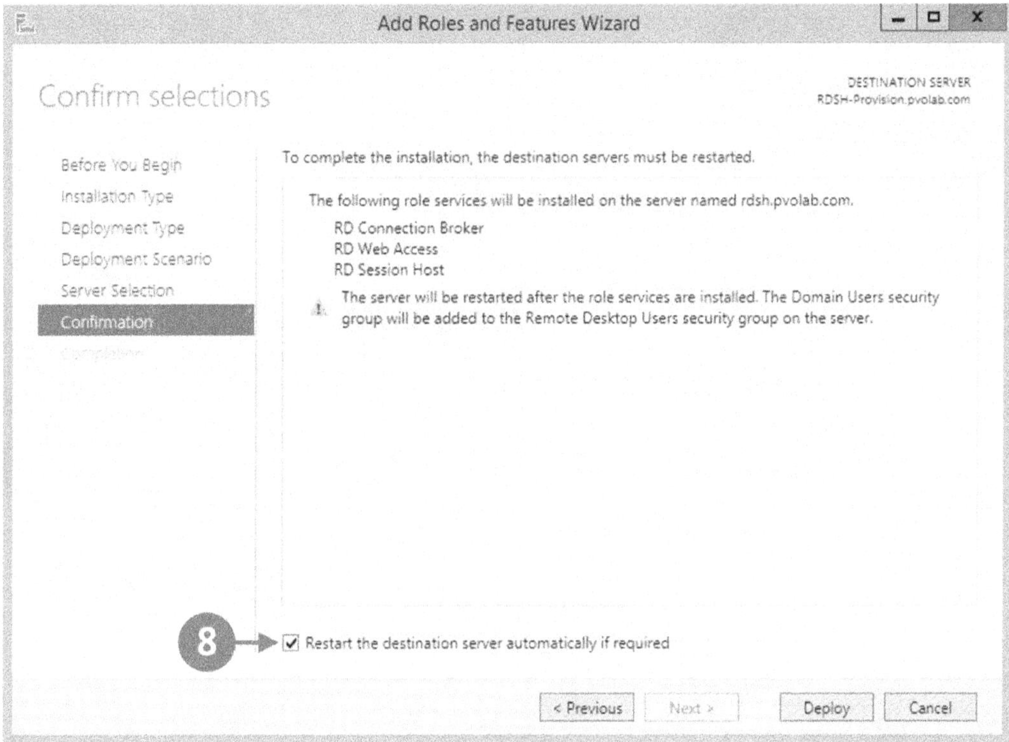

Check the **Restart the destination server automatically if required** box **(8)**, and then finally click the **Deploy** button. You will now see the **Completion** screen:

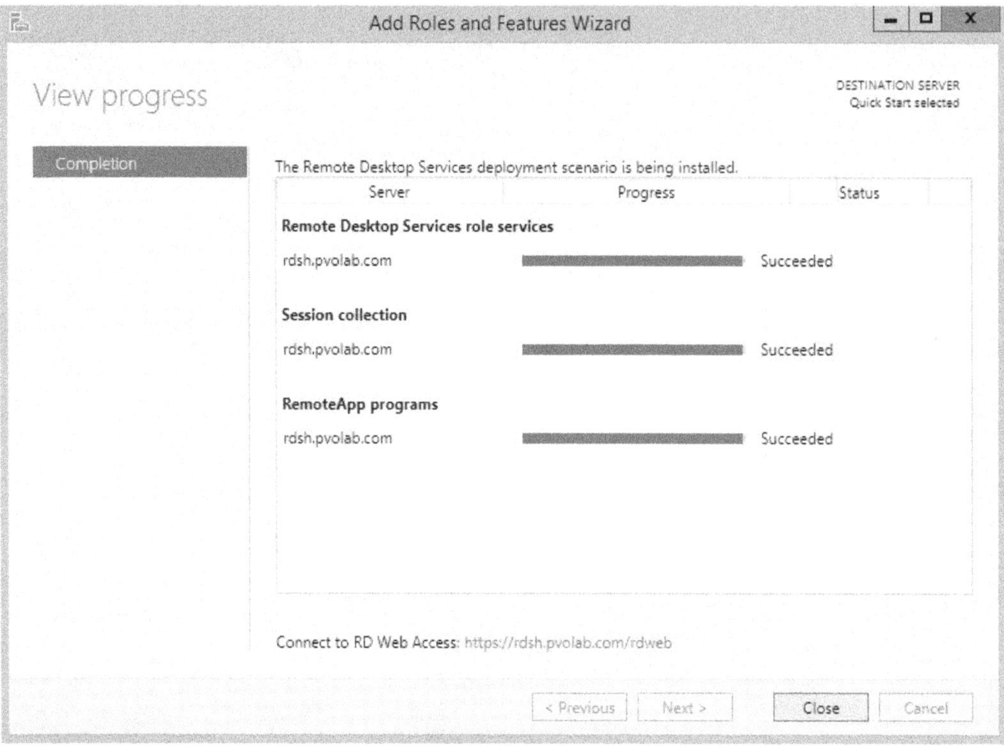

Check that the installation has completed successfully, and then click the **Close** button.

You will now return to the **Server Manager** screen, which will now show the roles for **Remote Desktop Services** and **IIS** have been added, as shown in the following screenshot:

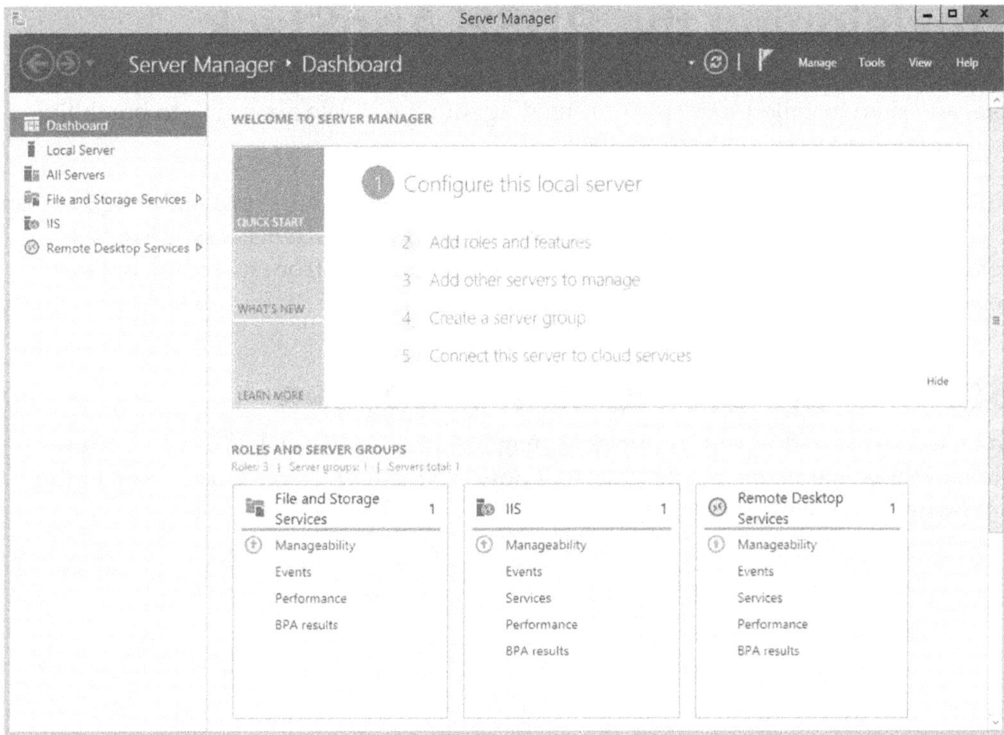

You should now have a server that has been configured as an RDSH host server.

The next step is to install the App Volumes Agent.

Installing the App Volumes Agent

The next part of the process is to install the App Volumes Agent onto the RDSH host server you are using for provisioning, so that it registers itself with the App Volumes Manager, which allows you to start using it for application provisioning.

We have already covered the installation process in the *Installing the App Volumes Agent* section of *Chapter 4, Installing and Configuring the App Volumes Software*, so please refer to that chapter on how to do this. The process is exactly the same for servers as it is for desktops.

Provisioning the RDSH AppStack

At this stage of the process, you have built a server and configured it with the RDSH role, and then installed the App Volumes Agent onto it. We are going to break the provisioning process into two stages.

Firstly, we will walk through a reminder of how to perform the provisioning process and then secondly, as we are installing applications on an RDSH server, we will detail the application installation process, as it is different from installing onto a desktop machine.

Starting the provisioning process

Open a console to the App Volumes Manager server and launch the App Volumes Manager management console. You will now see the login screen, as shown in the following screenshot:

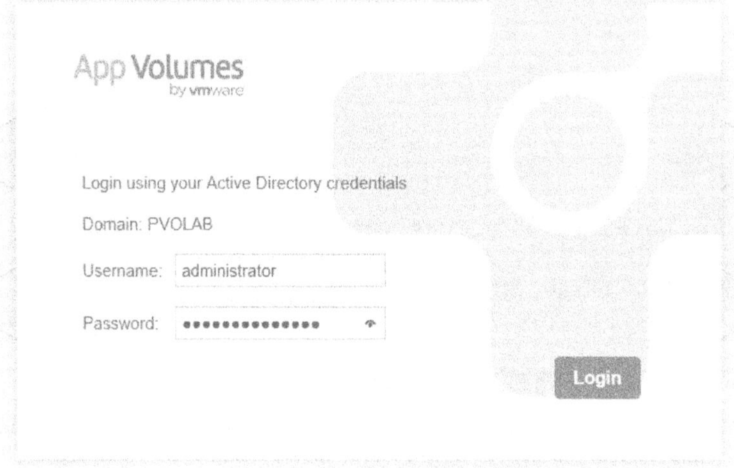

Enter the username and password of the administrator account and then click the **Login** button.

From the App Volumes Manager console, click the **VOLUMES** menu option **(1)**, and then click the **AppStacks** tab **(2)**.

Now click the **Create AppStack** button **(3)**, as shown in the following diagram:

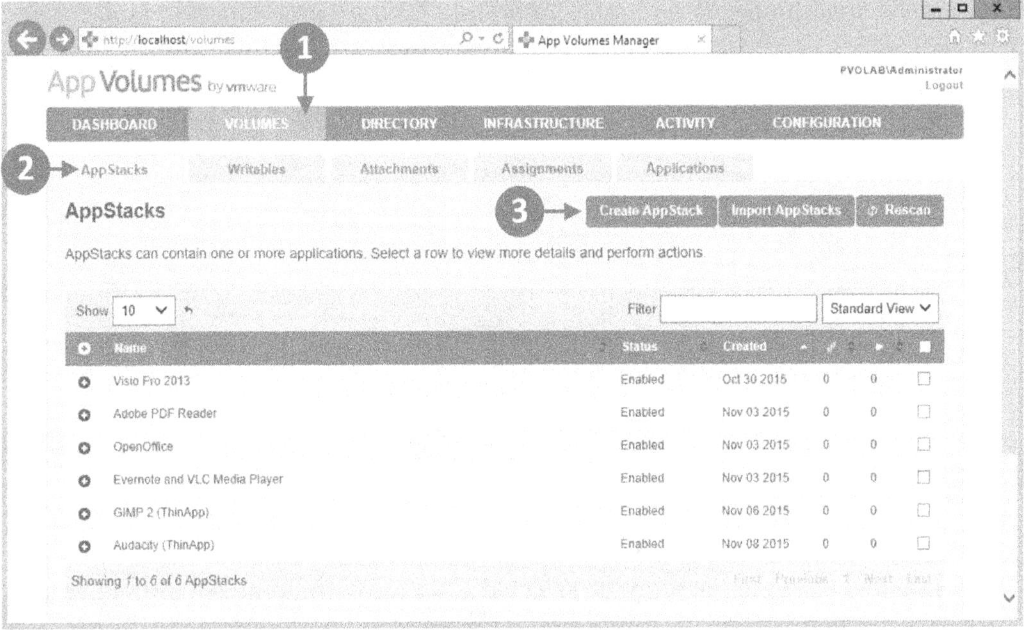

You will now see the **Create AppStack** screen, as shown in the following diagram:

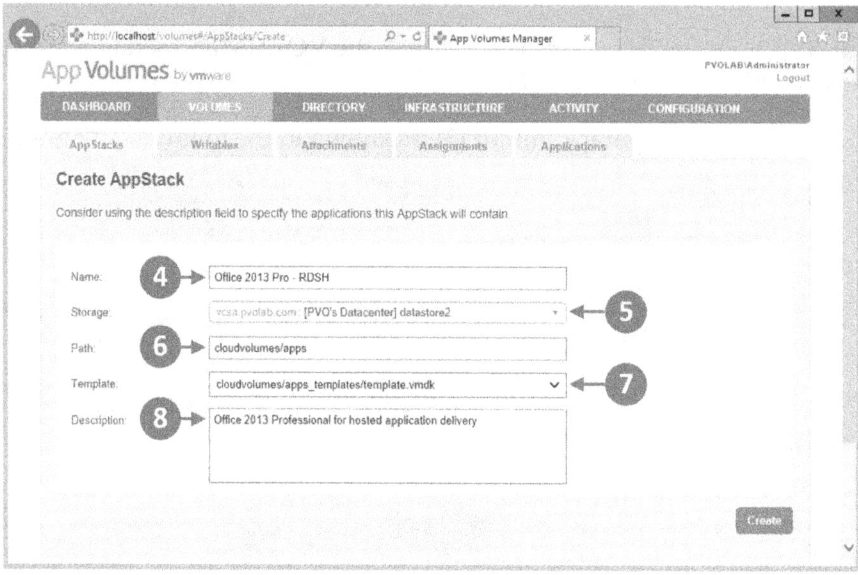

In the **Name:** box **(4)**, enter a name for the AppStack. In this example, we have called it `Office 2013 Pro - RDSH`.

Leave the **Storage:** box **(5)** and the **Path:** box **(6)** as the default settings.

Make sure that the **Template:** option selected is for **apps_templates/template.vmdk** **(7)**, and then finally in the **Description:** box **(8)**, enter a description of what this AppStack contains.

When you have completed this information, click the **Create** button.

You will now see the **Confirm Create AppStack** dialog box, as shown in the following diagram:

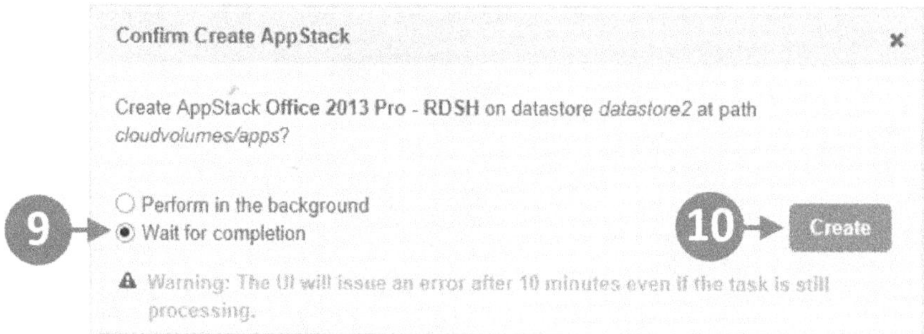

Click the radio button for **Wait for completion (9)**, and then click the **Create** button **(10)**.

The AppStack is now created and you will see the progress shown with the following message:

With the AppStack now created, you can start provisioning the applications. You will now see the AppStacks configuration screen, as shown in the following diagram:

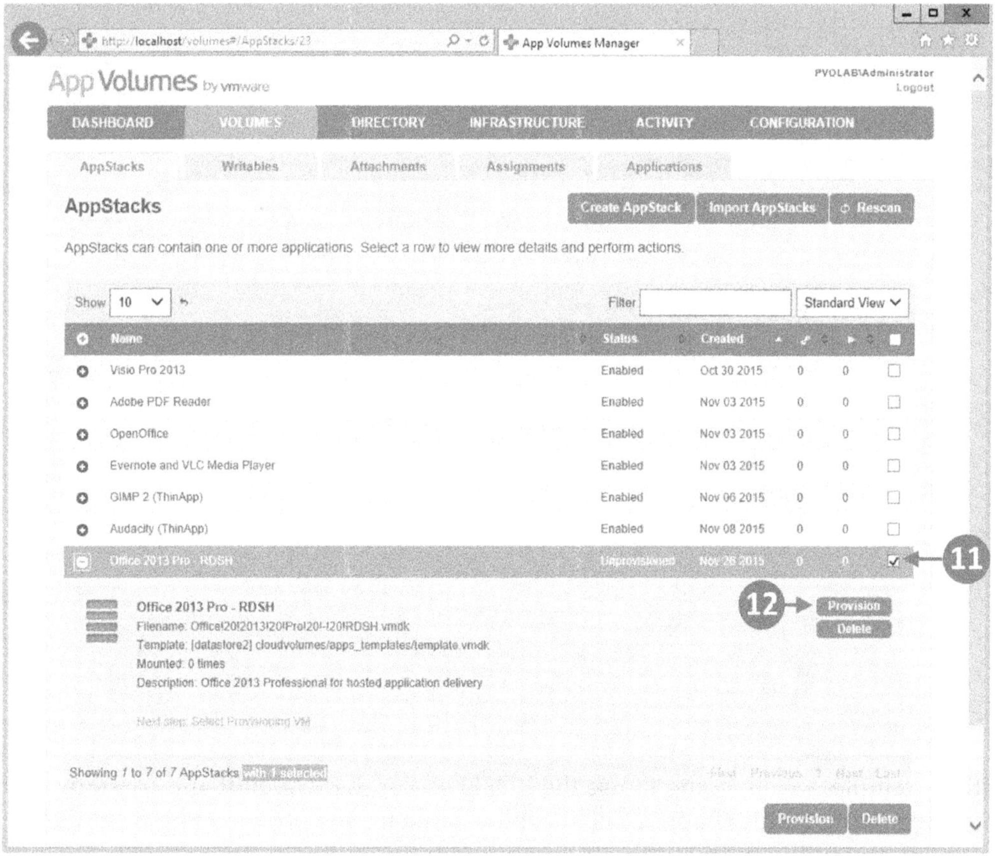

Select the AppStack that you just created by checking the tick box next to its entry on the inventory **(11)**. When selected, the entry will be highlighted in orange.

Now click the **Provision** button **(12)**.

Next you will see the **Provision AppStack: Office 2013 Pro - RDSH** screen, where you need to choose which virtual machine you are going to use to provision this particular AppStack.

This is shown in the following diagram:

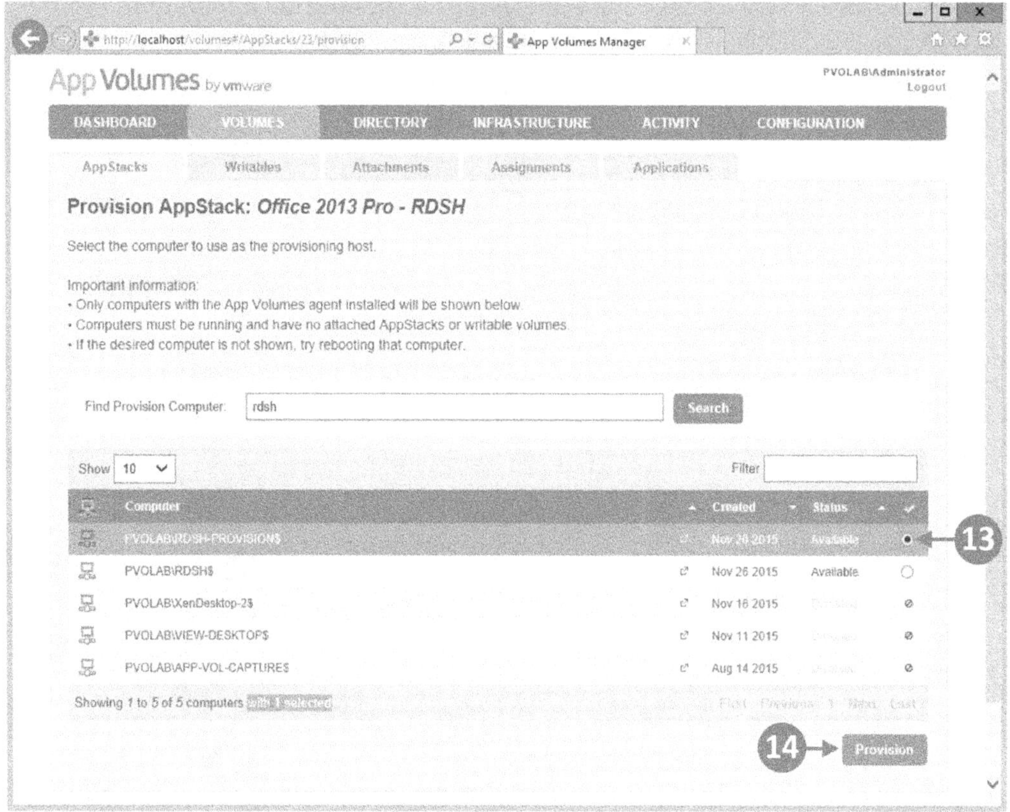

In this example, we are going to use the RDSH server that we built and configured at the beginning of this chapter. The machine name for the provisioning machine is `RDSH-Provision`.

Click the radio button next the entry for `PVOLAB\RDSH-PROVISION$` **(13)**, and then click the **Provision** button **(14)**.

You will now see the following dialog box:

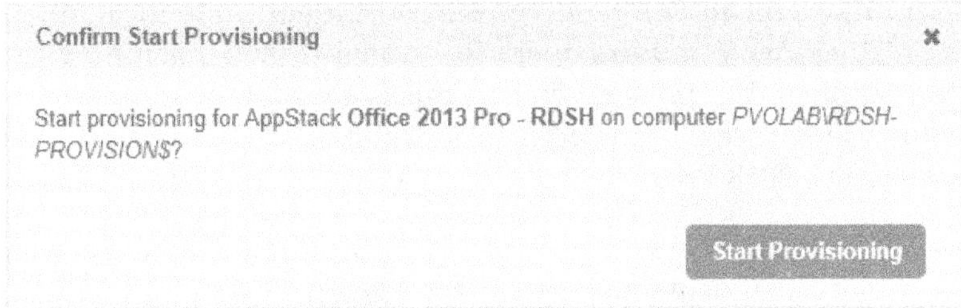

Click the **Start Provisioning** button to continue the process.

You will see the following message as the AppStack is attached:

The AppStack is now attached to the provisioning machine, as shown in the following screenshot:

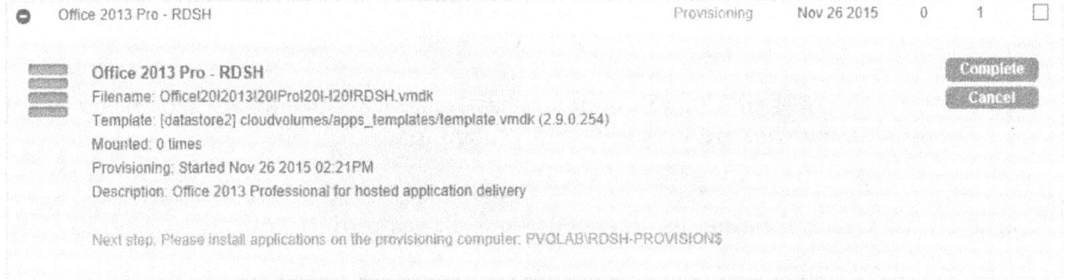

You can now start to install the applications on the provisioning machine.

> Remember, *DO NOT* click the **Complete** button until you have completely finished installing the applications.

In the next section, we are going to look at how to install applications on the provisioning machine, given the fact that it is an RDSH host.

Installing applications

Installing applications on an RDSH server is almost identical to installing applications on any other Windows operating system-based machine. However, there are a few subtle differences, given that this is a remote session host server. Let's run through the process of installing applications. In this example, we are going to install Office 2013 Pro.

Open a console to the RDSH server on which you want to install the applications; in this example, the machine name is `RDSH-Provision`.

First of all, ensure that the provisioning machine is in provisioning mode. When you switch to the console of the RDSH server, you should see the following dialog box:

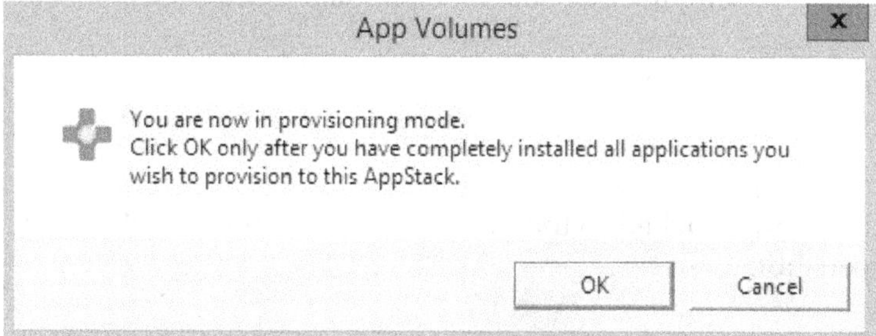
App Volumes
You are now in provisioning mode.
Click OK only after you have completely installed all applications you wish to provision to this AppStack.
OK
Cancel

DO NOT click on **OK** until you have completed the installation of all the applications you want included in this AppStack.

Next, open the **Control Panel**, as shown in the following diagram:

Control Panel
Programs
1
Uninstall a program
Get programs
Turn Windows features on or off

From the **Control Panel**, click on **Programs (1)**. The **Programs** dialog box opens, as shown in the following diagram:

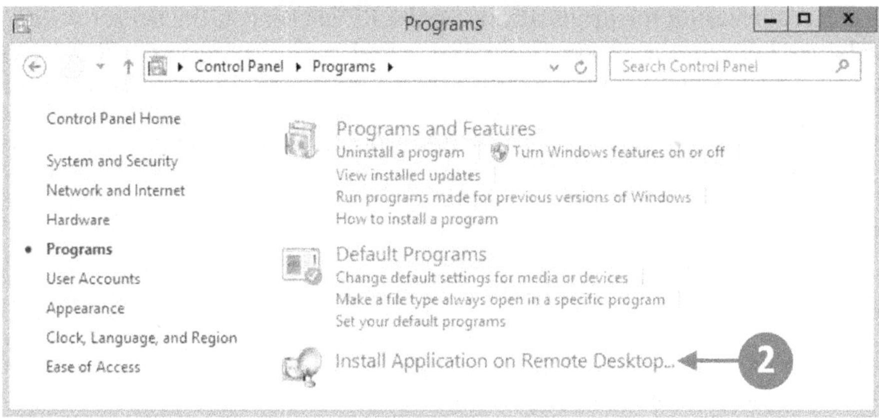

Click on **Install Application on Remote Desktop... (2)**.

You will now see the **Install Program From Floppy Disk or CD-ROM** dialog box, as shown in the following screenshot:

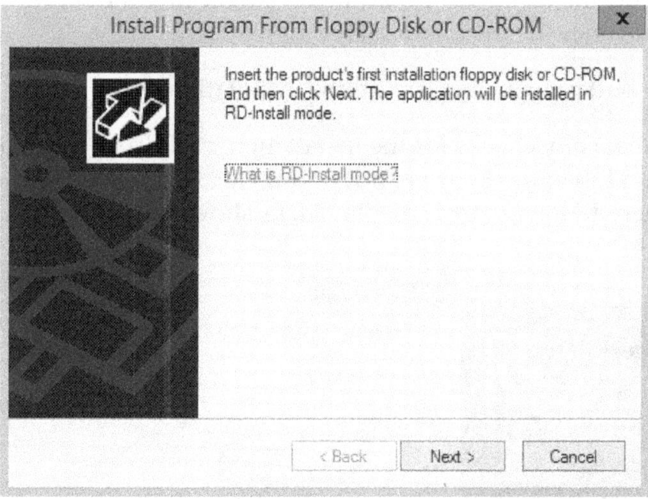

In this dialog box, you will see that it talks about something called **RD-Install mode**, with a link to **What is RD-Install mode?**

This is where the differences between a desktop installation and a server installation come into play. To install an application on an RDSH host server, the server needs to be switched to a special install mode known as RD-Install. This ensures that the applications are able to run in a multiuser environment, such as published applications where multiple users are running applications at the same time.

Once you have installed the applications on the RDSH server, the server needs to be switched back into normal mode, or what is called execution mode or **RD-Execute**, so that users can remotely connect to the server and the applications running on it.

This install mode change can also be initiated from the command line using the following commands:

```
change user /install
```

```
change user /execute
```

You can check the current install mode of your RDSH server from the command line using the following command:

```
change user /query
```

The easiest was to install applications is by installing them from the **Programs** option in **Control Panel**, which is how we are going to do it in this example. This option takes you through the installation process by automatically switching the server to RD-Install mode, installing the program, and switching the server back to RD-Execute mode once the installation is complete.

Click the **Next >** button to continue with the installation.

The server automatically checks for the installation media and installation files, first on the **A:** drive and then the **E:** drive. If it doesn't locate any media, then the **Run Installation Program** dialog box is displayed, as shown in the following screenshot:

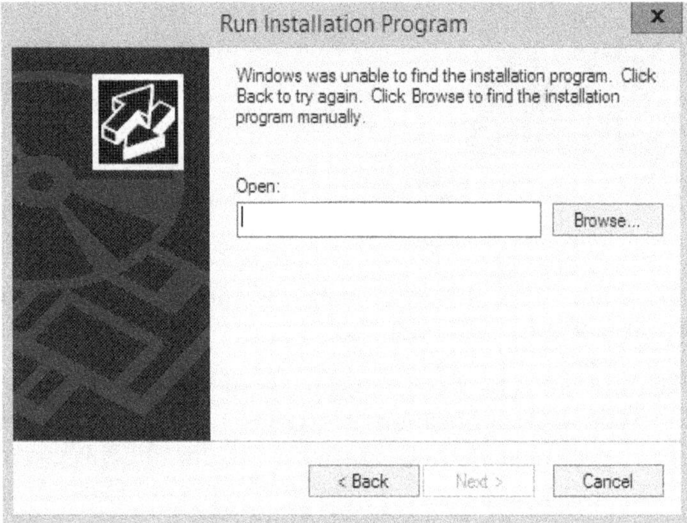

In the **Open:** box, type in the path to the application installer files if you know it. In this example, we are going to click on the **Browse...** button and, in the window that opens, we are going to navigate to the location where we have save the Office 2013 ISO file, which happens to be located in the shared folder.

Once located, click the **Next >** button, as shown in the following screenshot:

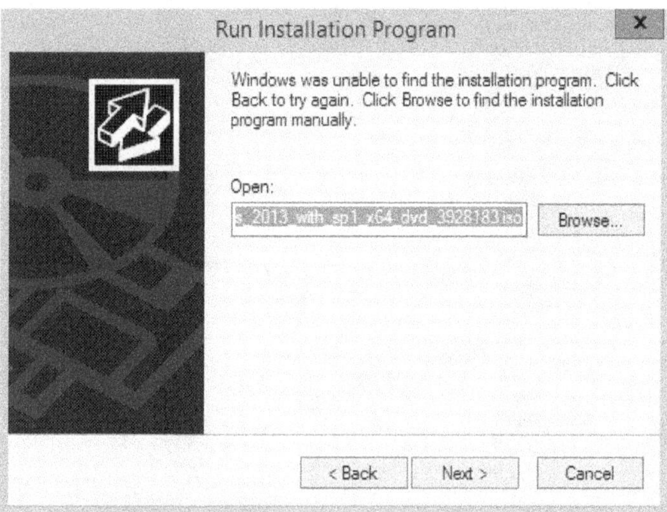

You will now see the **Finish Admin Install** dialog box, as shown in the following screenshot:

DO NOT click **Finish** until you have completed the application installation.

In the background, you will have also seen the ISO file we selected has been mounted as a DVD drive, and that the installation files on that disk image are now available, as shown in the following screenshot:

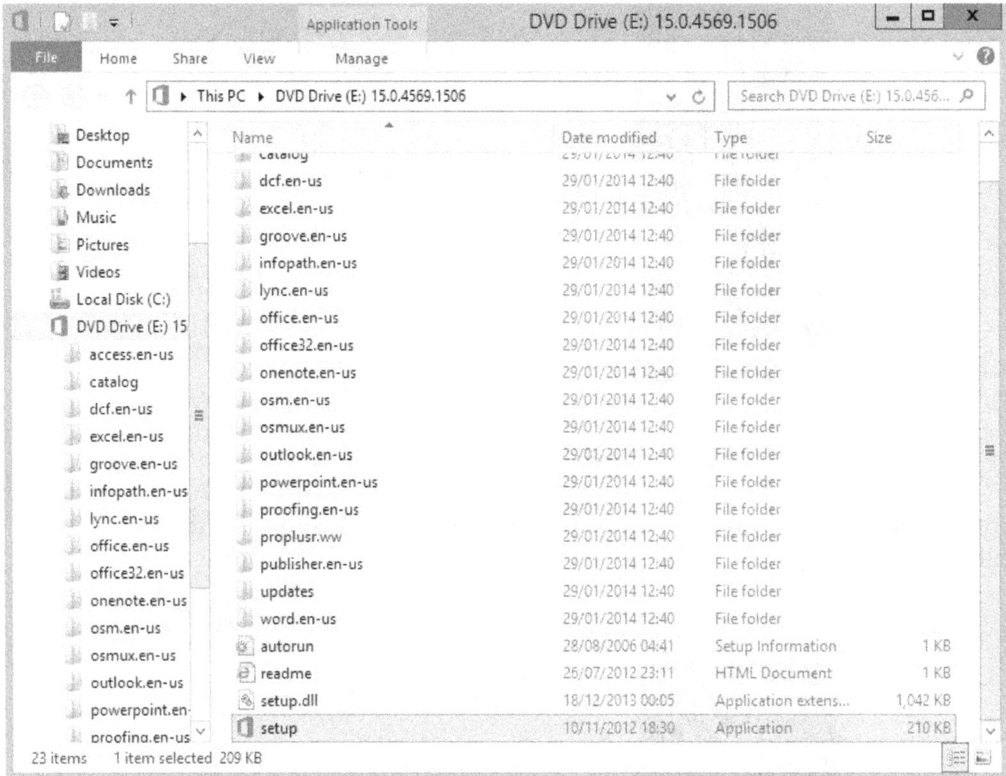

Locate and launch the setup program and start the installation of Office 2013. We are not going to go through that process, so continue and install Office as you would normally.

Make sure you have the appropriate license key, such as a **Volume License Key** (**VLK**), in order to be able to run Office on an RDSH server.

Once the installation has successfully completed and you have completed any additional configuration tasks, return to the **Finish Admin Install** dialog box and click **Finish**.

Next, return to the **App Volumes** dialog box and click **OK** to finish the provisioning process. You will see the following dialog box:

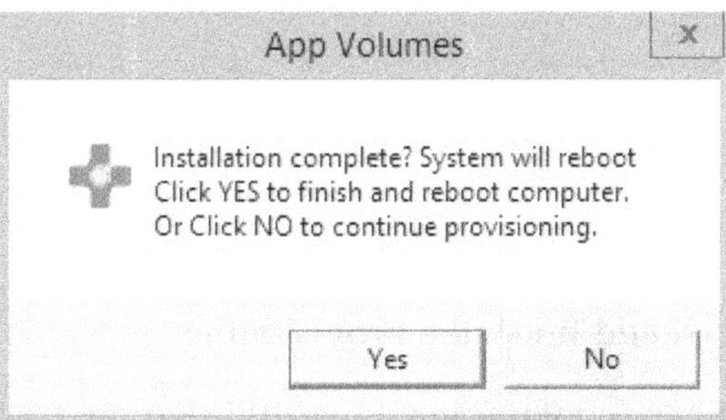
App Volumes
Installation complete? System will reboot
Click YES to finish and reboot computer.
Or Click NO to continue provisioning.
Yes
No

Click **Yes** to confirm that you have completed the application installation. You will now see the following dialog box:

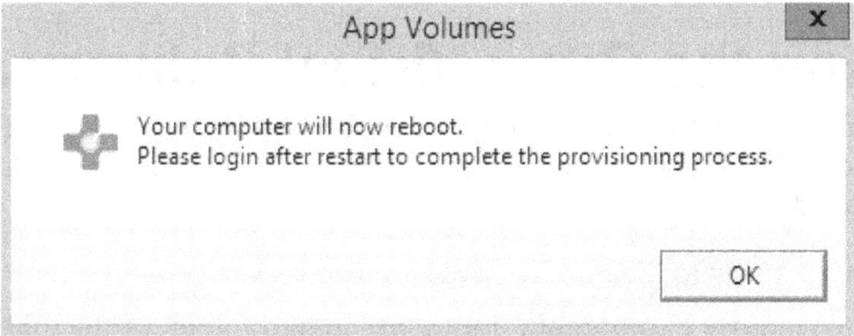
App Volumes
Your computer will now reboot.
Please login after restart to complete the provisioning process.
OK

Click **OK** to confirm the reboot. The provisioning machine will now reboot and in the process detach the newly created and provisioned AppStack.

Once rebooted, you will see the following dialog box:

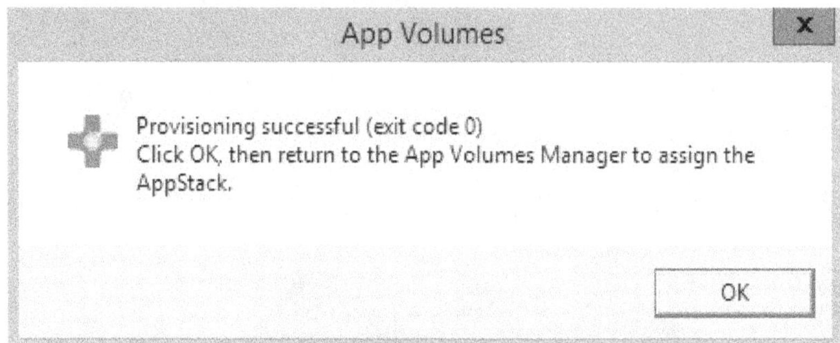

Click **OK** to close the box and finish the provisioning.

You now have an AppStack containing Office 2013 that can be attached to RDSH servers. In the next section, we are going to do exactly that, and attach the newly created AppStack to an RDSH server that is going to deliver applications with Citrix XenApp. We will start be installing the Citrix XenApp components.

Installing the Citrix Virtual Delivery Agent

In this section, we are going to install the Citrix **Virtual Delivery Agent** (**VDA**) components onto the RDSH server. The server we are going to use in this example is called `xenapp.pvolab.com`.

1. Open a console to the `xenapp.pvolab.com` server.
2. Open Windows Explorer and locate the shared folder, or the folder where you have stored the App Volumes and other software components, and locate the Citrix VDA installer files, as shown in the following screenshot:

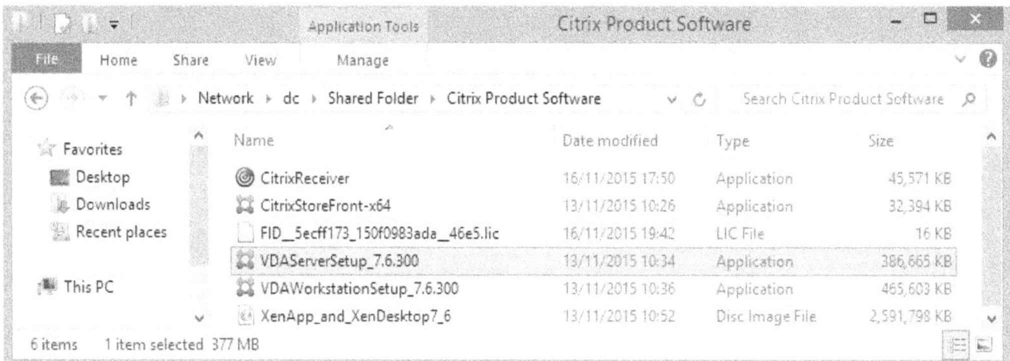

3. Launch the **VDAServerSetup_7.6.300** installer. You will now see the first configuration screen, as shown in the following diagram:

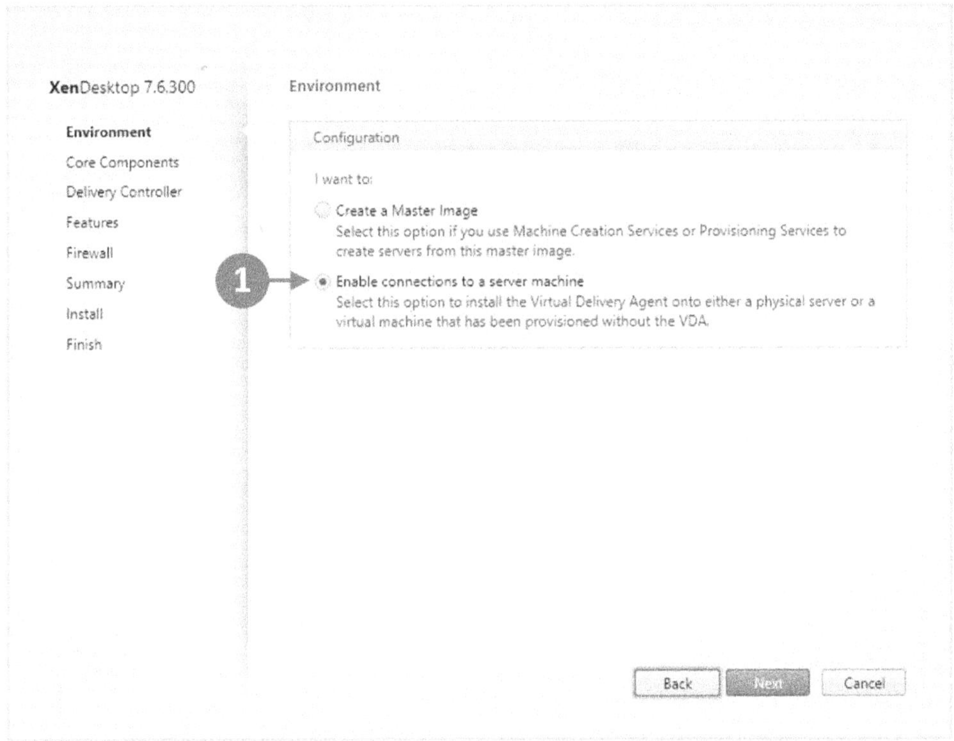

4. As you are going to build and configure a single XenApp Server, click the radio button for **Enable connections to a server machine (1)**.

   You can still use the option for creating a **Master image** and follow the same procedure.

Click the **Next** button. You will now see the **Core Components** configuration screen, as shown in the following screenshot:

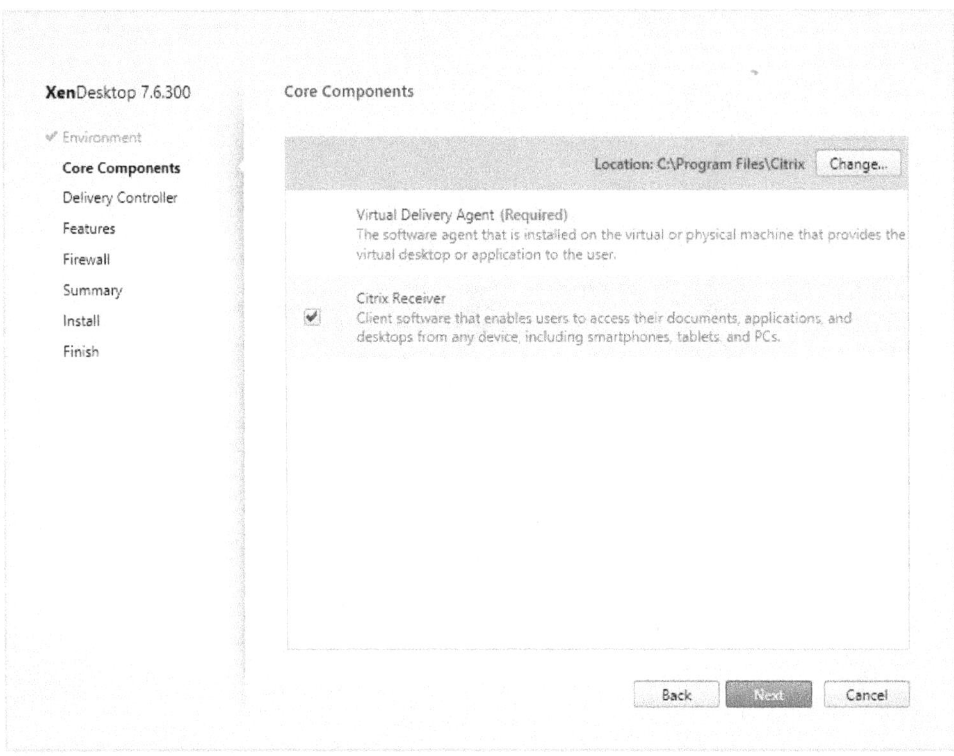

5. Click the **Next** button to continue the installation. In the next screen, shown in the following diagram, you configure the details of Delivery Controller:

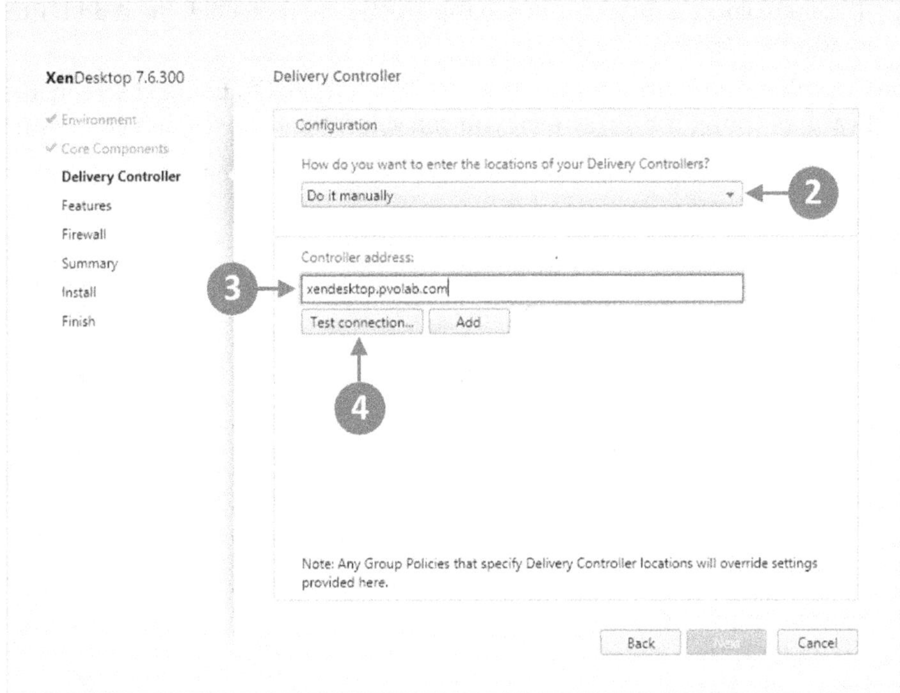

6. In the **How do you want to enter the locations of your Delivery Controllers?** box, click the dropdown menu **(2)** and select **Do it manually**.
7. Then in the **Controller address** box **(3)**, type in the details of the Delivery Controller for this server to use. In this example, the Delivery Controller is called `xendesktop.pvolab.com`.
8. Once you have entered the details, click **Test connection... (4)**, to ensure that the server can communicate with the Delivery Controller. If successful, you will see a green tick displayed **(5)**, as shown in the following diagram:

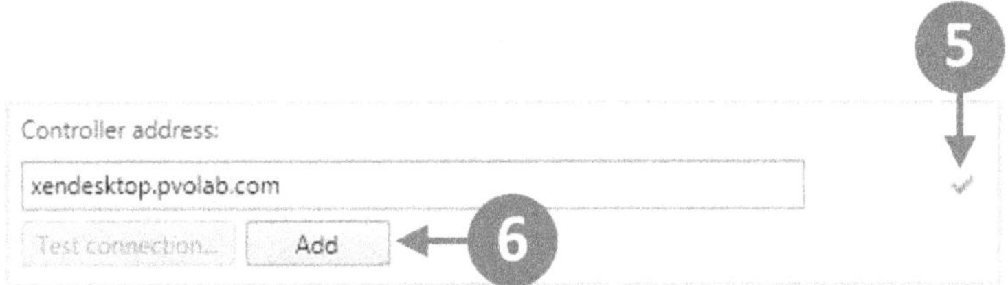

9. If you are successful and you see the green tick, then click the **Add** button **(6)** to add the Delivery Controller.
10. Click the **Next** button to continue the installation. On the next screen, the **Features** configuration screen, you can select the features that you want to install, as shown in the following screenshot:

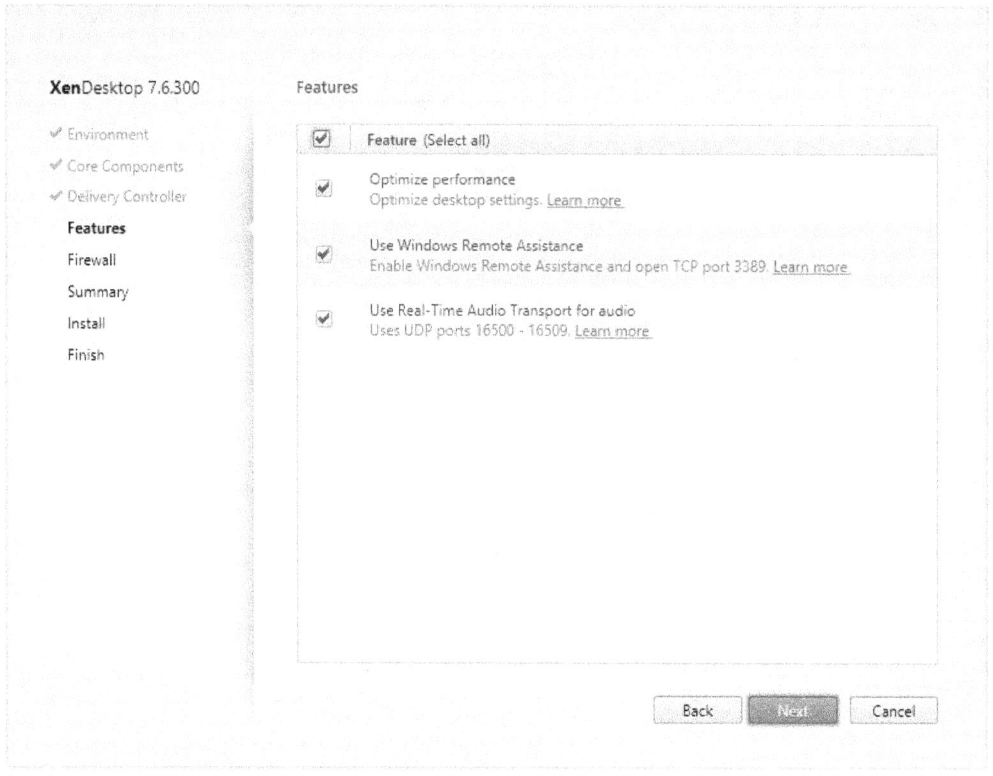

11. Check the box to add the features and then click the **Next** button. You will now see the **Firewall** configuration screen, as shown in the following diagram:

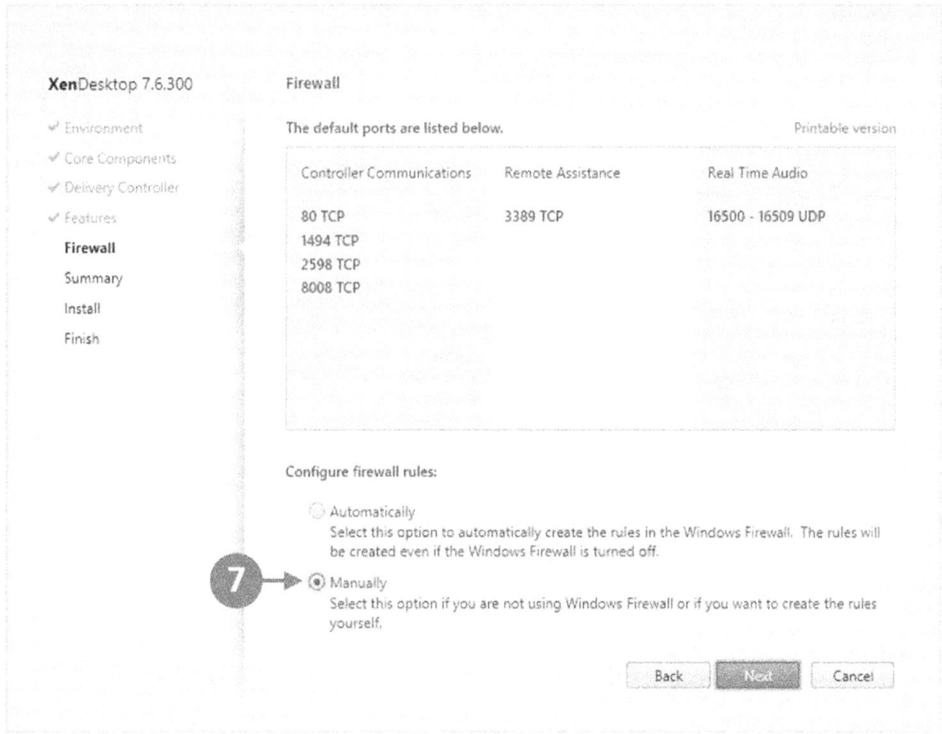

12. You have two options.

    The first option is to configure the firewall automatically and have the VDA create the firewall rules for you. The second option is to do it manually.

    In this example, click the radio button for **Manually (7)** and click **Next**.

    You will now see the **Summary** screen, as shown in the following diagram:

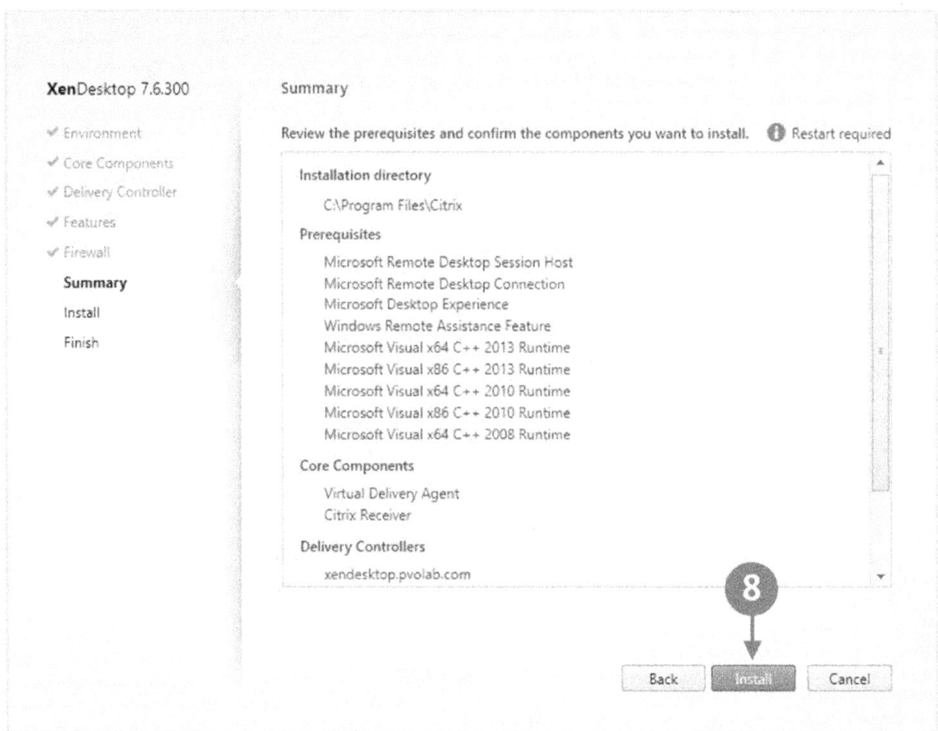

13. Click the **Install** button **(8)** to start the installation. You will now see the installation screen showing the progress of the components as they are being installed, as shown in the following screenshot:

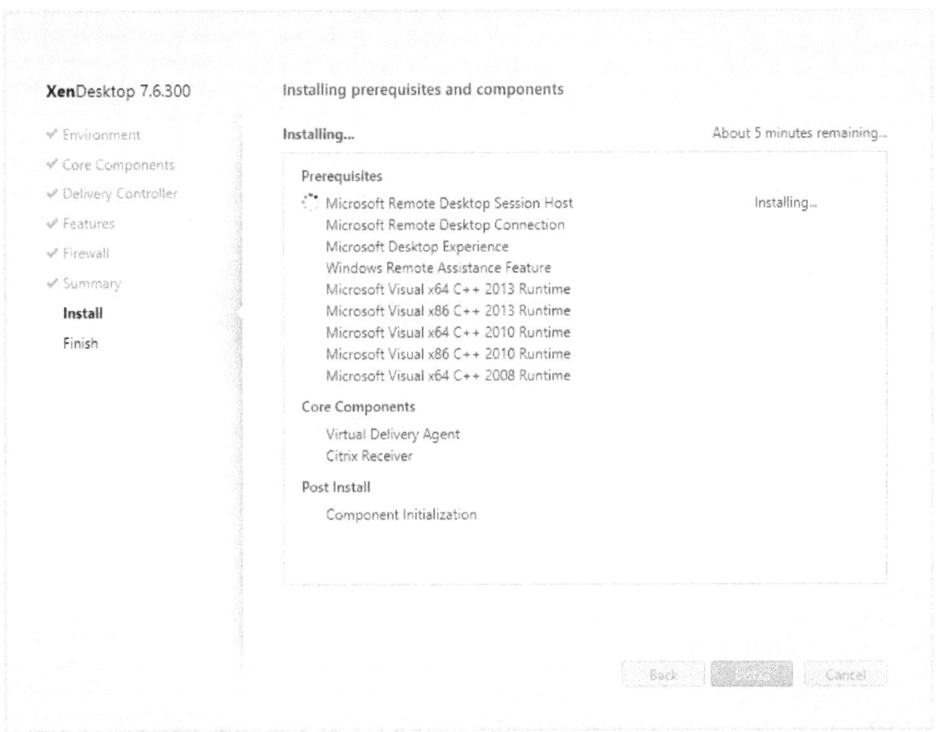

Once completed, you will see the **Finish** screen, as shown in the following diagram:

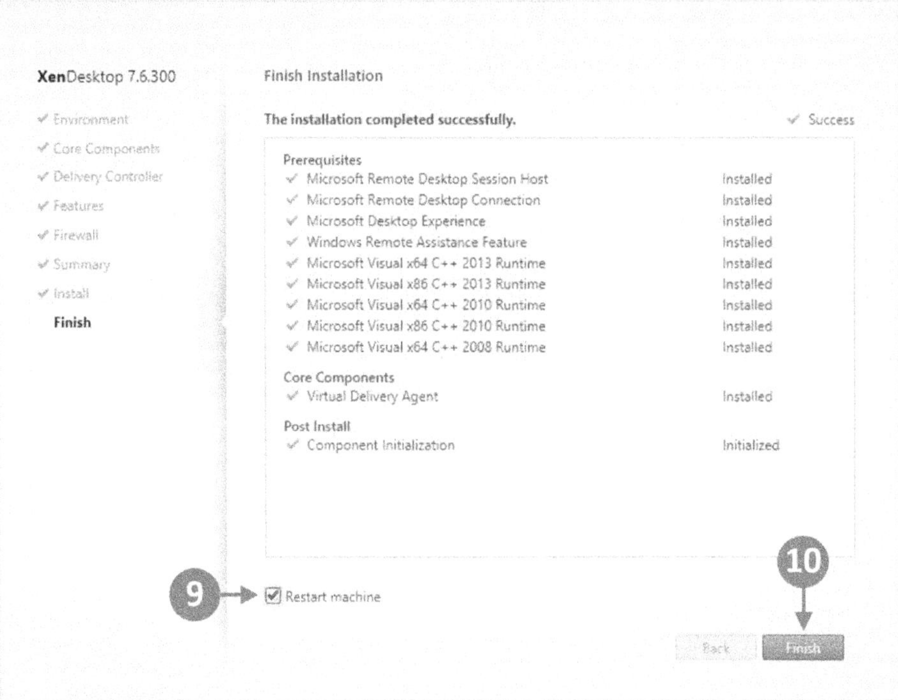

14. Check the **Restart machine** box **(9)**, and then click the **Finish** button **(10)**.

The server will now reboot.

Once rebooted, the next step is to install the App Volumes Agent so that you can attach the Office 2013 RDSH AppStack, before moving on to the Citrix-specific configuration tasks for delivering the applications.

Installing the App Volumes Agent

The next part of the process is to install the App Volumes Agent onto the RDSH host server you are using for provisioning, so that it registers itself with the App Volumes Manager, allowing you to start using it for application provisioning.

We have already covered the installation process in the *Installing the App Volumes Agent* section of *Chapter 4, Installing and Configuring the App Volumes Software*, so please refer to that chapter on how to do this. The process is exactly the same for servers as it is for desktops.

Assigning the AppStack to the XenApp RDSH Server

The next stage in the process is to assign and attach the Office Pro 2013 AppStack to the XenApp Server.

From there, you can then complete the Citrix-specific configuration tasks and select which applications are going to be published and who to.

Unlike our previous assignments when working with virtual desktop machines, in this scenario the AppStack is assigned directly to a virtual machine. In this case, the virtual machine in question is the XenApp Server that is already configured with the RDSH role and has the Citrix Virtual Delivery Agent installed.

1. If you are not still logged in, log in to the App Volumes Manager and click on the **VOLUMES** menu option, and then the **AppStacks** tab. You will now see the following diagram:

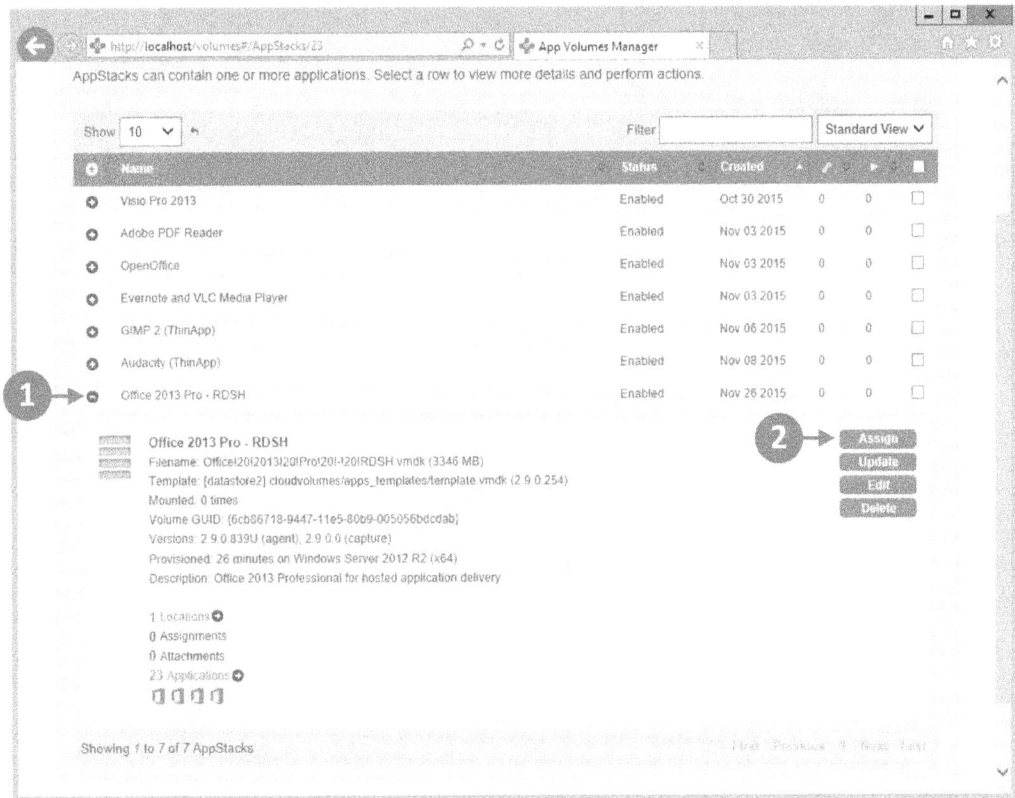

2. Click the **+/-** sign next to the **Office Pro 2013 - RDSH** entry **(1)** and then click the **Assign** button **(2)**.

   Youwill now see the **Assign AppStack: Office 2013 Pro - RDSH** screen, as shown in the following diagram:

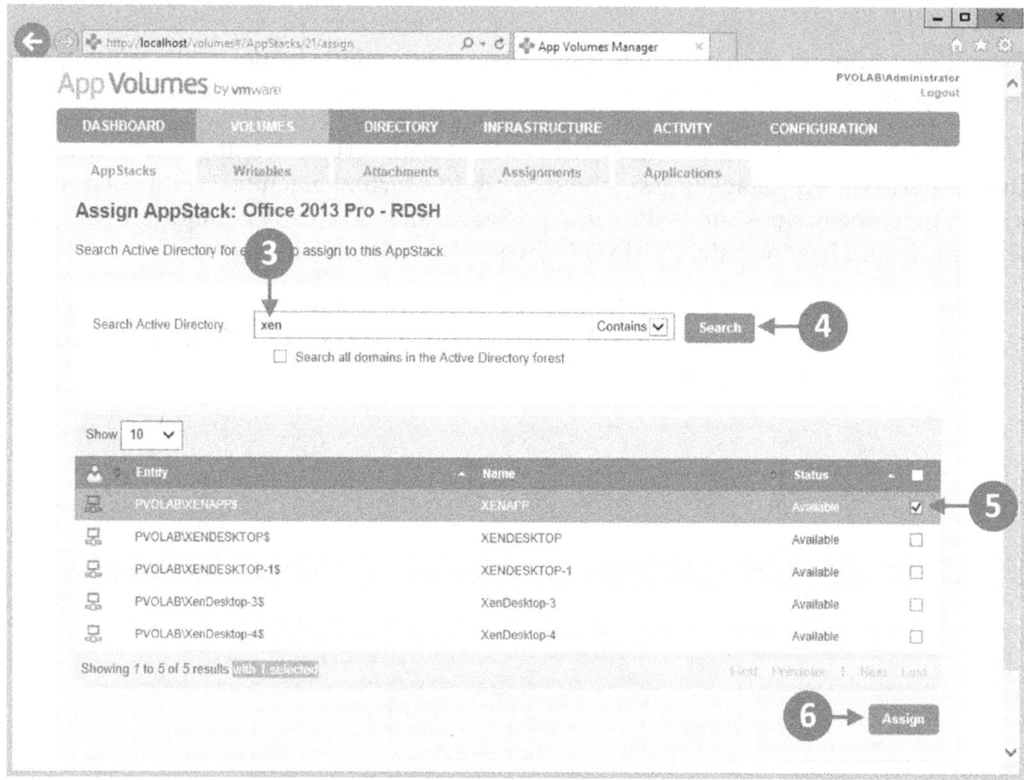

3. In the **Search Active Directory** box **(3)**, enter the name of the server to assign the AppStack to. In this example, the server we are searching for is **XenApp**, so type this or part of this name into the box and then click the **Search** button **(4)**.
4. You will see a list of results displayed. Check the box next to the server that you want to assign this AppStack to **(5)**. In this example, you are going to assign the AppStack to the XenApp Server listed as `PVOLAB\XENAPP%`.
5. Click the **Assign** button **(6)**. You will now see the **Confirm Assign** dialog box, as shown in the following diagram:

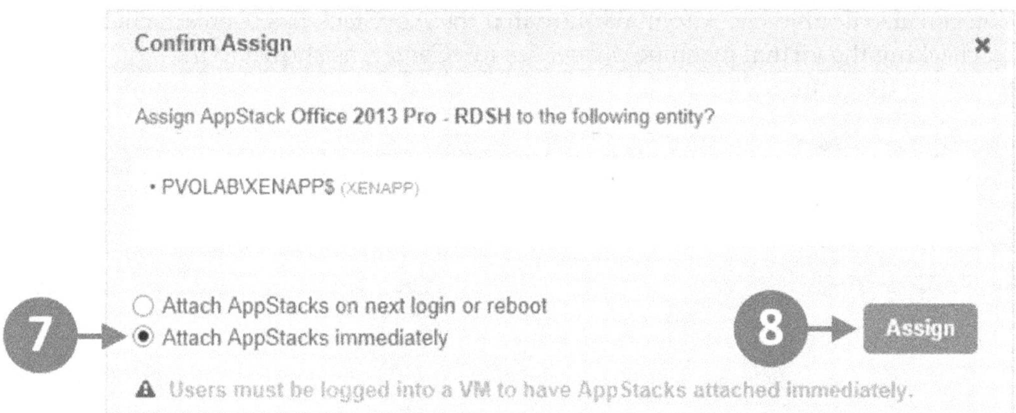

6. Click the radio button for **Attach AppStacks immediately (7)**, and then click the **Assign** button **(8)**. You will see the following message as the AppStack is assigned and attached:

Once the assignment has completed and the AppStack has been attached, you will see the following screenshot:

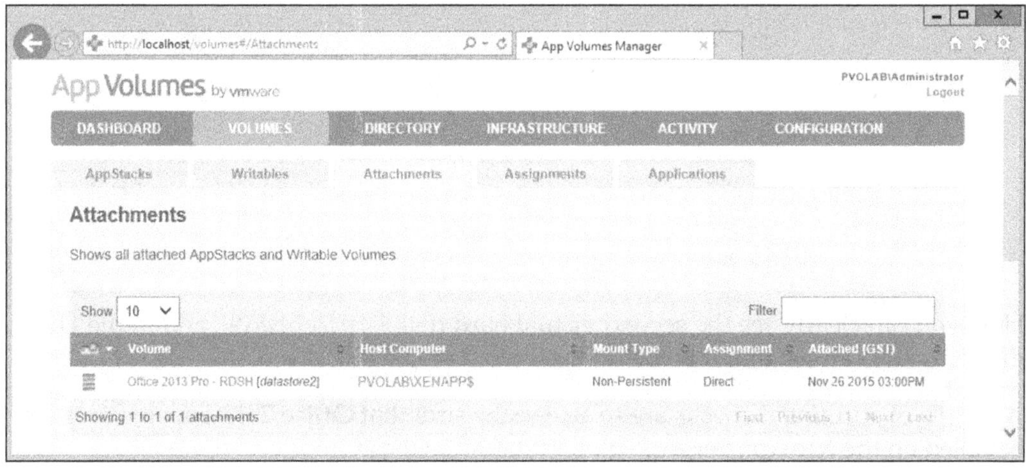

You can also double-check to make sure that the AppStack has been attached by checking the virtual machine properties in vCenter, as shown in the following diagram:

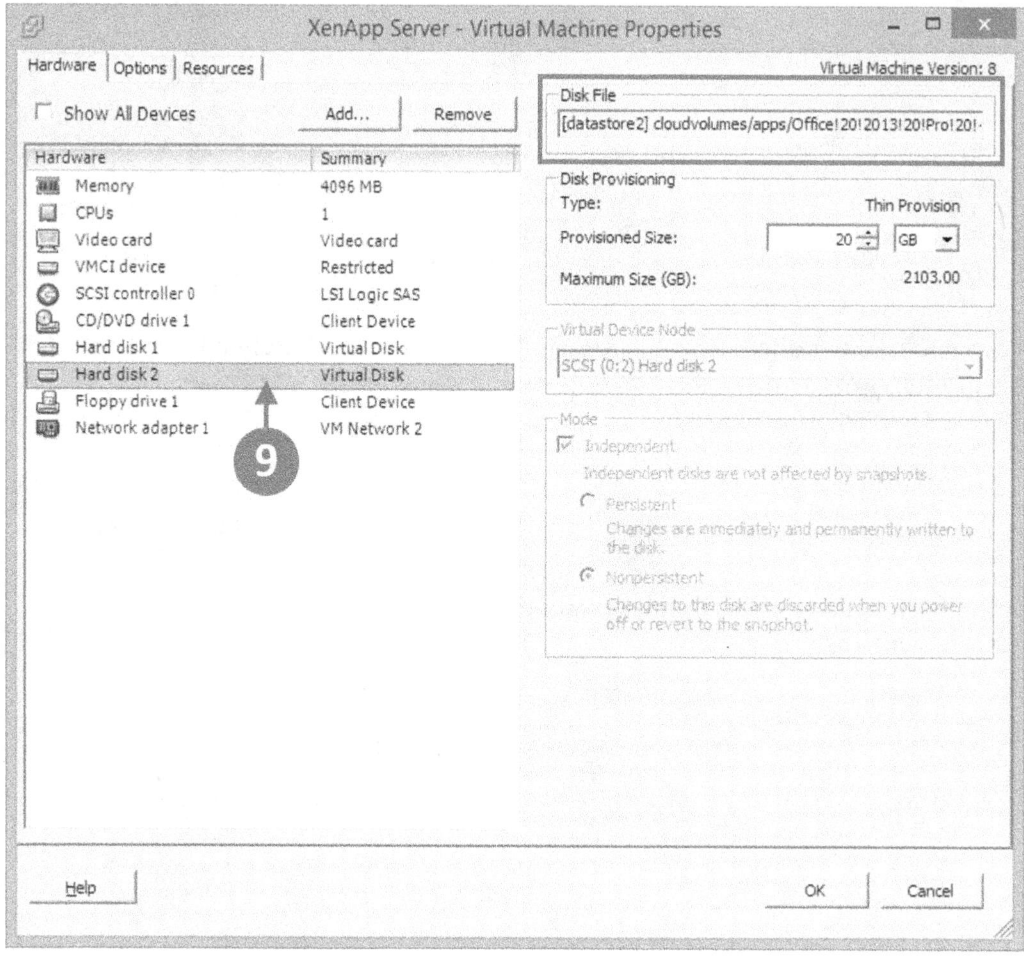

Here you can clearly see the second virtual hard disk is attached **(9)**, and in the **Disk File** box, you can see that it is the `Office 2013 AppStack`.

A couple of additional checks are to also make sure that Office 2013 appears as if it's installed on the XenApp Server. To do that, follow these steps:

1. Open a console to the XenApp Server.
2. Launch the **Control Panel** and then, from there, click **Programs** and then **Programs and Features**. This is shown in the following screenshot:

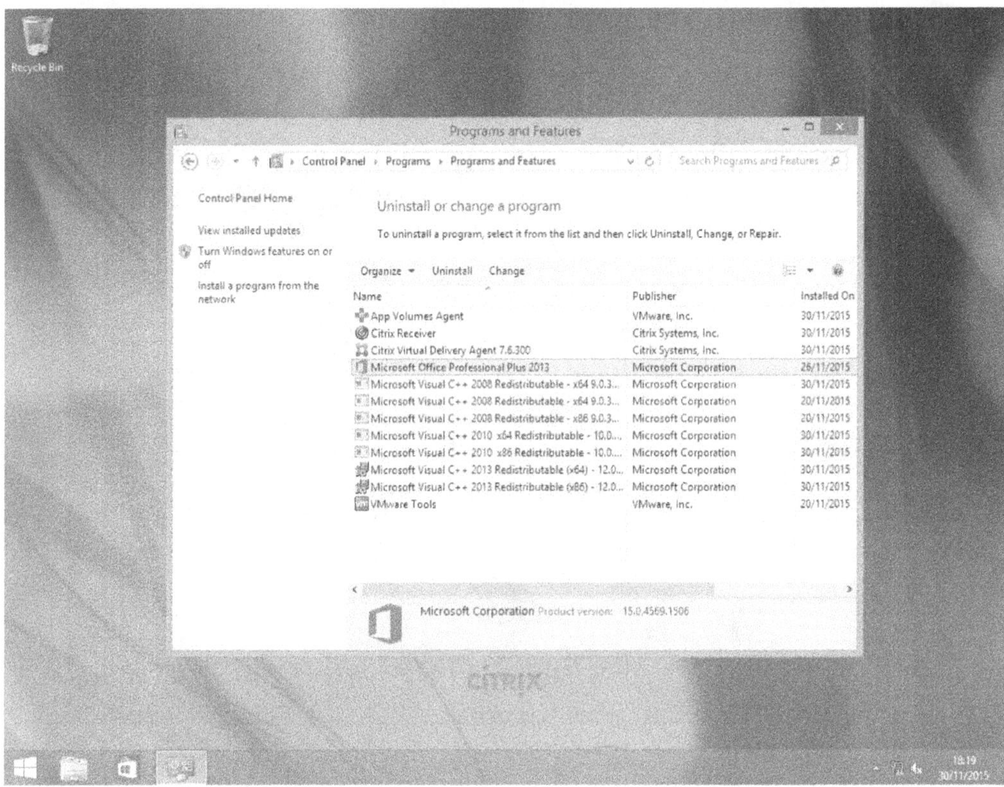

3. From the list of installed programs, ensure that there is an entry for **Microsoft Office Professional Plus 2013**.

The other check at this point is to make sure that the Office 2013 application appears on the Start menu of the server.

The reason this is important is that when you create the delivery group on the Delivery Controller, the applications are read directly from the **Start** menu. As a consequence, you also need to ensure that the user account that you log in to this server with has the appropriate user rights to be able to do this.

So to check from the desktop of the XenApp Server, simply click the **Start** button and then click the arrow displayed on the bottom-left of the screen.

You will see the following screenshot:

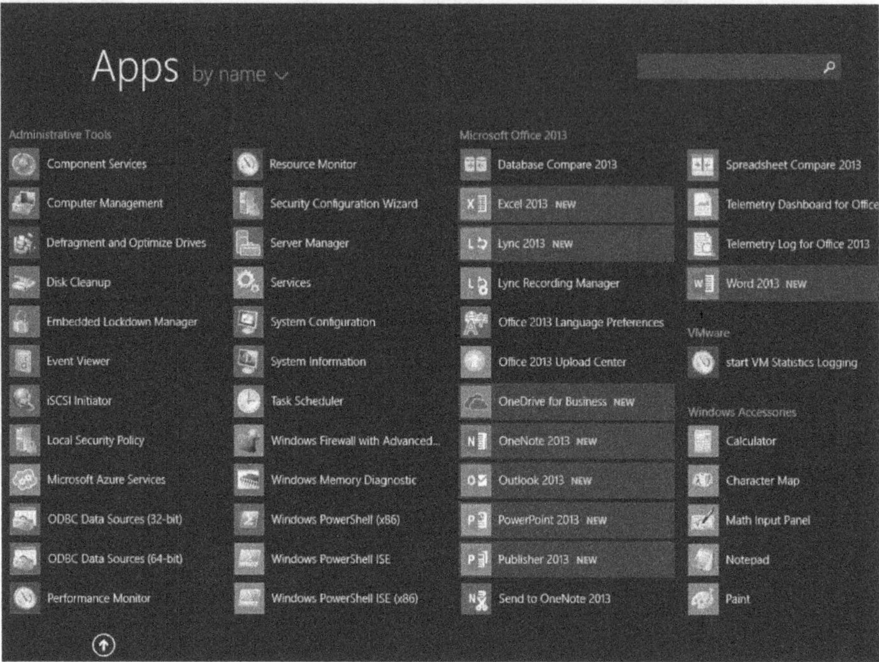

As you can see, the various Office 2013 components are listed on the App screen and, having not been launched yet, are listed as new.

You have now completed the installation and configuration of the XenApp Server. In the next section, you will configure the application delivery components, starting with creating a machine catalog.

Creating a machine catalog

Now that you have created a XenApp host server and assigned and attached the AppStack containing Office 2013, the next stage of the process is to configure the delivery components. In this section, you will walk through this process:

1. On the server where you installed the XenDesktop Delivery Controller, launch Citrix Studio. This is the **Microsoft Management Console** (**MMC**)-based console. You would have used this to complete the configuration stage when you built and configured the infrastructure components, and also if you created a catalog for virtual desktop machines in *Chapter 10, Deploying App Volumes in a Citrix XenDesktop Environment*. You will see the following diagram:

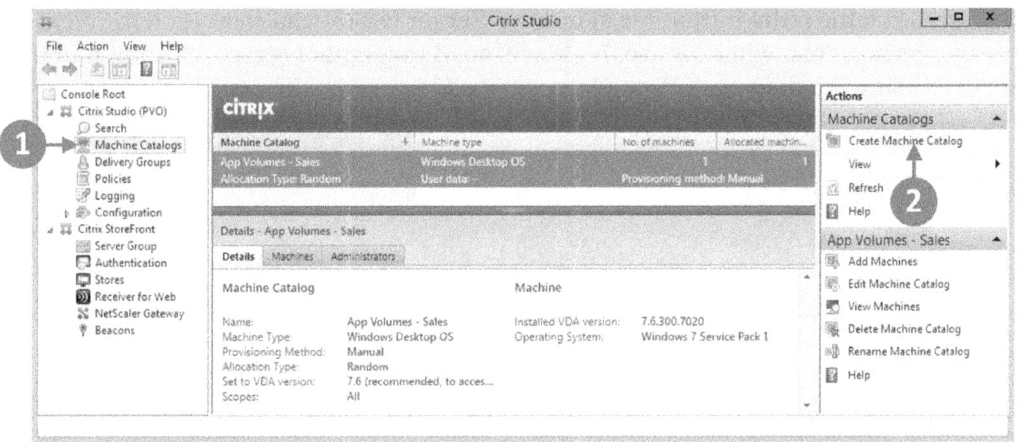

2. Click on **Machine Catalogs (1)**, and then click on **Create Machine Catalog (2)**.
3. Click the **Next** button on the **Introduction** screen to continue. You will now see the **Operating System** screen, as shown in the following diagram:

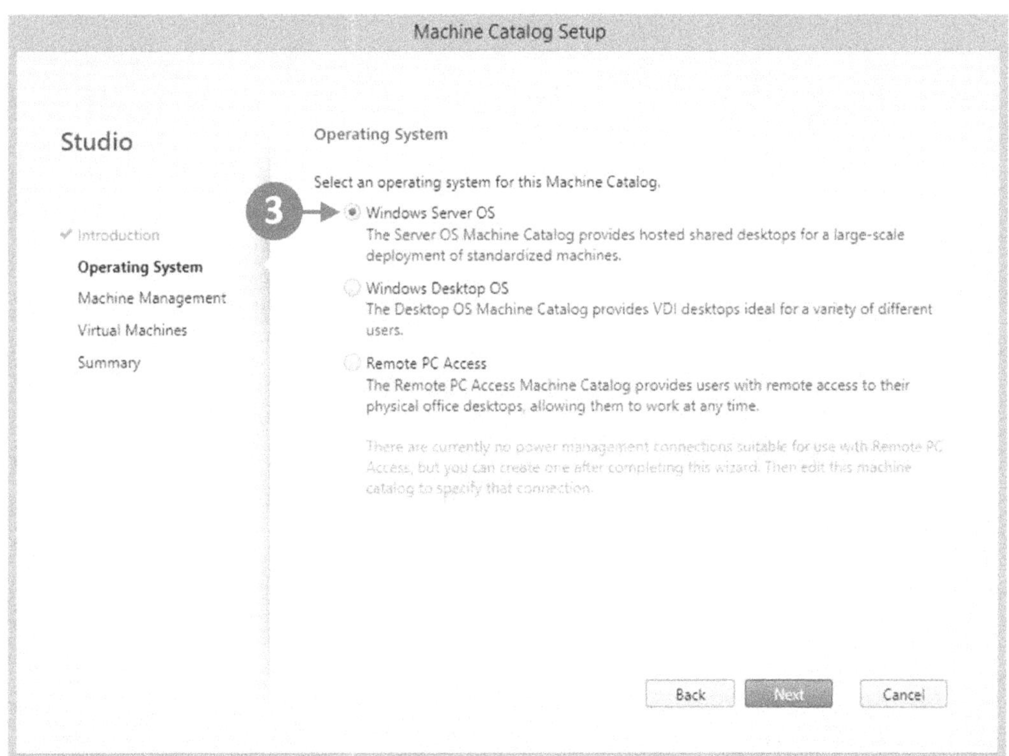

4. Click the radio button for **Windows Server OS (3)** and then click the **Next** button. You will now see the **Machine Management** screen, as shown in the following diagram:

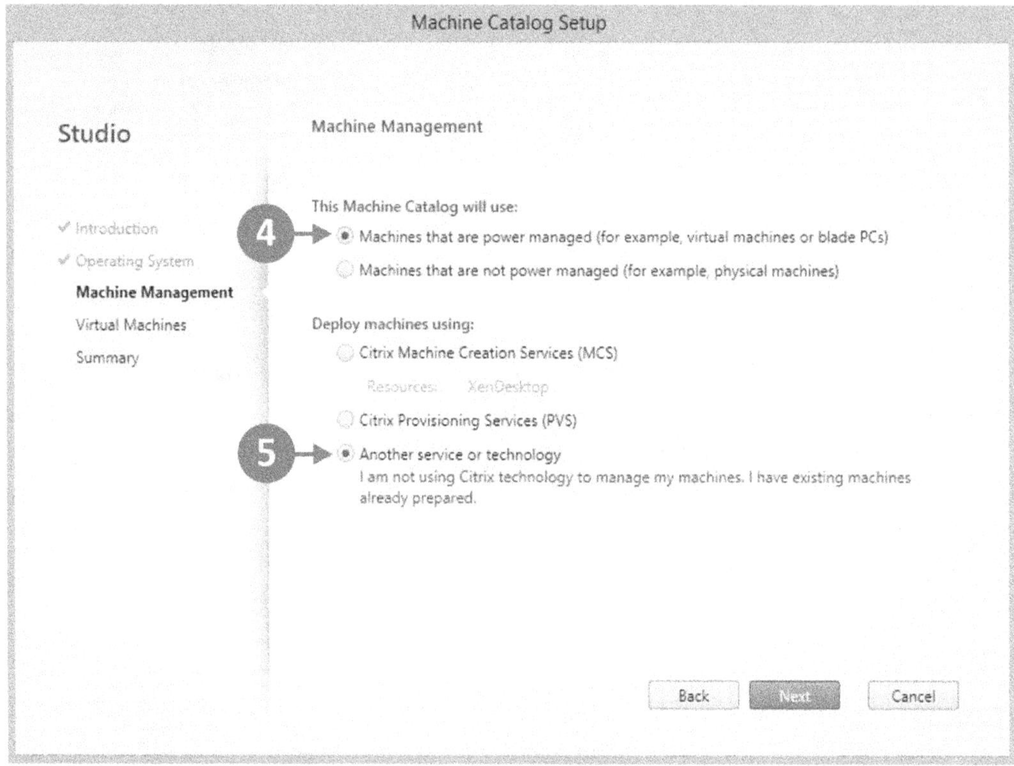

5. Click the radio button for **Machines that are power managed (for example, virtual machines or blade PCs) (4)**.
6. As you are using a server that has already been built and configured as the XenApp Server, then also click the radio button for **Another service or technology (5)**.
7. Click the **Next** button to continue. You will now see the **Virtual Machines** screen, as shown in the following diagram:

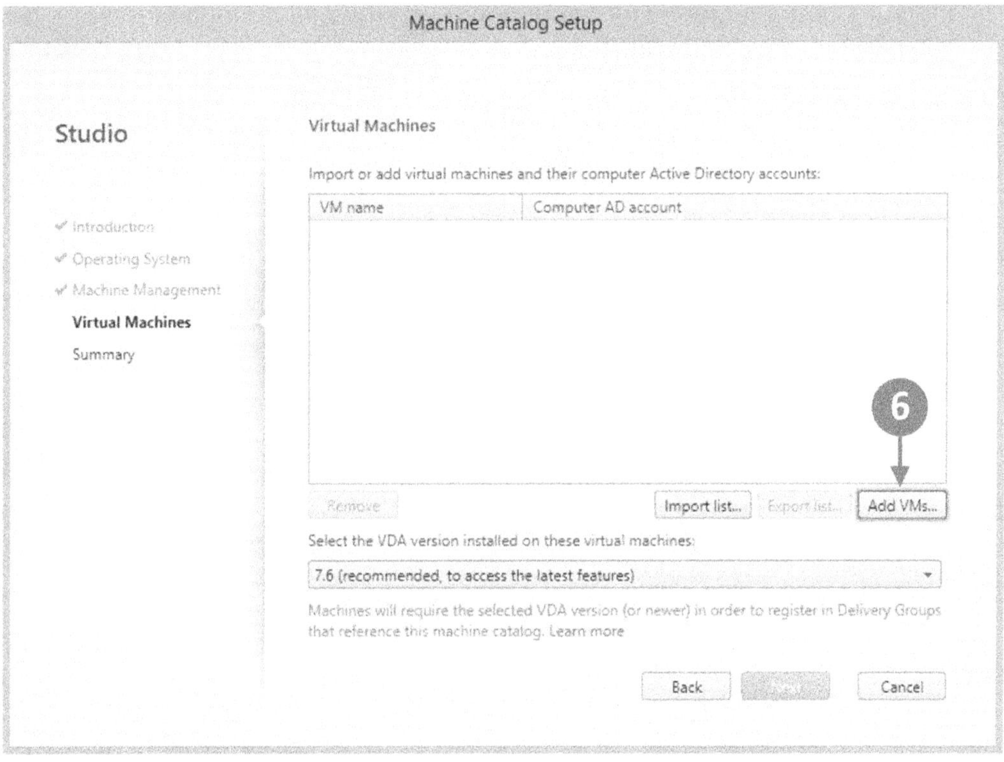

8. Click the **Add VMs...** button **(6)**.
9. In the **Select VMs** dialog box that is now displayed, we are going to select the XenApp Server previously built.
10. From the option, expand **vSphere | PVO's Datacenter | 192.168.0.23**. Scroll down until you find the entry for **XenApp Server**, and then check the box **(7)**.

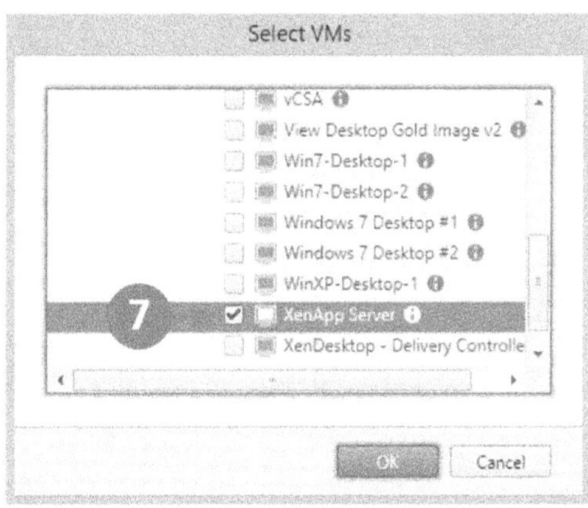

11. Click **OK** to continue. The server name is now displayed in the inventory list, as shown in the following diagram:

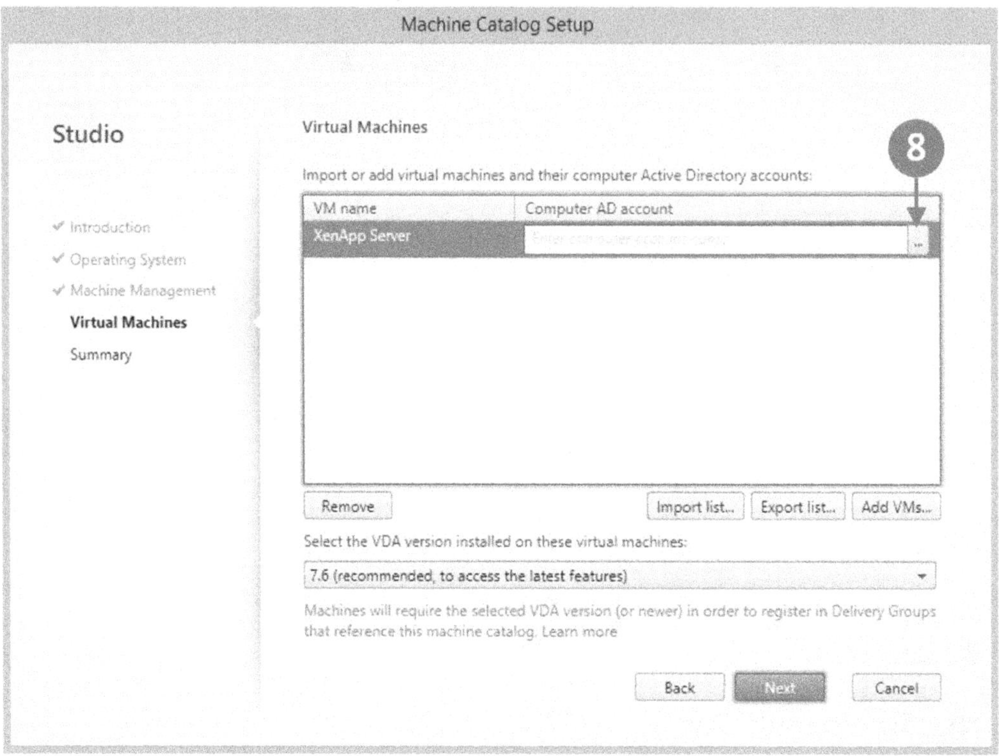

12. Before we can continue, you have to add the details of the Active Directory machine account for the XenApp Server. To do this, click the **...** box **(8)**.

13. From the **Select Computer** dialog box, in the **Enter the object name to select** box, type `xen` and then click the **Check Names** box **(9)**, as shown in the following diagram:

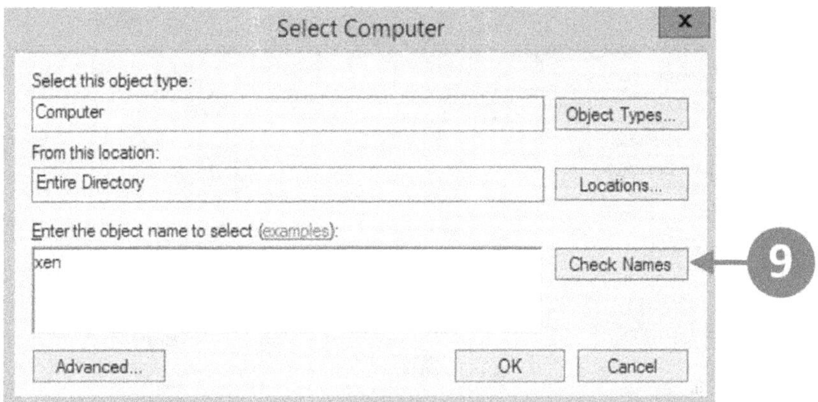

You will now see the **Multiple Names Found** dialog box, as shown in the following diagram:

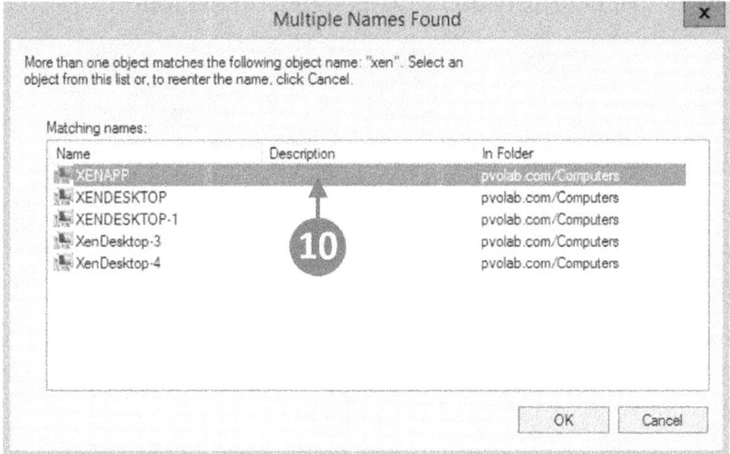

14. Select the entry for **XenApp (10)** and then click **OK**. You will now return to the **Select Computer** dialog box, which now shows the XenApp Server, as shown in the following screenshot:

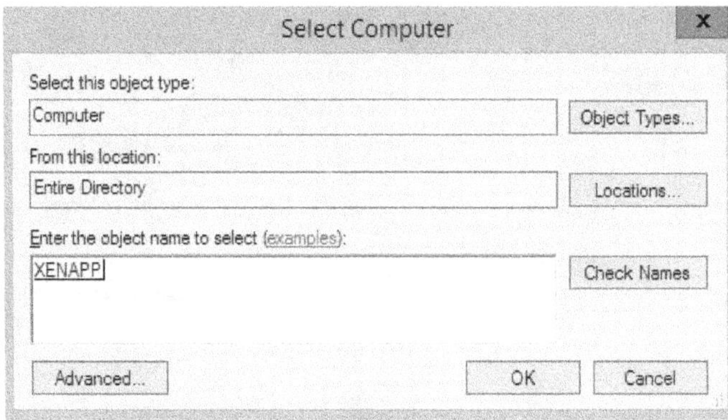

15. Click **OK** to select and close the **Select Computer** dialog box.

    You will now return to the **Citrix Studio** screen and the **Virtual Machines** screen. You will see that the XenApp Server now appears on the list, along with its Active Directory account, as shown in the following screenshot:

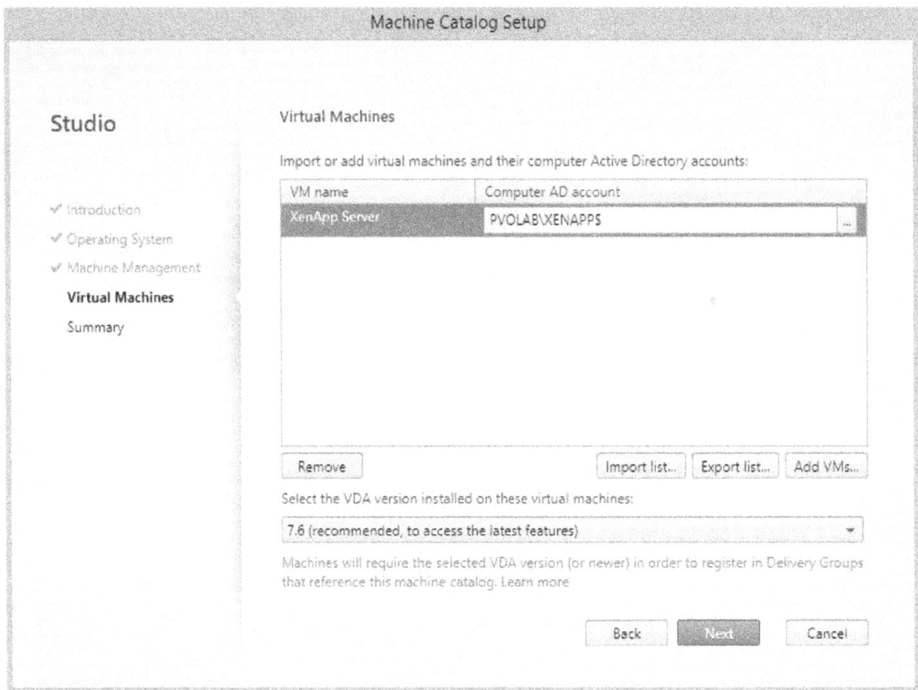

16. Click the **Next** button to continue. You will now see the **Summary** screen:

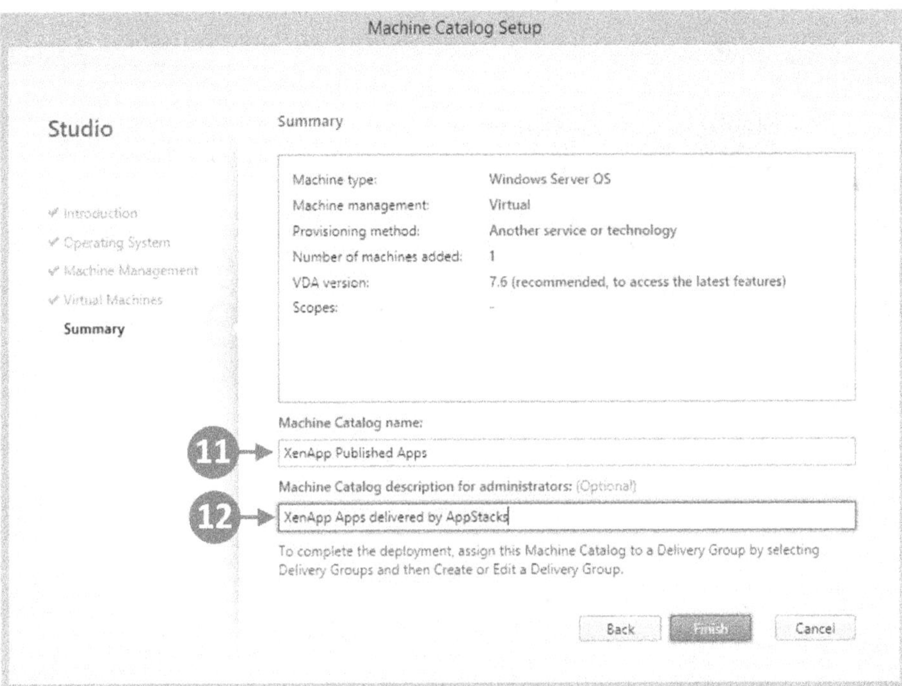

Even though this is the final **Summary** screen, there a couple of final things to configure:

- First, in the **Machine Catalog name** box **(11)**, enter a name for this machine catalog. In this example we are going to call it `XenApp Published Apps`.
- Lastly, in the **Machine Catalog description for administrators** box **(12)**, enter a description to identify this machine catalog. In this example, we are going to provide the description `XenApp Apps delivered by AppStacks`.

17. Click the **Finish** button to complete the configuration and close the machine catalog setup. You will now see the following screenshot:

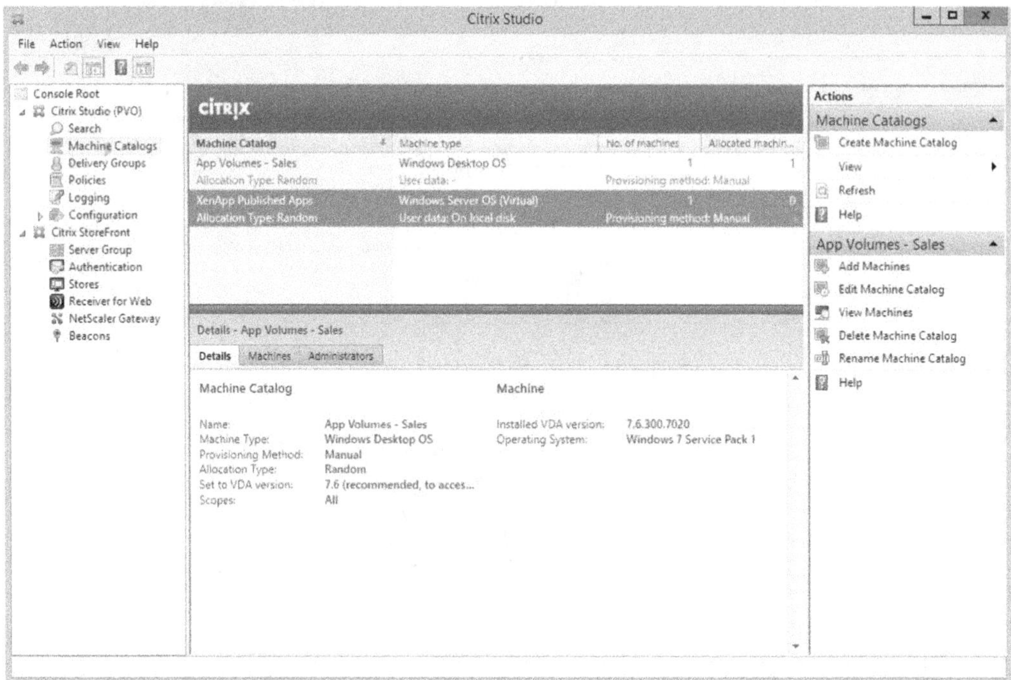

You have now successfully configured the machine catalog. The next step is to create a Delivery Group.

Creating a Delivery Group

Now we have created the machine catalog, the next step is to create a Delivery Group where we can configure the applications for publishing, as well as choosing which users are entitled to the applications.

1. From the Citrix Studio click on **Delivery Groups (1)**, and then click on **Create Delivery Group (2)**, as shown in the following diagram:

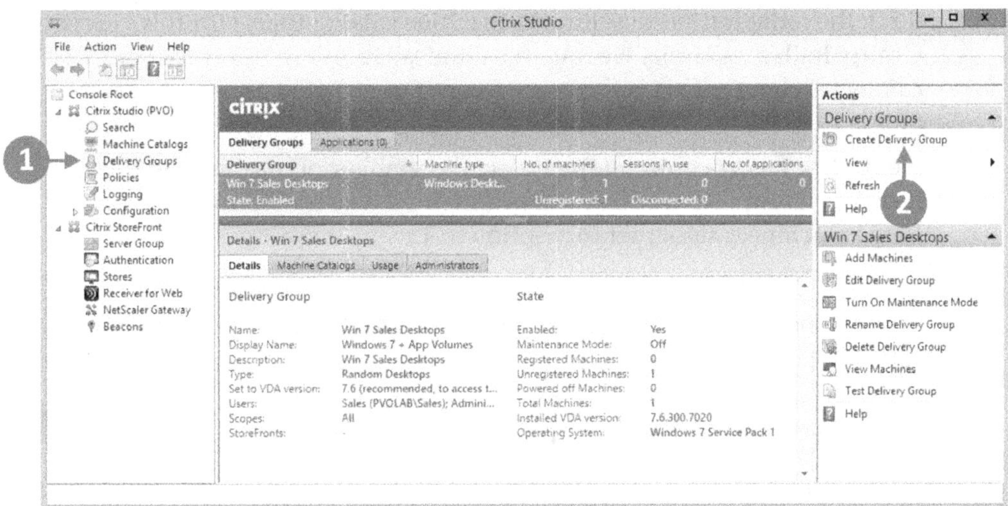

2. Click the **Next** button on the **Introduction** screen to continue. You will now see the **Machines** configuration screen, as shown in the following diagram:

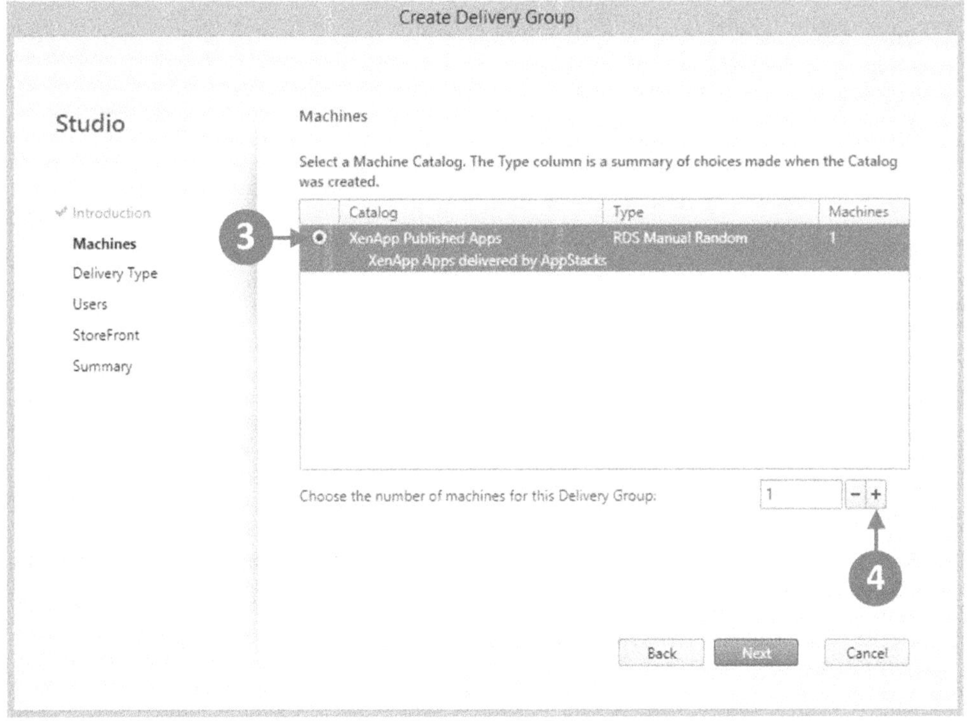

3. Click the radio button to select the machine catalog to use for this Delivery Group. In this example, we only have the `XenApp Published Apps` catalog to choose. This is the one we configured in the previous section of this chapter.
4. Next, click the **+/-** button **(4)** to select the number of machines in this Delivery Group. As we have only configured a single XenApp Server in the machine catalog, set this option to **1**.
5. Click the **Next** button to continue.

   You will now see the **Delivery Type** configuration screen, as shown in the following diagram:

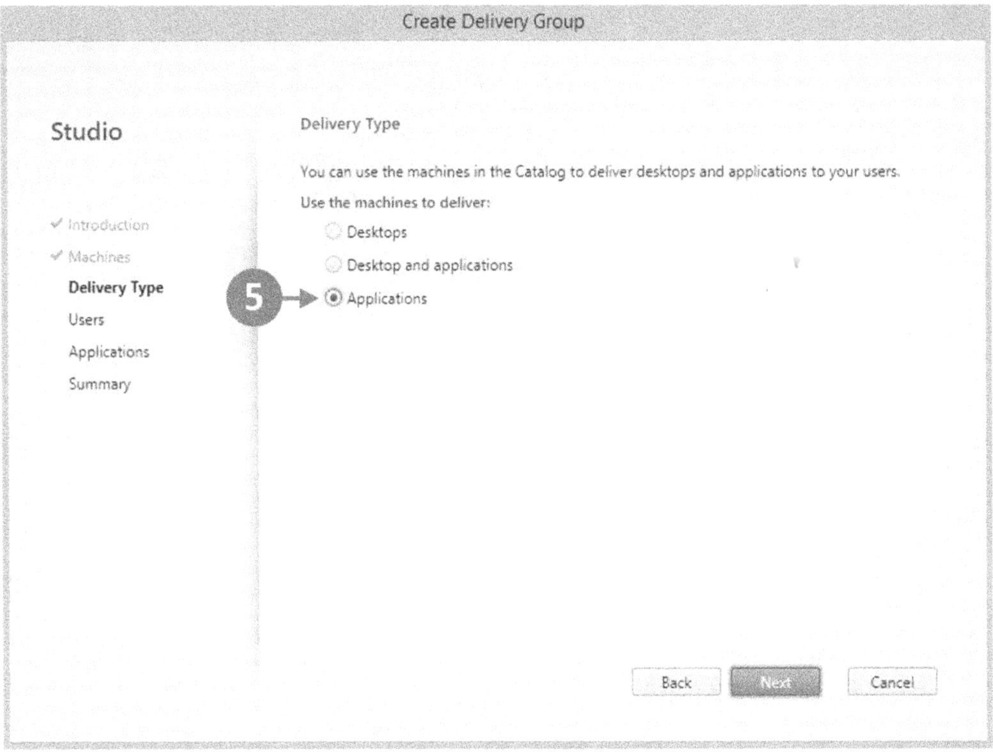

6. As we are just going to be delivering published applications, click the radio button for **Applications (5)** and then click the **Next** button to continue.

   You will now see the **Users** configuration screen, as shown in the following diagram:

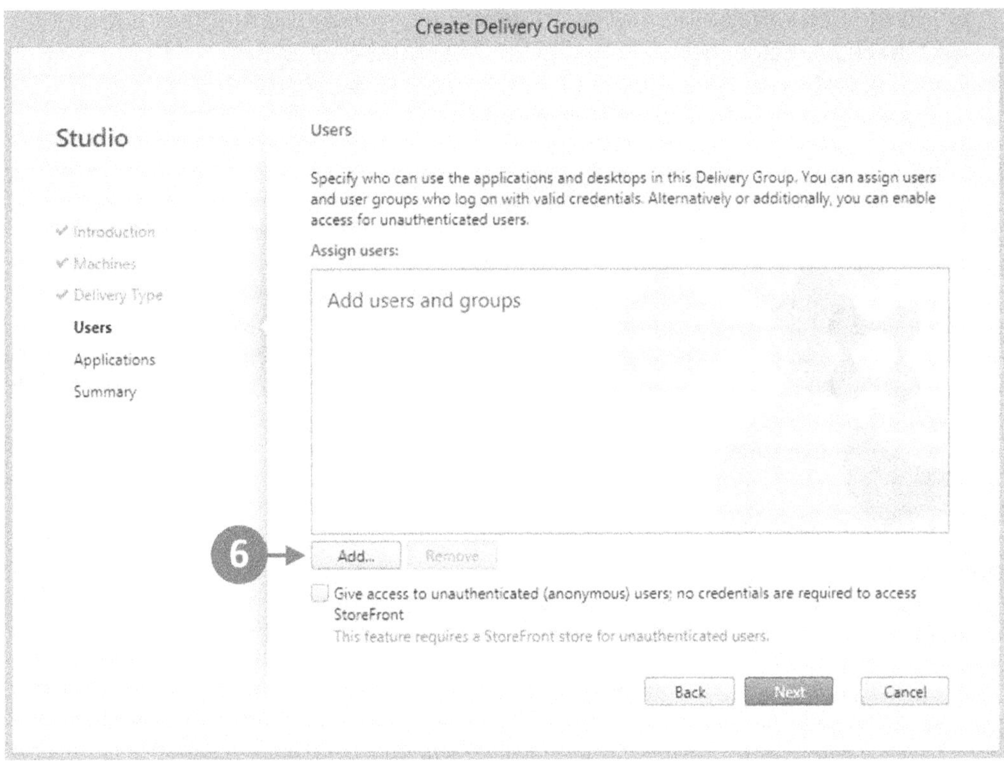

7. Click the **Add...** button **(6)** to add users. You will now see the **Select Users or Groups** dialog box, as shown in the following screenshot:

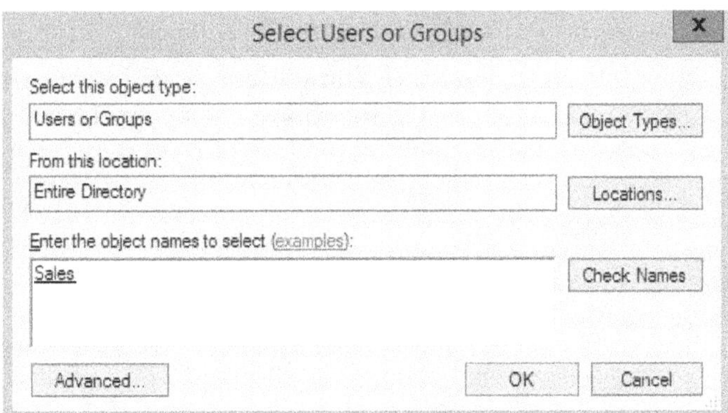

In this example, we are going to add a group to the entitlement.

8. In the **Enter the object names to select** box, type `sales` and then click the **Check Names** button. The **Sales** group should now appear.
9. Click **OK** to close the dialog box and return to the Citrix Studio screen, as shown in the following screenshot:

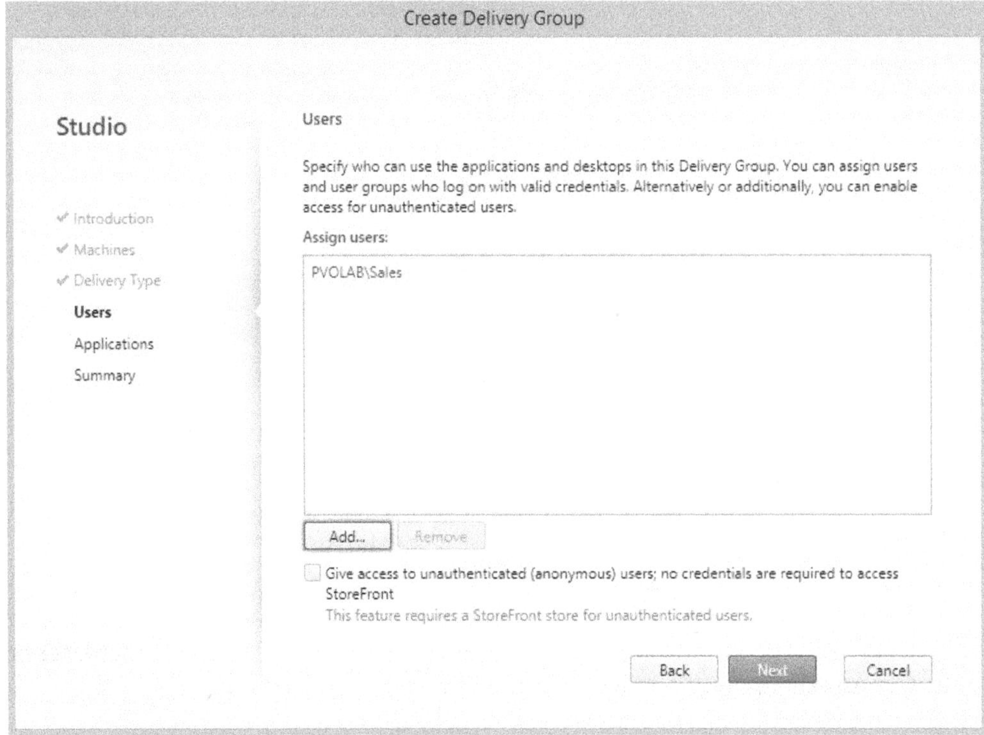

10. Click the **Next** button to continue. You will now see the **Applications** configuration screen, as shown in the following screenshot:

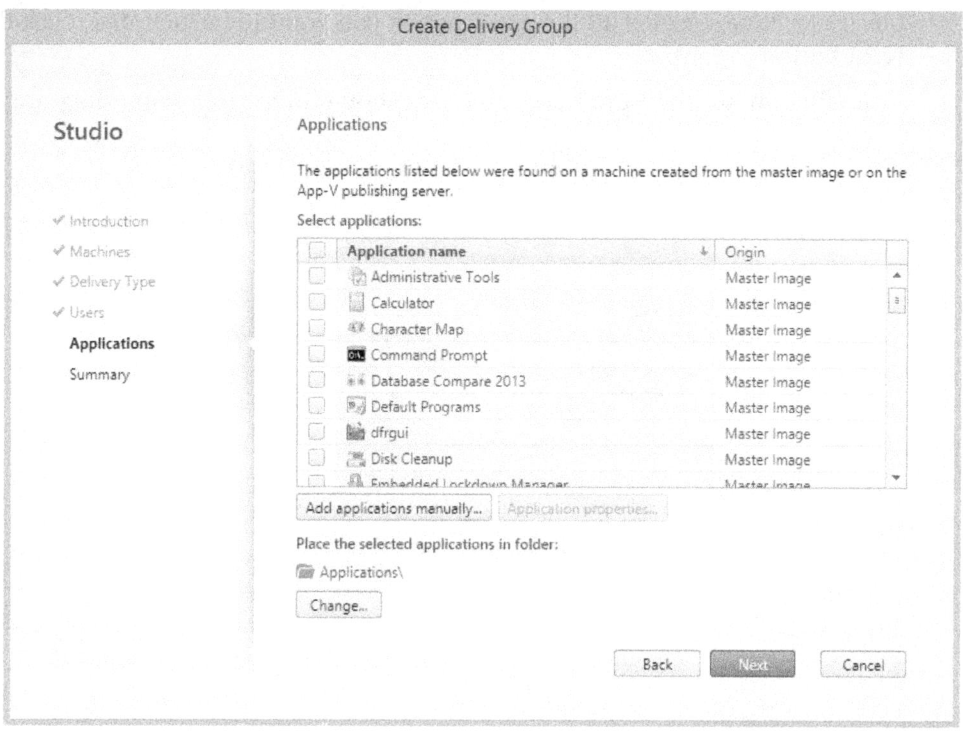

From the list of applications displayed, check the box next to those that you want to be included in this Delivery Group. In this example, select the following applications:

- **Calculator**
- **Excel 2013**
- **OneNote 2013**
- **Paint**
- **PowerPoint 2013**
- **Publisher 2013**
- **Word 2013**

Once you have selected all the applications you want to be included, click the **Next** button to continue.

You will now see the **Summary** screen, as shown in the following diagram:

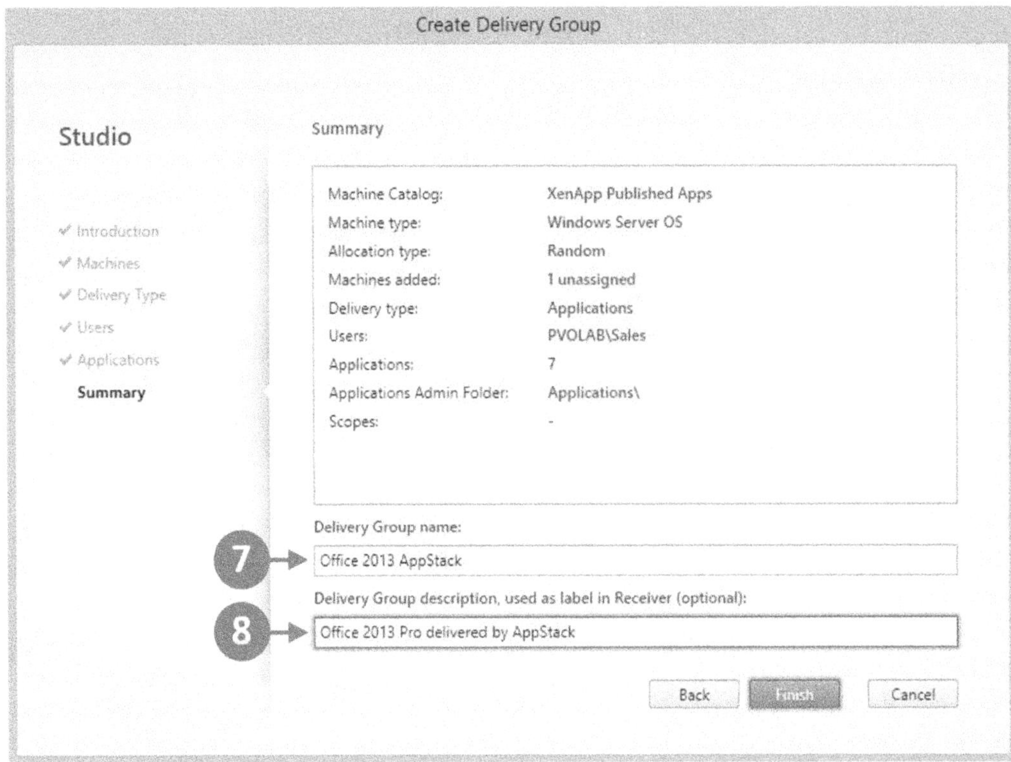

Even though this is the final **Summary** screen, there a couple of final things to configure:

- First, in the **Delivery Group name** box **(7)**, enter a name for this Delivery Group. In this example, we are going to call it `Office 2013 AppStack`.
- In the **Delivery Group description, used as label in Receiver (optional)** box **(8)**, enter a description to identify this Delivery Group. In this example, we are going to provide the description `Office 2013 Pro delivered by AppStacks`.

11. Click the **Finish** button to complete the configuration and close the Delivery Group setup. You will now see the following screenshot:

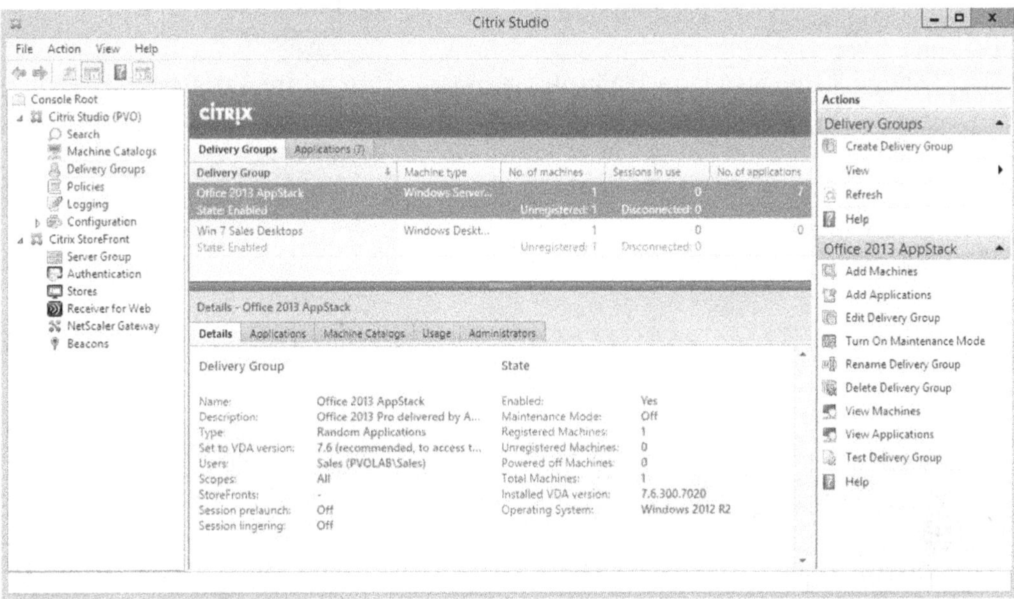

You have now successfully configured the Delivery Group.

Now that you have completed all the configuration steps for building a XenApp environment with applications being delivered using App Volumes AppStacks, the next step is to test that everything works as expected.

Launching AppStack-based XenApp applications

You have now completed the required configuration steps, built an AppStack for use with RDSH servers, created a machine catalog, and finally created a Delivery Group.

The next step is to log in to XenApp and test that end users can access their applications.

We are going to use one of the example user desktop machines to log in from, along with one of the users who is part of the Sales group that we configured in the Delivery Group. You will also need to ensure that Citrix Receiver is installed on this desktop machine.

1. The first step is to launch a browser and enter the address of the StoreFront server. In the Example Lab, a separate StoreFront server wasn't built and we will use the default address, so enter `http://xendesktop.pvolab.com/Citrix/SoreWeb/` as the address.

   You will now see the **Citrix Receiver** login screen, as shown in the following screenshot:

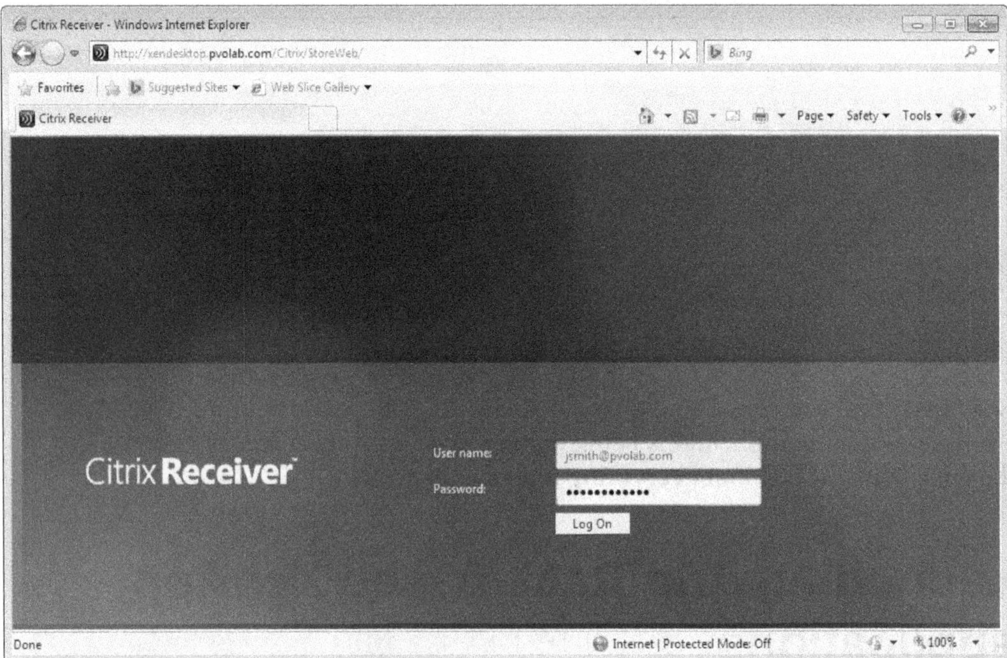

2. Enter the username `jsmith@pvolab.com` and their password.
3. Click the **Log On** button. You will now see the following screenshot:

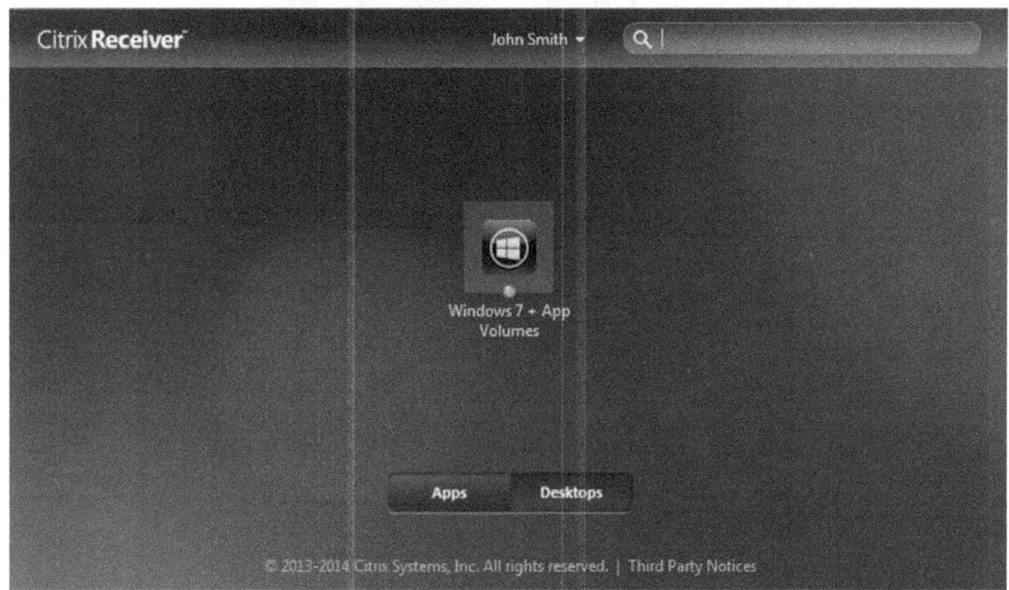

4. On the **Citrix Receiver** screen, click the **Apps** button. You will now see the following screenshot:

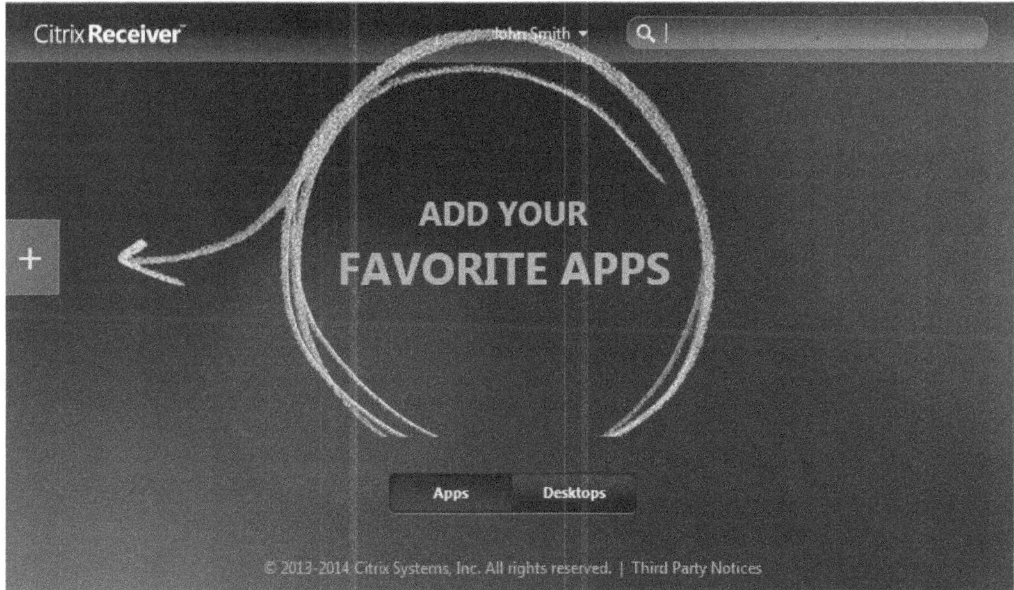

5. Click the **+/-** button, as directed in the screenshot. You will now see the following diagram:

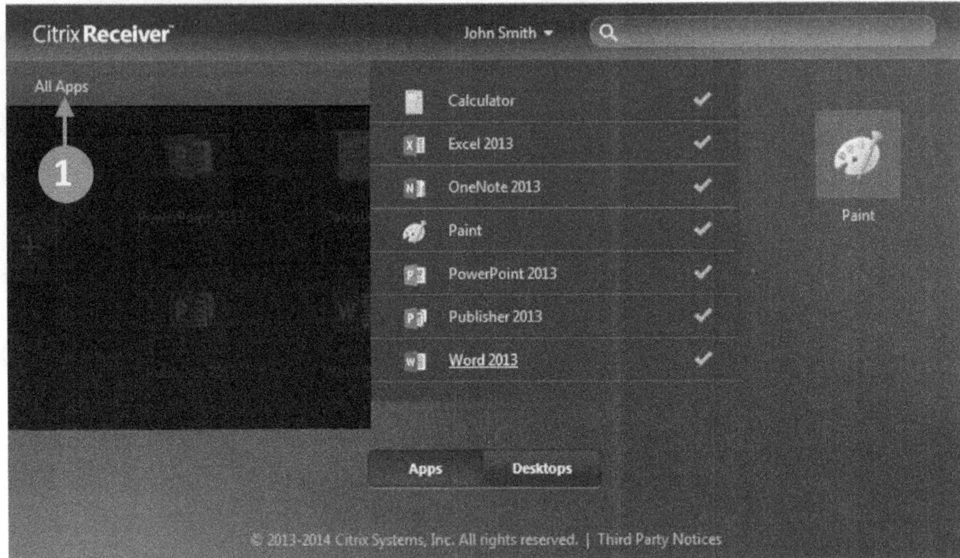

6. Click on **All Apps (1)**. You will then see all the available applications listed. Click on each one that you want to add, so that that they are ticked.

   Once completed, return to the **Citrix Receiver** main screen, as shown in the following screenshot:

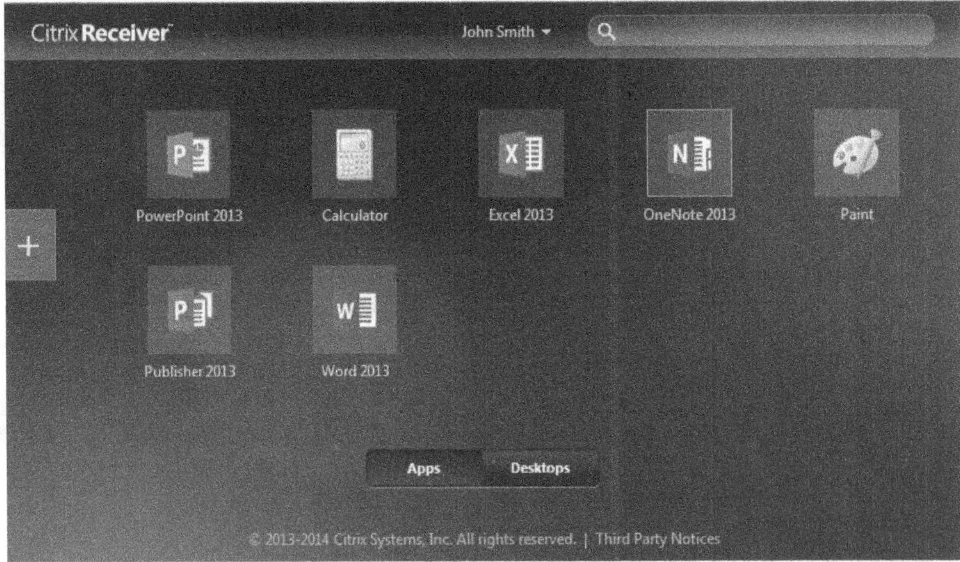

7. To make sure that applications launch and work as expected, we are going launch PowerPoint, so double-click on the PowerPoint icon. You will see the following message appear as the application launches:

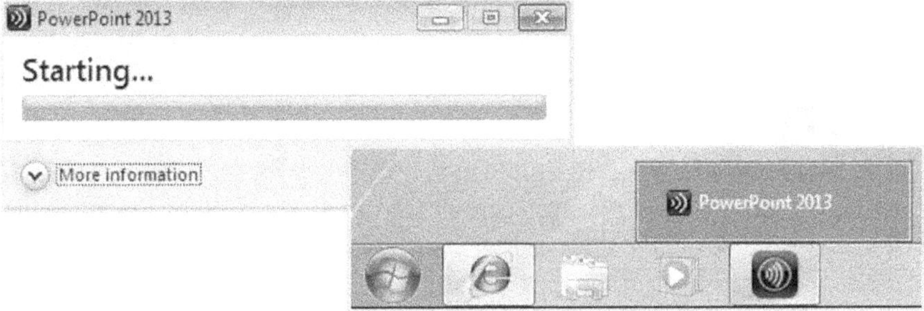

You will also see the Citrix Receiver icon appear on the task bar.

You will now see that PowerPoint has launched successfully, as shown in the following screenshot:

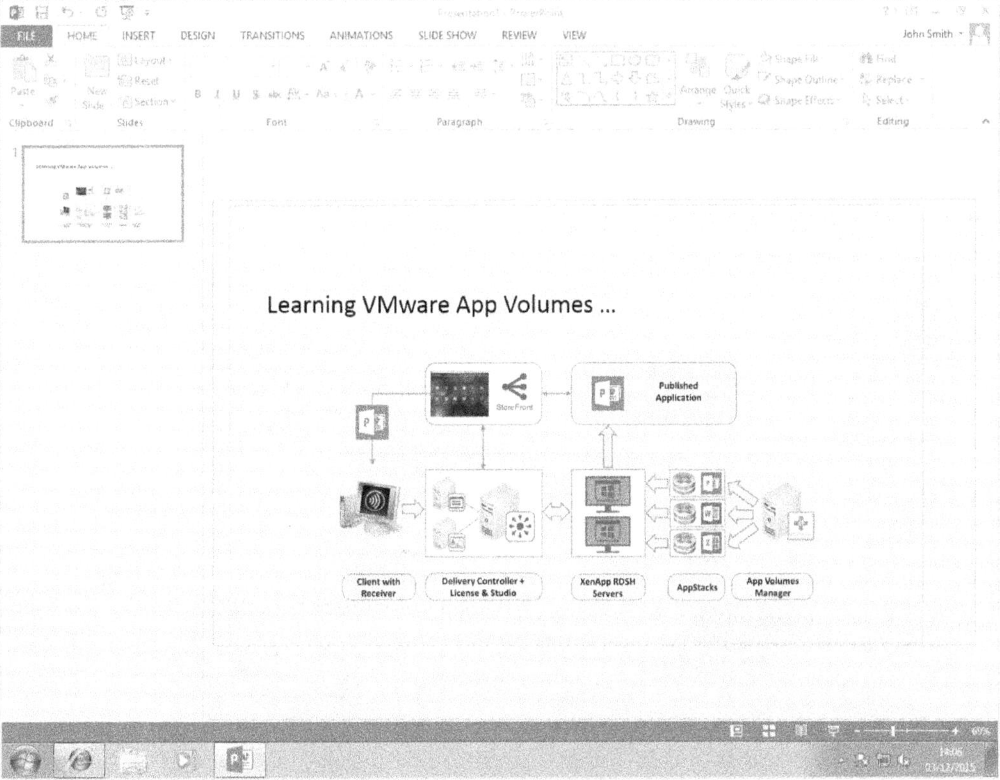

Once you are happing that everything is working as expected, quit PowerPoint and log off from Citrix Receiver.

You have now successfully set up a XenApp environment and delivered applications using App Volumes.

Summary

In this chapter, we have worked through the complete process of how to deploy App Volumes within a Citrix XenApp environment, in order to deliver applications that are part of an AppStack rather than being installed on the server. As we discussed, the use case for doing this enables you to build stateless XenApp farms, making it far easier to scale up, scale down, and, more importantly, be able to manage the applications as one entity.

We started by looking at the architecture of how it all fits together. Once familiar with the architecture, we went on to build a provisioning machine to provision our RDSH AppStack for Office 2013, before going on to build a XenApp Server, which was assigned the Office AppStack and then configured to publish some of the core Office applications.

Finally, we tested the solution to make sure it behaved as expected and that end users could log in and launch their applications.

In the next chapter, we are going to continue the theme of publishing applications, and this time take an in-depth look into how App Volumes works within a VMware Horizon View Hosted Application environment.

13
Deploying App Volumes in a Horizon View Hosted Apps Environment

In the last three chapters, we have looked in detail at how to build and configure Microsoft and Citrix environments, both for published applications and virtual desktop environments, to take advantage of the App Volumes technology in delivering just-in-time applications.

This penultimate chapter is going to focus back on VMware technology and look at how you build and configure a Horizon View environment designed to deliver hosted applications to end users with the applications being configured as AppStacks and delivered by Horizon View.

The Horizon View hosted applications solution is not too dissimilar to the Microsoft or Citrix environments for published applications that we have covered previously, as it uses the Microsoft RDSH as its foundation. Horizon View then provides the connection broker elements, the same broker that is used to broker Horizon View virtual desktop machines, to connect end users to published applications.

Therefore, the architecture and the process will seem somewhat familiar if you have already read those chapters.

Let's start with the architecture. The following diagram illustrates how App Volumes works within a Horizon View published application architecture:

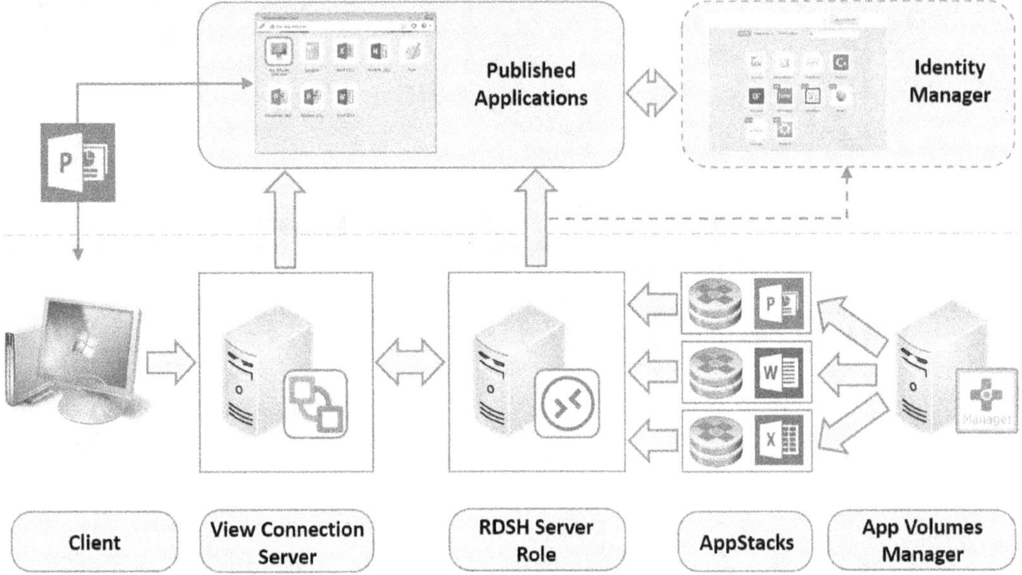

As we discussed previously, the Horizon View hosted application solution builds upon the Microsoft standard RDSH role, by adding the Horizon View Connection Server.

Users log in to the Horizon View Connection Server using the Horizon View Client, a web browser, or optionally the VMware Identity Manager solution. The AppStack containing the applications is attached to the RDSH server, and then the applications that you want to publish are read from the RDSH server and appear in the Horizon View Connection Server, from where you can then configure application pools for end users to connect to.

In the following sections, we are firstly going to walk through the process for creating the AppStack, then go on to configure the RDSH, before finally configuring the Horizon View Connection Server to deliver the published applications that are installed in the AppStack.

Building and configuring an AppStack for Horizon View hosted applications

Now that we have described the architecture of how App Volumes fits into a Horizon View hosted application environment, we can start to build and configure the environment.

There are a number of steps involved in creating the environment, which are illustrated in the following diagram:

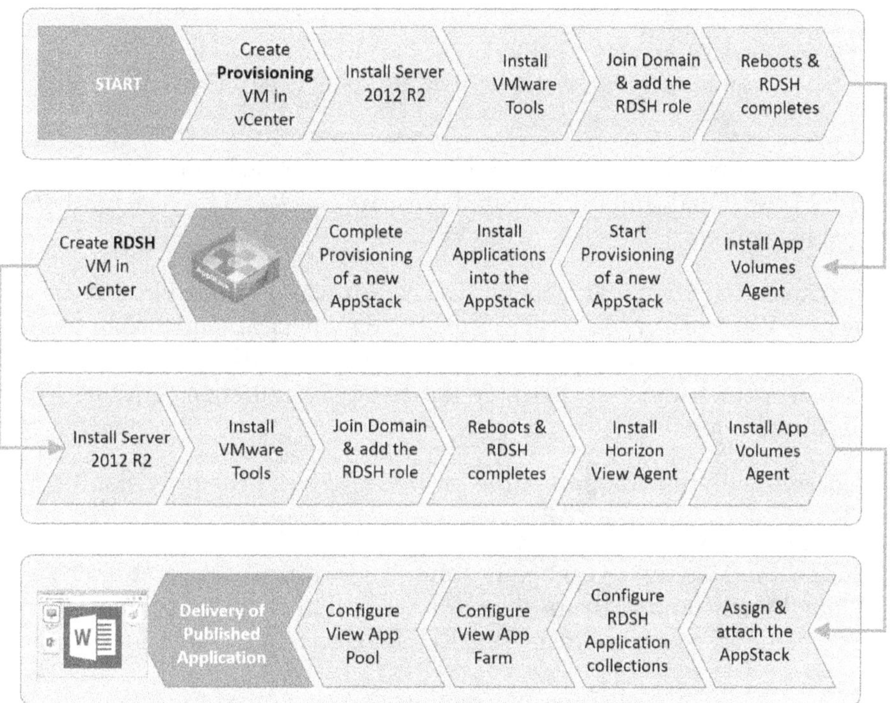

In this chapter, we are going to cover the complete scenario of building an AppStack for Office 2013 Professional, and then deliver this using the Horizon View hosted application feature. For this chapter, you will use two RDSH host servers (`RDSH-Provision` and `RDSH-View`) and the Horizon View Connection Server.

The steps described in the previous diagram are in the order in which they should be completed. It is important to note when to install the App Volumes Agent in particular, and this will become more important in other chapters when we come to installing VMware Horizon View.

As with the process described for building AppStacks for use with virtual desktop machines, the first part of the process is to build a provisioning machine from which you can create AppStacks from.

If you have already completed the AppStack provisioning process described in *Chapter 11, Deploying App Volumes in a RemoteApp Environment,* then you can skip these steps and go directly to the *Installing the Horizon View Agent* section of this chapter.

We are going to use this AppStack as our applications for publishing in Horizon View.

As a reminder, AppStacks need to be provisioned using the same operating system as they are going to be delivered to.

The provisioning machine will be used to create an AppStack containing Microsoft Office 2013 Professional, and once created, this AppStack can then be used on other RDSH-enabled servers.

So the AppStack that you will create in this chapter was also used in *Chapter 11, Deploying App Volumes in a Microsoft RemoteApp Environment,* and also in this chapter to deliver the applications within those environment scenarios. If you have already created this AppStack, then you can skip these steps. If not, then continue with the process outlined below.

Let's get started with the first part of the process and build the provisioning machine.

In the Example Lab, we have already built a Windows 2012 R2 server called `RDSH-Provision`. This server is already running VMware Tools, and is also joined to the domain, and in the next section we will pick up the configuration steps from the point where we install the RDSH role.

Installing the RDSH role on the provisioning machine

The first thing we are going to do is add the RDSH role to the `RDSH-Provision` machine.

Open a console to the server and launch the **Server Manager**. From the main screen, under **Configure this local server**, select the option for **Add roles and features (1)**, as shown in the following diagram:

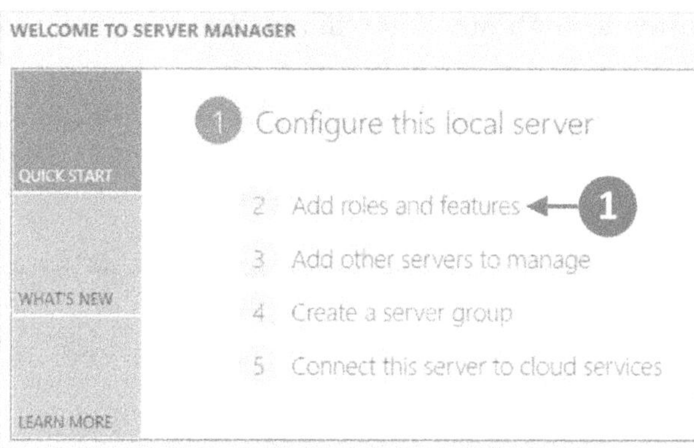

You will now see the **Before You Begin** screen. Click the **Next >** button to continue.

On the **Installation Type** screen, click the radio button for **Remote Desktop Services Installation (2)**, as shown in the following diagram:

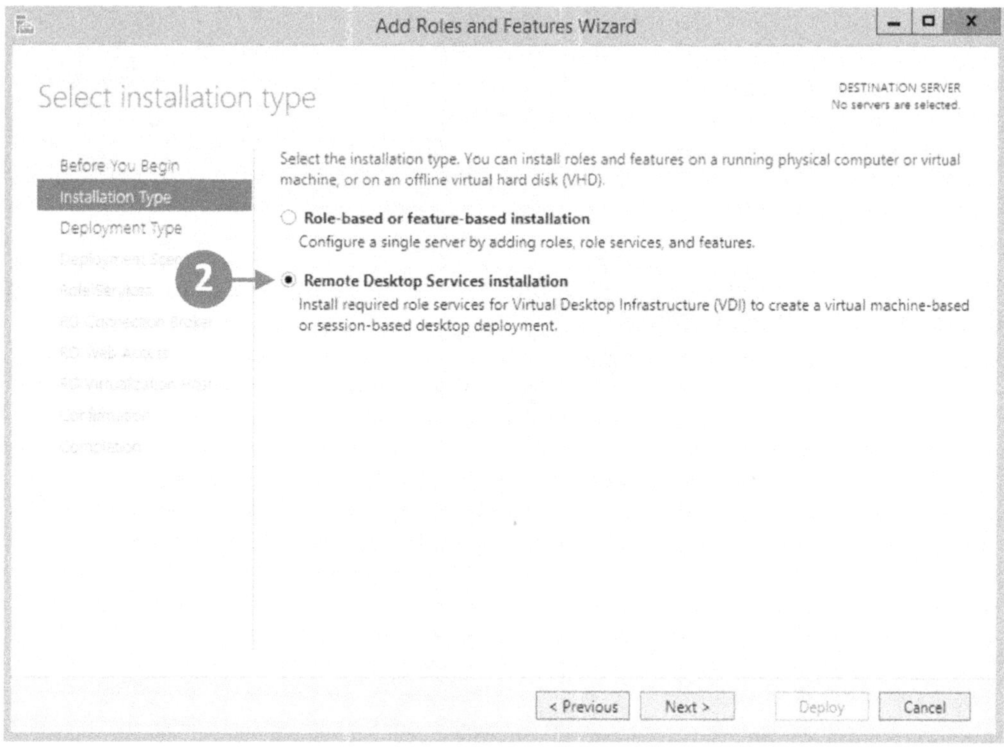

Click the **Next >** button to continue. You will now see the **Deployment Type** screen:

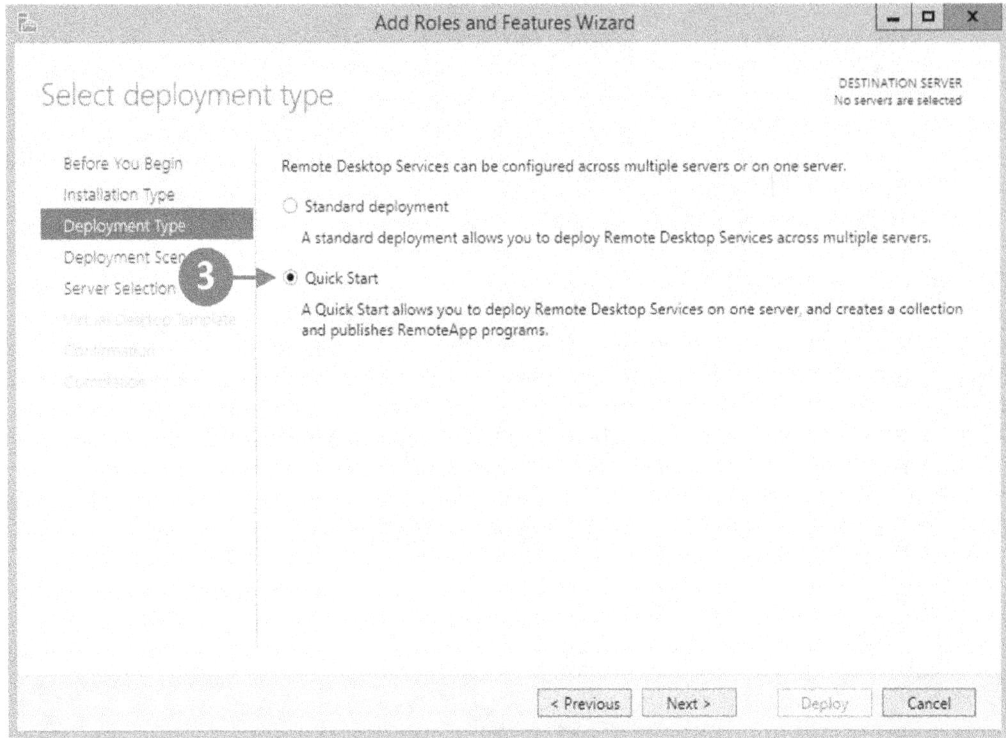

On the **Deployment Type** screen, click the radio button for **Quick Start (3)**, and then click the **Next >** button to continue.

You will now see the **Deployment Scenario** screen, as shown in the following diagram:

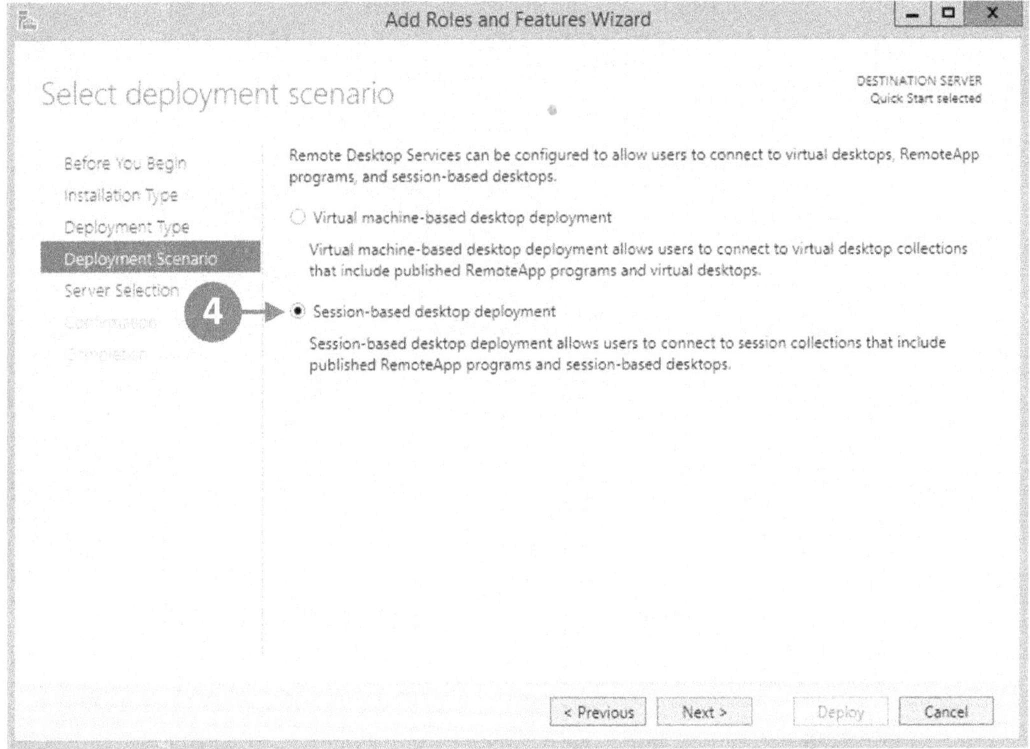

Click the radio button for **Session-based desktop deployment (4)**, and then click the **Next >** button to continue.

You will now see the **Server Selection** screen, as shown in the following diagram:

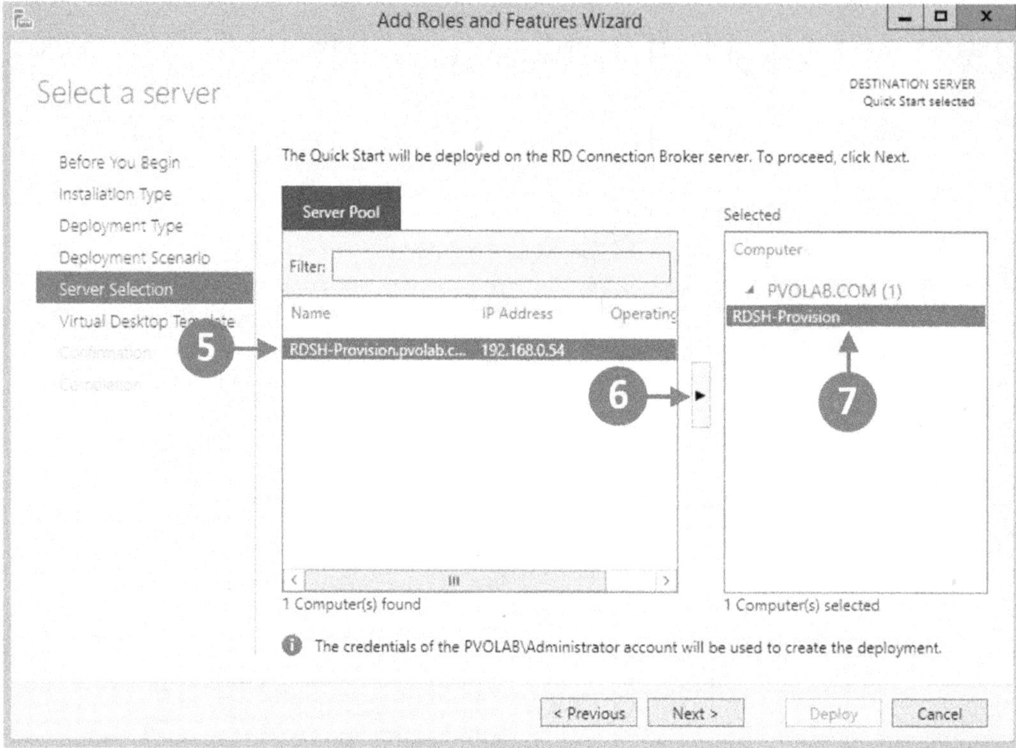

Select the server that you want to add the RDSH role to and use as the provisioning virtual machine. In this example, the machine name is **RDSH-Provision.pvolab.com**.

Highlight the server name in the **Server Pool** box **(5)**, and then click the arrow **(6)** to add it to the **Selected** box **(7)**.

Once complete, click the **Next >** button to continue.

You will now see the **Confirmation** screen, as shown in the following diagram:

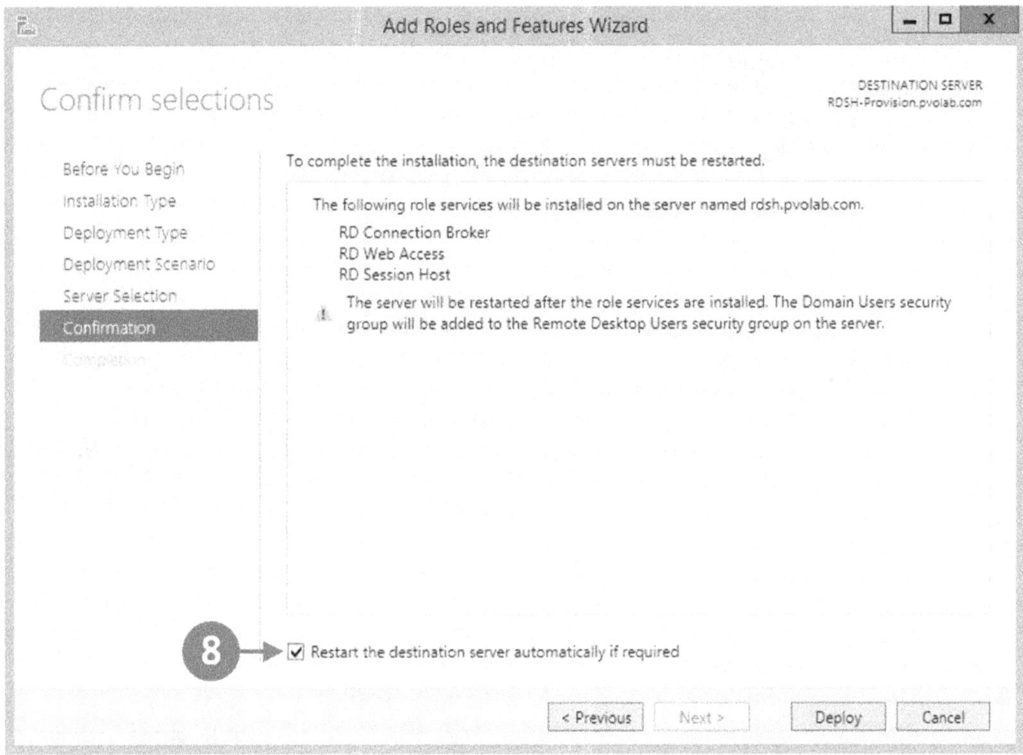

Check the **Restart the destination server automatically if required** box **(8)**, and then finally click the **Deploy** button. You will now see the **Completion** screen:

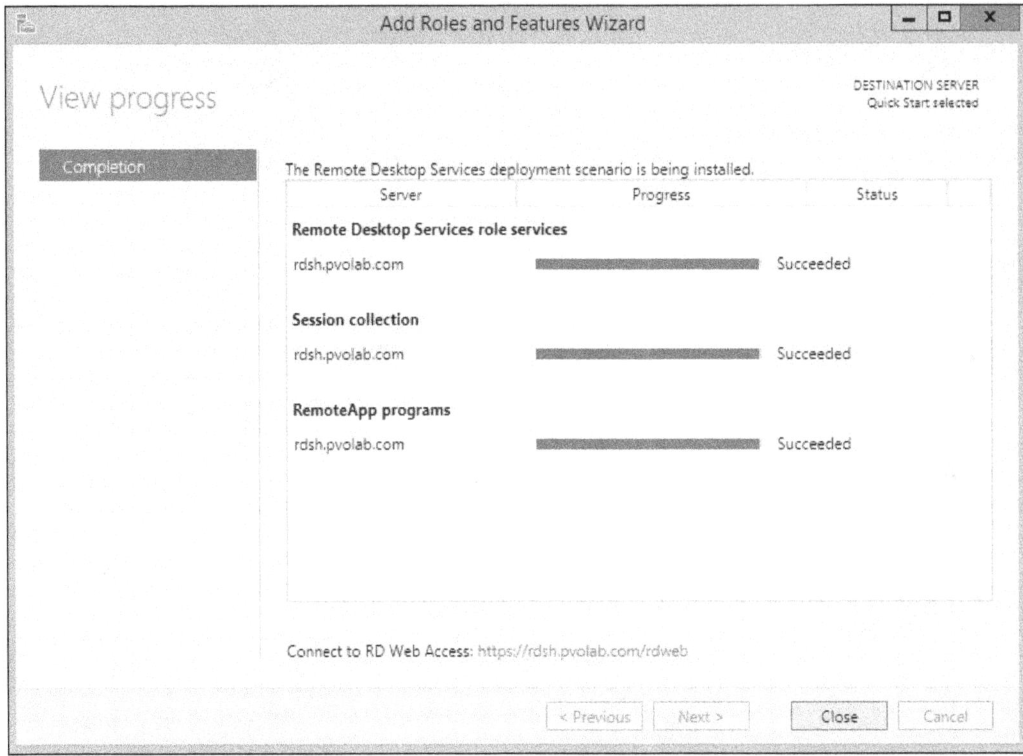

Check that the installation has completed successfully, and then click the **Close** button.

You will now return to the Server Manager screen, which will now show the roles for **Remote Desktop Services** and **IIS** have been added, as shown in the following screenshot:

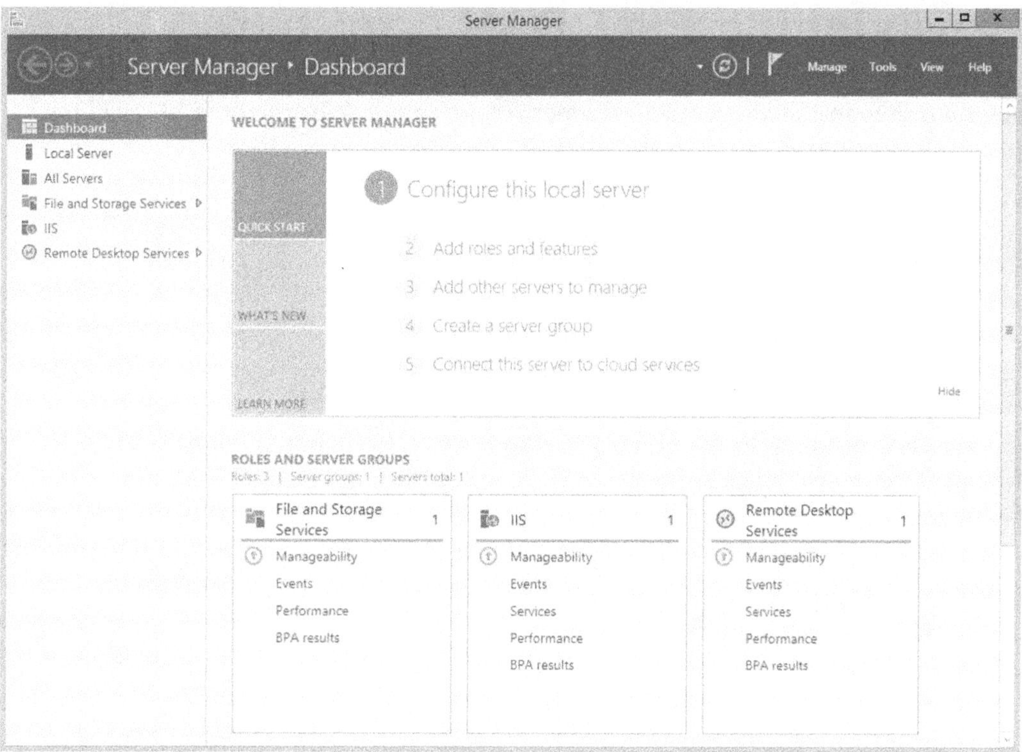

You should now have a server that has been configured as an RDSH host server.

The next step is to install the App Volumes Agent.

Installing the App Volumes Agent

The next part of the process is to install the App Volumes Agent onto the RDSH host server you are using for provisioning so that it registers itself with the App Volumes Manager, allowing you to start using it for application provisioning.

We have already covered the installation process in the *Installing the App Volumes Agent* section of *Chapter 4, Installing and Configuring the App Volumes Software*, so please refer to that chapter on how to do this. The process is exactly the same for servers as it is for desktops.

Provisioning the RDSH AppStack

At this stage of the process, you have built a server and configured it with the RDSH role, and then installed the App Volumes Agent onto it. We are going to break the provisioning process into two stages.

Firstly we will walk through a reminder on how to perform the provisioning process and then secondly, as we are installing applications on an RDSH server, we will detail the application install process, as it is different from installing onto a desktop machine.

Starting the provisioning process

Open a console to the App Volumes Manager server and launch the App Volumes Manager management console. You will now see the login screen, as shown in the following screenshot:

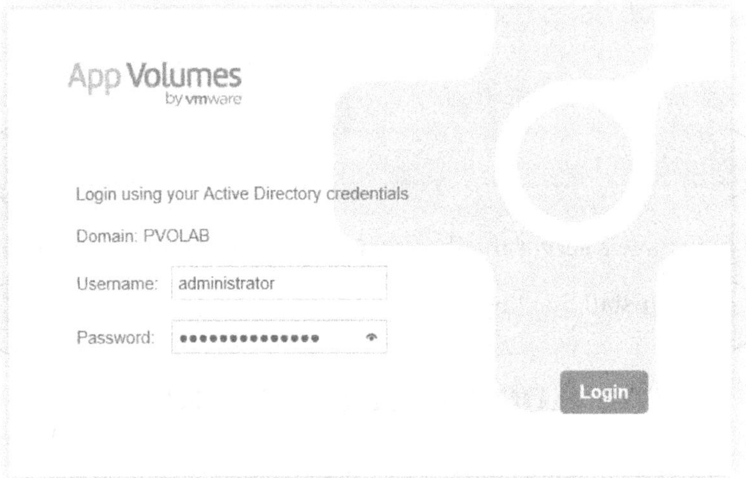

Enter the user name and password of the App Volumes administrator account and then click the **Login** button.

From the App Volumes Manager console, click the **VOLUMES** menu option **(1)**, and then click the **AppStacks** tab **(2)**.

Now click the **Create AppStack** button **(3)**, as shown in the following diagram:

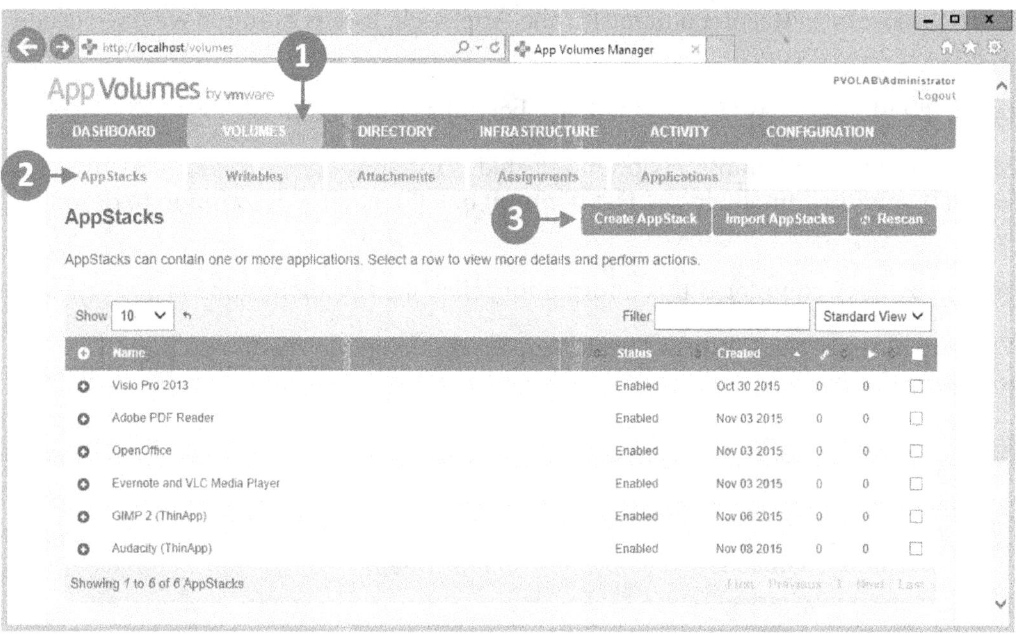

You will now see the **Create AppStack** screen, as shown in the following diagram:

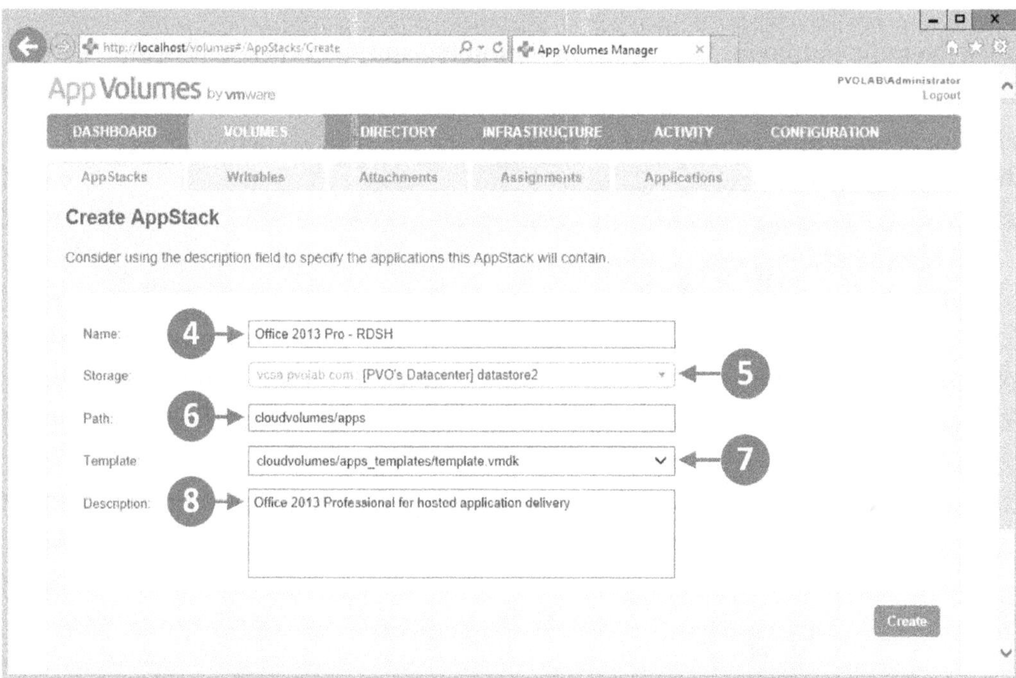

In the **Name:** box **(4)**, enter a name for the AppStack. In this example we have called it `Office 2013 Pro - RDSH`.

Leave the **Storage:** box **(5)**, and the **Path:** box **(6)** as the default settings.

Make sure that the **Template:** option selected is for `apps_templates/template.vmdk` **(7)**, and then finally in the **Description:** box **(8)**, enter a description to describe what this AppStack contains.

When you have completed this information, click the **Create** button.

You will now see the **Confirm Create AppStack** dialog box, as shown in the following diagram:

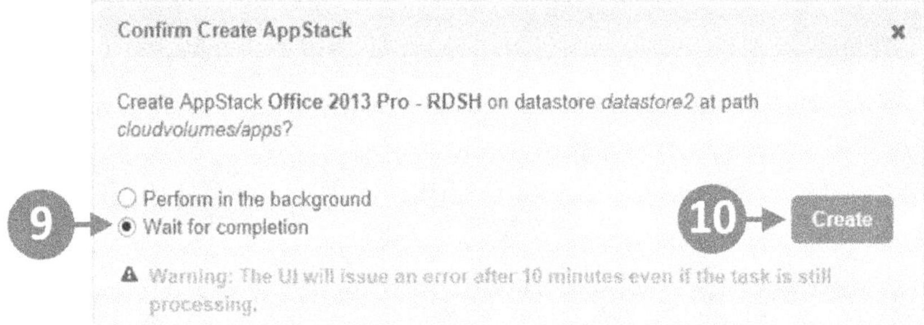
Confirm Create AppStack
Create AppStack Office 2013 Pro - RDSH on datastore datastore2 at path cloudvolumes/apps?
Perform in the background
Wait for completion
9
10
Create
Warning: The UI will issue an error after 10 minutes even if the task is still processing.

Click the radio button for **Wait for completion (9)**, and then click the **Create** button **(10)**.

The AppStack is now created and you will see the progress shown with the following message:

Creating AppStack

With the AppStack now created, and remember at this point the AppStack is just an empty container, the next step is to attach it to the provisioning machine.

You should have returned to the AppStacks page after the AppStack creation was completed, as shown in the following diagram:

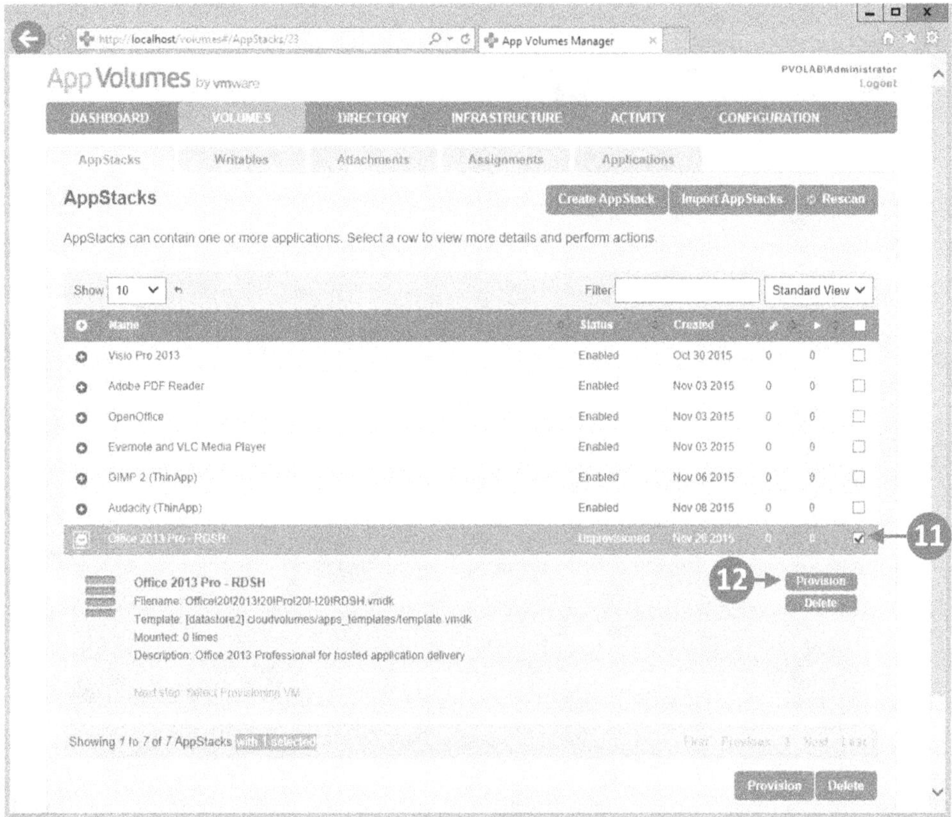

Select the AppStack that you just created by checking the tick box next to its entry on the inventory **(11)**. When selected the entry will be highlighted in orange.

Now click the **Provision** button **(12)**.

Next you will see the **Provision AppStack: Office 2013 Pro - RDSH** screen where you need to choose which virtual machine you are going to use to provision this particular AppStack.

This is shown in the following diagram:

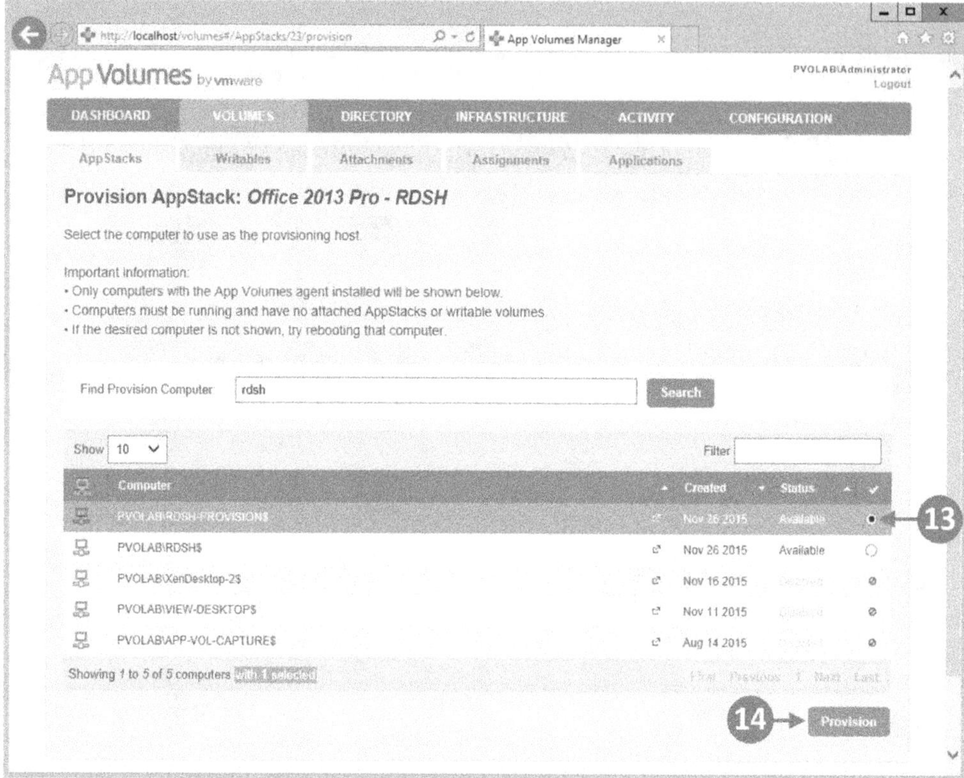

In this example, we are going to use the RDSH server that we built and configured at the beginning of this chapter. The machine name for the provisioning machine is `RDSH-Provision`.

Click the radio button next the entry for `PVOLAB\RDSH-PROVISION$` **(13)**, and then click the **Provision** button **(14)**.

You will now see the following dialog box:

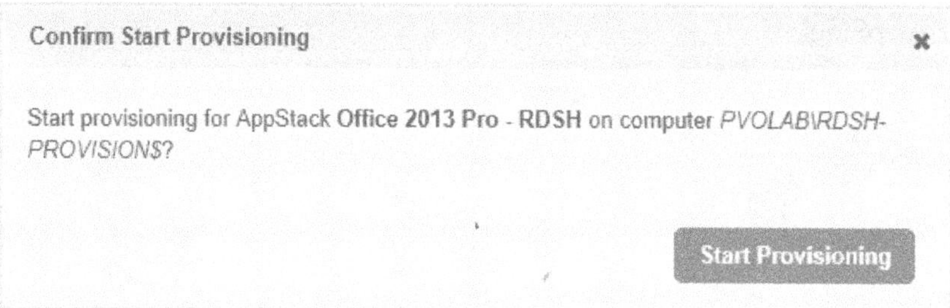

Click the **Start Provisioning** button to continue the process.

You will see the following message as the AppStack is attached:

The AppStack is now attached to the provisioning machine, as shown in the following screenshot:

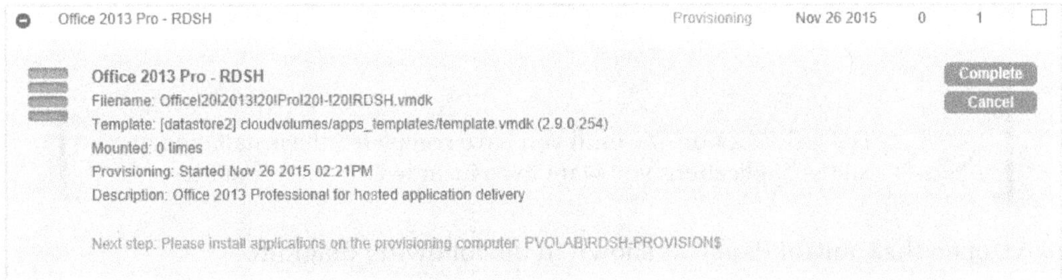

You can now start to install the applications on the provisioning machine.

> Remember, *DO NOT* click the **Complete** button until you have completely finished installing the applications.

In the next section, we are going to look at how to install applications on the provisioning machine, given the fact that it is an RDSH host.

Installing applications

Installing applications on an RDSH server is almost identical to installing applications on any other Windows operating system-based machine. However, there are a few subtle differences, given that this is a remote session host server. Let's run through the process of installing applications. In this example we are going to install Office 2013 Pro.

Open a console to the RDSH server on which you want to install the applications; in this example the machine name is `RDSH-Provision`.

First of all, ensure that the provisioning machine is in provisioning mode. When you switch to the console of the RDSH provisioning server, you should see the following dialog box:

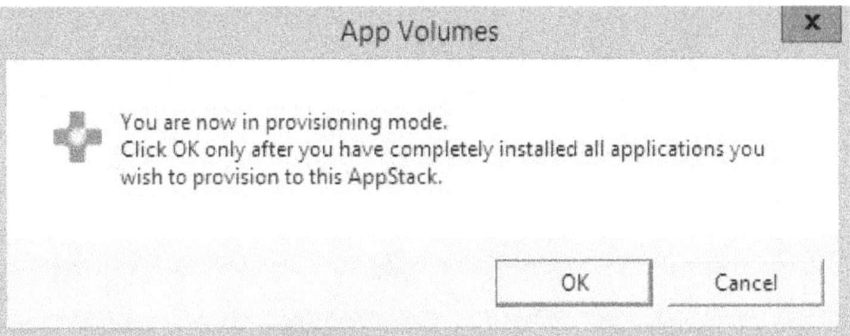

DO NOT click on **OK** until you have completed the installation of all the applications you want to be included in this AppStack.

Next, open the **Control Panel**, as shown in the following diagram:

From the **Control Panel**, click on **Programs (1)**. The **Programs** dialog box opens as shown in the following diagram:

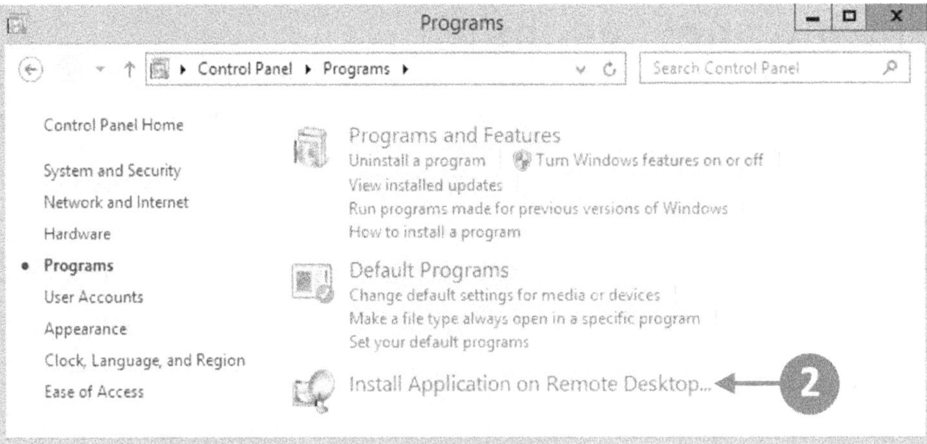

Click on **Install Application on Remote Desktop... (2)**.

You will now see the **Install Program From Floppy Disk or CD-ROM** dialog box, as shown in the following screenshot:

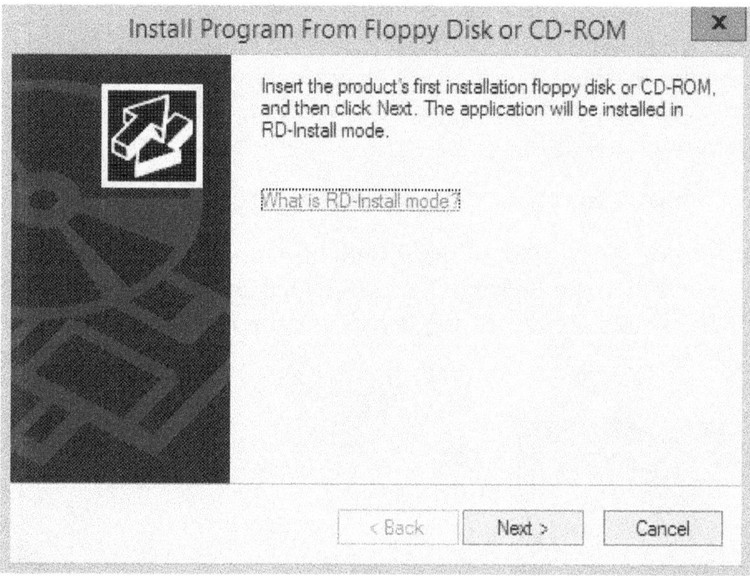

In this dialog box, you will see that it talks about something called RD-Install mode, with a link to **What is RD-Install mode?**

This where the differences between a desktop install and a server install come into play. To install an application on an RDSH host server, the server needs to be switched to a special install mode known as RD-Install. This ensures that the applications are able to run in a multiuser environment, such as published applications where multiple users are running applications at the same time.

Once you have installed the applications on the RDSH server, the server needs to be switched back into normal mode, or what is called execution mode or RD-Execute, so that users can remotely connect to the server and the applications running on it.

This install mode change can also be initiated from the command line using the following commands:

```
change user /install
```

```
change user /execute
```

You can check the current install mode of your RDSH server from the command line using the following command:

```
change user /query
```

The easiest way to install applications is by installing them from the **Programs** option in **Control Panel**, which is how we are going to do it in this example. This option takes you through the installation process by automatically switching the server to RD-Install mode, installing the program, and switching the server back to RD-Execute mode once the installation is complete.

Click the **Next >** button to continue the installation.

The server automatically checks for the installation media and installation files, first on the **A:** drive and then the **E:** drive. If it doesn't locate any media, then the **Run Installation Program** dialog box is displayed, as shown in the following screenshot:

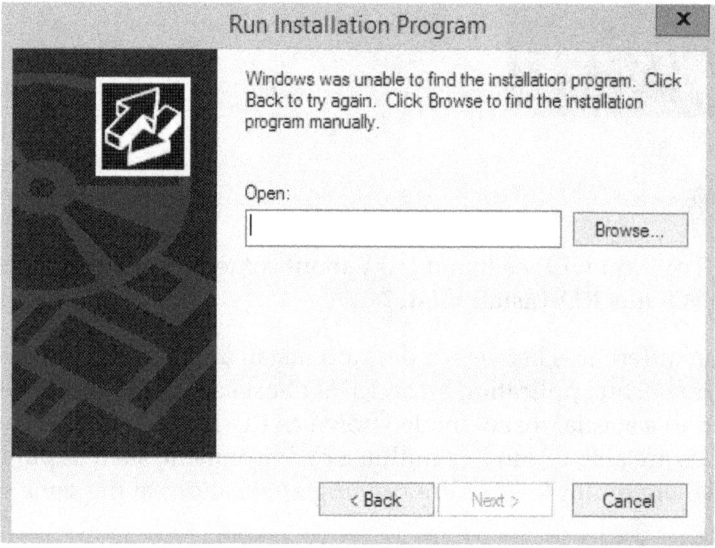

In the **Open:** box, type in the path to the application installer files if you know it. In this example, we are going to click on the **Browse...** button and in the window that opens, we are going to navigate to the location of where we have save the Office 2013 ISO file, which happens to be located on the shared folder.

This is shown in the following screenshot:

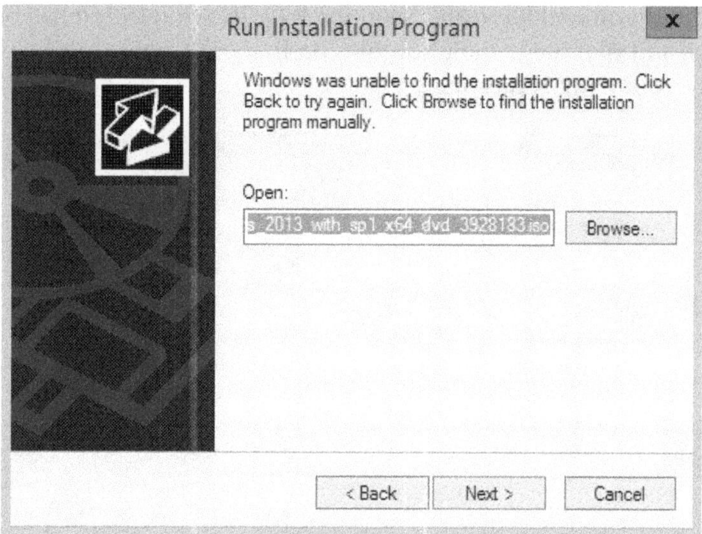

Click the **Next >** button.

You will now see the **Finish Admin Install** dialog box, as shown in the following screenshot:

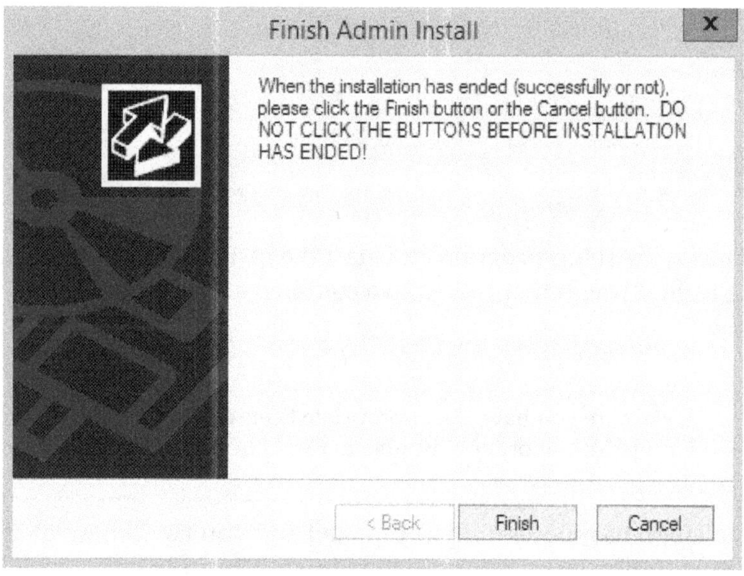

DO NOT click **Finish** until you have completed the application installation.

In the background you will have also seen the ISO file we selected has been mounted as a DVD drive and that the installation files on that disk image are now available, as shown in the following screenshot:

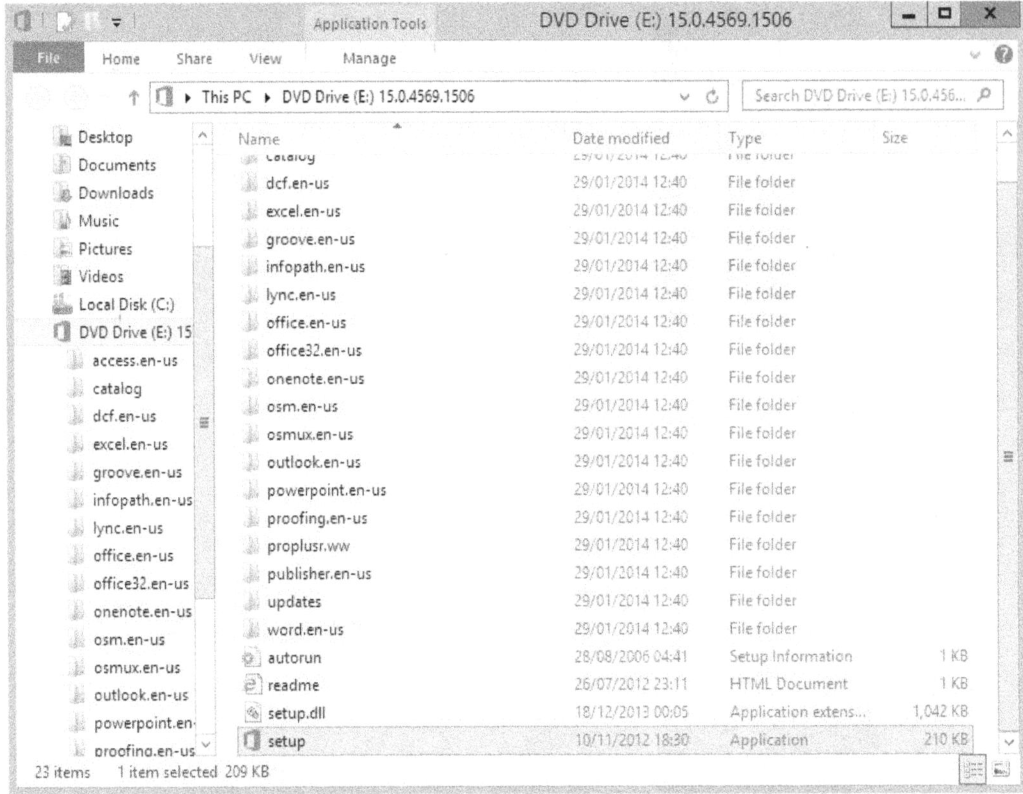

Locate and launch the setup program and start the installation of Office 2013. We are not going to go through that process, so continue and install Office as you would normally.

> Make sure you have the appropriate license key, such as a Volume License key, in order to be able to run Office on an RDSH server.

Once the installation has successfully completed and you have completed any additional configuration tasks, return to the **Finish Admin Install** dialog box and click **Finish**.

Next, return to the **App Volumes** dialog box and click **OK** to finish the provisioning process. You will see the following dialog box:

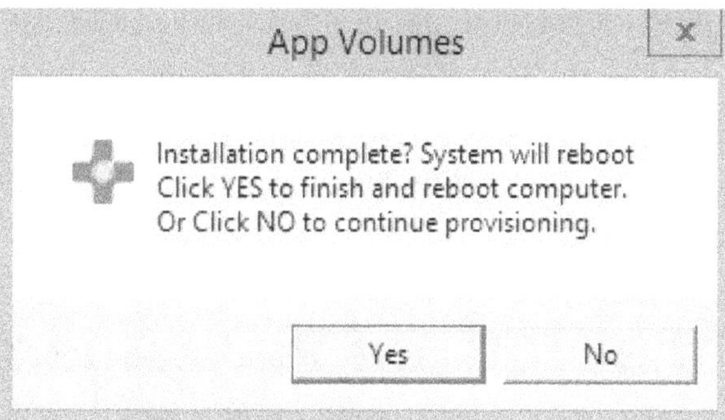
App Volumes
Installation complete? System will reboot
Click YES to finish and reboot computer.
Or Click NO to continue provisioning.
Yes
No

Click **Yes** to confirm that you have completed the application installation. You will now see the following dialog box:

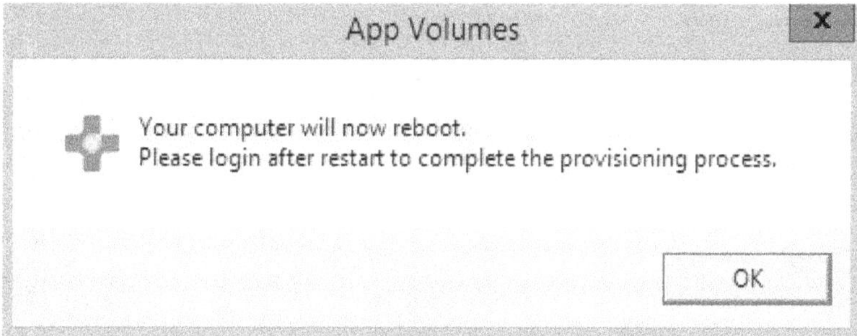
App Volumes
Your computer will now reboot.
Please login after restart to complete the provisioning process.
OK

Click **OK** to confirm the reboot. The provisioning machine will now reboot and in the process detach the newly created and provisioned AppStack.

Once rebooted, you will see the following dialog box:

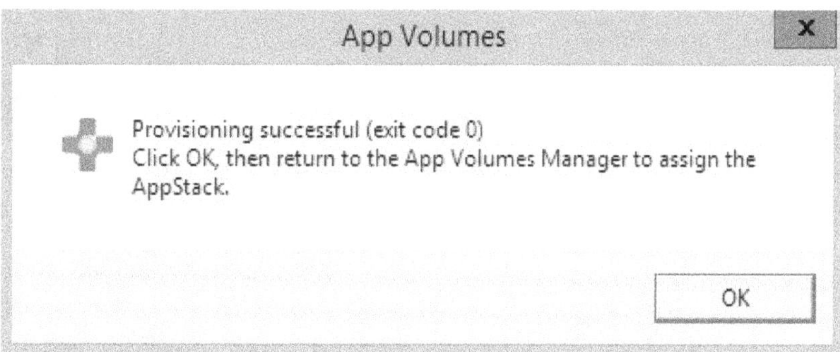
App Volumes
Provisioning successful (exit code 0)
Click OK, then return to the App Volumes Manager to assign the AppStack.
OK

Click **OK** to close the box and finish the provisioning.

You now have an AppStack containing Office 2013 that can be attached to RDSH servers.

In the next section, we are going to do exactly that, and attach the newly created AppStack to an RDSH server, but before we do, we need to configure the RDSH server that we are going to use, and add the Horizon View components.

Installing the Horizon View Agent

The next step we need to complete is to install the Horizon View Agent onto the RDSH server that we are going to use to host the applications.

In this example, we already have an RDSH server built with VMware Tools installed, and it is joined to the domain. The machine name for this server is `RDSH-View.pvolab.com`.

1. Open a console to the `RDSH-View` virtual machine.
2. Locate the shared folder or folder where you have stored the App Volumes and other software components and locate the Horizon View Agent installer, as shown in the following screenshot:

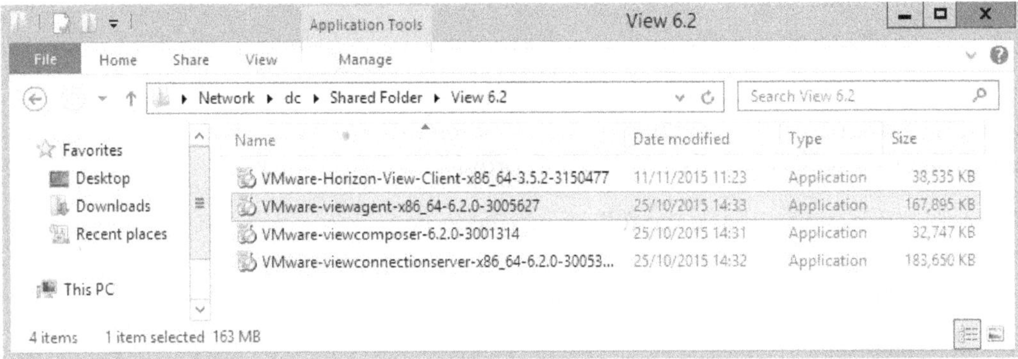

3. Launch the **VMware-viewagent-x86_64-6.4.2-3005627** installer. You will now see the welcome screen, as shown in the following screenshot:

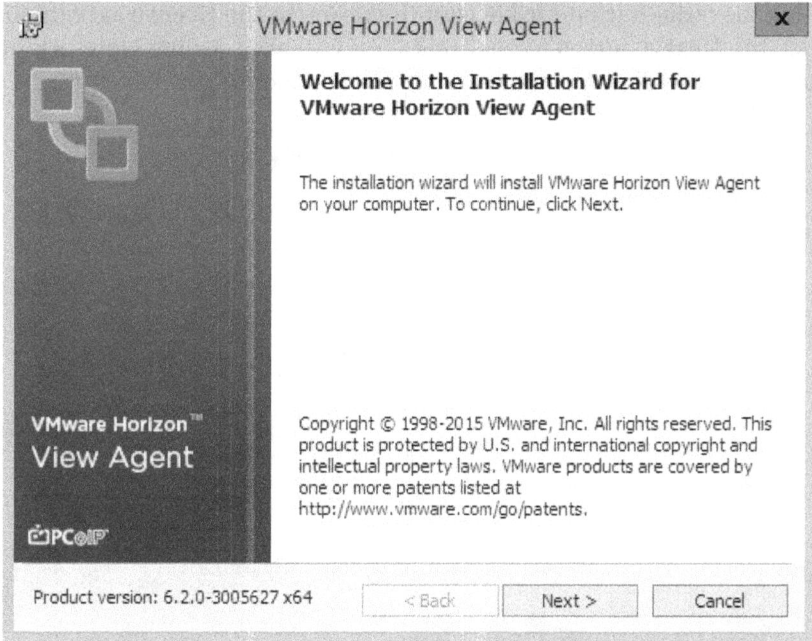

4. Click **Next >** to start the configuration and installation. You will now see the **License Agreement** dialog box, as shown in the following screenshot:

5. Click the radio button for **I accept the terms in the license agreement**, and click the **Next >** button to continue. You will now see the **Network protocol configuration** dialog box, as shown on the following screenshot:

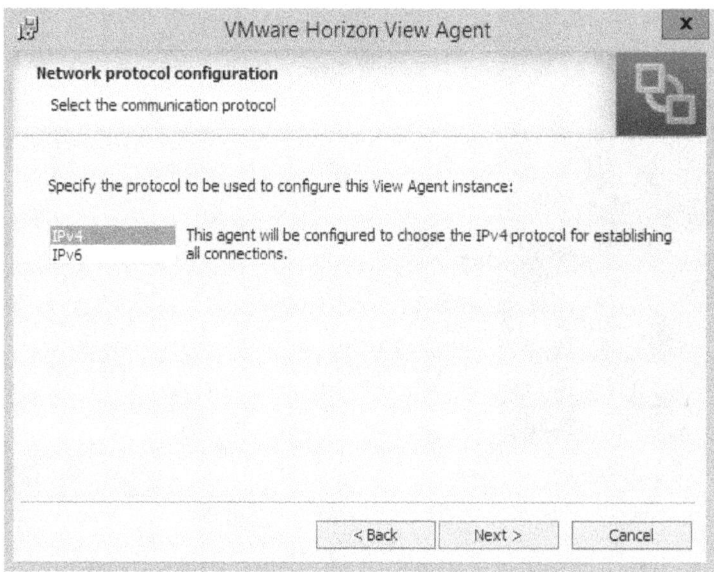

6. Click on **IPv4** and click the **Next >** button to continue. Next you will see the **Custom Setup** dialog box, as shown in the following screenshot:

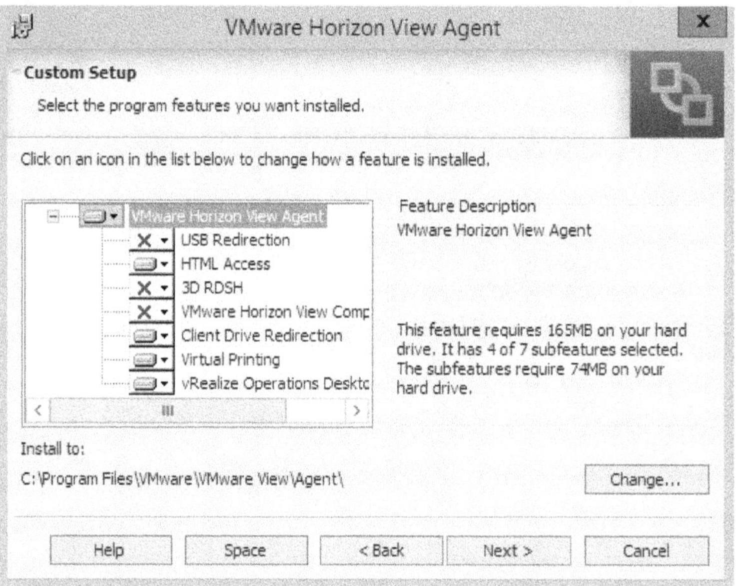

7. Leave the settings as default and click the **Next >** button to continue.
   In the next dialog box, **Register with Horizon View Connection Server**, you need to enter the details of the connection broker, as shown in the following screenshot:

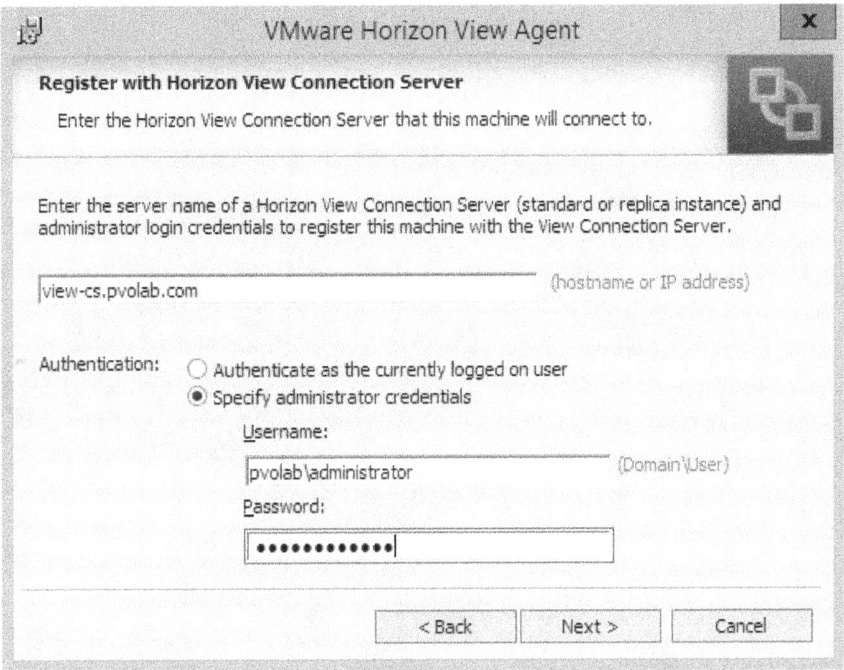

8. In the hostname or IP address box, enter the name of the Horizon View Connection Server. In this example, the name is `view-cs.pvolab.com`.
9. Then click the radio button for **Specify administrator credentials** and in the **Username** box, type in the details of the administrator account in the format `Domain\User`. In the Example Lab, you would enter `pvolab\administrator`.

10. Type in the password for this account and click the **Next >** button to continue. The last configuration dialog box, **Ready to Install the Program** is now displayed, as shown in the following screenshot:

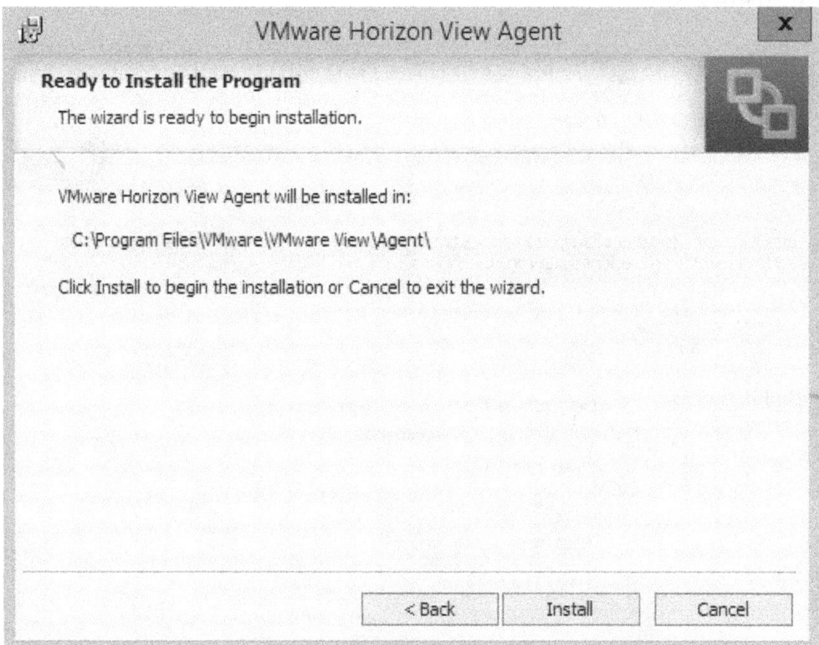

11. Click the **Install** button to continue.
12. You will now see the **Installing VMware Horizon View Agent** dialog box showing the progress of the installation, such as copying new files. Once this has completed, you will see the **Installer Complete** dialog box.
13. Click the **Finish** button to complete the installation and close the installer application.

Finally, you will be prompted to reboot the machine. Click **Yes** to reboot the server.

Once rebooted, the next step is to install the App Volumes Agent, which we will cover in the next section.

Installing the App Volumes Agent

The next part of the process is to install the App Volumes Agent onto the RDSH host server you are using for running the Horizon View hosted applications, so that it registers itself with the App Volumes Manager and you can assign AppStacks to it.

> You need to make sure that you install the App Volumes Agent after the installation of the Horizon View Agent. If you get the installation order wrong, then the Horizon View Agent will not load.

We have already covered the installation process in the *Installing the App Volumes Agent* section of *Chapter 4, Installing and Configuring the App Volumes Software*, so please refer to that chapter on how to do this. The process is exactly the same for servers as it is for desktops.

Assigning the AppStack to the RDSH server

Now that we have our Office 2013 AppStack and have an RDSH server configured, complete with the Horizon View Agent installed, you can assign and attach the AppStack containing Office 2013 to the `RDSH-View.pvolab.com` virtual machine:

1. If you go back to the App Volumes Manager console, you will see the Office 2013 AppStack listed, as shown in the following diagram:

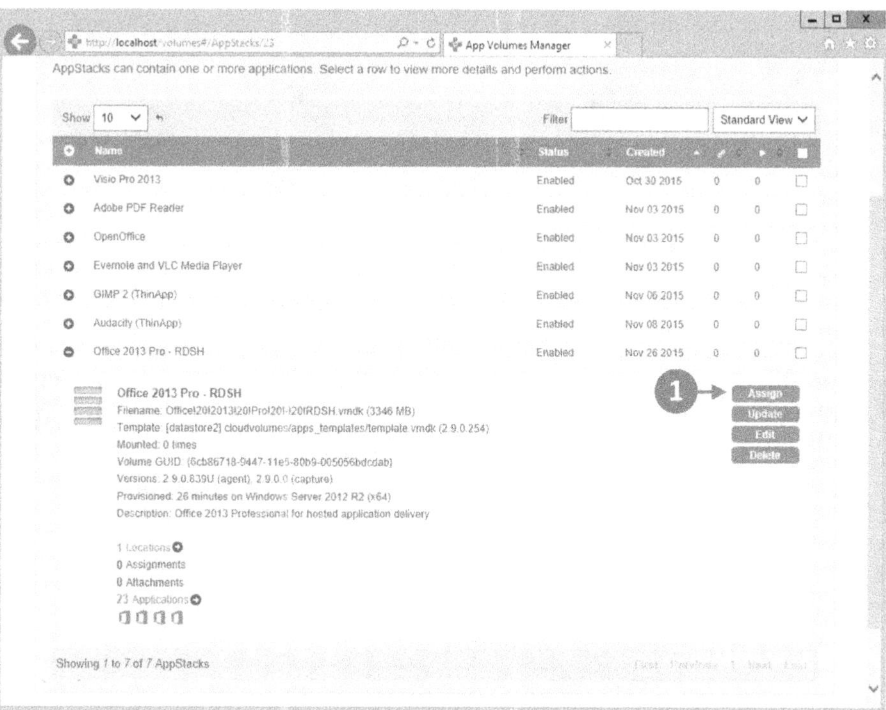

2. On the inventory, expand the entry for **Office 2013 Pro - RDSH** and then click the **Assign** button **(1)**. You will now see the **Assign AppStack: Office 2013 Pro - RDSH** configuration screen, as shown in the following diagram:

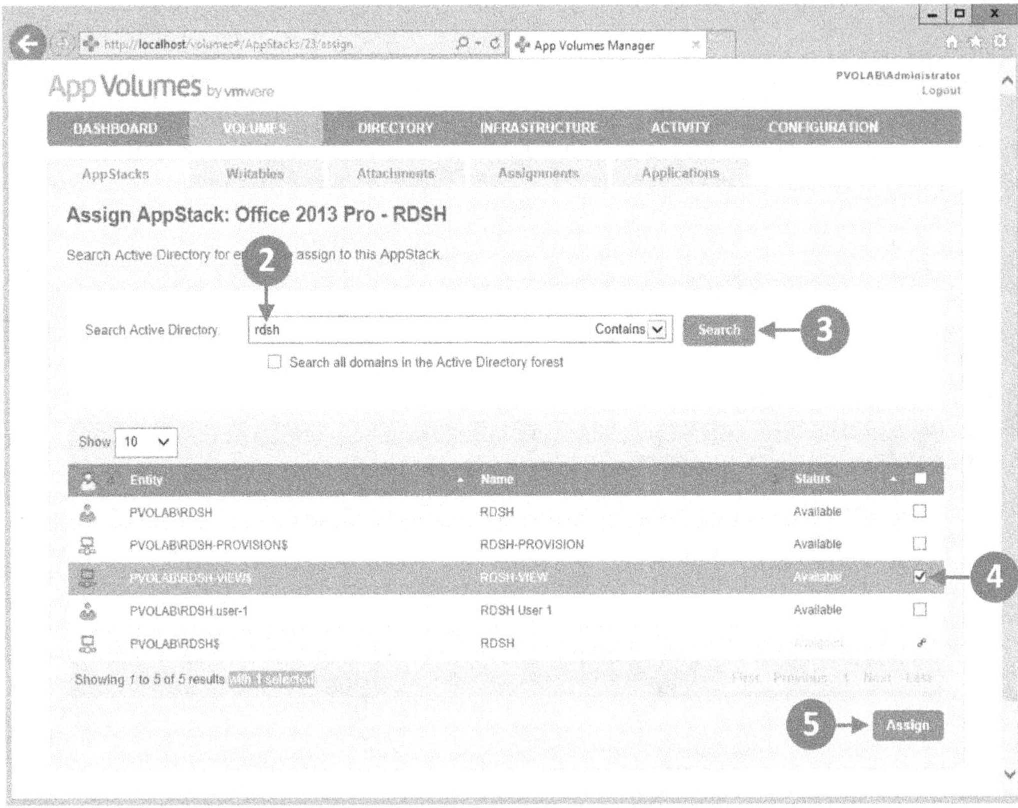

3. In the **Search Active Directory** box **(2)**, enter the details of the server name to which you want to attach the Office 2013 AppStack. In this example, type `RDSH` and then click the **Search** button **(3)**.
4. From the list of results, check the box for the `PVOLAB\RDSH-VIEW$` entry **(4)** and then click the **Assign** button **(5)**. You will now see the **Confirm Assign** dialog box, as shown in the following diagram:

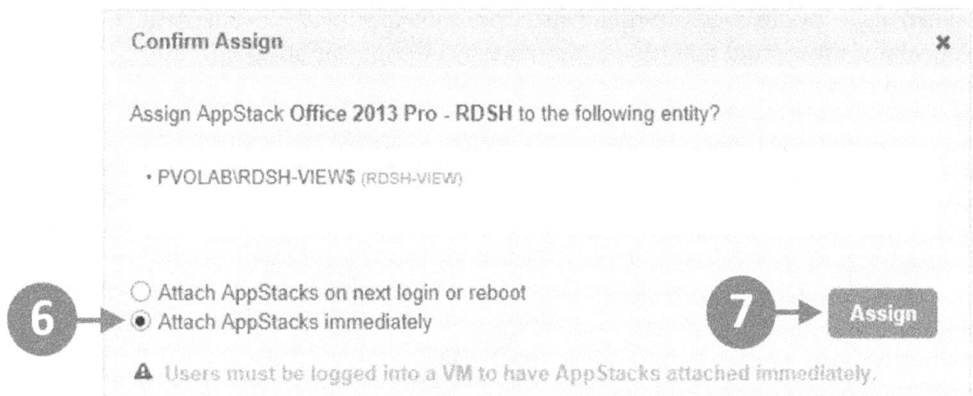

5. Click the radio button for **Attach AppStacks immediately (6)**, and then click the **Assign** button **(7)**. You will see the following message as the AppStack is assigned and attached to the virtual machine:

Once attached you will see the AppStack is now attached to the `RDSH-View` virtual machine, as shown in the following screenshot:

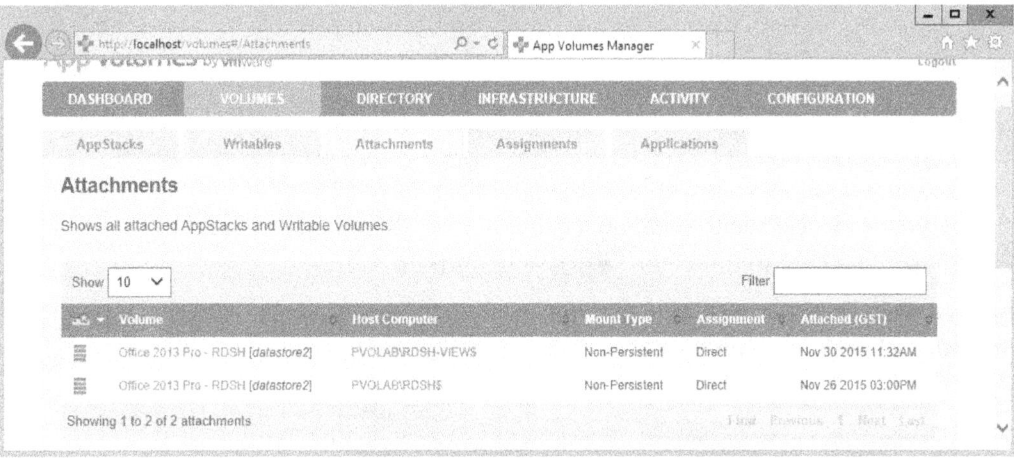

You can also double check to make sure that the AppStack has been attached by checking the virtual machine properties in vCenter, as shown in the following diagram:

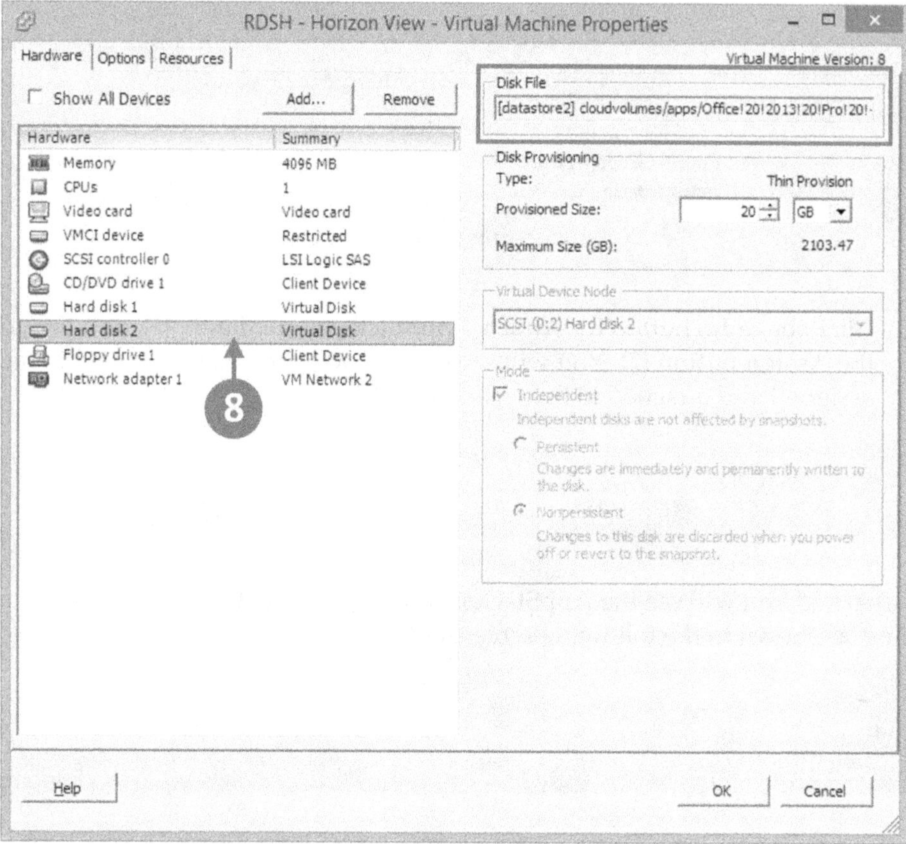

Here you can clearly see the second virtual hard disk attached **(8)** and in the **Disk File** box you can see that it is the Office 2013 AppStack.

In the next section we are going to configure the applications that you are going to publish and deliver using Horizon View.

Configuring applications for publishing

Before we continue, let's just quickly take stock of where we are in the process.

Let's quickly take stock of where we are in the process. So far we have built and configured an RDSH provisioning machine including the App Volumes Agent, and provisioned an AppStack that contains Office 2013 which can be used in remote application environments. In the last step, we assigned that AppStack to our second RDSH server, `RDSH-View`, and then made sure that it was attached.

The next step is to go back to the Remote Desktop Services configuration screen on the RDSH server and publish the applications by creating an application collection:

1. Open a console to the RDSH server and then launch **Server Manager**, as shown in the following diagram:

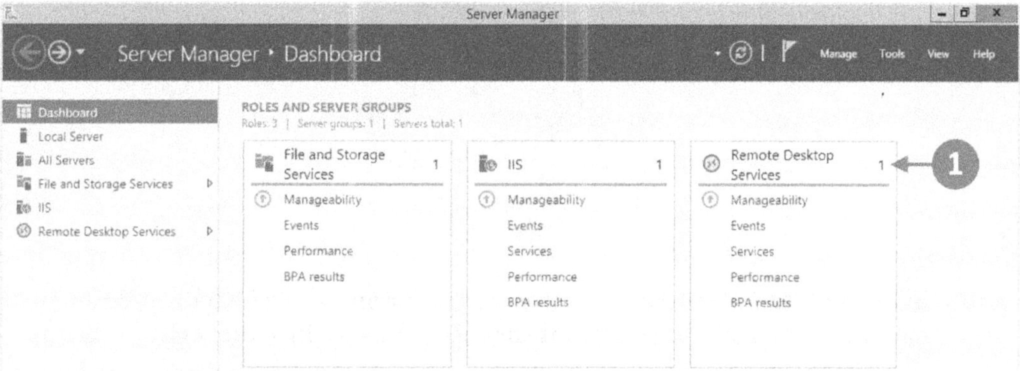

2. Click on **Remote Desktop Services (1)**. You will see the following diagram:

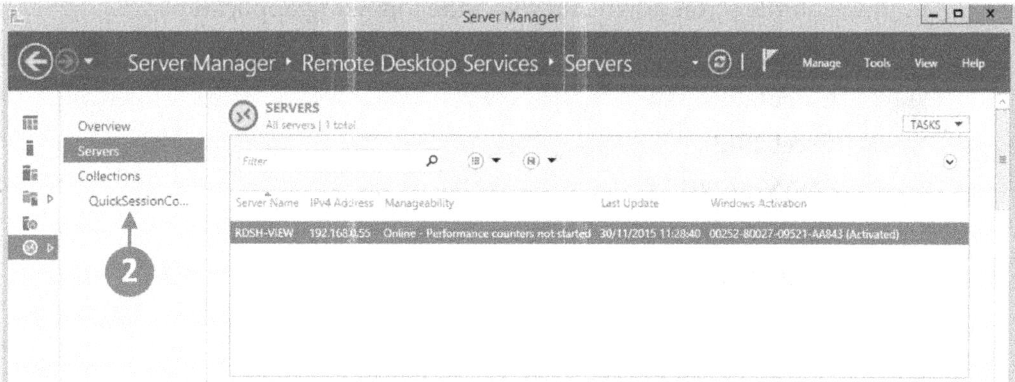

3. Ensure that the correct server is highlighted, in this example the RDSH server, and then click on **QuickSessionCollection (2)**. You will now see the **QuickSessionCollection** configuration screen, as shown in the following diagram:

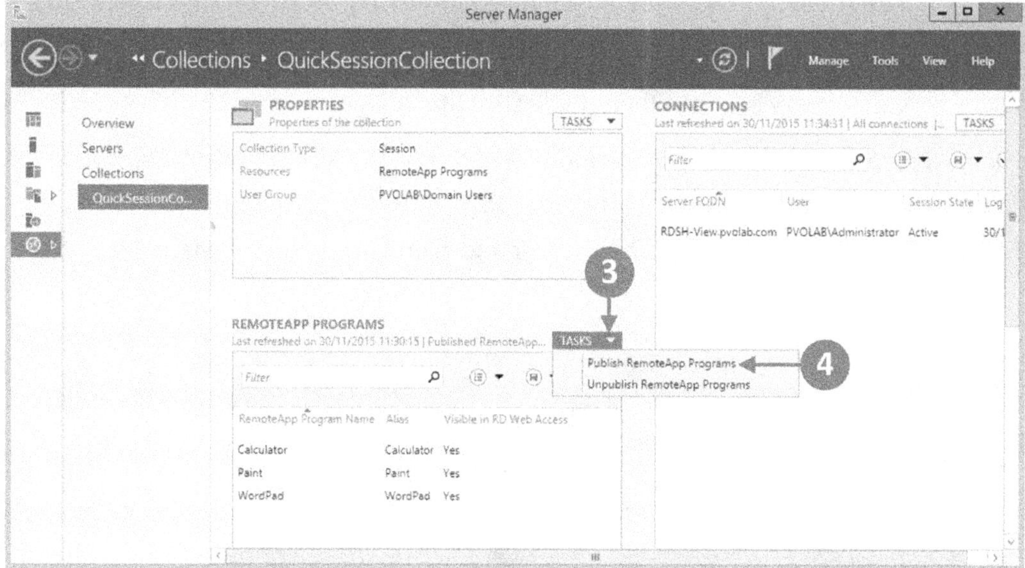

4. In the **REMOTEAPP PROGRAMS** box, click on the **TASKS** drop-down menu box **(3)**, and then select **Publish RemoteApp Programs (4)**.

   You can see that the default programs such as **Calculator** and **Paint** have already been published. In this example, we will leave that as it is.

   On the next screen you can select which applications you want to publish. In this example scroll down and select the following applications:

   - **Paint**
   - **Calculator**
   - **Excel 2013**
   - **OneNote 2013**
   - **PowerPoint 2013**
   - **Publisher 2013**
   - **Word 2013**

This is shown in the following screenshot:

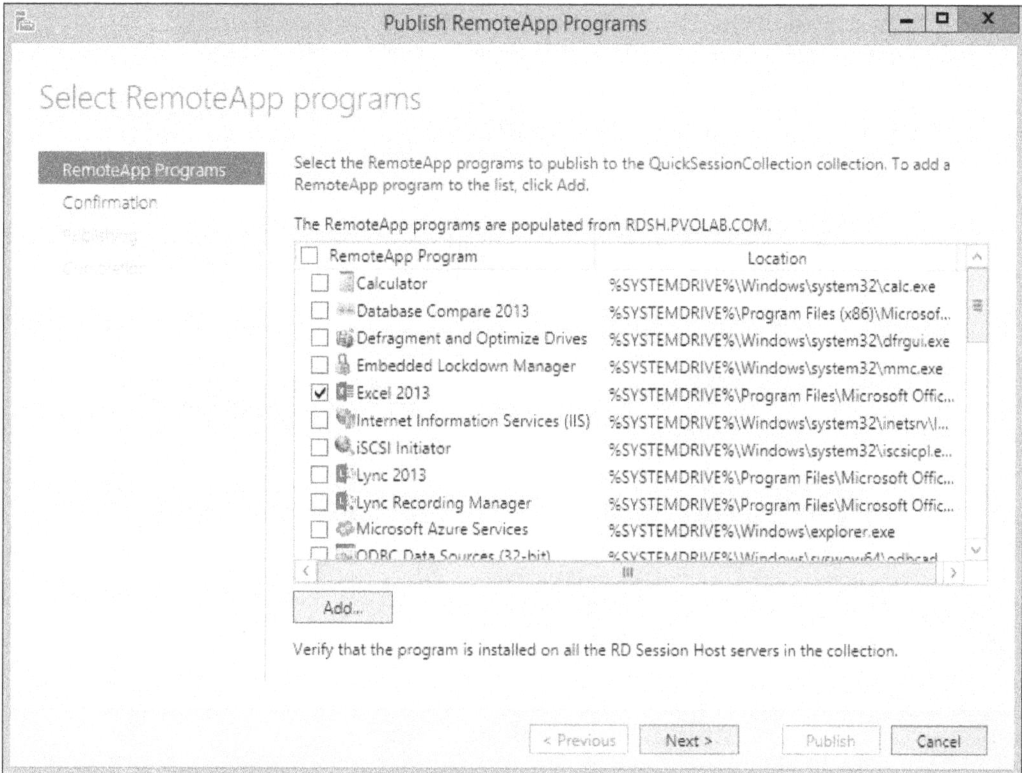

5. You will see that the list of applications also includes the Office 2013 components that are part of the AppStack we created at the beginning of this chapter. Those applications are not physically installed on this server, however the App Volumes Agent and the filter driver make them appear as if they were installed.

6. Once you have selected the applications that you want to publish, click the **Next >** button. You will now see the **Confirmation** screen, listing the applications that are going to be published, as shown in the following screenshot:

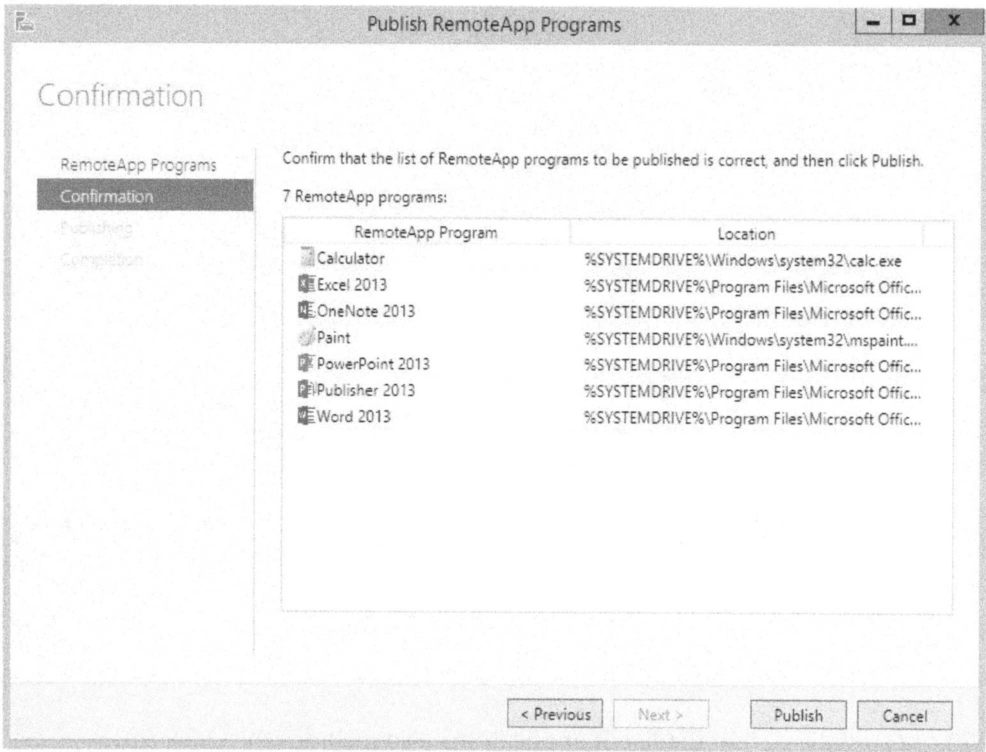

7. Click the **Publish** button.

You will now see the **Publishing** screen with a progress bar showing the process executing.

Once completed, you will see the final screen, the **Completion** screen. Click the **Close** button to close the dialog box and return to the **Server Manager** screen.

If you look again at the **REMOTEAPP PROGRAMS** box, you will see the new applications that have been added, as shown in the following screenshot:

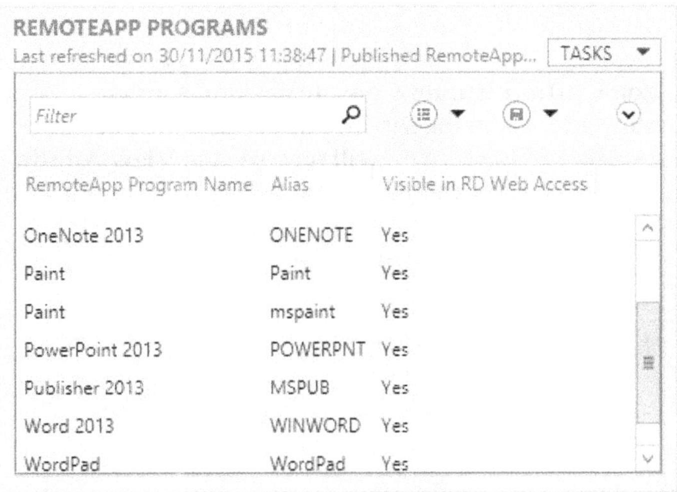

You have now successfully completed all the configuration steps and have a working RemoteApp solution that can deliver Office 2013 from an AppStack to the end users.

In the next section we are going to configure the Horizon View application Farm to publish these applications.

Configuring a Horizon View application Farm

Now that we have our remote applications configured, the next step is to configure Horizon View to deliver these remote applications. In Horizon View terms we configure what's known as a **Farm**. A Farm is basically a collection of RDSH servers that Horizon View can access in order to deliver the applications from those RDSH servers.

1. Open a console to the Horizon View Connection server and double click on the **Horizon 6 Administrator Console** desktop shortcut, or open a browser and enter the address to the server. In this example you would type `https://view-cs/admin`. You will now see the **View Administrator** console, as shown in the following diagram:

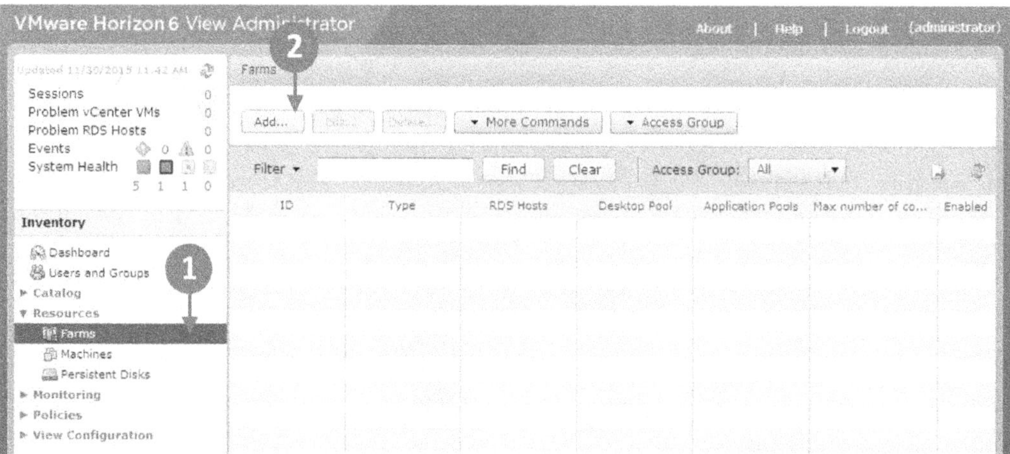

2. From the **Inventory** menu on the left hand side of the console, expand the **Resources** option and then click **Farms (1)**.

3. Now click the **Add...** button **(2)**. You will see the **Add Farm** configuration page, as shown in the following diagram:

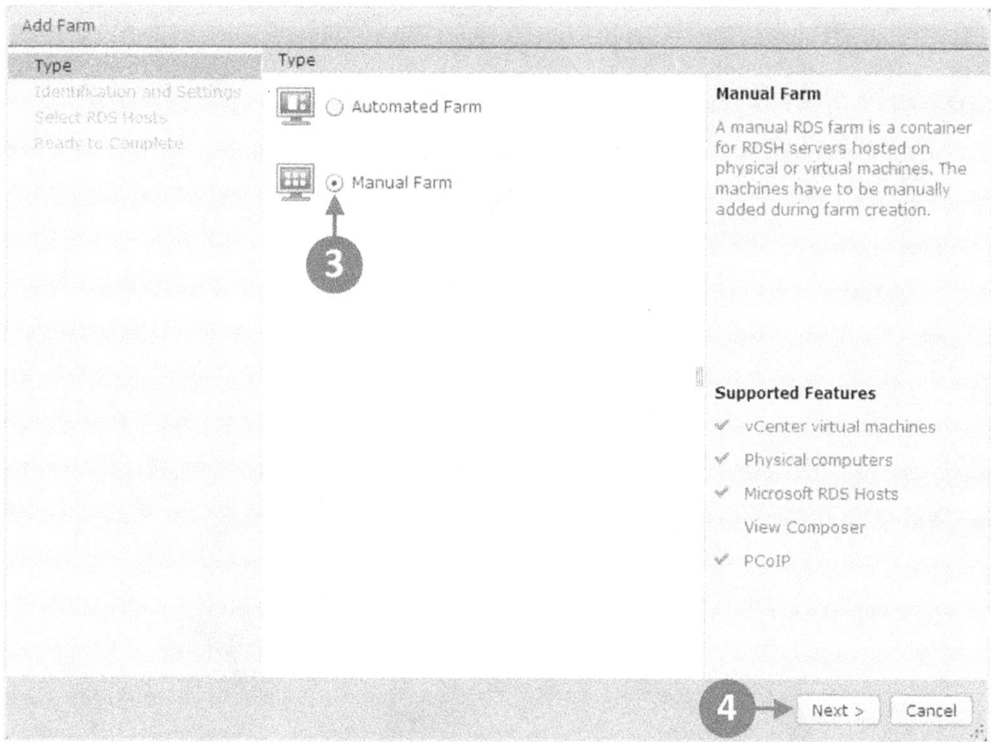

4. Click the radio button for **Manual Farm (3)**, and then click the **Next >** button **(4)**.

   You could choose the **Automated Farm** option, which would allow virtual machines to be provisioned automatically as you create the Farm, but in this example, we have already prebuilt an RDSH host server to use with our hosted applications.

You will now see the **Identification and Settings** page, as shown in the following diagram:

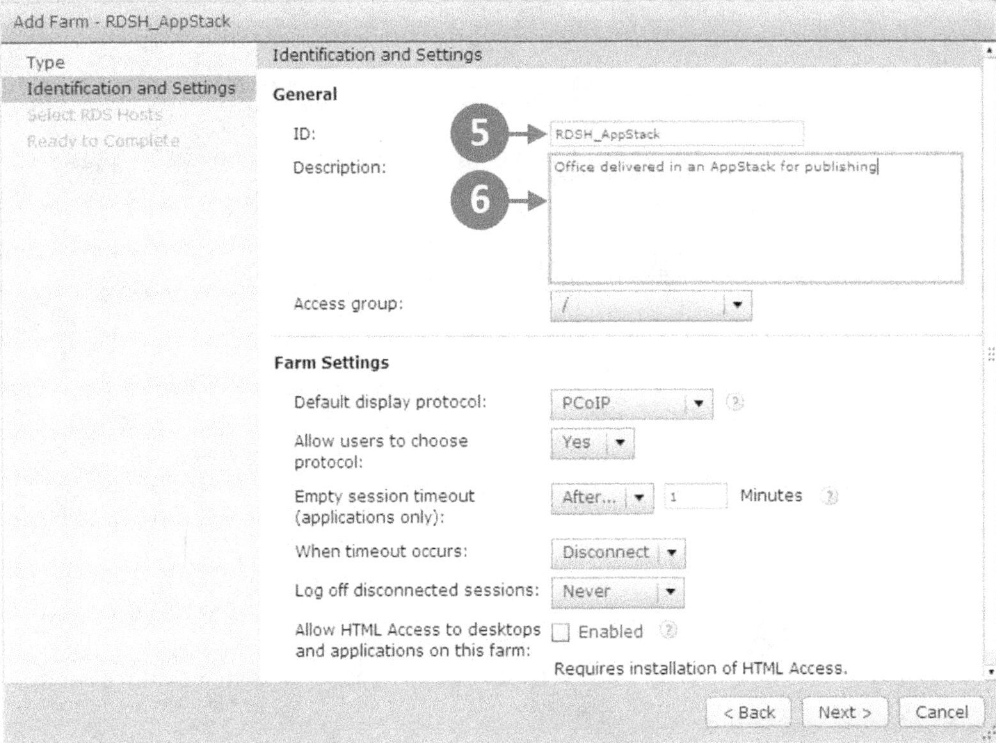

5. In the **ID:** box **(5)**, enter an ID or name for this Farm. In this example we have given the Farm the ID of `RDSH_AppStack`.
6. Then, in the **Description:** box, type in a description that describes what this Farm is going to be used for. In this example we have entered the description - `Office delivered in an AppStack for publishing`.

7. When you have completed the details click the **Next >** button.

   The next screen is the **Select RDSH Hosts** page, as shown in the following diagram:

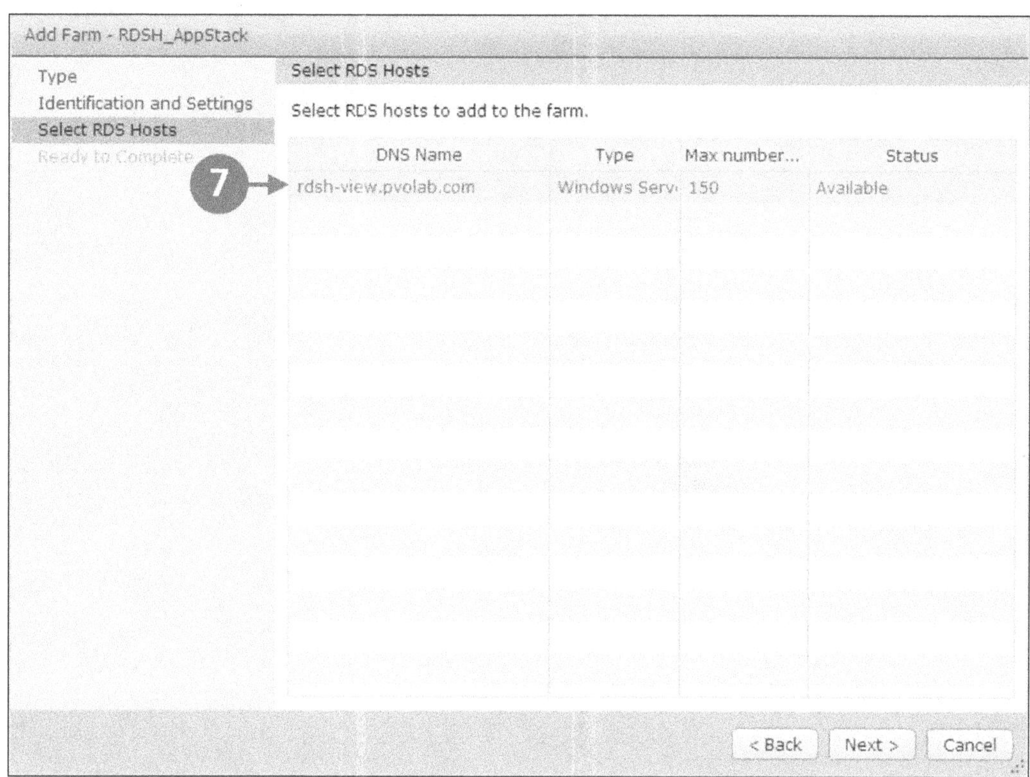

8. Select the RDSH server to be used **(7)**, and then click the **Next >** button.

   In this example the server is the `rdsh-view.pvolab.com` server and is running the Horizon View Agent.

The final configuration screen is the **Ready to Complete** screen, which summarizes the configuration details you have just entered and is shown in the following screenshot:

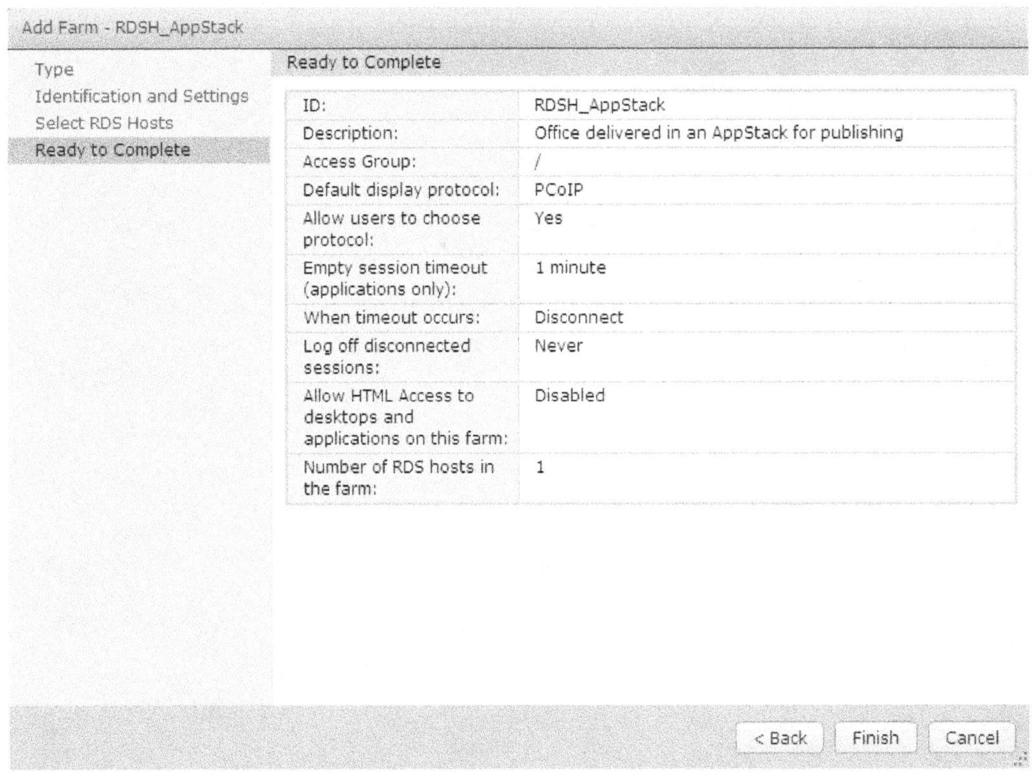

9. If you are happy that everything is configured correctly, click the **Finish** button. You will now return to the View Administrator console, as shown in the following screenshot, which shows the newly configured Farm:

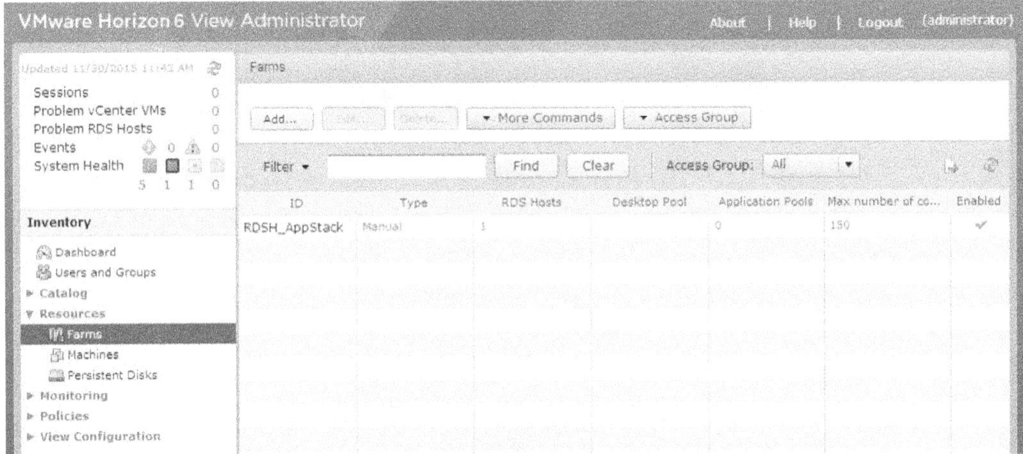

Now we have our Farm configured, the next step is to configure an application pool.

Configuring a Horizon View application pool

The next stage is to create an application pool. The application pool is going to contain all the applications that we want Horizon View to allow users to access:

1. From the **Inventory** menu on the left-hand side of the console, expand the **Catalog** option and then click **Application Pools (1)**.

2. Now click the **Add...** button **(2)**:

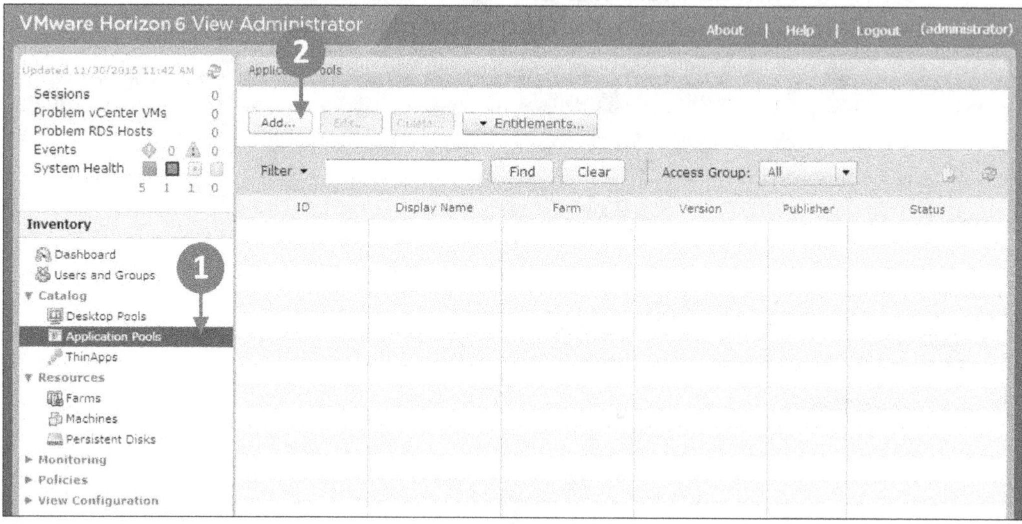

You will see the **Add Application Pools** configuration page, as shown in the following diagram:

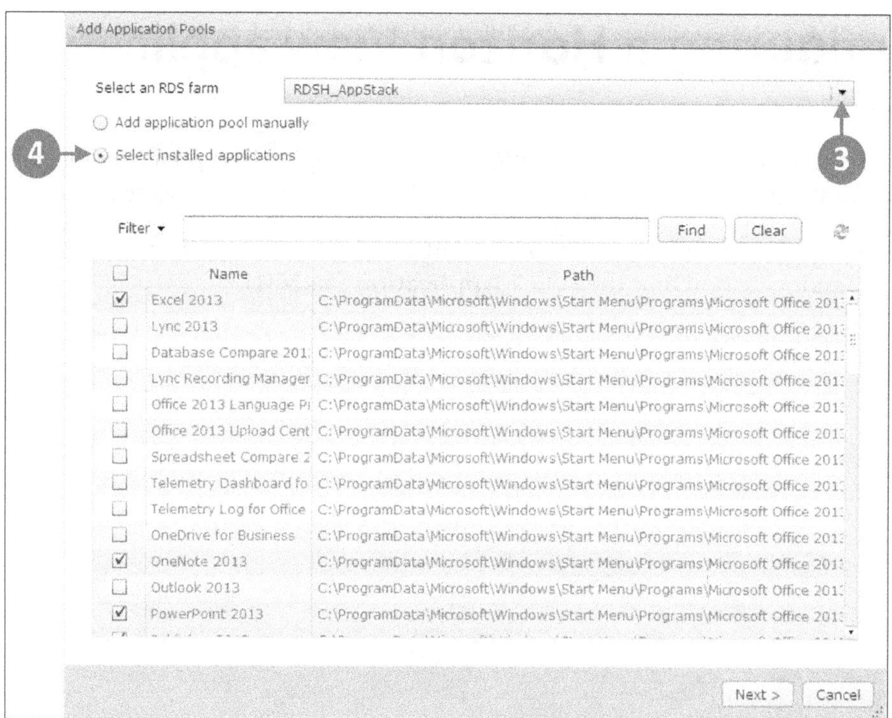

3. From the **Select an RDS farm** menu, click the dropdown arrow **(3)** and select the Farm that you configured in the previous section. In this example, it is the Farm called `RDSH_AppStack`.
4. Then click the radio button for **Select installed applications**. You will then see a list of the applications. This list has been populated directly from those applications that have been published on the RDSH host server and are read by the Horizon View Agent.

   Scroll down the list and select the following applications:

   - **Paint**
   - **Calculator**
   - **Excel 2013**
   - **OneNote 2013**
   - **PowerPoint 2013**
   - **Publisher 2013**
   - **Word 2013**

5. Once selected, click the **Next >** button. You will see the following diagram listing the chosen applications:

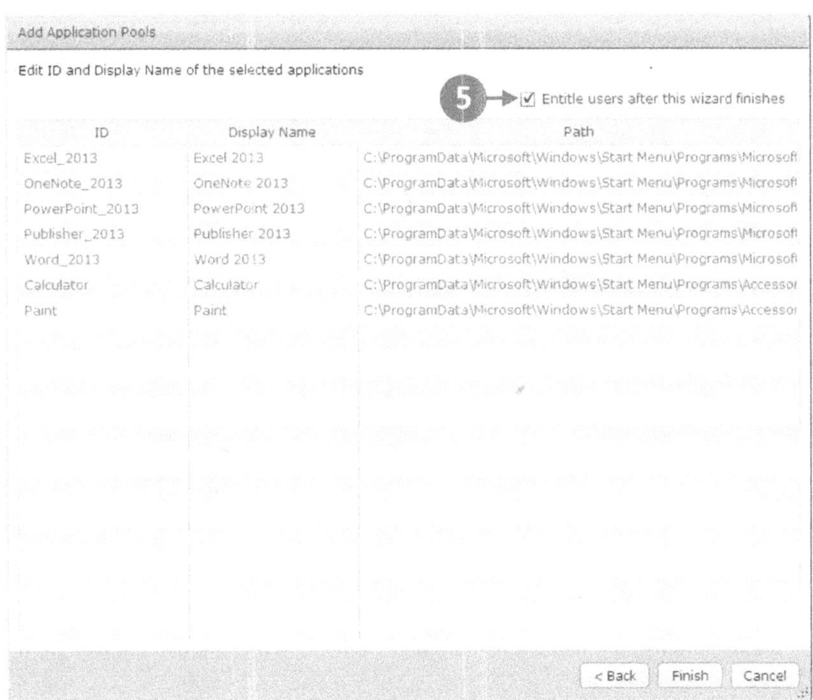

6. Check that all the applications are listed, and also check the tick box for **Entitle users after this wizard finishes**. This will take you automatically to the screen where you can entitle users to the applications.

Entitlement to applications is now done at the View Connection Server level rather than at the App Volumes Manager level. Remember, in the case of RDSH servers and AppStack assignments, AppStacks are now assigned to the RDSH host servers and not to users and groups.

7. Now click the **Finish** button. The application pool is now created and you are taken to the **Add Entitlements** screen, as shown in the following diagram:

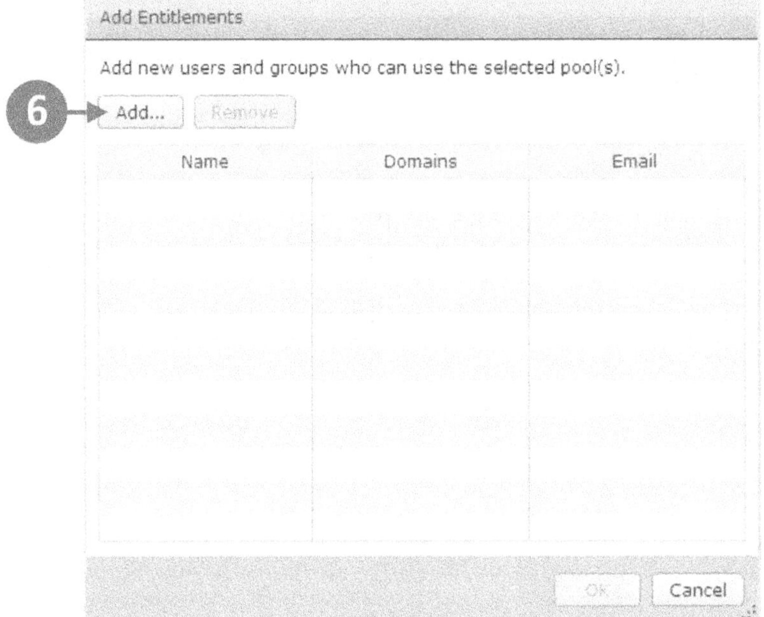

8. Click the **Add...** button **(6)**. You will now see the **Find User or Group** screen, as shown in the following diagram:

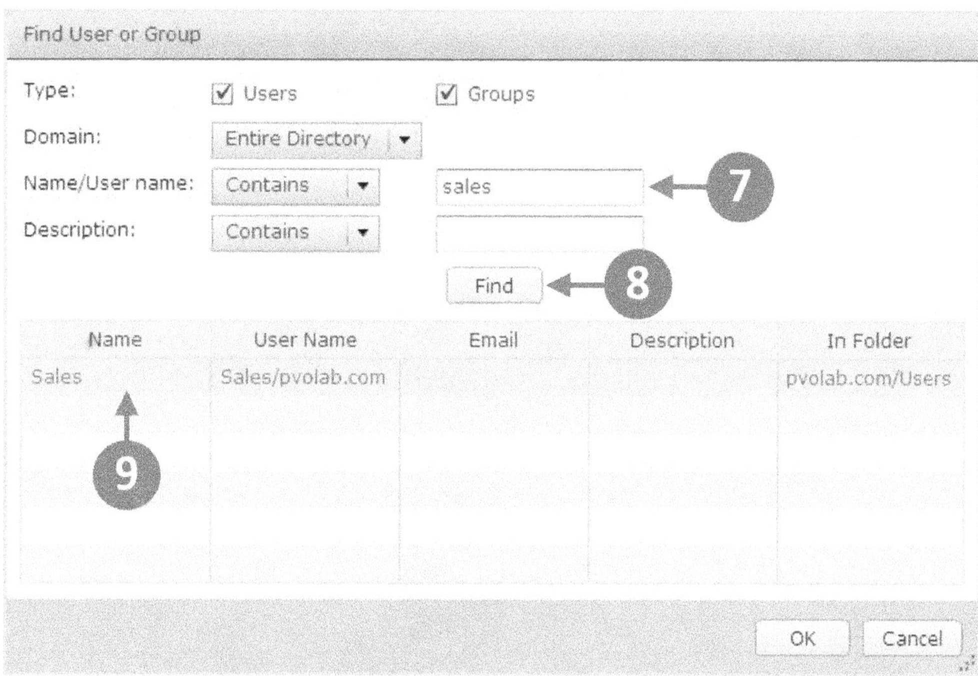

9. In the **Name/User name** box, ensure you choose **Contains** from the dropdown menu and then in the box **(7)**, type the name of the group or user you want to entitle to the application Farm.
10. In this example we are going to entitle the Sales group, so type **Sales** in the box. Click the **Find** button **(8)**.

11. You will then see the Sales group appear in the results. Click the entry for the Sales group to highlight it and then click **OK**. You will now see the following screenshot:

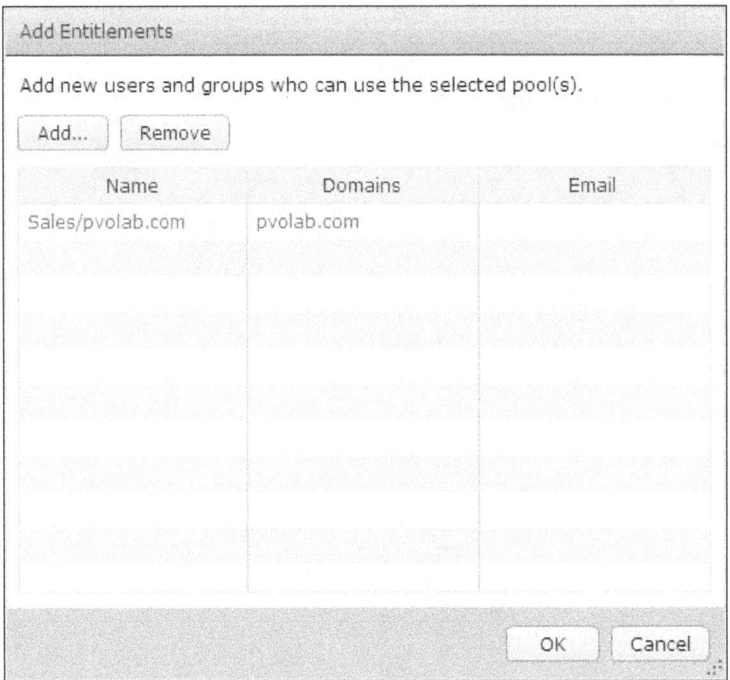

12. With the group now selected, click **OK** to complete the entitlements and close the configuration screen.

You will now return to the Horizon View Administrator console, which will show the newly created application pool and the applications within that pool.

This is shown in the following screenshot:

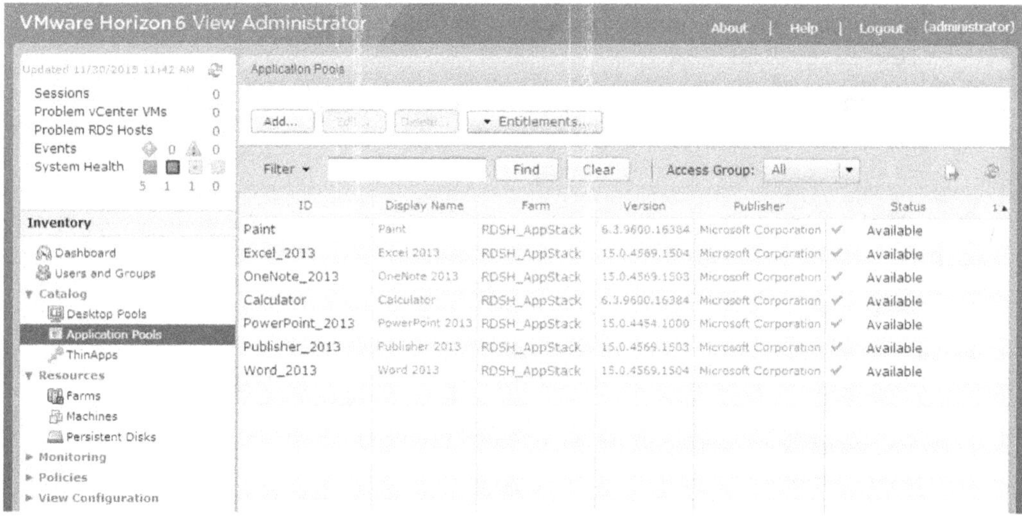

Once complete, you can log out of the Horizon View Administrator console.

You have now completed all the configuration tasks and should now have a working solution. We are going to put that to the test in the next section, where we are going to log in to the Horizon View Connection Server and launch one of the hosted applications.

Launching AppStack-based Horizon View hosted apps

In this final section, we are going to test the solution that we have built in this chapter, by delivering Horizon View hosted applications that are contained within an AppStack:

1. Open a console to one of the example desktop machines. Before you can test anything, the first thing you need to do is make sure you have the Horizon View Client software installed onto that machine. You can download the software from the following link:

   `www.vmware.com/go/viewclients`

We are not going to cover the installation of the Horizon View Client software, but during the installation it will ask you to enter the details of the Horizon View Connection Server. In this example, the server is called `view-cs.pvolab.com`.

Once installed, launch the Horizon View Client, as shown in the following screenshot:

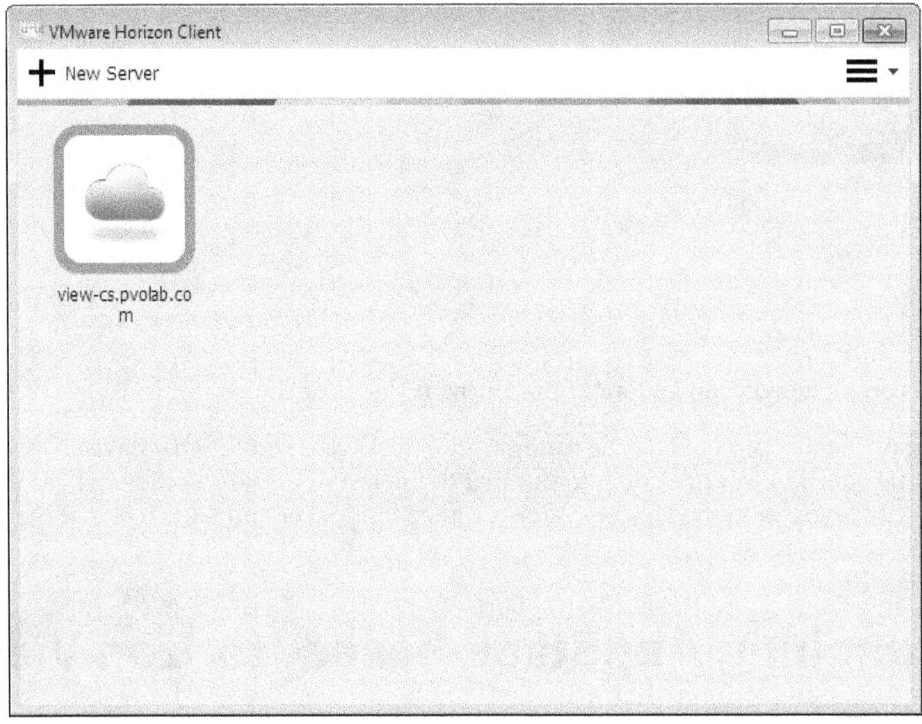

2. Double-click the icon for the Horizon View Connection Server. In this example, there just a single server. You will then see the **Login** box, as shown in the following screenshot:

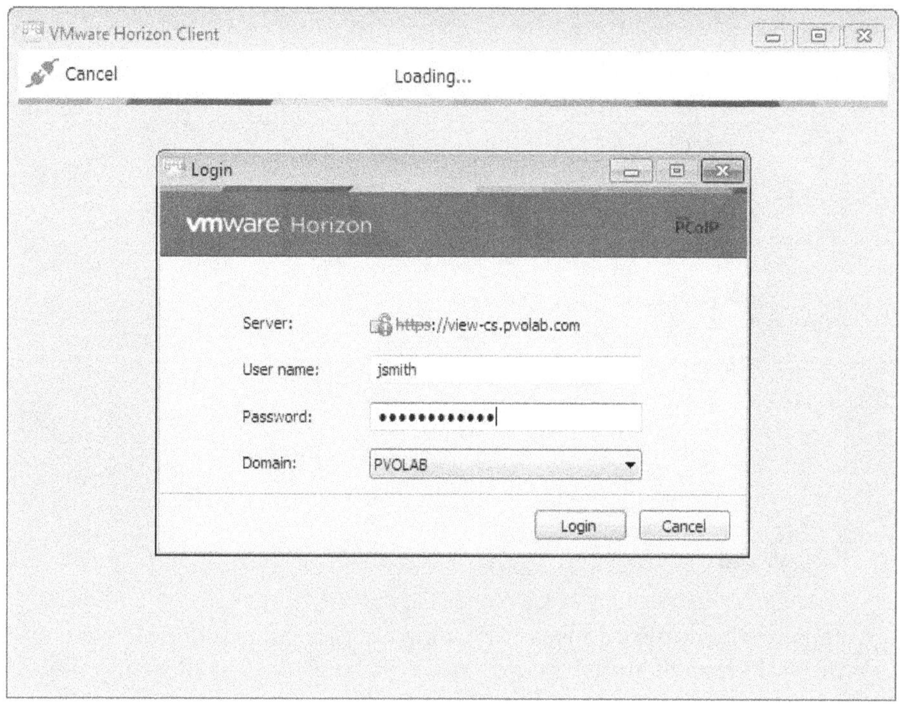

3. As you entitled the Sales group to this application pool, log in as a user in that group. In this example, we are going to log in as `jmsith`, so enter this into the **User name** box, followed by the password, and ensure the correct domain is shown in the **Domain:** box.

4. Now click the **Login** button.

   Once logged in, you will be presented with the applications that you selected to be published, along with the virtual desktop machine that was created in a previous chapter:

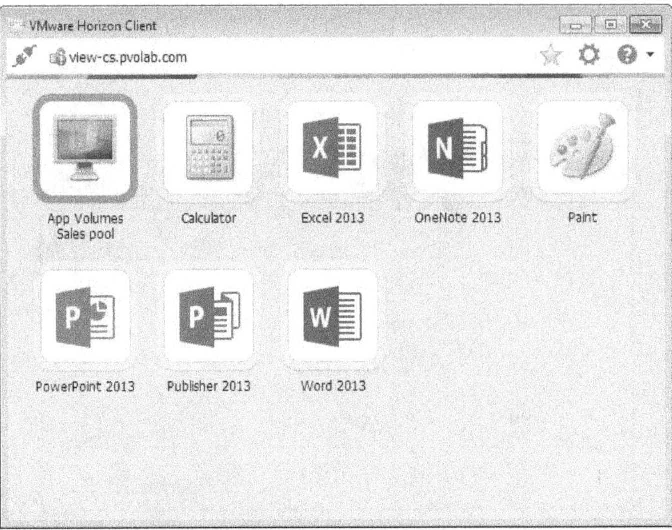

5. To ensure the applications launch and run as expected, double-click on the Word 2013 icon to launch Word. You will now see the following message as the application is prepared:

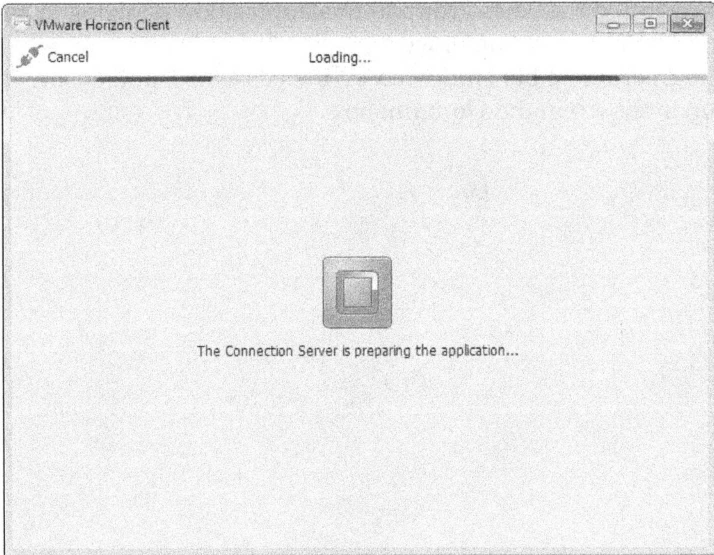

Once the connection has been established, the application will load, as shown in the following screenshot:

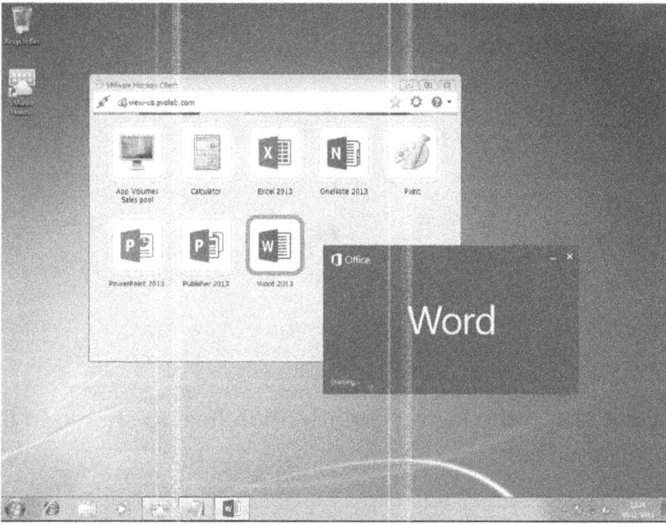

6. To complete the testing and to make sure that Word is working as you would expect it, try creating a document and typing some text:

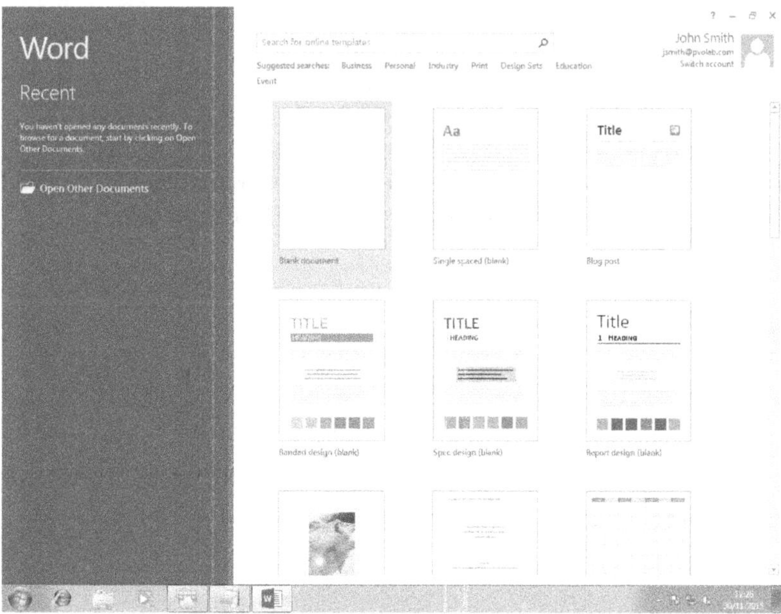

Once you are happy that Word is functioning correctly, you can exit the application.

7. Then disconnect from the Horizon View Connection Server by clicking the icon **(1)**, as shown in the following diagram:

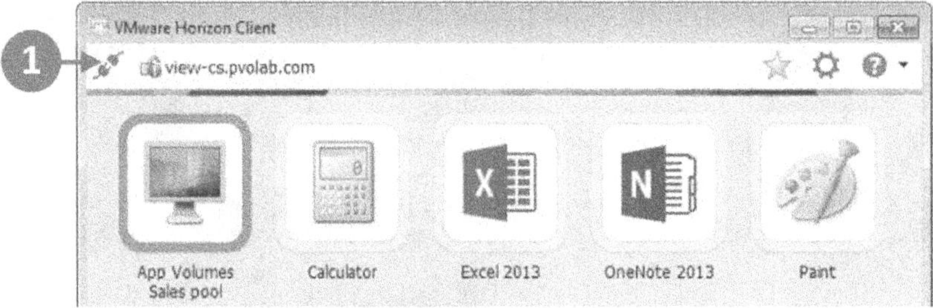

8. Finally, click **OK** in the log off confirmation box, as shown in the following screenshot:

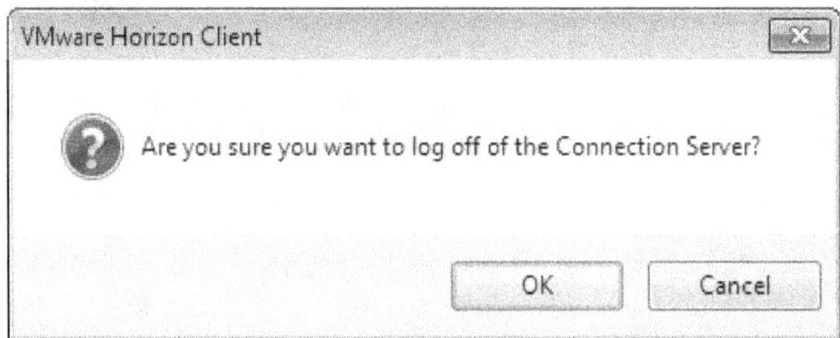

You have now successfully built and tested a Horizon View hosted application environment, with applications being delivered using AppStacks.

Summary

In this chapter, we started by talking about the use case for deploying App Volumes in an RDSH/Horizon View hosted application environment. We then went on the look at the architecture and how it all fits together.

Once familiar with the solution, we went on to build a provisioning machine to provision our RDSH AppStack for Office 2013, before building RDSH server, which was assigned the Office AppStack and then configured to publish some of the core Office applications. As these published applications were going to be brokered using Horizon View, the Horizon View Agent was also installed on the RDSH server.

The final piece of configuration was to create an application Farm and application pool using the Horizon View Administrator Console, before then entitling end users to the applications.

Finally, we tested the solution to make sure it behaved as expected and that end users could log in and launch their applications.

In the final chapter, we are going look at some of the advanced and additional features available with App Volumes.

Summary

14
Advanced Configuration and Other Options

In this final chapter, we are going to take a look at some of the advanced configuration options, such as batch script files and App Volumes Agent configuration, as well as some other additional administrations tasks, such as how to customize the App Volumes templates used for creating AppStacks and Writable Volumes, and how you can create your own template sizes.

Let's start with how to customize the AppStack templates.

Customizing AppStack templates

When you create a new AppStack or Writable Volume, the starting point is to take a copy of the existing templates previously attached to the provisioning machine or user's virtual desktop machine.

VMware App Volumes ships with four different types of template as standard, which are:

- AppStack application template (20 GB)
- Writable Volumes template for user-installed applications (10 GB)
- Writable Volumes template for user profiles only (10 GB)
- Writable Volume for user profiles and user installed applications (10 GB)

The standard template for creating AppStacks is by default configured to be 20 GB in size. Although this is thin provisioned, it might not make sense to use a 20 GB disk if you are just deploying an application that is a few MB's in size for example.

On the flip side, you may also have a more complex application, where 20 GB is not big enough to accommodate updates and patches going forward.

In this section, we are going to look at how to customize the size of your AppStack templates and then import this new template into the App Volumes Manager.

The process we are going to following is illustrated in the following diagram:

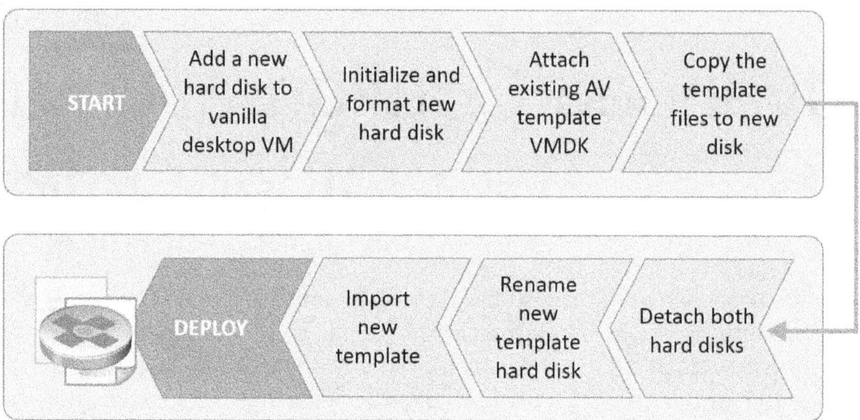

The first step is to create a new virtual hard disk and then attach it to a virtual desktop machine. In the Example Lab environment, there is a machine already built for this purpose called **Admin Desktop** which has been built and configured with Windows 7. Do not install any App Volumes components on to this machine.

Creating new virtual hard disk

Follow these steps to create a new virtual hard disk:

1. From the vSphere Client (you can use the vSphere Web Client), highlight the **Admin Desktop** virtual machine, right-click on it, and choose **Edit Settings... (1)** from the menu as shown in the following diagram:

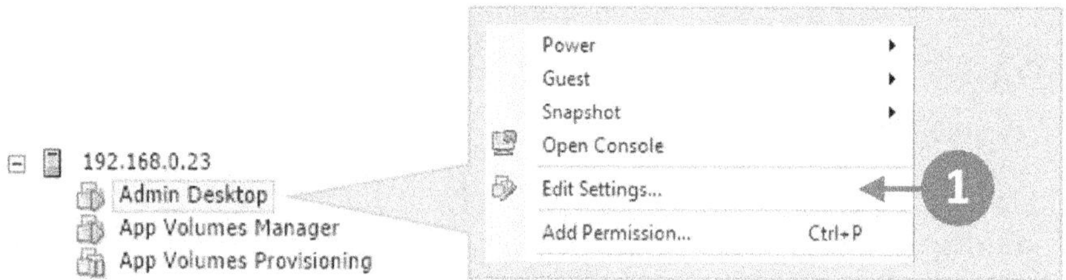

You will now see the **Admin Desktop - Virtual Machine Properties** screen as shown in the following diagram:

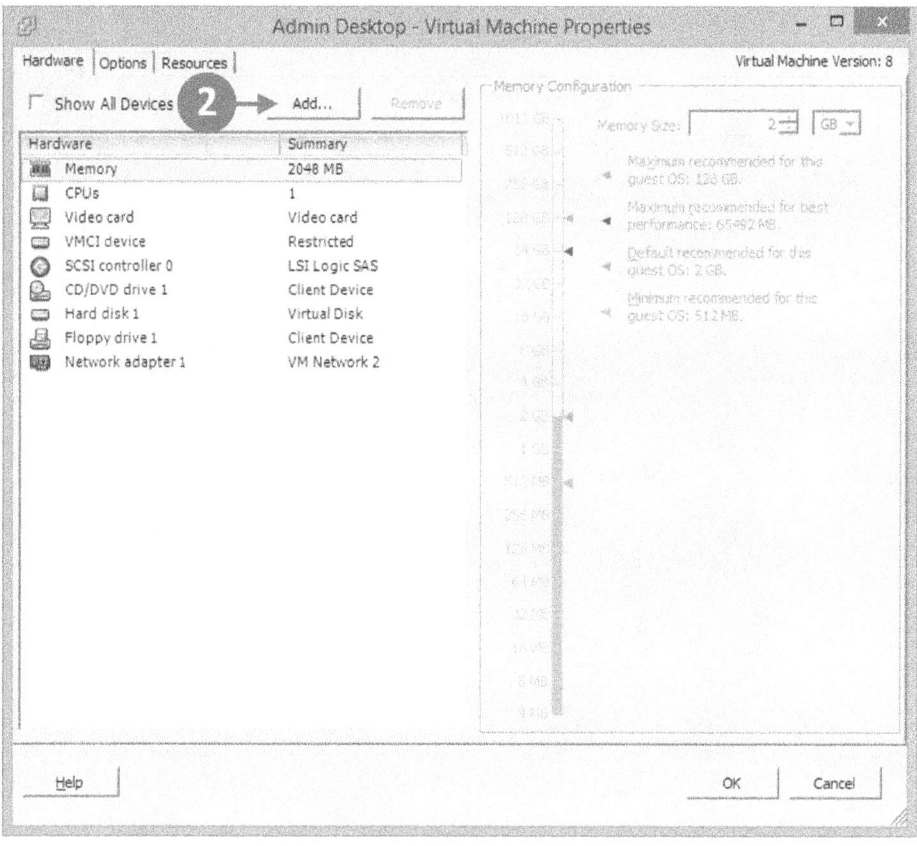

2. Click the **Add...** button **(2)**. You will now see the **Add Hardware** dialog box and the **Device Type** selection as shown in the following diagram:

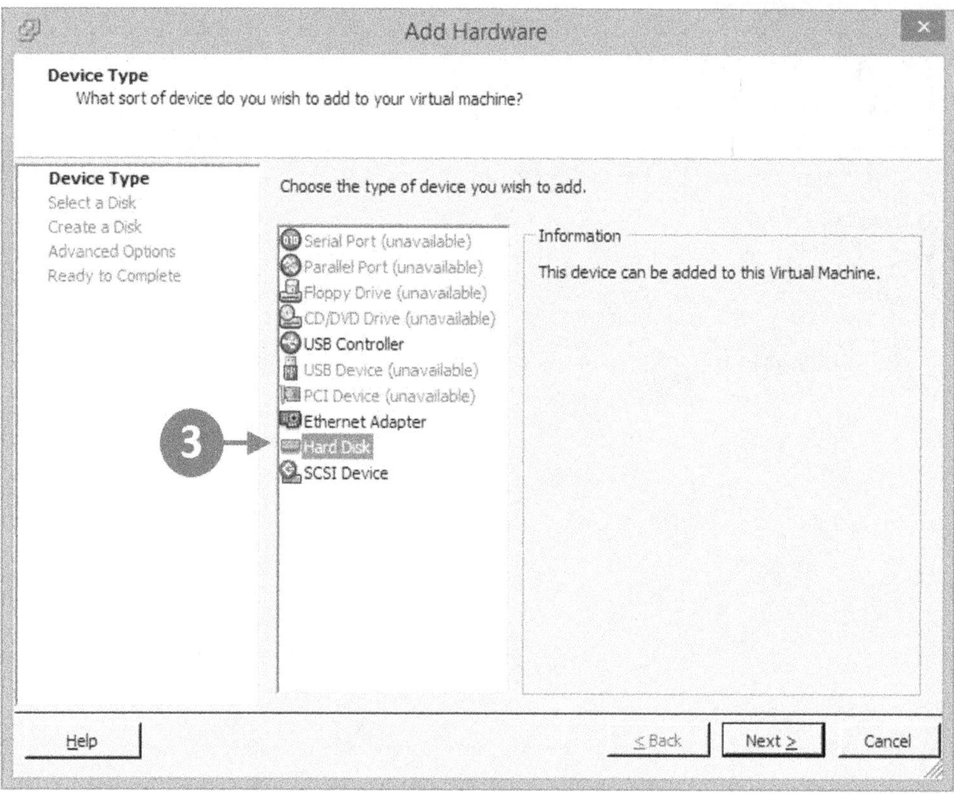

3. Click on **Hard Disk (3)** and then click the **Next >** button. You will now see the **Select a Disk** dialog box as shown in the following diagram:

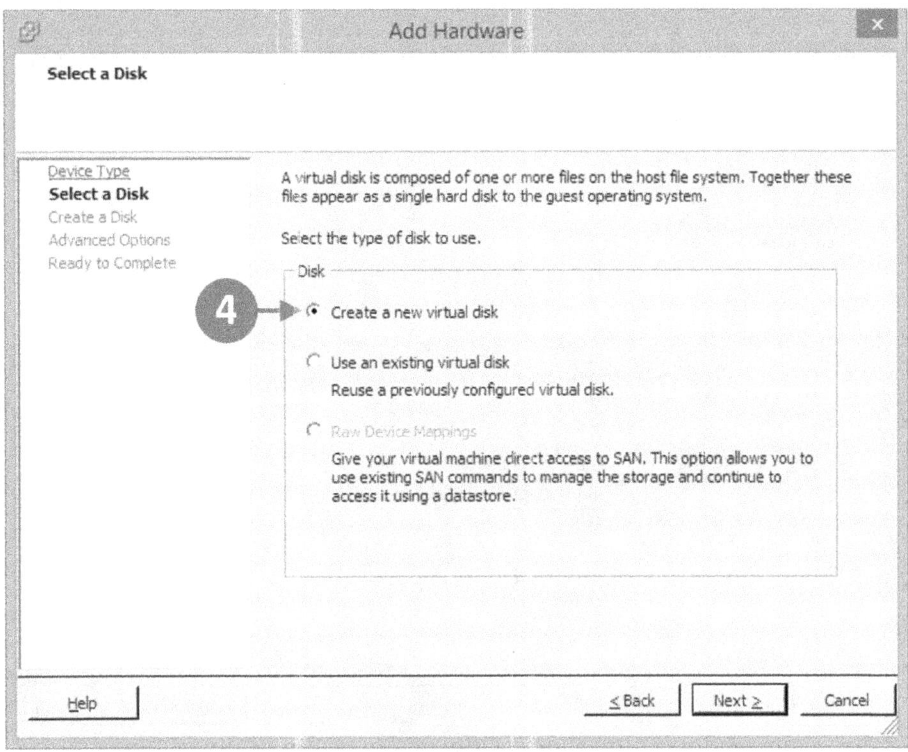

4. Click the radio button for **Create a new virtual disk (4)** and click the **Next >** button. You will now see the **Select a Disk** dialog box as shown in the following diagram:

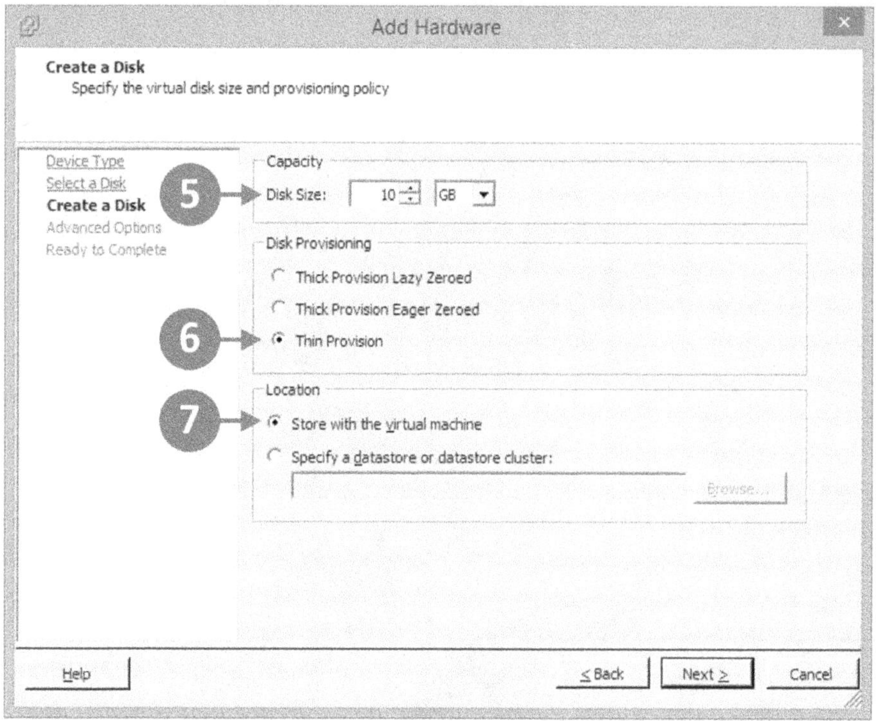

5. In the **Capacity** box **(5)**, enter a **Disk Size** for this new virtual hard disk. In this example we are going to create a virtual hard disk that is 10 GB.

Make sure you create a disk size that is going to meet the requirements of your AppStacks, especially if the applications are going to require numerous updates or patches.

6. In the **Disk Provisioning** box, click the radio button for **Thin Provision (6)**, and in the **Location** box, click the radio button for **Store with the virtual machine (7)**. We will move the newly created virtual hard disk later on.
7. Click the **Next >** button.
8. On the **Advanced Options** screen, accept the default configuration and click the **Next >** button.

9. Finally, on the **Ready to Complete** box, review the options you have configured and then click the **Finish** button to create the new virtual hard disk.

Initializing and formatting the new hard disk

Follow these steps to initialize and format the new disk:

1. With the new virtual hard drive created and attached to the Admin Desktop, open a console to the **Admin Desktop** virtual machine and launch the **Computer Management** console as shown in the following screenshot:

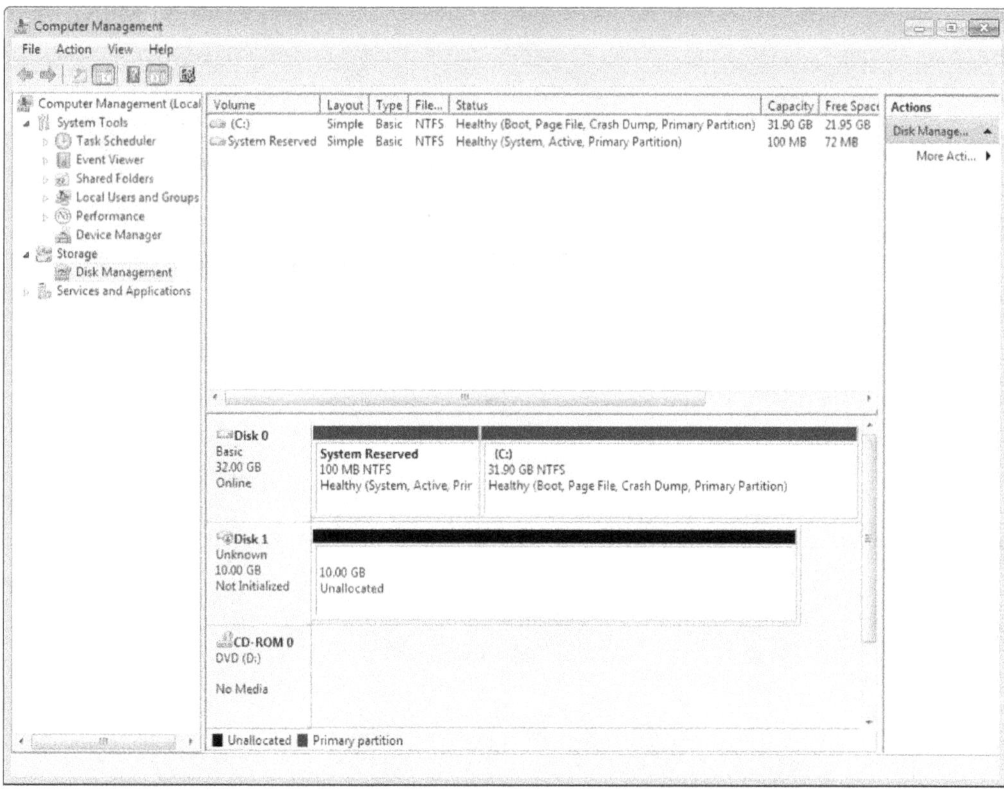

If the newly created virtual hard disk is not shown then click and select the **Disk Management** option from the left hand pane, right-click on it, and then select **Rescan Disks (1)** as shown in the following diagram:

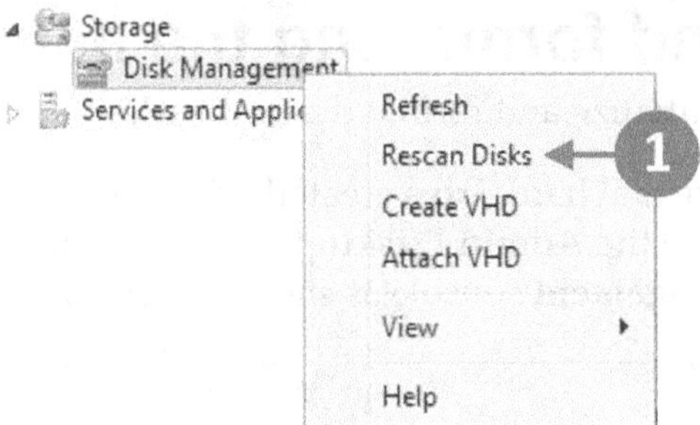

2. Next, click on the newly created **Disk 1** to highlight it **(2)** and then right-click on it. From the menu options displayed, click **Initialize Disk (3)** as shown in the following diagram:

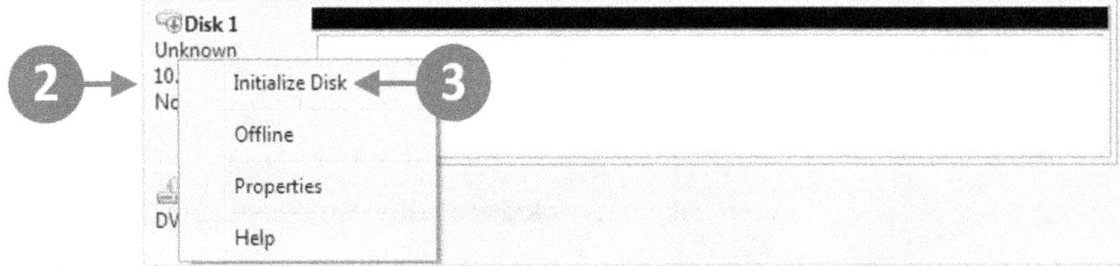

You will now see the **Initialize Disk** dialog box as shown in the following diagram:

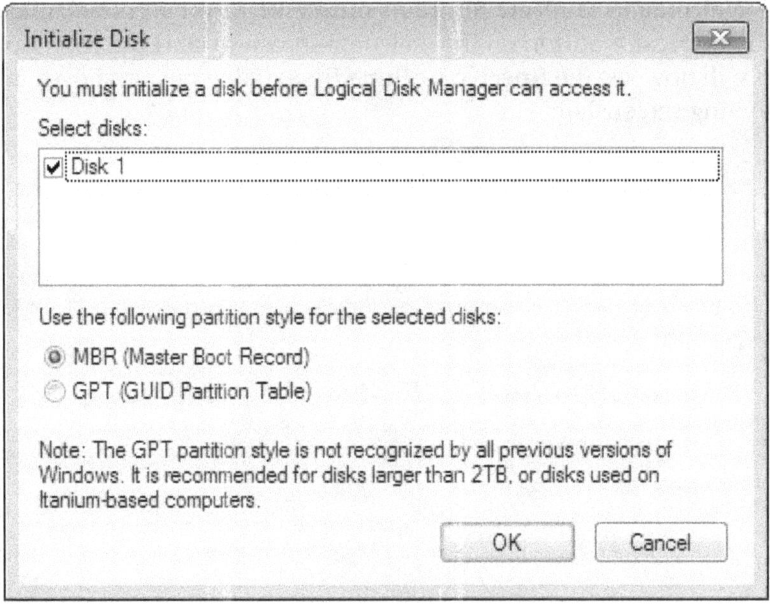

3. Click **OK** to continue. The disk is now initialized.
4. Next, click the new disk to highlight it **(4)**, right-click on it, and then from the menu click on **New Simple Volume... (5)**. This is shown in the following diagram:

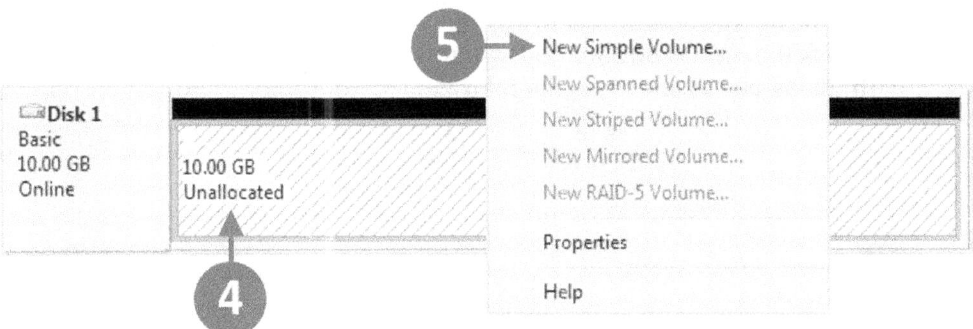

5. The **Welcome to the New Simple Volume Wizard** will now launch. Click the **Next >** button on the welcome screen to start the configuration. You will now see the **Specify Volume Size** dialog box as shown in the following screenshot:

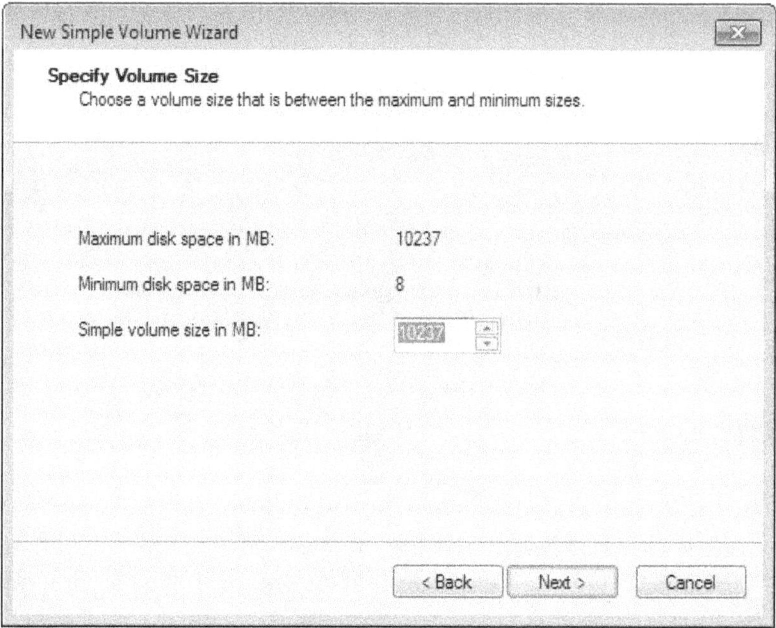

6. Leave the default setting, ensuring that you use the maximum volume size and click the **Next >** button. You will now see the **Assign Drive Letter or Path** dialog box as shown in the following screenshot:

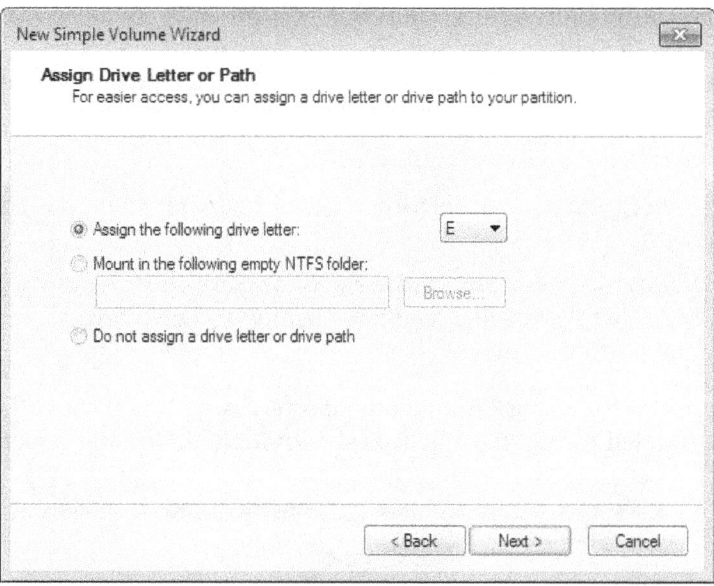

7. Again, leave the default settings and click the **Next >** button. You will now see the **Format Partition** dialog box as shown in the following diagram:

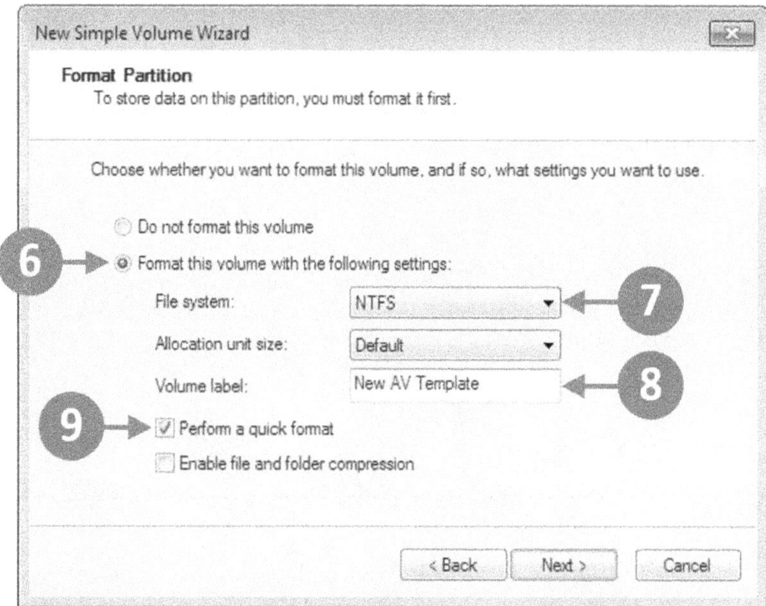

8. Click the radio button for **Format this volume with the following settings: (6)**, and on the **File system** box **(7)**, from the dropdown menu select **NTFS** and leave the next setting, **Allocation unit size**, as the default setting.
9. In the **Volume label** box **(8)**, enter a name for this volume. In this example we have called it `New AV Template`.
10. Finally, check the box for **Perform a quick format (9)**, and then click the **Next >** button.
11. You will now see the **Completing the New Simple Volume Wizard** dialog box. Check that the settings you have configured are correct and then click the **Finish** button.

You will now return to the Disk Management screen which will show the newly created and formatted virtual hard disk as shown in the following screenshot:

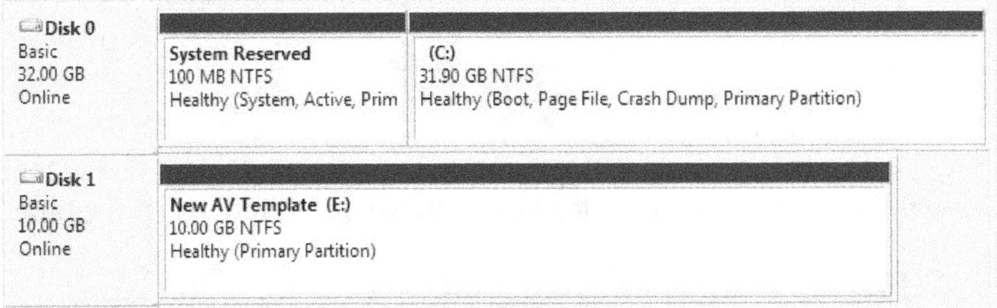

Next, we are going to attach the existing App Volumes AppStack template to the Admin Desktop virtual machine.

Attaching the existing virtual hard disk template

The next step is to attach the existing virtual hard disk template to the Admin Desktop virtual machine in preparation for copying the template files. Follow these steps:

1. From the vSphere Client (you can use the vSphere Web Client), highlight the **Admin Desktop** virtual machine **(1)**, right-click on it, and choose **Edit Settings.... (2)**.

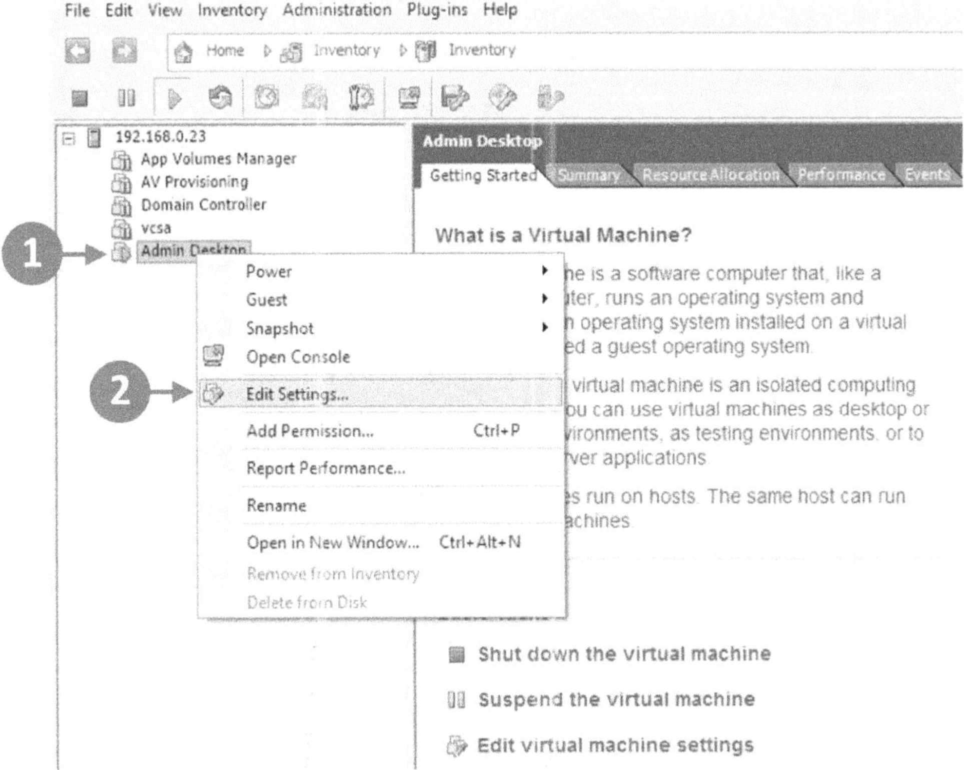

2. You will now see the **Admin Desktop – Virtual Machine Properties** screen.
3. Click the **Add...** button **(3)**, as shown:

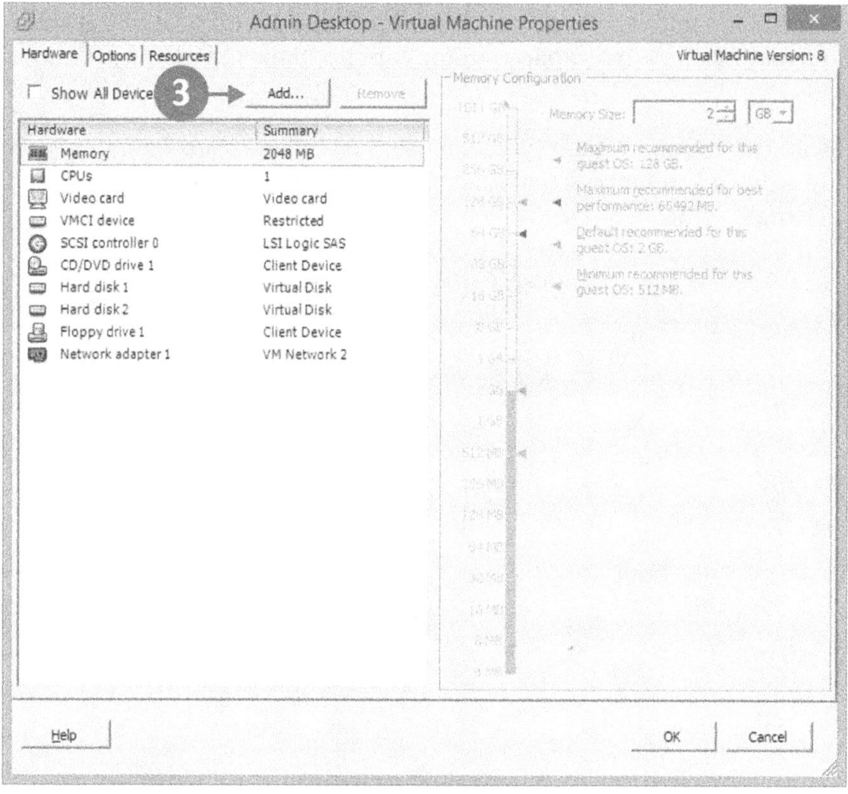

4. You will now see the **Add Hardware** dialog box and the **Device Type** selection screen.
5. Click on **Hard Disk (4)** and then click the **Next >** button:

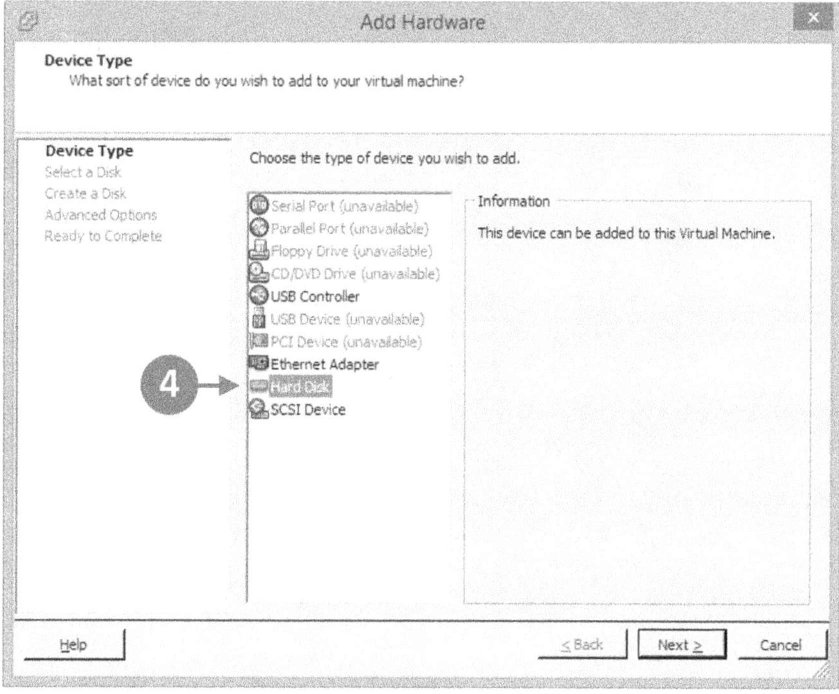

You will now see the **Select a Disk** dialog box as shown in the following diagram:

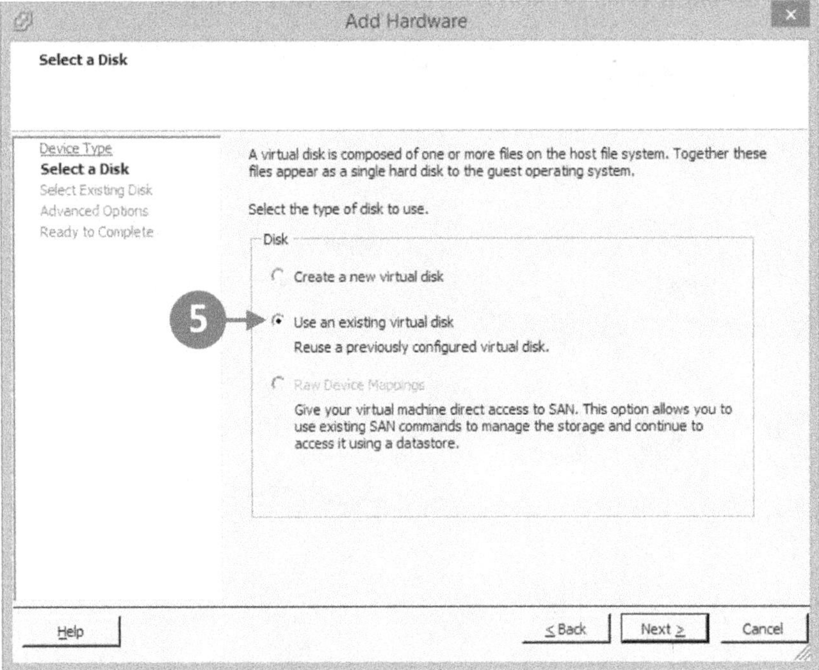

6. Click the radio button for **Use on existing virtual disk (5)** and then click the **Next >** button. You will now see the **Select Existing Disk** dialog box as shown in the following diagram:

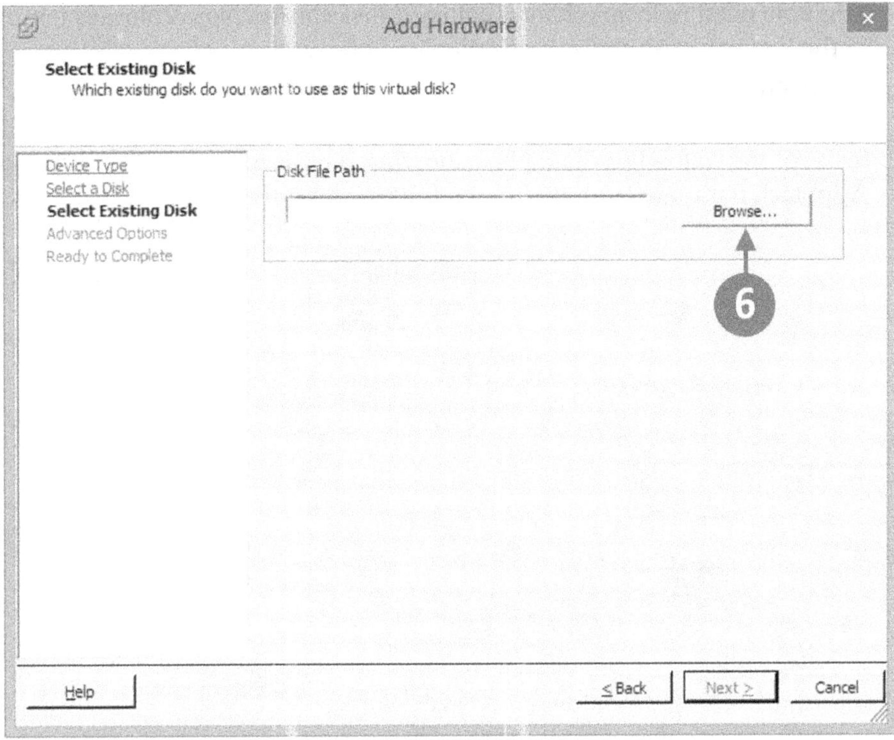

7. Click the **Browse...** button **(6)**. You will now see the **Browse Datastores** dialog box as shown in the following screenshot:

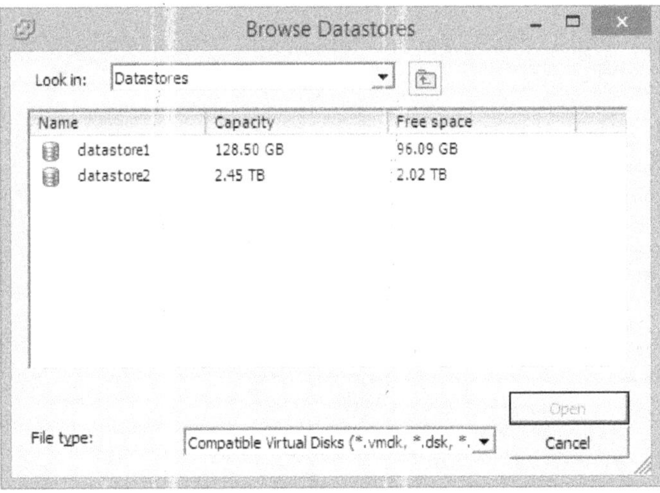

8. You now need to locate the virtual hard disk for the App Volumes template. In the Example Lab this is located on `datastore2`.
9. The default location is `datastore2` | `cloudvolumes` | `apps_templates`, so in the datastore browser dialog box navigate to that location. You will then see the following dialog box showing the `template.vmdk` file for the AppStack template as shown in the following screenshot:

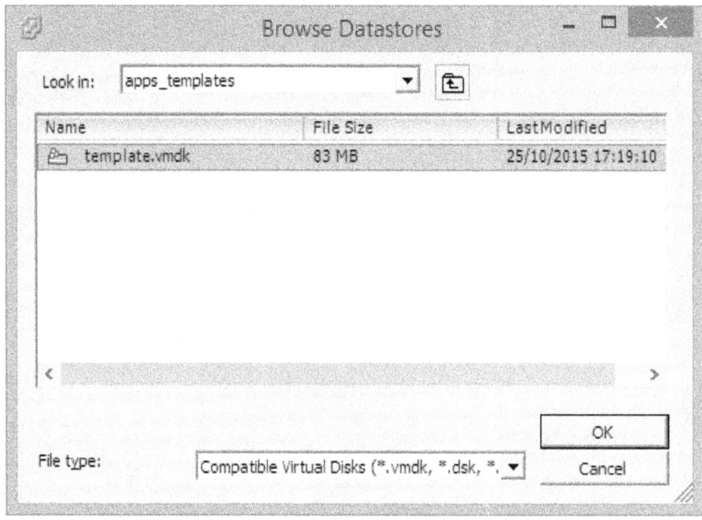

10. Highlight the file and then click **OK**. You will then return to the **Select Existing Disk** dialog box. You will see that the path to the template is now shown in the **Disk File Path** box as shown in the following screenshot:

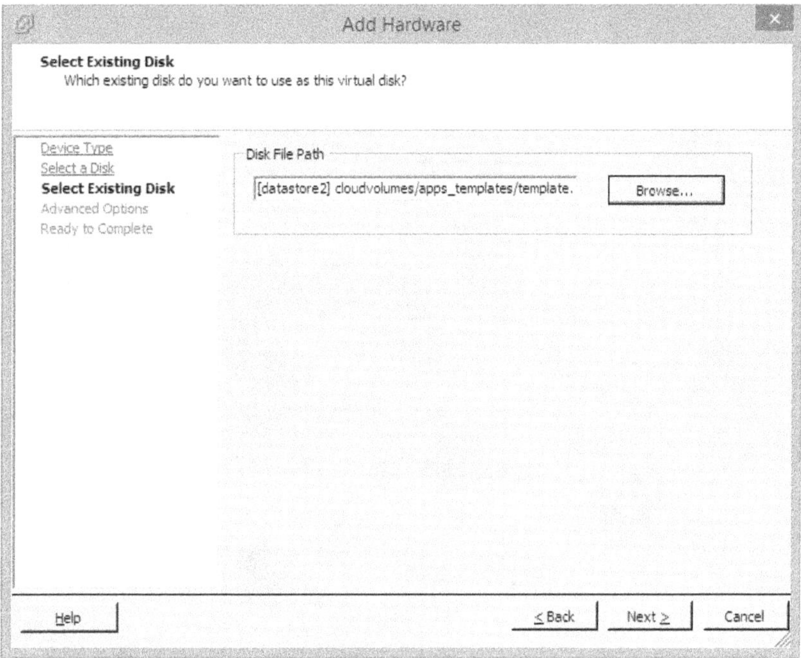

11. Click the **Next >** button to continue.

12. On the **Advanced Options** dialog box, keep the default setting and then click the **Next >** button:

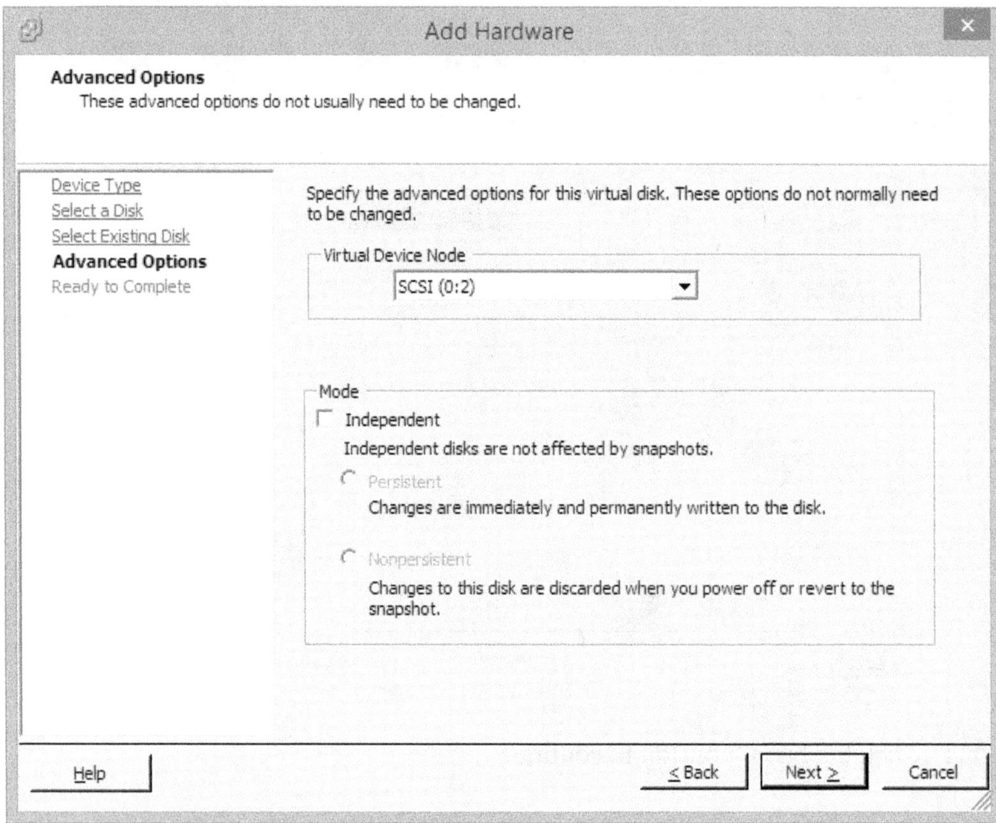

13. Finally, you will see the **Ready to Complete** dialog box. Check the options have been selected correctly and then click the **Finish** button:

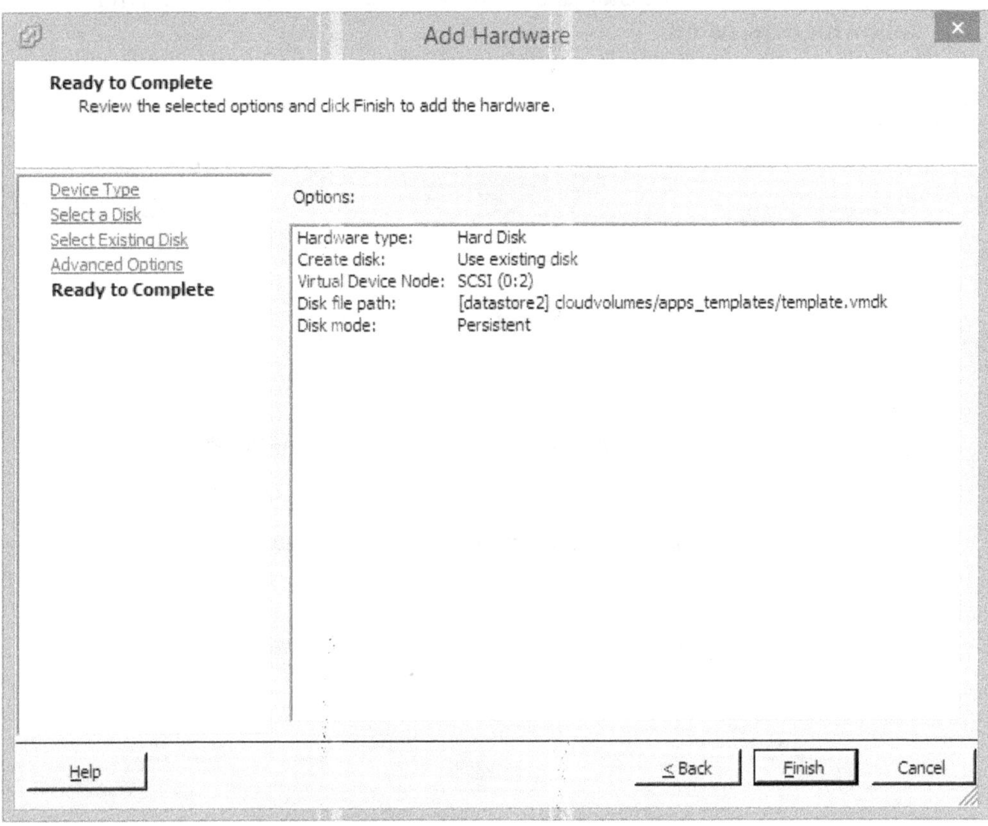

Now switch back to the console of the **Admin Desktop** virtual machine and check the **Disk Management** console. You should now see that the existing template virtual hard disk has been attached and is visible a shown in the following screenshot:

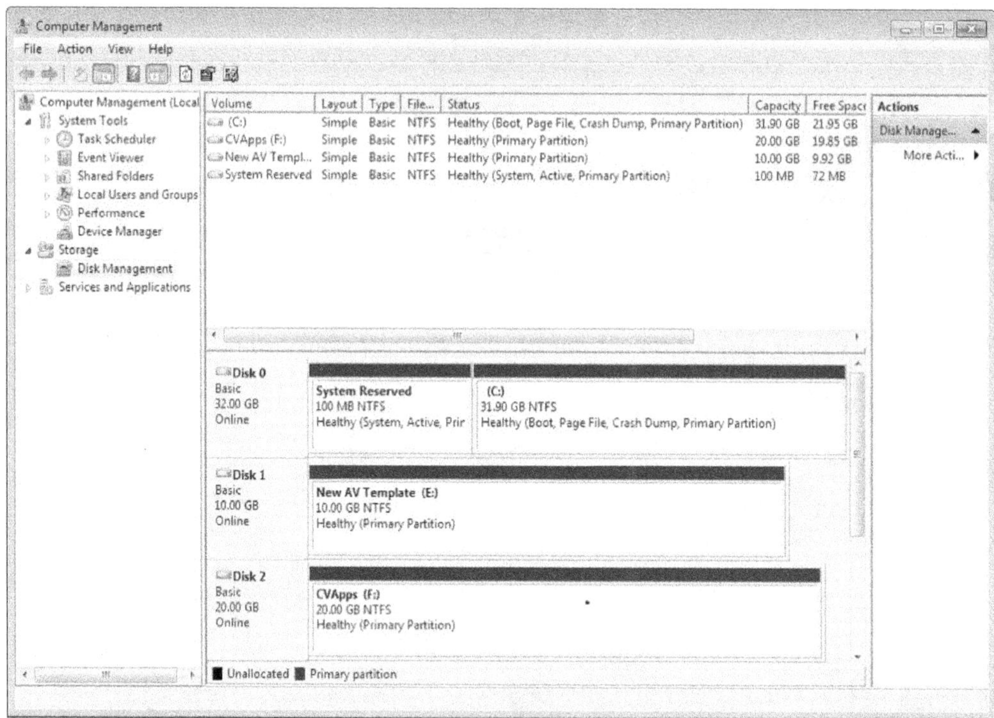

As you can see the existing virtual hard disk is listed as the **F:** drive, with the volume label **CVApps**. The new virtual hard disk listed as **E:**

The next step is to copy the template files from the current virtual hard disk to the new one.

Copying existing template files

In this next step we are going to copy the template files from the existing template to the newly created template. The files that are stored in the template are some of the batch files that we will cover later on in this chapter.

Before you start the copy process, just ensure that your Windows Explorer in the Admin Desktop virtual machine is set to show all files.

To do this first of all open Windows Explorer.

1. Click on **Organize (1)** and then from the menu options select **Folder and search options (2)** as shown in the following diagram:

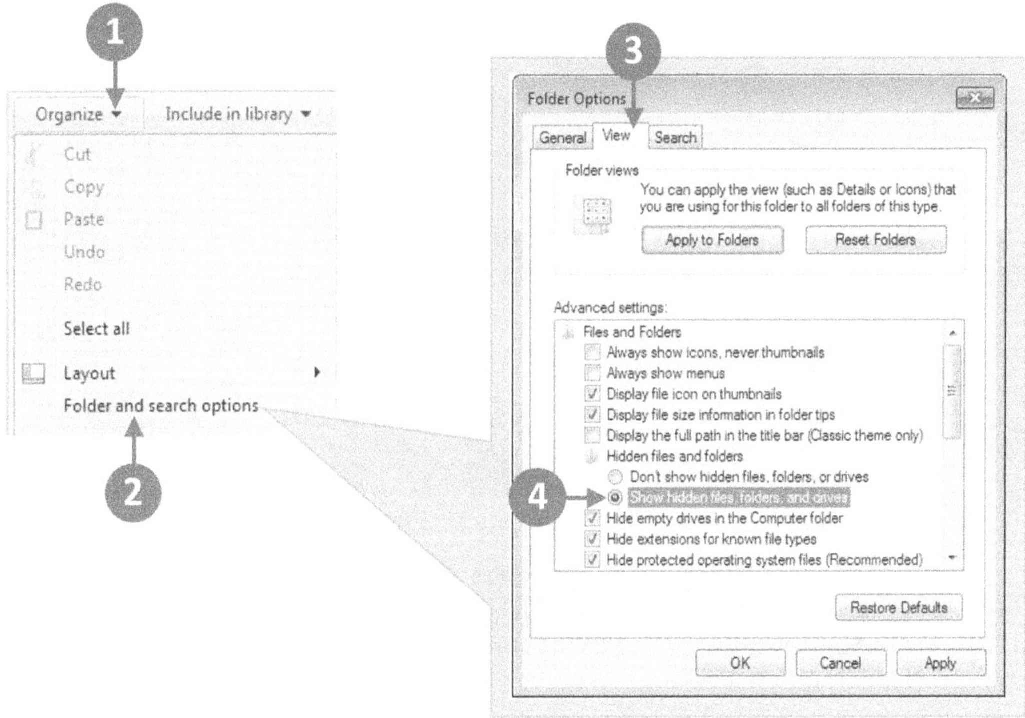

2. In the **Folder Options** dialog box, click the **View** tab, and then the radio button for **Show hidden files, folders, and drives (4)**.
3. Click the **Apply** button and then the **OK** button to close the dialog box.

   From Windows Explorer, browse to the **F:** drive, and select all the files within the folder as shown in the following diagram:

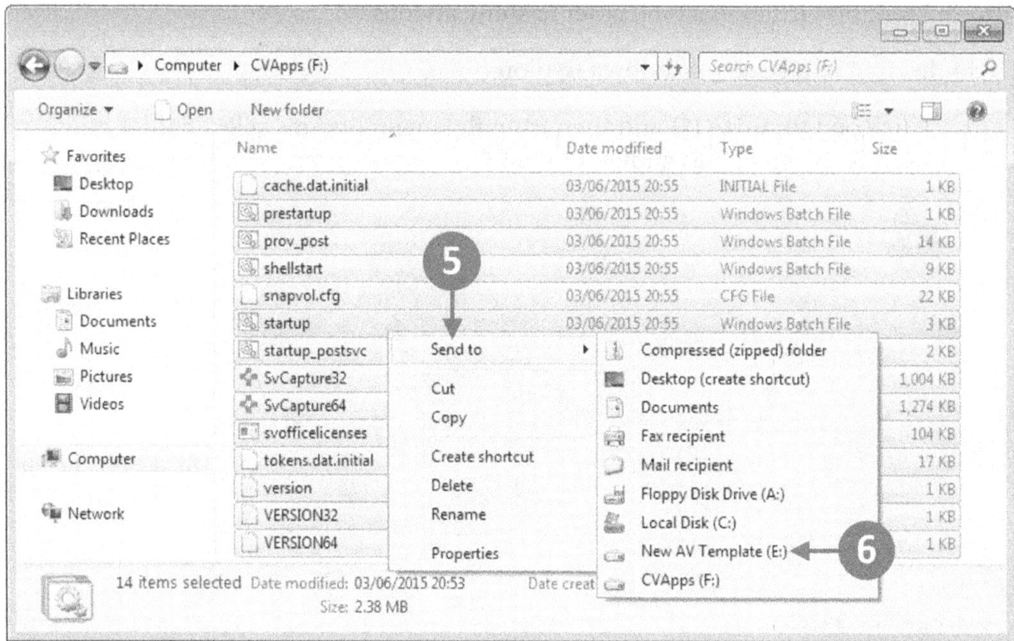

4. Right-click on the files and then from the menu select the **Send to** option **(5)**. From the list select **New AV Template (E :) (6)**.

Once the copy process has completed, check the **E:** drive to make sure all the files are there. If you are happy that the files have been successfully copied, then you can detach each of the virtual hard drives (existing template and new template) from the Admin Desktop virtual machine.

1. To do this, from the vSphere Client (you can use the vSphere Web Client), highlight the **Admin Desktop** virtual machine, right-click on it, and choose **Edit Settings...**.

You will now see the **Admin Desktop - Virtual Machine Properties** screen as shown in the following diagram:

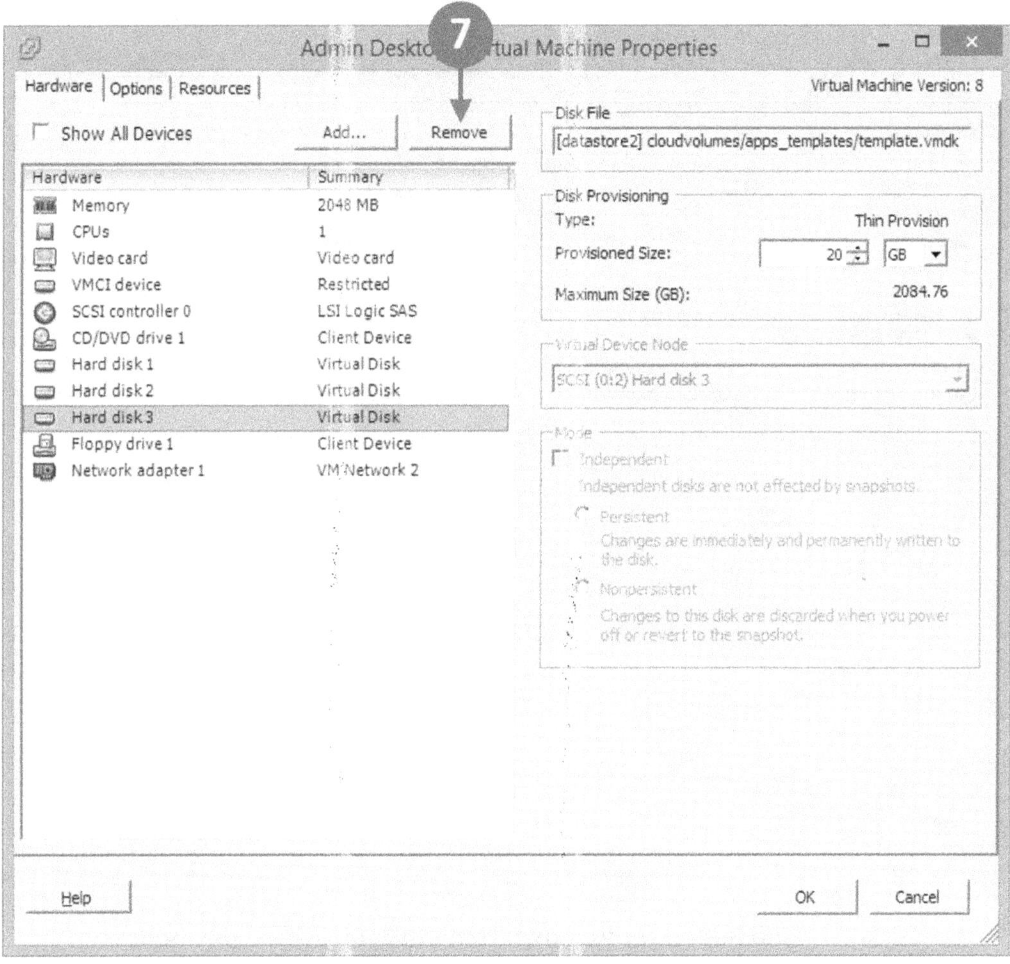

2. Click the **Remove** button **(7)**. You will now see the following diagram:

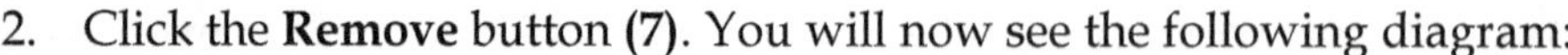

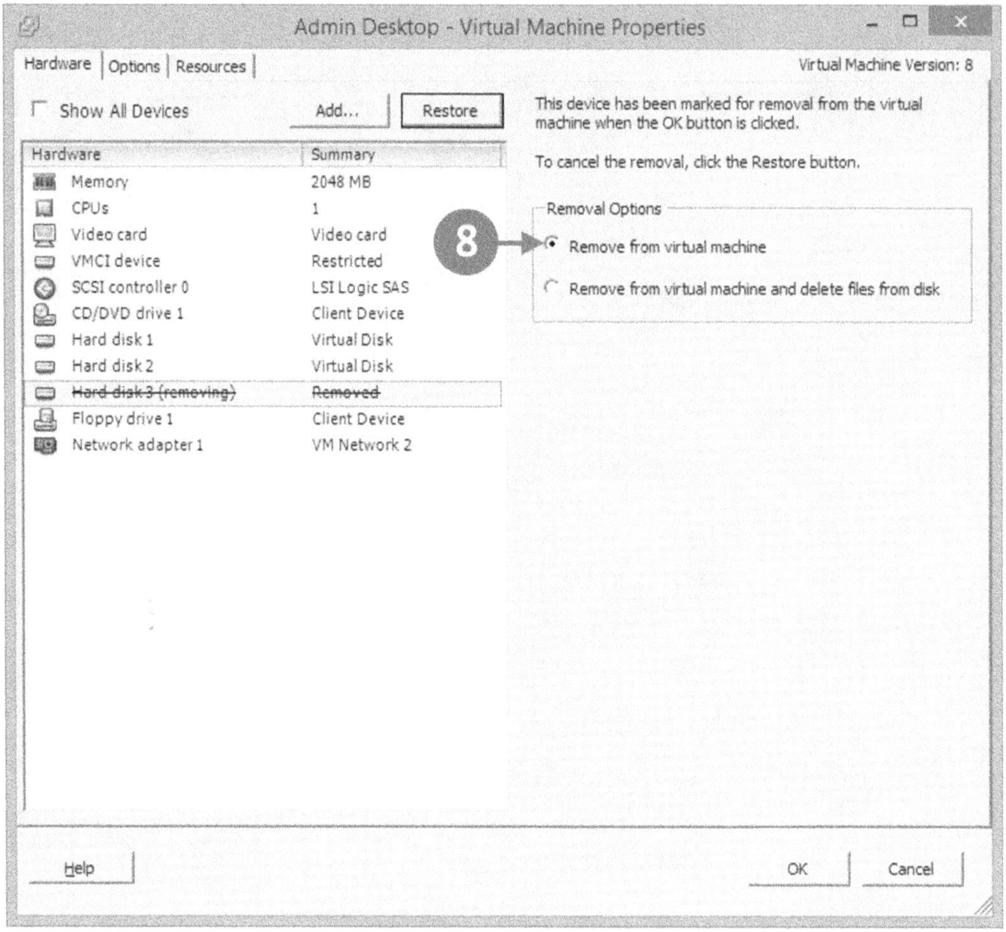

3. Click the radio button for **Remove from virtual machine (8)** and then click **OK**.

Repeat the process to detach Hard disk 2 from the Admin Desktop virtual machine.

Next we will move the newly created virtual hard disk template to the `AppVolumes` folder in the datastore.

Copying new template to App Volumes datastore

The next step is optional; however, it makes management easier if all the AppStack templates are stored in one location.

Therefore, we are going to move the new template into the same directory as the original template.

To do this follow these steps:

1. First of all, open the **Datastore Browser** window, and locate the new template you created in the previous section. As this was created as a new virtual hard disk for the Admin Desktop virtual machine, you will find the virtual disk in the folder for that virtual machine as shown in the following screenshot:

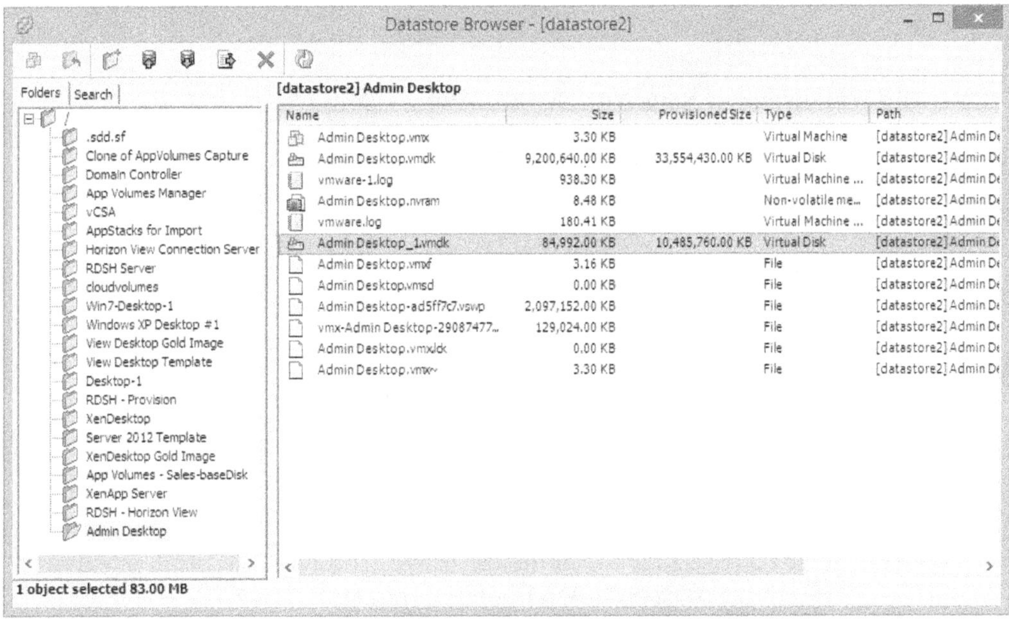

2. Click on the `Admin Desktop_1.vmdk` file to select it and then right-click on it. From the pop-up menu select the **Move to...** option **(1)** as shown in the following diagram:

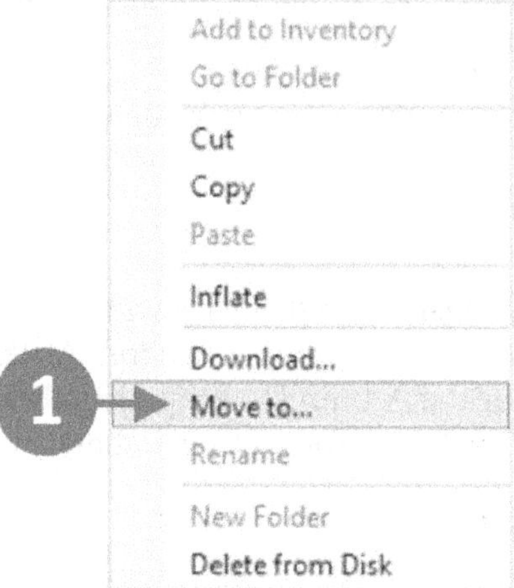

You will now see a **Confirm Move** warning box as shown in the following screenshot:

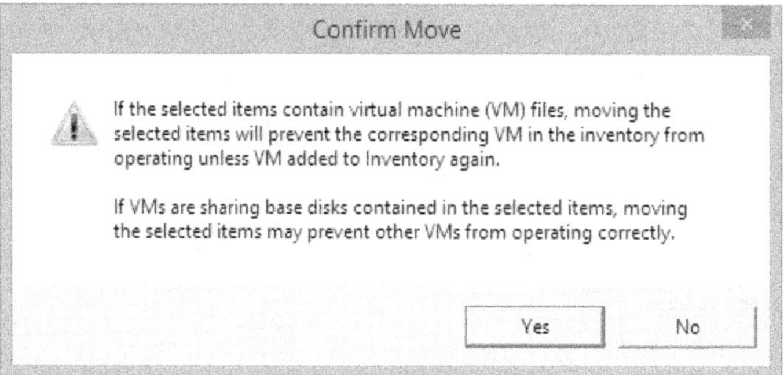

Click the **Yes** button to confirm the file move. You will now see the **Move Items To...** dialog box as shown in the following diagram:

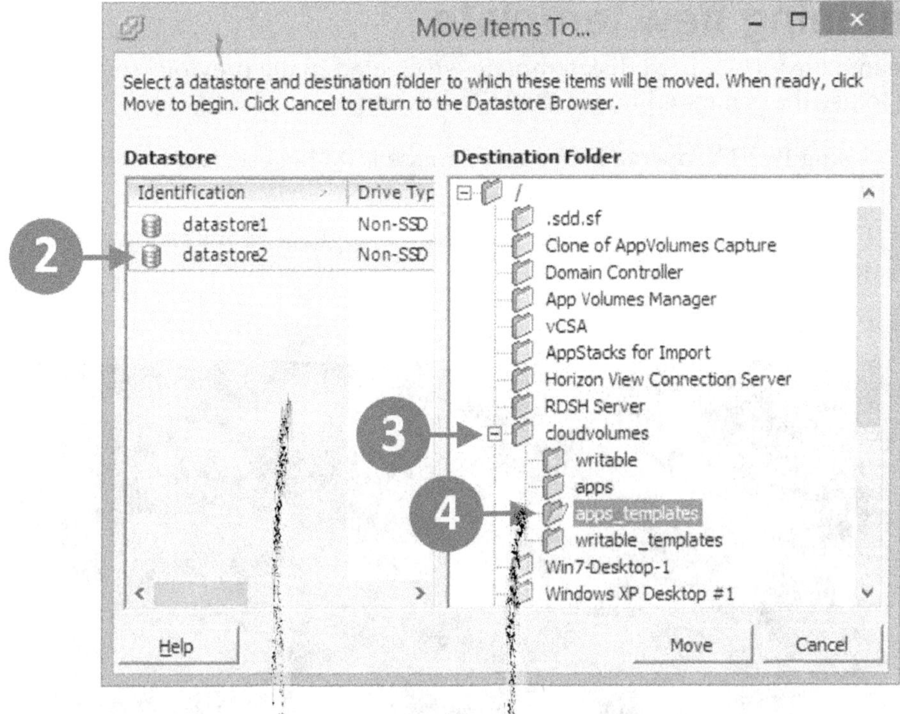

3. Navigate to the App Volumes folder, by clicking `datastore2` **(2)** and then expanding the `cloudvolumes` folder **(3)**, before clicking on the `apps_templates` folder **(4)**.
4. Click the **Move** button to move the VMDK file.

The new virtual hard disk template will now be moved to the `apps-templates` folder ready for import, however before we import it we are going to rename it to something more obvious as to what he virtual hard disk represents rather than using the name of the virtual machine from where it was created.

Renaming new template

To rename the virtual hard disk template we created in the previous section, we are going to use the command line of the ESXi host server.

1. Using **PuTTY**, open a SSH session to the ESXi host server. In this example we are going to connect to `192.168.0.23`.

   Once you have a SSH session established, login as **root** as shown in the following screenshot:

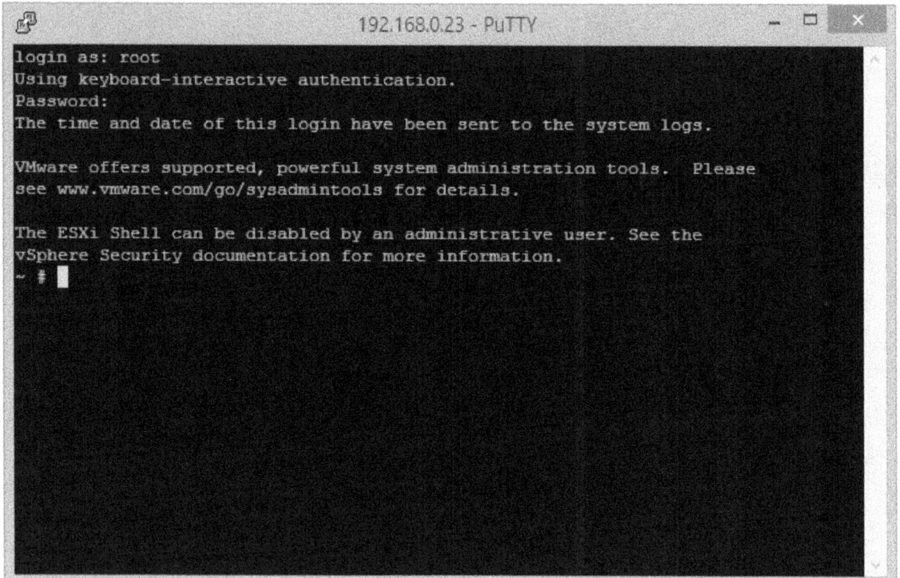

   From the command line change to the `apps-templates` directory. The path to this folder is `/vmfs/volumes/datastore2/cloudvolumes/apps_templates`.

2. Type `ls -lah` to show the contents as shown in the following screenshot:

```
192.168.0.23 - PuTTY
/vmfs/volumes/56279421-50d67ecf-30ce-bc305bf0cb80/cloudvolumes/apps_templates # ls -lah
total 170000
drwxr-xr-x    1 root     root          840 Dec  6 18:09 .
drwxr-xr-x    1 root     root          840 Nov  3 20:16 ..
-rw-------    1 root     root        10.0G Dec  6 18:02 Admin Desktop_1-flat.vmdk
-rw-------    1 root     root          502 Dec  6 18:09 Admin Desktop_1.vmdk
-rw-------    1 root     root        20.0G Dec  6 17:55 template-flat.vmdk
/vmfs/volumes/56279421-50d67ecf-30ce-bc305bf0cb80/cloudvolumes/apps_templates #
```

3. Now you are in the correct directory you can rename the file. At the command line type the following command:

   ```
   vmkfstools -E Admin\ Desktop_1.vmdk AV_10GB_Template.vmdk
   ```

   You have now renamed the file to something more meaningful, in this case we have called it `AV_10GB_Teamplate`.

The next step is to import the new template into the App Volumes Manager.

Importing the new template

Now we have created a new template virtual hard disk, copied it into the App Volumes templates directory, and renamed it, we can now import it.

1. Login to the App Volumes Manager console as shown in the following screenshot:

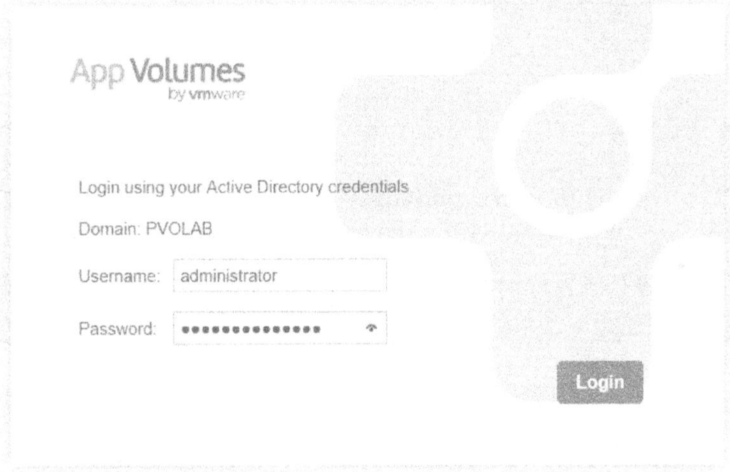

2. Once successfully logged in, click the **VOLUMES** menu option **(1)**, and then click the **AppStacks** tab **(2)** as show in the following diagram:

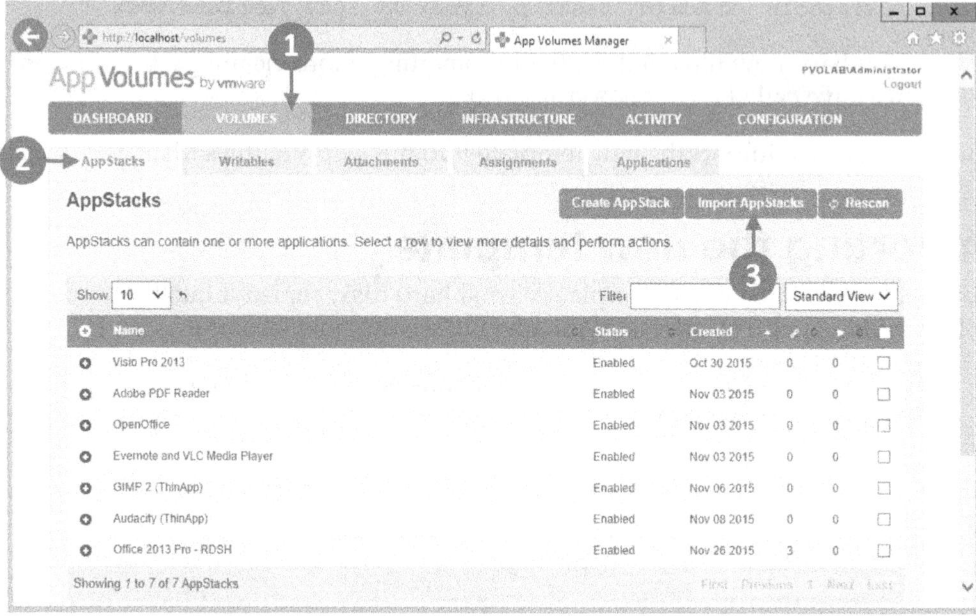

3. Now click on the **Import AppStacks** button **(3)**. You will now see the **Import AppStacks** screen as shown in the following diagram:

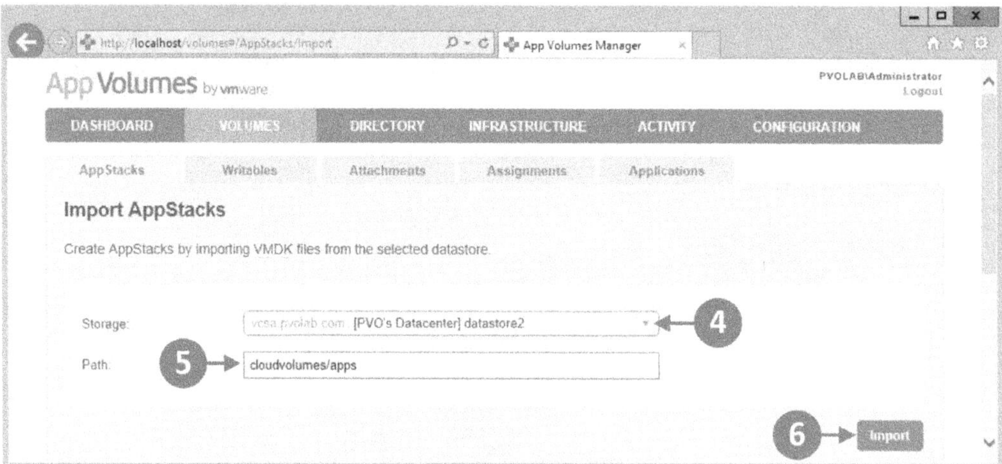

4. In the **Storage** box **(4)**, ensure that `datastore2` is selected and in the **Path** box **(5)**, ensure that the path is set to `cloudvolumes/apps`, the location of the new template.
5. Click the **Import** button **(6)** to start the import process. You will now see the **Confirm Import AppStacks** dialog box as shown in the following diagram:

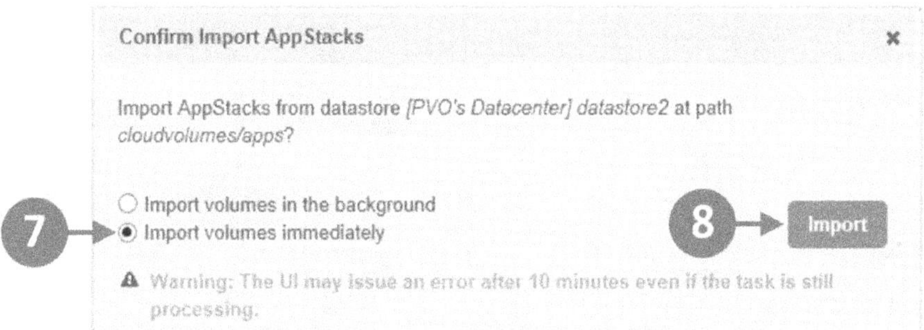
Confirm Import AppStacks
Import AppStacks from datastore [PVO's Datacenter] datastore2 at path cloudvolumes/apps?
Import volumes in the background
Import volumes immediately
7
8
Import
Warning: The UI may issue an error after 10 minutes even if the task is still processing.

6. Click the radio button for **Import volumes immediately** **(7)**, and then click the **Import** button **(8)**. You will see the following message as the AppStacks are imported:

Importing AppStacks

You have now successfully imported the new AppStack template.

To test that the AppStack template is available, let's quickly start the process for creating an AppStack:

1. From the **AppStacks** page on the App Volumes Manager console, click the **Create AppStack** button **(9)** as shown in the following diagram:

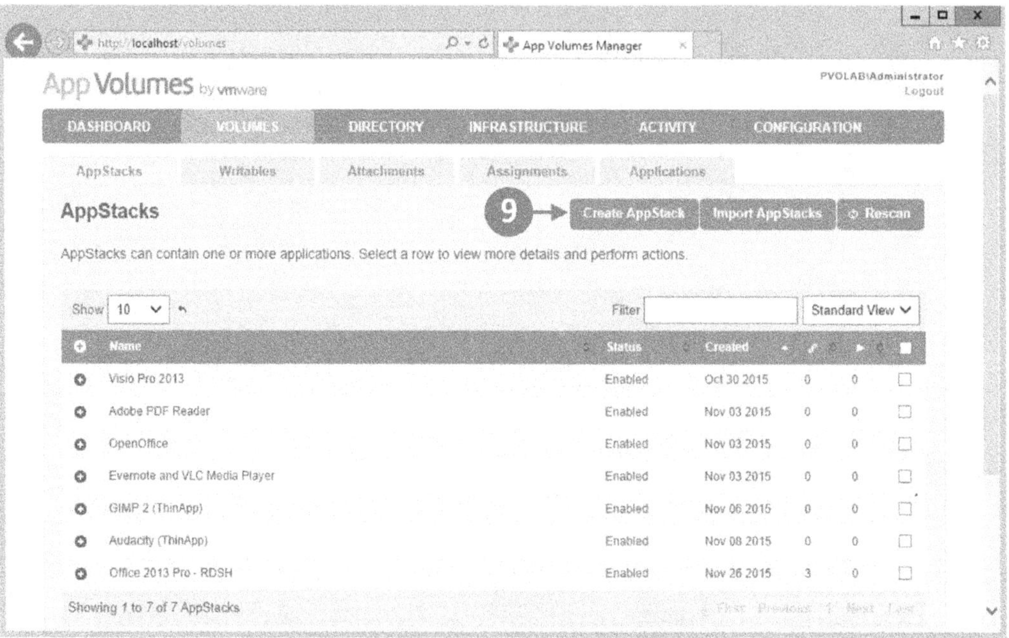

2. On the **Template** box, click the dropdown menu and check that the new template is available to select **(10)**, as shown in the following diagram:

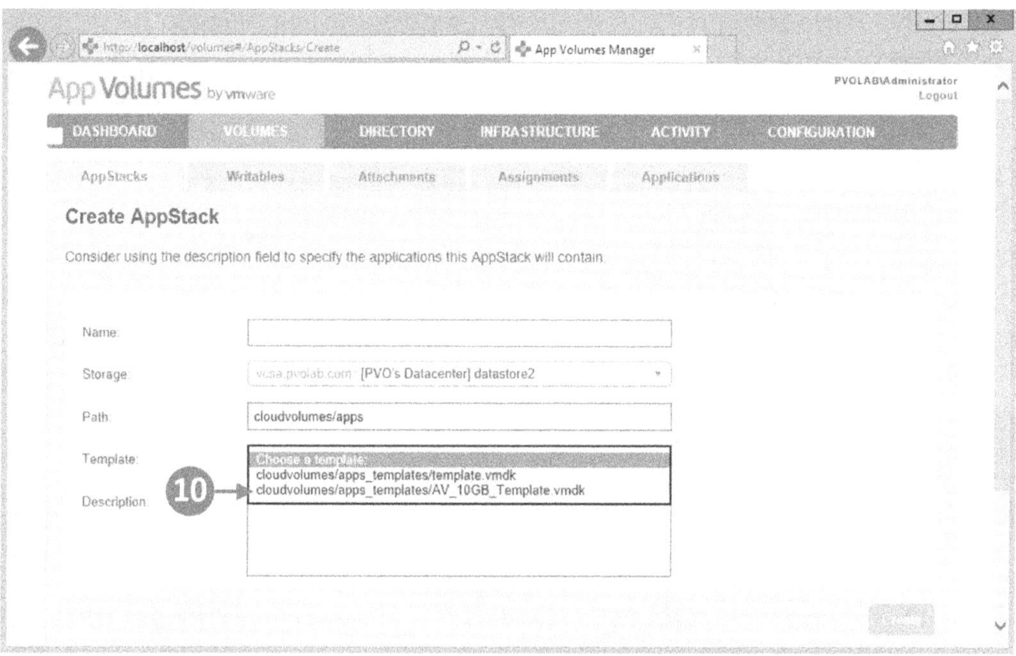

You have now successfully created a customized AppStack template.

Customizing Writable Volumes

As we stated at the beginning of the previous section, VMware App Volumes ships with four different types of template as standard:

- AppStack application template (20 GB)
- Writable Volumes template for user installed applications (10 GB)
- Writable Volumes template for user profiles only (10 GB)
- Writable Volume for user profiles and user installed applications (10 GB)

The standard template for creating Writable Volumes is by default configured to be 10 GB is size. Although this is thin provisioned, and as with the AppStack sizing, it might not make sense to use a 10 GB disk if you have users installing just a handful of small applications that are only a few MB's in size.

As with the resizing of AppStacks, the process for resizing and customizing Writable Volumes is exactly the same. The key difference is the location of the templates in the datastore, and also there is a separate tab in the App Volumes Manager console for importing the new Writable Volumes templates.

The other thing to bear in mind is at the copy stage. Remember there are three different Writable Volumes templates so make sure you copy the files that are appropriate for the Writable Volume template that you are creating.

On the flip side you may have users that have more complex applications to install, or developers that keep multiple version and therefore 10 GB is not big enough to accommodate their requirements.

App Volumes has a feature where you can increase the size of a Writable Volume from the App Volumes Manager console.

To do this follow below mentioned steps:

1. First of all, login to the App Volumes Manager.
2. Then click on the **VOLUMES** menu option, and then the **Writables** tab. You will now see the following diagram:

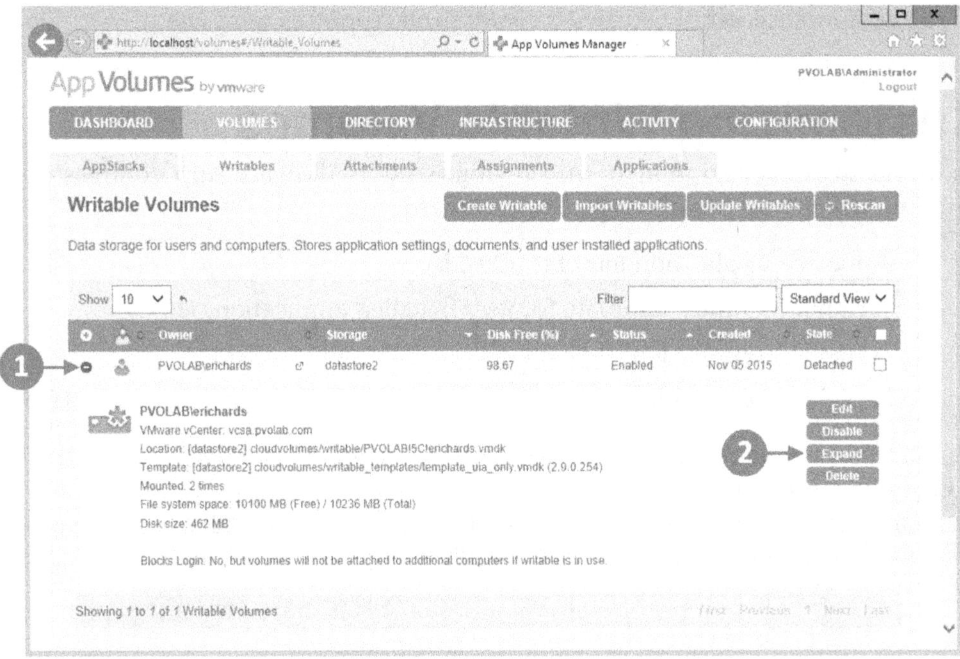

3. Click the **-** button **(1)** next to the Writable Volume that you want to change, and then click the **Expand** button **(2)**. You will now see the **Confirm Expand** dialog box as shown in the following diagram:

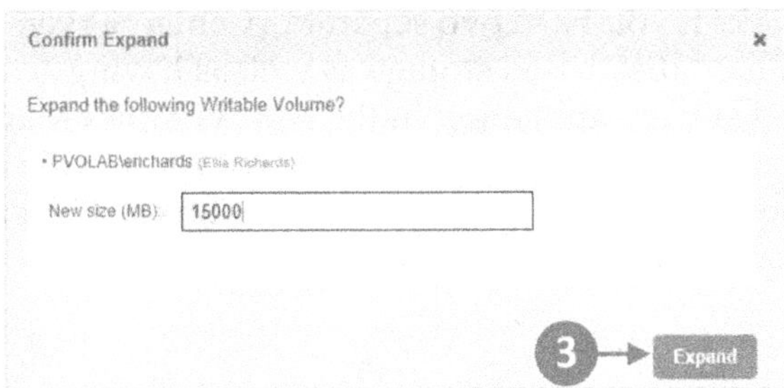

4. In the **New size** box, enter the new size you want for this Writable Volume. Note, the size entered is in MB. Then click the **Expand** button **(3)**. You will see the following message as the volume is expanded.

Creating and working with Storage Groups

Storage Groups are designed to automatically replicate AppStacks and to distribute Writable Volumes across multiple datastores. You can also define a group of datastores that should all contain the same AppStacks.

Some of these group attributes will only apply when you use a storage group to distribute Writable Volumes. This would include things such as the template location and also the distribution strategy.

The distribution strategy setting controls how volumes are distributed across a Storage Group. There are two options for distribution:

- **Spread** - This distributes files evenly across all storage locations. When a file is created, the storage with the most available space is selected.
- **Round-robin** - This distributes files by sequentially using the storage locations. When a file is created, the storage with the oldest used time is selected.

App Volumes can also effectively give you a basic level of storage tiering by managing which storage you can use by allowing the use of some datastores and not others.

So how does that work? If you have two separate vCenter Servers, with each one having its own local hard disk based storage as well as having access to flash-based external shared storage appliance. In the App Volumes Manager, you have the ability to mark the less performant storage as **Not Attachable** meaning that it is ignored when mounting volumes and can therefore be used just for replicating AppStacks. The following screenshot shows this option:

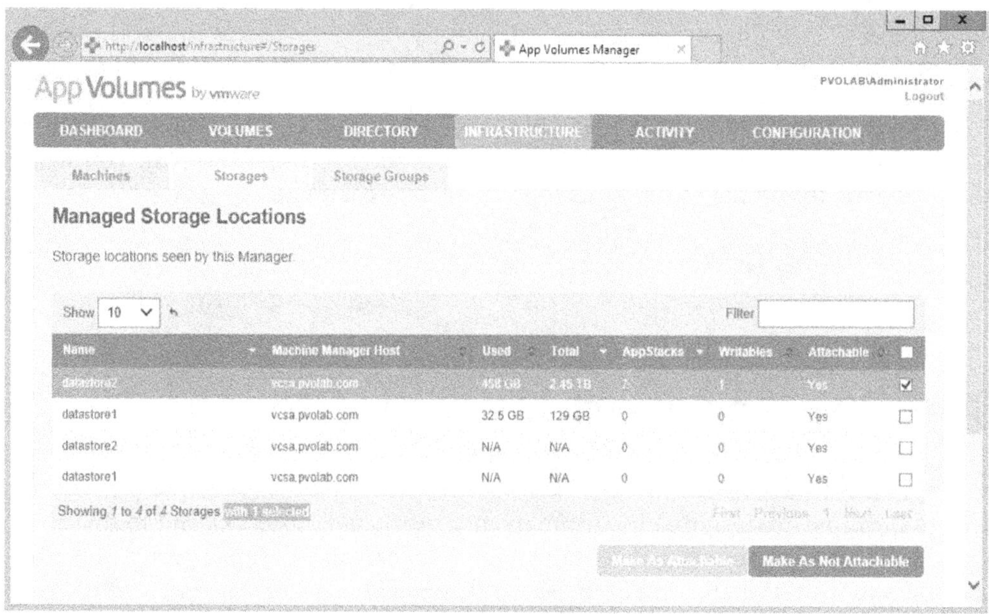

In this example `datastore2` has been selected and then by clicking the **Make As Not Attachable** button this datastore will now be ignored.

Now we have described the Storage Groups feature, let's create and configure a Storage group for example. Let's follow the following steps:

1. Login to the App Volumes Manager and then click on the **INFRASTRUCTURE** menu option **(1)**, and then the **Storage Groups** tab **(2)** as shown in the following diagram:

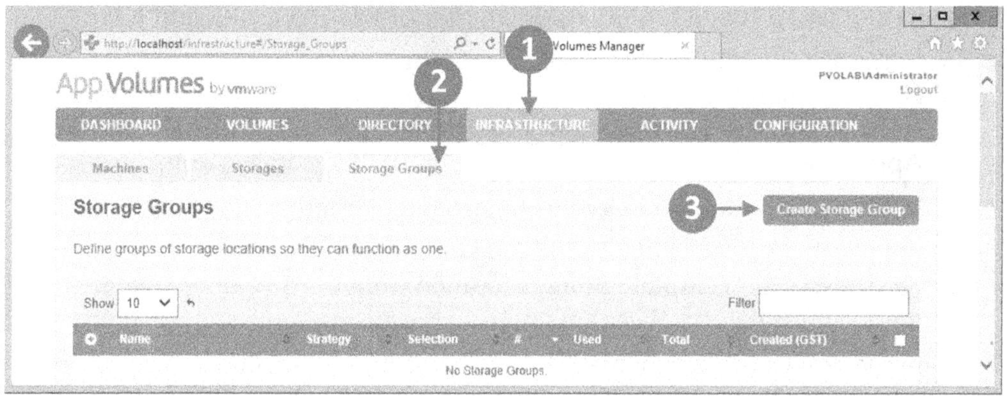

2. Click the **Create Storage Group** button **(3)**. You will now see the **Create Storage Group** screen as shown in the following:

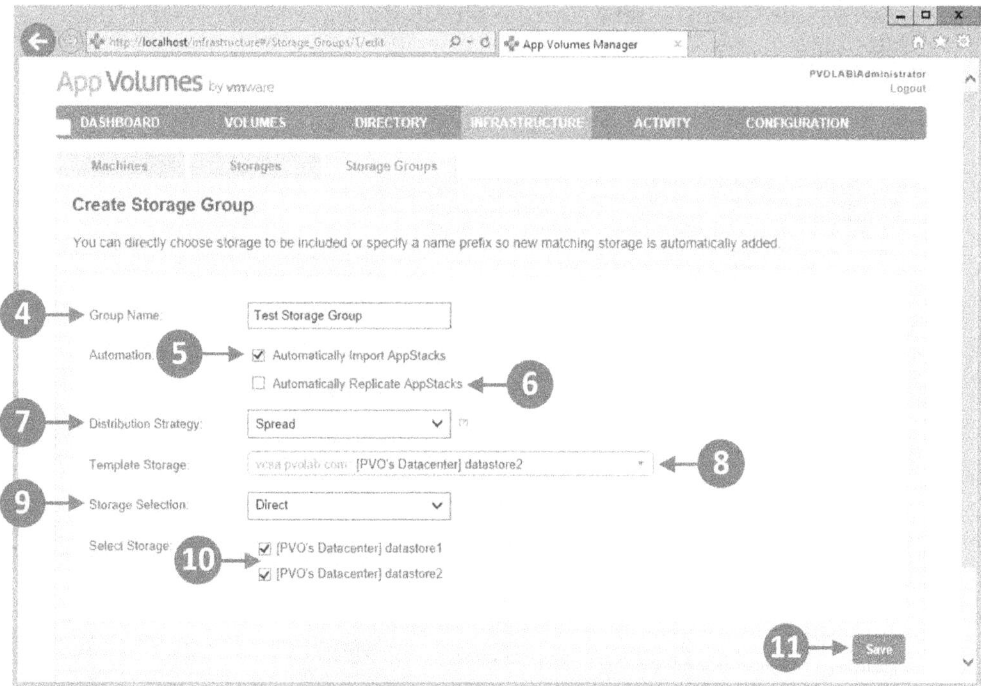

3. In the **Group Name** box **(4)**, enter a name for this Storage Group.
4. In the **Automation** section, check the **Automatically Import AppStacks** box **(5)** if you want to automatically place AppStacks into this Storage Group, and also check the **Automatically Replicate AppStacks** box **(6)** if you want AppStacks replicated across the datastores in this Storage Group.
5. In the **Distribution Strategy** box **(7)**, from the dropdown menu select either **Spread** or **Round-robin**.
6. Next, select the **Template Storage** location from the dropdown menu **(8)**. In this example the templates are on `datastore2`.
7. In the **Storage Selection** box **(9)**, from the dropdown menu select the **Direct** option, and then in the **Select Storage** section **(10)**, check the box for each datastore you want to include as part of this Storage Group. In this example we are going to select both `datastore1` and `datastore2`.
8. Finally click the **Save** button **(11)** to complete the configuration. You will now see the **Confirm Save Storage Group** dialog box as shown in the following diagram:

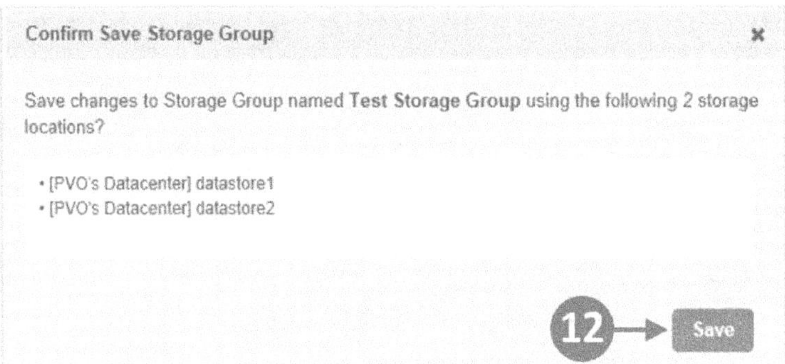

9. Click the **Save** button **(12)**. You will now see the following message to show the Storage Group has been created:

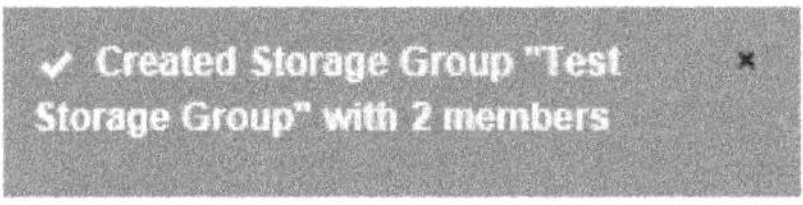

You will also now see the Storage Group in the App Volumes Manager console as shown in the following screenshot:

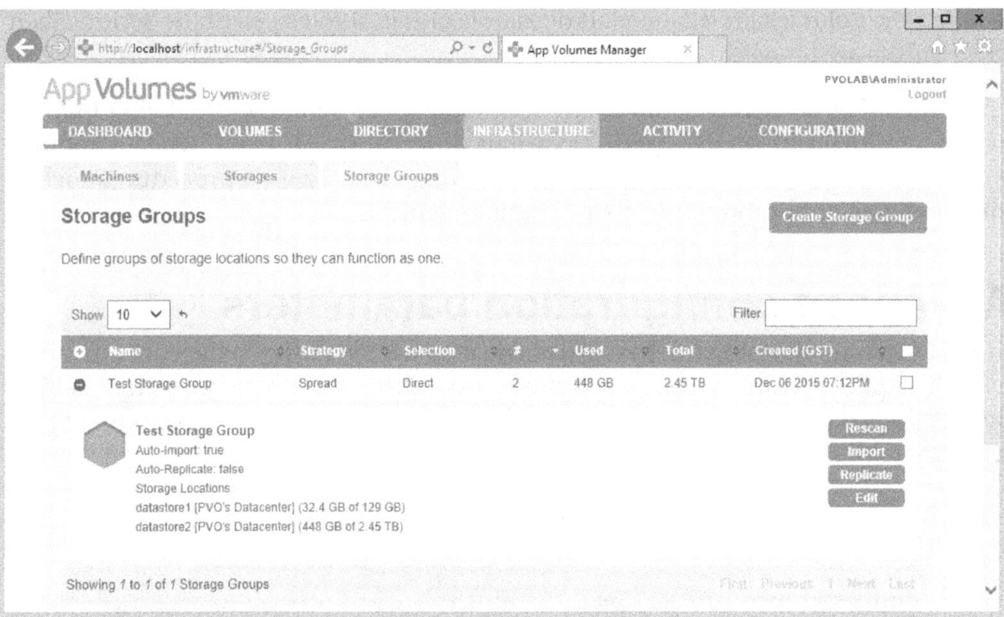

You have now successfully created a new Storage Group.

Advanced Agent configuration

The App Volumes Agent is made up from two different specific elements. Each one responsible for different tasks within the environment.

First off we have the **SVdriver**, which is responsible for the virtualization of volumes into the operating system and ensures that applications within AppStacks appear as though they were locally installed for example.

Secondly there is the **SVservice**. This is responsible for how the volumes are controlled as well as for the communication with the App Volumes Manager.

You can configure App Volumes Manager by selecting configuration options such as batch script files which are called at various points during system startup and login, as well as registry options for services, drivers, and other parameters.

Working with batch script files

App Volumes Agent executes batch script files either when an AppStack or a Writable Volume is attached dynamically or at various points during system startup and login.

If, when the volumes are attached, it does not contain some or all of the scripts, then these scripts are ignored.

The scripts themselves can contain any scriptable action with the idea being that. You can script an action to execute at various different points either when a volume is attached to a virtual machine or when executing virtualization procedures such as integrating an application into an operating system.

Advanced configuration parameters

In total there are thirteen different scriptable actions, the files of which are contained with the AppStack and Writable Volumes virtual disk files. If you remember back to the previous section where we customized a template and copied files from the old template to the new template, these are the different scripts.

These are listed in the following table:

Script	Description	Run As	Wait Time Parameter
prestartup.bat	Called when a volume is dynamically attached, or on during system startup but before virtualization is activated.	System Account	WaitPrestartup (default do not wait)
startup.bat	Called when a volume is dynamically attached, or when system starts up	System Account	WaitStartup (default do not wait)
startup_postsvc.bat	Called as and called after services have been started on the volume (not called if there are no services on volume)	System Account	WaitStartupPostSvc (default do not wait)
logon.bat	Called at log in and before Windows Explorer starts	User Account	WaitLogon (default wait until it finishes)
logon_postsvc.bat	Called after services have been started (not called if there are no services on volume)	User Account	WaitLogonPostsvc (default do not wait)
shellstart.bat	Called when a volume is dynamically attached or when Windows Explorer starts	User Account	WaitShellstart (default do not wait)
shellstop.bat	Called when the user is logging out before Windows Explorer is closed	User Account	WaitShellstop (default do not wait)
logoff.bat	Called at log out and Windows Explorer has terminated.	User Account	WaitLogoff (default do not wait)
shutdown_presvc.bat	Called when the computer is shutting down before services are stopped	System Account	WaitShutdownPresvc (default do not wait)
shutdown.bat	Called when the computer is shutting down after services are stopped	System Account	WaitShutdown (default do not wait)
allvolattached.bat	Called after all volumes are processed (so if user has 3 AppStack, this will be called after all 3 have loaded)	User Account	WaitAllvolattached (default do not wait)
post_prov.bat	Called at the end of provisioning to do any one-time steps that should be performed at the end of provisioning. Invoked when clicking the provisioning complete pop-up window while the volume is still virtualized.	System Account	WaitPostProv (default wait forever)
prov_p2.bat	Invoked at phase 2 of the provisioning process. After the machine is rebooted but before App Volumes Manager has been notified that provisioning is complete. This is the last chance to perform any actions on the provisioned volume with virtualization disabled.	System Account	WaitProvP2 (default wait forever)

SVdriver configuration parameters

As we discussed previously, the SVdriver is responsible for the virtualization of volumes into the operating system.

The SVdriver can be configured in the registry by entering values under the following registry key:

`HKLM\SYSTEM\CurrentControlSet\services\svdriver\Parameters`

You can configure the following options:

Parameter	Description
LogFileSizeInKB	The size of the log file before rotating the log file. The default value is 51200 (50 MB).
ReorderTimeOutInSeconds	Defined in seconds, how long to wait for all volumes to be attached and processed based on Order Precedence set from within App Volumes Manager.
MinimizeReplication	If this value is 1, only changes to data are preserved in a writable volume. If this value is 0, changes to data and file attributes (hidden, Read Only, and so on) permissions are preserved in writable volume.
EnableShortFileName	For legacy AppStacks created earlier than 2.3 set this parameter to 0 to disable DOS short names
EnableRegValueMerging	If this value is 1, merge certain registry values such as AppInitDlls across volumes . This is action is additive across the volumes.
DriveLetterSettings	The value for DriveLetterSettings is in a hexadecimal format, and any number of flags might be combined to implement multiple parameters.

DriveLetterSettings

The App Volumes Agent interacts with mapped volumes using a system path to the volume, without mapping it to a drive letter.

Although most applications are compatible with not having a drive letter associated with them, there are some applications that may still need to access a drive letter to launch applications. App Volumes provides a feature to resolve this issue by hiding the drive letter from Windows Explorer once it has been mapped.

You can define this behavior using the **DriveLetterSettings** registry value, and one of the values shown in the following table:

Value	Description
0x0000001	DRIVELETTER_REMOVE_WRITABLE. Do not assign drive letter for writable volumes
0x0000002	DRIVELETTER_REMOVE_READONLY. Do not assign drive letter for AppStack volumes
0x0000004	DRIVELETTER_HIDE_WRITABLE. Hide drive letter for writable volumes
0x0000008	DRIVELETTER_HIDE_READONLY. Hide drive letter for AppStack volumes

The setting value for DriveLetterSettings is a hexadecimal number, and allows any number of flags to be combined for multiple settings.

For example, if you want to use the **0x00000001** and **0x00000008** settings, then you would enter the value **0x00000009**.

SVservice configuration parameters

As we discussed previously, the SVservice is responsible for how the volumes are controlled, as well as for communication with the App Volumes Manager.

Like the SVdriver, the SVservice can be configured in the registry by entering values under the following registry key:

```
HKLM\SYSTEM\CurrentControlSet\services\svdriver\Parameters
```

You can configure the following options:

Parameter	Description
LogFileSizeInKB	The size of the log file before rotating the log file. The default value is 51200 (50 MB).
MaxDelayTimeOutS	The maximum wait for a response from the App Volumes Manager, in seconds. If set to 0, wait forever. The default is 2 minutes.
ResolveTimeOutMs	Defined in milliseconds for name resolution. If resolution takes longer than the timeout value, the action is canceled. If undefined, default is to wait for completion.
ConnectTimeOutMs	Defined in milliseconds for server connection requests. If a connection request takes longer than this timeout value, the request is canceled. If undefined, the default is 10 seconds.
SendTimeOutMs	Defined in milliseconds for sending requests . If sending a request takes longer than this timeout value, the send is canceled. If undefined, default is 30 seconds.
ReceiveTimeOutMs	Defined in milliseconds to receive a response to a request. If a response takes longer than this timeout value, the request is canceled. If undefined, the default is 5 minutes.
ProvisioningCompleteTimeOut	Defined in seconds to keep trying to contact the App Volumes Manager after provisioning is completed. If undefined, default is 120.
DomainNameWaitTimeOut	Defined in seconds how long to wait for the computer during startup to resolve Active Directory domain name. On machines that are not joined to any domain, you can set the value to 1 for faster llogin. If undefined, the default is 60.
WaitInstallFonts	Defines how long to wait in seconds for fonts to be installed. If undefined, the default is to not wait for completion.
WaitUninstallFonts	Defines how long to wait in seconds for fonts to be removed. If undefined, the default is to not wait for completion.
WaitForFirstVolumeOnlyValue	Defined in seconds, only hold logon for the first volume. After the first volume is complete, the rest are handled in the background, and the logon process is allowed to proceed. To wait for all volumes to load before releasing the logon process, set this value to 0. If undefined, default is 1.

Volume behavior parameters

Volume behavior parameters are values that need to be configured for SVservice configuration:

Parameter	Description
VolWaitTimeout	Defined in seconds. Time required to wait for a volume to be processed before ignoring the volume and proceeding with the logon process. The default value is 180.
VolDelayLoadTime	Defined in seconds. Time required after logon process to delay volume attachments. This value is ignored if a writable volume is used. Writable volumes must be attached prior to any AppStacks. If the value is greater than VolWaitTimeout, it will be reduced to the value of VolWaitTimeout. This might speed up the login time by delaying the virtualizing of applications until after logon is complete. The default value is 0 (do not delay load time).
CleanSystemWritable	If set to 1 and no writable volumes are attached, SVservice will clear any changes saved to the system during operation after a reboot. If set to 0, changes are stored in c:\SVROOT on system volume.

General behavior parameters

You need to configure services, drivers, and general behavior parameters values for SVservice configuration:

Parameter	Description
RebootAfterDetach	If set to 1, automatically reboot the system after a user logs off. If undefined, default is 0.
DisableAutoStartServices	If set to 1, do not automatically start services on volumes after attach. If undefined, default is 0.
HidePopups	If set to 1, svservice.exe does not generate pop-up messages. If undefined, default is 0.
DisableRunKeys	If set to 1, applications in the Run key will not be called. If undefined, default is 0.

Using VHD In-Guest operation mode

We have talked in previous chapters about the ability of App Volumes to integrate into other technology solutions, but in this section we are going to look at that from a different perspective and look at how App Volumes supports disk formats other than VMware VMDK virtual disk files, in this case by supporting VHD files.

In this section, we are going to demonstrate how to set up an App Volumes environment that uses VHD.

In order to use VHS disk files, you need a separate App Volumes Manager instance. You cannot run both VMDK and VHD-based environments on the same App Volumes Manager.

So in this section, we are going to run through the process of setting up such an environment.

Before starting, make sure you have configured a shared folder that can be used to store the AppStacks and has the appropriate permission levels:

1. In this example, we have created a new virtual Windows 2012 R2 Server and named it `app-vol-mgr-VHD.pvolab.com`. We will install the new instance of the App Volumes Manager onto this server.

To install the App Volumes Manager software, please refer to *Chapter 4, Installing and Configuring the App Volumes Software* and the *Installing App Volumes Manager* section.

2. Once installed, launch the App Volumes Manager by double-clicking on the icon on the desktop. We are now going to perform the initial configuration tasks.
3. On the **Welcome to App Volumes Manager** screen, click on the **Get Started** button.
4. On the **License Information** screen, click on the **Next** button.
5. The next page is for configuring **Active Directory**. In the **Domain Name** box, enter the fully qualified name of the domain. In the Example Lab, the entry would be `pvolab.com`.
6. In the **Domain Controller Host Name** box, enter the fully qualified name of the domain controller. In the Example Lab, type in **dc.pvolab.com**.
7. Once you have completed the configuration of this page, click on the **Next** button. You will see that the connection is tested and, if successful, you will now see the **App Volumes Administrator Group** screen.

8. In the **Search Groups** box, start to type in the name of the administrators group. This is the group that contains the App Volumes administrators that we set up as part of the prerequisites in *Chapter 1, Introduction to App Volumes*. The group is called `AppVol Admin`, so just type in the word `app` and click on the **Search** button.
9. The results of the search are displayed in the **Choose Group** box. In the Example Lab, we will see the option for `PVOLAB\AppVol Admin`, so select that and then click on the **Next** button.
10. You will now see the **Machine Managers** screen and this is where things differ from the previous installation, as we are now going to configure App Volumes to use VHD files. This is shown in the following diagram:

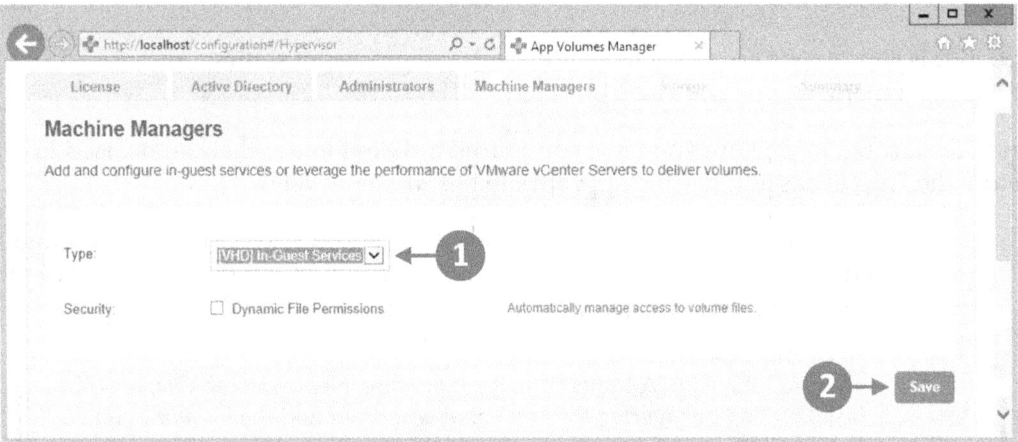

11. In the **Type** box **(1)**, from the dropdown menu, select the option for **[VHD] In-Guest Services** and then click on the **Save** button **(2)**.

    You will now see the **Machine Managers** screen with the newly added machine, as shown in the following diagram:

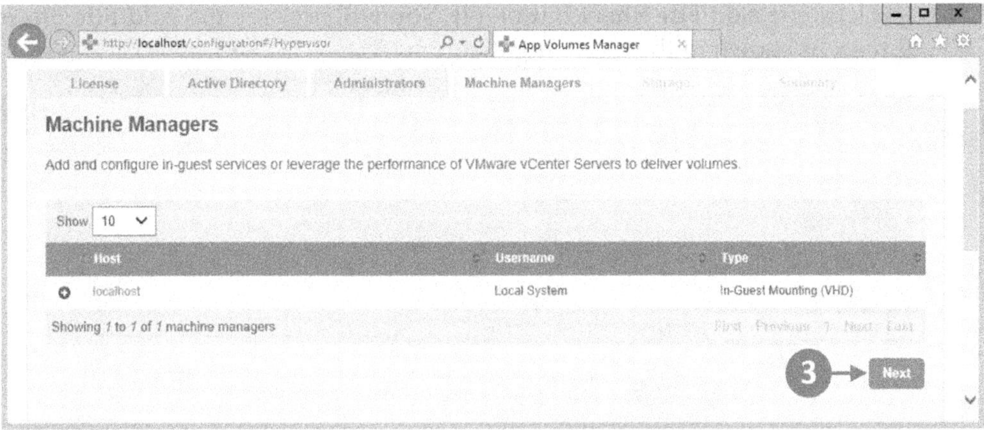

12. Click on the **Next** button **(3)** to continue. You will now see the **Storage** screen, as shown in the following diagram:

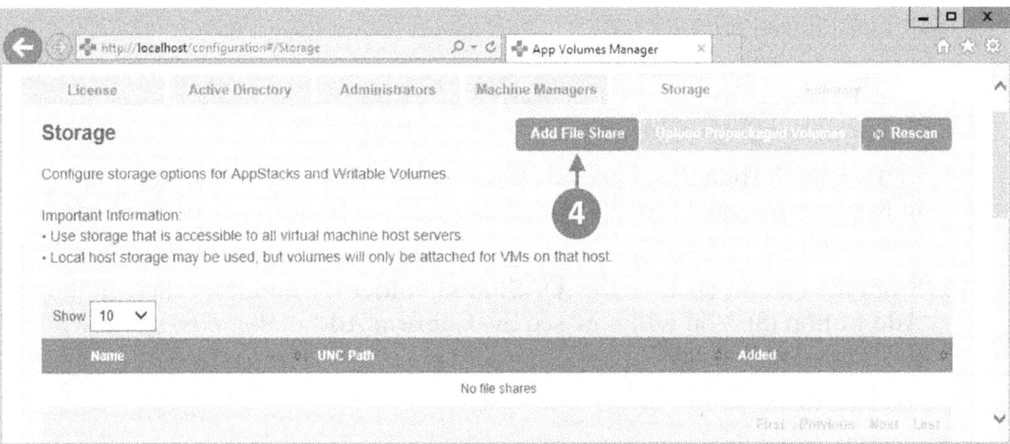

13. Click on the **Add File Share** button **(4)**. You will now see the **Add File Share** screen, as shown in the following diagram:

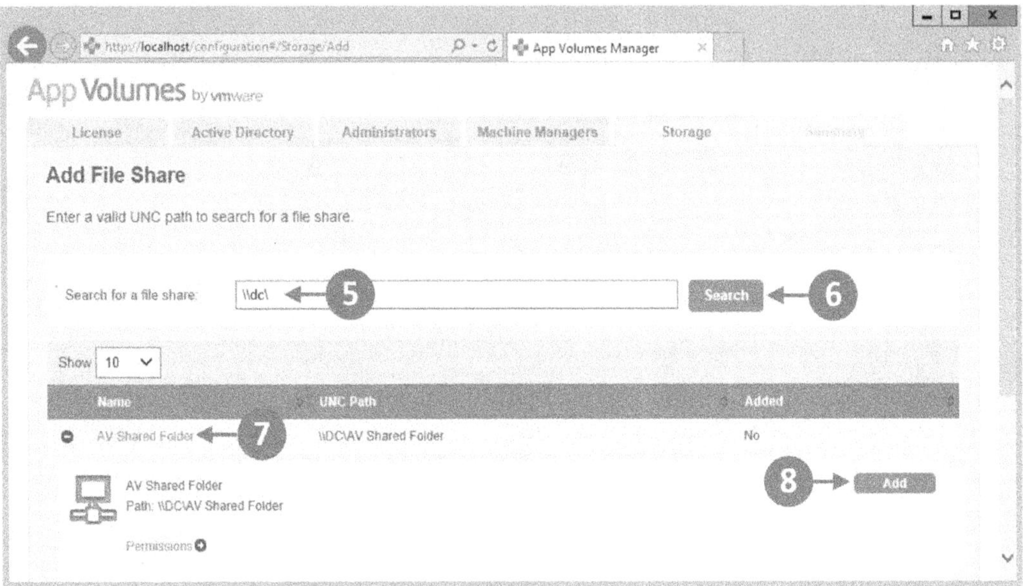

14. In the **Search for a file share** box **(5)**, enter the path to the shared folder. In this example, just type the first part, `\\dc\` and then click on the **Search** button **(6)**.
15. From the results, click on the **AV Shared Folder (7)**, and then click on the **Add** button **(8)**. You will now see the **Confirm Add** dialog box, as shown in the following diagram:

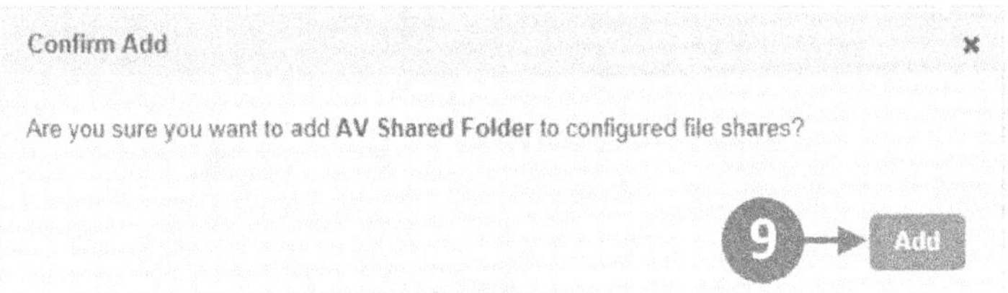

16. Click on the **Add** button **(9)**. Now the shared folder has been added, you need to configure the location to store the AppStacks and Writable Volumes, as shown in the following diagram:

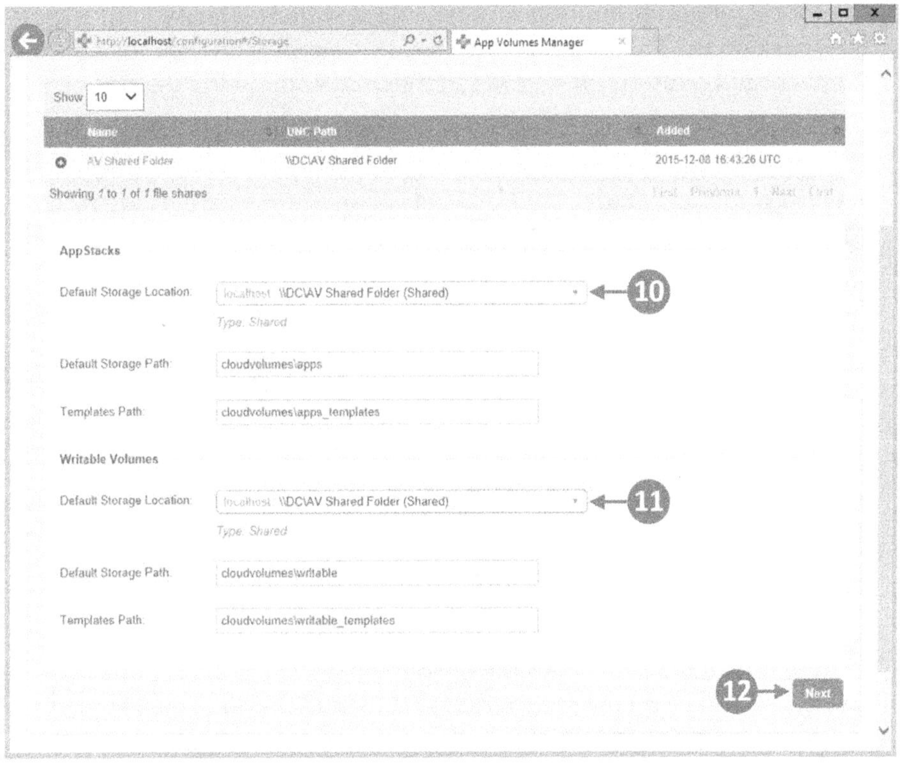

17. In the AppStacks section, from the **Default Storage Location** dropdown **(10)**, select the **\\DC\AV Shared Folder (Shared)** option.
18. In the Writable Volumes section, from the **Default Storage Location** dropdown **(11)**, select the **\\DC\AV Shared Folder (Shared)** option.
19. Click on the **Next** button **(12)**. You will now see the **Confirm Storage Settings** dialog box, as shown in the following diagram:

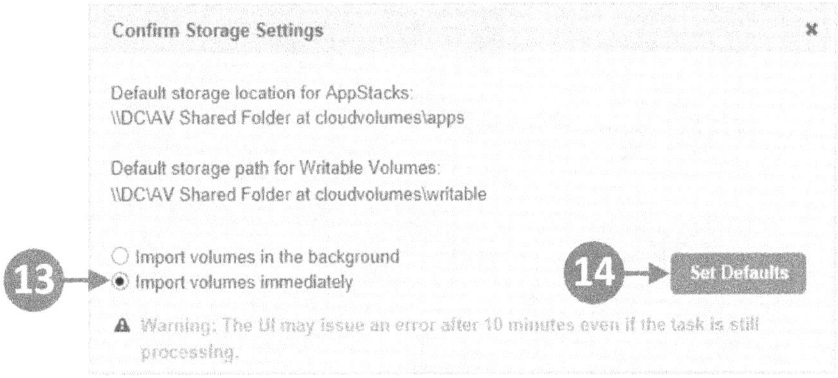

20. Click on the radio button for **Import volumes immediately (13)**, and then click on the **Set Defaults** button **(14)**. You will now see the **Upload Prepackaged Volumes** screen, as shown in the following diagram:

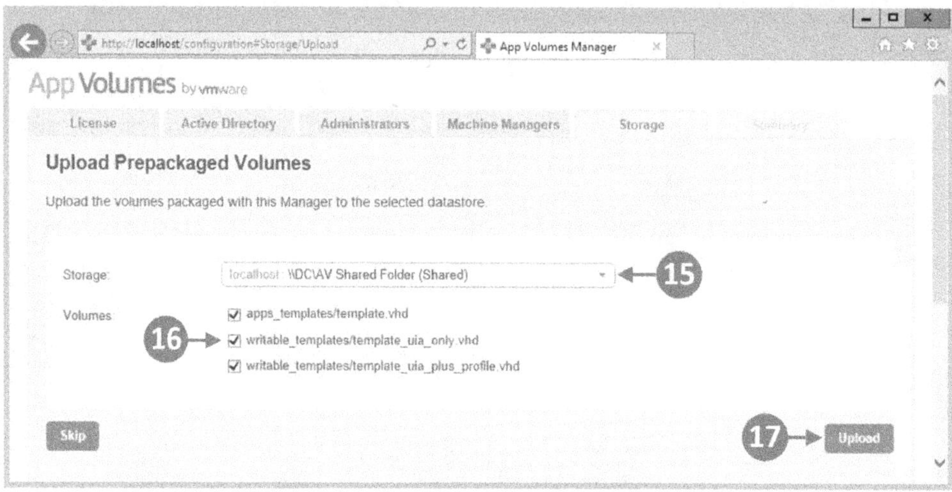

21. In the **Storage** box **(15)**, from the dropdown menu, select the shared folder **\\DC\AV Shared Folder (Shared)** and then in the **Volumes** section **(16)**, check the boxes for the templates that you want to upload.
22. Once completed, click on the **Upload** button **(17)**. You will now see the **Confirm Upload Prepackaged Volumes** screen, as shown in the following diagram:

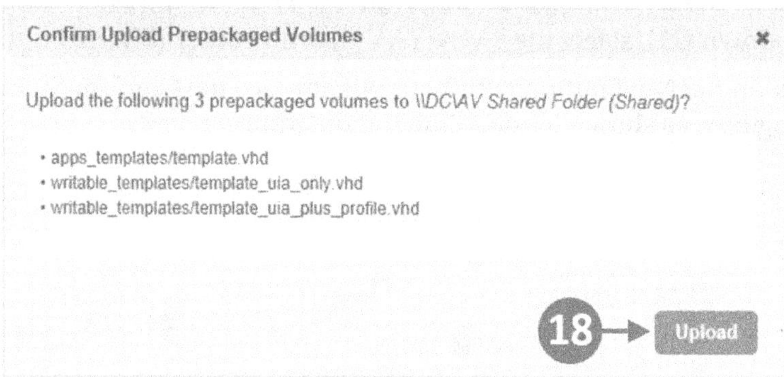

23. Click on the **Upload** button **(18)**.

Finally, you will see the **Summary** screen. Confirm that everything is configured correctly and then click on the **Next** button. You will return to the Manager console.

You have now successfully configured an App Volumes Manager to use VHD storage.

Upgrading to a new version of App Volumes

In this section we are going to look at the process and steps for upgrading to a new version of App Volumes. There is no direct upgrade process, and to upgrade to a new version, you first need to uninstall the current version.

In the next couple of sections, we are going to look at how to upgrade the App Volumes Manager and the App Volumes Agent.

Upgrading the App Volumes Manager

The process for upgrading to a new version of the App Volumes Manager, is illustrated in the following diagram:

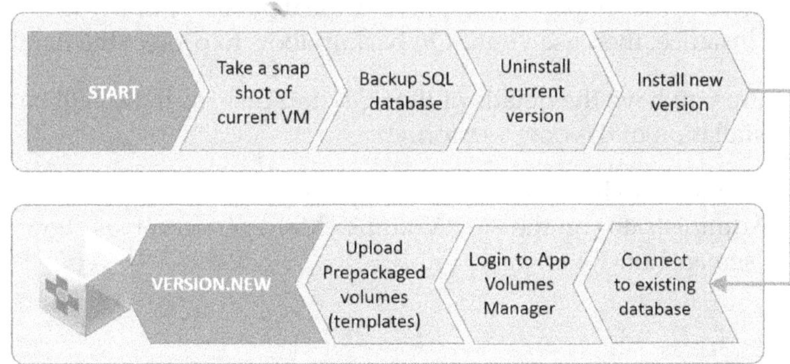

Before we start any upgrade, you need to back up the current environment. You need to back up the current App Volumes Manager, but more importantly you need to back up the SQL database.

In the Example Lab, we took a snapshot of the current App Volumes Manager, as shown in the following screenshot:

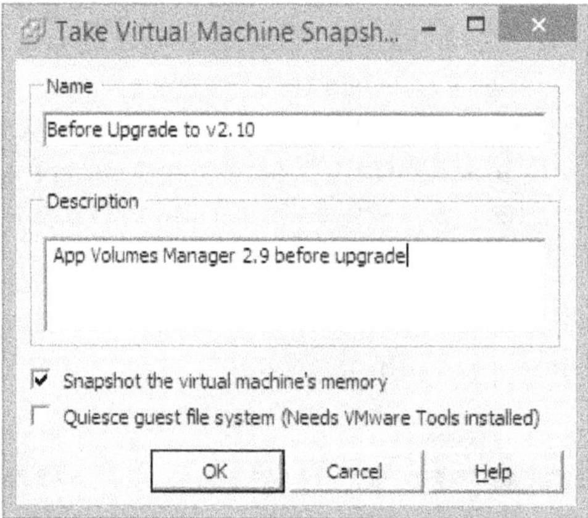

As we are running the SQL database on the same server in the Example Lab environment, taking the snapshot also protects the database, but if you are using a separate SQL instance, then use your SQL backup tools to protect the database.

Next, make sure you have the details of the SQL database, as these will be required during the installation of the new version.

If you don't have them to hand, then you can quickly check using the ODBC Data Source Administrator on the App Volumes Manager server, as shown in the following screenshot:

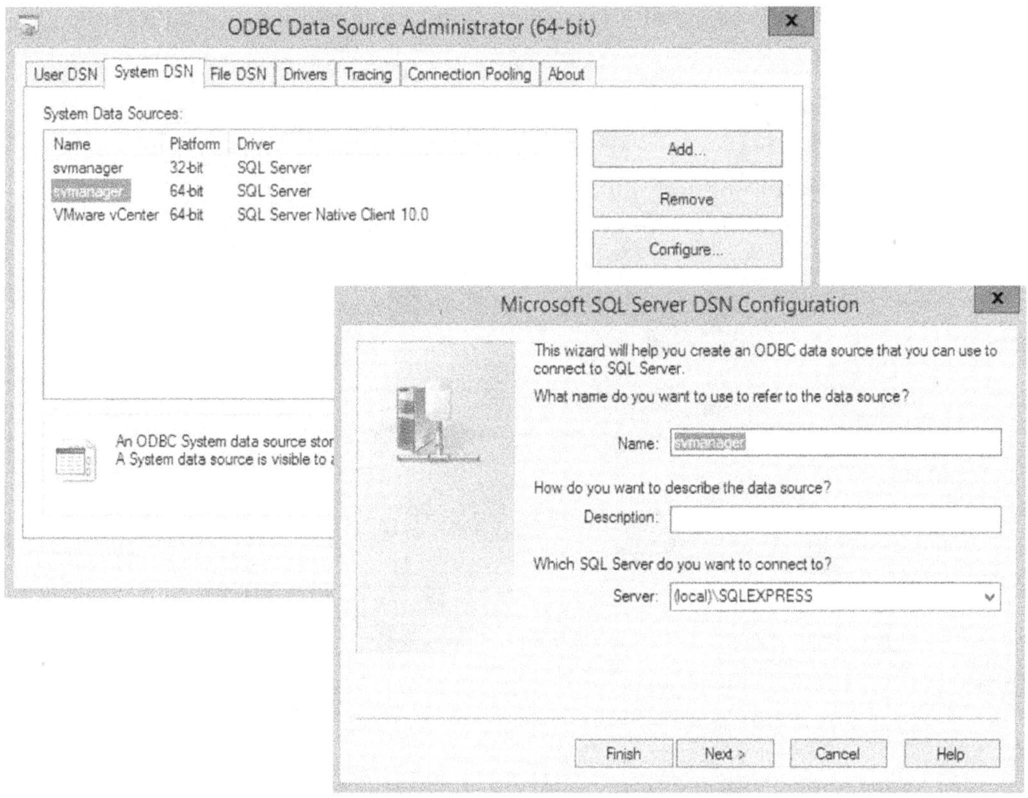

As you can see, the database name is `svmanager` and the SQL server is `SQLEXPRESS`.

So now we are ready to uninstall the current App Volumes Manager. Follow the these steps to uninstall it:

1. Open a console to the App Volumes Manager server and open the **Control Panel**.
2. Then click on **Programs** and then **Programs and Features**, as shown in the following diagram:

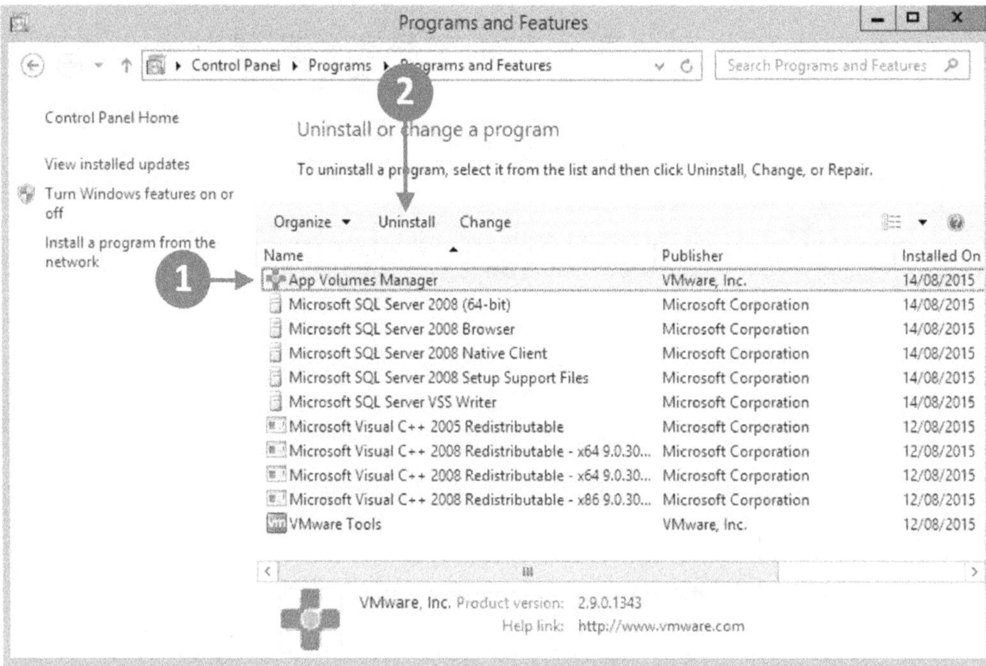

3. Click on **App Volumes Manager (1)** and then click on **Uninstall (2)**.
4. You will now see the **App Volumes Manager Installer** dialog box. Click on the **Next >** button to start the removal.
5. Then next dialog box is the **Remove the Program** dialog box. Click on the **Remove** button to remove the current version of App Volumes Manager.
6. Once removed, you will see the **App Volumes Wizard Completed** dialog box. To complete the uninstall process, click on the **Finish** button.

   You have now successfully removed this version of the App Volumes Manager and are ready to install the new version.

   Locate the shared folder, or folder where you have stored the new version of the App Volumes software, as shown in the following screenshot:

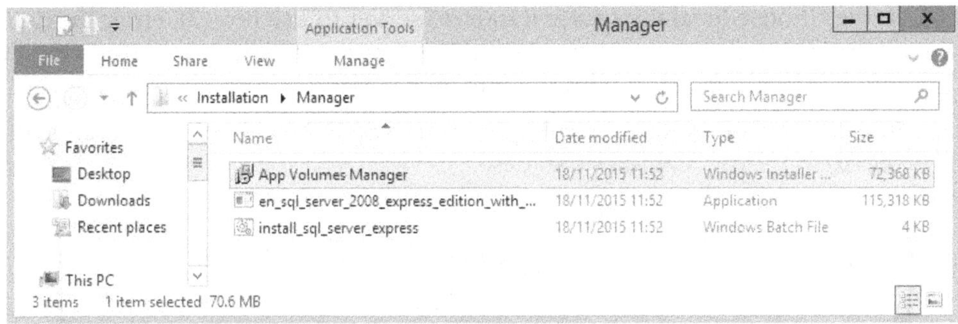

7. Double-click on the **Installation** folder, then the **Manager** folder, and then launch the **App Volumes Manager** Windows installer file. The **App Volumes Manager Installation Wizard** launches.
8. Click on **Next >** to start the installation.
9. You will now see the **VMware End User License Agreement** screen. Click on the radio button to accept the license agreement and then click on the **Next >** button.

   The next screen is the **Database Server** screen, as shown in the following diagram:

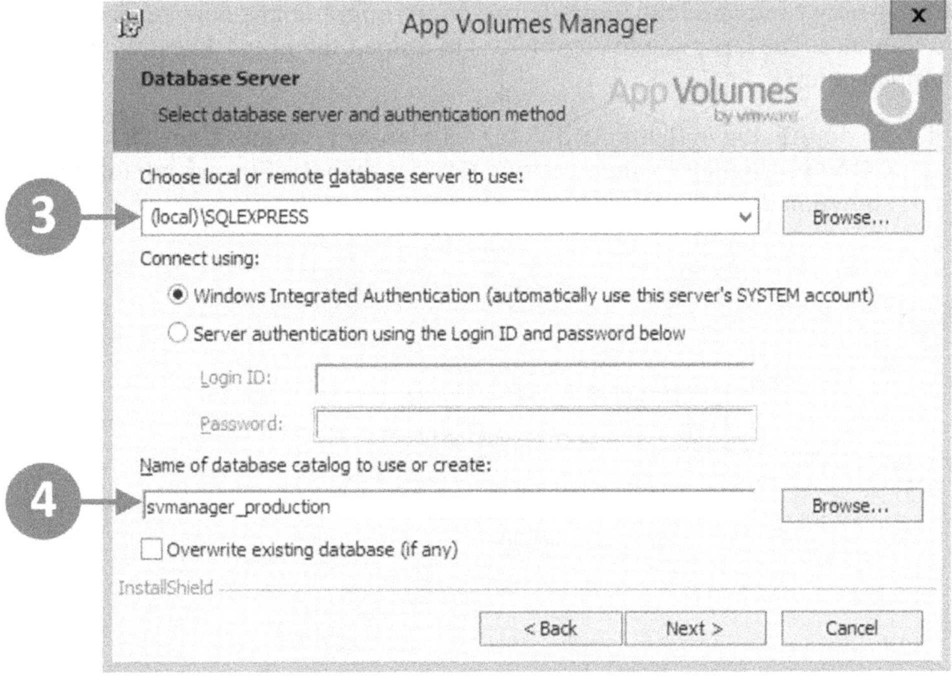

10. In the **Choose local or remote database server to use** box **(3)**, enter the details of the SQL server that you made a note of previously. This is the existing SQL database that was used with the previous version of App Volumes.
11. In the **Name of database catalog to use or create** box **(4)**, enter the name of the existing App Volumes database.

DO NOT check the **Overwrite** box or you will lose all your previous App Volumes information.

12. Click on the **Next >** button to continue.
13. You will now see the **Choose Network Ports** screen. Accept the defaults and then click on the **Next >** button.
14. On the **Destination Location** screen, accept the defaults and then click on the **Next >** button.
15. Click on the **Install** button on the **Ready to Install the Program** screen to start the installation.
16. Finally, on the **App Volumes Wizard Completed** screen, click on the **Finish** button to complete the installation and close the installer.

You have now completed the upgrade process to upgrade to a new version of App Volumes. The last piece to complete is to upload the prepackaged volumes or template files:

1. To do this, log in to the App Volumes Manager console, then click on the **CONFIGURATION** menu option **(5)**, and then the **Storage** tab **(6)**, as shown in the following diagram:

App Volumes by vmware

PVOLAB\Administrator
Logout

DASHBOARD VOLUMES DIRECTORY INFRASTRUCTURE ACTIVITY CONFIGURATION

License Active Directory Administrators Machine Managers Storage

Storage

Upload Prepackaged Volumes Rescan

Configure storage options for AppStacks and Writable Volumes.

Important Information:
• Use storage that is accessible to all virtual machine host servers.
• Local host storage may be used, but volumes will only be attached for VMs on that host.

AppStacks

Default Storage Location: vcsa.pvolab.com [PVO's Datacenter] datastore2
Type: VMFS - Share Mode: Local

Default Storage Path: cloudvolumes/apps

Templates Path: cloudvolumes/apps_templates

Writable Volumes

Default Storage Location: vcsa.pvolab.com [PVO's Datacenter] datastore2
Type: VMFS - Share Mode: Local

Default Storage Path: cloudvolumes/writable

Templates Path: cloudvolumes/writable_templates

Cancel Save

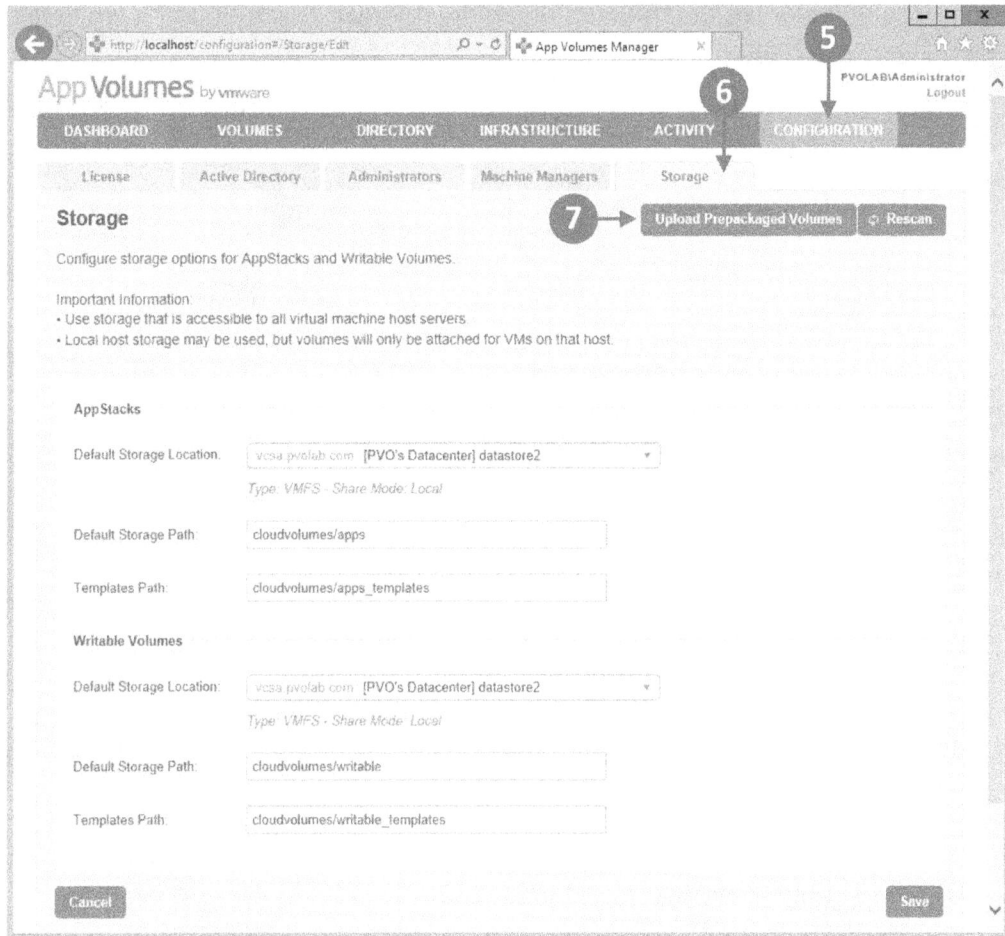

2. Click on the **Upload Prepackaged Volumes** button **(7)**.

You may find that the datastores are shown as being inaccessible. If this is the case, then click on the **Rescan** button to rescan the storage.

You will now see the **Upload Prepackaged Volumes** screen, as shown in the following diagram:

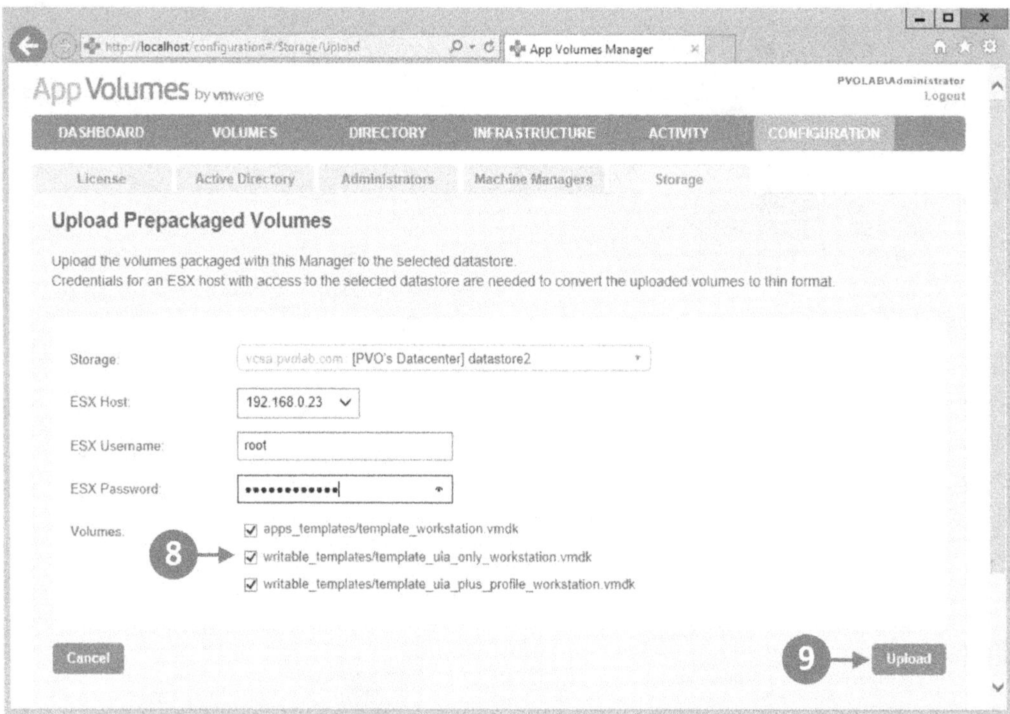

Ensure the correct address details for the ESXi host server are entered and then type in the username and password to connect to the ESXi host.

3. Check **Volumes: (8)** by checking the box next to each volume that you want to upload, and then click on the **Upload** button **(9)**.

   You will now see the **Confirm Upload Prepackaged Volumes** dialog box, as shown in the following screenshot:

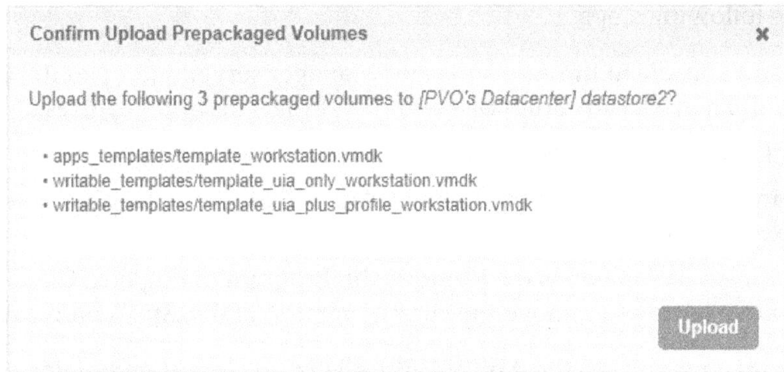

4. Click on the **Upload** button to complete the upload.

You have now successfully upgraded the App Volumes Manager.

Upgrading the App Volumes Agent

In this section, we are going to upgrade the App Volumes Agent on one of the virtual desktop machines. As with the App Volumes Manager, the first part of the process is to uninstall the current version.

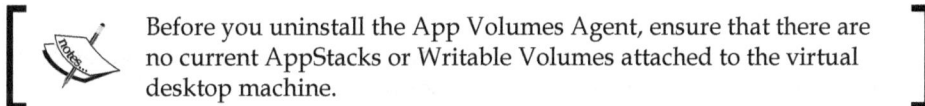

Before you uninstall the App Volumes Agent, ensure that there are no current AppStacks or Writable Volumes attached to the virtual desktop machine.

The upgrade process is pretty straightforward and is illustrated in the following diagram:

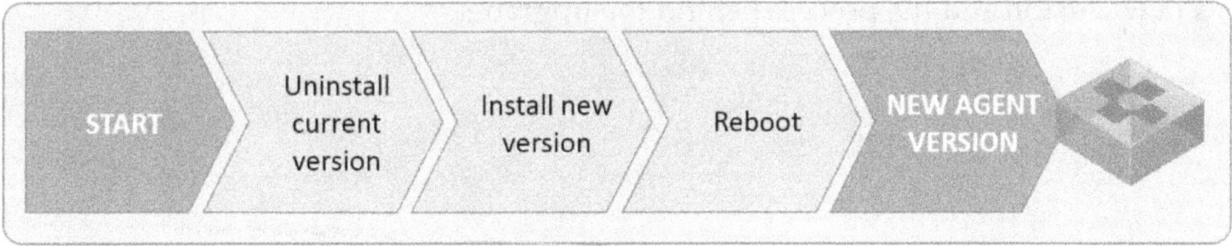

Perform the following steps:

1. Open a console to the App Volumes Manager server and open the **Control Panel**. Then click on **Programs** and then **Programs and Features**.
2. Click on **App Volumes Agent** and then click on **Uninstall**.
3. You will now see the **App Volumes Agent Installer** dialog box. Click on the **Next >** button to start the removal.
4. Then next dialog box is the **Remove the Program** dialog box. Click on the **Remove** button to remove the current version of the App Volumes Agent.

Once removed, you will see the **App Volumes Wizard Completed** dialog box. To complete the uninstall process, click on the **Finish** button. You will be prompted to reboot the virtual desktop machine. Click on **Yes** to reboot.

You have now successfully removed this version of the App Volumes Agent and are ready to install the new version.

The installation process of the App Volumes Agent is exactly the same as we covered in *Chapter 4, Installing and Configuring the App Volumes Software*, so please refer to that chapter to install the App Volumes Agent.

Summary

In this chapter, we have covered some of the more advanced features available with App Volumes, such as scripting and registry settings.

We also covered some of the additional features that don't necessarily fall into other chapters but are equally important to cover. These features include how to customize templates, configuring Storage Groups, and how to upgrade from an existing version to a new version and the process behind the upgrade.

Index

A

B

C

T

U

V

W

X